STUDENTS' RIGHT TO THEIR OWN LANGUAGE

STUDENTS' RIGHT TO THEIR OWN LANGUAGE

A Critical Sourcebook

EDITED BY

Staci Perryman-Clark
Western Michigan University

David E. Kirkland
New York University

Austin Jackson
Michigan State University

WITH A FOREWORD BY

Dr. Geneva Smitherman
Michigan State University

Published in cooperation with the National Council of Teachers of English/Conference on College Composition and Communication
1111 W. Kenyon Road
Urbana, Illinois 61801-1096
www.ncte.org

BEDFORD / ST. MARTIN'S   Boston   •   New York

For Bedford / St. Martin's

Publisher for Composition: Leasa Burton
Developmental Editor: Rachel C. Childs
Publishing Services Manager: Andrea Cava
Production Supervisor: Victoria Anzalone
Senior Market Development Manager: Karita France dos Santos
Project Management: DeMasi Design and Publishing Services
Text Design: Anna Palchik
Cover Design: Donna Lee Dennison
Composition: Jeff Miller Book Design
Printing and Binding: RR Donnelley and Sons

NCTE Stock No. 41299
Published in cooperation with the National Council of Teachers of
English/Conference on College Composition and Communication
1111 W. Kenyon Road
Urbana, Illinois 61801-1096
www.ncte.org

Manufactured in the United States of America.

9 8 7 6 5 4
f e d c b a

For information, write: Bedford / St. Martin's, 75 Arlington Street,
Boston, MA 02116 (617-399-4000)

ISBN 978-1-4576-4129-9

FOREWORD

1969 marked my first talk at a Conference on College Composition and Communication convention. It was held in Miami, Florida. My talk was a remix of a speech I had given in 1968, "Black Power is Black Language." By 1971, as a social activist and a pioneer in Black Studies, and with the Black Freedom Struggle on the ropes, I had decided to cast my lot with CCCC, or "4Cs," as insiders dubbed it. Reflecting back to what seems like another lifetime, I had done come a long way from the doo-wop days of our lives in Southside Chi-town and the East Side of the D, where, despite our girlish fantasies of "success" and our keep on keepin on ethos, there was always a lingering undercurrent of doom, despair, and dreams deferred. For me and my generation, the questions were many. Is God dead? What is liberation and empowerment for descendants of enslaved Africans? What is liberation for women? In a democracy, what is Free Speech—in ivory and ebony towers and beyond? Are university students "niggers"—slaves to their masters/professors—as civil rights activist and professor Jerry Farber argued in his 1960s essay, "The Student as Nigger"? It was an era during which many teacher-scholars—those involved in the business of 4Cs, as well as those in activist and revolutionary struggle in the world outside of 4Cs—were keenly aware, as Frantz Fanon taught, that "each generation must, out of relative obscurity, discover its mission, fulfill it, or betray it."[1]

For many of us, the assertion of student language rights was inextricable from our national and international quest for social justice. As the editors of *Students' Right to Their Own Language: A Critical Sourcebook* eloquently put it: "SRTOL is not about language. . . . It is about people and about respecting their rights and identities, particularly in public spaces, such as classrooms, workplaces, and the like. It is about understanding people and embracing, affirming, valuing, and bearing witness to who they are, have been, and shall become." Those of us in the Struggle realistically acknowledged that the *Students' Right to Their Own Language* would not be sufficient to achieve our vision of language rights in the pursuit of social justice. But our mission was to call the Question. Since the fall of 1971, when our 4Cs committee began its labor in the language rights vineyard, countless teacher-scholars have taken up the

Question. *Students' Right to Their Own Language: A Critical Sourcebook* is a brilliantly conceived collection that continues that tradition. It consolidates, in a single resource, works that provide critical conversations about SRTOL, its history, and its impact across the decades. In addition, it includes something else that is critical, and that, to my knowledge, cannot be found in current scholarship: the full *Students' Right to Their Own Language* background document. The version included here has minor twenty-first-century editorial emendations, but there is no significant departure from the original thirty-two-page publication that appeared in the fall of 1974 as a special issue of *College Composition and Communication*. Props and big ups to the editors for the inclusion of this primary source. This is invaluable not only for a new generation of teacher-scholars and graduate students in rhetoric and composition studies, but also for seasoned veterans in the field as well as readers outside the field—all can now read both the one-paragraph resolution and the background document for themselves. Over the decades since 1974, supporters and naysayers alike have defended or denounced the conception of "students' right to their own language" without having read these historical documents. In fact, at the mere mention of the phrase "students' right to their own language," it be on and poppin—and ain nobody up in the mix done read nothin!

As our Committee on CCCC Language statement was conceptualizing the monograph that would put flesh on the bones of the *Students' Right to Their Own Language* one-paragraph resolution, we focused on language although we did not envision the monograph as a mini-linguistics course. However, the field of linguistics was undergoing a major paradigm shift owing to the theoretical formulations of Chomsky[2] and the socially constituted linguistics of Hymes.[3] The new paradigm had major implications for instruction in composition and rhetoric, English language arts, and literacy. Thus the monograph concentrated on two major areas: 1) language appropriateness, or, following the fundamental contribution of anthropologist and linguist, the late Dell Hymes, what I've come to call the Hymesian Question: who can say (or write) what to whom under what conditions and with what consequences? and 2) Latinate and prescriptivist grammar teaching (e.g., classroom drills on *who-whom*, the conjugation of verbs, not ending sentences with prepositions, etc.), or, following the contribution of linguist Donald Lloyd, "the national mania for correctness," which shackles student writers and inhibits their production of clear, cogent, lively writing. The background document supporting the resolution was critical to enhancing the knowledge base of teachers, who had raised questions and issues about SRTOL from its inception. The Committee drew on our experience with teachers in classrooms, workshops, and conferences, and written and verbal responses to the resolution that had been coming our way since 1972 when the 4Cs executive committee adopted the resolution we had drafted. These experiences, responses, and reactions informed our organization of the monograph into fifteen critical topic areas, phrased as questions we had heard over the years from teachers and colleagues: "What do we mean by dialect?" (Linguists these days use "variety" instead of "dialect.") "Why do some dialects have more prestige than others?" "Does dialect affect the ability to read? To write? To think?" "How can students be offered dialect options?" How does dialect affect employability?"

And no, Virginia, those topical areas (fifteen in the original version, as mentioned above) did not apply to Blacks only. Let me quick, fast, and in a hurry here dispel the myth that the SRTOL policy and subsequent background document were constructed only for students who spoke African American Language (also known as "Ebonics" and "African American English"). Rather, as I note elsewhere, 4Cs was in the vanguard of language and literacy profes- sional bodies whose membership was coming to grips with the changing na- ture of the college student population. White working-class urban and rural students were becoming the first of their families to attend college, bringing their class and regional dialects to the campus. In the 1950s, Professor Donald Lloyd of the Structural Linguistics School came to their defense in the pages of *College Composition and Communication*:

> You discover . . . that dialects you have grown up to despise are rooted in respectable antiquity and still reflect the vicissitudes of pioneer life. If you respect American traditions, you find these traditions best embodied in the language of the illiterate back-country farm families, whether they still stand on their own land or congeal in uneasy clots in our industrial cities. You come therefore to describe with respect. You give information; you do not devise new decalogues.

Our committee was keenly aware that the Question we had called applied to an ethnically and racially diverse student population. SRTOL was a clarion call on behalf of the language rights of ALL students in composition classes, including the currently emerging population of speakers of English varieties from nations and communities outside of the United States.

Nonetheless, it is the case that a number of the real-world language examples in the monograph reflect features of African American Language (AAL), e.g., *Mary daddy home; Phillip mother in Chicago; Yesterday they look at the flood damage.* Two sociolinguistic factors account for this. First, of all varieties of U.S. English, AAL has the most fundamental differences—in syntax, pro- nunciation, lexicon, rhetorical and semantic strategies, discourse patterns— from "Edited American English" (to use the label our committee employed in 1971; today I use the label Language of Wider Communication, or LWC[4]). J. L. Dillard and other language historians[5] attribute these differences to the Creole history of AAL, in which African language patterns mixed with En- glish. These major and significant differences in language structure and lan- guage use are why some linguists contend that Black speech constitutes a language, not a dialect.[6] Second, because of these major linguistic differences, AAL was, and continues to be, the most studied and showcased U.S. English variety, resulting in numerous publications and broad-based exposure in aca- demic and popular venues. Hence, illustrative examples were handy and readily available.[7] I think these same sociolinguistic factors account, in large measure, for a section devoted to what the editors call "The Special Case of African American Language" in this volume.

Although English has now become a global *lingua franca*, our world remains linguistically diverse. Most citizens around the globe speak more than one language. The "English only" and "English is enough" mind-set of the United States is provincial, parochial, and out of step with the rest of the world. The next level of the language rights struggle calls for a policy mandating that all U.S. students become proficient in one or more languages in addition to English. Such an official language policy would bring the United States in line with other nations of our world. Our neighbor Canada, for instance, has for decades had two official languages—English and French. Enshrined in the Constitution of post-apartheid South Africa are eleven official languages—English, Afrikaans, and nine indigenous African ("Black") languages. And South Africa's language in education policy promotes the use of the official languages for teaching and learning (the specifics of implementation to be determined by local communities and schools).

Here in the United States several professional organizations, 4Cs among them, have adopted language policies of bi/multilingualism. The tripartite National Language Policy (NLP), formulated by the 4Cs Language Policy Committee in 1988, is now the official language policy of CCCC:

1. To provide resources to enable native and non-native speakers to achieve oral and literate competence in English, the language of wider communication.

2. To support programs that assert the legitimacy of native languages and dialects and ensure that proficiency in one's mother tongue will not be lost.

3. To foster the teaching of languages other than English so that native speakers of English can rediscover the language of their heritage or learn a second language.

I long for the day when the following joke will be outdated:

> What do you call a person who speaks three languages?
> Answer: Trilingual
>
> What do you call a person who speaks two languages?
> Answer: Bilingual
>
> What do you call a person who speaks one language?
> Answer: American.

* * *

> And although it seems heaven sent,
>   we ain't ready to see a Black president.
>   —TUPAC SHAKUR, "Changes," 1992

Had hip-hop artist Tupac Shakur not been killed in 1996, he would have lived to witness Barack Hussein Obama being democratically elected to the U.S. presidency—not once but twice. Now, doan git it twisted, I ain sayin that this momentous act, in and of itself, means that the United States is now a post-racial society. But what it does mean is that change is possible even in what hip-hop artist Eminem called the "Divided States of Embarrassment" ("White America," 2002). In 1974, *Students' Right to Their Own Language* laid the foundation for a national policy of multilingualism. I just stopped by to tell yall, the Struggle continues—but we can win.

Victory,

Geneva Smitherman, Ph.D., aka Dr. G
University Distinguished Professor Emerita of English
Co-founder and Adjunct Professor, African American and African Studies
Michigan State University
October, 2013

NOTES

1. From Frantz Fanon's *The Wretched of the Earth* (French edition, 1961, English translation, New York: Grove Press, 1963). Fanon, born in Martinique (in the French Caribbean), was a psychiatrist and revolutionary whose ideas were, and continue to be, influential in social justice struggles.

2. Linguist Noam Chomsky raised the issue of understanding human nature and the structure of human intellect through the study of language and forced deep considerations of language beyond mere surface notions of grammatical correctness promoted in the nation's schoolrooms. He rejected mid-twentieth-century behaviorist conceptions of language as response to environmental stimuli and established that human language is an inherent, species-specific mental trait that provides a unique capacity for the creation of an unlimited variety of expressions from a limited set of linguistic elements. Chomskyan linguistics has, of course, evolved since the publication of his *Syntactic Structures* in 1957, a slim but powerful book. That work as well as his *Cartesian Linguistics* (1966) and *Language and Mind* (1968; 1972) were critical in launching the paradigm shift. Linguist Steven Pinker provides a contemporary (and highly readable) update to the Chomsky School. See, for instance, his *The Language Instinct* (New York: Harper Perennial Edition, 1994).

3. Late linguist and anthropologist Dell Hymes introduced what he deemed "communicative competence" into our conception of language. This is the ability to use language in social context and social interaction. What a competent speaker needs is not the narrow notion of "good grammar," but good linguistic sense in knowing what to say to whom, under what conditions, and with what consequences. Communicative competence—language appropriateness—is not universal but varies from one speech community to another. A pioneer in the field of sociolinguistics, Hymes's ideas are represented in his "Ethnography of Speaking" chapter in Gladwin and Sturtevant's *Anthropology and Human Behavior* (1962) and his *Foundations in Sociolinguistics: An Ethnographic Approach* (1974).

4. I borrowed this label from language studies of multilingual societies, particularly those on the African continent, and adapted it to sociolinguistic conditions in the United States. See my 1979 article, "Toward Educational Linguistics for the First World" (*College English,* November).

5. See J. L. Dillard's landmark work, *Black English: Its History and Usage in the United States* (1972). For a contemporary update of the Creolist School, see John and Russell Rickford, *Spoken Soul: The Story of Black English* (2000).

6. See, for example, Arthur L. Palacas, "Liberating American Ebonics from Euro-English," *College English* (2001); Ralph Fasold, "Ebonic Need Not Be English," *Georgetown University Round Table on Languages and Linguistics 1999,* Georgetown University Press, 2001; H. Samy Alim and Geneva Smitherman, *Articulate While Black: Barack Obama, Language, and Race in the U.S.* (2012); Geneva Smitherman, "African American Language: So Good It's Bad," in *Word From the Mother: Language and African Americans* (2006).

7. In addition to Dillard's *Black English,* publications on AAL from 1960 through the early 1970s include Ruth I. Golden, *Improving Patterns of Language Usage* (1960); Dillard's "Negro Children's Dialect in the Inner City," in *The Florida Foreign Language Reporter* (Fall, 1967); Joan Baratz and Roger Shuy, *Teaching Black Children to Read* (1969); William Labov, "The Logic of Nonstandard English" (1970) and *Language in the Inner City* (1972); Walt Wolfram, *Detroit Negro Speech* (1970).

CONTENTS

*African American language as a lens for helping students make sense
of how language practices changed from one context or assignment to
the next. In essence, Perryman-Clark provides an example of how the
Students' Right to Their Own Language Resolution translates from
pedagogical theory to pedagogical practice.*

*language attitudes for in-service and preservice teachers. She posits the
formation of a reflexive language policy by helping teachers develop a
sociolinguistic knowledge base that provides students "a rationale from
which to make informed decisions."*

*Zuidema suggests that teaching students about various linguistic myths
can help dispel language prejudices. She provides examples of different
assignments that encourage students to be more conscious of linguistic
differences and prejudices. She also argues that SRTOL should go beyond
teaching students whose first language isn't Standard English, because
all students should learn about student rights. Also included is a
recommended bibliography of readings on "the grammar, vocabulary,
and rhetoric of Ebonics and other stigmatized language systems."*

*Wible's essay examines a Brooklyn College research project that placed
African American Language and culture as the focus of a composition
curriculum during the SRTOL era. Wible argues, however, that
"[b]ecause of charged political and educational discourses of the mid-
1970's . . . publishers shied away from adopting the [research] group's
textbook manuscript." He adds: "In most present-day work around issues
of linguistic diversity and language policy, then, compositionists seem to
agree that the conversations informing the 'Students' Right' theory did
not lead to pedagogical transformation inside the classroom."*

*Lovejoy, Fox, and Wills use the language experiences of three language
teachers to describe various classroom practices that reflect linguistic
diversity in college composition. They stress the need to increase teacher
awareness of linguistic diversity, and advocate ways that this can be
achieved when teachers reflect on their own experiences with language.
Such insight, they maintain, can provide teachers with useful strategies
for integrating policies and practices that affirm students' own language
varieties.*

STUDENTS' RIGHT TO THEIR OWN LANGUAGE

Understanding the Complexities Associated with What It Means to Have the Right to Your Own Language

In the fall of 1971, the officers of the Conference on College Composition and Communication (CCCC) charged a group of courageous and enlightened scholars (the Committee on CCCC Language) to fill a quiet room and begin drafting a language policy resolution that would reverberate through the chambers of history. Their voices, flowing and unified, unfiltered and bold, searched in unison for a message that could define a moment and articulate a rationale for broader language freedoms in education (and beyond) capable of emancipating the many fugitive dialects, which until then found no pardon in universities, colleges, and schools. After months of intense debate and rigorous scholarly work, in March 1972 these appointed and determined scholars presented the CCCC Executive Committee with a document, which in plain language exhorted the organization to adopt a position on language that supported the liberation of dialects and other linguistic variants intimately linked to the lives of people. In doing so, they outlined a new and broad ideological statement that called for teachers to affirm all students' right to exist (e.g., read, write, think, understand, and so on) in their own languages—or whatever language varieties (e.g., dialects, sociolects, argots) students were bringing with them to class. Their efforts, finally recognized at the 1974 CCCC Annual Meeting, led to the now historic Students' Right to Their Own Language (SRTOL) Resolution.[1]

Upon its adoption, SRTOL became one of the most controversial position statements passed in the history of CCCC. The document was intended to respond to questions concerning what educational institutions should do "about the language habits of students who come from a wide variety of social, economic, and cultural backgrounds" (p. 20 in this book*). Questions included but were not limited to: How should teachers instruct students whose heritage languages differ from the more hegemonic varieties traditionally endorsed by

---

*Cross-references to material printed in this volume are identified by "p. xx in this book" at the first instance in each part and "p. xx" for subsequent instances. References to sections not included in this book carry only a page number.

schools? What interventions and policies should be in place to ensure linguistic justice, language preservation, and healthy language development for all youth, regardless of cultural heritage or economic background? And finally, how might educators evolve language instruction in ways consistent with ever-evolving understandings of language, communication, and literacy? While it supposedly addressed the "problem" of language diversity, to many SRTOL failed to fully engage these important questions.

Despite the Committee's attempt to address these questions, the issue of students' rights to their own language in classroom spaces across the country and beyond has remained a complicated one because the policy never answered the question of how to "affirm" student language right, and do so in ways that might lead to learning. Yet, it seemed clear to the Committee that making sense of the complexities and diversities of language required a careful understanding of the nature of language itself. In this light, we reopen the doors to the room that the Committee filled back in 1971, offering readers a unique and critical glimpse of SRTOL's historical and legal basis in relationship to the Resolution's enduring impact on conversations about learning and inclusion across many fields that broadly focus on the study of languages, texts, and cultures. Further, by offering this volume, we hope that readers will gain a greater understanding of SRTOL's theoretical purposes and the theoretical challenges of these purposes, and an understanding of its explicit application and transformation to specific pedagogical practices and classroom research.

There have, of course, been other books written in the last thirty-five or so years that deal with SRTOL from varying angles. Perhaps chief among them is Scott, Straker, and Katz's 2009 volume *Affirming Student's Right to Their Own Language*, an edited collection of essays and research reports that provides a brief but important survey of the legal, cultural historical, and evolutionary topics on language rights in the United States. While their book examines SRTOL and its potential implications across a number of vectors, offering new and needed perspectives in the areas of theory/practice and law/globalization, it was not meant to archive in any exhaustive way the decades-long debates on language rights since the CCCC endorsed SRTOL. This volume, however, examines the implications of the CCCC endorsement in addition to moving critically in the direction of archiving in one place the various research studies, position statements, arguments, commentaries, and practical perspectives borne of or directly and indirectly influenced by SRTOL.

It has now been nearly forty years since SRTOL was first drafted and adopted by the CCCC. Many in fields that examine languages, texts, and cultures find themselves asking similar, if not the same, questions as those asked in 1971 by the Committee on CCCC Language: How might instructors within and across these fields teach across multiple lines of linguistic and cultural difference to help students broker effective communication skills? What frameworks, both theoretical and practical, might be available to guide these various fields in fostering just policies and enhanced practices that respect, value, use, and affirm the linguistic resources that *all* students bring with them to class? How might shifting notions of language, text, space, and culture, particularly as each catalyze linguistic hybridity and pluralism, inform and expand how language and literacy are understood, arranged, and facilitated at sites of inquiry and study?

As scholars of SRTOL, we well understand how an archive of central literature on the Resolution can be a critical resource for the academy, particularly as many academic fields struggle to address questions of language rights in twenty-first-century classrooms. To that point, this collection recognizes the historical and legal implications informing the CCCC's ability to ratify and affirm SRTOL. It also considers the sociocultural and political climate surrounding the Resolution's adoption as a position statement born in the context of the 1970s—a decade of figurative and literal war and radical social and political upheaval following the seismic cultural quakes of the civil rights movement, the antiwar movement, and the initial years of second-wave feminist movements. By 1974 (a year before the Vietnam War would "officially" end and in the fervent heat of the Black Power movement), SRTOL would be adopted by CCCC and its members, challenging long held yet unspoken modernist and sometimes discriminatory approaches to language in communication and composition studies in the United States.

At the time of SRTOL's ratification, many colleges offered open admissions programs—a physical manifestation of the rebalancing of modernity through a postmodern project undertaken to foster greater equity in American education. These programs altered the linguistic landscape of many colleges and universities, and as a result, many colleges and universities were forced to deal with populations of students with which they had never before dealt. These *new* students were linguistically different from the traditional college student at that time.[2] According to Stephen Parks, a history fashioned by war and struggle motivated the creation of the Resolution "as a means to politicize the student population into what might largely be represented as Black Power or New Left ideologies. A desire to learn the 'standard' [was] seen as either politically suspect or a sign of consciousness not fully enlightened" (*Class Politics* 85). At the time of its release, SRTOL seemed as radical as Parks's description. Not only was it suspicious of the primacy of some supposed (or imposed) standard, it rejected it, offering a more democratic framework that represented linguistic pluralism in its place.

Acknowledging key figures who played a part in the adoption of SRTOL offers yet another way of understanding the various implications surrounding the Resolution. Keith Gilyard suggests that African American compositionists in league with the National Council of Teachers of English (NCTE) Black Caucus played a significant role in the adoption of SRTOL. According to Gilyard:

> In November 1971, [Melvin] Butler [chair of the SRTOL language resolution] was named by the CCCC Executive Committee to head a group that would prepare a position statement on students' dialects. African Americans serving with Butler on the committee were Adam Casmier, Richard Long, and Geneva Smitherman. They combined with Ninfa Flores, Jenefer Giannasi, Myrna Harrison, Robert Hogan, Richard Lloyd-Jones,

Elisabeth McPherson, Elizabeth Martin, Nancy Pritchard, and Ross Winterowd to author one of the most important documents ever published by CCCC, the monograph *Students' Right to Their Own Language*. ("Contributions" 638–39)

While SRTOL gained wide-ranging support from many (but certainly not all) African American languages, texts, and cultures scholars, the legal basis of its ratification was also questioned across language, literacy, and composition studies by scholars—either due to lingering cultural ignorance or academic cowardice—who were fearful of the swift tide of reform destabilizing the linguistic status quo. This added to the complexities surrounding the Resolution's upholding. As multiple sources in this volume acknowledge, the voter turnout for the entire organization was only 79–20 (Gilyard "Contributions"; Smitherman "CCCC's Role" p. 58; Parks *Class Politics*; Wible "Pedagogies" p. 353). Hence, while it would gain far-reaching acceptance in the years following its ratification, during the time of its adoption SRTOL wasn't a very popular resolution, even at CCCC. Many other organizations, including the NCTE, refused to affirm the Resolution because of the organization's then conservative stance on language, thus contributing to the lack of widespread support surrounding SRTOL's passage and adoption. In this light, Lawrence Freeman suggested:

> [The] right to the language of one's nurture claimed in the resolution does not, narrowly speaking, have explicit protection under the Federal Constitution and statutes nor under the State constitution nor statutes. However, the First, Ninth, and Fourteenth Amendments of the Federal Constitution appear to offer substantial bases for the claimed right, and Title VII of the Civil Rights Act of 1964 (as amended) in clarifying portions of the Fourteenth Amendment provides yet other bases for the right and policies advocated by the resolution. ("Legal Bases" p. 115)

While neither state nor federal constitutions protect the right to communicate in one's home language varieties, such constitutions, as Freeman suggests, do appear to protect users of nondominant language varieties from various forms of discrimination. However, given present-day amendments to many state constitutions that propose to adopt "English Only"[3] laws, the legal bases surrounding the ratification of SRTOL continue to add layers of texture to the conversation of student language rights. For example, Arizona's controversial and much debated English as an Official Language law has emboldened state school districts to double down on English Only policies that penalize language diversity in classrooms. Other policies that limit linguistic pluralism have also been put forth in Arizona (i.e., banning [or boxing] books written across language lines, firing teachers with accented Englishes, remediating students who are emerging bilinguals, and so on). While some of the more egregious cases of linguistic backslides have been committed in Arizona, Arizona is far from alone when it comes to legalizing linguistic narrowness. Laws passed in states from California to Florida, from Tennessee to Texas have also moved passionately to restrict students' language rights (*Affirming Students'*

Rights), thus relegating SRTOL to the margins of the political debate and to the bottom of many educational institutions' priority lists.

Data, however, consistently veers on the side of student language rights advocates. Studies have too often suggested that home (or native) language fluency is key to language and literacy learning—and increasingly we are learning that home language fluency is also key to learning in general. Hence, we exist in a climate of conflict, where the politics of language and the sciences of language and learning don't always match. The broad affirmation of students' language rights remains complicated today because it requires that language and literacy instructors consider the circumstances under which students should receive rights to their own language (within classrooms and beyond) and whether such rights benefit or inhibit students' success in classrooms and in life, in spite of the emerging politics of linguistic regress.

Although many composition teachers recognize that no one language variety is inherently or naturally superior to another, and that differences "in dialects derive from events in the history of the communities using the language, not from supposed differences in intelligence or physiology" (CCCC "Students' Right" p. 24), many still debate the rhetorical contexts in which language varieties other than what Geneva Smitherman calls the Language of Wider Communication (LWC)[4] are most useful or, worst, appropriate. The argument is consistently the same—that students need to be familiar with the conventions associated with LWC, especially since many employers supposedly desire employees with LWC proficiency even when LWC is not requisite to or necessary for the job. (See Smitherman "A Retrospective"; Gilyard and Richardson; and Alim in this volume for a discussion on language as a gatekeeping mechanism, governing employability and determining who does and does not get to work.) Parks writes that when defending SRTOL, the SRTOL language committee was forced to respond "with an argument about the relationship between linguistic theory and economic reality" (p. 97). For many teachers of writing, theories that inform SRTOL are met with scrutiny because they don't easily address the aforementioned economic critique and have, as a result, faced overwhelming resistance.

Notwithstanding, many scholars on the other side of the economic fence maintain that, unless students' rights are affirmed in full in classrooms and beyond, students will be unfairly positioned in our academies and our economies to fail. That is, these scholars see a direct relationship between language awareness, rights, and respect and social, academic, and economic outcomes. Students whose languages are valued in classrooms perform better in school and in life. Conversely, students whose languages are devalued perform less well in school and in life. Other scholars also speculate that by affirming sociolinguistic hierarchies in classrooms, instructors of writing become complicit in reifying these hierarchies in society, thus helping to reproduce levels of discrimination at work by employers and other nonacademic power structures. Then to even the economic playing field, to more rightly (or righteously) distribute opportunity, these scholars suggest that enforcement of SRTOL is a prerequisite to preparing students for employment after college in two ways:

(1) by providing direct opportunities for learning and success in the class-room, and (2) by indirectly helping to create the conditions of tolerance and cultural celebration so that opportunity isn't angled in just one linguistic direction.

Other critics of SRTOL are not as critical of its economic value. Rather they challenge the document's ability to articulate clearly the relationship between the document in theory and its explicit manifestations in pedagogi-cal practice. The question here isn't how students' right to their own language can lead to a job; it is about how language rights can leverage learning and help instructors of writing teach more effective communication in the class-room. When returning to the question concerning what to do about the lan-guage habits of students who come from a wide variety of social, economic, and cultural backgrounds, many in language, literacy, and composition find themselves longing for specific classroom strategies, activities, and approaches that affirm students' rights to their own languages while also affirming a cur-riculum that has very specific aims. These aims are not always supportive of theories of language learning that SRTOL implies. For instance, Geneva Smitherman recalls that the CCCC Executive Committee established the "Selection and Editorial Committee for Activities Supporting Students' Right to Their Own Language." This group was tasked with collecting teaching materials, lesson plans, curricula, and classroom exercises that teachers could use in their own teaching practices. The group spent four years collecting material but CCCC refused to publish it. Smitherman attributes this startling decision to a change in political climate, from the heady progressive and radi-cal milieu of the early 1970s to the rightward, conservative shift that culmi-nated with the election of Ronald Reagan in 1980 ("A Retrospective" p. 140). As Scott Wible also argues, "In most present-day work around issues of lin-guistic diversity and language policy, then, compositionists seem to agree that the conversations informing the 'Students' Right' theory did not lead to peda-gogical transformation inside the classroom" ("Pedagogies" p. 354). Given this, critics who question what it means to have the right to your own lan-guage in the classroom and what these rights look like in pedagogical practice stand on solid ground in their critiques.

Like composition teachers longing for more specific pedagogical strate-gies for moving SRTOL theory to practice, classroom researchers are also invested in identifying how SRTOL policies support the learning opportuni-ties of students whose home languages differ from LWC. As editors of this collection, we have asked similar questions: How does SRTOL support ESL, EL, ESD, L1, L2, and bilingual students in the classroom? How does it include non-English language varieties, such as the Spanishes, Manderins, Arabics, First Nations languages, and so on, that have increasingly become part of the linguistic stew of American languages? And finally, what empirical research (both from within and from outside classrooms) supports the theoretical pur-poses for and presuppositions of SRTOL? Research on the classroom benefits of SRTOL matter not only for students whose language patterns differ from LWC, but for all students regardless of sociolinguistic location. As Perryman-

Clark argues, all students should be encouraged to make overt connections between their own communicative practices and alternative cultural traditions ("Writing" p. 258).

The texts in this collection each consider the many complexities associated with SRTOL with regard to the historical and political contexts surrounding its adoption, its ideological assumptions and critiques, its relationship between theory and pedagogical practice, and its relationship between theory and research. The aim of the book, then, is to provide examples of groundbreaking texts published on SRTOL beginning with the adoption and publication of the CCCC position statement on SRTOL to present. We include conversations that consider lingering questions for educators—questions that potentially encourage further dialogue in relation to SRTOL and the continuing struggle for student rights.

In Part One, "Foundations," we explore the origins of SRTOL to provide a historical overview and background information pertinent to the manifestation of SRTOL. Texts included in this section create a conversation that traces a historical and, at times, theoretical thread surrounding the adoption of SRTOL by CCCC. The first contribution, "Students' Right to Their Own Language," is the completed version of the Resolution as adopted by CCCC. It includes a brief historical overview of SRTOL within the context of CCCC governance, background regarding the theoretical rationale for its affirmation, and a bibliography of additional readings concerning pedagogical strategies for actualizing SRTOL theories in practice. While SRTOL provides a brief historical overview in relationship to CCCC governance and policy, additional contributions in this section include a behind-the-scenes look at key players who participated in its adoption and historical and sociocultural implications surrounding this participation. These contributions include Geneva Smitherman's "CCCC's Role in the Struggle for Language Rights" and Stephen Parks's "The Students' Right to Their Own Language, 1972–1974."

Two additional contributions in this section contextualize SRTOL beyond the historical context surrounding CCCC and participants in the organization. Lawrence D. Freeman's "The Students' Right to Their Own Language: Its Legal Bases" situates the language policies informing SRTOL within the context of Title VII of the Civil Rights Act of 1964. The legal perspective offered by Freeman deserves attention in this collection because "portions of the Fourteenth Amendment [provide] . . . bases for the right[s] and policies advocated by the resolution" (p. 115). Ann E. Berthoff and William G. Clark's "In Response to the Student's Right to Their Own Language" offers a perspective from scholars who opposed SRTOL because its bibliography did not include texts from scholars associated with the New Criticism of Literary Studies. In short, the texts we offer in this section provide readers with foundational perspectives needed to understand the historical framework guiding the document's adoption and opposition.

In Part Two, "The Politics of Memory: Linguistic Attitudes and Assumptions Post-SRTOL," we offer texts that explore competing theories in language pedagogy and policy both within the academy and beyond it. These theories, as we understand them, transcend SRTOL's direct impact on the composition classroom. For example, contributions made by John Trimbur and Geneva Smitherman examine composition instructors as activists who help students understand the far reach of language beyond the classroom. Their perspectives are key here, as each reminds us that classroom language is never just classroom language but intersecting fields of historical, social, and political inputs/outputs that exist in no neutral relationship to one another or in the orders of thought and knowledge both enhanced as generative cultural products. Implications for this type of transformative work tie well to the civil rights and Black Power movements and situate the work of the composition teacher along political trajectories where intellectual and social work bear real and lasting consequences for rethinking and remaking opportunities for learning and life.

Contrasting the philosophies of composition educators who promote alternative language varieties in the classroom, Allen N. Smith, in "No One Has a Right to His Own Language," argues in support of dominant language standards if students are to be respected and successful in larger society. Smith further suggests that, while there is no such thing as Standard English, the Resolution poses significant contradictions in its message when it promotes the idea of "pay[ing] homage to the vocational needs of our students" by adopting an ideological stance that requires students to "learn to speak and write in a manner acceptable to those who guard the entry points . . . to upward mobility" (p. 164). Smith's argument is about more than the Resolution's contradictions, however. He contends that while students have no "right" to language, teachers on the other hand *do* have a responsibility to teach students how to best approach an audience in a given context. The task then, from his perspective, is to learn how to be flexible enough to accomplish this and to master the kinds of language required to do so most effectively.

Jeff Zorn takes a position similar to Smith's, arguing less against the egalitarian spirit informing SRTOL than with the way SRTOL has been applied. Like Smith, Zorn takes issue with assumptions about terms such as "rights" and "dialects" and in such a way that students (and teachers) are still given the message that they must abandon other Englishes in the classroom. The rub with Smith's and Zorn's stances is that each assumes a "best" approach to language, setting in motion a hierarchy of means that ultimately end in the murky quagmire of political and cultural chaos maintained by the politics of power and the hegemony of dominant language histories. Then, the debate at large offers a vision of success on one hand tied to struggle (i.e., the struggle to accommodate multiple yet contingent status quos and the struggle to resist language acculturation for the local vernaculars of one's own heritage) and on the other tied to pluralism (i.e., defined by "best" approaches to many language, appropriateness, or respect for all languages—these are not the same). Both perspectives seem important to include in this volume, however, because they endure in debates about language rights in the field of composition and beyond and they offer assailable and, we think, fair critiques of the limits of the Resolution.

Joining this conversation is also Patrick Bruch and Richard Marback's "Race, Literacy, and the Value of Rights Rhetoric in Composition Studies." Unlike Smith and Zorn, Bruch and Marback critique monolingualist notions of language in their focus on the relationship between language rights and civic action. Indeed, there are far more voices represented here in favor of linguistic pluralism than perspectives favoring a monolingual approach to student success. This is perhaps because SRTOL does not directly address English-only policies. However, in this section we have tried to place SRTOL broadly in this particular policy debate to highlight the implications that English-only policy has in relationship to SRTOL. In this way, we find arguments by Bruch and Marback compelling, as they encourage compositionists to examine the historical implications surrounding rights rhetoric in the United States. In so doing, they further argue that a multidimensional understanding of language rights supports composition teachers in affirming language policies that "redefine the meanings of literacy and the meanings of inclusion, that composition studies stands to regain in heeding Smitherman's call to begin to celebrate, through engagement, the legacy of rights rhetoric in composition studies" (p. 186). Then, a central piece of Bruch and Marback's argument seems to be unpacking the difference between "struggle for rights" and "struggle over rights." By this and unlike other contributors to this section, Bruch and Marback are suggesting that the struggle of whether we should affirm language rights or not is decided. However, there is a new urgency that deals less with convincing people language rights are important and more with vying for those important rights in the present-day political trenches. Thus, this new urgency underwrites, if you will, a central question of this book: How do we struggle for and achieve that which we deem necessary in vapid climates of political hostility toward language diversities?

In Part Three, "The Special Case of African American Language," we direct attention toward the contributions of scholars who explore SRTOL's impact on student speakers and writers of African American Language[5] (AAL). Here we feature Smitherman's landmark articles "African American Student Writers in the NAEP, 1969–88/89" and "The Blacker the Berry, the Sweeter the Juice" to contextualize the relationship of AAL to SRTOL by explaining in rich detail how and why SRTOL matters to African American student writers. Indeed, while SRTOL was meant to challenge narrow notions of language in composition, in many ways it was aimed specifically at valuing the educational capital that students, and particularly African American students, bring to class. We see this framework of valuing students' linguistic assets, in this case AAL, highlighted throughout the SRTOL literature. In "Students' Right to Possibility: Basic Writing and African American Rhetoric," Keith Gilyard and Elaine Richardson offer a justification for such a framework for implementing SRTOL into practice as they found that "African American students who used more Black discourse scored higher [on essay exams] than those students who did not" (p. 223). Carmen Kynard in her essay "'I Want to Be African': In Search of a Black Radical Tradition/African-American-Vernacularized Paradigm for 'Students' Right to Their Own Language,' Critical Literacy, and

'Class Politics'" examines AAL as well, revisiting Lisa Delpit's notion of the "culture of power" as a trope that has often been used as a rationale for requiring students to learn LWC for upward mobility. Kynard also revisits the works of the National Council of Teachers of English and the Conference on College Composition and Communication's Black Caucus, and the "radical rhetorics" associated with the Black Panthers during the SRTOL era, to critique Steven Parks's discussion of Black Power/Black English. In revisiting each of these works, Kynard hopes to draw parallels between how inadequate responses to social justice in the 1960s and 1970s are similar to inadequate responses to placing SRTOL pedagogical theories into practice in composition classrooms. The balance that she advocates given the prolonged "social inadequacy of nonstandard forms" seems decisive so that students aren't analyzing structures of oppression through mimicry of them.

Additional texts in this section offer specific strategies for promoting SRTOL as a culturally responsive frame for the teaching of African American students in composition classrooms. In this light, Perryman-Clark offers an Afrocentric language-focused course design of a first-year composition curriculum. Featured in this design are sample assignments that engage both linguistic diversity and AAL, and encourage all students to think more critically about both linguistic diversity and the contributions that African American Language scholars have made with regard to the struggle for language rights. Perryman-Clark further emphasizes the concept of language rights by permitting all students "to choose the language varieties that *they* determine most appropriate for each writing situation" (p. 260). Unlike Gilyard and Richardson, who offer justification for a cultural model valuing the linguistic assets students bring with them to class, Perryman-Clark offers a nonexperimental (thus practical) pedagogical model that focuses on the role of African-centered writing curriculum as a means of developing proficient Black writers.

In Part Four, "Pluralism, Hybridity, and Space," we include contributions that examine policy-related implications in relationship to SRTOL. The intent of this section is to update the conversation on SRTOL based on significant scholarship that boldly treads new pathways for where and how issues of language rights should be taken up and understood. Here, the issue of space becomes significant, as SRTOL emerges as a document that frames the issue of space and language as much as it captures the issue of culture and language. By space, we mean the fluid and subtle yet contingent linguistic locations— the linguistic geographies (broadly conceived)—where language is itself relative to relative space, where both can be seen as malleable and contingent. Thus, the issue of space, particularly (but not exclusively) as it relates to culture, in relation to SRTOL organizes what we feel is a fascinating conversation as to the merits of SRTOL in glocal (i.e., the global/local dialogic unitary) contexts.

To this point, some of the contributions in this section critique notions of SRTOL that reinforce tensions that educators often express in discussions of SRTOL. For example, Canagarajah's essay "The Place of World Englishes: Pluralization Continued" complicates the Resolution's emphasis on linguistic dialects by offering a global critique of monolingualistic assumptions of English taught in composition classrooms and their wide-spreading implications for language policy:

> [A]s a teacher of writing for ESL and multilingual students, I am left with the question: what can I do to promote this pedagogical vision in my classroom now? I am concerned about the implications of this policy change for the texts produced by students in my current writing courses. Though the policy changes . . . are admittedly "long term ideals," teachers don't have to wait till these policies trickle down to classrooms. (p. 279)

Canagarajah's concern implies a "new" dynamic in the language/space rights debate that speaks to the swiftly changing, hybridizing, and pluralizing linguistic demography of college campuses. Such spaces, like our globe itself, are increasingly filled by students who transit continents and nations. Here, the issue of geography—specifically critical globalization—demands scholarly attention because it broadens the scope for interpreting SRTOL beyond the situation of the United States.

This is the issue that Gail Okawa takes up in her essay "From 'Bad Attitudes' to(ward) Linguistic Pluralism: Developing Reflective Language Policy among Preservice Teachers." In so doing, she encourages educators to think more broadly about student language rights by identifying and making informed decisions about language policies in education with regard to linguistic knowledge, attitudes, and students' complex backgrounds. Hence, we offer Okawa's contribution here because we acknowledge that the decision to affirm students' language rights is complicated, requiring significant education and research, particularly for preservice teachers and policy makers confronted with vast sociocultural shifts in language learning dynamics due to geo-migrations and other forms of postmodern sociocultural contact.

While globalization sets the stage for new conversations on SRTOL and linguistic pluralism, the stubborn issue of linguistic pluralism within the U.S. borders remains a vexing one. Perhaps chief among scholars looking at local language continuity/discontinuity is Django Paris, whose work examines youth language habits across ethnic lines. In his very informative essay "'They're in My Culture, They Speak the Same Way': African American Language in Multiethnic High Schools," Paris explores the use by vastly different groups of students of AAL within a multiethnic context. Central to Paris's examination of student language is its suggestion that SRTOL might mean students' right to all language varieties, even historically stigmatized varieties, available across socially and culturally bleeding linguistic locations. Here again, the issue of space is addressed, not so much as an artifact of global expansion but as a topic of local coalescence. That is, as different groups more and more collapse lives within shared spaces, the question of language sharings emerge. Importantly, a question at the heart of SRTOL also gets reimagined—what might we in fields of languages, texts, and culture studies learn from these sharings in organically brokered and migratory spaces of linguistic hybridity and pluralism?

In Part Five, "Critical Language Perspectives and Reimagining SRTOL in Writing Classrooms," we offer additional perspectives on language in relation to SRTOL in the composition classroom. These texts reveal the far-reaching impact of SRTOL on college writing students, and the need for all students—not just students of ethnic minority and working-class backgrounds—to learn about the implications of linguistic diversity in educational contexts both inside and outside the classroom. We consider this section one of the most important in the collection, considering that one continued critique of SRTOL lies in its inability to provide explicit pedagogical strategies (Smitherman "CCCC's Role" p. 58; Kinloch p. 429; Ball and Lardner p. 464; Lovejoy et al. p. 381). In some ways, we've already begun to touch on this through the Gilyard and Richardson, Kynyard, and Perryman-Clark articles. The articles in this section are distinct, however, in that they go beyond the case of Afrocentric classrooms. Contributors selected for this section identify specific strategies for general composition classrooms and composition teachers alike. These contributors include Leah Zuidema's "Myth Education: Rationale and Strategies for Teaching against Linguistic Prejudice," which provides specific strategies and resources that not only affirm linguistic diversity in the classroom, but also affirm the need to teach all students about linguistic diversity.

Scott Wible's "Pedagogies of the 'Students' Right' Era: The Language Curriculum Research Group's Project for Linguistic Diversity" also applies the framework of SRTOL to a broader curriculum experience. Wible offers a glimpse inside pedagogical and curricular materials related to a Brooklyn College research project that placed AAL and culture as the focus of a composition curriculum during the SRTOL era. The Brooklyn College research group sought to develop curricula in response to critics who challenge traditional bidialectalism and the complicated relationships it created between students and teachers. They also sought to develop curricula in response to the "back to basics" backlash, where critics charged that traditional bidialectalism lacked a focus on material (in addition to cultural) conditions. While the focus of these works seems to tread to AAL, Wible's framework bears implications for language pedagogy writ large because it imagines how cultural linguistic relevance and its material base can support student learning in the classroom. Although "[b]ecause of charged political and educational discourses of the mid-1970's . . . publishers shied away from adopting the [research] group's textbook manuscript" (p. 354), Wible's Language Curriculum Research Group's Project for Linguistic diversity still provides present-day implications for the continued necessity of pedagogical resources that, in fact, place SRTOL theories into pedagogical practice.

Other contributions in this section offer specific examples of how students write about and respond to SRTOL and linguistically diverse topics. These include Kim Lovejoy et al.'s "From Language Experience to Classroom Practice: Affirming Linguistic Diversity in Writing Pedagogy." Lovejoy et al. provide space for students to draw upon their own language rights as they manipulate linguistic choices in various writing situations and contexts. Their work also emphasizes the teacher—not just teacher experience but the general dissonance between supposed tolerance of linguistic diversity and assessment that is sensitive to it.

Other texts in this section focus more directly on programmatic policy and curricular resources than the students themselves. Stuart Barbier's essay "The Reflection of 'Students' Right to Their Own Language' in First-Year Composition Course Objectives and Descriptions" studied twenty-four Michigan community college first-year composition learning objectives in order to determine whether these course objectives supported SRTOL. Barbier provides key historical insights, contextualizing his findings from the twenty-four colleges. According to Barbier, eight possessed an explicit Standard English (SE) requirement; three possessed an academic discourse/educated policy statement; three had an appropriate conventions statement; four had a grammar/mechanics statement; and six possessed no statement at all (p. 409). Given the history that Barbier lays out, readers understand that, while SRTOL maintains a rethinking of language policy in the classroom, relatively little has changed in terms of how these institutions have chosen to write their goals. The point here is that SRTOL has had marginal if any impact on these institutions at all.

Responding to the constancy of institutional language programs post-SRTOL, H. Samy Alim's essay "Critical Language Awareness in the United States: Revisiting Issues and Revising Pedagogies in a Resegregated Society" calls for educators and administrators to create a "critical language awareness pedagogy" that not only affirms students' rights to their own languages, but also acknowledges the ways that language shapes and impacts larger "sociohistorical" forces that help those from dominant groups exert power over nondominant groups. In making this argument, Alim also acknowledges the need to revisit cultural awareness since language is cultural. Because many critical language awareness courses are often not required for teacher certification in teacher education programs ("CCCC Language Knowledge and Awareness Survey"), Alim also calls for critical language awareness programs in the United States as one important strategy for impacting classroom instruction, where teachers not only take students' languages into account but also account for the interconnectedness of languages with "the larger sociopolitical and sociohistorical phenomena that help to maintain unequal power relations in a still-segregated society" (Barbier p. 420). Here, Alim suggests that social reform is related to, and not the author of, classroom reform. Then the critical projects of educational equity and social justice, as Alim would have them, are related to classrooms and the teachers we prepare to teach in them.

In a similar way, Kinloch examines the complexity of language but among urban youth. She explores their varied and complex perceptions of race, language, and performance within classroom spaces. In so doing, she raises important issues beyond the rights conversation traditionally associated with SRTOL literature. For Kinloch, urban youth, particularly urban Black youth, exist in micropolitical ecologies, where affirming AAL, while not always a right, is an underaddressed social and cultural requirement.

In all, the articles in this section brings us closer to answering those "how to" questions, in addition to the "why's," that so many in fields of language, texts, and culture studies hold. This section writes itself into this volume around theories of critical pedagogical pragmatism, a direction where SRTOL points but where composition instructors still find themselves searching.

The final section in this collection, Part Six, "Lingering Questions," encourages composition teachers to revisit the original and intended purposes of the SRTOL Resolution. It also encourages educators to consider and reconsider existing and newer pedagogies, professional development opportunities, and policy decisions in relationship to student rights. Indeed, the conversation is a continuation of conversations offered in other sections of this book. Yet, in this section, we privilege big questions either left unanswered in other sections or newly put forth due to current debates on language and education. Such considerations suggest that educators reassess the pedagogical effectiveness of SRTOL in a present-day educational context. We conclude with this section because we acknowledge the need to revisit the purpose of the Resolution and the need to respond to the question of what schools "should do about the language habits of students who come from a wide variety of social, economic, and cultural backgrounds" ("Students' Right" p. 20). In addressing this issue, the contributions in this section provide implications for how composition educators may begin and continue responding to questions surrounding language rights in twenty-first-century educational contexts.

The questions and related answers being offered are far from new. But what these perspectives on language and rights offer is a space to continue the conversation. Stanley Fish has helped to fill the ellipse by asking, "What Should Colleges Teach?" in the final part of his three-piece *New York Times* editorial series of that title. Here, Fish addresses the question of how we should teach students to write with regard to SRTOL. For Fish, in order to affirm students' rights educators must equip them with "the tools that speak to its present condition." While different ideological stances concerning where we go from here function in relationship with SRTOL, Fish isn't alone in offering responses of what composition teachers should teach in their classrooms and how they should teach it. H. Samy Alim asks a related question, "What If We Occupied Language?" By occupying language, Alim means controlling public and private discourses, particularly discourses of power, by controlling (in the Marxist sense) the means of understanding (i.e., the meaning itself). Alim argues that tropes of oppression are maintained through nomenclature; hence, we (as scholars, teachers, and students of language) must inhabit language— taking new responsibility beyond our rights to it—to transform the social, cultural, material, and political conditions that plague society.

The final contribution in this collection responds more generally to the question of where to go from here. To address this question, we excerpted a chapter from Arnetha Ball and Ted Lardner, who provide recommendations for both K–12 administrators and writing program administrators for "extra-role" activities intended to serve as additional professional development opportunities for promoting linguistic diversity in schools and university writing programs. Ball and Lardner also provide strategies and recommendations for linguistic diversity within teacher education training programs in order to respond to the question of how we should teach students of marginalized populations, one of the purposes of SRTOL.

It seems appropriate that the book ends with a series of articles that pose enduring questions related to (student) language rights. Those questions fit in an ever-expanding room filled with flowing voices. Each voice responds to a critical question or set of questions raised toward the beginning of this introduction. Of course, the responses to these questions are not always the same. Perhaps the only thing that they have in common is their interest in and insights about SRTOL and the questions it continues to raise about human (language) rights. Some have interpreted those rights as limiting—either as obfuscating the human will toward progress through standardization or as not progressing humanity far enough toward the many distinctions of pluralism that splinter language beyond composites of English. As we hope you will understand after reading this book, SRTOL is not about language. It is about people and about respecting their rights and identities, particularly in public spaces, such as classrooms, workplaces, and the like. It is about understanding people and embracing, affirming, valuing, and bearing witness to who they are, have been, and shall become.

Indeed, this ever-expanding room of flowing voices will be as large or as small as we render it. Nevertheless, it is a room relentlessly fought for, furnished with the eclectic faces of what gets revealed in light but also the pain and prostration, melody and music of a diverse humanity blighted by a politics of intolerance that too often gets hidden in the dark. With this book, we simply hope to have opened the doors to the room, sharing the company of some of its many guests. Surely, as time continues, many more guests will fill the room; we are certain of this. Conversations will continue. New voices heard. New rights fought for. Still, today we take inventory of what has been said and hope that you, as we have, find these voices enlightening.

NOTES

1. We use the labels "SRTOL," "the Resolution," and "the policy" interchangeably throughout this document to refer to the 1974 Students' Right to Their Own Language Resolution.

2. While the United States was populated by a number of historically Black colleges and universities, particularly in its southern states, the historic norm for most American colleges was an overwhelmingly white demographic. This does not mean that students of color (i.e., Native Americans, Latino/as, Asians, and African Americans) did not attend colleges and universities in the United States; it means that such populations had been and continue to be in most cases grossly underrepresented.

3. "English Only" refers loosely to a political perspective/movement aimed at legalizing English as the official language of the United States. The consequences of such legislation would mean that some relative version of the English language would govern all government/public operations and, thereby, outlaw the use of other (American) languages in the conduct of public and government affairs.

4. While terms and phrases such as Language of Wider Communication, Standard(ized) English, Edited American English, and so on reflect intellectual nuances, such items, to our mind, represent and demarcate as a group the dominant or maintained discourse. As such, the terms may be referred to interchangeably throughout this introduction, shifting only in the context of a particular discussion and only as necessary. Contributors to this volume also draw on various

terminologies to describe this dominant (though not easily labeled) discourse. Please refer to their definitions to understand how and why contributors use a particular variant to refer to the dominant discourse.

5. The literature uses various terminology to refer to African American Language (or some understanding of its existence)—Ebonics, African American Vernacular English, Black English, and so on. While these terms represent various intellectual and political distinctions, we use African American Language here to refer to those families of African American discourse that originate from African American (as opposed to Black) culture. Though we make a distinction here, the terms mentioned above may be referred to interchangeability throughout this volume, shifting in the context of a particular discussion as the authors deem necessary. Contributors to this volume, in this way, will draw on various terminologies to delineate languages borne in African American culture. Please refer to their definitions to understand how and why contributors use a particular variant.

WORKS CITED

Barbier, Stuart. "The Reflection of 'Students' Right to Their Own Language' in First-Year Composition Course Objectives and Descriptions." *TETYC* 30.3 (2003): [pp. 404–414 in this book]. Print.

CCCC Language Policy Committee. *Language Knowledge and Awareness Survey.* Urbana: NCTE Research Foundation, 2000. Print.

Gilyard, Keith. "African American Contributions to Composition Studies." *CCC* 50.4 (1999): 626–44. Print.

Lovejoy, Kim Brian, Steve Fox, and Katherine V. Wills. "From Language Experience to Classroom Practice: Affirming Linguistic Diversity in Writing Pedagogy." *Pedagogy* 9.2 (2009): [pp. 381–403 in this book]. Print.

Parks, Stephen. *Class Politics: The Movement for the Students' Right to Their Own Language.* Urbana: NCTE, 1999. Print.

Scott, Jerrie Cobb, Dolores Y. Straker, and Laurie Katz, eds. *Affirming Students' Right to Their Own Language: Language Policies and Pedagogical Practices.* New York: Routledge, 2009. Print.

PART ONE

Foundations

1 Students' Right to Their Own Language

CONFERENCE ON COLLEGE COMPOSITION AND COMMUNICATION COMMITTEE ON LANGUAGE POLICY

EXPLANATION OF ADOPTION
(The following appeared as a Special Issue of *CCC*, Fall, 1974, Vol. XXV.)

To Readers of *CCC*:
This special issue of *CCC* includes the resolution on language adopted by members of CCCC in April 1974; the background statement explaining and supporting that resolution; and the bibliography that gives sources of some of the ideas presented in the background statement; besides offering those interested in the subject of language some suggested references for further reading. This publication climaxes two years of work, by dedicated members of CCCC, toward a position statement on a major problem confronting teachers of composition and communication: how to respond to the variety in their students' dialects.

A first draft of the resolution on language was presented to the Executive Committee at its meeting in March 1972, by a committee specially appointed by the officers in the fall of 1971 to prepare a position statement on students' dialects. After some amendments adopted by the Executive Committee at its meeting in November 1972, the resolution reads:

> We affirm the students' right to their own patterns and varieties of language—the dialects of their nurture or whatever dialects in which they find their own identity and style. Language scholars long ago denied that the myth of a standard American dialect has any validity. The claim that any one dialect is unacceptable amounts to an attempt of one social group to exert its dominance over another. Such a claim leads to false advice for speakers and writers, and immoral advice for humans. A nation proud of its diverse heritage and its cultural and racial variety will preserve its heritage of dialects. We affirm strongly that teachers must have the experiences and training that will enable them to respect diversity and uphold the right of students to their own language.

From *College Composition and Communication* 25.3 (1974): 1–32.

Realizing that the resolution would be controversial, and that it contained many assertions that could best be explained by reference to current research on dialects and usage, the Executive Committee appointed a special committee to draft a statement that would offer this explanatory background. The special committee reported at its New Orleans meeting in 1973, where its initial draft statement was thoroughly discussed. A revised draft was presented to and accepted by the Executive Committee at the Philadelphia NCTE meeting in November 1973. The resolution and background statement were then distributed to members of CCCC, and the resolution was considered at the regular business meeting in Anaheim in April 1974. It was adopted as the policy of CCCC by a vote of 79–20.

Because of the interest generated by the resolution and background statement, the officers decided that it should be sent to members in durable form, as a special issue of CCC, and should be made available to anyone interested in obtaining copies.

All members of CCCC, I think, owe much to the members of the committee that wrote this perceptive statement, which has won the praise of many linguists and rhetoricians. Special thanks are due to Richard Lloyd-Jones, who synthesized the contributions of different committee members into the final text you now have. Special thanks are due, also, to Melvin Butler of Southern University, chairperson of the special committee, whose untimely death prevented him from seeing the publication of the statement on which he and his fellow committee members worked so faithfully. This issue of CCC will be, we hope, a lasting tribute to his efforts.

Richard L. Larson
1974 Chair, CCCC

INTRODUCTION

American schools and colleges have, in the last decade, been forced to take a stand on a basic educational question: what should the schools do about the language habits of students who come from a wide variety of social, economic, and cultural backgrounds? The question is not new. Differences in language have always existed, and the schools have always wrestled with them, but the social upheavals of the 1960's, and the insistence of submerged minorities on a greater share in American society, have posed the question more insistently and have suggested the need for a shift in emphasis in providing answers. Should the schools try to uphold language variety, or to modify it, or to eradicate it?

The emotional nature of the controversy has obscured the complexities of the problem and hidden some of the assumptions that must be examined before any kind of rational policy can be adopted. The human use of language is not a simple phenomenon: sophisticated research in linguistics and sociology has demonstrated incontrovertibly that many long held and passionately cherished notions about language are misleading at best, and often completely erroneous. On the other hand, linguistic research, advanced as much of it is, has not yet produced any absolute, easily understood explanation of how people acquire language or how habits acquired so early in life that they defy conscious analysis can be consciously changed. Nor is the linguistic information that is available very widely disseminated. The training of most English teachers has concentrated on the appreciation and analysis of literature, rather than on an understanding of the nature of language, and many teachers are, in consequence, forced to take a position on an aspect of their discipline about which they have little real information.

And if teachers are often uninformed, or misinformed, on the subject of language, the general public is even more ignorant. Lack of reliable information, however, seldom prevents people from discussing language questions with an air of absolute authority. Historians, mathematicians, and nurses all hold decided views on just what English teachers should be requiring. And through their representatives on Boards of Education and Boards of Regents, businessmen, politicians, parents, and the students themselves insist that the values taught by the schools must reflect the prejudices held by the public. The English profession, then, faces a dilemma: until public attitudes can be changed—and it is worth remembering that the past teaching in English classes has been largely responsible for those attitudes—shall we place our emphasis on what the vocal elements of the public think it wants or on what the actual available linguistic evidence indicates we should emphasize? Shall we blame the business world by saying, "Well, we realize that human beings use language in a wide variety of ways, but employers demand a single variety"?

Before these questions can be responsibly answered, English teachers at all levels, from kindergarten through college, must uncover and examine some of the assumptions on which our teaching has rested. Many of us have taught as though there existed somewhere a single American "standard English" which could be isolated, identified, and accurately defined. We need to know whether "standard English" is or is not in some sense a myth. We have ignored, many of us, the distinction between speech and writing and have taught the language as though the *talk* in any region, even the talk of speakers with prestige and power, were identical to edited *written* English.

We have also taught, many of us, as though the "English of educated speakers," the language used by those in power in the community, had an inherent advantage over other dialects as a means of expressing thought or emotion, conveying information, or analyzing concepts. We need to discover whether our attitudes toward "educated English" are based on some inherent superiority of the dialect itself or on the social prestige of those who use it. We need to ask ourselves whether our rejection of students who do not adopt the dialect most familiar to us is based on any real merit in our dialect or whether we are actually rejecting the students themselves, rejecting them because of their racial, social, and cultural origins.

And many of us have taught as though the function of schools and colleges were to erase differences. Should we, on the one hand, urge creativity and individuality in the arts and the sciences, take pride in the diversity of our historical development, and, on the other hand, try to obliterate all the differences in the way Americans speak and write? Our major emphasis has been on uniformity, in both speech and writing; would we accomplish more, both educationally and ethically, if we shifted that emphasis to precise, effective, and appropriate communication in diverse ways, whatever the dialect?

Students are required by law to attend schools for most of their adolescent years, and are usually required by curriculum makers to take English every one of those years, often including "developmental" or "compensatory" English well into college if their native dialect varies from that of the middle class. The result is that students who come from backgrounds where the prestigious variety of English is the normal medium of communication have built-in advantages that enable them to succeed, often in spite of and not because of, their schoolroom training in "grammar." They sit at the head of the class, are accepted at "exclusive" schools, and are later rewarded with positions in the business and social world. Students whose nurture and experience give them a different dialect are usually denied these rewards. As English teachers, we are responsible for what our teaching does to the self-image and the self-esteem of our students. We must decide what elements of our discipline are really important to us, whether we want to share with our students the richness of all varieties of language, encourage linguistic virtuosity, and say with Langston Hughes:

> I play it cool and dig all jive
> That's the reason I stay alive
> My motto as I live and learn
> Is to dig and be dug in return.

It was with these concerns in mind that the Executive Committee of the Conference on College Composition and Communication, in 1972, passed the following resolution:

> We affirm the students' right to their own patterns and varieties of language—the dialects of their nurture or whatever dialects in which they find their own identity and style. Language scholars long ago denied that the myth of a standard American dialect has any validity. The claim that any one dialect is unacceptable amounts to an attempt of one social group to exert its dominance over another. Such a claim leads to false advice for speakers and writers, and immoral advice for humans. A nation proud of its diverse heritage and its cultural and racial variety will preserve its heritage of dialects. We affirm strongly that teachers must have the experiences and training that will enable them to respect diversity and uphold the right of students to their own language.

The members of the Committee realized that the resolution would create controversy and that without a clear explanation of the linguistic and social knowledge on which it rests, many people would find it incomprehensible. The members of the Executive Committee, therefore, requested a background statement which would examine some common misconceptions about language and dialect, define some key terms, and provide some suggestions for sounder, alternate approaches. What follows is not, then, an introductory course in linguistics, nor is it a teaching guide. It is, we hope, an answer to some of the questions the resolution will raise.

UNDERSTANDING LANGUAGE VARIETIES

A dialect is a variety of a language used by some definable group. Everyone has a personal version of language, an idiolect, which is unique, and closely related groups of idiolects make up dialects. By custom, some dialects are spoken. Others are written. Some are shared by the community at large. Others are confined to small communities, neighborhoods, or social groups. Because of this, most speakers, consciously or unconsciously, use more than one dialect. The need for varying dialects may arise from a speaker's membership in different age or educational groups. Or, it may arise from membership in groups tied to physical localities. The explanation of what a dialect is becomes difficult when we recognize that dialects are developed in response to many kinds of communication needs. And further complications occur because the user of a specific dialect, as a function of habit, can choose alternate forms which seem effective for given situations.

A dialect is the variety of language used by a group whose linguistic habit patterns both reflect and are determined by shared regional, social, or cultural perspectives. The user of a specific dialect employs the phonological (pronunciation), lexical (vocabulary), and syntactic patterns (word arrangement) and variations of the given "community." Because geographical and social isolation are among the causes of dialect differences, we can roughly speak about regional and social dialects. Regional differences in phonology may become quite evident when one hears a Bostonian say "pahk the cah" where a Midwesterner would say "parrk the car." Regional differences in vocabulary are also quite noticeable as in the words used throughout the country for a carbonated drink. Depending on where one is geographically, you can hear "soda," "soda water," "sweet soda," "soft drink," "tonic," "pop," or "cold drink." Regional differences in syntactic patterns are found in such statements as "The family is to home," and "The family is at home." Social differences can also be detected. Social differences in phonology are reflected in "goil" versus "girl." Social differences in vocabulary are reflected in the distinctions made between "restaurant" and "cafe." Syntactic phrases such as "those flowers" tend to have more prestige than "them flowers," and "their flowers" has more prestige than "they flowers."

It is not surprising to find two or more social dialects co-existing in a given region. In small towns where a clear social cleavage exists between the wealthier, more educated portion of the population and the mass of people, the difference may be reflected in their speechways. The local banker whose dialect reveals his group allegiance to the statewide financial community still is able to communicate easily with the local farmhand who may rarely cross the county line and whose linguistic habit patterns reveal different allegiances.

In many larger American cities people of the same ethnic origins tend to live in a single neighborhood and have a common culture and thus share a dialect. Through their clothing, games, and holidays they may preserve the values and customs of the "old country" or "back home." And in their restaurants, churches, schools, and homes, one may hear the linguistic values and customs of their heritage preserved. For example, a neighborhood group's cultural orientation may encourage its members to differentiate between action and intention in the immediate future and in a still-further immediate future through "I'm a-do it" and "I'm a'gonna do it." Yet, a neighborhood is not a country, so speakers of several dialects may mingle there and understand each other. Visitors with yet another heritage may render an approximation of such differentiation through "I'll do it now" and "I'll do it soon." Pride in cultural heritage and linguistic habit patterns need not lead either group to attack the other as they mingle and communicate.

Differences in dialects derive from events in the history of the communities using the language, not from supposed differences in intelligence or physiology. Although they vary in phonology, in vocabulary, and in surface grammatical patterns, the differences between neighboring dialects are not sufficiently wide to prevent full mutual comprehension among speakers of those dialects. That is to say, when speakers of a dialect of American English claim not to understand speakers of another dialect of the same language, the impediments are likely to be attitudinal. What is really the hearer's resistance to any unfamiliar form may be interpreted as the speaker's fault. For example, an unfamiliar speech rhythm and resulting pronunciation while ignoring the content of the message. When asked to respond to the content, they may be unable to do so and may accuse the speaker of being impossible to understand. In another situation, vocabulary differences may require that the hearers concentrate more carefully on contextual cues. If the word "bad" is being used as a term of praise, the auditor may have to pay unusual attention to context. Although the usual redundancies of speech ordinarily will provide sufficient cues to permit a correct interpretation, still the auditor has to work harder until he becomes accustomed to the differences. The initial difficulties of perception can be overcome and should not be confused with those psychological barriers to communication which may be generated by racial, cultural, and social differences and attitudes.

The manner in which children acquire language (and hence dialect) competence is unknown in spite of some research and much speculation on the subject. Theories ranging from the purely behavioristic to the highly metaphysical have been proposed. What is demonstrable, and hence known, is that children at very early ages begin to acquire performance skills in the dialect(s) used in their environment, and that this process is amazingly rapid compared to many other types of learning.

Before going to school, children possess basic competence in their dialects. For example, children of six know how to manipulate the rules for forming plurals in their dialects. In some dialects children add an "s" to the word to be pluralized as in "book/books." In some other dialects, plurality is signaled by the use of the preceding word as in "*one* book/*two* book." But in either instance children have mastered the forms of plurality and have learned a principle of linguistic competence. It is important to remember that plurality signals for the nurture dialect reflect children's reality and will be their first choice in performance; plurality rules for another dialect may simply represent to them the rituals of someone else's linguistic reality.

In a specific setting, because of historical and other factors, certain dialects may be endowed with more prestige than others. Such dialects are sometimes called "standard" or "consensus" dialects. These designations of prestige are not inherent in the dialect itself, but are *externally imposed*, and the prestige of a dialect shifts as the power relationships of the speakers shift.

The English language at the beginning of its recorded history was already divided into distinct regional dialects. These enjoyed fairly equal prestige for centuries. However, the centralization of English political and commercial life at London gradually gave the dialect spoken there a preeminence over other dialects. This process was far advanced when printing was invented; consequently, the London dialect became the dialect of the printing press, and the dialect of the printing press became the so-called "standard" even though a number of oral readings of one text would reveal different pronunciations and rhythmic patterns across dialects. When the early American settlers arrived on this continent, they brought their British dialects with them. Those dialects were altered both by regional separation from England and concentration into sub-groups within this country as well as by contact with the various languages spoken by the Indians they found here and with the various languages spoken by the immigrants who followed.

At the same time, social and political attitudes formed in the old world followed to the new, so Americans sought to achieve linguistic marks of success as exemplified in what they regarded as proper, cultivated usage. Thus the dialect used by prestigious New England speakers early became the "standard" the schools attempted to teach. It remains, during our own time, the dialect that style books encourage us to represent in writing. The diversity of our cultural heritage, however, has created a corresponding language diversity and, in the 20th century, most linguists agree that there is no single, homogeneous American "standard." They also agree that, although the amount of prestige and power possessed by a group can be recognized through its dialect, no dialect is inherently good or bad.

The need for a written dialect to serve the larger, public community has resulted in a general commitment to what may be called "edited American English," that prose which is meant to carry information about our representative problems and interests. To carry such information through aural-oral media, "broadcast English" or "network standard" has been developed and given precedence. Yet these dialects are subject to change, too. Even now habit patterns from other types of dialects are being incorporated into them. Our pluralistic society requires many varieties of language to meet our multiplicity of needs.

Several concepts from modern linguistics clarify and define problems of dialect. Recent studies verify what our own casual observation should lead us to believe—namely, that intelligence is not a factor in the child's acquisition of a basic language system. In fact, only when I.Q. is at about fifty or below does it become significant in retarding the rate and completeness with which children master their native spoken dialect. Dialect switching, however, becomes progressively more difficult as the speaker grows older. As one passes from infancy to childhood to adolescence and to maturity, language patterns become more deeply ingrained and more a part of the individual's self-concept; hence they are more difficult to alter.

Despite ingrained patterns characteristic of older people, every speaker of a language has a tremendous range of versatility, constantly making subtle changes to meet various situations. That is, speakers of a language have mastered a variety of ranges and levels of usage; no one's idiolect, however well established, is monolithic and inflexible. This ability of the individual speaker to achieve constant and subtle modulations is so pervasive that it usually goes unnoticed by the speaker and the hearers alike.

The question, then, is not whether students can make language changes, for they do so all the time, but whether they can step over the hazily defined boundaries that separate dialects. Dialect switching is complicated by many factors, not the least of which is the individual's own cultural heritage. Since dialect is not separate from culture, but an intrinsic part of it, accepting a new dialect means accepting a new culture; rejecting one's native dialect is to some extent a rejection of one's culture.

Therefore, the question of whether or not students *will* change their dialect involves their acceptance of a new—and possibly strange or hostile—set of cultural values. Although many students *do* become bidialectal, and many *do* abandon their native dialects, those who don't switch may have any of a number of reasons, some of which may be beyond the school's right to interfere.

In linguistic terms the normal teenager has *competence* in his native dialect, the ability to use all of its structural resources, but the actual *performance* of any speaker in any dialect always falls short of the totality implied by competence. No one can ever use all of the resources of a language, but one function of the English teacher is to activate the student's competence, that is, increase the range of his habitual performance.

Another insight from linguistic study is that differences among dialects in a given language are always confined to a limited range of *surface* features that have no effect on what linguists call *deep structure*, a term that might be roughly translated as "meaning." For instance, the following groups of sentences have minor surface differences, but obviously share meanings:

Herbert saw Hermione yesterday.
Herbert seen Hermione yesterday.

Mary's daddy is at home.
Mary's daddy is to home.
Mary daddy home.

Bill is going to the circus.
Bill, he's going to the circus.
Bill he going to the circus.

Preference for one form over another, then, is not based on meaning or even "exactness" of expression, but depends on social attitudes and cultural norms. The surface features are recognized as signs of social status.

LANGUAGE VARIETIES AND LEARNING

The linguistic concepts can bring a new understanding of the English teacher's function in dealing with reading and writing skills. Schools and colleges emphasize one form of language, the one we called Edited American English (EAE). It is the written language of the weekly news magazines, of almost all newspapers, and of most books. This variety of written English can be loosely termed a dialect, and it has pre-empted a great deal of attention in English classes.

If a speaker of any dialect of a language has competence (but not necessarily the ability to perform) in any other dialect of that language, then dialect itself cannot be posited as a reason for a student's failure to be able to read EAE. That is, dialect itself is not an impediment to reading, for the process of reading involves decoding to meaning (deep structure), not decoding to an utterance. Thus, the child who reads

Phillip's mother is in Chicago.

out loud as

Phillip mother in Chicago.

has read correctly, that is, has translated the surface of an EAE sentence into a meaning and has used his own dialect to give a surface form to that meaning. Reading, in short, involves the acquisition of meanings, not the ability to reproduce meanings in any given surface forms.

Reading difficulties may be a result of inadequate vocabulary, problems in perception, ignorance of contextual cues that aid in the reading process, lack of familiarity with stylistic ordering, interference from the emotional bias of the material, or combinations of these. In short, reading is so complicated a process that it provides temptations to people who want to offer easy explanations and solutions.

This larger view should make us cautious about the assumption that the students' dialect interferes with learning to read. Proceeding from such a premise, current "dialect" readers employ one of two methods. Some reading materials are written completely in the students' dialect with the understanding that later the students will be switched to materials written in the "standard" dialect. Other materials are written in companion sets of "Home" version and "School" version. Students first read through the "dialect" version, then through the *same* booklet written in "school" English. Both methods focus primarily on a limited set of surface linguistic features, as for example, the deletion of -*ed* in past tense verbs or the deletion of -*r* in final position.

To cope with our students' reading problem, then, we cannot confine ourselves to the constricting and ultimately ineffectual dialect readers designed for the "culturally deprived." We should structure and select materials geared to complex reading problems and oriented to the experience and sophistication of our students. An urban eight-year-old who has seen guns and knives in a street fight may not be much interested in reading how Jane's dog Spot dug in the neighbor's flower bed. Simply because "Johnny can't read" doesn't mean "Johnny is immature" or "Johnny can't think." He may be bored. Carefully chosen materials will certainly expose students to new horizons and should increase their awareness and heighten their perceptions of the social reality. Classroom reading materials can be employed to further our students' reading ability and, at the same time, can familiarize them with other varieties of English.

Admittedly, the kinds of materials we're advocating are, at present, difficult to find, but some publishers are beginning to move in this direction. In the meantime, we can use short, journalistic pieces, such as those found on the editorial pages of newspapers, we might rely on materials composed by our students, and we can certainly write our own materials. The important fact to remember is that speakers in any dialect encounter essentially the same difficulties in reading, and thus we should not be so much interested in changing our students' dialect as in improving their command of the reading process.

The ability to write EAE is quite another matter, for learning to write a given dialect, like learning to speak a dialect, involves the activation of areas of competence. Further, learning to write in any dialect entails the mastery of such conventions as spelling and punctuation, surface features of the written language. Again, native speakers of *any* dialect of a language have virtually total competence in all dialects of that language, but they may not have learned (and may never learn) to punctuate or spell, and, indeed, may not even learn the mechanical skill of forming letters and sequences of letters with a writing instrument. And even if they do, they may have other problems in transferring ease and fluency in speech to skill in writing.

Even casual observation indicates that dialect as such plays little if any part in determining whether a child will ultimately acquire the ability to write EAE. In fact, if speakers of a great variety of American dialects do master EAE—from Senator Sam Ervin to Senator Edward Kennedy, from Ernest Hemingway to William Faulkner—there is no reason to assume that dialects such as urban black and Chicano impede the child's ability to learn to write EAE while countless others do not. Since the issue is not the capacity of the dialect itself, the teacher can concentrate on building up the students' confidence in their ability to write.

If we name the essential functions of writing as expressing oneself, communicating information and attitudes, and discovering meaning through both logic and metaphor, then we view variety of dialects as an advantage. In self-expression, not only one's dialect but one's idiolect is basic. In communication one may choose roles which imply certain dialects, but the decision is a social one, for the dialect itself does not limit the information which can be carried, and the attitudes may be most clearly conveyed in the dialect the writer finds most congenial. Dialects are all equally serviceable in logic and metaphor.

Perhaps the most serious difficulty facing "non-standard" dialect speakers in developing writing ability derives from their exaggerated concern for the *least* serious aspects of writing. If we can convince our students that spelling, punctuation, and usage are less important than content, we have removed a major obstacle in their developing the ability to write. Examples of student writing are useful for illustrating this point. In every composition class there are examples of writing which is clear and vigorous despite the use of non-standard forms (at least as described by the handbook)—and there are certainly many examples of limp, vapid writing in "standard dialect." Comparing the writing allows the students to see for themselves that dialect seldom obscures clear, forceful writing. EAE is important for certain kinds of students, its features are easily identified and taught, and school patrons are often satisfied when it is mastered, but that should not tempt teachers to evade the still more important features of language.

When students want to play roles in dialects other than their own, they should be encouraged to experiment, but they can acquire the fundamental skills of writing in their own dialect. Their experiments are ways of becoming more versatile. We do not condone ill-organized, imprecise, undefined, inappropriate writing in any dialect; but we are especially distressed to find sloppy writing approved so long as it appears with finicky correctness in "school standard" while vigorous and thoughtful statements in less prestigious dialects are condemned.

All languages are the product of the same instrument, namely, the human brain. It follows, then, that all languages and all dialects are essentially the same in their deep structure, regardless of how varied the surface structures might be. (This is equal to saying that the human brain is the human brain.) And if these hypotheses are true, then all controversies over dialect will take on a new dimension. The question will no longer turn on language *per se*, but will concern the nature of a society which places great value on given surface features of language and proscribes others, for any language or any dialect will serve any purpose that its users want it to serve.

There is no evidence, in fact, that enables us to describe any language or any dialect as incomplete or deficient apart from the conditions of its use. The limits of a particular speaker should not be interpreted as a limit of the dialect.

Just as people suppose that speakers who omit the plural inflection as in "six cow" instead of "six cows" cannot manipulate the concept of plurality, so also some believe that absence of tense markers as in "yesterday they *look* at the flood damage" indicates that the speaker has no concept of time. Yet these same people have no difficulty in understanding the difference between "now I *cut* the meat / yesterday I *cut* the meat," also without a tense marker. The alternative forms are adequate to express meaning.

And experience tells us that when speakers of any dialect need a new word for a new thing, they will invent or learn the needed word. Just as most Americans added "sputnik" to their vocabularies a decade or more ago, so speakers of other dialects can add such words as "periostitis" or "interosculate" whenever their interests demand it.

LANGUAGE VARIETIES AND EDUCATIONAL POLICY AND PRACTICE

Since the eighteenth century, English grammar has come to mean for most people the rules telling one how to speak and write in the best society. When social groups were clearly stratified into "haves" and "have-nots," there was no need for defensiveness about variations in language—the landlord could understand the speech of the stable boy, and neither of them worried about language differences. But when social and economic changes increased social mobility, the members of the "rising middle class," recently liberated from and therefore immediately threatened by the lower class, demanded books of rules telling them how to act in ways that would not betray their background and would solidly establish them in their newly acquired social group. Rules regulating social behavior were compiled in books of etiquette; rules regulating linguistic behavior were compiled in dictionaries and grammar books. Traditional grammar books were unapologetically designed to instill linguistic habits which, though often inconsistent with actual language practice and sometimes in violation of common sense, were intended to separate those who had "made it" from those who had not, the powerful from the poor.

Practices developed in England in the eighteenth century were transported wholesale to the New World. Linguistic snobbery was tacitly encouraged by a slavish reliance on rules "more honored in the breach than the observance," and these attitudes had consequences far beyond the realm of language. People from different language and ethnic backgrounds were denied social privileges, legal rights, and economic opportunity, and their inability to manipulate the dialect used by the privileged group was used as an excuse for this denial. Many teachers, moved by the image of the "melting pot," conscientiously tried to eliminate every vestige of behavior not sanctioned in the grammar books, and the schools rejected as failures all those children who did not conform to the linguistic prejudices of the ruling middle class. With only slight modifications, many of our "rules," much of the "grammar" we still teach, reflects that history of social climbing and homogenizing.

Many handbooks still appeal to social-class etiquette and cultural stasis rather than to the dynamic and creative mechanisms which are a part of our language. They attempt to show one public dialect (EAE) which generates its own writing situations and its own restraints. By concentrating almost exclusively on EAE, such handbooks encourage a restrictive language bias. They thus ignore many situations which require other precise uses of language. We know that American English is pluralistic. We know that our students can and do function in a growing multiplicity of language situations which require different dialects, changing interconnections of dialects, and dynamic uses of language. But many handbooks often present only the usage of EAE for both written and spoken communication. Usage choices are presented as single-standard etiquette rules rather than as options for effective expression. This restrictive attitude toward usage is intensified by the way school grammar is presented as a series of directives in which word choice, syntax, surface features of grammar, and manuscript conventions are lumped together in guides of "correctness." These restrictive handbooks, by their very nature, encourage their users toward imitation, not toward generation of original written statements. By appealing to what is labeled "proper," they encourage an elitist attitude. The main values they transmit are stasis, restriction, manners, status, and imitation.

Teachers who are required to use such handbooks must help their students understand the implied restrictions of these texts. At best they are brief descriptions of the main features of EAE, and they clearly point out the limits of their own structures. Students should be encouraged to think of the handbook simply as a very limited language resource, and to recognize that its advice usually ignores the constraints of the situation. We alter our choices to create appropriate degrees of social intimacy. You don't talk to your kids as if they were a senate committee. A personal letter is not a technical report. Students use different forms of language in talking to their friends than they use in addressing their teachers; they use yet another style of language in communications with their parents or younger children; boys speak differently to boys when they are in the presence of girls than when the boys are alone, and so on — the list can be expanded indefinitely by altering the circumstances of time, place, and situation.

The man who says, "He had a pain in his neck, the kind you get when you've suffered a bore too long," is creating an emotional bond with his hearers. Using the handbook rule, "avoid unnecessary shifts in person," to criticize the speaker's choice denies a very important language skill, a sense of how to adjust the tone to the situation.

Furthermore, students need to recognize the difference between handbook rules and actual performance. When, after a half hour's work on pronoun reference practice, carefully changing "everyone/their" to "everyone/his," the teacher says, "Everyone can hand in their papers now," students can recognize the limits of the rule. They can compare the handbook's insistence on "the reason that" with the practice of the national newscaster who says, "the reason for the price increase is because. . . ." They can go on to consider what assumption underlies the claim that "he does" is always clearer than "he do."

By discussions of actual student writing both students and teachers can learn to appreciate the value of variant dialects and recognize that a deviation from the handbook rules seldom interferes with communication. The student who writes, "The Black Brother just don't believe he's going to be treated like a man anyway," is making himself completely clear. Students and teachers can go on to discuss situations in which adherence to handbook rules might actually damage the effectiveness of the writing. Through such discussions of tone, style, and situation, students and teachers can work together to develop a better understanding of the nature of language and a greater flexibility and versatility in the choices they make. The handbook in its clearly limited role can then be serviceable within the framework of a flexible rhetoric.

Teachers need to sensitize their students to the options they already exercise, particularly in speaking, so as to help them gain confidence in communicating in a variety of situations. Classroom assignments should be structured to help students make shifts in tone, style, sentence structure and length, vocabulary, diction, and order; in short, to do what they are already doing, better. Since dialects are patterns of choice among linguistic options, assignments which require variety will also open issues of dialect.

Role playing in imaginary situations is one effective way of illustrating such options, especially if the situations are chosen to correspond with a reality familiar to the students. Materials that demonstrate the effective use of variant dialects are also useful. A novel like John O. Killens' *Cotillion*, for instance, combines an exciting, coherent narrative structure with a rich, versatile range of Black speech patterns used in various social situations, and thus can be used to show both literary and linguistic artistry.

Discussions must always emphasize the effectiveness of the various options, and must avoid the simplistic and the patronizing. Tapes, drills, and other instructional materials which do nothing more than contrast surface features (the lack of *-s* in third person singular present tense verbs, or *-ed* in past tense verbs, for instance) do not offer real options. Instead, because they are based on a "difference-equals-deficit" model, they imply that the students' own dialects are inferior and somehow "wrong" and that therefore the students' homes, the culture in which they learned their language, are also "wrong." Such simplistic approaches are not only destructive of the students' self-confidence, they fail to deal with larger and more significant options.

Linguistic versatility includes more than handbook conformity. Becoming aware of a variety of pitch patterns and rhythms in speech can reduce failures in understanding caused by unfamiliarity with the cadence another speaker uses. Listening for whole contexts can increase the ability to recognize the effect of such ponderous words as "notwithstanding" or "nevertheless" as well as pick up the meaning of unfamiliar names of things. Recognizing contradictions and failures in logic can help students concentrate on the "sense" of their communication rather than on its form. Identifying the ways language is used in politics and advertising can help students see when they are being manipulated and reduce their vulnerability to propaganda. Practice in exercising options can make students realize that vividness, precision, and accuracy can be achieved in any dialect, and can help them see that sloppiness and imprecision are irresponsible choices in any dialect—that good speech and good writing ultimately have little to do with traditional notions of surface "correctness."

By building on what students are already doing well as part of their successes in daily living, we can offer them dialect options which will increase rather than diminish their self-esteem, and by focusing on the multiple aspects of the communication process, we can be sure we are dealing with the totality of language, not merely with the superficial features of "polite usage."

Standardized tests also create special kinds of problems for students and educators. These tests depend on verbal fluency, both in reading the directions and in giving the answers, so even slight variations in dialect may penalize students by slowing them down. Not only are almost all standardized tests written in test jargon and focused on EAE, they also incorporate social, cultural, and racial biases which cannot hold for all students. Rural Americans may not know much about street life, and urban students will know little about the habits of cows. Words like "punk," "boody," or "joog," if they appeared in tests, would favor one dialect group over others. Tests which emphasize capitalization, punctuation, and "polite usage" favor one restrictive dialect. Even literature tests which emphasize the reading lists of the traditional anthologies favor one kind of school literature. Consequently, those students fluent in test jargon and familiar with the test subject matter are excessively rewarded.

Another problem of standardized tests is that they may further restrict the students' worlds and ultimately penalize both those who do well and those who "fail." Those who succeed may become so locked into the rewarding language patterns that they restrict their modes of expression and become less tolerant of others' modes. Those who do not succeed may be fluent in their own dialects but because they are unable to show their fluency, get a mistaken sense of inferiority from the scores they receive.

Some test makers have recognized these biases and are trying to correct them, but theories governing test construction and interpretation remain contradictory. At least four major theories begin with different images and assumptions about genetic and environmental forces or verbal fluency and differences. To some extent the theory of test construction controls test results. In a sense, what goes in also comes out and thus tests tend to be self-validating. Furthermore, test results are reported in terms of comparisons with the groups used for standardizing and thus unless the purpose in giving the test is properly related to the comparison group, the results will be meaningless. For instance, a test intended to measure verbal ability for purposes of predicting probable success in reading difficult textual material is improperly used if it is part of the hiring policy for electrical technicians or telephone repairmen, as is being done in one major American city.

Ideally, until standardized tests fair to all students from all backgrounds can be developed, they should not be used for admitting, placing, or labeling students. Since they are built into the system, however, those who use and interpret the test results must recognize the biases built into the tests and be aware of the theory and purpose behind the tests. Used carelessly, standardized tests lead to erroneous inferences as to students' linguistic abilities and create prejudgments in the minds of teachers, counselors, future employers, and the students themselves.

Resolutions of the Annual Meetings of NCTE in 1970 and 1971 challenged the present forms and uses of standardized tests. Because our schools and colleges continue to administer them, we must continue to deal with the effects of such testing on students and curricula. In response to the problem, we can employ caution in using and trusting test results, and seek positive ways to neutralize the negative effects. We should develop and employ alternative methods for the measurement of our students' performance. Various types of written and oral performance-in-situation testing can be done in the classroom. Various forms of in-class study of dialect can lead students to understand what is common to all dialects and what is particular to individual dialects, and can determine, through discussion, which alternatives most effectively represent the intentions of the speaker or writer.

Tests should not be focused on whether students can think, speak, or write in the institutional dialect, but on whether they can think, speak, and write in their own dialects. If it is also necessary to know whether students have mastered the forms of EAE, that should be tested separately.

Teachers from other fields who view English as a service course, one which will save them the labor of teaching writing, often implicitly define writing as the communication of information within a limited social context. Perhaps when they (and some English teachers) fuss about spelling and usage, they are merely avoiding difficult problems of writing or, at least, avoiding talking about them. Sometimes, what they see as incompetence in writing is merely a reflection that the student doesn't understand the materials of the history or sociology course. But often they see the student's skill only in terms of limited needs. Whatever the reason for the complaint, courses which limit themselves to a narrow view of language in hopes of pleasing other departments will not offer a view of dialect adequate to encourage students to grow more competent to handle a fuller range of the language, and thus will defeat their own purpose.

What is needed in the English classroom and in all departments is a better understanding of the nature of dialect and a shift in attitudes toward it. The English teacher can involve the entire teaching staff in examining sample essays and tests from the various departments to determine whether a student's dialect in an essay examination from Mr. Jones in Geography *really* obscures clarity, whether Mary Smith's theme for Mr. Rogers is *really* worthless because of the "she don'ts" and because "receive" is spelled with an "ie." Such activities would help everyone in defining the areas which are vitally important to us.

We can also provide help for students who find themselves in courses whose teachers remain unreasonably restrictive in matters of dialect. In business and industry, secretaries and technical writers rescue the executive and engineer. Science professors have been known to hire English teachers to rewrite their articles for publication. Even a popular technical magazine, such as *QST*, the journal for ham radio operators, offers services which will "standardize" a variant dialect:

> Have you a project which would make a good *QST* story? We have a technical editing staff who can *pretty up* the words, should they need it— *ideas are more important for* QST *articles than a finished writing job.* (Italics added) (*QST*, April, 1971, p. 78)

We must encourage students to concentrate on crucial exactness of content, and we must persuade our colleagues to forget their own biases about dialect long enough to recognize and respect this better kind of exactness. Students—all of us—need to respect our writing enough to take care with it. Self-expression and discovery as much as communication demand care in finding the exact word and phrase, but that exactness can be found in any dialect, and the cosmetic features of polite discourse can be supplied, when needed for social reasons.

All English teachers should, as a minimum, know the principles of modern linguistics, and something about the history and nature of the English language in its social and cultural context. This knowledge can be acquired through reading, through course work, through experience, or through a combination of these. All teachers should know something about:

A. *The Nature of Language as an Oral, Symbolic System by which Human Beings Interact and Communicate:* If teachers understand that the spoken language is always primary and the written language is a separate and secondary or derived system, they will be able to recognize that students inexperienced in the written system may still have great competence and facility in the spoken language. Because both systems are arbitrary, there is no necessary connection between the words of a language and the things those words symbolize (leche, lait, milk, etc.) nor is there any necessary connection between the sounds of the word "milk" and the alphabetic symbols we use to represent those sounds. Once a teacher understands the arbitrary nature of the oral and written forms, the pronunciation or spelling of a word becomes less important than whether it communicates what the student wants to say. In speech, *PO*lice communicates as well as *po*LICE, and in writing "pollice" is no insurmountable barrier to communication, although all three variations might momentarily distract a person unfamiliar with the variant.

B. *The History of English and How It Continually Changes in Vocabulary, in Syntax, and in Pronunciation:* Teachers should understand that although changes in syntax and pronunciation occur more slowly than lexical changes, they do take place. The language of the King James Bible shows considerable syntactic variation from modern English, and linguists have demonstrated that speakers even as recent as the eighteenth century might be nearly unintelligible to modern ears. Vocabulary changes are easier for both teachers and students to observe. As we develop new things, we add words to talk about them—jet, sputnik, television, smog. From its earliest history, English has borrowed words from the other languages with which it has come in contact—French, Latin, Spanish, Scandinavian, Yiddish, American Indian—from sources too numerous to list. Because many of these borrowings are historical, teachers recognize and respect them as essential parts of the language. Teachers should be equally as willing to recognize that

English can also increase the richness of its word stock by a free exchange among its dialects. If teachers had succeeded in preventing students from using such terms as "jazz," "lariat," and "kosher," modern English would be the poorer. Such borrowings enlarge and enrich the language rather than diminish it.

C. *The Nature of Dialects:* A dialect shares similarities of pronunciation, syntax, or vocabulary that differentiates it from other dialects. These similarities within a dialect and differences between dialects are the product of geographical, social, cultural, or economic isolation. Our perception of the difference between an acceptable and unacceptable dialect depends on the power and prestige of the people who speak it. We tend to respect and admire the dialect of people who are wealthy or powerful. The planter's daughter who asks in a pronounced drawl to be "carried" home from the dance is charming, the field hand who says "That's shonuff a purty dress" becomes an object of amusement or scorn. The teacher who realizes that the difference is not in the superiority of either dialect, but in the connotation we supply, can avoid judging students' dialects in social or economic terms.

D. *Language Acquisition:* Although little hard evidence is available about how an individual acquires language, it is known that in learning a language, we must filter out those sounds that have no significance in that language and use only those that do; then we learn to put those sounds into structures that are meaningful in the language. Babies experiment with a multitude of possible sounds, but by the time they begin to talk they have discarded sound combinations that don't appear in the dialects they hear. If, later on, they learn a second language, they encounter problems in hearing and producing sounds and sound combinations that do not exist in their first language. For instance, native speakers of English who learn Spanish as adults have trouble distinguishing "pero" and "perro" because the double "r" sound does not appear in any dialect of English. Although phonemic differences between dialects of English are not as great as differences between English and a foreign language, differences do exist and it is unreasonable for teachers to insist that students make phonemic shifts which we as adults have difficulty in making.

E. *Phonology:* Phonology deals with the sound system of a language and the variations within that system. Teachers who understand phonology will not try to impose their own sound systems upon their students. They will not make an issue of whether the student says /hwayt hwel/ or /wayt weyl/ (white whale), nor will they be disturbed by shair-chair, warsh-wash, dat-that. They will not "correct" a student who says "merry" like "Murray" because they themselves may say "hairy" so that it is indistinguishable from "Harry." They will realize that even though a student says "ten" and "tin" exactly alike, nobody will be confused because context makes the meaning clear.

F. *Morphology:* Morphology deals with the elements of grammatic meaning in a language—tense, aspect, person, number—and the devices the language employs for indicating them. Just as context prevents homophones from confusing the listener, so context prevents morphological variations from becoming an obstacle to communication. The variations between foot and feet in "6 foot tall," "6 feet tall," or between "Mary" and "Mary's" in such phrases as "Mary hat" and "Mary's hat" make no difference in our ability to grasp the meaning. Teachers who recognize that morphological forms vary from dialect to dialect, but that within each dialect the morphology follows a system, will be less likely to challenge a student whose morphology is different on the ground that such variations represent "mistakes."

G. *Syntax:* Syntax refers to the arrangement of words within an utterance. Syntactic patterns are not the same in all languages (in English, the *red* dress; in the Chicano dialect of Spanish, el vestido *colorado*), nor are the syntactic patterns always the same in different dialects of the same language. The syntactic patterns, however, are systematic within each dialect, and seldom interfere with communication between speakers of different dialects within a language. "That girl she pretty" is just as understandable as "That girl is pretty" and "Don't nobody but God know that" is not only just as clear as "Only God knows," but in some circumstances its meaning is more emphatic.

H. *Grammar and Usage:* Teachers often think grammar is a matter of choosing between lie and lay, who and whom, everybody/his and everybody/their. Actually these are usage choices, in the same way as deciding whether to say "I done my work" or "I did my work" is a usage choice. Grammar, on the other hand, is a description of the system by which a language conveys meaning beyond the sum of the meanings of the individual words. It includes phonology, morphology, and syntax. The grammar of one American dialect may require "he is" in the third person singular present tense; the grammar of another dialect may require "he be" in that slot. The confusion between usage and grammar grows out of the prescriptive attitude taken by most school handbooks since the 18th century. Modern linguists see grammar not as prescriptive but as descriptive, and teachers who approach the study of grammar as a fascinating analysis of an intensely important human activity, rather than as a series of do's and don'ts, can often rid their students of the fear and guilt that accompanied their earlier experiences with "grammar." Perhaps such teachers can even help their students to find the study of grammar fun.

I. *Semantics:* Teachers should know that semantics is the study of how people give meaning to words and the way many of those meanings affect us emotionally rather than rationally. Teachers well grounded in modern semantics can help their students examine their word choices, not from the standpoint of right or wrong, proper or improper, but by analyzing the impact possible choices will have on listeners or readers. In some areas, for instance, some listeners will be turned off by the word "belly," whereas other listeners will find "stomach" affected and feel more comfortable with "gut." Students can be led to see why many newspaper readers could support a "protective reaction strike" but would have been upset by a "bombing attack."

J. *Lexicography:* Knowing that many words have strong connotative meanings will help teachers regard dictionaries not as authorities but as guides. Knowing that words are only arbitrary symbols for the things they refer to, teachers will realize that dictionaries cannot supply the "real" meaning of any word. Knowing that language changes, they will realize that expressions labeled "nonstandard" or "colloquial" by the dictionaries of fifty years ago may be listed without pejorative labels in an up-to-date dictionary. Knowing that pronunciations vary, they will use the pronunciation information in a dictionary as a starting point for class discussion on how most people in the students' own area pronounce that word. In short, teachers will help their students to realize that dictionaries describe practice rather than legislate performance. Dictionaries cannot give rules for using the words of a language; they can only give information about how words have been used.

K. *Experience:* Teachers need to ratify their book knowledge of language by living as minority speakers. They should be wholly immersed in a dialect group other than their own. Although such an opportunity may be difficult for some to obtain, less definitive experience may be obtained by listening to tapes and records as well as interviewing sympathetically speakers who use minority dialects. Empathy with the difficulties often faced by such speakers can be appreciated in indirect analogies with other situations which make one an outsider. But the most vivid sense of the students' problem is likely to come from direct experience.

L. *The Role of Change:* The history of language indicates that change is one of its constant conditions and, furthermore, that attempts at regulation and the slowing of change have been unsuccessful. Academies established to regulate language by scholarly authority have little effect on the dynamic processes of language. Moreover, there is little evidence that languages "evolve" in the sense that they become more expressive or more regular; that is, they simply change, but they do not, it seems, become better or worse. Dialect is merely a symptom of change. Paradoxically, past change is considered normal, but current change is viewed by some as degradation. From Chaucer to Shakespeare to Faulkner, the language assuredly changed, and yet no one speaks of the primitive language of Chaucer or the impoverished language of Shakespeare. Few complain that French and Spanish developed from camp-Latin. Literary scholars might dispute endlessly over the absolute merits of neo-classical versus romantic poetry, but no one would argue that literature would be richer if one or the other did not exist. In fact, there are positive esthetic reasons for arguing in favor of diversity. Such is the case with dialects; just as variety in modes of poetic perception enriches literature, so variety in dialects enriches the language for those who are not unreasonably biased in favor of one dialect. Diversity of dialects will not degrade language nor hasten deleterious changes. Common sense tells us that if people want to understand one another, they will do so. Experience tells us that we can understand any dialect of English after a reasonably brief exposure to it. And humanity tells us that we should allow every man the dignity of his own way of talking.

LANGUAGE VARIETIES, LINGUISTIC PROFILING, HOUSING, CIVIL RIGHTS, AND EMPLOYABILITY

English teachers should be concerned with the employability as well as the linguistic performance of their students. Students rightly want marketable skills that will facilitate their entry into the world of work. Unfortunately, many employers have narrowly conceived notions of the relationship between linguistic performance and job competence. Many employers expect a person whom they consider for employment to speak whatever variety of American English the employers speak, or believe they speak. Consequently, many speakers of divergent dialects are denied opportunities that are readily available to other applicants whose dialects more nearly approximate the speech of the employer. But a plumber who can sweat a joint can be forgiven confusion between "set" and "sat." In the same way, it is more important that a computer programmer be fluent in Fortran than in EAE. Many jobs that are normally desirable—that are viewed as ways of entering the American middle class—are undoubtedly closed to some speakers of some nonstandard dialects, while some of the same jobs are seldom closed to white speakers of nonstandard dialects.

Spoken dialect makes little difference in the performance of many jobs, and the failure of employers to hire blacks, Chicanos, or other ethnic minorities is often simply racial or cultural prejudice. One of the exceptions is the broadcast industry, where most stations at least used to require that almost all newscasters and announcers speak "network standard," but ethnic stations that broadcast "soul" (black), or country, or western, or Chicano programs tend to require the appropriate dialect. A related social bias is implied by certain large companies which advertise for receptionists who speak BBC (British Broadcasting Company) dialect, even though British English is a minority dialect when it is spoken in this country. For them prestige requires the assumption that Americans are still colonials.

The situation concerning spoken dialect and employability is in a state of change; many speakers of minority dialects are now finding opportunities that five or ten years ago would have been closed to them. Specific data is understandably difficult to find, yet it would seem that certain dialects have a considerable effect on employability. Since English teachers have been in large part responsible for the narrow attitudes of today's employers, changing attitudes toward dialect variations does not seem an unreasonable goal, for today's students will be tomorrow's employers. The attitudes that they develop in the English class will often be the criteria they use for choosing their own employees. English teachers who feel they are bound to accommodate the linguistic prejudices of current employers perpetuate a system that is unfair to both students who have job skills and to the employers who need them.

Teachers should stress the difference between the spoken forms of American English and EAE because a clear understanding will enable both teachers and students to focus their attention on essential items. EAE allows much less variety than the spoken forms, and departure from what are considered established norms is less tolerated. The speaker of a minority dialect still will write EAE in formal situations. An employer may have a southern drawl and pronounce "think" like "thank," but he will write *think*. He may say "y'all" and be considered charming for his quaint southernisms, but he will write *you*. He may even in a "down home" moment ask, "Now how come th' mail orda d'partment d'nt orda fo' cases steada five?" But he'll write the question in EAE. Therefore it is necessary that we inform those students who are preparing themselves for occupations that demand formal writing that they will be expected to write EAE. But it is one thing to help a student achieve proficiency in a written dialect and another thing to punish him for using variant expressions of that dialect.

Students who want to write EAE will have to learn the forms identified with that dialect as additional options to the forms they already control. We should begin our work in composition with them by making them feel confident that their writing, in whatever dialect, makes sense and is important to us, that we read it and are interested in the ideas and person that the writing reveals. Then students will be in a much stronger position to consider the rhetorical choices that lead to statements written in EAE.

BIBLIOGRAPHY

This bibliography of 129 entries is keyed to the statements made in the four sections of *Students' Right to Their Own Language*. It is, therefore, sociolinguistic in intent; that is, language as a vehicle of socio-cultural interaction is its concern. It is designed for the classroom teacher who deals with the uses of language variety and who teaches oral and written composing processes. Pedagogical treatments are balanced against theoretical statements so that immediate needs can be answered from two points of departure and so that further study may be undertaken as desired.

Because it is designed to appeal to a varied audience of teachers with differing interests and preparation, elementary, intermediate, and advanced considerations of the sociolinguistic problems surveyed in the statement itself are included. Items reflect problems spanning child-adult sociolinguistic concerns and the elementary-college educational spectrum. Annotations attempt to identify items for simplicity or complexity and for practical or theoretical concerns.

Though items reflect primarily those sociolinguistic concerns of the 1960's and 1970's, some earlier publications have been included to provide background and/or situational context for understanding the present controversy. Wherever decisions, directions, and concerns of pedagogy and research have not yet been resolved, variant perspectives have been included. Many essay collections have been included (1) to demonstrate the multiplicity of views available and (2) to provide easy access to source materials. Many entries are themselves distinguished by further-study bibliographies. Items known to exist unrevised in several sources are cross-referenced. Necessarily, the bibliography reflects those areas of sociolinguistic research and pedagogy in which the greatest amount of work has been conducted and published.

UNDERSTANDING LANGUAGE VARIETIES

Arthur, Bradford. "The Interaction of Dialect and Style in Urban American English," *Language Learning*, 21 (1971), 161–174. The interaction of dialect and style is defined and illustrated, and the implications of this for teaching acquisition of more formal variants are investigated. Understanding and acceptance of informal styles is urged.

Bernstein, Basil, and Dorothy Henderson. "Social Class Differences in the Relevance of Language to Socialisation," *Sociology*, 3 (January, 1969), 1–20. A discussion of a study of ways in which mothers' orientations to language help to determine children's responses to language codes and world views is presented.

Fickett, Joan G. "Tense and Aspect in Black English," *Journal of English Linguistics*, 6 (March, 1972), 17–20. An identification of tense and aspect of the Black English verb system shows how they reflect cultural attitude and value.

Fishman, Joshua A. *Sociolinguistics*. Rowley: Newbury House, 1970. Definitions of idiolect, dialect, and language (see Section II) are contained within a larger sociolinguistic definition which considers such areas as linguistic change, constraints, and repertoire range.

Hymes, Dell. "Models of the Interaction of Language and Social Setting," *Journal of Social Issues*, 23 (April, 1967), 8–28. Also in Gumperz and Hymes (1972). A "guide to analysis of speech socialization" is offered as a way of categorizing social units, components, and rules in order to understand the functional codes and roles of language. Such a guide can help the perceiver to understand how dialects differ.

John, Vera P., and Leo S. Goldstein. "The Social Context of Language Acquisition," *Merrill-Palmer Quarterly*, 10 (July, 1964), 265–275. The acquisition of labeling and categorizing words is discussed. Rate and breadth of shift from one to the other varies with social context and availability of mature speakers and affects cognitive development in different ways.

Kochman, Thomas. "Cross-cultural Communication: Contrasting Perspectives, Conflicting Sensibilities," *Florida FL Reporter*, 9 (Fall/Spring, 1971), 3–16, 53–54. Types of interference and communication failure are discussed. These are shown to result from lack of understanding of the ramifications of dialect, i.e., the cultural codes which determine the value to be given to linguistic habit patterns in situational context.

Labov, William. "Hypercorrection by the Lower Middle Class as a Factor in Linguistic Change," in Bright, William, ed. *Sociolinguistics*. The Hague: Mouton & Co., 1971. Hypersensitivity to prestige markers and codes is discussed. The role of hypercorrection in the propagation of linguistic change as speakers respond to pressures from above and below the level of conscious awareness is considered.

Labov, William. "The Logic of Non-Standard English," in Alatis, James, ed. *Linguistics and the Teaching of Standard English to Speakers of Other Languages or Dialects*. Monograph Series on Languages and Linguistics, No. 22. Washington, D.C.: Georgetown University Press, 1969. Also in Aarons (1969), Bailey and Robinson (1973), and Williams (1970). This carefully illustrated article argues that nonstandard English is not an illogical variety of speech. While showing its habit-pattern organization, Labov also argues against the verbal deprivation theory.

Labov, William. *The Social Stratification of English in New York City.* Washington, D.C.: Center for Applied Linguistics, 1966. This in-depth analysis of one multi-level speech community outlines the continuous social and stylistic variation of language influenced by socio-economic stratification and the transmission of prestige patterns. The nature of social control of language variety is considered.

Lenneberg, Eric H. *Biological Foundations of Language.* New York: John Wiley & Sons, 1967. Language as an aspect of the biological nature of human beings is studied. See especially Chapter Four for a discussion of language acquisition in the context of growth and maturation.

Lenneberg, Eric H., ed. *New Directions in the Study of Language.* Cambridge: The M.I.T. Press, 1967. Eight contributors investigate language acquisition problems from the viewpoints of maturation, social anthropology, human biology, and psychology.

Lenneberg, Eric H. "On Explaining Language," *Science,* 164: 3880 (May, 1969), 635–643. Also in Gunderson (1970). The argument that "the development of language in children can best be understood in the context of developmental biology" is introduced. Major problems in language acquisition are pinpointed.

Lieberson, Stanley, ed. *Explorations in Sociolinguistics.* The Hague: Mouton & Co., 1967. This collection of thirteen articles represents several views of the purposes of language/dialect. Through discussions of elaborated and restricted codes, social stratification and cognitive orientations, social status and attitude, and uniformation, the collection exposes those components which contribute to prestige or nonprestige forms.

Malmstrom, Jean. "Dialects-Updated," *Florida FL Reporter,* 7 (Spring/Summer, 1969), 47–49, 168. Also in Bentley and Crawford (1973). The nature of dialect (components and variables, socio-economic and geographical determinants) is outlined and discussed.

McDavid, Raven I., Jr. "The Dialects of American English," in Francis, W. Nelson. *The Structure of American English.* New York: Ronald Press, 1958. This chapter-article surveys dialect through discussion of dialect differences and causes, dialect geography, linguistic atlases, forces underlying dialect distribution, principal dialect areas (providing samples), foreign-language influences, class dialects, and literary dialect.

McDavid, Raven I., Jr. "Dialect Differences and Social Differences in an Urban Society," in Bright, William, ed. *Sociolinguistics.* The Hague: Mouton & Co., 1971. This article discusses the class markers by which speakers are tagged by their listeners and the resulting prestige (or lack of it) which is attributed to the speakers and their linguistic utterances.

McDavid, Raven I., Jr. "A Theory of Dialect," in Alatis, James, ed. *Linguistics and the Teaching of Standard English to Speakers of Other Languages* or *Dialects.* Monograph Series on Languages and Linguistics, No. 22. Washington, D.C.:

Georgetown University Press, 1969. This definition of dialect points up misuses of the designation and redefines the functions and limitations of the dimensions of language varieties.

McDavid, Raven I., Jr. "Variations in Standard American English," *Elementary English*, 45 (May, 1968), 561–564, 608. This article describes historical and current variations in phonology, vocabulary, and syntax which reflect regional differences yet represent Standard American English.

Troike, Rudolph C. "Receptive Competence, Productive Competence, and Performance," in Alatis, James, ed. *Linguistics and the Teaching of Standard English to Speakers of Other Languages or Dialects*. Monograph Series on Languages and Linguistics. No. 22. Washington, D.C.: Georgetown University Press, 1969. This discussion of receptive competence and its importance in developing productive competence encourages greater concern for such components in the development of materials and methods for second-dialect teaching.

Wolfram, Walt, and Nona H. Clarke, eds. *Black-White Speech Relationships*. Washington, D.C.: Center for Applied Linguistics, 1971. Eight viewpoints are represented through eight articles discussing the possible social and historical influences in the development of black-white varieties of English.

LANGUAGE VARIETIES AND LEARNING

Baratz, Joan C., and Roger W. Shuy, eds. *Teaching Black Children to Read*. Washington, D.C.: Center for Applied Linguistics, 1969. This collection of eight articles by reading specialists and dialectologists suggests that the "problem" in the learning-to-read process is generally attributable to the teacher, not the student. Discussion of reading difficulties is illustrated through problems of speakers of Black English. Especially recommended is William Labov's article. His discussion is applicable to reading classrooms at all levels.

Braddock, Richard, Richard Lloyd-Jones, and Lowell Schoer. *Research in Written Composition*. Champaign: NCTE, 1963. This survey considers the present state of knowledge about composition and outlines the case-study method of analysis. Part III emphasizes the factors influencing composition and measurement.

Cohen, Rosalie A. "Conceptual Styles, Culture Conflict, and Nonverbal Tests of Intelligence," *American Anthropologist*, 71 (October, 1969), 828–856. Conceptual styles (rule sets and constraints) which can be identified through linguistic and attitudinal behavior are investigated. It is argued that one must identify the conceptual style in order to understand interference problems. It is shown that such styles affect responses to standardized testing.

Emig, Janet. *The Composing Processes of Twelfth Graders*. Research Report No. 13. Urbana: NCTE, 1971. This report investigates the writing process and attempts "to identify the student's feelings, attitudes, and self-concepts which form the invisible components of the 'composition' which the teacher sees as a product." Especially valuable are Chapter 1 which reviews the literature and Chapter 3 which outlines the mode of analysis.

Friedrich, Richard, and David Kuester. *It's Mine and I'll Write It That Way.* New York: Random House, 1972. This freshman composition text combines an understanding of the nature of language with a demonstration that almost all students, when they write naturally about things meaningful to them, can learn to write well.

Gunderson, Doris V., ed. *Language & Reading.* Washington, D.C.: Center for Applied Linguistics, 1970. A survey of reading and language theories, reading research concerns, reading disability problems, and current instructional practices is developed through the statements of seventeen contributors.

Harrison, Myrna. *On Our Own Terms.* Encino: Dickenson, 1972. In this collection of forceful, effective student writing, many of the selections illustrate that having something to say, and saying it well, is not affected by dialect or spelling.

Kavanagh, James F., and Ignatius G. Mattingly, eds. *Language by Ear and Eye.* Cambridge: The M.I.T. Press, 1972. An overview of current knowledge of similarities and differences in the processing of language by ear and by eye is developed through twenty-two contributor statements. Language vehicles (speech and writing), speech perception and reading, and learning problems are considered.

Labov, William. "Statement and Resolution on Language and Intelligence," *LSA Bulletin,* 52 (March, 1972), 19–22. "On the Resolution on Language and Intelligence," *LSA Bulletin,* 53 (June, 1972), 14–16. "More on the Resolution on Language and Intelligence," *LSA Bulletin,* 54 (October, 1972), 24–26. These three statements reflect the most recent stances taken by socio-linguists on the "heritability of intelligence theory." They advance the argument that linguistic variables and language varieties are not being taken into consideration in attempts to measure intelligence and cognitive ability.

Macrorie, Ken. *Uptaught.* New York: Hayden Press, 1970. This discussion considers how conventional English classes have failed and offers some suggestions for a writing approach that emphasizes respect for students and the honesty of their expression.

Quay, Lorene C. "Language Dialect, Reinforcement, and the Intelligence-test Performance of Negro Children," *Child Development,* 42 (March, 1971), 5–15. The influence of motivation (with reinforcement) and communication (Standard English/Black English dialects) on responses and scores is evaluated. It is argued that the deficit/difference theories are based on speech production, not language comprehension.

Scarr-Salapatek, Sandra. "Race, Social Class, and IQ," *Science,* 174: 4016 (December 1971), 1285–1295. This discussion-definition outlines the environmental disadvantages hypothesis and the genetic differences hypothesis, demonstrating their interactions, and presenting their implications for the determination of IQ.

Smitherman, Geneva. "God Don't Never Change: Black English from a Black Perspective," *College English*, 34 (March, 1973), 828–834. This article argues for the uniqueness of Black expression which lies in the situational context from which the style of the Black Idiom develops. The argument is placed in historical context.

Williams, Frederick, ed. *Language and Poverty: Perspectives on a Theme.* Chicago: Markham Publishing Co., 1972. The linguistic deficit-difference controversy is surveyed through eighteen overview and position papers which attempt to explain the interrelationships of language, linguistic variety, and poverty settings.

Wolfram, Walt, and Marcia Whiteman. "The Role of Dialect Interference in Composition," *Florida FL Reporter*, 9 (Spring/Fall, 1971), 34–38. Interference problems which arise in written composition due to dialectal differences in grammatical and pronunciation features are discussed and manifestations of hypercorrection illustrated. Black English is used for illustration.

LANGUAGE VARIETIES AND EDUCATIONAL POLICY AND PRACTICE

Aarons, Alfred C., Barbara Y. Gordon, and William A. Stewart, eds. *Linguistic-Cultural Differences and American Education.* Special Issue. *Florida FL Reporter*, 7 (Spring/Summer, 1969). Multiple viewpoints, classroom projects and research results of forty-three contributors are arranged to focus on the cultural role of the school, on linguistic pluralism, on English teaching, on theory, and on curriculum development in this overview of current concerns.

Abrahams, Roger D., and Rudolph C. Troike, eds. *Language and Cultural Diversity in American Education.* Englewood Cliffs: Prentice-Hall, 1972. This introductory reader organizes its thirty-five articles to consider the interactions of cultural pluralism, linguistic knowledge, sociolinguistic approaches, and educational applications to our present understandings. Several articles illustrate these considerations through responses to Black English.

Allen, Harold, ed. *Readings in Applied English Linguistics.* Second Edition. New York: Appleton-Century-Crofts, 1964. Sixty-two articles are organized to represent the spectrum of linguistic thought and application through 1960. Historical background, current viewpoints, linguistic geography, usage, dictionary development, and linguistics' contributions to the teaching of grammar, composition, and literature are considered.

Allen, Harold B., and Gary N. Underwood, eds. *Readings in American Dialectology.* New York: Appleton-Century-Crofts, 1971. This introductory reader presents forty-one research statements arranged for the study of regional and social dialects.

Bailey, Richard W., and Jay L. Robinson. *Varieties of Present-Day English.* New York: The Macmillan Company, 1973. This introductory reader investigates the causes, differences, and persistence of varieties of English and considers teaching strategies through the statements of eighteen contributors. Study problems are included.

Baratz, Joan C. "Should Black Children Learn White Dialect?" *ASHA,* 12 (September, 1970), 415–417. Also in Smith (1972). It is argued that "standard English" is not "white dialect" but the *lingua franca* of the "American mainstream" culture to which the Black student has a right. A definition is attempted.

Barth, Carl A. "Kinds of Language Knowledge Required by College Entrance Examinations," *English Journal,* 54 (December, 1965), 824–829. Knowledge of traditional grammar is found not necessary for success on such standardized national tests as the SAT, ACT, College Board Achievement Test. Knowledge of usage and linguistic sensitivity gained through modern language teaching are adequate preparation.

Baugh, Albert C. *A History of the English Language.* Second Edition. New York: Appleton-Century-Crofts, 1957. This standard language history traces the changes that have taken place over 1500 years and relates those changes to the political and social events of English history.

Bentley, Robert H., and Samuel D. Crawford, eds. *Black Language Reader.* Glenview: Scott, Foresman and Company, 1973. This arrangement of twenty-nine statements from research, media, and classroom sources represents a self-contained introductory course for teachers in the origins, uses, and misuses of Black English.

Bolinger, Dwight. *Aspects of Language.* New York: Harcourt, Brace & World, 1968. This introductory text is designed to familiarize the reader with the terms and concepts of linguistics. Ways of talking about language are developed through careful definitions and question-application sequences after each chapter.

Budd, Richard W., and Brent D. Ruben, eds. *Approaches to Human Communication.* New York: Spartan Books, 1972. The viewpoints of twenty-four contributors provide a survey of theories and attitudes toward communication in fields such as art, history, zoology. Each position statement reflects the world view within which each type of communicator conceptualizes and is, therefore, able to accept statements about his field.

Burling, Robbins. *English in Black and White.* New York: Holt, Rinehart and Winston, 1973. This systematic explanation of major facts of nonstandard English dialects is designed for teachers and nonspecialists. Each chapter answers a practical question such as "What is the problem?" or "How is it used?" and offers study-discussion topics of use in the classroom.

Burling, Robbins. "Standard Colloquial and Standard Written English: Some Implications for Teaching Literacy to Nonstandard Speakers," *Florida FL Reporter*, 8 (Spring/Fall, 1970), 9–15, 47. An investigation of differences between written and spoken varieties of English and of some of the ways in which they interact is balanced against the cautionary advice that teacher attitudes toward, and knowledge of, nonstandard habit patterns is the real factor in teaching literacy. Problems in teaching language usage are clarified.

Cassidy, Frederick. "American Regionalisms in the Classroom," *English Journal*, 57 (March, 1968), 375–379. This article is a discussion of the regional variations existent in Standard English and a description of available dialect resources for classroom exploration of the language varieties which the student and the community use.

Cattell, N. R. *The New English Grammar: A Descriptive Introduction.* Cambridge: The M.I.T. Press, 1969. This introduction to generative transformational grammar presents a nontechnical description of the features of English grammar and the design of language.

Cazden, Courtney B., Vera P. John, and Dell Hymes, eds. *Functions of Language in the Classroom.* New York: Teachers College Press, 1972. Focusing on early education, the twenty contributors consider language problems which affect all classrooms—supplying perspectives on nonverbal communication, discussions of varieties of language and verbal repertoire, and of varieties of communicative strategies. They attempt an ethnography of communication in classrooms.

Chase, Stuart. *The Tyranny of Words.* New York: Harcourt, Brace, 1938. A discussion of how the words we select can distort our views is presented in a highly readable way.

Chomsky, Noam. *Aspects of the Theory of Syntax.* Cambridge: The M.I.T. Press, 1965. A study of developments in transformational generative grammar reviews, extends, and modifies earlier theory. Emphasis is on syntactic rather than phonological or semantic aspects of language.

Crowell, Michael G. "American Traditions of Language Use: Their Relevance Today," *English Journal*, 59 (January, 1970), 109–115. Nineteenth and twentieth century usage attitudes are considered as they relate to (1) growth and creativity in language and (2) maintenance of the *status quo* and as these attitudes have been affected by the prescriptive-descriptive discussions of usage. Crowell stresses that the maintenance of creativity and *status quo* attitudes encourages a healthy tension in our thinking and discussions of language.

Davis, A. L., ed. *Culture, Class, and Language Variety.* Urbana: NCTE, 1972. Ten articles are offered as a resource-reference for teachers who must plan classroom activities in such areas as grammar, syntax, and nonverbal communication. Included are transcriptions of children's speech (a tape cartridge of that speech accompanies the text).

Davis, Philip W. *Modern Theories of Language.* Englewood Cliffs: Prentice-Hall, 1973. Nine twentieth century theories of language (i.e., the theories of Saussure, Hjelmslev, Bloomfield, the Post-Bloomfieldians, and the Prague School; tagmemics; Firthian linguistics; stratificational grammar; transformational generative grammar) are characterized and discussed for the linguistically knowledgeable reader.

Derrick, Clarence. "Tests of Writing," *English Journal,* 53 (October, 1964), 496–499. This article criticizes the efficiency and reliability of national essay and objective "writing" tests designed for group testing. The essay tests are dismissed as unreliable; the objective tests are consigned to having reliability in producing information about skills related to writing. Derrick feels the answer to the problem lies in careful classroom testing and evaluating of writing samples.

Dillard, J. L. *Black English: Its History and Usage in the United States.* New York: Random House, 1972. The ramifications of Black English, its historical development, and its cultural validity and the implications of such information for teacher training and classroom practices are explained by the author. (See Chapter VII for his discussion of the harm done Black students by failing them on the basis of dialect.)

Elgin, Suzette Haden. *What Is Linguistics?* Englewood Cliffs: Prentice-Hall, 1973. This elementary text provides an introduction to phonology, syntax, semantics, historical linguistics, psycholinguistics, sociolinguistics, stylistics, applied linguistics, and field linguistics.

Evertts, Eldonna L., ed. *Dimensions of Dialect.* Champaign: NCTE, 1967. Various aspects of dialect-oriented problems are considered by fourteen linguists and teachers. Dialect features and their implications for the classroom are discussed. Raven McDavid's article contains a checklist of nonstandard dialect features.

Falk, Julia S. *Linguistics and Language.* Lexington: Xerox College Publishing, 1973. An introductory survey of basic concepts and applications of linguistics moves the reader through consideration of words, sounds and sound systems, writing, speaker control of language, grammar, dialect, language acquisition, and teaching issues.

Fasold, Ralph W., and Roger W. Shuy, eds. *Teaching Standard English in the Inner City.* Washington, D.C.: Center for Applied Linguistics, 1970. The biloquialist perspective is presented in this collection of six articles by educators attempting to deal with the problems of inner city teaching.

Fishman, Joshua A., ed. *Readings in the Sociology of Language.* The Hague: Mouton & Co., 1968. This reader is designed to give a socio-linguistic perspective through forty-five articles which consider language in small-group interaction, in social strata and sectors, through socio-cultural organization, and within the scope of multilingualism, language shift, and planning.

Francis, W. Nelson. *The English Language.* New York: Norton, 1965. An analysis of how English works is developed from the structuralists' viewpoint.

Fries, Charles C. *American English Grammar.* New York: Appleton-Century-Crofts, 1940. This descriptive grammar which concentrates on uses of word form, uses of function words, and uses of word order draws its data and conclusions from contemporary social discourse (i.e., personal letters). It also considers the role of the school in grammar and language teaching.

Funkhouser, James L. "A Various Standard," *College English,* 34 (March, 1973), 806–827. A discussion of how nonsituational handbook rules may be superseded in the classroom by situational rules for effective communication in writing is presented. Rule consistency is illustrated through Black English writing samples.

Goslin, David A. "What's Wrong With Tests and Testing," *College Board Review* Nos. 65/66 (Fall/Winter, 1967), 12–18, 33–37. These statements discuss the types and uses of tests, influences which scores exert, criticisms of validity, concern for their self-fulfilling prophecy, and the implications for group social structure, membership selection, and society.

Greenbaum, Sidney, and Randolph Quirk. *Elicitation Experiments in English.* (Miami Linguistics Series No. 10). Coral Gables: University of Miami Press, 1970. This report is a description of linguistic testing methods by which types of sociolinguistic acceptability may be identified and categorized. Differences between attitudes and beliefs about usage and actual usage habits are investigated through elicited items of linguistic behavior.

Grinder, John T., and Suzette Haden Elgin. *Guide to Transformational Grammar.* New York: Holt, Rinehart and Winston, 1973. This elementary text introduces the basic concepts of transformational grammar through thirteen chapters, each of which presents some aspect of the history, theory, and practice of that grammar. Teaching exercises with answers are provided.

Gumperz, John J., and Dell Hymes. *Directions in Sociolinguistics.* New York: Holt, Rinehart and Winston, 1972. An ethnography of communication is presented through nineteen articles which explain (1) the socio-cultural shaping of ways of speaking, (2) procedures for discovering and stating rules of conversation and address, and (3) origin, persistence, and change of varieties of language.

Hackett, Herbert. "Three Against Testing," *College Composition and Communication,* 15 (October, 1964), 158–163. This article reviews *The Brain Watchers, They Shall Not Pass,* and *The Tyranny of Testing* and finds their authors guilty of the same pretentiousness and carelessness which the authors found in the designers and users of standardized tests. The charges are specific and illustrate those authors' misconceptions by focusing on what such tests can and cannot do. It points out that validity, not reliability, is the problem area in standardized testing.

Hall, Richard. "A Muddle of Models: The Radicalizing of American English," *English Journal*, 61 (May, 1972), 705–710. The proliferation of models by which to determine one's usage is considered. Such pluralism forces the teacher to consider language options, to teach about the shifts in language values which are occurring, and to aim for greater student consciousness in the making of decisions about usage.

Hartung, Charles V. "Doctrines of English Usage," *English Journal*, 45 (December, 1956), 517–525. Also in Laird and Gorrell (1961). The four main "propriety of language usage" doctrines (of rules, of general usage, of appropriateness, of linguistic norm) which have influenced our thought are discussed. Hartung concludes that the doctrine of the linguistic norm with its concern for "maximum expression" would seem suitable for the classroom.

Hayakawa, S. I. *Language in Thought and Action.* Third Edition. New York: Harcourt Brace Jovanovich, 1972. This discussion of semantics provides an introduction to the study of the role and uses of language in modifying behavior, transmitting information, developing social cohesion, and expressing the imagination.

Herndon, Jeanne H. *A Survey of Modern Grammars.* New York: Holt, Rinehart and Winston, 1970. This handbook enables the reader to survey developments and concerns of modern grammars (structural and transformational-generative) and of varieties of American English. Implications of linguistics for the teaching of literature and composition are also surveyed.

Holt, Grace Sims. "Changing Frames of Reference in Speech Communication Education for Black Students," *Florida FL Reporter*, 9 (Spring/Fall, 1971), 21–22, 52. An argument for the role *affect* has in Black communication and its importance in linguistic-cultural patterns is presented. Classroom activities for the study of affect are provided.

Huddleston, Rodney D. *The Sentence in Written English.* Cambridge: Cambridge University Press, 1971. Working within the theoretical framework of transformational grammar, this syntactic study describes the grammar of written scientific English using a limited corpus of 135,000 words. However, "common-core" English grammar concerns are investigated through that corpus.

Imhoof, Maurice L., ed. "Social and Educational Insights into Teaching Standard English to Speakers of Other Dialects," *Viewpoints.* Bloomington: Indiana University Press, 1971. This overview considers system and order in varietal differences, effects of cultural attitudes toward given varieties, teacher attitudes, design and system of learning activities, competencies needed by ghetto teachers.

Jacobson, Rodolpho, ed. *Studies in English to Speakers of Other Languages & Standard English to Speakers of a Non-Standard Dialect.* Monograph No. 14, New York State English Council, 1971. This collection of twenty-four articles argues against the melting-pot theory and for the linguistic-cultural pluralism theory. Many viewpoints are represented as contributors approach the problem through discussion of attitudes toward language varieties, bidialectalism, bilingualism, the "Pygmalion effect," and testing.

Jacobs, Roderick A., and Peter S. Rosenbaum. *English Transformational Grammar.* Waltham: Blaisdell Publishing Company, 1968. This elementary text is based on a transformational model and moves from a description of principles of linguistic universals through discussion of constituents and features, transformations, embedding, and conjunction.

Jacobs, Roderick A., and Peter S. Rosenbaum. *Readings in English Transformational Grammar.* Waltham: Xerox College Publishing, 1970. Theoretical statements by thirteen transformational-generative linguists present current research in the concept of deep and surface structures.

James, Carl. "Applied Institutional Linguistics in the Classroom," *English Journal*, 59 (November, 1970), 1096–1105. It is suggested that the classroom study of English be focused on "distinctive features." This format considers language variety through those permanent (dialectal) and transient (diatypic) features by which we identify types of speakers and writers along a usage spectrum.

Jespersen, Otto. *Essentials of English Grammar.* Tuscaloosa: University of Alabama Press, 1964. This "signal" grammar of the spoken language investigates the development of sound systems, word classes, syntax, word form, and habits in language varieties. Other-language grammatical comparisons are made wherever feasible.

Joos, Martin. *The Five Clocks.* New York: Harcourt, Brace & World, 1967. This discussion of the five styles of spoken and written English encourages a tolerant view of varying linguistic habit patterns by illustrating the complexities of usage.

Katz, Jerrold J. *The Philosophy of Language.* New York: Harper & Row, 1966. This systematic approach to a philosophy of language provides for explanation of language from a twentieth century perspective, discussion of the current theory of language, and consideration of the implications of that theory for understanding conceptual knowledge.

Katz, Jerrold J. *Semantic Theory.* New York: Harper & Row, 1972. This depth study of semantic theory attempts an integrated body of definitions of meaning, sameness/difference of meaning, and multiplicity of meaning, and of the constraints at work in the development of meaning.

Kerr, Elizabeth M., and Ralph M. Aderman, eds. *Aspects of American English.* New York: Harcourt, Brace & World, 1963. Thirty statements are arranged to allow the reader to consider the developing and changing attitudes toward principles and sociolinguistic aspects of language. Historical, regional, social, and literary aspects are considered.

Kochman, Thomas. "Culture and Communication: Implications for Black English in the Classroom," *Florida FL Reporter*, 7 (Spring/Summer, 1969), 89–92, 172–174. Communication channels, mechanisms, networks, audience dynamics, goals and assumptions for language programs, and speech styles are discussed.

Kochman, Thomas, ed. *Rappin' and Stylin' Out: Communication in Urban Black America.* Champaign-Urbana: University of Illinois Press, 1972. A study of communication in the urban Black situation is presented through the views of twenty-seven contributors. The reader reviews the spectrum of Black communication from nonverbal to verbal, from expressive uses of language to expressive role behavior, and through vocabulary and culture. Visual and verbal illustrations are abundant.

Labov, William. *Language in the Inner City: Studies in the Black English Vernacular.* (Conduct and Communication No. 3.) Philadelphia: University of Pennsylvania Press, 1972. Nine essays (three previously unpublished) present a reorganization and rewriting of several earlier statements into an organized study of the structure, social setting, and uses of the Black English vernacular.

Labov, William. *Sociolinguistic Patterns.* (Conduct and Communication No. 4.) Philadelphia: University of Pennsylvania Press, 1972. Two new statements on contextual style and subjective dimensions of change are added to revisions of earlier statements on social change and motivation in language in this nine-essay collection.

Labov, William. *The Study of Nonstandard English.* Champaign: NCTE, 1970. This statement surveys the theoretical and educational issues surrounding the controversy over nonstandard English. Nonstandard English is considered within the context of the nature of language, sociolinguistic principles, educational implications, and needed in-school research. Space is given to informal and formal approaches to testing for varieties of language in order to determine presence of differences, perceptual competence in varieties, grammatical competence, and speech competence.

Laird, Charlton, and Robert M. Gorrell, eds. *English as Language: Backgrounds, Development, Usage.* New York: Harcourt, Brace & World, 1961. A collection of sixty statements is arranged to demonstrate changing attitudes over several centuries toward language, dialect, grammar, dictionaries, and usage.

Langacker, Ronald W. *Language and Its Structure.* Second Edition. New York: Harcourt, Brace & World, 1968. This introduction to language presents modern views of the nature, structure, and components of language and language variety. Language change, language families, and linguistic systems are considered.

Lederman, Marie Jean. "Hip Language and Urban College English," *College Composition and Communication* (20 October, 1969), 204–214. The value of employing, investigating, and defining "hip" language in the classroom is considered and seen as a "matter of human rights" to discuss varieties of language. All views are backed by classroom teaching illustrations.

Lehmann, Winfred P. *Descriptive Linguistics: An Introduction.* New York: Random House, 1972. This survey text presents the data of language through chapters dealing with phonetics, syntax and analysis, inflection and derivation. Also included are explanatory chapters on semantics, language theory, psycho- and sociolinguistics, and applied linguistics.

Liles, Bruce L. *An Introductory Transformational Grammar.* Englewood Cliffs: Prentice-Hall, 1971. This elementary text fuses transformational theory and application throughout its treatment of phrase structure, transformations, and phonological components.

Lloyd, Donald. "Structure in Language," *College English,* 24 (May, 1963), 598–602. In discussing the "social structuring of usage," Lloyd reiterates that all speakers adjust language to fit specific social situations by responding to situational cues.

Lloyd, Donald J., and Harry R. Warfel. *American English in Its Cultural Setting.* New York: Alfred A. Knopf, 1956. This descriptive introduction to how English works in American society treats speech and writing in terms of language learning and the role of the individual in society.

Long, Ralph B., and Dorothy R. *The System of English Grammar.* Glenview: Scott, Foresman and Company, 1971. The structure of contemporary standard English prose is described and demonstrated in this traditional grammar. It is a "grammar of sets" which explains grammatical functions, clause types, parts of speech, and word formation and is concerned with pedagogical considerations.

Marckwardt, Albert H., and Randolph Quirk. A *Common Language: British and American English.* London: Cox and Wyman, Ltd., 1966. A discussion of the differences and similarities between British and American English is rendered through twelve dialogues. The varietal differences in each have resulted from the demands of history, politics, economics, social and cultural change. Emphasis is on positive changes in response to the needs of situational context.

McKnight, George. "Conservatism in American Speech," *American Speech,* 1 (October, 1925), 1–17. An illustrated discussion of the history of linguistic conservatism in America to 1925 points out the various influences and groups which have not recognized the positive movements of linguistic change but have attempted to maintain a dichotomy between correctness and natural idiom.

Osenburg, F. C. "Objective Testing, the New Phrenology," *College Composition and Communication,* 12 (May, 1961), 106–111. This review of measurement problems inherent in vocabulary, multiple-choice reading, and English battery tests also touches on some of the ways in which students "learn" to answer test questions without really understanding what they're doing with language.

Pooley, Robert C. *The Teaching of English Usage.* Second Edition. Urbana: NCTE, 1974. Background and facts about usage are balanced against teaching procedures. Problems raised by concern for correctness and propriety are investigated. The requirements of language variety, attitude, and historical developments are considered.

Pyles, Thomas. *The Origins and Development of the English Language.* Second Edition. New York: Harcourt Brace Jovanovich, 1971. This descriptive history of the language is concerned with a chronological treatment of the phonological and grammatical development of English.

Quirk, Randolph, and Sidney Greenbaum. *A Concise Grammar of Contemporary English.* New York: Harcourt Brace Jovanovich, 1973. This transformational grammar (a shorter version of *A Grammar of Contemporary English*) provides a model and data for understanding varieties of English, elements of grammar, phrasal and syntactic patterning, and kinds of prominence (i.e., focus, theme, and emotive emphasis).

Roberts, Paul. *English Sentences.* New York: Harcourt, Brace & World, 1962. Chapters 1 and 2 make a clear distinction between a nongrammatical English sentence (Henry some flowers his mother brought) and a grammatical English sentence (Henry brung his mother some flowers) and discusses the social implications of dialect differences.

Schroth, Evelyn. "Some Usage Forms Die Hard—Thanks to College Entrance Exams," *English Journal*, 56 (January, 1967), 97–102. This article argues that College Board tests still test as substandard certain usage items which authorities on usage consider to have been accepted within the boundaries of current acceptable usage.

Shuy, Roger. *Discovering American Dialects.* Champaign: NCTE, 1967. This simplified introduction to dialects discusses regional and social varieties of American dialects, how and why they differ, foreign language influence, and literary dialects.

Shuy, Roger, ed. *Social Dialects and Language Learning.* Champaign: NCTE, 1964. Twenty statements by linguists and educators provide an overview of social dialectology, field projects, teaching programs, social factors affecting learning of Standard English and behaviorists reactions, and research implications. Many viewpoints—sometimes conflicting—are offered on such problems as acquisition of Standard English, usage problems and attitudes, dialect and multi-dialect behavior, and programs for the English classroom.

Sledd, James. "On Not Teaching English Usage," *English Journal*, 54 (November, 1965), 698–703. This argument against teaching English usage presents new views of language use which help to develop broader definitions of usage based on responsible judgment.

Smith, Alfred G., ed. *Communication and Culture.* New York: Holt, Rinehart and Winston, 1966. Signals, codes, and meanings of human communication are investigated through a sequential arrangement of fifty-five contributors' statements dealing with theory, syntactics, semantics, and pragmatics.

Smith, Arthur L., ed. *Language, Communication, and Rhetoric in Black America.* New York: Harper & Row, 1972. This collection of twenty-nine essays by communications specialists and educators discusses the communication process in its totality, i.e., dialect, styles, tone, situational context, rhetorical intention. Several case studies and F. Erickson's comparison of white and Black college students in rap sessions contribute to the illustration of the theme.

Smith, Holly. "Standard or Nonstandard: Is There an Answer?" *Elementary English*, 50 (February, 1973), 225–235. This research report-survey summarizes the controversy of school attitudes toward dialect and acceptability, a controversy which must be faced before staff can react to students' needs.

Smitherman, Geneva. "English Teacher, Why You Be Doing the Thangs You Don't Do?" *English Journal*, 61 (January, 1972). This article, written in the Black, suggests teaching technologies for inner-city English classrooms.

Steinberg, Danny D., and Leon A. Jakobovits, eds. *Semantics: An Interdisciplinary Reader in Philosophy, Linguistics, and Psychology.* Cambridge: Cambridge University Press, 1971. This collection of thirty-three articles representing several fields of study deals with the nature, source, and dimensions of linguistic meaning.

Stockwell, Robert P., Paul Schachter, and Barbara Hall Partee. *The Major Syntactic Structures of English.* New York: Holt, Rinehart and Winston, 1973. This survey of transformational grammar and theory is based on Fillmore's Case Grammar framework and is comprehensive in its treatment.

Whorf, Benjamin Lee. *Language, Thought and Reality.* Ed. John B. Carroll. Cambridge: The M.I.T. Press, 1967. These selected writings present Whorf's linguistic examination of the ways in which thinking is dependent on language and the ways in which language affects one's vision of the world.

Wilkinson, Andrew, ed. *The Context of Language.* (Volume 23 of *Educational Review*). Birmingham: University of Birmingham, 1971. Five articles concentrate on considering language in its situational context. Language is seen as a matter of options.

Wilkinson, Andrew, ed. *The State of Language.* (Volume 23 of *Educational Review*). Birmingham: University of Birmingham, 1969. Nine contributor statements present recent views on the state of grammar, language models and coding, kinds and registers of English, and reading acquisition.

Williams, Frederick, et al. "Ethnic Stereotyping and Judgments of Children's Speech," *Speech Monographs*, 38 (August, 1971), 166–170. Working with the "Pygmalion effect" (attitudes which language characteristics may elicit in listeners), the researchers investigate biases which lead to stereotypes. Implications for teacher training are considered.

Williams, Frederick et al. *Sociolinguistics: A Crossdisciplinary Perspective.* Washington, D.C.: Center for Applied Linguistics, 1971. A survey of interactions of the five fields of speech/communication, psychology, education, sociolinguistics, and linguistics/anthropology is presented through eleven contributors' statements-responses about social dialect.

Williamson, Juanita V., and Virginia M. Burke, eds. *A Various Language.* New York: Holt, Rinehart and Winston, 1971. This introductory reader surveys the history and scope of dialect studies through the statements of fifty contributors.

Wolfram, Walt. "Sociolinguistic Premises and the Nature of Non-standard Dialects," *Speech Teacher,* 19 (September, 1970), 177–184. Also in Smith (1972). This article is a discussion of sociolinguistic considerations which affect teacher evaluation of speech behavior and teacher attitudes toward nonstandard speech behavior. Verbal options as arbitrary and established by custom, dialect adequacy as a communicative system, and language as learned in community context are considered.

LANGUAGE VARIETIES, LINGUISTIC PROFILING, HOUSING, CIVIL RIGHTS, AND EMPLOYABILITY

Billiard, Charles, Arnold Lazarus, and Raven I. McDavid, Jr. *Identification of Dialect Features Which Affect Both Social and Economic Opportunity among the Urban Disadvantaged.* Final Report. Washington, D.C.: Office of Education, 1969. (EDRS-ED 038 483). The authors undertook a study to determine (1) dialect features associated with three ethnic groups (Anglo, Black, Latin American) and four social classes which were unacceptable to a dominant, urban culture (Fort Wayne, Indiana), (2) social markers which might handicap such speakers socio-economically and culturally, and (3) the implications of this for teacher preparation and classroom teaching. The results offer specific illustrations of code markers which may affect socio-economic mobility.

O'Neil, Wayne. "The Politics of Bidialectalism," *College English,* 33 (January, 1972), 433–439. A linguist considers the underlying ideology of school language programs and argues that they are informed by economic-political requirements. Bidialectalism is viewed as "part of the social and political machinery meant to control."

Sledd, James. "Bi-Dialectalism: The Linguistics of White Supremacy," *English Journal,* 58 (December, 1969), 1307–1315. A linguist argues against bidialectalism as a politically oriented move to control minorities and as an answer to economic mobility needs.

Sledd, James. "Doublespeak: Dialectology in the Service of Big Brother," *College English,* 33 (January, 1972), 439–457. Also in Smith (1972). A dialectologist discusses the racial and political implications of the controversy over minority dialects, stating that "doublespeak" is used as a political, economic weapon for control.

- Melvin A. Butler, Southern University, Chairman
- Adam Casmier, Forest Park Community College
- Ninfa Flores, Harvard University
- Jenefer Giannasi, Northern Illinois University*
- Myrna Harrison, Laney Community College
- Robert F. Hogan, NCTE, ex officio
- Richard Lloyd-Jones, University of Iowa
- Richard A. Long, Atlanta University
- Elizabeth Martin, Odessa College
- Elisabeth McPherson, Forest Park Community College, Past Chair, CCCC
- Nancy S. Prichard, NCTE, ex officio
- Geneva Smitherman, Wayne State University
- W. Ross Winterowd, University of Southern California

*Jenefer M. Giannasi compiled the annotated bibliography with members of the Committee on the CCCC Language Statement.

In August of 2006 the CCCC Language Policy Committee updated the original annotated bibliography. The 2006 version can be found at http://www.ncte.org/library/NCTEFiles/Groups/CCCC/NewSRTOL.pdf.

The Conference on College Composition and Communication reaffirms the students' right to their own language and language varieties. Realizing the continued need to preserve our Nation's diverse heritage of languages and language varieties, the CCCC reaffirms and upholds its 1974 position statement, "Students' Right to Their Own Language." November 23, 2003

2   CCCC's Role in the Struggle for Language Rights

GENEVA SMITHERMAN

A mong the language arts crowd, the Conference on College Composition and Communication (CCCC) has become famous (or infamous, depending on your vantage point) for its 1974 *Students' Right to Their Own Language* resolution. However, virtually since its inception, CCCC has served as the site of dialogues about language controversies. Poring over nearly 50 years of back issues of *CCC*, I realized that through its journal—initially called its "official bulletin"—CCCC has consistently provided a forum for scholars and activists to raise up the issue of language rights. While the central focus here will be on two organizational policies of CCCC, the "Students' Right" resolution of 1974 and the National Language Policy of 1988, my historical narrative incorporates articles and commentaries on language in *CCC*. These contributions by members and leaders in the field highlight CCCC's historical role in the struggle for language rights. While the organization has not always stepped decisively and swiftly to the challenge, its past record as advocate for those on the linguistic margins is, on balance, one in which CCCC can take pride.

DONALD J. LLOYD AND THE "NEW LINGUISTICS"

We begin this journey back in linguistic time with the words of linguist Donald J. Lloyd.

> The [article] is an expression at the very least of a frivolous obscurantism, or at the most of a vigorously cultivated ignorance . . . Failure to know [the factual studies of language] and what they mean . . . is responsible for the fact that the educational heart of darkness . . . is the English course . . . Emphasis on "correctness"—at the expense . . . of a fluid, knowledgeable command of our mother tongue—is responsible for the incompetence of our students in handling their language, for their embarrassment about their own rich . . . dialects, for their anxiety when

From *College Composition and Communication* 50.3 (1999): 349–76.

they are called upon to speak or write . . . and for their feeling that the study of English is the study of trivialities which have no importance or meaning outside the English class. . . .

In our day, to make statements about English and about language which do not square with linguistics is professionally reprehensible. Yet it is an indulgence arrogantly and willfully permitted themselves by many English teachers, not decently hidden in class, but in open publication in the journals of our field and in the concoction of the dreariest collection of ignorantly dogmatic textbooks that dominates any discipline in the schools. (10–12)

Thus Lloyd launched the first debate in *CCC*.[1] It was February 1951, and CCCC was just two years old. Lloyd was replying to "The Freshman is King; or, Who Teaches Who?" published in the December 1950 issue of *CCC* by Kenneth L. Knickerbocker of the University of Tennessee-Knoxville. In his scathing critique, with its signifyin title, "Darkness is King," Lloyd took Knickerbocker to task for coming to conclusions about the actual use of 19 "controversial" expressions (for example, Who did you meet?) based on an opinion survey by a lay person that had been published in *Harper's Magazine.* Lloyd argued that the "disputed expressions" had all been studied and "found to be in good use in this country," and he stated unequivocally that "the language of a person who uses none of these expressions is not superior to the language of one who uses some of them, or indeed, to that of one who uses all of them" (10). Not content with just knocking Knickerbocker upside the head, Lloyd also slammed the journal and the organization: "The appearance [of this article] in the bulletin of the CCCC is a little shocking," and "The assertion or implication that the language of a person who uses none of these expressions is superior on that account is a professional error which no English teacher should commit in print, and no editor should permit him to make" (10).

Surprisingly, Knickerbocker seemed not to be offended and even gave Lloyd props for his rhetorical skills: "This is a highly literate reply to my 'frivolous obscurantism.' It indicates that somewhere along the line Mr. Lloyd has been concerned with correctness. (I should like to teach my students to write as well as he does.) It may be that my little paper did not deserve to reap such a fine whirlwind, but since it did, let it blow" (footnote, Lloyd, "Darkness," 1951, 10). And blow it did! Although Knickerbocker was not heard from again on the subject, Martin Steinmann Jr. came into the fray, accusing Lloyd of lapses of logic that led him to "exhortations to action" (12). He and Lloyd did battle in three issues of *CCC*. Steinmann's obtuse writing style makes his critique difficult to follow, but in the main he appears to be arguing that Lloyd has invoked linguistics as a science to tell us what people should say based on what they do say. Actually, Lloyd's argument does not take this route at all. Rather, he points out Knickerbocker's fundamental error in accepting what people think they say for what they do say. Space does not permit a detailed analysis of this debate nor the reply to the reply to the reply. Suffice it to say that Steinmann's critique may be summed up as a "misguided foray into irrelevant tediousness and willful misconstruction of Lloyd's meaning" (Sheridan).

Clearly, from the jump, then, CCCC was a forum for linguistic debates and language issues of various kinds. To a great extent, this is attributable to the parallel development of Composition-rhetoric and Linguistics in the 1950s and 1960s, as both fields sought to reinvent themselves and stake intellectual claim to distinct identities among the established disciplines of the academy. Indeed, in those early years, linguistics was breaking away from anthropology and philosophy and formulating new grammars truly reflective of how English works (Structural, Transformational), grammars which were replacing the misfit Latinate-based models of old. At the time, there was a good deal of excitement about the "New Grammar," and linguistics seemed to hold out great promise to resolve a host of problems in the human sciences: language teaching and learning, the mystery of the structure of human cognition—and the teaching of literacy. Thus the most frequently cited authors in *CCC* articles from 1950–64 were linguists: Charles C. Fries (with 13 cites), Kenneth Pike (11), Paul Roberts (10), Donald Lloyd (8), Noam Chomsky (7), Phillips et al. (452). These early articles generally focused on the relevance, for Composition Studies, of the theories and research coming out of Linguistics, and within this general concern, their focus was most often on the specific issue of usage and the teaching of writing to those students who used nonstandard forms and who did not (as Charles Fries had put it in 1940) "carry on the affairs of the English-speaking people" (12–13). In this early period, those students were typically not students of Color, but rural and/or working-class whites. Lloyd spoke for these white regional and social class dialects quite poignantly:

> You discover . . . that dialects you have grown up to despise are rooted in respectable antiquity and still reflect the vicissitudes of pioneer life. If you respect American traditions, you find these traditions best embodied in the language of the illiterate back-country farm families, whether they still stand on their own land or congeal in uneasy clots in our industrial cities. You come therefore to describe with respect. You give information; you do not devise new decalogues. ("English Composition" 41)

Some scholars argued that composition courses should be built around Linguistics, that the English language itself, when studied from the vantage point of the new grammatical paradigms, could well serve as the content of the composition curriculum. Titles of articles from this early period are illustrative: John Carroll's 1956 "Psycholinguistics and the Teaching of English Composition," Mary Elizabeth Fowler's 1956 "Using Semantic Concepts in the Teaching of Composition," a 1957 Panel report on "From Literacy to Literature: The Pedagogical Use of Linguistics," a 1957 Workshop Report on "Applying Structural Linguistics in the Classroom" and a 1960 panel Report on "Linguistics in the Composition-Communication Course."

Beginning with the proposition that "an English composition course around linguistics" would "take the English language as a social instrument expressing, conditioning, and . . . conditioned by the society that uses it,"

Lloyd even goes so far as to say that linguistics "is a promised land for the English teacher" ("English Composition" 40, 43). Linguist and longtime CCCC leader Harold B. Allen, however, was quite cautious about the possibilities of language-based curricula for composition. He argued that research was needed in order to ascertain the applicability of linguistic knowledge to the production of powerfully written essays:

> It is my present conviction that power in the use of language, rather than mere skill, derives from sensitive awareness of the manifold resources of language, in structure as well as in vocabulary. This conviction rests on *a priori* grounds; but so does the belief of those who omit linguistic content and rely upon dogma. We need evidence that comes from research. ("Linguistic Research" 57)

Still, Ralph B. Long was not only cautious but caustic in his review of two texts for the "Freshman English" course. In "Grammarians Still Have Funerals," Long questions the usefulness of the "New Grammar" for composition instruction, indicts linguists for their "odd romantic primitivism" when it comes to speech and writing, and lambastes one for declaring that "a person would just as soon call himself a con man or an alchemist as a grammarian." Long rebuts:

> I have called myself a grammarian for many years ... Until Roberts' book came along, it would not have occurred me to compare grammarians—or even New Linguists, in spite of the extravagant claims many of them make for their work—with con men and alchemists ... the grammar Lloyd and Warfel and Roberts give at great length—at greater length than seems desirable for Freshman English—is about as vulnerable as the school grammar these men scorn ... It is unlikely that the New Linguists have really achieved immortality. (211–216)

Linguist James Sledd, however, seems to have put the lie to Long's assertion. Often referred to as "the conscience of the field" (see Olson 298), Sledd has been a regular on CCCC and NCTE conference programs over the decades, during which time he has consistently challenged compositionists and other language arts theorists and practitioners on behalf of linguistically marginalized and economically disenfranchised voices. In 1956, in his first appearance in *CCC*, Sledd asserted that while subordinate clauses are grammatically subordinate, this should not be confused, as it often is even today, with being logically subordinate. Thus, some teachers' admonition to put the main idea in the main clause and the subordinate idea in the subordinate clause doesn't always work. While this essay doesn't deal directly with language rights issues—a theme that Sledd would, in the coming decades, write about eloquently and powerfully—"Coordination (Faulty) and Subordination (Upside-Down)" is important in our historical narrative because it offered a precise and accurate linguistic description as a corrective for the misassumptions about language that many writing teachers held (and perhaps still hold?). Thus Sledd, a stalwart of the language rights struggle, here exemplifies the contributions of the New Linguists to the then-emerging field of Composition Studies.

Concerning standards of usage, in 1957 Charles Hartung echoed other progressive linguists in making a case for the value of linguistics in establishing usage norms for composition students. He argued that usage should be governed by "the doctrine of the linguistic norm," a standard derived from balancing "the intention of the speaker, the nature of the language itself, and the probable effect on the audience" (62). But while throughout the 1950s and 1960s, linguists and other CCCC scholars advocated the legitimacy and adequacy of all language variations, they also consistently called for composition instructors to toe the line in terms of teaching the social inadequacy of nonstandard forms. "If a new doctor or minister says 'you was,' confidence in him is lowered. Educated people should talk like educated people, no matter who is listening or what the occasion may be" (Ives 154). In his 1952 "Preparing the Teacher of Composition and Communication—A Report," based on his visit to 47 different colleges and universities, where he interviewed department heads, graduate deans, full and part-time faculty, and graduate students, Harold Allen argued strongly that the composition instructor should possess linguistic knowledge and sophistication. Despite what appears to be a progressive position on language differences, however, he went on to advocate that instructors should "help students to substitute one set of language practices for another set . . . to teach standard usage to freshmen who do not have command of it" (11). This is essentially a philosophy of subtractive bilingualism and is exactly the kind of contradictory position that Ernece Kelly would lambaste the entire CCCC organization for in her 1968 "Murder of the American Dream" speech. Even Lloyd, often considered a linguistic radical, acknowledged that instructors would find that they had to make a "change" in their students. However, in contrast to his contemporaries, Lloyd explicitly advocated an additive bilingualism, that students respect and retain their home languages:

> If we find anything that we have to change—and we do—we know that we are touching something that goes deep into [a given student's] past and spreads wide in his personal life. We will seek not to dislodge one habit in favor of another but to provide alternative choices for freer social mobility. We seek to enrich, not to correct . . . By respecting their traditions and the people from whom they come, we teach them to respect and to hold tight to what they have as they reach for more. ("English Composition" 42)

By 1962, as evidenced in his "On Not Sitting Like a Toad," Lloyd had refined his pedagogy for using "New Grammar" concepts (for example, pattern practice drills) to teach alternative language habits while simultaneously promoting retention of the mother tongue. In a class all by himself in the first years of CCCC, Lloyd anticipated the thinking that would lead to the "Students' Right" resolution two decades later.

"MURDER OF THE AMERICAN DREAM"

One major result of the social movements of the 1960s and 1970s was the creation of educational policies to redress the academic exclusion of and past injustices inflicted upon Blacks, Browns, women, and other historically marginalized groups. Programs and policies such as Upward Bound, open enrollment, Educational Opportunity Programs (EOPs), preferential/affirmative action admissions, and the development of special academic courses ("basic" writing) brought a new and different brand of student into the college composition classroom. Unlike the returning military veterans and other working class white students of the 1950s and early 60s, this new student spoke a language which not only reflected a different class, but also a different race, culture, and historical experience.

The symbolic turning point was 1968. The assassination of Dr. Martin Luther King, Jr., which occurred while the CCCC Convention met in Minneapolis, brought the organization "shockingly to an awareness of one of its major responsibilities" (Irmscher 105). In his memorial to King in the May 1968 issue of *CCC*, editor William Irmscher indicated that the organization now had a "new demand" placed upon it. Although he did not put it in these terms, for the first time, race/Color as a central component of linguistic difference became an in-yo-face issue that the organization could no longer ignore. Not that race/Color was a new issue that had somehow just fallen from the sky. Rather, the organization had heretofore simply proceeded as if racial differences did not exist and as if race did not need to be taken into account in the life of CCCC. In a sense, Irmscher's half-page homage to King symbolizes CCCC's loss of innocence.

Ernece B. Kelly's speech, "Murder of the American Dream," was delivered at the annual meeting in Minneapolis after the news of King's assassination and reprinted in the May 1968 issue of *CCC*. In this brief but powerful work, Kelly reproached CCCC for the lack of Black representation in the program, rebuked the organization for the exclusion of Black intellectual and literary products in anthologies, and took it to task for the way it deals with Black Language. Kelly states:

> Here we meet to discuss the dialects of Black students and how we can upgrade or, if we're really successful, just plain *replace* them ... Why aren't there Blacks here who will talk about the emergence of an image among Blacks which does not permit them to even bother with the question of whether or not the white man understands their dialect? ... Why aren't there Blacks ... [dealing] with the richness and values of the language of the Black ghetto? ... such ideas have been dealt with and their complexities examined. Why weren't these papers presented here? (107)

Subsequently, and as a direct response to her "Murder of the American Dream" speech, Kelly was invited to co-edit an issue of *CCC*, which appeared later that year, in December 1968. That issue includes articles by four African American writers, a first for *CCC*.

The late Sarah Webster Fabio poses the questions, "What is Black?" (also the title of her article) and "What is Black language?" Indicating that these questions were frequently being asked during that time, she defines Black Language as

> direct, creative, intelligent communication between black people based on a shared reality, awareness, understanding which generates interaction; it is a rhetoric which places premium on imagistic renderings and concretizations of abstractions, poetic usages of language, idiosyncrasies—those individualized stylistic nuances . . . which . . . hit "home" and evoke truth. (286)

James Banks's "Profile of the Black American" deals with a range of cultural issues, one of which is language. His brief comments on language and composition assert the legitimacy of Black students' language and downplays the need to master "standard English":

> When evaluating their compositions, the teacher must realize that these students emanate from a different culture . . . which possesses a language with a different structure and grammar, but nevertheless a valid structure and grammar. Thus the teacher must concentrate on the quality of ideas in the composition rather than on the student's use or misuse of standard American English grammar. Our mission is to teach these students how to think, to describe their environment, and to encourage their creativity . . . Grammar is incidental; the student will later pick up standard English grammar if he sees a need for it and if we have succeeded in developing his reflective and problem-solving skills. (296)

In the same issue, Leonard Greenbaum's "Prejudice and Purpose in Compensatory Programs" predicts an Orwellian nightmare for those seeking to suppress African American speech and other language varieties.

> Dialect has positive aspects . . . that are not part of standardized English . . . The desire to eliminate dialect is an egocentric solution proposed out of power and out of traditional modes of education that have always shunned the experimental in favor of the pragmatic. This was how the "system" dealt with immigrants at the turn of the century and just prior to and during World War II, and it is how, similarly, some propose it should deal with rural or inner-city dialects in the 1960's. This desire, no doubt, will win out. I can predict what lies in our future—a uniform society, most likely in uniform . . . we are hastening to our meeting with Orwell. (305)

It is interesting that several of the articles in this special issue touch on the question of language even when that is not a particular article's central focus. The late Elisabeth McPherson's brilliant, thoughtful piece, "Hats Off—or On—to the Junior College," employs, as a point of departure, a controversy about male students wearing their hats inside a community college building. "There was more involved than a possibly out-of-date, middle-class custom. There was a racial issue, too; it was only the Negro students for whom the hats, very narrow-brimmed and often very expensive, were a badge and a symbol" (317). In the course of her discussion, she touches on the matter of language as a mark of identity and culture, citing the work of linguist Benjamin Whorf and invokes the hat metaphor to address the question of dialects:

> The question of usage . . . is very much like the question of hats. Which is the more important status symbol for the student: leaving his hat on and keeping his own identity? Taking it off and learning to be an imitation WASP? This is a decision only the student can make . . . If changing his dialect is not the student's own idea . . . we have no right to insist on it simply because we prefer the sound of our own. If we are a college, and not just defenders of the status quo, we've more important business than worrying about dialect changes. (322)

Three years after the publication of this essay, McPherson would become a crucial member of the "Students' Right to Their Own Language" Committee. Nearly two decades later, in 1987, she accepted appointment to the Language Policy Committee, on which she continued to serve despite a lingering and debilitating illness.

STUDENTS' RIGHT TO THEIR OWN LANGUAGE

> We affirm the students' right to their own patterns and varieties of language—the dialects of their nurture or whatever dialects in which they find their own identity and style. Language scholars long ago denied that the myth of a standard American dialect has any validity. The claim that anyone dialect is unacceptable amounts to an attempt of one social group to exert its dominance over another. Such a claim leads to false advice for speakers and writers, and immoral advice for humans. A nation proud of its diverse heritage and its cultural and racial variety will preserve its heritage of dialects. We affirm strongly that teachers must have the experiences and training that will enable them to respect diversity and uphold the right of students to their own language.
>
> —CCCC, *Students' Right*, inside front cover

The *Students' Right* resolution followed logically on the heels of the dramatic 1968 annual meeting of CCCC and the subsequent December 1968 special issue of *CCC*, which were themselves affected by the social movements, political events, and assassinations in the world beyond Academe. The resolution is grounded in the sociolinguistic branch of linguistics, a natural affinity for CCCC. When the 1970s split in linguistics occurred, dividing the Cartesian/theoretical school (associated with Noam Chomsky) from the socially constituted school (associated with Joshua Fishman), CCCC followed the latter.

As an organizational position, the *Students' Right* resolution represented a critical mechanism for CCCC to address its own internal contradictions at the same time as marching, fist-raising, loud-talking protesters, spearheaded by the Black Liberation Movement, marred the social landscape of "America the beautiful." Some language scholars had begun to question bidialectalism as a goal for the linguistically marginalized (see Sledd's 1969 "Bi-Dialectalism").

They argued that the bidialectalism philosophy was only being promoted for those on the margins. Further, since linguistic research had demonstrated the linguistic adequacy of "nonstandard" dialects, why wouldn't the "system" accept them? To reject them was tantamount to making difference into deficiency all over again. From this viewpoint, it was clear that the charge to intellectual-activists was to struggle for the wider social legitimacy of all languages and dialects and to struggle, wherever one had a shot at being effective, to bring about mainstream recognition and acceptance of the culture, history, and language of those on the margins. It was this line of thinking that moved me to get involved in CCCC and the *Students' Right* struggle; it also moved many of my peers in other fields to become involved in their respective professional organizations. Most of us had been baptized in the fire of social protest and street activism. No romantic idealists, we knew the roadblocks and limitations involved in trying to effectuate change within the system. But we also knew that without "vision, the people perish." Besides, as I commented to a fellow comrade (a psychologist, who was one of the founders of the Association of Black Psychologists), what else was we gon do while we was waitin for the Revolution to come?

In this socio-historical climate, in the fall of 1971, the CCCC officers appointed a small committee to draft a policy resolution on students' dialects. I was a member of that committee and by the time of the 1972 vote, also a member of the CCCC Executive Committee. In March 1972, we presented the CCCC Executive Committee with the *Students' Right* position statement, a fairly terse, but highly controversial (some said "explosive") paragraph. The CCCC Executive Committee passed the resolution at its November 1972 meeting, promptly enlarged the Committee, and charged it with developing a background document to elaborate on the meaning and implications of the *Students' Right* policy. The Executive Committee realized that this resolution would stir up controversy and that many language arts professionals, including those teaching composition, held a variety of myths and misconceptions about language and dialects. Our job was to amass the latest scholarship and research on language diversity and on language matters relevant to the teaching of composition. The document we produced would be distributed to the membership in preparation for a vote. At the annual meeting in Anaheim, California, in April 1974, the *Students' Right to Their Own Language* was passed by a wide margin and subsequently became organizational policy. That fall, the resolution and supporting background document were published as a special issue of *CCC*.

CCCC was not merely being trendy, nor politically correct, in passing the *Students' Right* resolution. Rather, the organization was responding to a developing crisis in college composition classrooms, a crisis caused by the cultural and linguistic mismatch between higher education and the nontraditional (by virtue of color and class) students who were making their imprint upon the academic landscape for the first time in history. In its quest to level the playing field, U.S. society was making it possible for these students from the margins to enter colleges and universities. Most of these students, however bright, did not have command of the grammar and conventions of academic discourse/"standard English." Yet they often had other communicative strengths—creative ideas, logical and persuasive reasoning powers, innovative ways of talking about the ordinary and mundane. How was this contradiction to be resolved? What professional advice could ecce provide to frustrated composition instructors charged with teaching this new and different student clientele how to write? What could be done to help these students succeed in the composition classroom? And in the long view, how could the composition classroom, as part of the higher education of these students, prepare them for life beyond Academe? The Introduction to the *Students' Right* indicates that CCCC was sharply and painfully cognizant of these issues:

> Through their representatives on Boards of Education and Boards of Regents, businessmen, politicians, parents, and the students themselves insist that the values taught by the schools must reflect the prejudices held by the public. The English profession, then, faces a dilemma: until public attitudes can be changed—and it is worth remembering that the past teaching in English classes has been largely responsible [or those attitudes—shall we place our emphasis on what the vocal elements of the public think it wants or on what the actual available linguistic evidence indicates we should emphasize? (p. 21 in this book)

In the *Students' Right* resolution and in the subsequent background document, we sought to accomplish three broad goals: (1) to heighten consciousness of language attitudes; (2) to promote the value of linguistic diversity; and (3) to convey facts and information about language and language variation that would enable instructors to teach their non-traditional students—and ultimately all students—more effectively. In pursuit of these goals, the Introduction of the background document posed questions that composition professionals might ask themselves:

> We need to discover whether our attitudes toward "educated English" are based on some inherent superiority of the dialect itself or on the social prestige of those who use it. We need to ask ourselves whether our rejection of students who do not adopt the dialect most familiar to us is based on any real merit in our dialect or whether we are actually rejecting the students themselves, rejecting them because of their racial, social, and cultural origins. . . . Our major emphasis has been on uniformity, in both speech and writing; would we accomplish more, both educationally and ethically, if we shifted that emphasis to precise, effective, and appropriate communication in diverse ways, whatever the dialect? (pp. 21–22)

To convey facts and information about the latest research on language and language diversity, the background document was structured in the form of 15 discussion sections, each beginning with a question implicit in the resolution. All of the fifteen questions were similar in content, if not form, to areas of concern about which members of the profession were agonizing as they sought to understand what it means, in practice, to advocate, in theory, that students have a right to their own language. The questions were:

(1) What do we mean by dialect?

(2) Why and how do dialects differ?

(3) How do we acquire our dialects?

(4) Why do some dialects have more prestige than others?

(5) How can concepts from modern linguistics help clarify the question of dialects?

(6) Does dialect affect the ability to read?

(7) Does dialect affect the ability to write?

(8) Does dialect limit the ability to think?

(9) What is the background for teaching one "grammar"?

(10) What do we do about handbooks?

(11) How can students be offered dialect options?

(12) What do we do about standardized tests?

(13) What are the implications of this resolution for students' work in courses other than English?

(14) How does dialect affect employability?

(15) What sort of knowledge about language do English teachers need?

Finally, the background document concluded with an annotated bibliography of 129 entries keyed to the answers to the fifteen questions.

BEHIND THE SCENES

Both supporters and detractors have assumed that the "Students' Right" Committee was comprised of like-minded individuals. Although all of us were committed to addressing the language crisis facing the new wave of students in composition classrooms, and to helping resolve this crisis, there was a wide range of personal styles and great diversity in political ideologies among us. On one level, one might have considered us "progressives," but we clearly had our own internal contradictions. And so in the production of the resolution and the supporting monograph, our long hours of scholarly work were accompanied virtually every step of the way by intense political and ideological struggle.

One of our early debates occurred over the use of *his*. "The Student's Right to His Own Language" was the wording of the original resolution, and while a couple of the women in the group put forth strong objections to the masculinist tone, one of the men thought the whole argument was silly and a waste of time because the generic "he" had been used for centuries, and everybody knew it included women too. He then began to quote several historical examples, going way back to the Bible. One of the women interrupted this filibuster-like strategy and suggested that we should call it "student's right to her own language" since "her" was just as generic as "he." Then we tried "his or her," but someone objected to this on grounds of verbosity. We even tried using "people," but someone remarked that we were dealing with "students," not "people." Whereupon a lengthy debate ensued over whether or not the labels "people" and "students" could be used interchangeably. At the time, my womanist consciousness was just developing, and so I was not very vocal in this hours-long debate, for which I was soundly blessed out by one of the women when we took a bathroom break, who wanted to know what kind of linguist was I who was "afraid" to challenge male hegemony? The debate was finally resolved when Elisabeth McPherson, genius that my girl was, proposed that we cast the wording in the third-person plural. We had all been so locked into our linguistic prisons that we hadn't even thought of this quite simple solution to the problem. While this issue seems old hat now as we head for the 21st century, lest we forget, concerns about sexism in language did not always exist—even among many women.

Nor were we of identical persuasion on the issue of America's linguistic ills and the solutions to them. Hey, some members were even opposed to the use of four-letter words among us, not just the big, bad ones, but even the little ones like "damn" and "hell." (I report with pride that I was the first to introduce "cussing" into Committee discourse, to the relief of one of my male comrades.) The debates that were going on in the society, in the profession, and in CCCC about how to address America's social and sociolinguistic problems went on among us, filtered through the prism of language. Why should linguistic minorities have to learn two languages and majority members of society get by on one? That's linguistic domination. Why not accept a student paper with "nonstandard" surface features of language if the message was clear and the argument well-supported? That's what the "right" to their own language means. No, giving two grades, one for content, one for grammar, is a cop-out, you are still saying there is something "wrong" with the writer. Let's make the medium the message and write this monograph in a combination of Black English, Spanglish and standard English. And so it went. Then, as now, for some of us, the final document is seen as equivocating; it doesn't go far enough. For others, then as now, it is perceived as too permissive.

It has been said that politics is the art of compromise. And compromise we did. After the lengthy debates and verbal duels, we finally produced a document that we all felt we could live with. Credit for blending the multiple writing styles into a readable document goes to the talented editorial hand of Richard Lloyd-Jones and the skillful diplomacy of the late Melvin Butler, linguist and Committee Chair, whose untimely death prevented him from witnessing the fruits of his labor.[2]

REACTIONS TO THE *STUDENTS' RIGHT*

The fall-out was tremendous. Stringent, vociferous objections were put forth. There were calls for the resolution to be rescinded and the background document recalled. Some blasted CCCC for abdicating its responsibility and pandering to "wide-eyed" liberals in the field. Others accused CCCC of a "sinister plot" to doom speakers of "divergent" dialects to failure in higher education by telling them that their stigmatized language was acceptable. A few simply said that CCCC had done lost they cotton-pickin minds.

On the other hand, there were many who embraced the spirit of the resolution. They thanked CCCC for the supporting document, which many found extremely helpful, even as they acknowledged its flaws. Some complimented the organization for its "moral and professional courage." Others stepped to the challenge of developing writing assignments to "tap the potential" of their marginalized students. A few simply asked CCCC why it took yall so long.

Ideas about student-centered approaches to composition instruction and about sensitivity to students' language/dialects have by now become fairly commonplace in the discourse community of composition and in the language arts profession generally. Which is not to say that everyone subscribes to these ideas today, just that talk about them is no longer perceived as "weird." However, in the context of the 1970s, to promulgate ideas about students' right to anything was a bold, new style of pedagogy. Such ideas elicited strong reactions among CCCC professionals (irrespective of whether they supported the resolution or not) and moved the intellectual production of knowledge in the field to a whole nother level.

Articles and commentaries on the *Students' Right*, written in the years immediately following the resolution's passage, contain some of the most creative teaching ideas and are some of the most innovatively written essays published in *CCC* to date. In 1972 John R. Hendrickson wrote a response to the Executive Committee's resolution in "tibetan-American inglish" and critiqued the resolution through the device of parody. He argues that the resolution doesn't go "neer far enuff," that it should include language that exempts students from playing "musik" as it is written by classical composers and from learning about evolution since some "piple dont bleev" in it (301). David W. Cole employed the story of the Gileadites versus the Ephraimites as a metaphor to argue against the resolution. In the Biblical parable, the Ephraimites couldn't pronounce the word "shibboleth" in the correct Gileadite accent and could thus be prevented from crossing over the River Jordan. Similarly, Cole argued that non-mainstream dialect speakers will be prevented from crossing into the mainstream. Lawrence D. Freeman examined Constitutional Amendments and court cases that provide legal justification for students' right to their own language. Citing such cases as *Wisconsin v. Yoder* and *Griggs v. Duke Power*, Freeman argued that language rights can be seen as protected by custom and that there is a legal basis for hiring instructors who are skilled in the dialect/language of the students they will instruct (see p. 115). Seeking to devise teaching assignments grounded in the legitimacy of the students' language, Lou Kelly devised a method of "copyreading" which emphasizes clarity of meaning and expressiveness rather than grammatical correctness. Students can discover for themselves places where their writing should be edited for clarity and power, thus demonstrating, according to Kelly, that a composition instructor can facilitate students' competency in standard English while simultaneously respecting their own idiolects.

Louie Crew conducted an experiment with a class of Black English–speaking students in which they demonstrated creative capacity to "wrench" positive words and phrases from negative statements. He had students rephrase "white is ugly" and "black is beautiful" without using the words "white," "black," "ugly," or "beautiful." They came up with phrases like "ivory-faced honky" and "blue-eyed hookworms" (43–44). Allen N. Smith argued that "no one has a right to his own language" (p. 163), that the resolution is a contradiction in terms, for language is a social act. And William G. Clark critiqued the background document for what he deemed hypocrisy in its recommendation that teachers inform students preparing for certain occupations about the necessity of Edited American English. Clark asserted that this advice undermines "the resolution's claim about all dialects being equally valuable, implicitly valorizes standard English, and is a cop-out on the part of CCCC" (217).

The organization held its ground. It did not revoke the resolution, nor did it recall the background document. (In fact, that 25-year-old document is still in print and can be ordered from NCTE.) Some folk, ever-resistant to change, continued to rail against the policy. However, the initial hysteria faded, and fewer articles and commentary about the resolution appeared in *CCC* after about 1977. Instead, many in the field, fully cognizant that marginalized students were in higher education to stay—and would, in a matter of years, become the majority of the student population—began to direct their energies to creative and pedagogically responsible ways of implementing a *Students' Right* philosophy in their composition classes. As Donald Stewart would put it a few years later, the challenge is "how to respect the dialect the student brings to school yet not avoid the responsibility of teaching him or her alternative dialects and editing skills for coping with different language situations" (330).

The *Students' Right to Their Own Language* was a policy formulated to address the contradictions developed in the midst of a major paradigm shift in higher education, itself the result of a major paradigm shift in the social order. Language arts professionals across the Nation and on all levels were encountering the new brand of students and experiencing classroom crises similar to those of composition instructors. The CCCC *Students' Right* policy opened up a national dialogue about language diversity and professional responsibility. As Jix Lloyd-Jones, long-time CCCC leader and member of both the *Students' Right* Committee and the Language Policy Committee, has said:

> The statement had an intellectual base in sociolinguistics, but its energy came from support of social diversity. It forced a reconsideration of "correctness." It implied a model of language as "transactional" rather than as artifact. Behind the anger of the political oratory was acceptance of a thesis about the nature of language. (490)

In due course, other language arts organizations adopted policies reflecting the research and scholarship on language diversity coming out of sociolinguistics. But lest we forget, CCCC was the pioneer.

CCCC AND *CCC* DURING THE "SECOND RECONSTRUCTION"

Although many compositionists and other language arts professionals greeted the *Students' Right* policy with high enthusiasm, still a great degree of lingering confusion existed: "Well, then, if I don't correct the grammatical errors, what do I do?" as one well-meaning instructor queried. It seemed that the *Students' Right* background document was welcomed because it was informative in terms of theory; however, it did not go far enough in praxis. CCCC leadership acknowledged the need for something more in the form of explicit teaching materials, sample lesson plans, and a more practically oriented pedagogy. In 1976, the Executive Committee thus appointed the "Selection and Editorial Committee for Activities Supporting Students' Right to Their Own Language," on which three of the original *Students' Right* Committee members—Elisabeth McPherson, Jix Lloyd-Jones, and I—served. This new committee was charged with assembling, for publication, practical classroom assignments, activities, lectures, and teaching units that would show and tell how to apply the philosophy of the *Students' Right* resolution to the day-to-day experience of teaching and learning. By 1980, our committee had more than enough material for what we felt would be a valuable sequel to the *Students' Right* document. However, despite having spent nearly four years compiling and editing some excellent material, solicited from practitioners at all levels of language arts education, we were informed that CCCC had "reluctantly decided" not to publish the collection. What had happened since the passage of the original *Students' Right* resolution by CCCC Executive Committee (in 1972) and CCCC membership (in 1974) is attributable in great measure to the changed national climate of the 1980s.

Owing to the socio-political, educational, and economic decline in Black and other historically disenfranchised communities during the 1980s, political theorists such as Ronald Walters have dubbed the years from 1980 to 1992 as the "Second Reconstruction." The "first" Reconstruction had been launched in the late 1870s, with the Federal Government's abandonment of ex-slaves to Southern governments, which promptly rolled back the freedmen's political gains, and ushered in an era of lynchings and brutal assaults against Blacks which would not be redressed until the Black Freedom Struggle of the 1960s. After the promise and some fulfillment of the social movements of the 1960s and 70s, the U.S. moved to a more conservative climate on the social, political, and educational fronts—a move solidified in 1980 by the election of Ronald Reagan. By that time, the mood of CCCC, like the mood of America, seemed to have shifted from change and promise to stagnation and dreams deferred.

It was within the climate of the Second Reconstruction that Thomas J. Farrell's 1983 bombshell, "IQ and Standard English, "appeared in *CCC*. Farrell re-raised the old linguistic-cognitive deficiency theory about speakers of what was then still being called "Black English." (Although the term "Ebonics" was coined in 1973, it didn't catch on until the Oakland School Board's 1996 resolution.) Even though Farrell asserted that "mean IQ difference" between "black ghetto children" and speakers of "standard English" has "nothing to do with genetics or race, per se" (481), still he contended that:

> The non-standard forms of the verb "to be" in ... Black English may affect the thinking of the users ... Black ghetto children do not use the standard forms of the verb "to be" ... Many of those same black ghetto children have difficulty learning to read, and they do not score highly on measures of abstract thinking. ... I am hypothesizing that learning the full standard deployment of the verb "to be" is integral to developing Level II thinking because the deployment of that verb played a part in the development of abstract thinking in ancient Greece. (477, 479)

As shocking as it was to see Farrell's article in *CCC*, it has played a crucial role in the language rights debate for two reasons. First, it is a reminder that old arguments, which are assumed to be dead and long since buried, can resurface in new and potentially more dangerous forms which distort current research for "supporting" evidence. Second, despite my Lloydian reaction to this article's appearance in *CCC*, and notwithstanding my disillusionment about CCCC's rejection of the 1980 *Students' Right* follow-up publication, it is significant to note that by 1983 there had emerged a critical mass of compositionists who could and did provide solid, valuable rebuttals to Farrell, relying on research from sociolinguistics. And further, it is significant that *CCC* allowed the publication of four very lengthy "Counterstatement" essays in its December 1984 issue. One was from Karen Greenberg, who argued in her brilliant response that "be" verb constructions are simply applied according to different but identifiable rules of Black English, and that Farrell's terminology, such as "paratactic" and "hypotactic," was "pseudo-scientific," adding only the "gloss of respectability" (458). The other three valuable critiques in this *CCC* issue were offered by Patrick Hartwell, Margaret Himley, and R. E. Stratton.

"NATIONAL LANGUAGE POLICY"

In the 1998 celebration of African American History Month there was a television commercial for Mickey D's [gloss: Ebonics for McDonald's] which features a white father and his young son browsing through a gallery with paintings of African American heroes and she-roes. The father points to the work of Jacob Lawrence, and tells his kid "That's Jacob Lawrence, a famous painter." Next, they come upon a painting of Harriet Tubman, and the father says, "That's Harriet Tubman, a leader in the Underground Railroad." The kid exclaims, "Wow, that's cool" as a voice-over comes on saying, "It's not just Black History, it's *American* history" (emphasis Mickey D's).

The recognition that the story of Africans in America is the story of all Americans, that indeed, the history of other marginalized groups is also American history, marks the beginning of this nation's journey toward a mature social consciousness. Although the U.S. is comprised of diverse racial and ethnic groups, the common goal is to make this democratic experiment a success. In this quest the experience of one group is inextricably bound up with the experience of other groups. As Martin Luther King often said during his lifetime, we are one nation, and we must all learn how to live together, or we shall all die together.

Much like the theme of the Mickey D's commercial, and the legacy of King, CCCC's National Language Policy is a linguistic imperative for all groups—not just Blacks, Browns, the poor, and others on the margins. While addressed to and for all citizens, the National Language Policy is not a repudiation of the *Students' Right* resolution. That policy was the right move for that historical period, and it filled a deep pedagogical void. The National Language Policy symbolizes the evolution of CCCC sociolinguistic consciousness and was the next logical stage after the *Students' Right* campaign.

In the Fall of 1986, California passed its English Language Amendment to the State Constitution, making it the first state in contemporary times to establish, by law, a policy of "English Only." The late S. I. Hayakawa, then Senator from California, had introduced the first Constitutional Amendment on this issue in 1981, but it had stagnated in Congressional committees. The proponents of English Only had thus decided to take their campaign to various states with the goal of securing the requisite number of state language amendments to give English Only the status of an amendment to the U.S. Constitution. California, with its large number of Spanish speakers, and Asian and Mexican immigrants, had been selected as the test case.

A number of organizations and caucuses opposed California's measure and the growing formation of an English Only Movement. Within CCCC, the opposition came during the 1987 convention from the Progressive Composition Caucus (PCC). The Caucus described itself as a group of "composition instructors who view writing as a potentially liberating activity and teach from a socialist-feminist perspective. Our curriculum often emphasizes non-canonical literature and exposes sexist, racist, homophobic and corporate manipulation of language" (*PCC Newsletter*). Although PCC wanted CCCC to take a stand against English Only, there was also sharp tension at the time between PCC and the CCCC Executive Committee and leadership over the issue of conducting the Convention in a hotel involved in a labor action. Uncertain if they could trust CCCC to do the right thing, PCC decided that their sense-of-the-house motion should not only call for concerted opposition against English Only but should also include the name of someone they trusted to carry out the mandated opposition. The day before the Annual Meeting, PCC asked me if I would accept the charge and if I would allow my name to be included in their resolution. As I listened to their arguments, all I could think about was the dissin and doggin I had endured during the "Students' Right" years, and I kept saying "no way."

At the Annual Meeting in 1987, the PCC submitted the following sense-of-the-house motion:

> *Preamble:* As the leading professional organization dealing with language and literacy, the CCCC should be in the forefront of the effort to decide issues of language policy. *Resolved:* That the CCCC support the NCTE

resolution opposing English-only legislation by appointing a well funded task force, chaired by Geneva Smitherman, to articulate the issues and formulate and implement strategies to educate the public, educational policy-makers, and legislatures; further, that this issue receive major emphasis in the 1988 Conference theme. "Language, Self, and Society." (CCCC Minutes, 21 March 1987, pg. 5)

The motion passed. The task force that was appointed was called the "Language Policy Committee" (LPC).[3] Its charge was to develop a proactive response to the English Only Movement for consideration by CCCC Executive Committee, to compile information on English Only, and to network with other professional organizations and groups mounting English Only opposition campaigns.

CCCC kept its part of the bargain. The organization provided funding, full support and resources for the LPC to carry out its charge. Our Committee met over the summer of 1987 and developed the National Language Policy and a strategic implementation plan. We presented our work to the CCCC Executive Committee meeting and to the annual meeting in March 1988, and the following resolution passed unanimously:

Background

The National Language Policy is a response to efforts to make English the "official" language of the United States. This policy recognizes the historical reality that, even though English has become the language of wider communication, we are a multilingual society. All people in a democratic society have the right to education, to employment, to social services, and to equal protection under the law. No one should be denied these or any civil rights because of linguistic differences. This policy would enable everyone to participate in the life of this multicultural nation by ensuring continued respect both for English, our common language, and for the many other languages that contribute to our rich cultural heritage.

CCCC National Language Policy

Be it resolved that CCCC members promote the National Language Policy adopted at the Executive Committee meeting on March 16, 1988. This policy has three inseparable parts:

1. To provide resources to enable native and nonnative speakers to achieve oral and literate competence in English, the language of wider communication.

2. To support programs that assert the legitimacy of native languages and dialects and ensure that proficiency in one's mother tongue will not be lost.

3. To foster the teaching of languages other than English so that native speakers of English can rediscover the language of their heritage or learn a second language. (CCCC National Language Policy Brochure)

The National Language Policy stresses the need not just for marginalized Americans but all Americans to be bi- or multilingual in order to be prepared for citizenship in a global, multicultural society. More than a policy for students of one particular color or class, the National Language Policy recognizes that the ability to speak many tongues is a necessity for everybody.

This time the motion of history was on our side. Negative reaction to the National Language Policy has been minimal. Further, this organizational policy has not had to undergo the agonizing argumentation, contestation, debate—and denial—that the *Students' Right* resolution endured. By no stretch am I saying that compositionists have all been doing the right thing over the decade since the passage of the National Language Policy. What we are witnessing, though, is a developing sociolinguistic sophistication and political maturity about language rights issues. As the field of Composition-Rhetoric has evolved, so too has the language consciousness of CCCC professionals. Further, theorists now recognize the need to address realities relative to students' native language/dialect in the camp-rhetoric context, a posture that has, unfortunately, not always been the case.

Contributions to *CCC* in the period since 1988 clearly reflect a long-overdue recognition of the linguistic-cultural complexity of the composition classroom and of the writing instructor's task in that classroom. Terry Dean wrote of the pedagogical difficulties facing a "monocultural teacher" in a multicultural/multilingual composition classroom and proposes strategies for creative instruction in such a classroom. Howard Tinberg provided the example of a student who studied the speech of people on the island of Campobello, a community whose "customs and language seemed distinct," but whose "values and traditions were close enough to her own hometown's ways that she could feel a bond" (81). Drawing on her own multivocal competence across several linguistic and cultural traditions, CCCC leader Jacqueline Jones Royster challenged us to "construct paradigms that permit us to engage in better practices in cross-boundary discourse, whether we are teaching, researching, writing, or talking with Others, whoever those Others happen to be" (37–38). Analyzing the language and literacy practices of white students, Margaret Marshall makes a compelling argument for a broadened notion of "diversity," and contends that "we need a way of thinking about difference in student writing as more than a simple match between a set of predetermined divisions and uses of language" (232). A similar line of thought and conceptualization about the language and rhetorical complexity of students of Color—across linguistic traditions—appears in work published in *CCC* by scholars such as Lu, Soliday, Anokye, Canagarajah, and Bizzell. In sum, then, the spirit of CCCC National Language Policy—a broad-based challenge to address linguistic diversity throughout the body politic, not just among those who have historically been on the margins—is increasingly being reflected in the pages of *CCC* as the organization ends one half century and begins another.

CONCLUSION

If it is true, as CCCC leader Anne Ruggles Gere has asserted, that changing language attitudes is tantamount to changing a world view, then there may not be a lot that a policy from a professional organization can do about the myths and misconceptions about language that continue to plague the struggle for language rights. One cannot erase long-held attitudes and deeply entrenched biases and stereotypes with the stroke of a pen—you know, go henceforth and sin linguistically no more. On the other hand, those who (whether consciously or unconsciously) display the negative effects of *linguicism* are products of the school (and the college, though in fewer numbers) because everybody goes through school. The classroom, then, is a major player in shaping language attitudes, and the classroom that is particularly crucial for the formation of ideas about language is that of the K–12 level. And here is where CCCC, as a post-secondary organization, has very limited influence.

Although CCCC is politically autonomous, structurally, it is an institutional arm, operates under the broad umbrella, and shares the national headquarters of the National Council of Teachers of English (NCTE). In 1971, after the formation of what was to become the *Students' Right* committee, CCCC leadership and members began working within NCTE to promote the concept of the students' right to their own language. For three subsequent years, there was a concerted effort by CCCC to persuade NCTE to endorse CCCC language policy. However, this did not come to pass. Instead, at the 1974 NCTE Convention, NCTE membership passed a weak version of a language rights resolution. It was simply called NCTE Resolution #74.2, which carefully bypassed the label *Students' Right*. While Resolution 74.2 "accept[s] the linguistic premise that all these dialects are equally efficient as systems of communication," it goes on to "affirm" that students need to learn the "conventions of what has been called written edited American English." This was a posture that CCCC deliberately and consciously sought to avoid in its policy resolution because usage, spelling, punctuation, and other "conventions" of "written edited American English" were typically the only aspects of the writing process that teachers focused on. Thus, the *Students' Right* background document had asserted that

> Dialect . . . plays little if any part in determining whether a child will ultimately acquire the ability to write EAE. . . . Since the issue is not the capacity of the dialect itself, the teacher can concentrate on building up the students' confidence in their ability to write. . . . If we can convince our students that spelling, punctuation, and usage are less important than content, we have removed a major obstacle in their developing the ability to write. (pp. 28, 29)

Many people in the language arts field (and, I would wager, most of those outside the field) erroneously credit NCTE with the "Students' Right" resolution. I have repeatedly heard this from numerous people over the years since CCCC passed its resolution. This misattribution continues today. In a review published in the very pages of this journal in May 1997, Gary A. Olson states: "While the essays in this collection touch on a number of issues, the two pervasive concerns are bidialectalism, especially in relation to NCTE's [sic] "Students' Right to Their Own Language" (298). Recently in the *Journal of English Linguistics* special issue on Ebonics, linguist Walt Wolfram bemoans the persistence of negative language attitudes despite the efforts of professional organizations:

> Furthermore, the adoption of strong position statements on dialect diversity by professional organizations such as the National Council of Teachers of English (namely, the statement on Students' Right to Their Own Language) . . . barely made a dent on entrenched attitudes and practices with respect to language differences. (109)

But in order for a "dent" to be made in these attitudes and practices, the *Students' Right* would need to be embraced by K–12 teachers. Adoption by NCTE would have gone a long way towards building the K–12 support necessary to make such a "dent." The struggle waged by CCCC leaders and members to get NCTE support for the resolution was acrimonious and fierce—in-yo-face. (To date, some of them folk still don't speak to each other!) And so it is a bitter irony that NCTE is credited with passage of this progressive language policy. Let the record be clear: Despite the Faulknerian agony and sweat of the human spirit of many language warriors, NCTE never passed the *Students' Right to Their Own Language* resolution. In retrospect, this should not come as a surprise, because NCTE's sociolinguistic history is a mixed one. Back in 1917, it led a national promotion of "Better Speech Week," in which students recited the following pledge with regularity:

> I love the United States of America. I love my country's flag. I love my country's language. I promise:
> 1. That I will not dishonor my country's speech by leaving off the last syllable of words.
> 2. That I will say a good American "yes" and "no" in place of an Indian grunt "um-hum" and "nup-um" or a foreign "ya" or "yeh" and "nope."
> 3. That I will do my best to improve American speech by avoiding loud rough tones, by enunciating distinctly, and by speaking pleasantly, clearly, and sincerely.
> 4. That I will learn to articulate correctly as many words as possible during the year. (qtd. in Gawthrop 9–10)

Fortunately, the NCTE done come a long way, baby!

The other major reason that CCCC language policy pronouncements have not had broad-based impact has to do with the need to publicize these policies. One must do something, somehow actively engage in the process of language attitude change, organize language discussion panels and program events outside ivory—and ebony—towers, go out into the vineyards and speak the truth to the people, wherever one finds them—in the churches, the streets, the bars and pubs, at block club and other kinds of community meetings, on television talk shows, in one's personal social life, and on and on. This is the challenge of the membership of CCCC as we move into a multilingual/multicultural era of national and global life.

None of this should be construed as stating that CCCC's role in the language rights struggle has been insignificant. On the contrary, CCCC has had a significant impact as a language pioneer, initiating a national conversation on issues of dialect and language diversity. Whether you agreed with the *Students' Right* position or not, as an educator you were forced to address the issue. You could no longer ignore language and dialect diversity, whatever position you took, you had to reckonize (to put a slightly different twist on the Hip Hop term).

It is crucial to have organizational positions as weapons which language rights warriors can wield against the opponents of linguistic democratization. The *Students' Right* and the *National Language Policy* provide the necessary intellectual basis and rhetorical framework for waging language debates and arguments. Further, since intellectuals provide the ideological rationale for public policy, it was and is important for organizations like CCCC to go on record as supporting language rights. Organizational pronouncements about language can and do have influence and impact. A case in point: There was a time, up until around the mid-1970s, that speech tests were required to qualify for entry into university teacher education programs. People like me flunked these linguistically, culturally, and gender-biased tests and got forced into speech therapy. These tests have now been eradicated. This is a direct result of the intellectual and the activist wings of the social movements of the 1960s and '70s, manifested in the Academy in research that came out of sociolinguistics and in professional organizational positions like the *Students' Right to Their Own Language*.

The documented spirit of resistance in the *Students' Right* and CCCC *National Language Policy* is an important symbol that change is possible—even within the system. Of course the battle is not over; there is still work to be done in the vineyard. In the December 1997 issue of *CCC*, Arnetha Ball and Ted Lardner revisit the 1977–79 "Ann Arbor Black English case." In this Federal court case, I served as the chief advocate for a group of single Black women (most of them on welfare at the time) and their children (most of them boys), who sued the Ann Arbor, Michigan, School Board for its failure to educate their children, primarily its failure to teach them literacy skills. At the Martin Luther King, Jr. Elementary School the children attended, they had been classified as "learning disabled," primarily on the basis of their language (Ebonics). They were essentially educational cast-offs who were on their way to joining the already enormous pool of functional illiterates in too many African American communities in the U.S. The Judge ruled in the mothers' favor, acknowledging the legitimacy and systematicity of the children's home language—"Black English"—and mandating the School Board to devise a remedy to equip its teachers with literacy practices for these Ebonics-speaking children.

Ball and Lardner analyze the constructs underlying "teacher knowledge," using the teachers in *King* as a case study. They contend that teacher "lore" often substitutes for objective knowledge: "[teachers are] willfully ignorant of disciplinary knowledge" and "think they should be free . . . to ignore [for example] modern linguistic scholarship" (476). Further, they argue that teachers need a way of critiquing their own affective habits so as to develop "confidence in their ability to adapt" knowledge about linguistics in general, and in the case of *King*, about Ebonics in particular, to the literacy needs of students who speak Ebonics (AKA "Black English," "African American Vernacular English"). This recent Braddock Award winning essay recalls Donald J. Lloyd's battle for linguistic enlightenment 48 years ago, and says to CCCC and language warriors that the struggle for language rights continues.

In the same issue of *CCC*, there is another brilliant essay, this one by Charles F. Coleman. Using concrete examples taken from essays by what he terms ESD (English as a Second Dialect) students, Coleman demonstrates the ineffectiveness of traditional grammar approaches which result in what he calls "iatrogenic" effects (a borrowing from medicine, meaning that the so-called corrective creates new problems). His work, which is also applicable to ESL student writers, draws upon linguistic knowledge to pinpoint specific speech practices and to suggest ways of teaching that are informed by knowledge of those practices. Like Ball and Lardner's essay, Coleman's article also recalls Lloyd and the (now-old) "New Linguistics." However, Coleman's work says to us that although the struggle for language rights yet continues, CCCC can win.

Acknowledgments: I would like to express my gratitude and a special thanks to David Sheridan, PhD candidate in English at Michigan State University, for his most capable assistance and archival work. Also, a shout out to David Kirkland, undergraduate English major at Michigan State and my student assistant for his efforts to make me computer literate. Any shortcomings are entirely my own doing.

NOTES

1. Donald J. Lloyd, who taught for years at Detroit's Wayne State University, was a major figure in the early years of Composition Studies and Linguistics. His PhD in literature from Yale University hardly equipped him to teach literacy and language, and he notes that he learned, through trial and error over the years with his students, how to teach writing. He is co-author of *American English in Its Cultural Setting* (1962) and is credited with coining the phrase, the "national mania for correctness." On a personal note, while doing the research for this article, I remembered that Lloyd had taught me introductory linguistics at Wayne State. At the time, his ideas about language were profoundly shocking to most of his students—including me, who at the time was an untutored, fresh-from-the-ghetto very young teen-ager. Being the first of my family to go beyond the seventh grade—much less college—and on whom the family hopes for educational success were riding, I recall being highly attracted to—but at the same time fearful of—Lloyd's "heretical" challenge to prevailing language norms.

2. The other "Students' Right" Committee members were: Adam Casmier, Ninfa Flores, Jenefer Giannasi, Myrna Harrison, Richard Lloyd-Jones (who synthesized and edited our individually written sections), Richard A. Long, Elizabeth Martin, the late Elisabeth McPherson, and Ross Winterowd. Robert F. Hogan and Nancy S. Prichard served as NCTE *ex officio* members.

3. The other LPC members were: Elizabeth McTiernan Auleta; Ana Celia Zentella; Thomas Kochman; Jeffery Youdelman; Guadalupe Valdes; Elisabeth McPherson. Of the original group, Ana Celia Zentella, Elizabeth McTiernan, and I are still on the (now reconstituted) Language Policy Committee. Other current Committee members are: Richard Lloyd-Jones, Victoria Cliett, Gail Okawa, Victor Villanueva, Rashidah Muhammad, Elaine Richardson, Kim Lovejoy, and Jan Swearingen.

WORKS CITED

Allen, Harold B. "Preparing the Teacher of Composition and Communication—A Report." *CCC* 3.2 (1952): 3–13.

———. "Linguistic Research Needed in Composition and Communication." *CCC* 5 (1954): 55–60.

Anokye, Akua Duku. "Housewives and Compositionists." *CCC* 47 (1996): 101–03.

"Applying Structural Linguistics in the Classroom" (workshop). *CCC* 8 (1957): 159–62.

Ball, Arnetha and Lardner, Ted. 1997. "Dispositions Toward Language: Teacher Constructs of Knowledge and the Ann Arbor Black English Case." *CCC* 48 (1997): 469–85.

Banks, James A. "A Profile of the Black American: Implications for Teaching." *CCC* 19 (1968): 288–96.

Bizzell, Patricia. "The 4th of July and the 22nd of December: The Function of Cultural Archives in Persuasion as Shown by Frederick Douglass and William Apess." *CCC* 48 (1997): 44–60.

Canagarajah, A. Suresh. "Safe Houses in the Contact Zone: Coping Strategies of African American Students in the Academy." *CCC* 48 (1997): 173–96.

Carroll, John B. "Psycholinguistics and the Teaching of English Composition." *CCC* 7 (1956): 188–93.

Clark, William G. "In Responses to 'Students' Right to Their Own Language.'" *CCC* 27 (1975): 217.

Cole, David W. "An Ephraimite Perspective on Bidialectalism." *CCC* 23 (1972): 371–72.

Coleman, Charles F. "Our Students Write With Accents: Oral Paradigms for ESD Students." *CCC* 48 (1997): 486–500.

Conference on College Composition and Communication. *Students' Right to Their Own Language.* Special Issue. *CCC* 25 (1974). [Pages 19–57 in this book.]

Conference on College Composition and Communication. *The National Language Policy.* Urbana: NCTE, 1991 (brochure).

Crew, Louie. "Wrenched Black Tongues: Democratizing English." *CCC* 25 (1974): 42–45.

Dean, Terry. "Multicultural Classrooms, Monocultural Teachers." *CCC* 40 (1989): 23–37.

Fabio, Sarah Webster. "What is Black?" *CCC* 19 (1968): 286–87.

Farrell, Thomas J. "IQ and Standard English." *CCC* 34 (1983): 470–84.

Fowler, Mary Elizabeth. "Using Semantic Concepts in the Teaching of Composition." *CCC* 7 (1956): 193–97.

Freeman, Lawrence D. 1975, *"The Students' Right to Their Own Language: Its Legal Basis."* *CCC* 26 (1975): [pp. 115–20 in this book].

Fries, Charles Carpenter. *American English Grammar.* New York: Appleton, 1940.

"From Literacy to Literature: The Pedagogical Use of Linguistics" (Panel Report). *CCC* 8 (1957): 135–36.

Gawthrop, B. "1911–1929." *An Examination of the Attitudes of the NCTE Toward Language.* Ed. Raven McDavid, Jr.: Urbana: NCTE, 1965.

Gere, Anne Ruggles, and Smith, Eugene. *Attitudes, Language, and Change.* Urbana: NCTE, 1979.

Greenbaum, Leonard. "Prejudice and Purpose in Compensatory Programs." *CCC* 19 (1968): 305–11.

Greenberg, Karen. "Responses to Thomas J. Farrell 'IQ and Standard English.'" *CCC* 35 (1984): 455–60.

Hartung, Charles V. "Doctrines of English Usage." *CCC* 8 (1957): 55–63.

Hendrickson, John R. "Responses to CCCC's Executive Committee's Resolution on 'The Students' Right to His Own Language.'" *CCC* 23 (1972): 300–01.

Irmscher, William F. "In Memoriam: Rev. Dr. Martin Luther King, Jr. 1929–1968." *CCC* 19 (1968): 105.

Ives, Sumner. "Grammatical Assumptions." *CCC* 5 (1954): 149–55.

Kelly, Ernece B. "Murder of the American Dream." *CCC* 19 (1968): 106–08.

Kelly, Lou. "Is Competent Copyreading a Violation of the 'Students' Right to Their Own Language'?" *CCC* 25 (1974): 254–58.

Knickerbocker, Kenneth L. 1950. "The Freshman is King: Or, Who Teaches Who?" *CCC* 1.4 (1950): 11–15.

"Linguistics in the Composition/Communication Course" (Panel Report). *CCC* 11 (1960): 130–31.

Lloyd, Donald J. "Darkness is King: A Reply to Professor Knickerbocker." *CCC* 2.1 (1951): 10–12.

———. "An English Composition Course Built Around Linguistics." *CCC* 4 (1953): 40–43.

———. *American English in Its Cultural Setting.* New York: Knopf, 1962.

———. "On Not Sitting Like a Toad." *CCC* 13 (1962): 9–13.

Lloyd-Jones, Richard. "Who We Were, Who We Should Become." *CCC* 43 (1992): 486–96.

Long, Ralph B. "Grammarians Still Have Funerals." *CCC* 9 (1958): 211–16.

Lu, Min-Zhan. "Professing Multiculturalism: The Politics of Style in the Contact Zone." *CCC* 45 (1994): 442–58.

Marshall, Margaret J. "Marking the Unmarked: Reading Student Diversity and Preparing Teachers." *CCC* 48 (1997): 231–48.

McPherson, Elisabeth. "Hats Off—or On—to the Junior College." *CCC* 19 (1968): 316–22.

NCTE. 1974. Resolution #74.2. November, 1974.

Olson, Gary A. "Critical Pedagogy and Composition Scholarship." *CCC* 48 (1997): 297–303.

Phillips, Donna Burns, Ruth Greenberg, and Sharon Gibson. "College Composition and Communication: Chronicling a Discipline's Genesis." *CCC* 44 (1993): 443–65.

Progressive Composition Caucus Newsletter. April, 1987.

Royster, Jacqueline Jones. "When the First Voice You Hear Is Not Your Own." *CCC* 47 (1996): 29–40.

Sheridan, David. Unpublished essay, 1998.

Sledd, James. "Coordination (Faulty) and Subordination (Upside-Down)." *CCC* 7 (1956): 181–87.

———. "Bi-Dialectalism: The Linguistics of White Supremacy." *English Journal* 58 (1969): 1307–15.

Smith, Allen N. "No One Has a Right to His Own Language." *CCC* 27 (1976): [pp. 163–68 in this book].

Soliday, Mary. "From the Margins to the Mainstream: Reconceiving Remediation." *CCC* 47 (1996): 85–100.

Steinmann, Martin, Jr. "Darkness is Still King: A Reply to Professor Lloyd." *CCC* 2.2 (1951): 9–12.

Stewart, Donald. "Acting on the CCCC Language Resolution and Related Matters." *CCC* 31 (1980): 330–32.

Tinberg, Howard B. "Ethnography in the Writing Classroom." *CCC* 40 (1989): 79–82.

Walters, Ronald W. *Pan Africanism in the African Diaspora.* Detroit: Wayne State UP, 1993.

Wolfram, Walt. "Language Ideology and Dialect: Understanding the Oakland Ebonics Controversy." *Journal of English Linguistics* 26 (1998): 108–21.

3

The Students' Right to Their Own Language, 1972–1974

STEPHEN PARKS

We affirm the students' right to their own patterns and varieties of language—dialects of their nurture or whatever dialects in which they find their own identity and style. Language scholars long ago denied that the myth of a standard American dialect has any validity. The claim that any one dialect is unacceptable amounts to an attempt of one social group to exert its dominance over another. Such a claim leads to false advice for speakers and writers, and immoral advice for humans. A nation proud of its diverse heritage and its cultural and racial variety will preserve its heritage of dialects. We affirm strongly that teachers must have the experiences and training that will enable them to respect diversity and uphold the right of students to their own language.

"THE STUDENTS' RIGHT TO THEIR OWN LANGUAGE"

If the CCCC business meetings were becoming increasingly politicized and polemical, the Executive Committee continued to officially distance itself from the leftist political activity of the 1960s. For instance, at the November 1971 Executive Committee meeting, officers discussed what action should be taken concerning four sense-of-the-house motions passed at Cincinnati. . . . [T]hese motions had included strong statements concerning firing teachers for political activity, the "imperialist Vietnam War," support for the role of women in the profession, and the inclusion of African American interests in CCCC programs. Since the meeting, mail ballots had been sent concerning the first two resolutions. As reported by CCCC Chairperson Edward Corbett, "only 40 people responded to the mailing." A resolution was passed that "[i]n the light of the fact that only 40 people responded to the mail ballot, the results of the ballot cannot be considered representative and the Executive Committee can take no stand based on the responses, either approving or disapproving the resolutions" (CCCC Secretary's Report No. 65, 24 November 1971). As had

From *Class Politics: The Movement for the Students' Right to Their Own Language* (NCTE, 2000), 160–202.

happened at the MLA Convention in 1968, the policies of the NUC and the New Left had been blocked through a mail ballot.[1] Notably, the SRTOL would pass with just seventy-nine votes, only thirty more than the antiwar resolution had taken to pass and only thirty-nine more than the aforementioned mail ballots. As discussed later, however, the SRTOL would be sufficiently scrubbed of New Left policies; its low vote total would not be used to dismiss its passage.

THE SECOND SRTOL

Indeed, the whole SRTOL matter might have remained unresolved if Executive Committee member Richard Larson had not stated that the CCCC should "make another effort at a statement affirming the student's right to his own language." (The title had not yet been made gender neutral.) It is clear from the outset, however, that this new effort saw itself as principally opposed to the NCTE's previous statements. As recorded in the minutes, committee member Richard Lloyd-Jones "reminded the group that the Commission on Language had issued a very mild statement" (CCCC Secretary's Report No. 65, 24 November 1971). In response, Corbett appointed a new committee consisting of Richard Lloyd-Jones as chairperson, with Geneva Smitherman, Darnel Williams, Myrna Harrison, and Ross Winterowd, among others, as committee members. The committee was appointed "to examine the statements of the Commission on Language and the Commission on Composition [and] . . . to report to the Executive Committee in Boston [in November] its judgment about whether the CCCC should endorse an existing statement on language (from one of the NCTE Commissions) or propose its own" (CCCC officers meeting, 25 November 1971).

Even prior to Boston, however, Elisabeth McPherson reported at the CCCC officers meeting that the SRTOL committee was corresponding and "developing a CCCC statement on language." Further, McPherson reported that a subcommittee of Blyden Jackson, Walker Gibson, Betty Petola, and herself was recommending that CCCC "recommend acceptance of the [NCTE CEL "Statement on Usage," but only the] part stating that teachers should know about the nature and structure of language, including information about dialects, but that the Executive Committee [of CCCC] reject the rest of the report of the Commission and refuse to publish it" (CCCC officers meeting, 5 March 1972). It is important, then, that the subcommittee argued for an endorsement of only the general claim of a need for increased linguistic awareness. The subcommittee was not endorsing the CEL's argument about standard English nor its vision of how standard English should be used to supply students to the U.S. economy. That is, the subcommittee was leaving open what types of knowledge would be necessary to be linguistically aware, as well as the implications of the NCTE "Statement on Usage" for the writing classroom. The CCCC accepted these requests and, in effect, began the process of finding a new linguistic and nationalist paradigm through which teachers could understand dialect difference. Consequently, when approximately two weeks later Richard Lloyd-Jones reported to the full Executive Committee that the SRTOL committee believed its role was to decide whether the CCCC needed to develop its own language policy, it appears that the CCCC officers had already decided.

The Executive Committee's concern now focused on the makeup of the committee which would be writing the SRTOL. According to the minutes (CCCC Secretary's Report No. 66, 21 March 1972), Marianna Davis stated that the committee ought to include black linguists. This suggestion, however, seemed to be part of a larger concern about racial representation. Soon after this, the minutes reflect that both Davis and Douglass argued that the committee needed to represent a larger cross section of the CCCC constituency and to include a greater representation of minority groups. Additionally, they argued that a clearer committee charge was needed. Both of these objections were overridden. McPherson, who was now CCCC chairperson, is positioned in the minutes as arguing that any statement by the committee could be modified, rejected, or accepted; black linguists were not needed. Hogan, Nelson, and Campbell argued for the efficacy of a small group working on the project and then allowing the full Executive Committee to see its way through as a body. Consequently, McPherson ordered the committee, as currently organized, to report the next day (CCCC officers meeting, 21 March 1972).

The failure to produce a clearly stated charge, however, would come back to haunt the future status of the SRTOL, for the following day Lloyd-Jones reported that the committee now understood that the goal of the committee was to provide a brief statement on language, adding that such a statement would be *a guide to teachers on all levels and under a variety of local conditions*. In making the committee's mission include *all* teachers, the committee created the opportunity for future participants in the development of the SRTOL, such as Harold Allen, to argue that the SRTOL was properly under the domain of the NCTE. Furthermore, Lloyd-Jones added that the draft of the SRTOL statement about to be distributed "was not the report of his total committee nor did it represent consensus by the committee; it was being presented to determine if the ideas in it illustrated the general framework on the sort of statement the Executive Committee wanted" (CCCC Secretary's Report No. 66, 21 March 1972).

It is, of course, difficult to assess what transpired in the meeting. Nor is it possible to state positively what individual motivations shaped the document. Within the cultural, political, and historical context developed throughout this volume, however, it is possible to read how different versions of the resolution placed CCCC within the time period. It appears that faced with an unclear committee charge and an unclear consensus among its members, the SRTOL committee argued that the previously endorsed guidelines for junior college teachers be endorsed as the general policy of the CCCC. As recorded on a handwritten note, one of the original SRTOL's statements read as follows:[2]

> The Executive Committee of CCCC affirms the student's right to his own language—the dialect of his nurture in which he finds his identity and style. Claims that only one dialect is acceptable should be viewed as attempts of one social group to exert its dominance over another not as either true or useful advice to writers nor as moral advice to humans. A nation which is proud of its diverse heritage and of its cultural and racial variety ought to preserve its heritage of dialects. The Executive Committee affirms strongly the need for teachers to have such training to enable them to support this goal. (SRTOL [handwritten copy] n.d.)

This draft seems in line with the goals of the junior college guidelines as written by Gregory Cowan. . . . [T]hese guidelines had argued for the recognition "that all levels of language and all dialects are equally valuable and that academic insistence on a so-called 'standard' English for all situations is an unrealistic political and social shibboleth based on unsound linguistic information" (CCCC Secretary's Report No. 64, 24 March 1971). To that extent, the CCCC was not being placed in a position of endorsing a new viewpoint.

The initial revisions by the committee seem to further position the SRTOL within historical precedents. For instance, the committee moved to add spoken language as a protected right, yet the Dartmouth Conference had already articulated such a view. Given this strategy, the committee chose to speak on behalf of all CCCC members instead of just the Executive Committee. As amended, then, the resolution read as follows:

> We affirm the student's right to his own language—the dialect of his nurture in which he finds his identity and style. The claims that only one dialect is acceptable should be viewed as attempts of one social group to exert its dominance over another not as either true or sound advice to speakers or writers nor as moral advice to human beings. A nation which is proud of its diverse heritage and of its cultural and racial variety ought to preserve its heritage of dialects. We affirm strongly the need for teachers to have such training as will enable them to support this goal. (SRTOL [handwritten copy] n.d.)

Looking at the comments made on the draft, these changes appear to have occurred without much discussion or debate. This was not the case when it came to the role of the teacher, a role which had developed conflicting political significance as the 1960s progressed. As noted earlier, the Dartmouth Conference had created an image of the composition teacher simultaneously respecting a student's native dialect while teaching standard English. Citing Ellison, the Dartmouth Conference argued that such a pedagogy could lead to a lessening of social tensions and a greater opportunity for equality. Further, McPherson herself had stated to the Executive Committee that writing teachers needed to gain a background in linguistics if a student's dialect was to be understood. To this extent, the SRTOL was merely a weaving of a new linguistic paradigm into preexisting disciplinary insight and CCCC policy. The goal of the teacher appearing clear, "this goal" in the last line was amended to reiterate "this right":

We affirm strongly the need for teachers to have such training as will enable them to support this student's right to his own language.

Since 1966, however, the concept of student rights, particularly surrounding a person's dialect, had become permeated with issues of anticapitalism and Black Power. . . . Stokely Carmichael and the Black Panthers had tried to link Black English to a general critique of U.S. society. The amended last line, then, could appear to place teachers as potentially aligned with these more radical forces concerned with rights and language politics. To clarify the relationship, this right is placed under the rubric of cultural pluralism. Two different versions of this phrase exist:

> We affirm strongly the need for teachers to have such training as will enable them to support this part of our cultural pluralism.

> We affirm strongly the need for teachers to have such training as will enable them to support this feature of our cultural pluralism. (SRTOL [handwritten copy] n.d.)

Traditionally, *cultural pluralism* was a term intended to demonstrate a common American ethic beneath all the different ethnic and racial heritages. Given the strong rejection of the ethnicity paradigm then occurring, such language appeared to bring the concerns under an ethnicity paradigm which had been rejected by New Left forces. Additionally, through the use of "this part" or "this feature," the resolution is also indirectly endorsing standard English instruction as the "other" part or feature of a teacher's work. Thus, the language represented a deliberate attempt to distance the resolution from the more radical aspects of the 1960s. That is, the Executive Committee appeared to need language which would invoke the United States as a multiracial and multiethnic country but would not necessarily align teachers with the more radical implications of such language. Ultimately, however, it appears that invoking "cultural pluralism" went too far in the other direction. Consequently, the final language eliminates "cultural pluralism" entirely and settles for "diversity" at the same time that it reasserts the "students' rights."

> We affirm strongly the need for teachers to have such training as will enable them to support this goal of diversity and this right of the student to his own language. (SRTOL [handwritten copy] n.d.)

This phrasing merely reiterates the idea of "a nation proud of its diverse heritage." Since this "nation" is not named but merely an abstract idea, the CCCC effectively erases the resolution's immediate relationship to the competing images of the United States then occurring. That is, the SRTOL is not necessarily speaking about the history of the United States, but merely making a moral argument about diversity. Nor, despite its invocation of "students' rights," does the resolution invoke other loaded terms which would position the meaning of these rights within then-current debates. In effect, this gesture removed the teacher from the immediate terrain of the 1970s classroom. It offered no concrete meaning for teachers facing an increasingly varied and politically active student population. Nor did it offer a specific linguistic or nationalist paradigm through which to understand the resolution's intent. (It was this lack of specificity which would later spur CCCC to attempt to produce teacher guidebooks concerning the resolution.) The effect of such a revision, particularly if read as a revision of the NUC's original version, is to systematically translate the protest language of the 1960s into a seemingly ahistorical, unlocatable classroom. Or rather, to ensure the consent of the Executive Committee, the original NUC resolution had to be moderated and made into a general statement about student–teacher dynamics.

At the conclusion of the discussion, it was decided that the SRTOL committee should revise the statement as suggested.[3] As presented by Lloyd-Jones, the amended version of the SRTOL statement read as follows:

> We affirm the student's right to his own language—the dialect of his nurture in which he finds his identity and style. Any claim that only one dialect is acceptable should be viewed as attempts of one social group to exert its dominance over another, not as either true or sound advice to speakers and writers, nor as moral advice to human beings. A nation which is proud of its diverse heritage and of its cultural and racial variety ought to preserve its heritage of dialects. We affirm strongly the need for teachers to have such training as will enable them to support this goal of diversity and this right of the student to his own language. (CCCC officers meeting, 22 March 1972)

Gaining CCCC approval was risky. Composition teachers would not necessarily follow the Executive Committee's lead in endorsing a resolution which seemed to validate languages other than standard English. In fact, during discussions preceding the vote on the revised resolution, the minutes (CCCC Secretary's Report No. 66, 21 March 1972) reflect that it was agreed that any resolution would have to be part of a larger document which would explain to CCCC members the background of the statement, the necessary linguistics supporting it, and what its implementation would entail for teachers. This seemed crucial, since it was the role of teachers within the resolution which had created such trouble. Therefore, despite misgivings and the admitted need for further explanation, the resolution was passed by a vote of 22 to 1, with 1 abstention. Finally, Davis moved that McPherson appoint a subcommittee for the "purpose of working on an explanation and methods of implementing this statement and that such a group be given funds for travel" (CCCC Secretary's Report No. 66, 21 March 1972). The motion passed.

Beyond the passage of the resolution, this meeting also set in motion rule changes which would allow the ultimate approval of the SRTOL. That is, an attempt was made to alter the rules regarding what constituted a quorum at CCCC business meetings. At the Executive Committee meeting proper, Sophia Nelson had argued that the bylaws of the business meeting should be altered to allow fifty eligible representatives to constitute a quorum, as opposed to the current requirement of one hundred. After some discussion, the resolution failed by a vote of 7 to 14. Several months later, at the November 22, 1972, Executive Committee meeting, James Barry, who was in charge of a committee to develop guidelines for business meetings, gave his report. He proposed that two thirds of the voting members present should be necessary to pass any resolution and that one hundred eligible voters were necessary to pass any resolution. In the course of discussion, however, Larson recommended that, instead of two thirds, "[a] vote of the majority of members present constitutes adoption." This passed unanimously. Immediately afterward, Davis moved that "50 voting members will be considered a quorum." Cowan, who had earlier pushed through antiwar amendments concerning the "People's Peace Treaty," only to see them disputed through a mail ballot, seconded the motion (CCCC officers meeting, 22 November 1972). Although the vote total is not recorded, this motion also passed. Consequently, it was now possible to put the CCCC on record as endorsing a resolution with as few as twenty-six members voting in its favor. In contrast to the MLA, which through procedural moves had blocked the ability of small cadres of individuals from positioning it as a political organization, the CCCC was now open to a broad series of initiatives. As will be seen, a little over a year after the CCCC had decided to place its executive and business meetings at its conventions and open up the voting procedures, it would find itself subject to the type of politics the conservative elements of the MLA had tried assiduously to avoid.

WHEREAS IT IS AT LEAST ARGUABLE . . .

If the Executive Committee postponed a public discussion of how the SRTOL would impact teachers' duties, one possible formulation of these duties would be supplied by Wallace Douglass at the business meeting several days later. Anticipating the future rule changes, the first official act of those in attendance was to amend the quorum rules. It was moved and passed that the business meeting rules be amended to allow fifty members to constitute a quorum. The effect of this rule change was soon evident, for the amended quorum allowed resolutions concerning race to be approved which otherwise might have not been accepted. For instance, Marianna Davis, with the second of Wallace Douglass, presented a statement in support of the resolution of the College Language Association Black Caucus. While supporting the implementation of Black Studies programs, the resolution argued:

> We are distressed . . . at the apparent ease with which ill-conceived programs, directed by persons with limited experience with Black people and their history and often prompted by questionable academic and social motives, seem to receive ready approval. In contrast to this, Black institutions and their faculties are being by-passed in the general rush to redress an imbalance of which we are most direct witnesses.
>
> We are especially distressed by the funding policies of the major foundations, which are proceeding in this matter in a manner which can only be described as neopaternalistic. Accordingly we are calling upon the directors and trustees of these foundations to include knowledgeable

Black scholars at all levels in the formations of policies relating to Black people and studies based on them, and warn that many directions are now being pursued which are dangerous and will lead to disaster. (CCCC business meeting, 25 March 1972)

The second motion concerned the current role of publishers in printing African American writers:

The recent surge of interest in Black people in the United States has brought about, inevitably, an energetic redirection and expansion of activity in the world of publishing, particularly in the realm of textbook production. The members of the College Language Association, most of whom have spent many years teaching in predominantly Black institutions, have long been concerned, along with colleagues in other disciplines, with the Black experience. We now take note with some indignation that expansion into the field of Black studies has not entailed the abandonment of an essentially colonialist attitude held by the publishing industry in respect to Black teachers and scholars.

Many books now appearing have been prepared by "instant" experts and have apparently been seen only by such experts before they reach publication. CLA calls for nothing less than a decolonization in the field of publishing in which the talents, background, and experiences of those who have long labored, without reward, in this area will be drawn upon on the same favorable terms so readily available to white writers. (CCCC business meeting, 25 March 1972)

Both of these resolutions called for the larger publishing and academic communities to respect the historical role of the black college and black faculty. As had Stokely Carmichael and the Black Panthers, both of these resolutions invoke images of colonialism and decolonization. Rhetorically, at least, these resolutions appear to participate in larger social arguments concerning the role of African Americans in the United States, yet since neither of these resolutions called for the CCCC to take a stand on public policy concerning African Americans, neither generated much opposition. However, later in the same meeting, Wallace Douglass made a motion concerning "Executive Interference in Integration." The resolution stated:

Whereas it is apparent that the national executive has begun a formidable attack on the federal judiciary and

Whereas it seems that the Congress is likely to pass legislation prohibiting busing of children to achieve integration and

Whereas it is at least arguable that learning in English in its widest sense depends on children having as broad an experience with the various dialects or styles used in this country

Therefore be it resolved that the annual business meeting of the Conference on College Composition and Communication express its support of the Supreme Court decision in Brown vs. Board of Education of Topeka, Kansas, that furthermore it also express the hope that all deliberate speed may now, after eighteen years, be devised as including any and all means that are necessary to achieve the effective integration of the school systems of the United States. (CCCC business meeting, 25 March 1972)

While Executive Committee member Richard Clark spoke in support of the resolution, the minutes also reflect that some members stated that the motion was not the concern of CCCC. (. . . [E]arlier activities by the NUC had also been argued to be outside the CCCC mission; the ways in which the organization was having to confront its self-image as simply a teacher and researcher organization are evident here.) Mary Campbell stated that such a resolution would polarize the CCCC members. Another member spoke in favor of the resolution, stating that it was not about busing, but about achieving integration. Finally, Douglass himself argued that the resolution was aimed at deploring executive interference in the judicial process. In effect, however, Douglass was asking the CCCC to stand against the emerging conservative New Right forces taking control of the political debate in the United States.

Indeed, during the period in which the SRTOL was being developed within the CCCC, roughly from 1969 to 1974, the political climate was rapidly changing under Richard Nixon's presidency. During Nixon's administration, the southern states were given almost unprecedented political power. In an attempt to court favor with the South during his presidency, Nixon made efforts to reduce funds for school desegregation from $1 billion to $75 million as well as to block "enforcement of integration laws, even sending Justice Department lawyers down to sue for the suspension of court-ordered school integration in Mississippi" (Sale 1975, 244). In fact, Nixon aide Robert Haldeman ordered that "no official anywhere in his Administration was at any time for any reason to make a statement that might upset and antagonize the South" (Sale 1975, 244). His administration also argued against busing and against the Voting Rights Act, cut funds for Justice Department lawyers working on civil rights law enforcement, and decided "that all challenges to existing voting laws would have to be decided by protracted lawsuits" (Sale 1975, 244–246 passim).

Beyond his efforts to block busing, Nixon also attempted to influence the type of education that students would receive. Under the leadership of Sidney Marland, who was Nixon's Commissioner of Education, a series of academic reforms were implemented which would push for "career education." As discussed by Ira Shor in *Culture Wars* (1986), Marland's attempt to push career education in public schools and community colleges was an attempt to limit the number of students exposed to a liberal arts education and to slow the production of overeducated college students with no jobs to fit their degrees:

> Soft disciplines in the humanities, arts, and general studies, along with autonomous programs in experimental education, were undermined by the thrust towards courses most open to direct job-training. The broad critical learning possible in liberal arts, women's courses, minority programs, interdisciplinary studies, etc., represented the political problem of the 1960's which careerism in the 1970's helped to solve. Marland not

only saw career education as an antidote to campus unrest, but he also gladly agreed to its vocational character, despite his "career" tag. When one voc-ed advocate suggested that with career education vocationalism finally went "big time," Marland happily agreed. (35)

For instance, during Marland's tenure, community colleges received $850 million to fund occupational programs for three years. (This influx of money was occurring at the same time that Gregory Cowan was attempting to push for implementation of the junior college guidelines, which contained some elements of the SRTOL.) Notably, the guidelines moved English instruction away from a strictly utilitarian function. As a result of this increased funding, as well as Nixon's campaign against antiwar demonstrators, four-year colleges and universities also began to examine the relevance or appropriateness of programs.

Consequently, in offering the resolution on "Executive Interference," Douglass was attempting to get the CCCC to stand for its recent history of supporting the government's duty to ensure equality in educational access. The CCCC, he seemed to be saying, should not be seen as even implicitly supporting the sea change in civil rights policy and education. Furthermore, by linking this duty to language, Douglass also seemed to be indicating that the SRTOL and its endorsement of a heritage of diversity demanded a statement on social politics as well. Whereas the SRTOL held the students' language as a right which blocked some moves by a teacher in a writing classroom, Douglass's statement argued that to support diversity in dialects demanded that busing or school integration be supported and worked for by the CCCC. That is, whereas the SRTOL steered clear of taking a stance on public policy, Douglass's statement demanded that the very endorsement of dialect differences (and the need to increase students' awareness of those differences) demanded that school desegregation occur.[4] Despite its endorsement of an expanding role in the liberal welfare state, this particular resolution was thus in many ways more in the spirit of the NUC than the emerging SRTOL. Indeed, this resolution passed by a vote of 83 to 12. The SRTOL only had 79 votes in its favor. Notably, neither would have passed without the altered quorum rules.

The Third SRTOL

As CCCC chairperson, McPherson attempted to represent the SRTOL as a significant accomplishment. In her 1972 report to the NCTE (McPherson 1972a), she stated, "Perhaps the most important thing CCCC did this year was to adopt . . . 'The Students' Right to Their Own Language,'" yet she had to be aware that such a statement would not go unchallenged. To allay the fear of CCCC members, McPherson informed them that a longer report explaining the resolution and its meaning was being produced. In a memorandum addressed to CCCC members, McPherson (1972d) states:

> When the Executive Committee of the Conference on College Composition and Communication met in Boston at the end of March, the mem-

bers of that committee passed the following resolution on the Student's Right to His Own Language. . . . At the same meeting, on March 22, the Executive Committee agreed that a committee should be created to write a longer statement providing the members with the linguistic background on which the resolution rests. The committee is in the process of formation now, and we hope it will have at least a preliminary report when the Executive Committee meets in November.

The promise of a forthcoming report which would supply the linguistic background for the statement, however, could not blunt the negative reaction. In October, *CCC* began to print the reactions of CCCC members to the resolution. William Pixton (1972) criticized both the logic and the probable outcome of the resolution. In particular, Pixton indirectly demonstrates that the Executive Committee's attention to the language of diversity and cultural pluralism was well placed. Stating that it is sound advice to inform students of the need to learn standard English, Pixton wrote that the SRTOL, in contrast,

> will result in a chaos of dialects that will hamper communication and promote ignorance, a situation to be brought about by teachers who, abrogating their responsibility to teach English, substitute in its place the cultivation of individual verbal eccentricity. America will become Babel, and a man traveling from New York to California will be forced to seek the assistance of thirty translators. (300)

Beyond endorsing a belief in the power of English teachers slightly out of touch with rationality, Pixton is positioning the SRTOL as taking English teachers outside of their traditional roles of teaching standard English. The refusal of other CCCC members to take seriously the resolution's endorsement of the validity and logic of all languages is best demonstrated by John R. Hendrickson (1972):

> Praiz be for I hav liv to see grandpas personl-type tibetan-Amurican inglish vindikated. at last igdorence has took its riteful plas in the world if olny grandpa hadnt of bin in such a hury to check out he cood og got a job tiching inglish most anywheres from the plow tot the compozi9shyun clas in yoost won yump. . . . This is muy dilect and I'god its gonna be perservd even if itmeens the deth of the bestest anglo-imperialist fashistrtriting that was ever rote. Beowulf had his day and he coodnt even talk inglish but now its mine and what I say it teibetan-amunicans arise you aint got nuthin to loose but other piples funny inglish. (301)

This counterstatement continues Pixton's disdain for social or political attempts to counter linguistic prejudice toward other dialects. In fact, in this instance, the prejudice is so extreme that differences get translated into simple spelling errors (*olny* for *only*). In contrast to the work of Smitherman or Labov, Hendrickson does not even consider that nonstandard dialects might have their own logic or consistency. He also fails to consider how dialects might be usefully invoked in a classroom setting. Hendrickson's viewpoint demonstrates the refusal to consider how a teacher could reconfigure knowledge in

the classroom so that different dialects could lead to both an increased understanding of language *and* the acquisition of dialects of wider communication.

In part, both Pixton and Hendrickson assume that the right accorded to
students negates and invalidates the teacher's knowledge of standard English.
Following the militant image of the student then emerging, these writing
teachers seem to be unable to imagine a student who, while maintaining the
right to his or her own language, would also choose to learn the dialect of
wider communication. (. . . [E]ven Vernon of *It's Mine and I'll Write It That Way*
[Friedrich and Kuester 1972] had reasons for wanting to learn standard
English over Friedrich's objections.) Finally, in his invocation of imperialism,
Hendrickson also mocks the emphasis of the original motivation of groups
such as the NUC and thus participates in the larger social movement of the
New Right to discredit the language of the liberal and progressive left. That is,
in part, these responses demonstrate the extent to which the political and educational work of the 1960s was unable to fully dethrone the negative images
of dialect speakers and their ways of speaking; when the political climate
began to edge toward the right, these diffuse symbols could be rearticulated
with other conservative elements into a reinvigorated hegemonic structure.

In this environment, McPherson found herself having to argue that the
SRTOL's endorsement of all languages was supported by traditional academic
standards and was not an abandonment of standard English. For instance, in
a letter to an upset CCCC member (McPherson 1972c), she began her defense
by reiterating the SRTOL as a call for a higher standard of education for both
current students and future teachers:

> First, it is largely because the Executive Committee does feel strongly
> that, just as a chemistry major should understand chemistry thoroughly,
> so should an English major, and especially a major who plans to teach
> English, understand thoroughly the nature of language, the nature of
> dialects, and the way a student's language habits affect his view of him-
> self and of the world. Second, the committee feels strongly that if educa-
> tion is not to remain the privilege of an elitist few, we must recognize that
> dialect differences do not by themselves prevent students from getting
> on with the real business of a college education: the understanding of
> real chemistry, for instance, or indeed, the more important business of
> "English"—organization of ideas, specificity of expression, support for
> generalizations, appreciation of literature. Third, there is no real evidence
> that correcting student papers for so-called errors has any effect other
> than eliminating from a chance at education those students whose lan-
> guage choices differ from our own.

For McPherson, the SRTOL is a call for future teachers to become educated in
all aspects of the English language: literary forms, dialect forms, and so on.
Further, taking aim at those who value writing instruction only for its economic usefulness, she supports a view of education for all, not just the elite.
That is, much like Friedrich and Kuester's (1972) text, the English classroom
becomes a place where writing, in the sense of communication, dominates.
Echoing Smitherman's "Black Power Is Black Language" (1972), McPherson

also defines the effectiveness of communication as more important than whether that communication is written in standard English. It is significant that all of these individuals had spoken about the need to listen to students who want to learn standard English.

McPherson's letters, however, did not seem to be a forceful enough response. Facing criticism of the resolution for both its practical effects and scholarly support, the Executive Committee apparently decided to amend the resolution. Richard Larson states that at its November 22, 1972, meeting, the committee made several changes. After these amendments, the resolution reads:

> We affirm the students' right to their own patterns and varieties of lan-
> guage—the dialects of their nurture or whatever dialects in which they
> find their own identity and style. Language scholars long ago denied
> that the myth of a standard American dialect has any validity. The claim
> that any one dialect is unacceptable amounts to an attempt of one social
> group to exert its dominance over another. Such a claim leads to false
> advice for speakers and writers, and immoral advice for humans. A nation
> proud of its diverse heritage and its cultural and racial variety will pre-
> serve its heritage of dialects. We affirm strongly that teachers must have
> the experiences and training that will enable them to respect diversity
> and uphold the right of students to their own language. (CCCC "*Stu-
> dents' Right*," p. 19 in this book)

The most obvious change, which is not highlighted, is the removal of "his" for the gender neutral language of "their." More substantially, the resolution makes two key moves. First, instead of a right to one's *own language*, the resolution personalizes language to individual "patterns and varieties." If this right was not later put in terms of "one social group" dominating "another," this personalization might be seen as an attempt to remove any remnants of the group rights and identity which had characterized Black Power discussions of language politics. Instead, while group identity is maintained, the authority to claim group identity is now placed in the hands of linguists, who have proven the invalidity of any standard. That is, the statement's moral stance on language rights is now portrayed as the result of linguistic research. At the outset, "The claim that any one dialect is unacceptable" was written as "Any claim," but now the resolution precedes this phrase with backing from linguistic research ("Language scholars long ago . . ."). This gesture returns the SRTOL back to its mission of responding to the NCTE CEL. The rhetorical effect of such an addition, however, is to turn a general moral belief into a consequence of research (or as McPherson had written in her letter to CCCC members, the result of "linguistic background.") Such a move weakens the political and ethical strength of the resolution. Consequently, although the body of the resolution is significantly more aggressive in tone, the cumulative effect of these revisions is to weaken the moral impact of the statement. Ultimately, what had been a moral duty of teachers has become the moral outcome of academic research. Perhaps as important, the positions that advocates of the New Left and Black Power student activists were making about social justice in the classroom also are recoded as depending on academic research.

Obviously, the resolution had traveled far from its inception in the NUC. Much of the social and economic politics undergirding NUC efforts had been eliminated. Moral critiques of the liberal welfare state, Vietnam War polices, institutional racism, and class stratification also appeared to be left behind. The confrontational images of the student invoked by these organizations had been recast into a classroom where language scholars and teachers define students' rights, rights which had very little traction with the actual activities of student protesters. Douglass's attempts (CCCC business meeting, 25 March 1972) to link the resolution's intent with social movements such as busing seem to have failed.

Within the context of the NCTE and CCCC, however, the radical nature of this resolution should not be underestimated. That is, the resolution can be seen as a politically radical response to the CECs "Statement on Usage" (n.d.). That document . . . was clearly embedded within a linguistic tradition which supported the exclusion of Black English. It had clearly stated the need for teachers to recognize "economic reality" and prepare students in standard English. This version of the SRTOL (1974) is significant, then, for what it does not do: It does not position teachers as producers of future workers; it does not endorse the nationalist paradigm of Marckwardt or McDavid; it does not call for the necessity of standard English; it does not denigrate other ways of speaking. In that sense, its lack of specificity speaks volumes about what it was against: the CEL and figures such as Pixton and Hendrickson. Within this oppositional context, phrases such as "a nation proud of its linguistic and racial variety" clearly position the CCCC within a set of linguistics and politics which, if not radical, were certainly liberal. Even the more conservative version of the NUC's original prompting resolution, then, was progressive. That is, within the NCTE–CCCC dynamic, it represented a political and linguistic departure from the Cold War definition of composition, for it was, in fact, arguing for the right of students to refuse instruction by empowering student acts of civil disobedience.

The final meaning of the resolution, however, was not yet decided. With the language of the resolution now complete, the Executive Committee approved the drafting of a language statement which would make clear its "meaning and intent."

DEFENDING THE RIGHT

When the SRTOL was first passed by the Executive Committee, the committee also resolved to produce a longer document, a language statement, which would explain the resolution to CCCC members. The resolution had produced quite a bit of controversy. Consequently, it is not surprising that in McPherson's request to Melvin Butler to chair the SRTOL language statement committee, she argues that the committee's work "will be extremely important to college English instructors and to the students they teach" (McPherson

1972b). In effect, the SRTOL language statement committee needed to explain that the SRTOL resolution was not an abandonment of the traditional role of instructors to teach standard English and to secure an economic future for their students. It is not accidental, then, that the SRTOL language statement committee[5] focused its initial efforts on explicating the effects of the resolution on future graduates.

At the same Executive Committee meeting where the resolution was amended, the language statement committee reported that the audience for the statement should include "business people as well as professional educators." In particular, the committee decided that "post-schoolroom concerns (training of teachers, students' lives after they leave high school or college, concerns of business people)" would warrant their own section (CCCC Secretary's Report No. 67, 22 November 1972).

Indeed, in correspondence between March 1 and March 11, 1973, the SRTOL language statement committee, now under the guidance of Richard Lloyd-Jones,[6] began to discuss how the resolution situated students in relationship to the economy. That is, almost immediately, the committee was confronted with an argument about the relationship between linguistic theory and economic reality. Under the section titled "How Does Dialect Affect Employability," a draft of the document discussed the implications of spoken dialect:

> Many employers expect a person whom they consider for employment to speak whatever variety of American English the employers speak, or believe they speak. Consequently, many speakers of divergent dialects are denied opportunities that are readily available to the applicants whose dialects more nearly approximate the speech of the employer. But a plumber who can sweat a joint can be forgiven confusion between "set" and "sat." (SRTOL [handwritten copy] n.d.)

In response, Ralph Long stated that the initial draft of the resolution and background statement were "quite unsatisfactory." Long (1973) argued that the emphasis on

> dialects [is] quite out of proportion for teachers of composition. [I agree] that we should "leave" spoken language alone as much as possible— totally so in composition classes, but [for] the purposes of expository writing standard English is indispensable — even, sometimes, for plumbers, as the experience of an old friend long active in the plumber union showed. standard English is not "mythical"; it is absurd to regard EAE (Edited American English) as a reality but standard [English] as a myth.

On the same date, however, McPherson (1973) was writing to Lloyd-Jones that the document should not be read as an endorsement to teach standard English until employers become more tolerant. She writes,

> [One section] seems to say that until employers change their minds, we must continue to teach "standard," and that's not what anybody meant. Could it read something like: "As teachers determined to affirm the

students' right to their own language, we must work toward seeing that employers stop discriminating against prospective employees who speak a divergent dialect."

Expanding upon this idea, McPherson asks if the following paragraph might be included:

> The people who insist that English teachers must deliberately impose a new and different "school dialect" ignore the ways in which situation motivates versatility, and, perhaps, overrate the possibilities of external "teaching." When students move into new situations—other school classes, new jobs, community projects—the situations themselves will "teach" far more effectively than a classroom can, and students whose school experiences have given them a sense of confidence in themselves and their language, rather than a sense of ineptitude and inadequacy, will be ready to "learn" from the new situation.

Arguing that "this whole document is a strong protest" against the emerging social consensus, McPherson stated that the English classroom was not a just a site for turning students into marketable workers. In fact, turning the argument about the need for career education on its head, she appears to be arguing that it is up to the particular businesses to train their employees in the language of the job, a muted endorsement of similar claims made in NUC's *Open Up the Schools* (1972). To this extent, McPherson also shares common ground with Davidson's (1966) student syndicalist paper. Unlike Davidson, however, McPherson would not embark upon an argument that such practices make the students unproductive for the corporate economy. Instead, it would be the businesses' role to make the students "useful." That is, she would ask writing teachers to suspend their belief that the teaching of standard English was the goal of teachers and not of particular businesses. She was asking teachers to consider how writing instruction could be used to allow students to invent their own relationship to the larger society. Moving to summarize the implications of her additions within the same rubric, McPherson (1973) also suggested the following statement:

> We must encourage students to concentrate on the crucial exactness of words and ideas, and persuade our colleagues to discard their own biases about dialect long enough to recognize and respect this better kind of exactness.

The impact of these additions on the document was to frame the SRTOL statement as endorsing a composition classroom where the relationship between dialects (including standard English) and their individual usefulness were the topic. In doing so, McPherson gave body to the SRTOL resolution as a call for teachers to do more than participate in the production of future workers; instead, teachers would participate in the formation of individually empowered speakers and writers. Such a stance was in stark opposition to the emerging Nixon doctrine of career education and earlier NCTE documents (such as NITE), as well as against the wishes of the factions of CCCC previously discussed. Although little of McPherson's language is incorporated into the document, the moral dilemma she articulates is included:

> The attitudes that [tomorrow's employers] develop in the English class will often be the criteria they use for choosing their own employees. English teachers who feel they are bound to accommodate the linguistic prejudices of current employers perpetuate a system that is unfair to both students who have job skills and to the employers who need them. (CCCC "Students' Right," p. 39)

The potential for such statements, however, is muted by the nationalist landscape in which they are embedded. That is, much more in the spirit of the CEL than the NUC, the SRTOL language statement produces an image of the United States as a harmonious country. In particular, an initial reading of the completed document makes it appear as an endorsement of the ethnicity paradigm and integration politics that had earlier characterized the civil rights movement of Martin Luther King Jr. . . . King had argued that the Montgomery bus strike had produced a sense of the African American community which created a cross-class alliance representing the unfilled promise of the Declaration of Independence and the Constitution of the United States. With the African American as a symbol of such a possibility, King seemed to argue that a harmonious community was possible within a capitalist state if citizens lived up to the heritage and meaning of U.S. democracy. Differences could be accommodated by capitalism. In fact, capitalism could benefit from these differences.

As was evident in the CCCC's SRTOL resolution from its outset, the resolution is also a call for the United States to live up to a certain standard: "A nation proud of its diverse heritage and its cultural and racial variety will preserve its heritage of dialects" (p. 19). As noted earlier, however, the SRTOL as written does not actually claim that the United States has acted in accordance with this precept. Within the SRTOL language statement, however, the United States is represented as a place where, in everyday situations, tolerance and understanding are the norm. In particular, it is the relationship between a banker and a farmer through which this tolerance is announced:

> It is not surprising to find two or more social dialects co-existing in a given region. In small towns where a clear social cleavage exists between the wealthier, more educated portion of the population and the mass of people, the difference may be reflected in their speechways. The local banker whose dialect reveals his group allegiance to the statewide financial community still is able to communicate easily with the local farmhand who may rarely cross the county line and whose linguistic habit patterns reveal different allegiances. (pp. 23–24)

In NUC documents, such as the previously discussed "Who(m) Does Standard English Serve?" (Knowles et al. 1969), this recognition of a class-based linguistic difference was used to argue for an interracial class alliance among nontraditional students and workers. Here the difference is used to demonstrate a latent understanding which can be appealed to for the sake of linguistic

diversity. That is, the farmer does not take this difference as an alienating economic factor, but as an underlying confirmation of equality. Generalizing
from the interaction of these two individuals, the statement argues that a similar situation exists in the metropolitan United States as well.

> In many larger American cities, people of the same ethnic origins tend to
> live in a single neighborhood and have a common culture and thus share
> a dialect. Through their clothing, games, and holidays, they may pre-
> serve the values and customs of the "old country" or "back home." And
> in their restaurants, churches, schools, and homes, one may hear the lin-
> guistic values and customs of their heritage preserved. For example, a
> neighborhood group's cultural orientation may encourage its members
> to differentiate between action and intention in the immediate future
> and in a still-further immediate future through "I'm a-do it" and "I'm
> a'gonna do it." Yet, a neighborhood is not a country, so speakers of sev-
> eral dialects may mingle there and understand each other. Visitors with
> yet another heritage may render an approximation of such differentia-
> tion through "I'll do it now" and "I'll do it soon." Pride in cultural heri-
> tage need not lead either group to attack the other as they mingle and
> communicate. (p. 24)

Notably, such an image of U.S. cities can work only if the then-recent riots in
Watts, Harlem, and Newark are ignored. These riots, particularly for Bobby
Seale's vision of the Black Panthers, had led to an increased call by black activists for black economic empowerment. In the particular case of Stokely Carmichael, such empowerment was a direct critique of how class works in the
United States, yet the SRTOL language statement acts as if capitalism's recognition of differences will ameliorate fundamental class and social inequity.
Consequently, the rhetorical structure of the document works to minimize or
displace the NUC's attempt to link racial and class politics. As was seen earlier and will be reiterated later, in the SRTOL language statement, economic
concerns are cast principally in light of how to expand acceptable dialects
within corporate capitalism, not how to use dialects to question it.

Indeed, the SRTOL language statement creates an image of dialects as a
cultural problem which can be solved by the raised consciousness of its citizens. That is, the answer to the question of why different dialects are not
accepted is the personal attitudes of the listener. When "speakers of a dialect
of American English claim not to understand speakers of another dialect of
the same language, the impediments are likely to be attitudinal. What is really
the hearer's resistance to any unfamiliar form may be interpreted as the
speaker's fault" (p. 24). Given the endorsement of a traditional view of the
United States and its citizenry, the SRTOL is a call for individuals to live up to
the moral character which, the SRTOL language statement implies, has historically characterized U.S. citizens.

In addition, the SRTOL language statement also seems to be positioning
itself closer to the work of Marckwardt and McDavid than was implied by the
resolution alone. This is particularly evident in the final draft of the language
statement's discussion of American English and its historical development.

When tracing the development of English in the United States, the SRTOL language statement excludes many of the recently discovered African influences on American English. . . . [L]inguists such as Herskovitz argued that the roots of Black English were actually international. Dillard in particular represented Black English and its history as a way to reimagine American English, yet, as in the work of McDavid or Marckwardt, the SRTOL language statement argues for an essentially British origin of American English.

> When the early American settlers arrived on this continent, they brought their British dialects with them. Those dialects were altered both by regional separation from England and concentration into sub-groups within this country as well as by contact with the various languages spoken by the Indians they found there and with the various languages spoken by the immigrants who followed. (p. 25)

After recounting the development of New England English as the standard idiom, the section "The History of English and How It Continually Changes in Vocabulary, in Syntax, and in Pronunciation" of the document states:

> From its earliest history, English has borrowed words from the other languages with which it has come in contact—French, Latin, Spanish, Scandinavian, Yiddish, American Indian—from sources too numerous to list. (p. 35)

The language of Black English is reduced to "sources too numerous to list" and to several recorded instances within the text. Within the SRTOL language statement, then, a version of the ethnicity paradigm is reinvoked that serves to bracket out certain historical experiences (or linkages) through which dialects might gain oppositional meaning. While the document openly rejects the cultural deficit models endorsed by Deutsch and Bereiter, the document does not offer positive models of Black English's impact on standard American English.[7] That is, in a resolution and a document clearly initiated by NUC activists to speak on behalf of African American and working-class students, it would appear that there is little demonstration of what their culture, language, or history represents about the historical development of English in the United States. Here the conservative nature of the ethnicity paradigm, as diagnosed by Omi and Winant (1994), becomes evident, for with the invocation of that paradigm, an NUC attempt to create an argument of social and economic justice has been effectively eliminated from the meaning of the SRTOL.

The document's call for a respect of different cultures or dialects must be read within this overarching conservative paradigm. For instance, within a document painting the social fabric of the United States as harmonious, the statement reads, "Our pluralistic society requires many varieties of language to meet our multiplicity of needs" (p. 26). It further states, "Since dialect is not separate from culture, but an intrinsic part of it, accepting a new dialect means accepting a new culture; rejecting one's native dialect is to some extent a rejection of one's culture" (p. 26), yet the potential opening up of diversity along leftist lines, which was at least possible in the resolution, is effectively muted by the collapsing of a race-and class-based politics into the ethnicity paradigm. Within the potential pluralism of the United States, the activation of different dialects within a student's possibility can now safely be ascribed as the new goal of education: "No one can ever use all of the resources of a language, but one function of the English teacher is to activate the student's competence, that is, increase the range of his habitual performance" (p. 26). It is within this validation of the ethnicity paradigm that the SRTOL statement can ultimately endorse language as representing the pluralistic nature of U.S. society. While appearing to articulate the goal of many 1960s New Left and Black Power organizations, the SRTOL statement thus falls closer to the emerging New Right politics in its articulation of what those dialects represent about the United States or what questions they might cause the United States to ask about itself.

Ultimately, the angry student who protests the idea of a pluralist America from a New Left or NUC perspective is replaced by a student "eager to come to the aid of his country." That is, the SRTOL statement is careful to represent the ability and willingness of dialect speakers to learn standard English. In contrast to earlier rhetorical moments where the black-dialect speaker is brought in to validate a particular political position, here white men are brought in to validate the potential assimilation of urban black and Chicano students. The SRTOL language statement argues that minority dialect speakers are equally as capable of learning standard English as those with more classically recognized regional dialects, that is, southern or New England dialects. The section titled "Does Dialect Affect the Ability to Write" states,

> In fact, if speakers of a great variety of American dialects do master EAE—from Senator Sam Ervin to Senator Edward Kennedy, from Ernest Hemingway to William Faulkner—there is no reason to assume that dialects such as urban black and Chicano impede the child's ability to learn EAE while countless others do not. (p. 28)

Nonstandard speakers' acquisition skills are historically represented as part of a larger national Cold War effort:

> And experience tells us that when speakers of any dialect need a new word for a new thing, they will invent or learn that needed word. Just as most Americans added "sputnik" to their vocabularies a decade or more ago, so speakers of other dialects can add such words as "periostitis" or "interosculate" whenever their interests demand it. (p. 30)

In such a scheme, the nonstandard dialect speaker comes to represent both the ideal ability of a united citizenry participating in the utopic image of the United States and the international benefits such participation brings to the nation. To this extent, then, the document could be read as conservative. Unlike the political and economic motivations behind the NUC's attempts to recognize dialect differences as the first step to a social reformation of U.S. society, here recognition comes to stand for further incorporation of the nonstandard dialect speaker into traditional economic and cultural roles and into an emerging global responsibility.

Such a reading of the document necessarily leads to the SRTOL's invocation of Langston Hughes. For within the SRTOL language statement, it is the voice of Hughes who represents the proper attitude toward language difference. In particular, Hughes is brought in to support the traditional idea of the ethnicity paradigm. Through the protocols of the text, the image given of Hughes is similar to the representation of Ralph Ellison in Dartmouth Conference documents. . . . [I]n the work of Muller (1967) and Dixon (1966), the image of the English teacher was of someone who could manage different dialects within a writing classroom to produce social harmony. Within that dynamic, the voice of Ralph Ellison was cited as representing the possibility of relieving tension: "[I]f you can show me . . . how I can cling to that which is real in me, while teaching me the way into the larger society, then I will . . . drop my defenses and hostility" (cited in Dixon 1966, 19). Approximately ten years later, the SRTOL appears to use the voice of Hughes to argue that a proper tolerance toward language diversity will result in individuals who "dig all jive":

> I play it cool and dig all jive
> That's the reason I stay alive.
> My motto as I live and learn
> Is to dig and be dug in return. (p. 22)[8]

In citing Hughes, however, the SRTOL language statement appears to conclude the SRTOL resolution's long march from progressive politics to a traditional, nationalist statement about diversity, for it is important to note that the Hughes poem comes from his 1967 collection of poetry *The Panther and the Lash*. . . . [This collection] is an argument against the ethnicity paradigm. That is, in various poems, Hughes positions African Americans outside the parameters of the traditional U.S. history. In a poem called "American Heartbreak," Hughes writes:

> I am the American heartbreak—
> The rock on which Freedom
> Stubbed its toe—
> The great mistake
> That Jamestown made
> Long ago.

Commenting on the need to find heroes outside the American historical landscape, in a poem titled "Angola Question Mark," Hughes writes:

> Don't know why I
> Must turn into
> a Mau Mau
> And lift my hand
> Against my fellow man
> To live in my own land.

Reiterating and expanding on the idea of "digging jive," Hughes discusses the murder of James Powell. Written in the form of a riddle, "Death in Yorkville" asks "How many bullets does it take / To kill a fifteen-year-old kid" (15). The poem then goes on to retell the history of African Americans as the violent repression and murder of their race and culture. For Hughes, invoking U.S. history would not liberate African Americans; only an international understanding would accomplish this goal. As Hughes notes at the end of his poem concerning Powell, "Death aint No jive" (21). While African Americans may have to "play it cool / And dig all jive" to "stay alive," such conditions were not conducive to African American self-respect or long-term survival. That is, Hughes will only "dig all jive" if he is "dug in return"; otherwise, trouble will ensue.

This use of Hughes within a conservative argument must also be placed within one of the other moments when race is discussed. In the section titled "What Do We Do About Handbooks?" the following scene is represented:

> By discussions of actual student writing both students and teachers can learn to appreciate the value of variant dialects and recognize that a deviation from the handbook rules seldom interferes with communication. The student who writes, "The Black Brother just don't believe he's going to be treated like a man anyway," is making himself completely clear. Students and teachers can go on to discuss situations in which adherence to handbook rules might actually damage the effectiveness of the writing. (pp. 31–32)

As did Labov, this example uses a nonstandard writing example to express a social critique of the current status of African Americans. Unlike the utopic image of the United States, represented earlier, this example interrupts and argues that race is a category unrepresented and oppressed within the ethnicity paradigm of the United States. If race is used as the controlling metaphor for the United States, it seems to say, an image of injustice and oppression emerges. Using this image, one could imagine a critique of "handbook rules" which would lead to points very similar to Stokely Carmichael's English class: that is, only when the African American student gains control of the language defining American history will that student be able to reimagine a new, liberating subject position. Within such a paradigm, McPherson's argument about the need to alter the dynamics of business and dialect could have taken on a potentially more radical meaning, yet, similar to Sumner Ives's reaction to a student paper on the Vietnam War . . . , the document asks the teacher only to speak in terms of "effectiveness." Consequently, within the parameters of the SRTOL language statement, it is difficult to imagine any of this discussion occurring. That is, more confrontational or nontraditional approaches to race or the politics of dialects are effectively muted in the document. Ultimately, the inclusion of Hughes marks the absence of a radical economic educational critique more than its endorsement.

To say that the SRTOL language statement is a conservative document when placed next to the militant politics of the New Left, however, is not to denigrate its importance within the shifting relationship between teachers and students, NCTE and CCCC, or New Left and New Right debates about education. Just as the SRTOL resolution could be considered radical when placed next to the CEL statement, in the emerging conservative climate of the 1970s, any statement which appeared to accord students rights or dethrone standard English was "radical" at the moment of the New Right's emergence. That is, one reading of the SRTOL would be to see it as an instance of the radical margin being incorporated into a traditional center. While this is certainly true, it is also important to remember that political terrain upon which the imagined center–margin binary exists is constantly shifting. As a document created in the meantime between the New Left and the New Right, then, the SRTOL offers one attempt to negotiate the new emerging social context.

WE AFFIRM STRONGLY . . .

By November 1973, the SRTOL resolution and language statement were ready to be submitted to the Executive Committee. The committee's response to the language statement, however, was mixed and somewhat confrontational. According to the minutes, William Irmscher, who would later figure in the movement to overturn the SRTOL, stated that the language statement was meant to be a "means of understanding the resolution," yet in the discussion that followed, complaints were made that the statement was ambiguous:

> [Was it] an endorsement of bi-dialecticism or [an] endorsement of tracking in education; [it had] a glib treatment of handbooks; what language options [are meant]; young teachers [will be] hard put to know what to do with the document. (CCCC Secretary's Report No. 69, 21 November 1973)

Some unidentified members even argued that the "previous resolution as written is not acceptable." Committee members questioned "the rhetoric used [and] the political implications." In fact, "the controversial nature of the background statement [led to] Mr. Bain's question of whether the Language Committee had considered rewording the resolution." Ross Winterowd explained that it was not within the charge of the language committee since they had "no mandate to change it" (CCCC Secretary's Report No. 69, 21 November 1973). McPherson, however, argued that the committee should accept the language statement. In fact, it [was] argued by some that the language statement was more a "whereas" than an individual document. Consequently, the Executive Committee had an obligation to accept or reject the preamble to their own resolution. Initially, a motion was made that the Executive Committee "accept and transmit the Resolution and Background Statement to the membership of CCCC for their study and consideration and a vote on this resolution be taken at the Anaheim Conference in 1974" (CCCC officers meeting, 21 November 1973). This motion passed by a vote of 14 to 4, with one abstention. Cowan then moved that the resolution be embedded in the letter sent to

CCCC members, expressing the approval of the Executive Committee and encouraging acceptance. This motion passed by a 12–4 vote.

Consequently, soon after the Executive Committee meeting, Richard Larson, now CCCC chairperson, sent a letter to the CCCC members. In the letter, Larson . . . avoids the political beginnings of the SRTOL in New Left activism. Instead, he dates the beginning of the SRTOL with an oblique reference to "a series of discussions begun in 1969." Positioning the document as a linguistic, new rhetoric statement, Larson argues that it incorporates the "current findings of linguists and rhetoricians about dialects and usage." Further, Larson points out that the language statement, if not the resolution," has won the praise of linguists who have examined it; it is, in my judgment, a major accomplishment and probably the first extended statement prepared to assist the deliberations of members on a major issue since the CCCC was founded." . . . It was not possible, however, to use such a disciplinary argument to shield the SRTOL against political interpretations of its meanings.

Even prior to the SRTOL resolution and language statement's formal distribution, members of the CCCC community began reacting to the recent events on a grassroots level. For instance, in April, Constance Weaver, who would later serve on the committee to revise the SRTOL, would ask for copies of the SRTOL language statement. In doing so, she hoped to "persuade the Linguistics Committee of the Michigan Council of Teachers of English to introduce . . . a resolution that the MCTE endorse the CCCC resolution" (Weaver 1974). In June, Nancy Prichard (1974) circulated a statement of support from the Institute for Service and Education which argued that the statement does not grow out of a need to "smash tradition, rather it is a positive extension of the fundamental educational issue arising out of the 1960's: how can we effectively teach language skills to students who come from diverse backgrounds?" Consequently, she argues,

> The position statement is comprehensive and extraordinary in that it not only examines some of the assumptions underlying the teaching of English, but it provides some contemporary linguistic thought and findings concerning some of these assumptions. Clearly, if we have any commitment at all to providing educational opportunity, we have no alternative to our affirmation of the students' right to their own language. . . . [We] also hope that those who attend the convention in Los Angeles will not allow the fantasy of Disneyland to obscure the importance of affirming the students right to their own language. (Prichard 1974)

Other people, however, used the possible political associations created by an endorsement of the SRTOL to discredit it. In May, Evelyn Miller, of Manchester Community College (MCC), wrote to Richard Larson that "the Proposed Position Statement [is] totally unacceptable [since] it is based upon the tendentious assumption that what is called Standard English is merely a dialect" (Miller 1974a). In response to the statement, Miller (1974b) circulated a memorandum calling for her English Department "to take a firm stand in favor of Standard English in all our composition courses at MCC." In support of her position, Miller cites Stephen Koch's "Hard Times for the Mother Tongue." In the excerpt she provides, Koch attacks the politics of individuals who would draw moral conclusions from linguistic insight:

> Listening to the current polemics, one might gather that Standard English is somehow highly literate and the mandarin of upper-crust speech. It is nothing of the kind. It is simply more or less correct English. . . . Correctly spoken, it easily encompasses an internal array of regional dialects. . . . There is nothing fancy or overwhelming about it. Its fundamental structural habits are very simple, and (except perhaps for children born into the most extreme of the illiterate English dialects) there is no reason why it should not be second nature to anyone of normal intelligence by the age of fifteen. . . . it is the fundamental—and indispensable—basis for educated speech, writing, and thought in the English Language.
>
> Indispensable? The American universities are currently crammed with students who have no command over it whatsoever. And this fact, grounds for despair, is being promoted by some as grounds for celebration. . . . [T]he fact is that a grotesque proportion of students coming from the secondary schools are close to being functional illiterates. Even middle class students who speak Standard English habitually cannot write it: many remain stuck in the pre-literate language of infantilism. They are only slightly better off than their less-pampered conferees from outside the middle class, whose teachers sometimes seem divided between hostile hailers and people who think correct English (or almost any other kind of education) is a class insult. . . .
>
> Now as the universities drown in the inundating ignorance produced by these attitudes, their irritated and pressed staffs—the ranks of the professors swollen by many brilliant people who have absolutely no pedagogical or scholarly calling, but who are busy evading the "real world"—began to be infected with [America's historical anti-intellectualism] and to ramify it in more fancy versions. Standard English? Since it is possible to demonstrate that the illiterate dialects of English have their own coherent grammar and structure, that it is quite possible to "conceptualize" in them, who needs it? Not teaching [Standard English] is a viscous cultural imperialism, an arbitrary humiliation rigged by the middle class to flatter itself—and to baffle and stultify what are called its class and racial enemies. . . . Around the educational catastrophe swirls the numbing fog of a politicized and mysticized ideology of illiteracy. (cited in Miller 1974b)

It should be noted that Koch writes into his argument many of the racial stereotypes which had surrounded Black English. Speakers of nonstandard dialects are "stuck in pre-literate languages of infantilism." Individuals who cannot grasp the fundamentals of standard English are only those who come from the "most illiterate of households." Negating all the linguistic scholarship that demonstrated structural differences between Black English and standard English, Koch argues that the learning of standard English is easily acquired. The image of the nonstandard-dialect speaker that emerges is of either a lazy individual who refuses to learn or an individual so damaged by his or her culture that he or she is unable to learn. In addition, he attaches any opinion that would claim a legitimate status for Black English to the anti-imperialist or class-war ideologues. While he is certainly correct in drawing these two domains together, he obviously does so to further weaken the possibility of resolutions such as the SRTOL. Clearly this argument shows the weakening or near collapse of the legitimacy of the New Left rhetoric as the 1970s continued.[9] Further, it demonstrates that the CCCC and Larson were unable to contain the associations the SRTOL would accrue during its history.

Given the range of grassroots responses, it seemed that the business meeting at Anaheim would be packed and contentious. Unlike previous years, however, the Anaheim convention would have an attendance of only eight hundred people, lower than any other convention of the previous six years. Additionally, to a great extent, the "business" agenda of the CCCC, particularly the business meeting, was increasingly dominated by the need to respond to the changing political and social climate. Unlike in the 1960s, when the business meeting served as a forum to push forward a progressive and liberal agenda, that agenda was now under attack both politically and economically. As noted previously, Nixon had forcefully argued against the New Left, painting the "silent majority" as the true repository of social values. It was also his administration which "cut and impounded university funds for liberal arts, libraries, and scientific research, [and] eliminated most grants for graduate education (down from 51,400 to 6,600 in the Nixon years)" (Sale 1975, 250). The effect of the new rhetoric and government policies was to lead universities to cut back or remodel their liberal arts programs. This shift also led to the abandonment of full-time faculty for the cost effectiveness of part-time faculty. Consequently, it should not be surprising that the business meeting addressed the effects of these policies. Among the resolutions presented was one directly relating to the new economic troubles facing English departments:

Resolution III:

BACKGROUND: Lower enrollment, or the fear of lower enrollments; decreased budgets, or the threat of decreased budgets; community pressures; and legislative demands for economy and accountability have led some colleges and universities to dismiss faculty members with little or no notice, ignoring the obligations of tenure and bypassing the procedural safeguards intended to protect untenured faculty. Because English departments are especially vulnerable to such administrative retrenchment, the method by which these dismissals are handled becomes a special concern of CCCC.

RESOLVED, first that CCCC express its condemnation of the arbitrary abrogation of tenure, the mass dismissal of untenured staff, and the elimination of due process; and second, that CCCC strongly urge that all retention and tenure decisions, whether or not they involve a reduction

in staff size, be securely based on a thorough, balanced professional evaluation of teaching competence, and a consideration of each faculty member's contributions in creative, research, and professional work. (CCCC
business meeting, 6 April 1974)

The emphasis on "community pressures" as well as legislative pressures further indicates the extent to which the CCCC found its previously liberal business meetings out of step with the culture.

At the same time that Nixon continued his attacks upon "egghead" academics,[10] there was a growing movement to a "Back to the Basics Curriculum." This reform effort grew out of a conservative attempt to portray liberal
curriculum reforms as the reason for the United States' "social decline." They
argued for a return to a "traditional education" (Shor 1986, 78–79). According
to "Back to the Basics" advocates, proof of their position was the failure of
SAT scores to improve; according to New Right advocates, SAT scores were
declining. In response, the SAT added a section which would measure a student's ability to identify and correct standard English usage. At a CCCC business meeting at which the Executive Committee was asking the CCCC to
endorse the SRTOL, such a move was clearly antithetical. Consequently, the
following resolution was passed:

> BACKGROUND: Beginning in October, 1974, a new section will be
> added to the Scholastic Aptitude Test — a 30 minute test of English usage
> containing questions similar to the objective portion of the English Com-
> position Achievement Test. To make space for this section, fifteen min-
> utes will be taken from the verbal portions of SAT and fifteen minutes
> from the math portion. The new usage score will be recorded separately,
> along with the math score and the verbal score, which will be reported in
> two parts: reading comprehension and vocabulary. This new section was
> added without consultation or advice from the professional associations
> most closely concerned, NCTE and CCCC. Although the usage section is
> said to be an experiment, subject to re-evaluation after two years, the
> students who are rated by the test between 1974 and 1976 will be perma-
> nently labeled by their scores in this section.
>
> RESOLVED, first, that CCCC protest the inclusion of an objective usage
> test in Scholastic Aptitude Test, on the grounds that such tests are a
> measure of copy reading skill rather than a measure of student ability to
> use language effectively in connected discourse of their own composing;
> such tests place emphasis on mechanical matters of spelling, punctuation
> and conventions of usage, rather than on clarity, appropriateness, and
> coherence of thought; such tests tend to discriminate against minority
> students whose linguistic experiences often lead them to choose answers
> different from those expected by the test-makers; and the inclusion of
> such a test may encourage secondary English teachers to teach toward
> the test at the expense of matters more fundamental to effective writing
> and sophisticated reading; and second, that CCCC encourage members
> to resist the use of usage scores in the admission and placement of its
> students. (CCCC business meeting, 6 April 1974)

Unlike other New Left or NUC resolutions passed at a CCCC business meeting, the following day, the Executive Committee decided that Part One of the resolution "be sent to CEEB and ETS, to the Association of College Admissions Officers and the admissions officers of CEEB member schools; and Part Two should be included in Mr. Larson's report to the membership. In addition, the entire resolution should be sent to the CCCC Committee on Testing and the NCTE Task Force on Evaluation and Measurement" (CCCC officers meeting, 7 April 1974). Notably, these measures did not necessarily have as much support as previously passed New Left resolutions.

It is within this emergence of conservative politics that the SRTOL came to vote. Unlike the other resolutions, the SRTOL was not presented with a clear statement of its social or political background. If the language statement proper had provided such information, this would not be notable. In a context in which the right had achieved the political initiative nationally, it appears bringing up the New Left past of the SRTOL would be unwise. Consequently, those in attendance received only the resolution, without context, for discussion. As recorded in the minutes, the SRTOL was presented as follows:

> BACKGROUND: All CCCC members were sent by mail the explanatory statement and bibliography which serve as support for this resolution.
>
> RESOLVED, that CCCC affirm the students' right to their own language—the dialects of their nurture or whatever dialects in which they find their own identity and style. Language scholars long ago denied that the myth of a standard American dialect has any validity. The claim that any one dialect is unacceptable amounts to an attempt of one social group to exert its dominance over another. Such a claim leads to false advice for speakers and writers, and immoral advice for humans. A nation proud of its diverse heritage and its cultural and racial variety will preserve its heritage of dialects. We affirm strongly that teachers must have the experiences and training that will enable them to respect diversity and uphold the right of students to their own language. (CCCC business meeting, 6 April 1974)

Given the support of the previous two resolutions, it is not surprising that the SRTOL was passed by a vote of 79 to 20. What is noteworthy is that under previous rules, or perhaps in a better attended conference, the SRTOL could not have been voted on and probably would not have passed. As was noted previously, however, the meeting rules had been changed to allow only fifty members to constitute a quorum and majority vote for passage. The low vote total for the SRTOL would hurt its status. Seventy-nine votes were in the approximate range of previous votes endorsing the "People's Peace Treaty," anti–Vietnam War stands, and anti–usage standards measures. Furthermore, over the previous six years the business meeting had become the site of New Left and activist politics. The political context of the resolution, then, automatically made it appear to be a coup d'état by the radical minority rather than a stand taken by the Executive Committee that developed over the course of two years.

It is also unclear whether the resolution would have passed if the CCCC business meeting was held, as previously, at the NCTE Convention, for after the CCCC passed the SRTOL, the NCTE also passed a similar resolution. But perhaps in response to the growing criticism, the NCTE amended its resolution slightly:

> RESOLVED, that the National Council of Teachers of English affirm the students' right to their own language—to the dialect that expresses their family and community identity, the idiolect that expresses their unique personal identity; affirm the responsibility of all teachers of English to assist all students in the development of their ability to speak and write better whatever their dialects; affirm the responsibility of all teachers to provide opportunities for clear and cogent expression of ideas in writing, **and to provide the opportunity for students to learn the conventions of what has been called written edited American English;** and affirm strongly that teachers must have the experiences and training that will enable them to understand and respect diversity of dialects; and
>
> Be it further RESOLVED, that, to this end, the NCTE:
>
> make available to other professional organizations this resolution as well as suggestions for ways of dealing with linguistic variety, as expressed in the CCCC background statement of students' right to their own language; and promote classroom practices to expose students to the variety of dialects that comprise our multiregional, multiethnic, and multicultural society, so that they too will understand the nature of American English and come to respect its dialects. (NCTE 1988, emphasis added)

It is evident that the NCTE statement backs away from much of the moral tone and intent of the CCCC SRTOL. As opposed to a statement which speaks about the immorality and unsoundness of demanding that students learn another dialect, the NCTE statement offers assistance for students to broaden the parameters of individual dialect use. It also ensures that students are given the opportunity to learn "edited American English." To a great extent, the NCTE resolution most clearly matches the more conservative aspects of the CCCC's SRTOL language statement. The NCTE resolution noticeably calls for the NCTE to circulate its resolution, but the CCCC's language statement. The NCTE must have felt that its own resolution most clearly matched the intent of the statement.

CONCLUSION

In amending its SRTOL resolution, the NCTE was offering, inadvertently, the final requiem for the radical and progressive politics which had first brought students' rights into the CCCC arena. In fact, when the CCCC and NCTE SRTOL documents are combined, the total affect is not unlike the original CEL language statement. Ultimately, however, even the more sedate and restrained NCTE SRTOL would not go unnoticed.

NOTES

1. In fact, the use of mail ballots had so effectively blunted the ability of the business meeting to act as a catalyst for progressive politics that during the 1980s the Progressive Composition Caucus attempted to pass an amendment which would dictate that the Executive Committee must follow business meeting resolutions.

2. The original version of the SRTOL produced by the committee was approximately two pages long. During a break, however, the statement was edited down by members to approximately one paragraph. In a discussion with the author, Richard Lloyd-Jones stated that the original document contained additional emphasis on the linguistic knowledge needed by teachers. He also stated that he no longer owned a draft of the original two-page statement. Thus, I am more concerned with how the various cultural forces directed the language chosen for the final resolution than with any particular committee member's contribution. My argument, in part, is that the committee acted as a body rather than as individual members in response to the political and social terrain. The role of individual members in constructing the resolution is best left to their memory and their personal goals at that time.

3. At this meeting, Davis suggested that an ad hoc committee or a task force be appointed that would include people not on the Executive Committee. Apparently, there were still concerns that the SRTOL committee, in its makeup and consequent actions, was not strong enough in its support for the rights and concerns of minority members, or perhaps there was concern that the SRTOL was beginning to lose the political intent and focus originally articulated by advocates of the NUC. In any case, the idea of a task force was rejected.

4. The idea in the SRTOL resolution that students should gain experience with different dialects was translated in the SRTOL language statement, in part, into the idea that the teacher should visit the areas in which those students live but not necessarily endorse policies which would ensure their continued presence in a diverse classroom.

5. As detailed in the published SRTOL (1974), the full committee was chaired by Melvin Butler, and its members were Adam Casimer, Nina Flores, Jennifer [*sic*] Giannasi, Myrna Harrison, Robert Hogan, Richard Lloyd-Jones, Richard A. Long, Elizabeth Martin, Elisabeth McPherson, Nancy Prichard, Geneva Smitherman, and W. Ross Winterowd. (. . . it is interesting to note that Ken Macrorie was invited to be a member of the SRTOL committee but declined.)

6. Melvin Butler was killed during an attempted robbery of his home.

7. The SRTOL clearly positions itself against arguments that minority or underclass students are culturally deprived. In a direct response to the work of Bereiter and Deutsch, the statement argues,

> To cope with our students' reading problem, then, we cannot confine ourselves to the constricting and ultimately ineffectual dialect readers designed for the "culturally deprived." We should structure and select materials geared to complex reading problems and oriented to the experience and sophistication of our students. An urban eight-year-old who has seen guns and knives in a street fight may not be much interested in reading how Jane's dog Spot dug in the neighbor's flower bed. Simply because "Johnny can't read" doesn't mean "Johnny can't think." He may be bored. Carefully chosen materials will certainly expose students to new horizons and should increase their awareness and heighten their perceptions of the social reality. (p. 28)

8. As published in *The Panther and the Lash* (Hughes 1967), the poem is reproduced differently:

> I play it cool
> And dig all jive—
> That's the reason
> I stay alive
>
> My motto,
> As I live and learn
> Is
> *Dig and be dug*
> In return.

9. A less confrontational argument about the connection between social politics and linguistic insight was written by graduate students Warren Dwyer, Kent Baker, and Dennis McInerny (1974). They wrote that while the resolution is "in many ways laudable, we find a good deal of inconsistency and factitiousness in the supporting statements." These authors argue that from the

simple fact of dialect diversity, the concept of a rich language cannot be implied; the linguistic concept of dialects does not imply any judgment about their worth. Consequently, disputing the overlaid morality, they conclude, "The compassion that obviously motivates the Resolution is commendable, but we believe that any resolution regarding minority students that is not explicitly committed to teaching them standard English is an invitation to the cynicism and neglect that have for so long nourished separateness and deprivation in this country" (Dwyer et al. 1974).

10. This phrase is attributed by Sale (1975, 250) to John Mitchell of the Nixon administration.

WORKS CITED

Committee on the English Language (CEL). n.d. "Statement on Usage." NCTE Archives, Urbana, Ill.

Conference on College Composition and Communication (CCCC). Business meeting reports. NCTE Archives, Urbana, Ill.

———. Officers meeting minutes. NCTE Archives, Urbana, Ill.

———. Secretary's reports. NCTE Archives, Urbana, Ill.

Davidson, Carl. 1966. "A Student Syndicalist Movement: University Reform Revisited." *New Left Notes* (9 September): 2, 11.

Dillard, J. L. 1972. *Black English: Its History and Usage in the United States.* New York: Random House.

Dixon, John E. 1966. *Growth through English: A Report Based on the Dartmouth Seminar, 1966.* Reading, England: National Association for the Teaching of English.

Dwyer, Warren, Kent Baker, and Dennis McInerny. 1974. "Remarks on 'The Students' Right to Their Own Language,'" 3 April. NCTE Archives, Urbana, Ill.

Friedrich, Dick, and David Kuester. 1972. *It's Mine and I'll Write It That Way.* New York: Random House.

Hendrickson, John R. 1972. "Response to the CCCC's Executive Committee's Resolution "The Students Right to His Own Language.'" *College Composition and Communication* 21 (2): 191–192.

Herskovitz, Melville J. 1958. *The Myth of the Negro Past.* Boston: Beacon Press.

Hughes, Langston. 1967. *The Panther and the Lash: Poems of Our Times.* New York: Knopf.

Knowles, Mary Tyler, Betty Resnikoff, and Jacqueline Ross. 1969. "Who(m) Does Standard English Serve? Who(m) Does Standard English Hurt?" *NUC-MLC Newsletter* 1 (5): 4–6.

Labov, William. 1969. *The Study of Non-Standard English.* Urbana, Ill.: National Council of Teachers of English.

———. 1972. "The Logic of Nonstandard English." In *Language, Socialization and Subcultures,* ed. Pier Paolo Giglioli. New York: Verso Press.

Lloyd-Jones, Richard. 1973. Correspondence with Elisabeth McPherson, 7 December. NCTE Archives, Urbana, Ill.

Long, Ralph B. 1973. Correspondence to Richard Lloyd-Jones, 9 March. NCTE Archives, Urbana, Ill.

Marckwardt, Albert. 1958. *American English.* New York: Oxford University Press.

McDavid, Raven. 1971a. Memorandum to CEL. Madison, NCTE Archives, Urbana, Ill.

———. 1971b. "Planning the Grid." *American Speech: A Quarterly of Linguistic Usage* 46 (1–2): 9–26.

McPherson, Elisabeth. 1972a. Annual Report to the NCTE. NCTE Archives, Urbana, Ill.

———. 1972b. Correspondence with Melvin Butler, 8 May. NCTE Archives, Urbana, Ill.

———. 1972c. Correspondence to Richard Riel Jr., 15 November. NCTE Archives, Urbana, Ill.

———. 1972d. "Memorandum To: Members of the CCCC," 8 May. NCTE Archives, Urbana, Ill.

———. 1973. Correspondence with Richard Lloyd-Jones, 9 March. NCTE Archives, Urbana, Ill.

———. 1974. "Notes on Students' Right To Their Own Language." NCTE Archives, Urbana, Ill.

Miller, Evelyn. 1974a. Correspondence to Richard Larson, May 28. NCTE Archives, Urbana, Ill.

———. 1974b. Memorandum to English Department at Manchester Community College, May 28. NCTE Archives, Urbana, Ill.

Muller, Herbert J. 1967. *Uses of English: Guidelines for the Teaching of English from the Anglo-American Conference at Dartmouth College.* New York: Holt, Rhinehart, and Winston.

National Council of Teachers of English (NCTE). 1988. "Position Statement on Issues in Education from the National Council of Teachers of English." *NCTE Forum.* NCTE Archives, Urbana, Ill.

New University Conference (NUC). 1971. NUC Resolutions at CCCC. NUC Archives, Wisconsin Historical Society, Madison.

———. 1972. *Open Up the Schools: NUC Papers #3.* NUC Archives, Wisconsin Historical Society, Madison.

Omi, Michael, and Howard Winant. 1994. *Racial Formation in the United States: From the 1960s to the 1990s*, 2nd ed. New York: Routledge.

Pixton, William. 1972. "Response to the CCCC's Executive Committee's Resolution 'The Students Right to His Own Language.'" *College Composition and Communication* 21 (2): 192.

Prichard, Nancy. 1974. Correspondence with CCCC Officers, February. NCTE Archives, Urbana, Ill.

Sale, Kirkpatrick. 1975. *Power Shift: The Rise of the Southern Rim and Its Challenge to the Eastern Establishment*. New York: Vintage Books.

Shor, Ira. 1986. *Culture Wars: School and Society in the Conservative Restoration, 1969–1984*. Boston: Routledge.

Smitherman, Geneva. 1972. "Black Power Is Black Language." In *Black Culture: Reading and Writing Black*, ed. Gloria M. Simmons and Helene Hutchinson. New York: Holt, Rhinehart, and Winston.

"Students' Right to Their Own Language" [handwritten copy] n.d. NCTE Archives, Urbana, Ill.

"Students' Right to Their Own Language." 1974. *College Composition and Communication* 25 (3): [pp. 19–57 in this book].

Weaver, Constance. 1974. Correspondence with Nancy Prichard, 16 April. NCTE Archives, Urbana, Ill.

4

The Students' Right to Their Own Language: Its Legal Bases

LAWRENCE D. FREEMAN

The CCCC resolution concerning the right of students to the language of their nurture has raised the significant question whether the policies implicit in the resolution would enable speakers and writers of non-English languages or "nonstandard" dialects to survive in, or cope with, the mainstream culture and economy. While such policy considerations are important, they must be balanced against the individual "right" claimed for students. In its present form, the resolution alleges this right on linguistic, psychological, moral, and sociological or anthropological grounds. The words "identity," "moral advice," and "diverse heritages," for instance, might be taken as the "god" words of available psychological, moral, and sociological or anthropological theories to which a majority of the CCCC membership is attracted and perhaps are adherents. I intend to suggest that in addition to these apparent bases for the claiming of the individual student's right, there are other sources of support for the claim.

The CCCC resolution, viewed from a legal perspective, alleges on behalf of students a *right* and, in elaborating that right, urges on States (and by implication on the federal government) a policy of *neutrality* with respect to language. That is, the resolution not only claims a right but implies that in recognition of that right the State must, in its language policy (at least in the schools), neither deny a student his language or dialect nor disparage it, and cannot develop and pursue policies that classify students solely on the basis of linguistic (verbal and non-verbal) attributes without compelling reason. The right to the language of one's nurture claimed in the resolution does not, narrowly speaking, have explicit protection under the Federal Constitution and statutes nor under most State Constitutions or statutes. However, the First, Ninth, and Fourteenth Amendments of the Federal Constitution appear to offer substantial bases for the claimed right, and Title VII of the Civil Rights Act of 1964 (as amended) in clarifying portions of the Fourteenth Amendment provides yet other bases for the right[s] and policies advocated by the resolution.[1]

From *College Composition and Communication* 26 (1975): 25–29.

The first substantial basis for the claimed right of students to their own language is provided by the First Amendment's protection of the free exercise of speech. Of particular importance is the Supreme Court decision in *Tinker and Tinker v. Des Moines Independent School District*, a "free speech" case. In its decision, the Court held that the First Amendment right is protected for students even in the context of schools:

> Students in school as well as out of school are persons under our Constitution. They are possessed of fundamental rights which the State must respect.[2]

While this decision concerned non-verbal expression (the wearing of black armbands), in arriving at it, the Court described constraints on the State in its relation to students: "State-operated schools may not be enclaves of totalitarianism," and the State may not regard students as mere "closed-circuit recipients of only that which the State chooses to communicate."

This view of the application of the First Amendment right to free speech in the context of schools suggests that "students' right to their own patterns and varieties of language" is, in part, protected by the First Amendment. The right of free speech, which has been amplified to include non-verbal expression, has never been limited to protection of speech or writing employing a *specific* language or dialect. Thus, it appears that in so far as students employ their own language or dialect in the schools, their right to do so is protected, except, perhaps, if it creates substantial disruption of the school's order. And this right is more obviously protected in the case of the mono-lingual student who cannot reasonably be said to exercise free speech except by employing the language or dialect to which he or she has been acculturated. Except in specific contexts involving identifiable educational objectives and a showing of reasonable and substantial state interest, this right cannot be curtailed.

The issue we are addressing, however, is more profound than our consideration of the free-speech clause implies. For instance, the Treaty of Guadalupe Hidalgo can be interpreted as protecting the colonists' and their descendants' use of Spanish. The U.S. Civil Rights Commission has observed that this Treaty "guaranteed certain civil, political, and religious rights to the Spanish-speaking colonists and attempted to protect their culture and language."[3] The Treaty does not explicitly refer to either culture or language, though the transcripts of legislative debate on granting statehood to New Mexico and Arizona indicate that at least the residents of New Mexico regarded Article IX of the Treaty as offering protection of their use of Spanish. At least two provisions in the New Mexico constitution embodied this interpretation, one prohibiting restriction of participation in civic activities because of linguistic attributes and another requiring the legislature to provide training for teachers to render them proficient in both English and Spanish. Under this interpretation of the Treaty of Guadalupe Hidalgo—it is not the only possible interpretation—the descendants of the Spanish-speaking colonists appear to have their right to "their own patterns and varieties of language" protected. If this or a similar interpretation of the Treaty were upheld, it would compel those States ceded under the Treaty to remain neutral in language policy in the schools, at least with respect to Spanish language and dialects.

The right the CCCC resolution claims for students, however, extends beyond the right of free speech and beyond any right arguably conferred on some citizens under the Treaty of Guadalupe Hidalgo. It affirms a right for all American students and does not restrict that right to any specific languages or dialects. The resolution, it appears, can fairly be interpreted as requiring the schools neither to deny a student use of any language or dialect nor to disparage use of either. This extensive claim appears to have substantial basis in the little-noticed, seldom-invoked Ninth Amendment to the Federal Constitution, which provides that "the enumeration in the Constitution, of certain rights, shall not be construed to deny or disparage others retained by the people." Unless this amendment is regarded as mere surplusage, there exist unenumerated rights retained by the people. The questions that arise are, what are these unenumerated rights, and by what procedures are they to be determined?

The rather momentous Supreme Court decision in *Wisconsin v. Yoder* serves as a useful starting point in searching for answers to these questions. In this case, the Court exempted Amish children from the Wisconsin state law compelling school attendance after completion of the eighth grade. The Court's decision was grounded narrowly on the "free exercise of religion" clause of the First Amendment. The decision thus is not directly applicable to our considerations, but the Court's reasoning in balancing state interest and individual rights is relevant. The testimony of Dr. Donald A. Erickson, in the view of the Court, was persuasive:

> He . . . testified that the system of learning-by-doing was an "ideal system" of education in terms of preparing Amish children for life as adults in the Amish community. . . . As he put it, "these people aren't purporting to be learned people, and it seems to me that the self-sufficiency of the community is the best evidence I can point to.[4]

Subsequently the Court writes:

> Insofar as the State's claim rests on the view that a brief additional period of formal education is imperative to enable the Amish to participate effectively and intelligently in our democratic process, it must fall. The Amish alternative to formal secondary school education has enabled them to function effectively in their day-to-day life under self-imposed limitations on relations with the world, and to survive and prosper in a contemporary society as a separate, sharply identifiable, and highly sufficient community for more than 200 years. In itself, this is strong evidence that they are capable of fulfilling the social and political responsibilities of citizenship without compelled attendance beyond the eighth grade at the price of jeopardizing their free exercise of religious belief.[5]

The significance of this reasoning is that the court is led to reaffirm an old legal distinction between custom (*consuetudines*) and official law (*leges*).[6] The force of the opinion is to recognize, in the absence of any showing of rational and substantial state interest, the supremacy of the custom of the person or place over official law.

This reasoning is useful in illuminating the meaning of the Ninth Amendment, which appears to provide protection of rights not sanctioned by official law. The available judicial interpretation of this amendment is minimal, construction of it having been attempted only once by the Supreme Court.

In *Griswold vs. Connecticut*, a case involving a Connecticut law prohibiting the sale of contraceptives, the Court found the law unconstitutional, since it violated an unenumerated "right of privacy," protected in part by the Ninth Amendment. Justice Goldberg, in his concurring opinion, provides this commentary on the determination of unenumerated rights:

> In determining which rights are fundamental, judges are not left at large to decide cases in the light of personal and private notions. Rather they must look to the "traditions and collective conscience of our people" to determine whether a principle is "so rooted there . . . as to be ranked as fundamental." . . . "Liberty also gains content from the emanations . . . of specific guarantees" and "from experience with the requirements of a free society."[7]

Goldberg's methodology clearly depends on a distinction between official law and custom and holds that custom can function as the source of law and rights. One commentator, adumbrating Goldberg's position, has observed that human rights which are not enumerated in the Constitution will be revealed and become apparent in the future.[8] This amendment and Justice Goldberg's interpretation of it provide another and more extensive basis for a protected right to one's own patterns and varieties of language, to his own and his group's customary modes of expression, in which he and they find their identity or personhood and personal styles.

But merely claiming, or substantiating, a right does not resolve the issues raised by the resolution, for inevitably state interest and individual right must be balanced, particularly in the context of the schools. It is an obviously rational and substantial interest of the state to require instruction in English (including Educated American English), if only on the most utilitarian and pragmatic grounds. The question that arises is how the state can assure that its citizens will possess the linguistic attributes necessary to participate effectively in political and other civic arenas without jeopardizing the individual student's right.

I propose that this question can be resolved by compelling the schools to be neutral with respect to languages and dialects. Justice Clark in balancing state interest and individual rights with respect to religion illuminates the principle of neutrality:

> . . . it might well be said that one's education is not complete without a study of comparative religion or the history of religion and its relationship to the advancement of civilization. It certainly may be said that the Bible is worthy of study for its literary and historic qualities. *Nothing we have said here indicates that such study of the Bible or of religions when pre-*

sented objectively as part of a secular program of education may not be effected consistent with the First Amendment.[9]

With respect to language, the principle of neutrality would go as follows: there is nothing to *prevent* the teaching of language and dialects other than those possessed by the student so long as they are presented *objectively* as instruments of value and use in social and political intercourse and intellectual inquiry. Corollary to this principle of linguistic neutrality is the principle that a speaker or writer of a non-preferred language or dialect cannot be differentially incorporated into the activities of the school (or of society in general).

The legal bases of the resolution include more than those we have so far explored. In calling for more improved and appropriate education of teachers in matters of language, the CCCC appears cognizant of the existence of, and the implications of, Title VII of the Civil Rights Act of 1964 (as amended) and the related regulatory and legal developments it has occasioned. On its face, Title VII appears to be unrelated to the CCCC resolution, since it provides protection against employment and personnel practices which discriminate on the basis of, among other things, sex and race. Discrimination on the basis of language is not explicitly prohibited by this provision, but that does not render it irrelevant to the resolution. Under Guidelines for Selection of Employees promulgated by the Equal Employment Opportunities Commission, which has administrative jurisdiction over Title VII, criteria for selecting employees must have a manifest relationship to the job under consideration.

The Supreme Court in *Griggs vs. Duke Power* cites these guidelines approvingly and is moved to observe:

> The facts of this case demonstrate the inadequacy of broad and general testing devices as well as the infirmity of using diplomas or degrees as fixed measures of capability . . . diplomas and tests are useful servants, but Congress has mandated the common sense proposition that they are not to become masters of reality.[10]

The result of the Court's decision is that the licensing, hiring, and promotion of educational personnel will probably be considerably reshaped, voluntarily or under court order, and reshaped by establishing selection criteria for each process that is related to a specific teaching job. One civil-rights lawyer has argued that a two-pronged test of programs educating teachers will evolve: not only must the programs have a demonstrable effect on the teacher's acquisition of necessary knowledge, competency, and skill, but this knowledge, competence, and skill, when utilized by a teacher in an educational setting, must have a demonstrably benign effect on the achievement and well-being of children.[11] The second test is, of course, presently idealistic, since there is no substantial evidence regarding the effect of specific teaching competencies on specific children.[12] But even in the absence of research, I am persuaded that common sense would indicate that a teacher who cannot speak or understand the only language or dialect commanded by a monolingual child cannot have a sustained benign effect on the child. The implications of this common-sense proposition are substantial in light of the Commissioner of Education's estimate that in 1968 approximately six million children in America's schools were being taught by persons who "do not know their [students'] language."[13] Moreover, I cannot imagine how one would defend licensing or employing teachers who do not command their students' language or dialect as having its source in a rational and substantial state interest. The state assuredly has a substantial and rational interest in undertaking to insure that its citizens acquire linguistic skills necessary for effective participation in civic and political processes, but that interest, whether in licensing or other areas, cannot include denying or disparaging the students' use of the language or dialect of their nurture.

This discussion has been intended to describe briefly the substantial legal justification for the resolution on the students' right to their own language. But it also suggests some parameters which any further debate and discussion of the resolution might well observe. Before any objections to or attacks on the resolution are given recognition or serious attention, their authors should be required to demonstrate:

(1) That the requirement of state policy of linguistic neutrality is not obligatory;

(2) That the achievement and well-being of children is enhanced by licensing and hiring personnel who can neither speak, write, nor understand the patterns and varieties of language to which the student has been acculturated.

Office of the Superintendent of Public Instruction
Springfield, Illinois

NOTES

1. I ignore here Title VI of the Civil Rights Act; see Lau v. Nichols, ____ U.S. ____ (1974), 42 LW 4165. See also U.S. v. Texas, 342 F. Supp. 24 (1971).

2. 393 U.S. 503 (1969).

3. U.S. Commission on Civil Rights, *The Excluded Student: Educational Practices Affecting Mexican-Americans in the Southwest, Report III* (Washington, D.C.: GPO, 1973), p. 76.

4. 406 U.S. 205 (1972) at 223.

5. 406 U.S. 205 (1972) at 224.

6. On the history of this distinction, see Paul Vinogradoff, *Custom and Right* (Cambridge: Harvard University Press, 1925), particularly Chapter II.

7. 381 U.S. 479 at 493.

8. Bennett Patterson, *The Forgotten Amendment* (Indianapolis: Bobbs-Merrill, 1955). p. 51.

9. Abington School District v. Schempp, 374 U.S. 203 at 225; emphasis added.

10. 401 U.S. 424 (1971) at 433.

11. William Robinson, "The Power of Competency-Based Teacher Education: Views of a Civil Rights Lawyer," in *The Power of Competency-Based Teacher Education* by the Committee on National Program Priorities in Teacher Education, Benjamin Rosner, Chm. (Boston: Allyn and Bacon, 1972), pp. 278–279.

12. See Phyllis Hamilton, *Competency-Based Teacher Education* (Menlo Park: Stanford Research Institute, 1973), pp. 19–21.

13. *The Education Professions, 1968. . . .* (Washington, D.C.: GPO, 1969 [OE-58032]), p. 42.

5

In Response to "The Students' Right to Their Own Language"

ANN E. BERTHOFF AND WILLIAM G. CLARK

The views expressed in the Resolution and the Language Statement are the mirror image of those held in pre-Boas days. That old imperialist linguistics which claimed that allegedly muddy sounds imply imprecision of meaning and inadequacies of conceptual power has been supplanted by an anti-imperialist linguistics that devalues any notion of the special purpose or powers of the written word.

We have known for at least fifteen years that Structural Linguistics has nothing to tell us about composition or the composing process. It seems clear that the concepts of Transformational Grammar, *as they are deployed by the authors of the Language Statement*, have nothing to tell us about the reading process. "Reading," the Language Statement declares, "involves the acquisition of meanings, not the ability to reproduce meanings in any given surface forms." This attempt to employ the concept of language acquisition in the context of a discussion of reading creates a muddle: meanings are not acquired but are hypothesized and tested by developing significances and judging contexts, by acts of mind which are usually identified as *interpretation*. Understanding what we read is dependent on how we construe the "surface features," i.e., on how we apprehend relationships articulated by the words on the page. Interpretation requires that we critically evaluate these constructions by comparing them with alternative readings: a mystical plunge to "deep structures" is no substitute for this critical procedure. ("Deep structure" is certainly the most problematic of all Chomsky's notions. In any case, casual reference to undefined concepts cannot do the work of argument.)

Since the authors of the Language Statement have no conception of language other than as a "system" for "communication" (neither term being defined properly), it is foolhardy to expect this directive to be concerned with language as "the supreme organ of the mind's self-ordering growth," as I. A. Richards has called it. Of course, Richards is not listed in the Bibliography—the one critic who has the most to teach us about how to keep our famous

From *College Composition and Communication* 26.2 (1975): 216–17.

"tripod" of language, literature, and composition from collapsing before we discover what it might support. There are no philosophers of language listed—not a single item by Black, Whitehead, Langer, Cassirer; not a single psychologist not of the school from which the assumptions of the Language Statement are derived—nothing of Piaget, Bruner, Vygotsky, Werner. We are urged instead to read—Stuart Chase! Instead of Jacques Barzun or Patrick Creber, we have the General Semanticists. To claim that this selection of studies can assist our understanding of the issues is ridiculous. Like the Resolution and the Language Statement, the Bibliography is the product of sham scholarship.

It is our moral and professional responsibility to learn how to meet the challenge of illiteracy wisely and humanely and imaginatively. To that end, we do not need a declaration of principles, no matter how high-minded or tough-nosed, but a definition and critique of the pedagogical and curricular options. Appeal to obscure or highly problematical or simply irrelevant linguistic conceptions, in the name of cool, scientific assessment, won't get us off the hook.

Certainly, we need to admonish ourselves about the dangers of uncritical attitudes towards "standards" of "correctness," but it is fatuous to set aside the problem of illiteracy in the interest of cautionary sermonizing. Declaring that everyone has a "right" to his own "language" is sloganeering, very close in spirit and rhetorical form to anti-Communist manifestos and other varieties of response formulated according to a notion of "public relations." Some of my colleagues have dismissed the Resolution as "just political." But that is precisely what it is not: the Resolution and the supporting documents only distract us from the real issues, which are incomparably serious because they are at once pedagogical, philosophical, and political.

ANN E. BERTHOFF
University of Massachusetts
Boston

In the October 1974 issue of *CCC*, William Pixton fights the good fight for Standard English and against the resolution affirming Students' Right to Their Own Language. He must have been surprised if he read the *CCC* pamphlet containing the expanded version of that resolution, which CCCC members were asked to vote on at Disneyland, to learn that it asserts that English teachers should teach Standard English.

I know I was surprised. But there is no mistaking the meaning: ". . . it is necessary that we inform those students who are preparing themselves for occupations that demand formal writing that they will be expected to write EAE" (p. 39 in this book). EAE stands for Edited American English, which the pamphlet defines in terms that make clear that EAE is a euphemism for the soiled term Standard English.

I was not only surprised, I was disappointed. The whole project had from the beginning been so logical and so impossible and so noble: other dialects *are* as good as Standard English; no more than a handful of English teachers *would* have stopped worshipping at the shrine of Standard English whatever the resolution said; and teaching dialect speakers that their dialect is as good as any other is a *virtuous* act. But the committee in charge of the resolution lost their nerve and cost us a cause.

Doubtless the committee members decided in the end to trade nobility for students' employability; but they came to that decision very late in their document and very surreptitiously. They had for thirteen pages of their pamphlet argued persuasively that there is no reasonable basis for preferring one dialect to another and that the act of preferring one dialect is a devastating criticism of the others.

In fact, just before their argument self-destructs, they speak of dialect and employment in terms which point to a very different conclusion from the one they are about to reach: "Since English teachers have been in large part responsible for the narrow attitudes of today's employers, changing attitudes toward dialect variations does not seem an unreasonable goal, for today's students will be tomorrow's employers" (p. 39). That seems to say that our job as English teachers is to stop insisting on students' use of Standard English and to begin acquainting students with the facts about dialect variations so that when they become employers they will not discriminate on the basis of dialect.

Almost immediately thereafter comes the explosion—the endorsement of Standard English. The committee members slip it in quietly, as quietly as any explosion I've ever heard: William Pixton may not have heard it yet. But it's there and no mistake. They call it EAE; they urge us English teachers to stroke our dialect speakers a good bit so they will know it's nothing personal, and they tell us that *only* students who are going into occupations which require formal writing will need to master EAE. But the final message is unmistakable: "Be gentle with your students. Encourage them. Be interested in their ideas. But, by God, see to it that they write like white folks!"

WILLIAM G. CLARK
University of Iowa
Iowa City

PART TWO

The Politics of Memory: Linguistic Attitudes and Assumptions Post-SRTOL

6

Linguistic Memory and the Politics of U.S. English

JOHN TRIMBUR

According to Mary Louise Pratt, a common misconception regarding the American public's view of language is that the U.S. is hostile to multilingualism. Instead, Pratt says, Americans are *ambivalent* about the multiple languages spoken on the street, at work, in the schoolyard, and in the homes where 25 percent of the population speak a language other than English. The politics of language in the U.S. are a tug-of-war between English monolingualism (which, as Pratt notes, gives the U.S. the "well-earned nickname of *cemeterio de lenguas*, a language cemetery" [111]) and the linguistic reality that the U.S. is now, as it has always been, a multilingual society. The ambivalence that Pratt so acutely identifies has its own specific histories in lived experience and linguistic memory. My task here is to look for the roots of this ambivalence in the formation of U.S. English in the late colonial and early national period, roughly 1750 to 1850, just as the American colonists were breaking away from England and, in the matrix of the new nation, establishing the relationship of English to other languages. The design of this essay is first to trace the postcolonial politics of language in the United States. Then I suggest how the linguistic memory that emerges from decolonization and nation building continues, often in unsuspected ways, to influence the language policy of the modern U.S. university and U.S. college composition.

LANGUAGE POLICY AND THE FOUNDING FATHERS

One of the familiar liberal arguments about the politics of language in the United States, often taken up by opponents of the English Only movement, holds that the great wisdom of the Founding Fathers is that they made no national language policy, whether through legislating an official language or establishing a corpus-planning language academy along the lines of the Académie française, as John Adams and others proposed. The Founding Fathers' noninstitutional stance—their refusal to give official status to English—is seen accordingly as evidence of their enlightened tolerance of linguistic diversity

From *College English* 68.6 (2006) : 575–88.

and a multilingual citizenry. This refusal to institutionalize English, however, should not be taken to mean the United States did not have a national language policy. Rather, to use Harold F. Schiffman's term, language policy in the colonial and national period was "covert" (14–15), whereby the politics of language diffused throughout civil society, making language policy a matter of custom rather than law, operating through cultural formations instead of state mandate. According to Schiffman, we must look for the grounds of language policy, whether the overt type found in state edict and national planning or the covert type characteristic of the Founding Fathers' United States, in "linguistic culture"—what he defines as the "set of behaviours, assumptions, cultural forms, prejudices, folk belief systems, attitudes, stereotypes, ways of thinking about language, and religio-historical circumstances associated with a particular language" (5).

Locating the Founding Fathers in the linguistic culture of their time helps us see their language policy, in keeping with the political philosophy of the era, as laissez-faire in character. According to the laissez-faire spirit of the age, as Joseph Lo Bianco puts it, "a foundational liberty of the new republic, or the very *'privateness'* of the language domain, made it inappropriate for there to be state involvement with language" (52; emphasis added). For the Founding Fathers, the state must be neutral in matters of language, recognize no favoritism in policy nor accord official status to any language. The Founding Fathers' neutrality, however, not only restricted the power of the state by keeping language policy out of the political domain (thereby explaining their reluctance to recognize linguistic rights as a basic political liberty); it also assigned language to the private domain, where language policy enters all the more persuasively into the civic networks, relations of production, popular discourse, and everyday practices of U.S. linguistic culture.

To put it another way, a laissez-faire language policy, despite its ostensible neutrality, may be just as programmatic as overt forms of language policy. The suppression of African languages through the slave trade and the formation of a plantation labor force offers the most revealing evidence of how language policy operated covertly, yet systematically, in the colonial and national period. Slave traders routinely separated speakers of the same African languages as a means of social control, and plantation owners paid particular attention to purchasing slaves who spoke different African languages in order to restrict communication and the possibilities of insurrection. Under threat of harsh punishment, which included having their tongues cut out, slaves were prohibited from speaking their native languages or teaching them to their children. Instead, to manage work relations on the plantations, initially pidgin and eventually creolized versions of English were developed as linguistic innovations that, along with compulsory illiteracy laws that forbade teaching slaves to read and write, constituted the official and unofficial language planning of the planter class.

Looked at this way, the Founding Fathers' laissez-faire language policy amounted not so much to linguistic tolerance or, as Shirley Brice Heath argues, a historical precedent for bilingualism. Rather its very covert nature virtually guaranteed the inevitable Anglification of language in the United States through the workings of labor relations, the market, and civil society. During the late colonial and early national period, a politics of English *mainly* (as opposed to the later, more virulent politics of English Only) secured "unassailable" status in the salient domains of power—government, work, education, religion, commerce.

In his well-known study of English language planning and reform, *Grammar and Good Taste*, Dennis Baron says that during the eighteenth and nineteenth centuries "the major patterns of American language reform crystallized" (3). I agree that the late colonial and early national period offers a particularly telling moment for understanding the politics of English in the United States (and, as I've already suggested, the historical structures of American ambivalence about multilingualism). Still, once we identify the cultural logic in the language policy of the era, it becomes hard to accept Baron's claim that the efforts of American language planners and reformers in the eighteenth and nineteenth centuries "have always fizzled out" (2), no more than "exercise[s] in futility" (5). Rather, state neutrality, the privatization of language, and the accompanying absence of linguistic rights can be seen at work in a language policy that was not so much "futile" as productive. While in some instances settler colonies, such as European Jews in Palestine and the Dutch in South Africa, developed new national languages—modern Hebrew and Afrikaans—the United States held to the language of the mother country, rejecting proposals for a new national language (Greek, Hebrew, and French were put forward). It should not be surprising, then, that Baron says "the question of one English or two pervades discussions of language in America in the eighteenth and nineteenth century" (33). What I want to show, however, is that this installation of an Anglo-American dyad in U.S. linguistic culture produces a systematic forgetting of the multiple languages spoken and written in North America and thereby constitutes a key source of American ambivalence toward multilingualism.

POLITICS OF ENGLISH IN THE POSTCOLONY

In postcolonial theory, ambivalence is often identified with the liminality of the postcolonial subject. However, one of the difficulties with the very idea of postcolonialism, as Anne McClintock and others have pointed out, is that it's often employed as a singular ahistorical category—*the* postcolonial subject, *the* postcolonial condition, *the* postcolonial intellectual, postcolonial discourse, and so on. Accordingly, I must begin by saying it is critical to historicize ambivalence in order to identify its structures of feeling, to understand its historical processes and productions, and to clarify the potentialities for liberation entangled in its trajectories.

As I see it, postcolonial theory is a standpoint from which to analyze colonialism, anticolonial struggles, and the process of decolonization. To make good use of such a postcolonial standpoint, we need to draw distinctions between the displacements and settlements of historically specific colonial moments. If it is meaningful to think of the United States as a postcolony at all, we must recognize the term "postcolony" as an analytic one, rather than honorific or celebratory, an instrument to see what kind of colony was established in North America and what the process of decolonization signifies for the politics of U.S. English.

It is conventional to divide the colonial expansion of the European nations (and later the United States and Japan) into settler colonies and exploitation colonies. From this perspective, McClintock's characterization of the United States as a "breakaway settler colony" is pertinent and instructive. If it is true that the American colonists fought the first successful war of national liberation in the modern era, it is just as true that formal political independence from England resulted in shifting control of colonization from the metropolis to the colony itself. The United States as a new nation quickly turned to the project of forging a transcontinental empire, based on slavery and the relocation of American Indian tribes, by annexing the territories of the Louisiana Purchase and those that became Florida and Alaska through purchase, and conquering militarily the Mexican territories that now make up the states of Texas, New Mexico, Arizona, and California.

As may be evident, one definitive quality of the U.S. postcolony is the shallowness and limits of the process of decolonization. Consequently, in terms of the politics of language, the story of decolonization has been told by literary and cultural historians as largely a matter of the relation between British and American English—of whether the new nation would develop its own variety of English to bring out its "revolutionary truth" or defer to received London standards. To be sure, some of the ambivalence that accents the politics of English in the United States can be traced to the "linguistic insecurity" Baron notes in eighteenth- and nineteenth-century America. Still, representing the politics of language as the question of English (see Baron; Kramer; Simpson) amounts to a performance of the past that can be read symptomatically as a ritualized forgetting that the United States was then, as it is now, a multilingual society. To frame the politics of language in terms of Anglophiles and Anglophobes maintains a resolutely English-only perspective that pays no attention, or attention only in passing, to the multiplicity of languages in North America and their relation to English in the colonies and the new nation.

What I'm getting at here is that we need to decenter but not dismiss the Anglo-American linguistic dyad as the central focus of a politics of language in the U.S. postcolony, to relocate it instead in the wider circulation of peoples and languages in the geohistorical region of the circum-Atlantic world. This is the polyglot vortex that produced, as Paul Gilroy puts it, a "new structure of cultural exchange [. . .] built up across the imperial networks that once played host to the triangular trade of sugar, slaves, and capital" (157). To understand the cultural exchanges that shaped U.S. linguistic culture—its linguistic memory and its habits of forgetting—requires a transnational perspective that enables us to see how U.S. English took shape in relation to other languages.

THE ANGLO-SAXON SURROGATE

"Newness," Joseph Roach says, "enacts a kind of surrogation—in the invention of a new England or new France out of memories of the old" (4). Surrogation, as Roach explains it, involves a substitution for the missing original
that results in a systematic (and systematically incomplete) forgetting. When
"actual or perceived vacancies occur in the network of relations that constitutes the social fabric"—when, say, someone dies or retires from work or,
for our purposes, settles new lands or breaks ties with the old—then the
incumbents, according to Roach, "attempt to fit satisfactory alternates." However, since "collective memory works selectively, imaginatively, and often
perversely, surrogation rarely if ever succeeds." Whether through deficit or
surplus, the "intended substitute" is inevitably an inexact fit, a source of
ambivalence more than a resolution to the anxiety of displacement. Thus, as
Roach notes, "selective memory requires public enactments of forgetting,
either to blur the obvious discontinuities, misalliances, and ruptures of, more
desperately, to exaggerate them in order to mystify a previous Golden Age,
now lapsed" (2–3). In *Cities of the Dead: Circum-Atlantic Performance*, Roach
shows how circum-Atlantic memory, through such public spectacles as parades,
carnival, Wild West shows, auctions, funeral traditions, and blackface min-
strelsy, as well as works of British and American theater and literature, both
retains and tries to forget the consequences of the diasporic and genocidal
history of colonization and slavery.

In the politics of language, we can see how the settlement of the English
colonies and the War of Independence looked to the historical primacy of
Anglo-Saxon origins and linguistic memories of an older, pure English speech.
In the colonial and national period, thinkers such as Benjamin Franklin and
Noah Webster called up an ancestral, free-born Anglo-Saxon surrogate in
order to "erase evidence of diaspora and mixture" and to "promote myths of
monocultural autochthony" (Roach 109). The Anglo-American dyad Franklin
and Webster installed in linguistic memory, as surely as the selective memories Roach identifies in other cultural domains, involves an incomplete substitution and systematic forgetting. In part, this forgetting entails the conceptual
erasure of indigenous populations by representing American Indian languages as extinct or dying. In part, it denies the suppression of African languages and makes the inventive hybridity of African American language into
a deficient and disabling dialect of English. Most of all, the "genius of Anglo-
Saxonism," as Roach says (and Franklin and Webster demonstrate), is its
capacity "to perpetuate itself by simultaneously expanding its boundaries in
the name of freedom and disavowing its consequent affiliations in the name
of race" (109).

Benjamin Franklin's infamous tirade against Pennsylvania Germans in
his "Observations Concerning the Increase of Mankind," written in 1751,
presents a remarkable instance of Anglo-Saxon expansionism and its racialized identifications and divisions. Here is a key passage from Franklin's
"Observations":

> Why should the Palatine Boors be suffered to swarm into our Settle-
> ments, and by herding together establish their Language and Manners
> to the Exclusion of ours? Why should Pennsylvania, founded by the
> English, become a colony of Aliens, who will shortly be so numerous as
> to Germanize us instead of our Anglifying them, and will never adopt
> our Language or Customs, any more than they can acquire our Complex-
> ion [. . .]? (234)

As can be seen, for Franklin the English claim to Pennsylvania rests on priority of settlement and the purported originality of the English settler colonists.
The very notion that Pennsylvania could be "founded" by Europeans depends
in the first instance, of course, on the replacement of aboriginal sovereignty
and native patterns of land use by English settlement and the entitlement of
free-born subjects of the British Empire to expand the territory of "Anglo-
Saxon Liberty." By installing such an Anglo-Saxon surrogate in the gap
between the mother country and the new world, the displaced English settlers
in North America seized on a readily available fiction to represent themselves
as being at home in the colonies—a means of remembering and forgetting
that in turn erased native inhabitants and cast the "swarm" of Pennsylvania
Germans as illegitimate invading rivals.

Franklin's xenophobic fear of a "colony of Aliens" who threaten to "Ger-
manize us instead of our Anglifying them" certainly fits, as Heath suggests,
into a larger pattern in the United States, where the language of non-English-
speakers who are seen to pose a social, economic, or political threat becomes
the "focus of argument" about linguistic status and political legitimacy (10).
In a sequence of rhetorical moves that have become standard in the politics of
U.S. English, Franklin begins by asserting the linguistic priority of English
and its authenticity as the language of settlement. Then he constructs an
unbridgeable divide between English speakers and German speakers that is
warranted not only by linguistic and cultural difference but also, revealingly,
by the lack of a shared "Complexion."

Franklin's move from language to complexion leads him to disaffiliate
English settlers from Germans on the grounds of racialized identities. In a
now familiar gesture, language and race become proxies for each other as
Franklin divides the world between the "black or tawny" people of Africa,
Asia, and Native America, the "swarthy" people of Europe (which includes
not only the predictable Spaniards and Italians but also Swedes and Germans), and the Saxons and English alone who "make the principal Body of
White People on the Face of the Earth." Linguistic memory merges with natural history as Franklin maps a racialized taxonomy across the surface of the
globe. What is most troubling to Franklin is the recognition that, according
to the categories of his own invention, "the number of white People in the
World is proportionately very small." In Franklin's articulation of language
and race, the installation of an Anglo-Saxon surrogate in the multilingual and
multiethnic world of the circum-Atlantic provokes the realization that whiteness is surrounded and outnumbered. "I could wish their Numbers were
increased" (234), Franklin says, in one of those moments of Anglo-Saxon lin-

guistic and racial paranoia, when Empire, to use Michael Hardt and Antonio Negri's terms, becomes aware of the Multitude.

The diaspora of the circum-Atlantic world, as Roach says, puts "pressure on autochthony, threatening its imputed purity, both antecedent and successive, because it appears to make available a human superabundance for mutual assimilation" (43). In the case of Franklin, the founding myth of the English colonies, with its claims to priority of settlement, takes place in a geohistorical landscape in which the Anglo-Saxon minority is threatened by swarming multitudes and a Babel of languages. The overwhelming number—the "herd"—of racialized others threatens miscegenation and promiscuous liaisons of all sorts. Predictably, Franklin calls for a halt to immigration to Pennsylvania that might "darken its People." Nonetheless, Franklin's desire to bring forward an authorizing, autochthonous Anglo-Saxon origin of language and liberty kept colliding with the linguistic and cultural impurities of the circum-Atlantic world, the "alien double," as Roach puts it, who appears "in memory only to disappear" (6). The "whiteness" of Franklin's imagination, to use Roach's words, "could not exist even as perjury" without the necessary "failures of memory to obscure the mixtures, blends, and provisional antitypes necessary to its production" (6).

The pressures of the circum-Atlantic world, in other words, could not but provoke new and inventive strategies of linguistic memory and forgetting. In the case of Noah Webster, Franklin's rival German is no longer the source of linguistic, cultural, and racial anxiety but instead is assimilated and refigured in a shared Teutonic linguistic culture. As Thomas Paul Bonfiglio notes, "Webster believes in a profoundly Germanic infrastructure in the English language" (83) that reaches back to Biblical times before the separation of Noah's sons Shem, Ham, and Japheth. Vernacular words in Celtic and Teutonic languages—the foundation, for Webster, of an English rooted in antiquity—acquire a primacy and historical pedigree in their affinity with words that were part of a common language before the linguistic dispersion of Babel. According to Webster, while Shem and Ham are the sources of Semitic and Hamitic languages and cultures, Europeans are the descendants of Japheth. From these ancient roots, Webster argues, Teutonic influences shaped not only Greek and Latin but, more tellingly for his purposes, the English spoken in the United States and England.

In a stroke of linguistic nationalism, Webster makes American English historically antecedent to British English. As Webster says in his *Dissertations on the English Language*, published in 1789, there is a "surprising similarity between the idioms of the New England people and those of Chaucer, Shakespeare, Congreve, &c. who wrote in the true English stile" (108). Webster's linguistic nationalism hinges foremost, it is important to see, not on postcolonial innovation but on a restoration of the linguistic memory of an English that "seldom uses[s] any words except those of Saxon origin," a language free of the Latin contaminants of the Roman conquest and the Norman yoke. "[T]he people of America, in particular the English descendants," Webster says, "speak the most *pure English* now known in the world" (288). As Baron notes, "Webster recognizes that Americans owe their language to the mother country" (45). Nonetheless, for Webster, the English of the British Empire is a language in decline, a decadent and impure product of neologism, loss of standards, and intercultural contact. "Let it be observed," Webster says in 1816, "that so far as a difference between the language of Englishmen and of Americans consists in our use of words obsolete in the higher circles of Great Britain, the change is not in *our* practice but in that of Englishmen. The fault, if any is *theirs*" (qtd. in Baron 58). American English, as Webster sees it, "still adhere[s] to the analogies of the language, where the English have infringed them. So far therefore as the regularity of construction is concerned, we ought to retain our own practice and be our own standards" (129).

According to Webster, American English not only has a purity of origin but also a uniformity of expression that guarantees its function in binding the nation into a common speech community. In contrast to the linguistic situation in England, Americans are not divided by local dialects. "The people of distant counties in England," Webster says, "can hardly understand one another, so various are their dialects." In the United States, however, "in the extent of twelve hundred miles in America," he continues, "there are very few, I question whether a hundred words [. . .] which are not universally intelligible" (288–89). Perhaps, but only if you ignore the Plantation Creole spoken by slaves, who made up more than one-fifth of the population when Webster was writing, and the various linguistic hybrids spoken along the borders of the United States, where French, Spanish, and Native American languages interacted with English through annexation, trade, and diplomacy. Further, the pidgin spoken by the multiethnic crews aboard sailing ships in the circum-Atlantic triangle trade combined "nautical English," the " 'sabir' of the Mediterranean," the "hermeticlike cant talk of the 'underworld,' " and "West African grammatical construction" to shape a new language of the underclasses (Linebaugh and Rediker 153). The uniformity of English that Webster has in mind, as has so often been the case in the United States, is the language of the New England settlers, the Anglo-Saxon descendants whose own regional dialect became the surrogate for a missing English of national unity.

TOWARD A NATIONAL PUBLIC POLICY ON LANGUAGE

Webster's legacy, as Michael P. Kramer puts it, is having shaped "American linguistic history into a final, open-ended chapter of the Anglo-Saxon spirit" (62). Certainly this is the linguistic memory that has been institutionalized in English studies, U.S. college composition, and the modern U.S. university. Since the overturn of the classical curriculum and the establishment of graduate education on the German model in the late nineteenth and early twentieth centuries, the U.S. university has drastically curtailed the educational role of languages other than English—whether Greek and Latin in the old-time American pietistic colleges or German for those Americans who went to German universities to get PhDs. Instead, English has become the unquestioned medium of instruction and the vernacular of modernity, identified with science, technology, and the professions. First British and then American literature replaced the classics as the cultural heritage of university education, and English composition has become the single universal requirement in undergraduate education in the United States. In turn, the other modern languages have been territorialized in departments of French, German, Spanish, and so on, as national literatures, assigning to English only the status of a living language (Horner and Trimbur).

Along similar lines, from the late nineteenth century on, language policy took on a decidedly more overt English-only character in the political domain. For example, oral knowledge of English was required for naturalization by the Nationality Act of 1906 and English literacy by the Internal Security Act of 1950. Settlement house workers and other progressive reformers designed Americanization campaigns to assimilate new immigrants to English and to American culture. Beginning in the late 1880s, a number of cities and states proposed legislation, aimed mainly at German language schools, to restrict or ban altogether bilingual education and instruction in languages other than English, sometimes bringing forward "research" studies to show bilingual education is a harmful "*burden* for children" (Schiffman 236). With the entrance of the United States into World War I, anti-German sentiment intensified, and state Councils of Defense banned the use of German not only in schools, churches, and the press but also at work and in phone conversations. Such overt attempts to favor English and curtail other languages by way of state intervention have continued, of course, in the English Only movement and in more recent legal attacks on bilingual education.

What appear to be departures from the laissez-faire language policy of the early republic must be seen, Schiffman argues, as arising from and codifying ideas already prevalent in American linguistic culture rather than sharp breaks. I have shown some of the ways the "Anglo-Saxon spirit" that underwrites the linguistic culture of English monolingualism took root in the colonial and national period, from the 1750s, when Franklin was agitating against the Pennsylvania Germans, to the 1850s, when the publication of *Moby Dick* in 1850 and Matthew Perry's opening of Japan in 1853 marked symbolically the movement outward from the circum-Atlantic world to the trans-Pacific rim in the age of high American imperialism. Until quite recently, the Anglo-Saxon surrogate of Franklin and Webster's era fit reassuringly into a taken-for-granted narrative of American exceptionalism, where the Pilgrims strode forward on their "errand in the wilderness," toward the manifest destiny that loomed on the western horizon. By the late nineteenth century, however, fraught with Social Darwinist fears of immigration from southern and eastern Europe, race mixing, and the loss of Teutonic vigor, Anglo-Saxonism hardened in the imperialist ethos of the "white man's burden," as Rudyard Kipling urged on his fellow English speakers in the brutal pacification of the Philippines following the Spanish American War. Not surprisingly, the United States made English an official language for the first time in the conquered territories of Puerto Rico and the Philippines.

The issue here is not simply Anglo-Saxon hegemony in linguistic memory, the imposition of English on colonized people, or the Americanization campaigns directed at immigrants around the turn of the previous century. Rather what is crucial is the relentless monolingualism of American linguistic culture, the strategies by which English is meant to replace and silence other languages. If anything, this unidirectional monolingualism has been codified in melting-pot ideologies as a "natural" language shift to English only (with consequent loss of mother tongue) that occurs by the third generation in immigrant families, thereby making bilingualism and the maintenance of home languages appear to be aberrant and un-American. In other words, U.S. English inevitably figures as a loss of memory, a language of forgetting whose very ground of speech is the displacement of other languages. And yet, as Roach suggests, "the most persistent mode of forgetting is memory imperfectly deferred" (4). Linguistic memory—the incomplete forgetting of ancestral languages—virtually guarantees ambivalence about multilingualism in the United States, as traces of other languages—embedded residually in mundane rituals, ethnic and racial identifications, the names and taste of food, the sound of a word, a style of dress—collide with English monolingualism and its Anglo-Saxon heritage.

From a certain angle, it would appear that "memory imperfectly deferred" is compulsively resurfacing in the U.S. university, in the form of multiculturalism, postcolonial theory, and transnational studies. The emergence of this countermemory has indeed recast the study of history, literature, and culture, with works such as Roach's *Cities of the Dead*, among many others, that take as their unit of analysis not the nation-state and the national character of the old American exceptionalism but instead the circulation of people and intercultural exchange across national borders. Still, as Marc Shell and Werner Sollors have pointed out, there is a remarkable silence within this recent and important body of work, as well as across the university curriculum, about the multilingualism that the Anglo-American linguistic dyad has traditionally erased.

The primacy of English as the medium of instruction in the U.S. university retains a powerful hold on teaching and learning, curtailing the development both materially and programmatically of a multilingual curriculum. Take, for example, Hampshire College, surely known for its progressive education. In 1994, a third of the curriculum consisted of courses in "cultural diversity," and yet there were no "foreign" language courses at all. In contemporary English studies, while English-language writers across the global diaspora and works of world literature in English translation are widely read, there is no apparent institutional or critical space for the vast nonanglophone literature written in the United States. To test this point, check the table of contents of Shell and Sollors's groundbreaking *The Multilingual Anthology of American Literature*, with its original texts and English translations, to see how many writers you've ever heard of. Another instance of systematic forgetting is the reference volume *Asian-American Literature: An Annotated Bibliography* (Cheung and Yogi), which explicitly excludes "works written in Asian languages, unless they have been translated into English" (Sollors 14).

In the field of writing studies, until quite recently there has been very little discussion of writing in languages other than English in composition classrooms, and the writing that takes place in Spanish, French, German, Chinese, Arabic, and other language courses has remained largely invisible, both conceptually and programmatically. For this reason, the question "Should We Invite Students to Write in Home Languages? Complicating the Yes/No Debate," raised by Peter Elbow and coauthors (Bean et al.), is especially noteworthy because it focuses attention on potentially productive relations between English and other languages and dialects in composition. Nonetheless, the trajectory of writing instruction, for Elbow at least, remains largely unidirectional, with composing in a mother tongue represented not in terms of biliteracy but as a move toward a finished essay in English. In another recent experiment in cross-language relations, Isis Artze-Vega, Elizabeth Doud, and Belkys Torres have developed strategies for a bilingual composition pedagogy at the University of Miami, using bilingual texts, journals, freewriting, and class discussion in Spanish, and bilingual writing assignments in the style of Gloria Anzaldúa that call on students to embed Spanish (or other languages) in predominantly English compositions. To my mind, this latter work is particularly significant because, by figuring Spanish as a medium of writing equal to English, it begins to address explicitly the status of languages in the writing classroom and the problem of language policy in the writing curriculum.

The question traditionally asked in writing studies is how cross-language relations inhibit or facilitate students' mastery of academic literacy in English. I think the question needs to be changed, to ask instead how such available linguistic resources can be tapped to promote biliteracy and multilingualism. I want to imagine a new configuration of languages in the U.S. university and in U.S. college composition that realigns the old Anglo-American linguistic dyad, making English not the center but the linking language in multilingual writing programs, multilingual universities, and a multilingual polity. To do this would require a shift from the unidirectional and subtractive monolingualism that has long dominated writing programs in the modern U.S. university to an active and additive multilingualism in which a range of languages are involved as the medium of writing, as the medium of instruction across the university curriculum, and as the medium of deliberation in the public sphere.

I realize that the Anglo-American linguistic dyad is a coalition of the willing and that English monolingualism exerts a strong undertow on how we think about other languages. But it is precisely for this reason that, as Geneva Smitherman argued in 1987, academics in speech, language, and writing studies need to "take up the unfinished business of the Committee on the Students' Right to Their Own Language" by calling for a national public policy on language that would (1) teach standard edited English as the language of wider communication, (2) recognize the legitimacy of nonmainstream languages and dialects and promote mother tongues, along with English, as the medium of instruction, and (3) promote the learning of one or more additional languages, such as Spanish or other relevant languages. The exact configuration of languages to be studied and learned will depend on individual interest and local circumstances. The key point for Smitherman is that the "three-prong policy [. . .] constitutes an inseparable whole" (31) that is meant to change the status of languages in the United States by reconfiguring their relation to one another.

What Smitherman's proposal for a national language policy makes clear is that multilingualism does not mean simply affirming the linguistic rights of minority language groups to use their own language as they see fit. Certainly, a national public policy on language must defend such rights, which have never been fully recognized in the United States. As I see it, however, multi-lingualism signifies more than the tolerance of many languages. It also entails the status planning of languages and an additive language policy whereby all students as a matter of course speak, write, and learn in more than one language and all citizens thereby become capable of communicating with one another in a number of languages, code-switching as appropriate to the rhetorical situation. The goal of such a national language policy, I believe, goes beyond a discourse of linguistic rights to imagine the abolition of English monolingualism altogether and the creation in its place of a linguistic culture where being multilingual is both normal and desirable, as it is throughout much of the world. If anything, the multilingual language policy I'm advocating would loosen the identification of language with racialized and ethnic groups by putting multiple languages into circulation as means of participating in public life and linguistic resources of reciprocal exchange.

WORKS CITED

Baron, Dennis. *Grammar and Good Taste: Reforming the American Language.* New Haven: Yale UP, 1982.
Bean, Janet, Maryann Cucchiara, Robert Eddy, Peter Elbow, Rhonda Grego, Rich Haswell, Patricia Irvine, Eileen Kennedy, Ellie Kutz, Al Lehner, and Paul Kei Matsuda. "Should We Invite Students to Write in Home Languages? Complicating the Yes/No Debate." *Composition Studies* 31.1 (2003): 25–42.
Bonfiglio, Thomas Paul. *Race and the Rise of Standard English.* Berlin: Mouton de Gruyter, 2002.
Franklin, Benjamin. *The Papers of Benjamin Franklin.* Vol. 4. Ed. Leonard W. Labaree, et al. New Haven: Yale UP, 1959.
Gilroy, Paul. *"There Ain't No Black in the Union Jack": The Cultural Politics of Race and Nation.* Chicago: U of Chicago P, 1987.
Hardt, Michael, and Antonio Negri. *Empire.* Cambridge, MA: Harvard UP, 2000.
Heath, Shirley Brice. "English in Our Language Heritage. *"Language in the U.S.A.* Ed. Charles A. Ferguson and Shirley Brice Heath. Cambridge: Cambridge UP, 1981. 6–20.
Horner, Bruce, and John Trimbur. "English Only and U.S. College Composition." *CCC* 53 (2002): 594–630.
Kramer, Michael P. *Imagining Language in America: From the Revolution to the Civil War.* Princeton: Princeton UP, 1992.
Linebaugh, Peter, and Marcus Rediker. *The Many-Headed Hydra: Sailors, Slaves, Commoners, and the Hidden History of the Revolutionary Atlantic.* Boston: Beacon, 2000.
Lo Bianco, Joseph, "The Language of Policy: What Sort of Policy Making Is the Officialization of English in the United States?" *Sociopolitical Perspectives on Language Policy and Planning in the U.S.A.* Ed. Thom Huebner and Kathryn A. Davis. Amsterdam: Benjamins, 1999. 39–66.
McClintock, Anne. "The Angel of Progress: Pitfalls of the Term 'Post-colonialism.'" *Colonial Discourse and Post-Colonial Theory.* Ed. Patrick Williams and Laura Chrisman. New York: Columbia UP, 1994. 291–304.

Pratt, Mary Louise, "Building a New Public Idea about Language." *Profession 2003*. New York: MLA, 2003. 110–19.

Roach, Joseph. *Cities of the Dead: Circum-Atlantic Performance*. New York: Columbia UP, 1996.

Schiffman, Harold F. *Linguistic Culture and Language Policy*. London: Routledge, 1996.

Shell, Marc, and Werner Sollors. *The Multilingual Anthology of American Literature: A Reader of Original Text with English Translations*. New York: New York UP, 2000.

Simpson, David. *The Politics of American English 1776–1850*. New York: Methuen, 1986.

Smitherman, Geneva. "Toward a National Public Policy on Language." *College English* 49 (1987): 29–36.

Sollors, Werner. "For a Multilingual Turn in American Studies." *ASA Newsletter* 20.2 (1997): 13–15.

Webster, Noah. *Dissertations on the English Language*. Boston: Isaiah Thomas, 1789.

7   *"Students' Right to Their Own*
Language": A Retrospective

GENEVA SMITHERMAN

We affirm the students' right to their own patterns and varieties of language—the dialects of their nurture or whatever dialects in which they find their own identity and style. Language scholars long ago denied that the myth of a standard American dialect has any validity. The claim that any one dialect is unacceptable amounts to an attempt of one social group to exert its dominance over another. Such a claim leads to false advice for speakers and writers, and immoral advice for humans. A nation proud of its diverse heritage and its cultural and racial variety will preserve its heritage of dialects. We affirm strongly that teachers must have the experiences and training that will enable them to respect diversity and uphold the right of students to their own language.

> —Passed by the Executive Committee of the Conference
> on College Composition and Communication (CCCC),
> November, 1972, and by the CCCC Membership, April, 1974

It has now been well over a generation since Kwame Ture (then Stokely Carmichael) issued his clarion call for "Black Power" and thus charted a new course for the Civil Rights Movement in America. But his cry, horrendous and frightening as it seemed to be to some in 1966, was not without precedent in the annals of the African American struggle. For just twelve years earlier, Richard Wright had entitled his book on the emerging independence movements in Africa, *Black Power*. And surely Rosa Parks' historic refusal to give up her seat to whites and move to the back of the bus on December 1, 1955, paved the way for Kwame Ture's "Black Power"—a bold call for new directions and strategies. These actions and events from the Black Experience symbolize the motive forces that led to the unleashing of Brown Power, Woman Power, Poor Peoples Power, Gay Power, and other human energy sources that fundamentally altered American power relations in our time.

From *The English Journal* 84.1 (1995): 21–27.

THE HISTORICAL BACKDROP

As marching, fist-raising, loud-talking, and other forms of resistance marred the landscape of "America the beautiful," the power elites huddled to design reforms to acculturate the oppressed into the dominant ideology. The Unhip among researchers, scholars, and intellectuals assembled the data base upon which these reforms were built, arguing, for instance, that even though the linguistic-cultural differences of those oppressed by race, class, or gender were *cognitively* equal to those of the mainstream, they were *socially* unequal. Early on, some scholars—like James Sledd in his 1969 *English Journal* "Bi-Dialectalism: The Linguistics of White Supremacy," and me in my 1968 "Black Power is Black Language" (delivered in April, 1969 in Miami at my first CCCC Convention)—early on, such scholars tried to pull our coats (to enlighten) to the trickeration (deception) of the power brokers. They argued that it was purely academic to demonstrate, in Emersonian, armchair philosophizing style, the legitimacy of the oppressed's language and culture without concomitantly struggling for institutional legitimacy in the educational and public domains. If the patriarchally constituted social and economic structure would not accept non-mainstream speech varieties, then the argument for *difference* would simply become *deficiency* all over again.

Against this backdrop, enlightened academics saw their task clearly to struggle for such legitimacy. They were not romantic idealists; indeed, many of them had been baptized in the fire of social protest and street activism. No, not idealists, but those who know that without vision, people will perish. These progressive academics began working within their professional societies and organizations to bring about mainstream recognition and legitimacy to the culture, history, and language of those on the margins. And it was not only within NCTE and CCCC that this struggle was waged, but all across the alphabetic spectrum—the APA (American Psychological Association); the ASA (American Sociological Association); the MLA (Modern Language Association); the SCA (Speech Communication Association); the ABA (American Bar Association); the ASHA (American Speech and Hearing Association); and on and on across disciplines and throughout the Academy. Though the struggles were spearheaded by Blacks, it quickly became a rainbow coalition as Hispanics, women, Native Americans, and other marginalized groups sought redress for their ages-old grievances against an exploitative system.

Let us recall that the Cause was just if the methods awkward. The Enlightened were, after all, attempting to effectuate change WITHIN THE SYSTEM. And even those of us who were more revolutionarily inclined recognized the folly of doing *nothing* while waiting for the Revolution to come.

THE BIRTH OF "STUDENTS' RIGHT"

In this socio-historical climate, in the fall of 1971, the officers of CCCC appointed a committee to draft a policy resolution on students' dialects, and thus the first "Students' Right to Their Own Language" Committee was born.

After months of intense scholarly work and political struggle, both within and outside our Committee, in March, 1972, we presented the CCCC Executive Committee (of which I was also a member at the time), with the position statement which has come to be known as the "Students' Right to Their Own Language." When I say "intense struggle," it is not dramatic hyperbole; for instance, we debated for hours on the question of the student's right to *his* own language vs. *his* or *her* own language: remember, this was over twenty years ago.

In November of 1972, the CCCC Executive Committee passed the "Students' Right" resolution and began to pave the way to make this admittedly controversial resolution a matter of CCCC policy. They recognized that their membership, as well as other language arts professionals, would need to be educated about the current research on language variation, usage, and the history of American English. A Committee was appointed to develop a background document that would elaborate on the assertions in the brief "Students' Right" statement before presenting the resolution to the full body of CCCC and eventually to the profession at large. The background document was presented to the CCCC Executive Committee at the Philadelphia NCTE Convention in November, 1973. Subsequently, this document and the resolution itself were distributed to CCCC membership.

In April of 1974, at the CCCC business meeting in Anaheim, California, the "Students' Right to Their Own Language" became the official policy of CCCC. That fall, the complete background document was published as a full issue of CCCC's journal, *College Composition and Communication.* The "Students' Right" resolution appears on the inside cover of that issue. The document seeks to inform by presenting a set of 15 issues, in the form of questions, about language, dialect, and teaching-learning—e.g., "Does dialect affect the ability to write?" "Why do some dialects have more prestige than others?" Included also is a bibliography of 129 entries keyed to these 15 questions (pp. 19–57 in this book).

NCTE's Response to "Students' Right"

Although CCCC is politically autonomous, structurally, it is an institutional arm of NCTE, sharing some resources, headquarters, and, of course, concern for language education with NCTE. Further, many CCCC members, myself included, are members and workers of both organizations. In 1971, after the formation of what was to become the "Students' Right" Committee, CCCC leadership and its members began working within NCTE to promote the concept of the students' right to their own language. For the next three years, there was a concerted effort by CCCC to persuade NCTE to endorse the CCCC position statement. However, this did not occur. Instead, at its 1974 Convention, NCTE passed a weaker version of the CCCC's "Students' Right to Their Own Language." Although many of us on the "Students' Right" Committee and within CCCC were profoundly disappointed, we consoled ourselves by the thought that the action taken by NCTE was at least not a *negative* vote on the issue.

There are two crucial differences between the CCCC and the NCTE actions around "Students' Right to Their Own Language."

First, the NCTE resolution distinguishes between spoken and written language in relationship to students' dialects, and although it "accept(s) the linguistic premise that all these dialects are equally efficient as systems of communication," the resolution goes on to "affirm" that students should learn the "conventions of what has been called written edited American English" (NCTE Resolution #74.2, 1974). This was an issue that the CCCC "Students' Right" Committee struggled with and deliberately decided *not* to focus on. We recognized that spelling, punctuation, usage, and other surface structure conventions of Edited American English (EAE) are generally what's given all the play (attention) in composition classrooms anyway. Based on the ground-breaking linguistic research of scholars such as Chomsky (e.g., 1968), Labov (e.g., 1970, 1972), Halliday (e.g., 1973), Hymes (e.g., 1964, 1972), Dillard (e.g., 1972), Shuy (e.g., 1964, 1967), and Fishman (e.g., 1970), the CCCC background publication contends that:

> . . . dialect . . . plays little if any part in determining whether a child will ultimately acquire the ability to write EAE. . . . Since the issue is not the capacity of the dialect itself, the teacher can concentrate on building up the students' confidence in their ability to write . . . the essential functions of writing [are] expressing oneself, communicating information and attitudes, and discovering meaning through both logic and metaphor . . . [thus] we view variety of dialects as an advantage . . . one may choose roles which imply certain dialects, but the decision is a social one, for the dialect itself does not limit the information which can be carried, and the attitudes may be most clearly conveyed in the dialect the writer finds most congenial . . . [Finally] the most serious difficulty facing "non-standard" dialect speakers in developing writing ability derives from their exaggerated concern for the *least* serious aspects of writing. If we can convince our students that spelling, punctuation, and usage are less important than content, we have removed a major obstacle in their developing the ability to write. (pp. 28–29)

The second crucial difference between NCTE and CCCC around the "Students' Right" issue is that CCCC committed tremendous time and energy resources to the illumination of this language issue. For several years after the passage of the position statement by the 1972 CCCC Executive Committee, CCCC committees worked to produce two documents (although one was never published) to provide guidance to teachers on the meaning and implications of the "Students' Right" position and the impact of this policy on classroom practice.

Although NCTE did not come on board with the full vigor we in CCCC would have liked, it did agree in its version of the "Students' Right" resolution to make available to other professional organizations the suggestions and rec-ommendations in the CCCC background document and to

> promote classroom practices to expose students to the variety of dialects that occur in our multi-regional, multi-ethnic, and multi-cultural society, so that they too will understand the nature of American English and come to respect all its dialects. (NCTE Resolution #74.2, 1974)

IMPLEMENTATION OF "STUDENTS' RIGHT"

After the NCTE action, CCCC moved into the next phase of the "Students' Right" history. To be sure, there was high interest and enthusiasm, but unfor-tunately, there was also lingering confusion—you know, "Well, what they want me to *do*?" Although the CCCC background document was informa-tive in terms of theory, it did not go far enough in praxis. CCCC leadership acknowledged that there was a need for more explicit teaching materials, sample lesson plans, and a more specific pedagogy. The Executive Committee thus appointed the "Selection and Editorial Committee for Activities Support-ing Students' Right to Their Own Language," on which I also served.

This Committee was charged with assembling a publication of practical classroom assignments, activities, lectures, and teaching units that would show and tell how to apply the philosophy of the "Students' Right" resolu-tion to the day-to-day experience of teaching and learning. Many of the people who served on this Committee, as on the other "Students' Right" Committee, are well-known and active members of the profession. We spent nearly *four years* compiling and editing some excellent material, solicited from practi-tioners at all levels of education, only to be informed that CCCC had "reluc-tantly decided" not to publish the collection.

What had happened since the passage of the original "Students' Right" resolution some years earlier is that the nation was moving to a more conserv-ative climate on the social, political, and educational fronts. It was a move which would be solidified in 1980 by the election of President Ronald Reagan. Thus the mood of CCCC, as the mood of America, had shifted from change and promise to stagnation and dreams deferred.

PRODUCT AND PROCESS OF "STUDENTS' RIGHT"

We have overviewed the process; now let us look at the product in relation-ship to this process.

Even though earlier I generously labelled our group "progressive," we were not all of like minds about the "Students' Right" resolution, nor its implications. And we certainly were not of identical persuasion on the issue of America's linguistic ills and solutions to them. Hey, some of us even had reservations about the use of little four-letter words—not dem big, bad foe letter ones, with initial fricatives and sibilants; just the little ti-notchy ones like "damn" and "hell." (Apropos of this, I do hereby confess to being the first to introduce "cussing" into Committee deliberations, to the distinct relief of my old comrade, Ross Winterowd of the University of Southern California.) Yet despite our diverse ideologies and political perspectives, we shared a spirit of collective enlightenment on the language question.

The "Students' Right" background document is a compromise publication, born of the contradictions among radicals, moderates, and conservatives. It is, moreover, the consequence of the talented editorial hand of Richard (Jix) Lloyd-Jones from the University of Iowa and of the skillful diplomacy of late linguist Melvin Butler of Southern University, our Committee Chair, whose tragic, untimely death prevented him from witnessing the fruits of his labor. For some of us, then as now, the document is seen as equivocating; it doesn't go far enough. For others, then as now, it is perceived as too permissive.

Yet, short of totalitarianism and fascism on the one hand, or armed revolutionary struggle, on the other, compromise is what comes from working *within* the system. And so those of us who embrace the dialectical vision of history applaud the recently renewed momentum and interest in the "Students' Right to Their Own Language," for without struggle, there is no progress.

As should be obvious to all writing teachers worth their training, the "Students' Right" document is the product of multiple writing styles. After deciding to use the admittedly wack (corny) twenty-question format of the once-popular television quiz show, we divvied up the work and the writing. Although we critiqued each other's writing and despite the admirably awesome editing job done by Melvin, and later Jix, still it must be conceded that the document is stylistically uneven. Yet the final product is preferable to what any *one* individual might have written because it reflects a *collective* response to the language question: "What should the schools do about the language habits of students who come from a wide variety of social, economic, and cultural backgrounds?" (p. 20).

African Americans weren't the only "submerged minorities" (a term we wrestled with in Committee deliberations) forcing the question, as the "Students' Right" framed it: "Should the schools try to uphold language variety, or to modify it, or to eradicate it?" Yet, a good deal of the background document (i.e., examples, illustrations, bibliographic references, etc.) focus on *Black* speech. This is logical given not only the large numbers of African Americans among the oppressed, but also given that Blacks were the first to force the moral and Constitutional questions of equality in this country. Further, of all underclass groups in the U.S., Blacks are pioneers in social protest and have waged the longest, politically principled struggle against exploitation.

Finally—and this is an ironic footnote in American life—whenever Blacks have struggled and won social gains for themselves, they have made possible gains for other groups—e.g., Hispanics, Asians, gays, etc., even some white folks! For instance, the nineteenth-century emancipation of African slaves in this country paved the way for the first Women's Movement, during which, in fact, Black champions for the abolition of slavery, Frederick Douglass and Sojourner Truth, for example, fought vigorously for women's rights. In similar fashion, then, *Black* students' right to *their* own language has made possible *all* students' right to their own language.

THE NEED TO RECOGNIZE STUDENTS' LANGUAGE AND CULTURE

Let me remind you that those who do not learn from the past are doomed to repeat it. In spite of recently reported gains in Black student writing, chronicled by the NAEP and higher scores on the SAT, the rate of functional illiteracy and drop-outs among America's underclass is moving faster than the Concorde. A genuine recognition of such students' culture and language is desperately needed if we as a profession are to play some part in stemming this national trend. I write genuine because, in spite of the controversy surrounding policies like the "Students' Right to Their Own Language," the bicultural, bilingual model has *never* really been tried. Lip-service is about all most teachers gave it, even at the height of the social upheaval described earlier.

You see, the game plan has always been linguistic and cultural absorption of the Other into the dominant culture, and indoctrination of the outsiders into the existing value system (e.g., Sledd 1972), to remake those on the margins in the image of the patriarch, to reshape the outsiders into talking, acting, thinking, and (to the extent possible) looking like the insiders (e.g., Smitherman 1973). In bilingual education and among multilingual scholars and activists, this issue is framed as one of language *shift* vs. language *maintenance* (see Fishman 1966, 1980). That is, the philosophy of using the native language as a vehicle to teach and eventually *shift* native speakers *away from their home language*, vs. a social and pedagogical model that teaches the target language—in this country, English—while providing support for *maintaining the home language*—Spanish, Polish, Black English, etc. All along, despite a policy like the "Students' Right," the system has just been perping—engaging in fraudulent action.

I am a veteran of the language wars, dating to my undergraduate years when I was victimized by a biased speech test given to all those who wanted to qualify for a teaching certificate. I flunked the test and had to take speech correction, not because of any actual speech impediment, such as aphasia or stuttering, but because I was a speaker of Black English. Such misguided policies have now been eradicated as a result of scientific enlightenment about language and the renewed commitment to cultural pluralism that is the essence of the American experiment.

A few years after my bout with speech therapy, I published, in the pages of this journal, my first experimental attempt at writing the "dialect of my nurture": "English Teacher, Why You Be Doing the Thangs You Don't Do?" (Smitherman 1972). Encouraged by former *EJ* editor, Stephen Tchudi (then Judy), I went on to produce a regular *EJ* column, "Soul N Style," written in a mixture of Black English Vernacular and the Language of Wider Communication (i.e., Edited American English), and for which I won a national award (thanks to Steve Tchudi, who believed in me—Yo, Steve, much props!). In the 1977 edition of *Talkin and Testifyin: The Language of Black America*, I called for a national language policy, the details of which I had yet to work out. A decade later, I had come to realize that such a policy was needed, not just for African

Americans and other groups on the margins, but for the entire country, and that the experience of African Americans could well be the basis for what I called a tripartite language policy (Smitherman 1987). Like I said, I been on the battlefield for days.

CCCC's "NATIONAL LANGUAGE POLICY"

Over the years since 1971, CCCC has evolved its linguistic and social consciousness beyond the issue of students' right to their own dialect to encompass the students' right to multiple ways of speaking. In 1987, it established the Language Policy Committee to study the current "English-Only" Movement and to develop a position for CCCC on English-Only's call for a Constitutional amendment to make English the sole language of this country. That Committee, like its predecessor, the "Students' Right" Committee, formulated a CCCC position that has become organizational policy. In March 1988, CCCC adopted the "National Language Policy," which is as follows:

> There is a need for a National Language Policy, the purpose of which is to prepare everyone in the United States for full participation in a multicultural nation. Such a policy recognizes and reflects the historical reality that, even though English has become the language of wider communication, we are a multi-lingual society. All people in a democratic society have the right to equal protection of the laws, to employment, to social services, and to participation in the democratic process. No one should be denied these or any other civil rights because of linguistic and cultural differences. Legal protection, education, and social services must be provided in English as well as other languages in order to enable everyone in the United States to take full advantage of these rights. This language policy affirms that civil rights should not be denied to people because of linguistic differences. It enables everyone to participate in the life of the nation by ensuring continued respect both for English, the common language, and for the many other languages that have contributed to our rich cultural and linguistic heritage. This policy has three inseparable parts:
>
> 1. to provide resources to enable native and non-native speakers to achieve oral and literate competence in English, the language of wider communication.
>
> 2. to support programs that assert the legitimacy of native languages and dialects and ensure that proficiency in the mother tongue will not be lost; and
>
> 3. to foster the teaching of languages other than English so that native speakers of English can rediscover the language of their heritage or learn a second language.

The formulation of such a national language policy would mean that on *all* levels of education, every student would be required to develop competence in at least three languages. One of these would be, of course, the Language of Wider Communication, which everyone would learn. The second would be the student's mother tongue—e.g., Spanish, Polish, Black English, Italian, Arabic, Chinese, Appalachian English. The legitimacy of the home language would be reinforced, and students' ability to function in that language would be part of their expanded linguistic repertoire by the end of twelve years of schooling. Thirdly, every student would have command of at least one totally foreign language. That language would vary, depending on the options and social conditions in local communities and schools.

"Students' Right" and New Paradigm Shift

In retrospect, then, the "Students' Right to Their Own Language" served its historical time and paved the way for this next evolutionary stage. We're now in the period of a new paradigm shift, from a provincial, more narrowly conceived focus to a broader internationalist perspective. We thus are being forced to address the issue of multiple linguistic voices, not only here, but in the global family. NCTE and CCCC, having grappled with these issues through the "Students' Right" era [are], I think, well-positioned for a leadership role in formulating a national language policy for this nation. Not just a policy for the narrow confines of, say, composition classrooms, which was our more modest goal in developing the CCCC "Students' Right" resolution, but a language policy that would impact *all* levels of education in *all* school subjects and in *all* social and institutional domains.

This is what is needed to carry us into the next century, just six years away. I thus herein issue a call to all language arts educators and the entire NCTE membership to sign onto the CCCC National Language Policy. We—and your students—await your response.

NOTE

Kwame Ture, then Stokely Carmichael, first used the "Black Power" slogan in a speech in June, 1966, on a protest march in Greenville, Mississippi. The march, designed to go across the state of Mississippi, had been initiated by James Meredith, the first Black to be admitted to the University of Mississippi, who had been ambushed and shot early on during the march. Carmichael and other Civil Rights leaders had come to Mississippi to continue Meredith's march. The concept of empowerment, as well as the accompanying rhetorical strategy, had been carefully worked out by the leadership of the Student [Nonviolent] Coordinating Committee (SNCC), which was wailing for the opportune moment to introduce the slogan of "Black Power" into the discourse of the Civil Rights Movement. A few days before Stokely's speech, SNCC worker, Willie Ricks, had begun using the slogan in local meetings to rally the people. And it was actually Ricks who convinced SNCC leadership—and Carmichael—that this was the historical moment to drop "Black Power." In retrospect, Kwame Ture confessed that Stokely Carmichael "did not expect that 'enthusiastic response' from his audience of sharecroppers, farm workers, and other everyday Black people in Mississippi." "The Time Has Come, 1964–66," *Eyes on the Prize II: America at the Racial Crossroads (1965–1985).*

WORKS CITED

Chomsky, Noam. 1968. *Language and Mind.* New York: Harcourt, Brace, Jovanovich.
Conference on College Composition and Communication. 1974. "Students' Right to Their Own Language." *College Composition and Communication* 25.3 (Fall): [pp. 19–57 in this book].
Conference on College Composition and Communication. 1988. "National Language Policy." Urbana, IL: NCTE.

Dillard, J. L. 1972. *Black English: Its History and Usage in the United States.* New York: Vintage Books.

Eyes on the Prize II: America at the Racial Crossroads (1965–1985). 1990. PBS video series.

Fishman, Joshua A. 1966. *Language Loyalty in the United States.* The Hague: Mouton.

———. 1970. *Sociolinguistics.* Rowley: Newbury House.

———. 1980. "Bilingual Education, Language Planning, and English." *English World-Wide.* 1.1: 11–24.

Halliday, M. A. K. 1973. *Explorations in the Functions of Language.* London: Edward Arnold.

Hymes, Dell, ed. 1964. *Language in Culture and Society.* New York: Harper and Row.

———. 1972. "Introduction." *Functions of Language in the Classroom.* Eds. C. Cazden, V. John-Steiner, and D. Hymes. New York: Teachers College Press.

Labov, William. 1970. *The Study of Nonstandard English.* Urbana, IL: NCTE.

———. 1972. *Language in the Inner City.* Philadelphia: University of Pennsylvania Press.

National Council of Teachers of English. 1974. *NCTE Resolution #74.2.* Urbana, IL: NCTE.

Shuy, Roger. 1964. *Social Dialects and Language Learning.* Urbana, IL: NCTE.

———. 1967. *Discovering American Dialects.* Urbana, IL: NCTE.

Sledd, James. 1969. "Bi-Dialectalism: The Linguistics of White Supremacy." *English Journal* 58.9 (Dec.): 1307–1315.

———. 1972. "Doublespeak: Dialectology in the Service of Big Brother." *College English* 33.1 (Jan.): 439–457.

Smitherman, Geneva. 1972. "English Teacher, Why You Be Doing the Thangs You Don't Do?" *English Journal* 61.1 (Jan.): 59–65.

———. 1973. " 'God Don't Never Change': Black English from a Black Perspective." *College English* 34.3 (Mar.): 828–34.

———. 1977. *Talkin and Testifyin: The Language of Black America.* Boston: Houghton Mifflin.

———. 1987. "Toward a National Public Policy on Language." *College English* 49.1 (Jan.): 29–36.

8   *"Students' Right to Their Own Language": A Counter-Argument*

JEFF ZORN

DEDICATION

I learned to teach English at a Historically Black College in Alabama under the guidance of no-nonsense African American women. Studying "Students' Right to Their Own Language," a resolution affirming the legitimacy of dialect from the National Council of Teachers of English (NCTE), when it first appeared in the early 1970s, my mentors saw beneficent intent but blatant shortcoming. Betty Gates, my most inspirational colleague, said, and I am quoting exactly, "With friends like these, black children hardly need enemies."

"Students' Right to Their Own Language" remains the official position statement of the guild of college compositionists on dialect difference, lionized to this day as a first principle of "liberatory" English teaching. My mentors would be sorely disappointed to learn this. It is in respectful memory of these excellent English teachers — Betty Gates and Emma Cleveland in particular — that I offer my counter-argument.

STUDENTS' RIGHT TO THEIR OWN LANGUAGE": THE BEGINNINGS

The sound, kind impulse behind "Students' Right to Their Own Language" (SRTOL) was to support the aspirations of poor, nonwhite, and culturally marginalized students. The document itself, however, offered underachievement and provincialism to the students it purported to serve. Even its advocates concede that SRTOL reads as committee prose with the different hands not smoothly blended, but no one has said firmly enough, or demonstrated patiently enough, how little sense SRTOL makes.[1]

In 1973 the Conference on College Composition and Communication of the National Council of Teachers of English approved the SRTOL resolution. A special edition of *College Composition and Communication* then printed that resolution for general distribution, prefaced it with a rationale, and appended

---

From *Academic Questions* 23.3 (2010): 311–26.

fifteen sections of commentary. Even a cursory glance at the resolution itself makes plain why a full booklet was needed to begin explaining it to fellow professionals:

> We affirm the students' right to their own patterns and varieties of language—the dialects of their nurture or whatever dialects in which they find their own identity and style. Language scholars long ago denied that the myth of a standard American dialect had any validity. The claim that any one dialect is unacceptable amounts to an attempt of one social group to exert its dominance over another. Such a claim leads to false advice for speakers and writers, and immoral advice for humans. A nation proud of its diverse heritage and its cultural and racial variety will preserve its heritage of dialects. We affirm strongly that teachers must have the experiences and training that will enable them to respect diversity and uphold the right of students to their own language.[2]

Recently two books and at least five major articles have lauded SRTOL as a classic guide for the current generation of English compositionists, a first principle of enlightened professional praxis.[3] As one of its drafters and long-term defenders has stated, SRTOL "moved the intellectual production of knowledge in the field to a whole nother [sic] level."[4] The turn away from coaching all students in Formal Standard English toward "counter-hegemonic literacy training," i.e., reshaping writing classes into political conversion seminars, "was the next logical stage after the *Students' Right* campaign."[5] The stakes are high, then, in toppling SRTOL off the pedestal it has held for decades.

My critique develops six points, all with wide-ranging importance for English education, and more generally for U.S. education, today. STROL (1) never begins to examine a "right" to one's own language; (2) offers no consistent view on the importance of dialect; (3) wildly overrates its "sophisticated" knowledge in sociology and linguistics; (4) both draws on and feeds into a reactionary politics of ethnic-cultural chauvinism; (5) clumps people into homogeneous, internally undifferentiated groups, missing individuals (in particular, individual student-writers) entirely; and (6) tries to shame English teachers for professional work of which we should be proud.

All told, I will show that SRTOL is a shameful piece of work whose ongoing endorsement warps and stains language education in the United States.

SRTOL NEVER EXAMINES A "RIGHT" TO ONE'S OWN LANGUAGE

From the beginning SRTOL should have considered, seriously, the meaning of a "right" to one's own language. The absence of any such discussion suggests a general shortcoming of SRTOL advocacy to this day: conceptual carelessness.

Pursuant to the victories of the civil rights movement, "rights"-talk spread to desires and demands far beyond the prerogatives of citizenship. Some claims were justified under the heading of human rights, ethical treatment owed people as such. Others were justified as cultural rights afforded individuals by virtue of membership in a particular group. Still others, perhaps most, were rights justified only in the aggressive insistence with which they were claimed: my "right" to, apparently, whatever I want, irrespective of how I might be violating obligations with greater weight than what I just demanded out of the blue.

Note well, then, that the resolution's first verb "affirm" and last verb "uphold" suggest falsely that students already *had* the right to their own language. The more accurate phrasing here is: "We are now granting students a right that we just invented for them." For good reason, American students previously had been acceded no more "right" to use Farsi, German, Cantonese, Spanglish, Cajun, or Ebonics in their essays than to identify Bolivia as a river in Asia. SRTOL can point to no educational tradition, professional principle, or ethical rule prohibiting teachers from correcting student work. Teachers in every discipline at every grade level do that all the time.

School curriculum is a pervasively benign case of "one social group exerting its dominance over another," i.e., learned adults initiating the young into intellectual traditions, scholarly procedures, and forms of disciplinary knowledge. It may overstate its claim, but generally the school is correct to issue the same demands and offer the same rewards to students of every "identity and style." If a student comes from a culture that knows nothing and cares nothing about algebra, the school will set out to teach it to him. If a student comes from a culture that treats women as inferiors, the school will not allow him to act disrespectfully toward female students, instructors, and administrators.

SRTOL never acknowledges that the language of "rights" fits comfortably in no instructional setting. I have every right to play the piano as badly as I do. If I do go to a piano teacher, I have every right to dismiss everything he tells me, every right not to practice, every right to stagnate or get worse at the keyboard. But then why bother taking lessons? School is mandatory up to a certain age, but the principle is the same: In any class, I can claim the right not to learn what is being taught ("You can't make me!"). In doing so, however, I relinquish the role of student and will incur penalties unmitigated by my claiming the right not to learn.

Rights—actual, bona fide rights—invoke complementary obligations on the part of others. If I have the right to enter a building during its posted hours of operation, the person at the door must let me in. Anyone can claim the "right" to speak or write any way he pleases, but nothing in that assertion inhibits anyone else from judging the language unfit for the occasion. More than just blowing smoke, SRTOL plants the seeds of Pyrrhic victory in students; it tells them they *win* when they continue to speak and write their vernacular despite all appearances (low grades, low test scores, bad interviews, bad job performance ratings, etc.) to the contrary. This was my mentors' exact insight: the disadvantaged cannot afford Pyrrhic victories.

Throughout, SRTOL romanticizes failure as a heroic affirmation of personal identity and community culture. One key strategy here is to pooh-pooh differences like the following as merely "surface level":

Hermione saw Herbert yesterday.
Hermione seen Herbert yesterday.

The first version appears in every textbook, handbook, and style manual extant, while the second bespeaks great distance from books and the company of educated people.[6] Resisting segregation and marginalization may well be heroic, but treating the markers of segregation and marginalization as badges of honor is not. It is, rather, to put a politically correct spin on deficits imposed by the powerful on the unwilling.

Claims to a "right" to one's own language are trumped by the obligation to write well. If the assignment calls for writing in a language other than English or for capturing nonstandard dialect, fine. Otherwise, Formal Standard English remains the academic norm, and a student has no "right" not to employ it with excellence.

SRTOL OFFERS NO CONSISTENT VIEW ON THE IMPORTANCE OF DIALECT

SRTOL never settles on the importance of dialect. In the space of five pages, dialect goes from being a central feature of identity and intellection to something trivial.

Urging English teachers to keep our dirty hands off, SRTOL argues early on that dialects convey a unique worldview and guide speakers to unique registers of insight, perception, and feeling. To master a dialect, then, is to claim a culture and personal identity. On the cognitive level, dialect dictates how easily students can read Standard English materials. Cultural dissonance and the complexities of psycholinguistic processing make transfers between dialect codes very difficult, so even the slightest differences between a student's vernacular and a textbook's language will cause slow-down, confusion, and inability to comprehend.

Soon after, a very different picture emerges. Now SRTOL depicts the mastery of Edited American English as a piece of cake because dialects differ only in a few, easily identified surface-level features; this is precisely why students will be allowed to take Edited American English as an elective course late in their academic careers.

The contradiction here goes straight back to the definition of dialect as "a variety of language used by some definable group" and to the inclusion of "whatever dialects in which [students] find their identity and style" under the SRTOL purview. For no good reason and to no good effect, SRTOL subsumes and treats as co-equals the "dialect" challenges facing Ebonics-speaking schoolchildren, upper-class white Southerners, non-Anglophone immigrants, skinheads, surfers, and computer geeks spouting jargon.

And so, while SRTOL may sound high-minded and progressive in claiming, "A nation proud of its diverse heritage and its cultural and racial variety will preserve its heritage of dialects," this makes no sense whatsoever. Linguistic localism in the United States lost ground to progress, significant advances like the rise in educational attainment, the greater ease of transportation, developments in communication technology, and the reduction of social discrimination.[7] It was not *bad* when the South got less isolated, less Dixie. It is not *bad* when children can communicate perfectly with classmates and teachers with forebears from every corner of the planet. It will not be *bad* when dialects like Faux-Contrite Steroid Abuser disappear from our midst.

No individual, community, state, or nation is better off "preserving" the local color embodied in foot binding, dog fighting, child labor, elder abuse, bad hygiene, gay bashing, and language forms rooted in illiteracy and isolation. In "The Case Against Romantic Ethnicity," Gunnar Myrdal concluded, "What is obviously needed in America is a much higher identification with the nation as a whole."[8] SRTOL lurched woozily in the other direction, toward "preserving" under-education, provincialism, ethnic chauvinism, and political fragmentation.

SRTOL WILDLY OVERRATES ITS "SOPHISTICATED" KNOWLEDGE IN SOCIOLOGY AND LINGUISTICS

The rhetoric of SRTOL is that of forestalling disagreement through the tactics of shaming and bullying. Readers are led by the nose to select the obvious choice in a "dilemma" faced by English teachers: Should we continue to align our work with the American public's uninformed *prejudices*, or should we move forward with fresh *knowledge*? No one wants to be thought backward and bigoted, so the latter choice seems obvious — until the reader realizes that no substance accompanies the razzmatazz.

Claiming to center its argument on "sophisticated research in linguistics and sociology," SRTOL proceeds to make nothing but unsophisticated, unconvincing sociolinguistic claims, especially in its answers to the question "Who uses the dialect Standard English?" The authors successively identify as that dialect's speakers (1) the educated, (2) "those in power in the community," and (3) the middle class.

Clearly, no "identifiable group" of dialect speakers is marked off here. Educated people appear in all social classes and typically lack power in any community. Middle-class Americans may or may not have a higher education and may or may not use Standard English regularly. In many communities, the power-holders are not educated, middle-class, or speakers of Standard English. And aren't members of the hereditary upper class, not the middle class, those who typically have the most power, the most education, and the speaking style that most closely approximates the way books are written?

Denied its callow sociolinguistics, SRTOL is left to manipulate readers by equating support for Standard English with bigotry. People who reject classroom use of Ebonics, Hawaiian Pidgin, Spanglish, South Bostonese, etc., are depicted as having disdain if not hatred for the speakers of these dialects. They ascribe "inherent superiority" to the dialect of rich white people because they inordinately admire wealth, power, and whiteness.

SRTOL's plea to attend to "the distinction between speaking and writing" points the way to rebuffing this reckless attack on personal character. With perfect consistency, individuals can have respect if not outright love for speakers of nonstandard dialects and still press to require Formal Standard English in schools. Speakers *from* those dialect groups (like my Alabama mentors) have advocated ardently for Standard English, as have political activists *against* the hegemony of rich white people.[9]

In the quadrant of English devoted to on-the-record discourse, there is a single, non-mythical Formal Standard, a *level*, not a *dialect* of the English language as no "identifiable group" uses it except, by circular definition, the literate. No dialect competition exists for this "grapholect": no Spanglish economics textbooks, Surfer lab reports, Pidgin insurance contracts, or Cajun legal briefs. Insofar as the purpose of discourse is the careful, patient explication of ideas, Formal Written Standard does have "inherent superiority" over all vernaculars. The word choices available to educated writers, the phrases, sentences, paragraphs, and clusters of paragraphs they can configure, and the argumentative structures they can erect have but distant, weak echoes in vernacular—for all the lyricism, emotional resonance, and promising insights the vernacular might contain.

Feel the irony, then, in the level of English employed by SRTOL's most committed defenders:

> Counter-hegemonic literacy training would focus both on how the literacy training of some groups is not recognized and on how to withhold recognition, or question the recognition—and concomitant valuation—of the cultural capital of the literacy of dominant groups.[10]

> To [insist upon Standard English] would be to again hypostasize linguistic forms, as opposed to continuously weighing and challenging the material social conditions under which specific language forms are reified, elevated, and demoted. Our claim is that exclusive emphasis on acquiring competence in writing as a means to equality, freedom, and justice privatizes competence and so fails to maintain discursive conditions through which being a competent writer comes to mean equality, freedom, and justice.[11]

Defending street talk, the authors write the English farthest distant from street talk, because street talk never suffices for intellectual complexity and careful policy argumentation.

SRTO Draws on and Feeds into a Reactionary Politics of Ethnic-Cultural Chauvinism

In *Democracy in America*, Alexis de Tocqueville praised the forging of a new, uniquely American person, *novus homo*, out of the various stocks and strains of Europeans immigrating to our shores. The key for de Tocqueville was that the original settlers all spoke English: "The tie of language is, perhaps, the strongest and the most durable that can unite mankind. All the emigrants spoke the same tongue."[12] Later arrivals, non-Anglophones, regularly kept their original language alive, but Standard American English remained the "strongest and most durable tie" within an increasingly diverse polity.

Once linguistic multiplicity overwhelms the Standard, the center cannot hold, and the biggest losers will be those hustling in from the periphery. Sensing imminent loss, champions of Standard American English have sounded forth from within the African American community both before and after SRTOL's appearance.

A particularly powerful statement came in 1971 from the editorial board of *Crisis*, the magazine of the National Association for the Advancement of Colored People (NAACP):

> What our children need, and other disadvantaged American children as well—Indian, Spanish-speaking, Asian, Appalachian, and immigrant Caucasians—is training in basic English which today is as near an international language as any in the world. To attempt to lock them in a provincial patois is to limit their opportunities in the world at large. . . . Let our children have the opportunity, and be encouraged, to learn the language which will best enable them to comprehend modern science and technology, equip them to communicate intelligently with other English-speaking peoples of all races, and to share in the exercise of national power.[13]

Similar reactions were recorded to the Oakland Ebonics Resolution of 1997. Cynthia Tucker, syndicated columnist of the *Atlanta Constitution*, decried the board's making "sub-standard scholarship, including poor grammar and diction" into "a Black thing."[14] Like Tucker, film director Spike Lee was ridiculed as a child for "speaking white," and he has stated, "I'm not a fan of Ebonics. I understand that African Americans have this duality to operate in both worlds, but Ebonics shouldn't be taught in school."[15] In another context, Lee noted, "There's something very sick where if you speak well and you speak articulately, it's looked at as being negative. . . . That's crazy when intelligence is thought of as being white and all the other stuff is being black and being down."[16]

In " 'Students' Right to Their Own Language': A Retrospective," Geneva Smitherman contrasts all the "Unhip," who continued to press for Standard English, with the "Enlightened," who fought instead "to bring mainstream recognition and legitimacy to the culture, history, and language of those on the margins."[17] The unhip seek an equitable sharing of the bounties of contemporary life, but Smitherman detects a malicious "game plan" behind all such overtures: "linguistic and cultural absorption of the Other into the dominant culture, and indoctrination of the outsiders into the existing value system (e.g., Sledd 1972), to remake those on the margins in the image of the patriarch."[18]

Where Smitherman sees evil "absorption" and "indoctrination," others will applaud the long-overdue triumph of inclusion and worry more about the ethnic enclaves that the Smitherman/SRTOL "game plan" always brings to mind. The fantasy is idyllic, a tapestry of peace, love, and understanding in adjoining Meadows of Difference. The regular reality is ugly: distrusting, avoiding, and even despising the Others, who are not "our kind." Ethnic solidarity is about blood ties, not character virtues or moral principles. Given its long, sordid history, how can the championing of blood ties be *enlightened* or *progressive?*

It is very significant, very revealing, then, that the first person mentioned in Smitherman's "Retrospective," bathed in the most flattering light, is Kwame Ture (Stokely Carmichael), who in Smitherman's words "issued his clarion call for 'Black Power' and thus charted a new course for the Civil Rights Movement in America."[19] The testimonial sparks an immediate realization: channeled by Smitherman, James Sledd, et al., Ture's "clarion call" pervades SRTOL. And then a second realization: this is to SRTOL's great discredit, and to the great harm done in its name ever since.

How *tragic* it was that Kwame Ture charted African Americans' course away from gaining the same successes enjoyed by other Americans! Ture depicted integration as not worth trying; it was "a subterfuge, an insidious subterfuge, for the maintenance of white supremacy."[20] Promulgating "anti-racist racism," Ture concluded that "this country cannot justify any longer its existence" and "I do not want to be part of the American pie." Left for black Americans were separation within the United States—"We must cut ourselves off from white people. We must form our own institutions, credit unions, co-ops, political parties, write our own histories"—and third-world solidarity, "to hook up with black people around the world."[21]

In making Black Power militancy its political template, SRTOL marginalized other "definable groups," including integrationist African Americans, no less than Eurocentrism ever had. Everywhere else in America "anti-racist racism," like regular-old racism, continued to lose decisively to a principled veering toward color-blindness in both public and private life.[22]

SRTOL CLUMPS PEOPLE INTO RELENTLESSLY HOMOGENEOUS GROUPS

Difference is anything but slighted if we reject Romantic Ethnicity as an organizing principle in schools and society-at-large. As Richard Rodriguez observes in "Disunited We Stand," losses in group identification pave the way for gains in individuals' originality, creativity, and independent initiative. America organizes "around the first person, singular pronoun," Rodriguez writes, and the play of Difference among free-thinking, creative individuals is exponentially more productive than the play of Difference among clans, squadrons, and mobs of the like-minded.[23]

Anticipating and no doubt informing the dominant "Composition Theory" of today,[24] SRTOL sees no individuals and will permit teachers to see no individuals in front of them. It trades throughout in races, social classes, and crude ideological camps—the ruling, closed-minded, selfish, and bigoted versus the victimized, warm, altruistic, and open-minded.

Privy to the insights, casts of mind, and language capabilities of each student, writing instructors more than anyone on campus should appreciate the huge differences, person-to-person, within SRTOL's rigid, inviolable categories. To all English compositionists with eyes wide open, constructs on the order of "Black Language," "the oppressed," "Asian Americans," and "working-class culture" will seem overstated, reductive, and likely to lead to *terrible* curriculum planning and *terrible* classroom teaching.

I cringe, for instance, when I read Monique Brinson's description of Shel Silverstein as simply "a white male author," preparatory to "re-inventing" his poem "Boa Constrictor" in Ebonics for her students.[25] Reducing a creative artist to those categories is the most distorting and mis-educative of shorthands, as though it's all the same whether we read Silverstein or Richard Rorty, Kurt Vonnegut, Henry James, Dave Barry, Allen Ginsberg, Stephen King, Woody Allen, Walt Whitman, Zane Grey, William Faulkner, Robinson Jeffers, Elmore Leonard, Pat Buchanan, Hunter S. Thompson, John Cheever, John Updike, or Charles Bukowski—all pale-male Americans who therefore think and write *so* similarly.

Silverstein's art draws on many other categories of sociological description but mostly on his unique vision and creative talent. Brinson sees nothing like a *person* in Silverstein, just a *representative* of two groups to which he belongs. She sees her students exactly the same way, assuming in advance that *as* African Americans they all need to run Silverstein's simple, amusing poem through racially coded filters before they can get anything out of it. Brinson isolates her students even as Silverstein promises to include them, and her provincial small-mindedness comes straight from SRTOL's pages. Like hers, its spirit is insular, hostile to young people's wandering away from the crowd, hostile then to education itself.

In sharpest contrast, Kenneth Clark, the distinguished psychologist whose research informed *Brown v. Board of Education*, fondly recalled his own teachers in Harlem "who did not consider themselves social workers. . . . They were asked to teach reading, arithmetic, grammar, and they did." An eighth grade teacher, Miss McGuire, "taught me to understand the beauty of an English sentence. And she didn't do it by worrying about my background." Another, Mr. Mitchell, "a blue-eyed blond WASP, taught us Shakespeare. Those plays came alive, right in the center of Harlem. . . . It had nothing to do with color—the teacher's or ours."[26]

An integrationist to the end, Clark opposed Romantic Ethnicity and cultural nationalism as strains of "parochialism." In 1968 he wrote against opening an all-black dormitory at the University of Chicago and later resigned from the board of trustees of Antioch College protesting the plan for a racially exclusive Afro-American Institute there. In his own teaching, Clark tried to help students understand that "genuine pride in oneself can[not] be based on anything as external as color."[27] In line with these views, Clark favored teaching Standard English to all American students, regardless of social background. Debating the classroom use of Ebonics with a black Harvard graduate, Clark stated: "I would like these youngsters to speak the way you do, so that people will pay attention to them—even when they are speaking nonsense, as you are now."[28]

In his deep, mature, commanding voice—a golden trumpet to Ture's thin, wheezy kazoo—Clark issues a clarion call for setting high learning standards for all students, the *same* standards whatever the individual's race and cultural style. The clearest right of students—soon to chart courses for their own lives and the democracy's future—is to a well-delivered liberal education. Training no one to mindless orthodoxy, liberal education puts into doubt everything students think they know. If in the end students keep what they came with, it will be only after entertaining the live option of wholly different beliefs. This marks the "liberating" part of liberal education, the freeing of a mind to *decide* truth for itself, rationally. Rallying around dialect and immersing children in local group-thought are qualitatively less far-sighted.

SRTOL TRIES TO SHAME ENGLISH TEACHERS FOR FIRST-RATE PROFESSIONAL WORK

In the decades following SRTOL, English teachers have been censured as repressive and racist—often by our own "theorists"—just for doing our job competently. Instead of continuing to play the role of punching-bag we must again assert due pride in our vocation.

The worth of our professional contribution can be measured in the ease with which foundational civic documents and long-dead authors are still read today. Slang and population demographics change daily. In balancing the linguistic demands of the right-now, English teachers have allowed for yesterday's voices (the voices of oppositionality equally with those of assent) to speak with immediate comprehension. We have had a hand as well in great national gains in communication, knowledge, integration, social mobility, and economic productivity.

A student's "right" to semi-literacy is as hollow as his or her "right" to master no mathematics beyond adding and subtracting. To follow SRTOL in "preserving" nonstandard dialects is to welcome miscommunication, cultural isolation, political fragmentation, and strict limits on students' achievements in school and beyond. To follow SRTOL in overrating students' language proficiency, however heartfelt the desire to see the disadvantaged succeed, is to delay the inevitable for students and expose our entire guild to *correct* charges of dereliction of duty.

When English teachers provide purposeful instruction in Formal Written Standard, we are the opposite of racist, elitist, and classist, not keeping the gate closed but opening it wide. In his monumental study, *The Americans: The Democratic Experience*, Daniel Boorstin noted:

> As the schoolroom was expected to perform a remedial function, the temptations were increased for insecure, upward-mobile teachers to impose "Rules of Good English" on their insecure, upward-mobile students. But there was also the Democratic Temptation—to flatter the people by assuring them that whatever they were already doing was right and best.[29]

Boorstin's "Democratic Temptation" is surely one to avoid. As my Alabama mentors perfectly intuited, if flim-flam flattery serves no one well, it serves disadvantaged students especially poorly.

The one positive use today for SRTOL is as a negative heuristic, a road-map to the wrong-headedness of "liberating" students by adding to their underachievement and grievance. As a profession and as a nation, we would maximize this positive potential by repudiating SRTOL and the entire body of mis-educative "counter-hegemonic literacy training" that has followed in its wake.

NOTES

1. Theater critic John Simon had many keen insights into what was wrong with SRTOL. For Simon's scathing critique, see "Playing Tennis Without a Net," chapter 6 of *Paradigms Lost: Reflections on Literacy and Its Decline* (New York: C.N. Potter, 1976).

2. Conference on College Composition and Communication, *Students' Right to Their Own Language*, a special edition of *College Composition and Communication* 25 (Fall 1974), text available at http://www.ncte.org/library/NCTEFiles/Groups/CCCC/NewSRTOL.pdf. All references within the text refer to this version of SRTOL. [Page 19 in this book.—Ed.]

3. See Valerie Felita Kinloch, "Revisiting the Promise of *Students' Right to Their Own Language*: Pedagogical Strategies," *College Composition and Communication* 57, no. 1 (September 2005): pp. 429–52 in this book; Stephen Parks, *Class Politics: The Movement for Students' Right to Their Own Language* (Urbana, IL: National Council of Teachers of English, 2000); Patrick Bruch and Richard Marback, "Critical Hope, 'Students' Right,' and the Work of Composition Studies," in Patrick Bruch and Richard Marbeck, eds., *The Hope and the Legacy: The Past, Present, and Future of 'Students' Right to their Own Language'* (Cresskill, NJ: Hampton Press, 2005); Bruce Horner, " 'Students' Right,' English Only, and Re-Imagining the Politics of Language," *College English* 63, no. 6 (July 2001): 741–55; Geneva Smitherman, "Black English/Ebonics: What It Be Like?" in Theresa Perry and Lisa Delpit, eds., *The Real Ebonics Debate* (Boston: Beacon Press, 1998). Scott Wible, "Pedagogies of the 'Students' Right' Era: The Language Curriculum Research Group's Project for Linguistic Diversity," *College Composition and Communication* 57, no. 3 (February 2006): pp. 353–80 in this book.

An article with closely related sensibilities is Arthur L. Palacas, "Liberating American Ebonics from Euro-English," *College English* 63, no. 3 (January 2001): 326–52. Palacas has one shining moment of clarity: "The intentional move away from the teaching of grammar and sentence construction in composition graduate programs, for example, has unintentionally and ironically privileged the standard-speaking student to the detriment and exclusion of African American students and others from nonstandard language backgrounds, and it has truly hampered the effectiveness of teachers" (349).

4. Smitherman, "CCCC's Role in the Struggle for Language Rights," *College Composition and Communication* 50, no. 3 (February 1999): p. 70 in this book.

5. Ibid., p. 74.

6. Less than twenty years before SRTOL, NCTE publications still called all such phrasings as "Hermione seen Herbert" and "Mary daddy home" illiteracies and recommended that English teachers attend to these problems in student writing first. See National Council of Teachers of English, *The English Language Arts in Secondary School* (New York: Appleton-Century-Crofts, 1956), 379.

7. E. D. Hirsch, Jr., strikes just the right balance: "Therefore, without in the least discounting the losses incurred by the disappearance of small-group dialects, I find the conclusion inescapable that the benefits are greater than the costs." *The Philosophy of Composition* (Chicago: University of Chicago Press, 1977), 49.

8. Gunnar Myrdal, "The Case Against Romantic Ethnicity," *The Center Magazine* 10, no. 1 (July–August 1974): 27.

9. Antonio Gramsci, the Italian Communist who first gave "hegemony" theoretical prominence, anticipated SRTOL's exact error:

> Someone who only speaks dialect, or understands the standard language incompletely, necessarily has an intuition of the world which is more or less limited and provincial, which is fossilized and anachronistic in relation to the major currents of thought which dominate world history. His interests will be limited, more or less corporate or economistic, not universal. While it is not always possible to learn a number of foreign languages in order to put oneself in contact with other cultural lives, it is at least necessary to learn the national language properly. A great culture can be translated into the language of another great culture. . . . But a dialect cannot do this.

Antonio Gramsci, *The Antonio Gramsci Reader: Selected Readings 1916–1935*, ed. David Forgacs (New York: Schocken, 1988), 326–27. Unlike SRTOL's authors, Gramsci understood "fossilized and anachronistic" provincialism for what it is.

10. Horner, " 'Students' Right,' English Only," 753.

11. Bruch and Marback, "Critical Hope," 11.

12. Alexis de Tocqueville, *Democracy in America*, trans. Henry Reeve, vol. 1, rev. ed. (1835; New York: The Colonial Press, 1899), 28.

13. "Black Nonsense," quoted in Robbins Burling, *English in Black and White* (New York: Holt, Reinhart, and Winston, 1973), 109.

14. Cynthia Tucker, "Ebonics Is a Farce That Masks the True Nature of Poverty," syndicated column, reprinted in *Liberal Opinion Week*, January 13, 1997.

15. Jackie Corgan, "Spike Lee Casually Spells It Out," *Indiana Daily Student*, October 10, 2002, https://www.idsnews.com/news/story.aspx?id=24233&search=bob%20knight&section=search.

16. Leslie Williams, "Black Americans Already Have a Language—English," *San Francisco Examiner*, January 20, 1997, A-19. See also Bill Cosby, "Elements of Igno-Ebonics Style," *Wall Street Journal*, January 10, 1997, A-10.

For deeper, more scholarly discussion of Ebonics, see John Baugh, *Beyond Ebonics: Linguistic Pride and Racial Prejudice* (New York and Oxford: Oxford University Press, 2000); John McWhorter, *Doing Our Own Thing: The Degradation of Language and Music and Why We Should, Like, Care* (New York: Gotham, 2003); Theresa Perry, "I 'on Know Why They Be Trippin': Reflections on the Ebonics Debate," in *The Real Ebonics Debate*, 3–15; and Roger W. Shuy, "Bonnie and Clyde Tactics in English Teaching," in *Contemporary English: Change and Variation*, ed. David L. Shores (Philadelphia: Lippincott, 1972), 278–88.

To explore the educational connections between dialect difference and language difference, see Lucy Tse, *"Why Don't They Learn English?": Separating Fact from Fallacy in the U.S. Language Debate* (New York: Teachers College Press, 2001); Kathryn Au, *Multicultural Issues and Literacy Achievement* (Hillsdale, NJ: Erlbaum, 2006); Laurie Olsen, *Made in America: Immigrant Students in Our Public Schools* (New York: New Press, 1997); Dennis Baron, *The English-Only Question* (New Haven, CT: Yale University Press, 1990); James Crawford, *Hold Your Tongue: Bilingualism and the Politics of "English Only"* (Reading, MA: Addison-Wesley, 1992); and Ronald Schmidt, Sr., *Language Policy and Identity Politics in the United States* (Philadelphia: Temple University Press, 2000).

17. Geneva Smitherman, " 'Students' Right to Their Own Language': A Retrospective," *English Journal* (January 1995): p. 141 in this book.

18. Ibid., p. 146. See also Smitherman's "Black English/Ebonics," "CCCC's Role," and the introductions to *Black English and the Education of Black Youth* (Detroit, MI: Wayne State University Press, 1981) and *Talkin and Testifyin: The Language of Black Youth* (Detroit, MI: Wayne State University Press, 1986). The reference to SRTOL contributor James Sledd is very significant in that Sledd's writings, especially "Bidialectalism: The Linguistics of White Supremacy," deeply influenced SRTOL, subsequent SRTOL advocacy, and the general professional orientation toward political indoctrination in the classroom. "Bi-Dialectalism: The Linguistics of White Supremacy," *English Journal* 58, no. 9 (December 1969): 1307–15. See also "Doublespeak: Dialectology in the Service of Big Brother," *College English* 33 (January 1972): 439–57.

19. Smitherman, " 'Students' Right," p. 140.

20. Stokely Carmichael, "Black Power" (speech, Berkeley, CA. October 1966), text available at http://www.americanrhetoric.com/speeches/stokelycarmichaelblackpower.html.

21. Ibid. See also, the Student Nonviolent Coordinating Committee Statement on Black Power, http://www.answers.com/topic/student-nonviolent-coordinating-committee-founding-statement-1960.

22. In Hawaii, for example, cultural rights activists argued for making Pidgin the general language of instruction in local schools, with Standard English to be offered as an elective if at all. Those interested in reading arguments from both sides of the debate, see Bruce Dunford, "Hawaii Debates Classroom Pidgin," *San Francisco Chronicle*, November 27, 1999, A3, available at http://airwolf.lmtonline.com/news/archive/1128/pagea11.pdf; and Terri Menacker, "There's a Place for Ebonics and Pidgin, Too," *Honolulu Star-Bulletin*, February 1, 1997.

23. Richard Rodriguez, "Disunited We Stand," in *Creating America*, ed. Joyce Moser and Ann Watters, 4th ed. (Upper Saddle River, NJ: Pearson/Prentice Hall, 2005), 156.

24. In her tribute to James Berlin, for example, Linda Brodsky describes working hard to disabuse her students of the foolish notion that they are unique people and not "culturally constituted subjects." "Remembering Writing Pedagogy," *JAC* 17, no. 3 (Fall 1997), http://www.jacweb.org/Archived_volumes/Text_articles/V17_I3_Brodkey.htm. Susan Miller, who favors "a prose-lytizing intellectual agenda" in class, attacks traditional composition teaching in similar terms: "An isolated 'individual,' imagined even now, after Althusser, as independently experiencing 'life'

outside the language, rituals, and behaviors that construct it, becomes the imagined 'real' subject of the course." Miller's quotation marks around the words "individual," "life," and "real" tell most of the tale here. "Composition as a Cultural Artifact: Rethinking History as Theory," in *Writing Theory and Critical Theory*, ed. John Clifford and John Schlib (New York: Modern Language, Association, 1994), 29.

25. Monique Brinson, "Removing the Mask: Roots of Oppression Through Omission," in *The Real Ebonics Debate*, 135.

26. Nat Hentoff, *The Nat Hentoff Reader* (Cambridge, MA: Da Capo Press, 2001), 174–75.

27. Ibid., 208.

28. Ibid.

29. Daniel Boorstin, *The Americans: The Democratic Experience* (New York: Vintage, 1973), 455.

9

No One Has a Right to His Own Language

ALLEN N. SMITH

Although I consider myself a humanist in the intellectual sphere and a liberal in most social and political matters, I cannot swallow the official pronouncement of the Conference on College Composition and Communication that "Students Have a Right to Their Own Language." The very statement is a contradiction. No one has a right to "their own" language. Language, by definition, is common to all who use or attempt to use it, and the use of language is not an individual but a social act, particularly when the individual takes the trouble to set his words down on paper. Writing is not a form of self-expression, and anyone who teaches that it is is doomed to failure from the start. One of the great battles which takes place at the outset of every freshman comp course is to convince each student that there is an audience out there and that he or she must write for that audience at every step of the development: mechanically, grammatically, logically, and aesthetically.

If the resolution adopted by the CCCC Executive Committee in 1973 meant only that we should respect our students as individuals and recognize their infinitely varied family and social backgrounds and that our role as teachers demands constant courtesy in both the classroom and the conference, so few teachers would deny it that it would hardly have been worth the committee's trouble to pass it. But the question seems to go much deeper. The resolution apparently involves a question about the end product of our service: what should we be teaching and for what purpose?

The question is muddled further by the creation of a straw man—i.e., the debate over whether there is or is not a "standard American English" that should be the goal of composition teachers to inculcate. Many of those who advocate students' right to their own language argue, correctly, I think, that there is no such standard, that it is mythical. To me, this is obvious. No body of men, and no computer, can survey, analyze, and synthesize the speaking and writing habits of some 200 million delightfully varied American citizens, and if they could, the result hardly would be what any English teacher would want to teach. Nor is there any textbook or grammar which does in fact offer

From *College Composition and Communication* 27.2 (1976): 155–59.

the definitive and comprehensive standard to apply in each and every individual choice of expression.

The second complication arises when we pay homage to the vocational needs of our students. The argument runs that "every student has a right to his own language," but if he wants to get a job better than that of his parents and peers, he had better at some point, for purely practical reasons, learn to speak and write in a manner acceptable to those who guard the entry points to passageways to upward mobility. This leads to such contradictions as that which occurred in a frustrating regional conference of CCCC which I attended recently on the Eastern Shore of Maryland, an area fraught with local dialects. The conference opened with an amusing and thoughtful statement by Robert Hogan, Executive Secretary of NCTE, who advocated students' right to their own language. His keynote address was followed immediately by a panel which concerned itself with "How and When Do We Change the Student from His Own Dialect to Standard English?" The strange thing was that no one appeared to recognize that the panel's goal was at cross purposes with the basic thrust of the opening address. If a student has a right to his own language, we have no right to change it at any point, and if we suggest helping him change it solely for the practical purpose of getting and holding a job, we are advocating the cheapest form of hypocrisy and the most difficult sleight of hand act in the history of language, the development of a dual language for use at home and at work. It is true that success often is correlated with high vocabulary although which is the cause and which is the effect or what the relationship is is confusing, but if any English teacher were content to teach language skills used by the average bank president or airline pilot it would be a dereliction of duty. So long as English teachers catch themselves on the horns of the dilemma between asserting the right of students to their own language on the one hand and the need to teach them some mythical standard of good English on the other for employment purposes, they will continue to spin in the circles which were so obvious at the above-mentioned English conference, which I suspect was representative of similar debates across the nation. But if we simply deny both premises, things may get better: students do not have a right to their own language, and teachers do not have a primary duty to teach them how to get better jobs. This eliminates the conflict between the two, but it leaves us with the question of what it is that we should be doing.

Teachers, by definition, are custodians of the past. No matter how often we embrace the idea of "relevance" or "accountability" in education, our particular role in any society is to gather and disseminate the standards and values of the past for the coming generation in our respective chosen fields. This is true of science teachers, legal scholars, arts-and-crafts teachers, golf instructors, or any other teachers. All research is history, of course, and all teaching is based on research. Now, some teachers—accountants for example—do train students for a particular vocation (still using the standards and knowledge of the past), but other teachers, including those in the so-called "general education" fields, are much too general to offer a particular vocational advancement. Try as we may, we are never going to convince a state legislator or a parent of a student that the general-education requirements have an overriding practical value. The value is indirect, both to the individual student and to society. I cannot guarantee that he will be happier or wealthier if he learns to speak and write "well." He may make far more in a job which does not require high language skills, and he may be much better off in speaking in his own "dialect." But his education at my hands will offer him a slim, short-lived chance to escape from his own limited time and place in this present world to a mythical world composed of some of the biggest and most exciting ideas which have come down to us from the past. At my hands, he may learn to read more deeply and to write more effectively because of what he reads. Other sources will give him the flesh and blood of his own lifetime. My job is to give him range, even though I can never recreate that range in its own flesh and blood terms, try as I will. For certain jobs, this range will be useful, even if only as a status symbol. For many others, it may be a social or psychological impediment, as it has been for me in certain circumstances. Off the job, this same intellectual curiosity may or may not be useful to the individual. However, I feel certain that if it proves too expensive or time-consuming, the individual will quickly discard it after graduation. I offer him only a choice, which admittedly few of my students make permanently. But every student in a civilized society should be given the choice, and our solons decree that it should be roughly between their eighteenth and twenty-second years (except for veterans, of course). I might debate the particular value of specializing in that age group, but I cannot forsake the idea of introducing every individual in our society to history and logic and literature regardless of the outcome.

Now of what benefit is this all to society? The short-term benefits are debatable. The present, apparently widespread dissatisfaction with jobs in factories and offices undoubtedly is due in part to the higher volume of higher education at present. And the acquisition by the telephone companies and the automobile manufacturers of a coterie of well-educated specialists and humanists in place of individuals with natural drive and mechanical aptitudes may have a lot to do with their relative wastefulness and inefficiency. But, on the whole, a society produces only so much excellence in a single generation, far more, statistically, in a period of ten or twenty generations or more. To gradually forsake the heritage of the past (the best of the past) would certainly limit our enjoyment to the relatively smaller number of works of high quality in the single generation, and it would probably reduce the excellence of contemporary works through the loss of the examples of the past. And it certainly would further reduce the enjoyment of contemporary excellence by failing to produce a trained audience for them. I cannot say our society definitely would be less affluent if we gave up all but vocational training, but it would become poorer nevertheless. This is the only claim we can make for insisting that our students become "educated" in a general sense.

These are fine words, but how then do we teach the values of the past? How, for example, do we teach students to write well if there is no present standard of American English to go by and if we deny students a right to self-expression? We teach (or I teach anyway) by offering students examples of the best writing from the past (best because it has survived to our time) coupled with the pragmatic test of trying to please a present-day audience (their teacher and their fellow students). I teach mechanics by showing students that repeated spelling errors deny their thoughts a chance to be understood without interruption. I teach clarity by showing them the glazed eyes of their fellow students when they attempt to read an incomprehensible essay in class. I teach the value of concrete writing by showing them how the glaze gradually evaporates when they drive home their main point with a vivid illustration. I teach organization by showing them how an audience follows their argument only when there are clear benchmarks and divisions within it. But in order to develop the skills which will work in the classroom, in their own time, they must discover the basic principles which work in the literature of the past. And, therefore, we read a good deal in my writing class, and I try to analyze the techniques or principles employed by these readings. And they are free to use some of these principles in their own work. Some of these same principles are presented abstractly or concretely in textbooks. But I have never found a successful English textbook which grips the hearts and minds of most of my students. Nor have any of the twenty other freshman comp teachers in my own school. The reason is that even the best textbook is too fragmentary and too disjointed. It does not dwell on the great expression of a great idea for a long enough period to capture the imagination of a student. I think a textbook may serve as a teacher's guide or principle of organization for his course, but it probably never should be put into the student's hands. Rather, let the teacher himself create a course which leads students through these principles, using works of sufficient substance to have a chance to catch the minds of students. Why not then use a good anthology? I am less opposed to this, except that most anthologies also are fragmented, either a catch-all for all sorts of ideas or a book organized according to textbook principles rather than by content. It is better to organize a writing course according to certain major content themes which run through the course. You can teach a writing course about almost any subject under the sun, but you have to have a subject. You can't teach students to write about nothing. Nor can you teach them to write about themselves, because this violates the whole purpose of writing, which is to tell others something. I cannot tell a student that his personal expressions in a diary or journal are good, bad, or indifferent. But I can tell him that he has failed to produce a good intellectual biography of Confucius or Lord Bertrand Russell. The hardest thing in the world is to write about yourself in a way interesting to others. It should come last, long after freshman comp has been suffered through and mastered.

Thus, I teach writing by using examples of the past, examples ranging from the Bible to James Reston's latest column in the *New York Times* but always examples outside the student's own personal experience. And these examples do not represent standards, because there are no absolute standards in either the present or the past, only examples that have survived for the same reasons that some student essays survive in the classroom, because they are more interesting to an audience than others. The standard is success or excellence, and success or excellence can never be reduced to a set of absolute principles. There is an element of chance and an element of imagination in each attempt. This is what makes writing relevant in the sense of being "new." I cannot teach this, but, paradoxically, some of the best examples of the old are so strange to modern students that they sometimes seem strikingly "new" to them, and they sometimes catch on from this. Often, they don't.

And this brings me to the last and greatest question of motivation. Why do students write? Obviously they do so to get a grade or a credit. Why do they write well? They write well because they come to the class with a heavy load of high-quality reading and imitate it (which I have nothing to do with) or because they learn to care enough about ideas to learn the craft of writing well for the sake of expressing those ideas. Nothing can make a student care about his work or polish it or even carefully edit it, unless he is proud enough of what he has learned to want to get it across, not to emasculate it. The only motivation to good writing I know is passion, passion so strong that the student even is willing to control it artfully to achieve his effects.

What have I said here? Students do not have a right to their own language; they only have a right to learn a language which will produce the proper effects on whatever audience they may speak or write to. There is no correct standard of American English (beyond a certain number of completely negative rules), but there are certain techniques of tightness, clarity, precision, specificity, and logic which can be borrowed from the best surviving examples of the past and which may on occasion work in something the student is writing for a test audience in his classroom. We cannot defend our vocation on a short-term vocational basis because the values to both the individual and society are too debatable. We may be able to defend English as a vital part of a so-called general education in an affluent society which has enough time and money to permit some members of each generation to acquire the knowledge and techniques created laboriously over centuries of trial and error.

Teachers must realize and take some pride in the fact that they are custodians and purveyors of the past. They must accept the fact that other people—students and society in general—are not so concerned with the past as they are. There always is a healthy war between the past and the present and it goes on in my classroom every day. I see the looks of longing between boys and girls in my classroom (and cast a few myself). I see the students who bring their tennis rackets and shorts to class. I know that some cut classes to sign up for employer interviews at the placement service. That's understandable, and I do try to understand my students, even those who speak in a different dialect than my own. But my (professional) interest is different than their everyday interests. My job is to struggle to engage their minds in something more sweeping, though less concrete, than money or sex. I try to teach them the techniques which will give them range, give them the ability to read the record of the past and the ability to write to express to others what they have learned. I hope no one believes I am being too theoretical or idealistic about this or that I am ignoring the pressures of students or parents or legislators for something relevant. I am saying, as a totally practical measure, that we cannot survive or do what we have been trained to do by denying that we do it. We do not teach dialects which fail to bring one group together with another. We do not teach people to get jobs. We teach English as it has come down to us over many centuries of thought and effort. If we don't do this, I can guarantee you that we won't last long teaching dialectology or vocational skills. In a crisis, you have to throw your best pitch, and I know the only way to ward off the natural indifference and resentment and boredom of students in required English is to capture their imaginations. When I have that in hand, I no longer have to worry about absenteeism, grade complaints, or cries of "relevance." Until I have their imagination, they are going to complain about something because no one willingly sits on a hard chair on a sunny day because I am polite to him or because of some job he plans to take in the distant future. In advocating that we should teach from the past, I am surprisingly arguing that we should deal with the most immediate here and now: the here and now of a classroom which is exciting rather than dull. This is what I owe my students. I refuse to willingly bore them, and I refuse to teach them according to their own natural inclinations or interests. I take on the more difficult task of trying to acquaint them with that specialized, abstract, dated world of the past because that's where the greatest proportion of human genius resides.

10   Race, Literacy, and the Value of Rights Rhetoric in Composition Studies

PATRICK BRUCH AND RICHARD MARBACK

Commemorating its fiftieth year, Geneva Smitherman celebrated *CCC* as an "advocate for those on the linguistic margins" (p. 58 in this book). As Smitherman makes clear in both the title of her commemorative article— "CCCC's Role in the Struggle for Language Rights"—and in her opening reference to "Students' Right to Their Own Language," composition's advocacy for those on the linguistic margins has been most meaningful when it has been expressed through a rhetoric of rights. Drawing attention to the legacy of a rights rhetoric in composition studies, Smitherman demonstrates that the constitutive ambiguity of rights rhetoric continues to create contexts for exchange, deliberation, and progress. While rights rhetoric has served us in our search to understand and enact a just redistribution of literacy resources through the teaching of writing, the rights rhetoric of compositionists has not been without its problems. A rhetoric of rights is limited by the collision of shifting meanings of rights in American culture with the theorization of those meanings in composition studies. For at least the last twenty-five years, the use of a rights rhetoric in composition studies to advance the cause of racial equality contrasts with uses of rights rhetoric in public policy that limit the prospects for racial equality.

Nonetheless, we would not disagree with Smitherman's claim that "although the struggle for language rights yet continues, CCCC can win" (p. 80). In light of the transformation of rights rhetoric in popular culture and public policy, we would add that winning the struggle *for* language rights requires that we struggle *over* rights. Struggling for rights without struggling over rights leads to an empty victory in what Patricia Williams has called the "shell game" of racial equality in which "blacks who refuse the protective shell of white goodness and insist that they are black are inconsistent with the paradigm of goodness and therefore they are bad" (116). For compositionists, to struggle over language rights involves framing deliberation about the cultural, historical, and theoretical meanings and values of a right to literacy in terms of ongoing struggles for racial equality and social justice.

From *College Composition and Communication* 53.4 (2002): 651–74.

In what follows, we locate the language rights rhetoric of composition studies within larger struggles over the rhetoric of rights in public policy and perception and among critical legal-studies scholars such as Williams. Locating the profession in this way, we make problematic the prospects of a rhetoric of language rights. We do so not to obstruct the expansion of language rights but, rather, to cultivate the constitutive ambiguity of rights rhetoric, enriching and extending the senses in which compositionists can claim to win the struggle for language rights. We begin by outlining claims and contentions over rights, describing the possibilities and perils of rights rhetoric as it has taken shape in the United States over the last thirty years. We then locate the rights rhetoric of compositionists on this map, charting the ebbs of broader claims about equality and justice and rights within the flows of claims in composition studies about language rights. Charting the course of language rights in composition studies within the nation's struggle over rights, we conclude by echoing Smitherman's call to celebrate the rights rhetoric of CCCC. We amplify her call to encompass broader views of debates over rights to enable ourselves to better carry the struggles of the past into the future.

RIGHTS RHETORIC IN CONTEMPORARY AMERICAN CULTURE AND PUBLIC POLICY

A rhetoric of rights is fundamental to the U.S. Constitution and continues to frame debates over political conceptions of selfhood and citizenship. As a language central to political and public debate, rights rhetoric is at one and the same time an unambiguous expression of political truths and an indeterminate signifier for negotiating multiple civic and political values. For example, the rights to free speech and to bear arms are now recognized by most, if not all, Americans as inalienable personal possessions that neither individuals nor government can take away. But even though we may think of rights as possessions, as somehow ours, we do not have rights except in relation to others. With rights, then, come obligations of tolerance. Our claims to possess individual rights have merit only to the extent that we preserve and protect the rights claims of all individuals. We can have faith that our rights will not be violated because we accept that it is wrong to violate the rights of all others, even though the rights claims of others may either conflict with our own claims or appear to us as repugnant. In terms of free speech, people and governments are obligated to tolerate speech that is hateful or inflammatory or malicious because this toleration preserves both the freedom of speech as well as the ideals of personhood and citizenship such freedom makes possible. Fundamental to the constitution of rights in the United States, then, is a tension between rights we have by virtue of our personhood and obligations we have to the rights of others by virtue of our citizenship in a community.

The reconstruction and civil rights amendments added to the U.S. Constitution were attempts to expand definitions of personhood and citizenship to include ex-slaves and African Americans denied their rights on the basis of their skin color. Preference for expressing the struggle for racial equality in terms of the rights of all persons is clear in the 1946 summary report of the President's Commission on Civil Rights:

> The central theme in our American heritage is . . . that every human being has an essential dignity and integrity that must be respected and safeguarded. More over, we believe that the welfare of the individual is the final goal of group life. Our American heritage further teaches that to be secure in these rights he wishes for himself, each man must be willing to respect the rights of other men. . . . Thus, the only aristocracy that is consistent with the free way of life is an aristocracy of talent and achievement. The grounds on which our society accords respect, influence, or reward to each of its citizens must be limited to the quality of his personal character and of his social contribution. (*To Secure* 2–3)

Arguing for their personhood and citizenship. claiming an essential dignity and integrity for African Americans, the rights rhetoric of the civil rights movement directly extended the constitutional principles of rights outlined in the 1946 report. The boycotts, sit-ins, and marches of the early civil rights movement gave substance to an emergent African American rhetoric of civil rights, demonstrating to a nation the depth of human dignity and integrity of African Americans and the strength of their convictions to the constitutional principles of fundamental human rights. At the same time, violent reactions to the protests exposed the systematic intolerance of rights for African Americans and betrayed a lack of commitment among many white Americans to the full realization of constitutional principles.

The most prominent spokesperson for the civil rights movement, Martin Luther King, Jr., constantly and consistently claimed civil rights for African Americans on the grounds of constitutional legitimacy and in relation to the demonstrations of dignity of the civil rights protesters. In a March 14, 1965, *New York Times Magazine* article published during the congressional debate on President Johnson's voting rights bill, King affirmed the relationship of nonviolent protest to legislative action:

> In Selma, Ala., thousands of Negroes are courageously providing dramatic witness to the evil forces that bar our way to the all-important ballot box. They are laying bare for all the nation to see, for all the world to know, the nature of segregationist resistance. . . . Once it is exposed, and challenged by the marching feet of Negro citizens, the nation will take action to cure this cancerous sore. What is malignant in Selma must be removed by Congressional surgery so that all citizens may freely exercise their right to vote without delays, harassment, economic intimidation and police brutality. Selma is to 1965 what Birmingham was to 1963. (26)

In 1965, as in 1946, the rights denied African Americans are described as owed to them not because of their race but because it is only just that they, too, are accorded rights and privileges as humans and as citizens. But even more, denying to African Americans the rights of citizenship diminishes the principles of justice that extend citizenship to all. For King, the Jim Crow laws and informal tactics enabling southern whites to bar African Americans from voting were not simply illegal. They didn't merely contradict constitutional principles; Jim Crow laws and tactics were immoral. They violated the fundamental principles of rights to human dignity and self-determination on which constitutional justice is grounded and through which it is guaranteed. Exposing the injustices of American society and challenging racism through a rhetoric of rights and direct action, African Americans marched into a leadership role in the struggle over the meanings of justice in American public life.

King also understood that the persuasive force of the emerging African American rights rhetoric depended on the coercive use of state-sanctioned authority. For example, securing voting rights for southern blacks depended upon aggressive enforcement of the law. While the President could and did aggressively deploy National Guard troops for the purpose of safeguarding the right to vote of southern blacks, placing this force in the service of the legislative rhetoric of civil rights ultimately did not compel a culture of toleration. Early demands for formally equal access to public life that were framed in terms of civil rights did not directly address questions of how that life, nonetheless, remained structured to privilege whiteness.

As the victories of the civil rights movement began to mount, it became clear that they were, at least in part, victories in a shell game in which the terms of equality obliged African Americans to play an unwinnable game of catch up. In hindsight, it is clear that rights rhetoric meant different things to different people. The paradox of rights rhetoric was exemplified in a *Time* magazine report on the 1963 March on Washington:

> The march on Washington was a triumph. But after everybody agreed on that, the question was: Why? ... It was in the probable effects on the conscience of millions of previously indifferent Americans that the march might find its true meaning. The possibility of riot and bloodshed had always been there: and in the U.S.'s "open society" they would have been plainly visible for the whole world to see. But the marchers took that chance, and the U.S. took it with them. No one who saw the proceedings could come to any other conclusion than that those scores of thousands of marching Negroes were able to accept the responsibilities of first-class citizenship. (13–14)

Time magazine echoes King by emphasizing the potency of rights rhetoric to quicken the conscience of "previously indifferent" beneficiaries of racial injustice. But more importantly, *Time*'s rhetoric struggles to limit the semantic ambiguity of rights and the legitimacy of direct action. In contrast to King's representation of rights rhetoric as a means for African Americans to "expose" and "challenge" the "cancerous sore" of racism on the world stage, *Time* proposes that the "true meaning" of the March on Washington was that it demonstrated to white Americans that black Americans could responsibly exercise rights. The rights rhetoric of *Time* emphasizes peaceful inclusion of African Americans who have moved the conscience of white Americans by allaying white fears of black "riot and bloodshed." Embedded in this rhetoric is the assumption that black deviance, rather than white resistance, had historically made whites indifferent to equal rights. At the same time, the rights rhetoric used by *Time* glosses over the legacy of slavery and the persistent culture of racism that structured the exclusion of African Americans and necessitated the marches.

As would later become more apparent, for the mainstream society that *Time* represented, African American rights rhetoric was persuasive so long as it demonstrated willingness to both accept "the responsibilities of first-class citizenship" and to support (rather than expose or challenge) an "open society" that would prove over time to stubbornly maintain racial hierarchies. In *Time*, the rhetoric of rights is infiltrated by a semantics of formal access to institutions separated from relations of race that had always defined them.

Uses of rights rhetoric that simultaneously advocated for inclusion and resisted confronting the conditions and legacies of exclusion posed for civil rights legislation the problem of defining how far the government could go in the direction of engineering a culture of toleration and a well-defined commitment to racial equality. On June 4, 1965, in his commencement address at Howard University, entitled "To Fulfill These Rights," Lyndon Johnson introduced affirmative action with the analogy that

> You do not take a person who, for years, has been hobbled by chains and liberate him, bring him up to the starting line of a race and then say, "you are free to compete with all the others," and still justly believe that you have been completely fair. Thus it is not enough just to open the gates of opportunity. All our citizens must have the ability to walk through those gates. (126)

As Johnson makes clear, civil rights and voting rights legislation may remove the formal barriers to equality and justice, but they do not effectively enable equal participation in a nation where institutional circumstance and rhetorical habit informally perpetuate inequality.

Even though Johnson proposed using the government to redistribute opportunities and resources in order to excise the injustice and unfairness exposed by civil rights protesters, the legal rhetoric of affirmative action has failed to shift the social meanings of rights from a consideration of what we are owed as persons to what we owe each other as citizens. This is due in large part to the fact that civil rights and affirmative action rhetorics defined the meanings of racial equality much as *Time* magazine did, in terms of realizing the universal potential of human ability rather than in terms of dismantling the racist dynamics of American society. Stephen Steinberg has observed of Johnson's speech that it is an instance of "semantic infiltration" in which the rhetoric of rights is infiltrated by the interests of privilege, where the imperative of political compromise undermines the authority of critical insight. By the end of Johnson's speech, the chains of slavery and segregation that have structured society, hobbling African Americans and preventing them from participating on an equal footing, are refigured as having crippled the souls and psyches of individual African Americans. In these terms and under these conditions, racial equality was perceived as best achieved not by reengineering society but by improving black people. Rights rhetoric becomes infiltrated by a semantics of neutrality unresponsive to injustice. As Steinberg has argued, by phrasing antiracism in terms of social uplift, Johnson's speech opened the way for the subsequent "liberal retreat from race," creating the possibility for increasing skepticism regarding the competitive ability of African Americans (20–26).

Over the last thirty years, retreat from affirmative action initiatives has been justified through a rights rhetoric infiltrated by a semantics of self-interests and individual ability that increasingly expresses affirmative action as giving undue preference to minorities. In 1986, in a landmark decision striking down affirmative action considerations in the awarding of government contracts, Supreme Court Justice Antonin Scalia wrote in his concurring opinion, "The relevant proposition is not that it was blacks, or Jews, or Irish who were discriminated against, but that it was individual men and women, 'created equal,' who were discriminated against" (*City of Richmond* 528). Here, the African American version of rights rhetoric that persuaded a nation of the need for racial justice and that led Congress to pass sweeping civil rights legislation can only tolerate individual claims for rights. In the most unfortunate of ways, Johnson's hope to make the competition fair had been realized. The Supreme Court no longer considered African Americans hobbled by the chains of slavery or Jim Crow laws. Rather, the continued use of affirmative action initiatives were increasingly perceived more as giving African Americans a head start than as giving them a fair chance. Here, whites can and have and continue to claim privilege as their due through appeals to rights rhetoric.

As the emergence of the idea of reverse discrimination makes clear, the rhetoric of rights in and of itself fails to suggest a fair and just and unambiguous criterion for balancing competing rights against each other as well as against competing obligations. The most recent challenges to college admissions have succeeded to the extent that the rights of privileged white students are easily made more persuasive than either the rights of underprivileged minorities or our obligations to principles of racial equality and social justice. Critiquing rights rhetoric in these terms, communitarians characterize it as too centered on individual opportunities to take account of patterns of group behavior such as racial discrimination. Communitarians argue, instead, for a shift in attention away from what we are owed toward a consideration of what we owe others, a shift from a rhetoric of rights to a language of rightness. As "The Responsive Communitarian Platform" explains,

> The language of rights is morally incomplete. . . . Rights give reasons to others not to coercively interfere with the speaker in the performance of protected acts; however, they do not in themselves give me a sufficient reason to perform these acts. There is a gap between rights and rightness that cannot be closed without a richer moral vocabulary—one that invokes principles of decency, duty, responsibility, and the common good, among others. (19)

But in their advocacy of norms of rightness, communitarians are confronted with the dilemma of universalizing standards that may, in fact, violate individual rights. We may believe that it is without question indecent and irresponsible to engage in hate speech. But this does not mean that we believe it is, therefore, appropriate and acceptable to legally compel only decent and responsible speech. However, if we did decide to outlaw all speech that is not decent and responsible, how could such a decision be made? And what would we do about dissent? Samuel Walker argues that the communitarian vision does not offer a viable alternative to rights because communitarians fail to fully appreciate the constitutive ambiguity of rights rhetoric. As Walker points out, the advocacy and enforcement of rights do much to bring our attention to norms of rightness by encouraging our toleration of others; as difficult to enact and enforce as rights are, the social awareness of rights has made people more conscious of each other's claims for dignity and respect. For Walker, "the open, tolerant, and inclusive definition of community embodied in the rights revolution represents a preferable vision of a good society" (179). From this point of view, even though the gains of the civil rights movement have been compromised, important gains have been made nonetheless.

Critical legal studies scholars committed to exposing the privilege written into law consider the rights revolution too clouded by exclusionary dichotomies to provide a vision of the good society. Still, as troubled as she is by the rhetoric of rights, Patricia Williams refuses to abandon rights rhetoric because she recognizes its persuasive power for African Americans. Like Walker, Williams understands the persuasiveness of rights rhetoric lies in its ambiguity, its simultaneous claim for universality, and its promise of formal identity. She reminds us that rights rhetoric stakes out for powerless African Americans a claim against the unchecked power of white America, holding out hope for enacting principles of equality and justice that African Americans can experience in their day-to-day lives. But to make good on that promise, she argues, we need to let go of the prospect of an unambiguous rights rhetoric. We need to abandon a rights rhetoric that universalizes rights independently of the dynamics of enacting rights in specific conditions of unequal power. Where Walker counters the communitarian critique of rights in a manner that seems content with the semantic infiltration of rights rhetoric, Williams proposes that we need "not the abandonment of rights language for all purposes, but an attempt to become multilingual in the semantics of evaluating rights" (149). As Williams suggests, becoming multilingual in the semantics of evaluating rights is not an individual act but a social process of negotiation and struggle in which people attempt to see the often competing claims and obligations of rights "simultaneously yet differently" (150).

Proposing multiple, even contradictory, meanings for rights, Williams acknowledges the problem of rights rhetoric semantically infiltrated by a language of individual effort. Her proposal asks us to acknowledge that the competing meanings we assign to rights are finite and situated and so open to change. Bringing attention to our competing and contradictory uses of rights rhetoric opens vocabularies that either limit rights to individual claims or that avoid hard questions about social subjectivity. To be productive, confrontation among people with differing expectations of what others owe them as well as differing perceptions of what they owe others must take shape as a struggle over the differently situated meanings of appeals to rights rhetoric.

In summary, rights rhetoric unfolds as a struggle over whose interests will shape American democracy in what ways. This need not be bad. The rhetoric of rights remains persuasive and useful as long as we remain multilingual in the semantics of evaluating rights. To the extent that our rights rhetorics are semantically infiltrated, to the extent that they constitute a shell game constrained to a limited range of meanings that either fail to inspire or that encourage only self-interestedness, the rhetoric of rights betrays our best efforts at comprehending racial injustice and so enacting equality. Acknowledging the openness of meaning in rights rhetoric, we accept a constant process of struggle over rights and over the meanings of justice and equality. While these considerations demonstrate the ambiguity of rights rhetoric, they should not dissuade us from the prospects made available in composition studies through uses of rights rhetoric. However, we need to be wary of what we struggle over if we are to avoid the shell game of semantic infiltration and win the struggle for language rights.

RIGHTS RHETORIC IN COMPOSITION STUDIES

The legacy of rights rhetoric we have discussed thus far is significant for a discussion of rights rhetoric in composition studies. The introduction of rights into the discourse of composition drew its inspiration from the successes of the civil rights movement, to further advance the cause of racial equality by addressing the increasingly apparent injustices of traditional literacy education. As Smitherman and others have recently pointed out, however, despite more than three decades of struggle for language rights in composition studies, literacy education continues to institutionalize racial injustice. It would seem that by drawing inspiration through rights rhetoric, composition studies has allowed the semantic infiltration of its rights rhetoric. For this reason, the prospects of multilingualism in the semantics of evaluating rights is essential to a critical discussion of rights rhetoric in composition studies.

In what follows, we discuss uses of rights rhetoric in composition studies in terms of the struggles over rights already outlined. Our goal is to bring greater critical depth, and so greater meaningfulness and usefulness, to rights rhetoric in composition studies. We do this through close attention to the first significant adaptation of a national rights rhetoric in composition studies, "Students' Right to Their Own Language." Worked out over several years in the early 1970s, "Students' Right" takes full advantage of the rights rhetoric that had emerged through the civil rights movement. Specifically, "Students' Right" brings into composition the tensions of rights rhetoric already apparent in President Johnson's 1965 Howard University Commencement Address. Like Johnson's speech, "Students' Right" is torn between a commitment to the dignity of all persons, regardless of their language, and a responsibility to act on behalf of students marginalized because of their literacy, a responsibility to somehow use literacy education to make the race for education and employment a fair one.

The resolution, adopted by CCCC members in 1974, is worth quoting in full:

> We affirm the students' right to their own patterns and varieties of language—the dialects of their nurture or whatever dialects in which they find their own identity and style. Language scholars long ago denied that the myth of a standard American dialect has any validity. The claim that any one dialect is unacceptable amounts to an attempt of one social group to exert its dominance over another. Such a claim leads to false advice for speakers and writers, and immoral advice for humans. A nation proud of its diverse heritage and its cultural and racial variety will preserve its heritage of dialects. We affirm strongly that teachers must have the experience and training that will enable them to respect diversity and uphold the right of students to their own language. (p. 19)

The resolution makes several claims about the language rights of students that introduce into composition studies the fundamental difficulties of rights rhetoric. The resolution claims unqualified respect for the language use of all students. Language use is a right to be respected because the diversity of language styles and dialects is essential to individual self-formation. In terms of the rhetoric of rights discussed above, the resolution advocates a tolerance of differences that opens spaces for and establishes relationships of personhood and citizenship. For one group to impose criteria for language use on another amounts to an obstruction of their right to choose for themselves their identities. As the resolution makes clear, any attempts to limit a person's literacy skills amount to an intolerance that violates rights fundamental to all humans.

But for composition teachers, the resolution calls for more than tolerance. The language rights of students compel an obligation among teachers of writing not only to respect but also to actively "uphold the right of students to their own language." Through the obvious reference to African American vernacular and relations between black and white racial groups in the middle sentences of the resolution, the claim for universal respect for human rights is translated into a professional concern for using the teaching of writing to remedy linguistic prejudice and to resist specific past practices of social group dominance. Because teachers of writing are in the position of being able to use literacy education to advocate linguistic difference as well as promote assimilation to conventions, the resolution raises major rights conflicts: When we, as teachers, acknowledge the rights of others, how far must we go in order to protect or advocate for those rights? Should our advocacy aim at a kind of social engineering that works to shift the accepted status of mainstream conventions, marginalized conventions, or both? How do we weigh such affirmative action measures against all other rights and obligations? And is this what it means to claim to struggle for language rights?

The answers given to these questions in the background statement to "Students' Right" have framed subsequent receptions of the resolution and uses of rights rhetoric in composition, enabling a struggle for rights that has precluded sustained struggle over rights rhetoric as a resource for transforming literacy education. Introducing the joint publication of the resolution and background statement in 1974, CCCC Chair Richard Larson explains that the resolution was believed by the CCCC Executive Committee to be "controversial" and to contain assertions best "explained by references to current research on dialects and usage." Explaining the rights assertions of the resolution in terms of linguistic research, the background statement invites the kind of semantic infiltration of rights rhetoric discussed above by translating the resolution's rhetoric of rights—a rhetoric of what equity, fairness, and justice obligate us to do for those on the margins—into an unambiguous rhetoric of rightness: a rhetoric of what the research tells us we should do for all individuals in the interests of a neutral truth. Framing discussion of the resolution in terms of research into language usage and instruction, the background statement makes little mention of rights. It concentrates, instead, on debunking the myth of a standard American dialect, supporting the claim for linguistic equality, and outlining classroom practices that uphold the diversity of students while also teaching the conventions of edited American English. In retreat from the ambiguity of rights rhetoric and in search of firm semantic foundations for relating the teaching of writing to the struggle for rights, the background statement turns the resolution's strong language of "racial variety" and "social group dominance" into a language of individual freedom from externally imposed negative feelings and attitudes.

While the shift from rights rhetoric to a discourse of research may diffuse controversy and persuasively support the claims of the resolution, that semantic shift has important consequences for how compositionists enact in the classroom the concept of a right to language. Part of the reason for reframing a rights resolution in terms of the accuracy of research may have been the perception that the ambiguity of rights rhetoric is unhelpful, even counterproductive. Substituting the clarity of research for the ambiguity of rights, the background statement to "Students' Right" describes the racial dynamics of literacy as irrational infiltration of personal prejudices on what should be neutral and impartial interactions among citizens. As argued in the background statement, "the emotional nature of the controversy has obscured the complexities of the problem and hidden some of the assumptions that must be examined before any kind of rational policy can be adopted" (p. 20). In search of a rational policy, the background statement abandons rights rhetoric in favor of arguments made in terms of "sophisticated research in linguistics and sociology" (p. 20), justifying the importance of respecting diversity through a language of research that supercedes a language of emotion.

Abandoning rights rhetoric in order to overcome emotional investments in language controversies, the background statement opens itself to a kind of communitarian critique: its language fails to compel a continuing struggle over obligations to the language diversity of students. We may recognize, as the background statement explains, that the privilege of standardized English in schools and in the workplace brings more advantages to some and less to others. In and of itself, such recognition does not compel us to unlearn the privilege of standardized English. We can, in fact, tolerate and respect students' right to their own language as we teach them standardized English by promoting the use of distinct dialects in discreet settings. As many compositionists have read "Students' Right," we are obligated to promote standardized English in public and professional settings where it is required, at the same time respecting the appropriateness of diverse dialects within community and home settings. However, this is a rights rhetoric excessively weakened by semantic infiltration if it means simply respecting the already established hierarchies of dialects and boundaries of language use. The right to a language, like the right to free speech, is not a right unless it is universalized, unless it is a right in all situations and at all times that it does not interfere with the rights of others. To say that students have a right to the language of their identity in classrooms where we are teaching them and evaluating them on their use of a standardized English is to disregard the crucial public dimension of rights, that rights are meaningful only in our relations with others. As our discussion of rights rhetoric more generally has shown, successful struggle for rights requires a public redistribution of advantage that dislodges privilege. Successful struggle for rights further requires a public recognition of the differences that have organized inequality, a recognition that demands everyone's toleration and respect. A reasonably strong claim for the language rights of those on the linguistic margins must provide for both redistribution and toleration.

To its credit, the background statement does attempt to articulate the individual acquisition of literacy within the structural limits of privilege. It uses the language of research to address the problem of gaining recognition for nonstandard dialects that have been unjustly stigmatized. Identifying racism as irrational and emotional, the background statement recalls early civil rights appeals to a color-blind "aristocracy of talent and achievement." As the background statement explains, "when speakers of a dialect of American English claim not to understand speakers of another dialect of the same language, the impediments are likely to be attitudinal" (p. 24). Attitudes are not individualized and unstructured, they are learned. Overwrought emotional responses to illiteracy and misinformed attitudes about dialect variation are partially functions of how English has been taught, and so research can correct such attitudes by better informing teaching:

> Until public attitudes can be changed—and it is worth remembering that the past teaching in English classes has been largely responsible for those attitudes—shall we place our emphasis on what vocal elements of the public thinks it wants or on what the actual available linguistic evidence indicates we should emphasize? (p. 21)

The answer is clear. Teachers of writing must resist the common sense that "the values taught by the schools must reflect the prejudices held by the public" in favor of teaching, "what the actual available linguistic evidence indicates we should emphasize" (p. 21).

As a framework for guiding classroom practice, the research that prohibits the prejudice of misplaced attitudes does not discount the economic and social necessity of privileging standard English. In this case, to advocate for the rights of students on the linguistic margins involves recognizing "the need for a written dialect to serve the larger, public community has resulted in a general commitment to what may be called 'edited American English,' that prose which is meant to carry information about our representative problems and interests" (p. 25). While such recognition limits a student's right to his or her own language, it, nonetheless, involves redistributing the resources of edited American English so as to undo the linguistic privilege with which more affluent white students "sit at the head of the class, are accepted at 'exclusive' schools, and are later rewarded with positions in the business and social world" (p. 22). This version of advocacy for language rights does not challenge teachers (or anyone else) to unlearn the privilege of institutionally organized and publicly sanctioned mainstream literacy. The imperative of the "Students' Right" resolution to act on behalf of the rights of linguistically marginalized students demands that teachers unlearn their bias against marginalized differences in order to bring those students more fully into the linguistic mainstream.

As we described it in terms of rights rhetoric generally, the struggle for the right of inclusion falters on affirmative action claims that retreat from the social structures of racial privilege by focusing exclusively on improving the competitiveness of marginalized individuals. In the background statement to "Students' Right," struggle for the inclusion of linguistically marginalized students falters on claims that divorce consideration of the individual acquisition of standardized English from the racial dynamics of linguistic marginalization. Having let go the ambiguity of rights for the certainty of research, the background statement cannot develop a vocabulary that unites struggles for the rights of all students with struggles over what our obligation to those rights entails with respect to members of linguistically, culturally, and socioeconomically marginalized groups.

Respondents to the "Students' Right" resolution and background statement recognized the call to struggle for the rights of students. Yet, respondents rejected the struggle *for* rights by not engaging the struggle *over* rights. Instead of connecting the limitations of "Students' Right" to the limited use of rights rhetoric, they challenged the usefulness of rights rhetoric itself for compositionists thinking about dilemmas of race, equality, and privilege in literacy education. Respondents expressed frustration with the apparent semantic distance between rights and rightness—between the claim that professionals have a primary responsibility to citizens' rights to difference and efforts to redistribute literacy conventions that, as the background statement itself proposed, "serve the larger, public community" (p. 25).

For these compositionists, the paradoxical ambiguities of rights rhetoric unnecessarily inflame passions over false controversies. As Anne Berthoff observed, compositionists recognized a "moral and professional responsibility to . . . meet the challenge of illiteracy wisely and humanely and imaginatively" but, for her, "declaring that everyone has a 'right' to his own 'language' is sloganeering" (p. 122). Others agreed, pointing out that the language of rights had seemingly little to contribute to discussions of teaching writing because "the use of language is not an individual but a social act" and, therefore, has more to do with overcoming than protecting difference (Smith p. 163 in this book). For these scholars, the most rights rhetoric can do is remind us that the responsibility of teachers of writing is to provide the greatest possible access to opportunities to overcome exclusion or difference. The argument here is that the ambiguous rhetoric of the rights resolution actually detracts from the obvious resolution of important issues of literacy and equality because "students do not have a right to their own language; they only have a right to learn a language which will produce the proper effects on whatever audience they may speak or write to" (Smith p. 167), a right already well recognized in teaching writing.

Rejecting the resolution that rights rhetoric can deepen collective reflection and practice, these compositionists do not struggle over rights. Without a struggle over rights, compositionists have no language to ask questions like these: Under conditions of material inequality and linguistic marginalization, who decides the proper effects of language? Whose interests do those effects and that language serve? What role do compositionists play in deciding the effects of language and serving the interests of language users?

To the extent that responses to "Students' Right" do not struggle over rights, Berthoff's observation is accurate: rights rhetoric inflames passions rather than inspiring new connections and commitments. But it is the refusal to take up issues of language diversity and literacy education that reduces rights rhetoric to sloganeering. Rights rhetoric can inspire new commitments to language, literacy, and education, but only to the extent that its meanings are contested. Patricia Williams's call for us to become multilingual in the semantics of evaluating rights is crucial here. Doing so, we avoid the semantic infiltration of rights rhetoric. But we leave unresolved, and thus open to contestation, the issues of rights central to composition, issues of why and how language comes to matter and to signify differences, issues of hope and possibility.

In the decades of our retreat from the ambiguities of rights rhetoric, advocacy for those on the linguistic margins has manifested an enduring commitment to the universal right of persons to be recognized as citizens and humans. In composition research, teaching, and theory, we have remained steadfast that all citizens are capable of success and that our responsibility revolves around struggling to make, as one recent study phrased it, "conventions about which [students] have a fundamental and democratic right to know" equally available to all (Gray-Rosendale 62). But this struggle to respect the essential dignity and integrity of each individual's right of access has taken place in the absence of a rights rhetoric of struggle over the kinds of equality that literacy education might enact. The lack of a compelling, historically resonant, and politically robust vocabulary framing critical attention to the semantic infiltration of privileged interests into our discourse of advocacy and uplift diminishes the potency of both critique and advocacy.

This is not to say that progress has not been made through advocacy for those on the linguistic margins, nor is it to propose that our advocacy has not been the subject of critical reflection. To the contrary, as Smitherman highlights in her commemorative article, it is important to attend to the progress that has been made as we steel our resolve for continuing the struggle. The rhetoric of research continues to provide insights into best practices of advocacy for students' right of access. Parallel to progress in classroom advocacy, the rhetoric of research has opened the profession to insights of critical theory and political philosophy. But as valuable as these pursuits have been, they have not been able to inspire the broad-based departures from past practices and paradigms that will be central to professional struggle over racial equality and social justice.

Exemplary of the progress that has been made within the discourse of research, Catherine Prendergast has drawn from the insights of critical legal studies to call attention to the ways that race operates as an "absent presence" in composition studies (36). Specifically, Prendergast argues that discursive socialization, the dominant mode of pedagogical response to the exclusionary dynamics of literacy, is of limited value in addressing overarching racial inequalities. Paraphrasing the conclusions of critical legal studies, Prendergast points out that, although the discursive socialization paradigm is attractive because it seems to represent an unambiguous response to continuing inequalities, given the historical entrenchment of privilege in institutionally valued discourses, "it will not be simply enough to add women and people of color and stir. Without significant changes to the profession and pedagogy, women and people of color will continue to wind up on the bottom" (50). Walking through the gates of opportunity means transforming the features — racial, gendered — that make those gates always already less open to some and more open to others. Prendergast's insights return us to questions at the heart of the "Students' Right" resolution regarding rhetorical resources for inspiring a redefinition of literacy that acts on behalf of racial equality and social justice. Her insights also point up the potential significance of heeding Williams's imperative that we "become multilingual in the semantics of evaluating rights" (149). At present, the limited professional engagement with rights rhetoric as a rhetoric of opportunity and uplift is unable to support conditions for critical insights like Prendergast's to challenge the economy of compromises that constrains the horizons of classroom practices and social relations.

Arnetha Ball and Ted Lardner have recently drawn attention to the gulf between critical theories like Prendergast's and classroom practices. In "Dispositions toward Language: Teacher Constructs of Knowledge and the Ann Arbor Black English Case," Ball and Lardner argue that a continuing crisis of racial injustice in literacy instruction revolves around the glaring lack of progress in terms of the regard that individual teachers feel and, thus, the respect that classroom environments and practices exhibit for language diversity and cultural difference. Despite both decades of research exploring the formal linguistic equality of different dialects and the importance of dialect diversity in representing and enacting cultural diversity, Ball and Lardner point out that "teachers still continue to exhibit negative attitudes toward African American English, often stating that African American English has a faulty grammar system and that children who speak African American English are less capable than children who speak standard English" (473). For Ball and Lardner, the reason for this still continuing dilemma is that composition research has paid too little attention to the importance of the rhetorics through which teachers "encounter and contextualize the pedagogical ramifications of language diversity" (481–82).

Responding to this dilemma, Ball and Lardner emphasize the need for a rhetoric of "teacher efficacy." Teacher efficacy creates opportunities for teachers to reflectively examine "the emotional tone of classroom interactions" (478) as a way to engage the affective messages those interactions send to students and to become aware of unconscious negative attitudes. This attention to the need for a rhetoric through which to address ways that race, as a structure of unequal expectations, influences individual attitudes and institutional practices is valuable. As a research perspective, attention to affect encourages teachers to take responsibility for the implicit and explicit messages that they send to students about who is expected to succeed in school and society.

But affect does not compel us to reflect on the justness of institutionalized definitions of success. As a rhetoric of transformation, affect cannot dislodge the ways that practices and attitudes supportive of racial privilege are entrenched in institutions despite the attitudes of individual teachers. Affect cannot bridge the chasm between institutions whose "goal is to move urban youth in cities like Cleveland or Detroit into academic discourse communities" (Ball and Lardner 480) and insights such as Prendergast's that "the value of discursive socialization is contingent (on factors such as race) rather than universal" (49). This is not to discount the significance of linking a professional rhetoric of situated engagement with overarching structures influencing individual attitudes and practices. Instead, this example highlights the continuing need for a rhetoric of rights through which compositionists can link individual struggles for the rights of linguistically marginalized students to multilingual struggles over the semantic terms and conditions that have influenced institutionally dominant renderings of those rights.

The ebbs and flows of rights rhetoric in composition studies orient the profession within a broader motion in the United States between rights as a rhetoric central for nonwhite leadership to struggles over racial equality and rights as a rhetoric semantically infiltrated by the interests of white privilege. In the years since the first flurry of response to the "Students' Right to Their Own Language" resolution, the tide of multilingual engagement with the pedagogical implications of rights rhetoric shifted so profoundly that, as chair of the CCCC in 1996, Lester Faigley suggested "it no longer seems like we are riding the wave of history but instead are caught in a rip tide carrying us away from where we want to go" (32). What remains of the wave of rights rhetoric is an often unspoken assumption that, as teachers of writing, our primary classroom obligation must be to the right of students' access to privileged conventions. In light of broader efforts to rhetorically distance struggles for rights from struggles to overcome racial inequality and social injustice, the narrowing of appeals to rights rhetoric in composition studies has left untapped a rhetoric and legacy that have been and that can become a major resource for enabling and inspiring multilingual interpretations of literacy as a democratic cultural practice. In part, reconnecting to the rich legacy of rights rhetoric is made difficult by the perilous foothold that semantically infiltrated rights rhetoric allows to those on the linguistic margins who might use rights rhetoric to meaningfully contest what Prendergast calls "the limits of the kind of inclusion liberalism promises" (51). Within this context, the multiplicity of rights rhetoric, the potential within it to think "simultaneously yet differently" about rightness, frames the risks and rewards of the struggle.

THE FUTURE STRUGGLE FOR RIGHTS

W. E. B. DuBois recognized the problem of the twentieth century would be the problem of the color line. Though the clearly drawn color line and the policies of official discrimination that inscribed it have largely been erased by a rhetoric of rights, institutionalized group privilege still continues to present a major obstacle to the dream of democracy in the United States. The current conservative semantic infiltration of rights rhetoric threatens the value of rights as a vocabulary for further challenging and completely undoing institutionalized racial privilege. Educational programs from New York to California implemented to facilitate and support access to higher education are targeted by rights lawsuits and dismantled by lawmakers defending, in the coded language of contemporary semantic infiltration, taxpayers' rights. Crowning thirty years of such semantic infiltration, California's state ballot proposition 209, which by popular vote eliminated affirmative action in higher education admissions in the state, was labeled the California Civil Rights Initiative. In such a time, it is tempting to hold fast in our professional rhetorics to the gains that we have made through talk of how best to individually operationalize literacy's promise of open and equal access to all. But we must not hold so tightly to our gains that we let go needs and opportunities for further progress.

The future struggle for language rights will be the struggle over how literacy can contribute to a multicultural democracy committed to group equity and social justice. As Prendergast, Ball and Lardner, and Smitherman make clear, the dilemma of racialized group injustice continues to structure relations between and among compositionists and students from the linguistic margins and mainstreams. Drawing attention to the need for compositionists to transform everyday practices in writing classrooms, each of these scholars heeds the important warning of Becky Thompson and Sangeeta Tyagi, "in the face of conservative consolidations of power, it is both easy and dangerous to fall into the trap of becoming defensive, trying to hold the line on gains while losing energy to brainstorm about what can and must be done" (xxii). One avenue available to compositionists for building on the gains that have been made through struggles for rights is to attend more deeply to struggles over rights and, thus, to create conditions for our profession to become multilingual in the semantics of evaluating rights.

Even though the professional legacy of rights rhetoric that derives from responses to "Students' Right to Their Own Language" has faltered on the semantic infiltration of rights rhetoric, this does not prohibit the possibility for compositionists becoming multilingual in the semantics of evaluating rights. In multilingual terms, the untapped value of "Students' Right" lies in the opportunities that rights rhetoric makes available for professional practice to extend beyond struggles *for* every individual student's right to possess the currently dominant literacy. Becoming multilingual in the semantics of evaluating rights today involves examining how rights rhetoric has been contested by groups located in a history of power relations and recognizing that the meanings assigned rights are neither necessary nor permanent. As we have argued, in addition to a struggle for rights of individual opportunity, the history of rights rhetoric makes possible a struggle *over* rights, a struggle over literacy as a right, and an obligation to communicative practices that actively pursue racial justice through affirmation of the civil rights of those on the linguistic margins and through transformation of the privileges that have kept them there.

The multiplicity of rights rhetoric is had through recognition that rights claims are claims to inclusion not distinct from the right for recognition of differences. Reflecting on the previously unimaginable changes in social relations accomplished by the civil rights movement, Martin Luther King, Jr., highlighted the fact that, articulating their insights through a rhetoric of rights, young African Americans who had "traditionally imitated whites in dress, conduct, and thought in a rigid, middle class pattern . . . ceased imitating and began initiating. Leadership passed into the hands of [African Americans] and their white allies began learning from them. This was a revolutionary and wholesome development for both" (*Trumpet* 46). Exploiting the semantic ambiguity of rights, historically dominant and subordinate groups came to see themselves and others in new ways.

In light of the "revolutionary and wholesome" legacy that King points to, the "Students' Right" resolution is an amazing gesture. It imported into composition studies an ambiguous rhetoric through which African Americans and other marginalized groups established leadership roles in struggles over how best to transform dominant cultural practices, demonstrating "limits of the kind of inclusion that liberalism promises" (Prendergast 51). Calling upon the central principle of liberalism — rights — as a way of addressing literacy's limitations for particular groups, "Students' Right" encourages the profession to recognize that the semantics of rights both constrains relations among persons and opens those relations to redefinition. Through such a multilingual formulation of the implications of rights, compositionists can theorize the rights and obligations of writing relationally—in ways that account for the simultaneous yet different contributions of universal inclusion and positional difference to creating relationships of justice and equality. We can produce a struggle over rights that enhances the struggle for rights.

Struggling over rights means turning writing against the shell game of color blindness and neutrality. This professional agenda has implications in the classroom, in the curriculum, in institutional work, in research, and in public discourse. These implications are local rather than universal. For us, the struggle over rights is a lens through which to read our contexts and actions in them. In the past, emphasis has often been placed on struggling for the right of access. Reading the contexts and content of our work through those terms, we have made great strides. We have built conceptual tools and practical strategies like process approaches that have broadened access and deepened understandings of access. But when not accompanied by careful attention to local struggles over the terms of access, our good work has left unchallenged the negative effects of universality. As a result, the belief in group-level neutrality continues to make access to literacy a shell game. Undoing this shell game will involve defining learning writing around learning to struggle over rights. If all students and their teachers leave writing classes better able to struggle over rights, we might reasonably hope that future conversation about literacy and rights will break the cycle of miscommunication most recently evident in the Oakland Ebonics controversy.

At its best, rights rhetoric is an effort to use the master's tools to dismantle the master's house. Operating in this way, rights rhetoric has historically institutionalized a vocabulary invested and infused with the needs and claims of African Americans in particular and members of all marginalized groups in general. Following the civil rights movement, rights has, at times, made possible a rhetoric of powerful nonwhite public leadership and public redefinition in the interests of those disempowered by the rules of the shell game of race, opportunity, and achievement. It is this legacy and promise, the legacy and promise that King describes of multilingual and multiracial leadership in struggles to redefine the meanings of literacy and the meanings of inclusion, that composition studies stands to regain in heeding Smitherman's call to begin to celebrate, through engagement, the legacy of rights rhetoric in composition studies.

WORKS CITED

Ball, Arnetha, and Ted Lardner. "Dispositions toward Language: Teacher Constructs of Knowledge and the Ann Arbor Black English Case." *College Composition and Communication* 48 (1997): 469–85.

Berthoff, Ann E, and William G. Clark. "In Response to 'Students' Right to Their Own Language'." *College Composition and Communication* 26 (1975): [pp. 121–23 in this book].

City of Richmond v. J. A. Croson Co. 488 U.S. 469. U.S. Supreme Ct. 1989.

"Civil Rights: The March's Meaning." *Time Magazine* 6 Sept 1963: 13–15.

Faigley, Lester. "Literacy after the Revolution." *College Composition and Communication* 48 (1997): 30–43.

Gray-Rosendale, Laura. "Inessential Writings: Shaughnessy's Legacy in a Socially Constructed Landscape." *Journal of Basic Writing* 17.2 (1998): 43–75.

Johnson, Lyndon. Commencement Address. Rpt. in Lee Rainwater and William L. Yancey. *The Moynihan Report and the Politics of Controversy*. Cambridge: MIT P, 1967. 125–32.

King, Martin Luther, Jr. *The Trumpet of Conscience*. New York: Harper, 1968.

———. "Civil Right No. 1, The Right to Vote." *New York Times Magazine* 14 Mar. 1965: 26–27.

Prendergast, Catherine. "Race: The Absent Presence in Composition Studies." *College Composition and Communication* 50 (1998): 36–53.

"The Responsive Communitarian Platform: Rights and Responsibilities." *Rights and the Common Good: The Communitarian Perspective*. Ed. Amitai Etzioni. New York: St. Martins, 1995.

Smith, Allen N. "No One Has a Right to His Own Language." *College Composition and Communication* 27 (1976): [pp. 163–68 in this book].

Smitherman, Geneva. "CCCC's Role in the Struggle for Language Rights." *College Composition and Communication* 50 (1999): [pp. 58–82 in this book].

Steinberg, Stephen. "The Liberal Retreat from Race during the Post-Civil Rights Era." *The House That Race Built: Black Americans, U.S. Terrain*. Ed. Wahneema Lubiano. New York: Pantheon Books, 1997. 13–47.

Students' Right to Their Own Language. Spec. issue of *College Composition and Communication* 25 (1974): [pp. 19–57 in this book].

Thompson, Becky W., and Sangeeta Tyagi. Introduction. "A Wider Landscape . . . without the Mandate for Conquest." *Beyond a Dream Deferred: Multicultural Education and the Politics of Excellence*. Ed. Thompson and Tyagi. Minneapolis: U of Minnesota P, 1993. xiii–xxxiii.

To Secure These Rights: The Report of the President's Commission on Civil Rights. Rpt. in *The Civil Rights Reader: Basic Documents of the Civil Rights Movement*. Ed. Leon Friedman. New York: Walker, 1968.

Walker, Samuel. *The Rights Revolution: Rights and Community in Modern America*. New York: Oxford UP, 1998.

Williams, Patricia J. *The Alchemy of Race and Rights*. Cambridge: Harvard UP, 1991.

PART THREE

The Special Case of African American Language

11

African American Student Writers in the NAEP, 1969–88/89 [1992] and "The Blacker the Berry, the Sweeter the Juice" [1994]

GENEVA SMITHERMAN

The two articles which follow are research reports of a major study of writing by 17-year-old African American students in the National Assessment of Educational Progress (NAEP), from 1969 to 1988/89. My study was funded by grants from the National Council of Teachers of English. NAEP is a federally funded decennial evaluation program, mandated by Congress and initiated in 1969. The last full-scale, national Writing Assessment was done in 1988–9, the last year of my study. Since that time, focus has shifted gradually to state writing-assessment systems.

This twenty-year study, conducted with the assistance of colleagues and student research assistants, analyzed a total of 2,764 essays, which had been scored by teacher-raters trained by NAEP. My goal was to develop a profile of the written literacy accomplishments of African American youth, at the school-leaving age, over the span of a generation, at three different time periods— 1969, 1979, 1988–9. The first research report, "Black English, Diverging or Converging?" published in 1992, focuses on rater scores and syntax in the essays; the second report, "The Blacker the Berry, the Sweeter the Juice," published in 1994, focuses on rater scores, syntax, and discourse styles.

NATIONAL ASSESSMENT OF EDUCATIONAL PROGRESS (NAEP)

NAEP is a federally funded survey of the educational attainments of youth and adults at four age levels: nine, thirteen, seventeen, and twenty-six to thirty-five. Its purpose is to measure growth or decline in educational achievement in ten subject areas: writing, reading, literature, science, mathematics, citizenship, music, art, social studies, and career and occupational development. Administered at five- and ten-year intervals since its inception in 1969, NAEP offers the advantage of a scientifically selected national representative sample, uniform scoring procedures and guidelines, a nationally administered, standardized test format, and a high degree of reliability and validity.

From *Talkin That Talk: Language, Culture, and Education in African America* (Routledge, 2000), 163–91.

For example, the percentage of exact agreement on the rating of the 1984 papers from seventeen-year-olds ranged from 89 percent to 92 percent, with corresponding reliability coefficients of .89 and .91 (Applebee, Langer, and Mullis, 1985, 68). The writing task time is fifteen or sixteen minutes, depending on the task, and students submit first drafts. Previously administered by the Education Commission of the States, NAEP has been under the purview of the Educational Testing Service since 1984.

The students assessed reflect national, representative groups, in a random sample, stratified by race–ethnicity, social–educational class, region of country, urban–rural, gender, and other demographics. From 1969 to 1979, approximately 8,100 students were assessed. From 1984 to 1988–9, approximately 18,000 students were assessed.

NAEP's essay tasks represent three types of rhetorical modalities: (1) imaginative–narrative, (2) descriptive–informative, and (3) persuasive. For the *imaginative* modality, in the 1969 and 1979 NAEP, students were given a picture of a stork and told to make up a story about it. The prompt was comprised of three possible opening lines: (1) "I'm telling you, Henry, if you don't get rid of that thing, it's going to eat up the cat!"; (2) "But mother, I *am* telling the truth! It laid an egg in the Chevy"; and (3) "Last night a very odd-looking bird appeared in the neighborhood." In 1984, students were given a picture of a box with a hole in it and an eye peering out. They were told to "imagine" themselves in the picture, to describe the scene and their feelings about it, and to make their descriptions "lively and interesting." There was no imaginative task in 1988.

For the *descriptive–informative* task, the 1969 and 1979 students were asked to describe something they knew about, a familiar place or thing, in such a way that it could be recognized by someone reading the description. For 1984 and 1988, they were given the topic "Food on the Frontier" and asked to write an essay discussing reasons for the differences between food on the frontier and food today. Finally, for the *persuasive* modality, in 1984 and 1988 the students' task was to write a letter to the recreation department in their city or town, trying to convince the head of that department to buy either an abandoned railroad track or an old warehouse to create recreational opportunities. (We were unable to obtain the persuasive essays for 1969 and 1979; thus this longitudinal comparison was not possible.)

Black English: Diverging or Converging?

During the decades of the 1960s and 1970s, African Americans made great strides in educational and community development. The years from 1960–80 produced 80 percent of *all* the African American doctorates in our entire history in North America (Blackwell, 1981). Since 1960, we have witnessed a burgeoning Black middle class without parallel or precedence in the Black Experience. And finally, in an area closer to the subject of this article, the writing of African American students improved *twice* as much as that of their white counterparts in the decade from 1969 to 1979, as measured by the National Assessment of Educational Progress (NAEP, 1980). Thus William Labov's mid-1980s announcement that Black English was diverging from Standard White English shocked the scholarly and lay communities across the nation (Labov and Harris, 1986).

What has come to be called the "Divergence Hypothesis" posits that Black English Vernacular (BEV) is charting a separate course of development from that of white dialects in this post-modern era. Contrary to predictions about the impact of racial integration, of the media, of increased educational development and enhanced literacy, Black speech has not continued to de-creolize as we had anticipated back in the 1960s and 1970s — or so the divergence argument goes. Labov attributes divergence to racial isolation and foreshadows serious negative consequences for African American students who are now facing a language of instruction even more drastically different from their own language than was the case in their parents' day. While rebuttals to the Labovian Divergence Hypothesis have employed counter-examples from *speech* (e.g., Vaughn-Cooke, 1987; Wolfram, 1990), this article examines the issue from the vantage point of *writing*; using national samples of 17-year-old African Americans in the National Assessment of Educational Progress (NAEP), from 1969–88/89. This study seeks to illuminate the question of the frequency and distribution of Black English Vernacular in writing over a generational time span. If Labov is right and there has been divergence from Standard English (SE) in speech, has there been concomitant divergence in writing?

Issues in the Study

I first began this line of research in early 1981, with the release of the 1979 NAEP writing results. The test results indicated that the writing of African American students had improved *twice* as much as that of their white counterparts in the decade from 1969 to 1979. I sought to investigate whether these higher writing scores were accompanied by a decline in Black English Vernacular over the decade and a concomitant greater control of Edited American/Standard English. Results from this earlier research did indeed indicate a significant decline in BEV over the decade in the case of the imaginative-narrative essays. However, there was no parallel decrease in the descriptive/informative essay modality from 1969 to 1979 (Smitherman and Wright, 1983).

The question of the relationship between writing scores and the distribution of BEV in writing is a logical issue given assumed negative teacher attitudes and the stigma attached to features of Black English in writing. This earlier research shed some light on this question in that the narrative essays, which showed significant declines in BEV features from 1969–79, also were the essays which demonstrated the dramatic improvement in writing scores over the same time frame. Thus we concluded that the decrease in BEV in the narrative essays and the corollary increase in rater scores spoke "favorably for our efforts at teaching EAE" (Smitherman and Wright, 1983 NCTE Research Report). Further, we noted that the lack of increase in the descriptive essay scores and the concomitant lack of decline in BEV suggests that while writers may produce Standard English prose for one type of writing assignment, they may not exhibit the same level of control over SE in other types of assignment (9).

Although the 1988 writing assessment did not result in significantly increased writing scores from 1979–88/89, the issue of Black English in the essays was a natural outgrowth of discussions about divergence which first emerged in 1985 among national media accounts about the direction of BEV. Extending the analysis and methods of the first research, our recent study sought to examine not only the co-variation of BEV and rater scores. More critically, it examined the question of divergence vs. convergence over a 20-year time span.

Sample and Methods
The data set consists of 2,764 essays written by 17-year-old African Americans in NAEP for 1969, 1979, 1984, and 1988/89. Each essay has been given a primary trait and/or a holistic score by NAEP teacher-raters trained and experienced in holistic scoring and general writing assessment. A holistic score is an assessment of overall writing competency, what NAEP describes as "a global view of the ideas, language facility, organization, mechanics, and syntax of each paper taken as a whole" (Applebee et al., 1990, 84). Further, with holistic scoring, papers are evaluated relative to one another, rather than against specific criteria, as is the case with primary trait scoring. In 1969 and 1979, NAEP raters utilized a four-point scale for holistic scoring, and in 1984 and 1988, they used a six-point scale.

In primary trait assessment, papers are evaluated according to features of specific writing tasks. This score reflects the measure of student success of accomplishing the specific assigned purpose of the writing task. Here matters of mechanics, grammar, and syntax are subordinated to fluency and execution of the assignment. In all years under analysis here, NAEP raters utilized a four-point scale for primary trait scoring (although not the same scale across the 20-year span) (see Tables 11.1 and 11.2 for sample scales).

TABLE 11.1   NAEP primary trait scale

Score	
4	**Elaborated.** Students providing elaborated responses went beyond the essential, reflecting a higher level of coherence and providing more detail to support the points made.
3	**Adequate.** Students providing adequate responses included the information and ideas necessary to accomplish the underlying task and were considered likely to be effective in achieving the desired purpose.
2	**Minimal.** Students writing at the minimal level recognized some or all of the elements needed to complete the task but did not manage these elements well enough to assure that the purpose of the task would be achieved.
1	**Unsatisfactory.** Students who wrote papers judged as unsatisfactory provided very abbreviated, circular, or disjointed responses that did not even begin to address the writing task.
0	**Not Rated.** A small percentage of the responses were blank, indecipherable, or completely off task, or contained a statement to the effect that the student did not know how to do the task; these responses were not rated.

Table 11.2 NAEP holistic scale (imaginative essay modality)

Score	
6	A 6 story demonstrates a high degree of competence [appropriate for grade level] in response to the prompt but may have a few minor errors. A story in this category generally has the following features: • is well developed with a clear narrative structure • contains considerable detail that enriches the narrative • clearly demonstrates facility in the use of language • is generally free from errors in mechanics, usage, and sentence structure
5	A 5 story demonstrates clear competence in response to the prompt but may have minor errors. A story in this category generally has the following features: • is developed with a clear negative structure • contains details that contribute effectively to the narrative • demonstrates facility in the use of language • contains few errors in mechanics, usage, and sentence structure
4	A 4 story demonstrates competence in response to the prompt. A story in this category generally has the following features: • is adequately developed but may have occasional weaknesses in narrative structure • contains details that contribute to the narrative • demonstrates adequate facility in the use of language • may display some errors in mechanics, usage, or sentence structure but not a consistent pattern or accumulation of such errors
3	A 3 story demonstrates some degree of competence in response to the prompt but is clearly flawed. A story in this category reveals one or more of the following weaknesses: • is somewhat developed but lacks clear narrative structure • contains few details that contribute to the narrative • demonstrates inappropriate use of language • reveals a pattern or accumulation of errors in mechanics, usage, or sentence structure
2	A 2 story demonstrates only limited competence and is seriously flawed. A story in this category reveals one or more of the following weaknesses: • lacks development and/or narrative structure • contains little or no relevant detail • displays serious or persistent errors in use of language • displays serious errors in mechanics, usage, or sentence structure
1	A 1 story demonstrates fundamental deficiencies in writing skills. A story in this category reveals one or more of the following weaknesses: • is undeveloped • is incoherent • contains serious and persistent writing errors

The method for analyzing BEV in the essays was as follows. Each of the linguistic variables comprising Black English was analyzed and coded, based on the presence or absence of the variable in a specified environment (see Table 11.3). The percent of realization for each variable was computed. Then the data were statistically analyzed using analysis of variance. Pearson correlation was used for determining the co-variation of rater scores and BEV. Significance level was set at 0.05.

Although the same linguistic variables were analyzed across all four assessments, rating scales, as mentioned, differed from 1969/79 to 1984/88. Additionally, topics were different, and some differences in test administration and procedures occurred after NAEP moved to Educational Testing Service (ETS) in 1983. To adjust for these differences, comparisons were made from 1969 to 1979 and from 1984 to 1988. The 1969–79 results were then juxtaposed with the 1984–88/89 results.

TABLE 11.3   Black English variables

Variable	Example from NAEP essay
ED MORPHEME:	
Main-Verb Past (MV + Ø)	Frontier *use* corn and meat for there basic food.
Main-Verb-Perfect (Have/Had + MV + Ø)	They have *work* hard . . . to keep the crops growing good to eat.
Verbal Adjective (V + Ø)	I am writing because I am *concern* of the recreational project . . . in our town.
Passive (Be + MV + Ø)	I am *lock* in an apartment with darkness looking through this little hole.
S-MORPHEME:	
Noun-Plural (N + Ø pl)	Pioneers didn't have such *thing* . . . to keep their foods.
Noun-Possessive (N + Ø poss)	*Today* way is . . . easier.
Third Person-Singular (V + Ø)	But our environment of today *do* have refrigeration and things . . . can be stored.
HYPERCORRECTION	
(N pl + s)	But today *peoples* are able to get refrigeraters and food still spoil.
COPULA:	
Be + Main Verb (Ø + MV)	I feel like someone ___ *watching* me throwing at me.
Be + Noun (Ø + N)	He ___ a real good *citizen*.
Be + Adjective (Ø + Adj)	I think it ___ *great* to have some place to play.
Be + Preposition (Ø + Prep)	I feel really good about what ___ *around me*.
Be + Adverb (Ø + Adv)	But it *out door*.

SUBJECT-VERB
AGREEMENT-PRESENT
(Subj pl + is)   A bird and egg *is* in that car.

SUBJECT-VERB
AGREEMENT-PAST
(Subj pl + was)   The pioneers then *was* no different than what
                                        we do today.

PERFECTIVE DONE/HAVE
(Ø have/has/had + MV)   . . . the food to mostley allready ___ been
                                        cooked and caned for you . . .

IRREGULAR VERBS:
                                        But back then they *eat* a lot of heath food.

                                        So I *have gave* my opinions about what I think
                                        you should do.

MULTIPLE NEGATION
                                        Last night there was a straight-looking new
                                        bird in the neighborhood *no one never* seen
                                        before *nowhere.*

IT EXPLETIVE
(It + V + N)   *It* is a lot different things that would brighten
                                        up our community.

UNDIFFERENTIATED
THIRD-PERSON PLURAL
PRONOUN
                                        . . . soon are later they will quiet that job
                                        because they will have a lot of money in the
                                        bank for *they family* and *they self.*

PRONOMAL APPOSITION
(N Subj + P subj)   People in the old day *they* do not have
                                        refrigeration . . .

Results

First, one of the most significant results is that the frequency of BEV in *all*
essays for *all* years is generally low. This finding matches other studies of African American student writing in that BEV speech patterns are only minimally
reproduced in writing (see, e.g., Scott, 1981; Chaplin, 1987). Further, certain
prevalent BEV speech patterns occur very infrequently in writing, for example,
the classic *be* aspect, as in *They be tired.*

Now to summarize the results of the 1969–79 comparison reported in
Smitherman and Wright (1983 NCTE Research Report).

1. Black English *did decline* in the narrative essays from 1969 to 1979; however, this was not the case with the descriptive/informative essays.

2. In fact, with some features of BEV—e.g., irregular verbs, subject–verb agreement-past—there was an *increase* in the 1979 descriptive essays.

3. Copula patterns—strong indications of the African substratum that characterizes Black English—remained exactly the same over the ten-year period—i.e., 6 percent in both years.

4. There was a significant positive correlation between the amount of BEV and the rater score, even in the case of primary trait scoring (i.e., if the rater is following the scale, there should be minimal or no penalties for BEV).

In the 1984–8 comparison, juxtaposed with the 1969–79 results, the evidence emerges more clearly and unambiguously for convergence, not divergence. Significant results were found with the following linguistic variables:

1. *copula*;

2. *ED morpheme*;

3. *S morpheme*;

4. *it-expletive*.

All of these variables declined from 1984 to 1988 (see Table 11.4). Finally, in terms of the total sum of *all* Black English variables, the period from 1984 to 1988 showed a clear decline, unlike the unevenness of the 1969–79 decade (see Table 11.5).

TABLE 11.4   BEV patterns compared, 1984–88/89

Variable	Essay type and year	BEV mean
Copula	1984P	0.05
	1988P	0.04*
	1984I	0.06
	1988I	0.03**
–ED Morpheme	1984P	0.13
	1988P	0.10*
	1984I	0.18
	1988I	0.08**
–S Morpheme	1984P	0.10
	1988P	0.04**
	1984I	0.12
	1988I	0.07**
IT-Expletive	1984P	0.008
	1988P	0.04*
	1984I	0.06
	1988I	0.00**

P = Persuasive   I = Informative
* = Not statistically significant   ** = Statistically significant at 0.05 or lower

One other interesting result was made possible in 1988, a test of the interaction of essay modality and production of Black English. In the 1969–79 comparison, there was a trend toward a difference in the distribution of Black English in imaginative and informative essays. The imaginatives tended to have less Black English, both within and across years. The informatives had more BEV, and as mentioned, it actually increased in some subvariables and overall from 1969 to 1979 (see Table 11.5). We concluded then, and the statistical analysis supported this conclusion, that there is a correlation between essay modality and the production of BEV. We theorized that when the writer is familiar with the form, as in the case of the imaginative story-telling tradition in African American culture, he/she produces less Black English than is the case with culturally "foreign" essay forms. With ETS' innovation in the 1988 NAEP of having the same writers write on both the informative and persuasive topics, we were able to test this correlation further.

Results comparing the same writers' essays on "food" (informative/descriptive) and "recreation" (persuasive) were conflicting. That is, with some subvariables of Black English, there were *more* in the persuasive modality ("recreation") than in the informative ("food"), as in the case of the *ED morpheme*, for example. With others, as in the case of *It-expletive*, the Black English form occurred only in the informative (see Table 11.6). The results seem to suggest that modality might have no effect on BEV production. By using the same writers on two different tasks, NAEP's 1988 administration allowed for an analysis controlling for the effect of the writer, which we were unable to do in our 1969–79 analysis, where the writing was done by different writers on two different tasks. Yet the question of the interaction of essay modality and

TABLE 11.5   Overall BEV patterns compared, 1969–88/89

1969–79 Essay type	Year	BEV mean
Imaginative	1969	0.11
Imaginative	1979	0.09*
Informative	1969	0.10
Informative	1979	0.44**
Persuasive	Not available	Not available
1984–88/89 Essay type	Year	BEV mean
Imaginative	1984	0.11
	Not given in 1988	
Informative	1984	0.10
Informative	1988	0.06**
Persuasive	1984	0.09
Persuasive	1988	0.05**

* = Not statistically significant
** = Statistically significant at 0.05 or lower

TABLE 11.6   BEV patterns compared, same writer, persuasive
and informative essays, 1988

Variable	Persuasive	Informative
ED	0.22	0.11**
S	0.08	0.10*
COPULA	0.08	0.05
IT-EXPL	0.00	0.09*
OVERALL BEV	0.09	0.08*

* = Not statistically significant
** = Statistically significant at 0.05 or lower

BEV production still remains open because we do not yet have a comparison
of the same writers performing both *imaginative and informative (or persuasive)*
tasks (the basis of comparison that led to our conclusion about the 1969–79
NAEP essays). That is, it may very well be that the imaginative story-telling
rhetorical style is the ideal form for BEV writers. Certainly, this proposition
should be tested in future research.

We turn now to the results of rater evaluations and BEV distribution and
frequency in 1984 and 1988. With holistic scores, there continues to be what
we found in 1969–79, a significant correlation between the amount of BEV
and the rater score. As expected, it was a negative correlation (see Table 11.7).
That is, the more BEV, the lower the holistic score. This finding is not surprising, given the holistic method, which includes assessment of grammar,
mechanics, and syntax. With primary trait scores, however, a significant difference emerges in the 1984 and 1988 NAEP that we did not see earlier, no
statistically significant correlations between BEV and primary trait scores. In

TABLE 11.7   Correlations between BEV syntax and holistic or
primary trait scores, 1984 and 1988

Essay year and type	Scoring method	R-value	P-value
1984 Informative	H	−0.3192	0.0006**
1988 Informative	P	−0.0526	0.170*
1984 Persuasive	H	−0.3248	0.000**
1988 Persuasive	H	−0.1591	0.03**
1984 Imaginative	H	−0.2748	0.000**
	P	−0.0802	0.10*

H = Holistic Scoring   P = Primary Trait Scoring
* = Not statistically significant
** = Statistically significant at 0.05 or lower

the 1980s, only holistic scores proved to significantly correlate with the frequency of BEV. Further, the 1984 imaginatives, which were rated both holistically and with primary trait scoring, provide a good indication of how the same essay fares under two different rating scales. The amount of BEV syntax had a significant adverse effect on rater score only when holistic, but not primary trait, scoring was used to rate the essay (see Table 11.7). As mentioned, this contrasts sharply with the 1969 and 1979 results where BEV grammar had a significantly negative effect on rater score, *even in the case of primary trait scoring*. Ideally, if raters are assessing task accomplishment for specific features of discourse production, then features of grammar and syntax would count minimally or not at all in whether a writer accomplished the rhetorical demands of the task. This ideal was not achieved in either 1969 or 1979, but 1984 and 1988/89 NAEP raters accomplished this goal.

Finally, unlike the period from 1969 to 1979, writing scores of African American students did not exhibit any dramatic improvement over the decade from 1979 to 1988/89. However, if we look at 1984–1988, according to NAEP, "Black and Hispanic students appeared to show consistent improvements at all three grade levels, although the changes were not statistically significant" (Applebee et al., 1990, 9).

Conclusions and Implications

This analysis of Black English Vernacular in essays by African American 17-year-olds over a generational time span yields two significant conclusions: (1) BEV does not presently affect rater score in primary trait scoring; and (2) the use of BEV in writing has significantly declined since 1969.

The fact that writers are not penalized for BEV in terms of their accomplishment of specific writing tasks is testimony to the various educational and social forces that have served to sensitize teachers about dialects. We can note such movements and policies as the 1974 CCCC "Students' Right to Their Own Language"; language diversity seminars and training workshops and programs in teacher education and in school districts across the country, beginning in the 1970s; the internationally publicized *King* ("Black English") Federal Court Case in 1979; the numerous convention programs and presentations on linguistic diversity and nonstandard English since the 1970s; and the voluminous scholarly and lay publications and media attention to language issues over the past fifteen years. All of these forces and events have had an impact on the linguistic liberation of African American students in the nation's schools and classrooms. The clear implication is that teachers now seem comfortable with and demonstrate the competence to divorce success in writing modality from attention to features of grammar.

The fact that there is a pattern of decline in BEV in the NAEP essays raises questions about the Divergence Hypothesis, at least in Black *writing*, over the past twenty years. Although there was a slight, but not statistically significant, increase from 1969 to 1979, in the informative essay modality, this increase did not hold for the imaginative essays where the trend was toward a decline. More importantly, there were significant decreases in both essay

202 THE SPECIAL CASE OF AFRICAN AMERICAN LANGUAGE

types from 1984 to 1988. In the informative category, BEV *decreased* from 10 percent to 6 percent ($p = 0.0004$), *interestingly the exact number of percentage points of the increase from 1969–79*. Although NAEP raters did not code for specific BEV variables, as this study did, NAEP's conclusions about Black students' grammar may be considered as matching the general direction of the present findings. NAEP states: "For the nation as a whole, students' control of the mechanics of written English was comparable in 1984 and 1988. However, Black students showed small gains in grammar, punctuation, and spelling relative to their White counterparts" (Applebee et al., 1990, 9). This result, in combination with the present study's findings about the decline in Black English production over time, strengthens the case for BEV convergence in the direction of Edited American/Standard English over the past twenty years, at least in writing, if not in speech.

Objectively, empirically, there seems to be a case for convergence. What is the explanation for this? One possibility is today's students' increased facility in code switching, i.e., from Black to Standard English, as the situation warrants, in comparison to their counterparts in the previous generation. African American students seem to have become more adept in their command of Edited American English [standard US English that has been edited for errors in grammar, punctuation, etc.] perhaps due to increased literacy, schooling, media exposure, and heightened awareness of the importance of education. Thus the predictions of the 1960s and 1970s about eventual complete *de-creolization* (i.e., the de-Africanizing of BEV in the direction of Standard English) were not so far off the mark, as Divergence theorists have argued. It may simply be that the manifestation of de-creolization is to be found in *writing* (and other school-based language tasks), not in the oral repertoire of the African American speech community. Here the rich verbal and linguistic traditions are thriving, changing, even "diverging," and charting new paths in American popular culture forms (e.g., BEV in Rap music). I see this as a healthy state of affairs.

"THE BLACKER THE BERRY, THE SWEETER THE JUICE" [1994]

Written literacy among African American students continues to be of major concern to educators, policy makers, researchers, and the lay community. African American students have consistently scored lower than their European American counterparts in all rounds of the National Assessment of Educational Progress (NAEP) since its inception in 1969 (NAEP, 1980; Applebee, Langer, and Mullis, 1985). And even in that decade of remarkable progress for African American student writers, 1969 to 1979, where 1979 NAEP results indicated that they had improved *twice* as much as their white counterparts, African American students still were not writing on a par with white students, as the 1979 NAEP results also indicated.

The upward surge first evidenced in 1979 continued in the 1980s, though not with the same dramatic level of improvement. According to NAEP, from 1984 to 1988, "Black and Hispanic students appeared to show consistent improvements at all three grade levels, although the changes were not statistically significant" (Applebee et al. 1990, 9). Although black students' scores still do not parallel those of whites, there is some slight encouragement in NAEP's finding, particularly in light of their conclusion that generally in 1988 the nation's students "continued to perform at minimal levels on the writing assessment tasks, and relatively few performed at adequate or better levels" (Applebee et al., 1990, 6).

The topic of the African American Verbal Tradition—both its discourse modalities and its grammar—is frequently at the heart of discussion and concern about African American student writing. Of particular significance is the extent to which Black English Vernacular (BEV) patterns of syntax and discourse are reproduced in writing. A significant related issue concerns the potential correlation between a student's use of such BEV patterns and evaluation of his or her essay by writing instructors. This aspect of the study addresses both issues by focusing on BEV *discourse* patterns.

Issues in the Study

Work by researchers such as Whiteman (1976), Scott (1981), Wright (1984), Chaplin (1987), and my own earlier work on NAEP (Smitherman, 1985 NCTE Research Report) raised issues concerning comparisons of African American and European American student writers, methodological concerns about differential topics, audiences, task conditions for speech and writing, the importance of BEV discourse over BEV syntax in writing, and the relationship between the "students' right to their own language" and teacher ratings of student writing. The following crucial questions are examined here.

1. Can black student writing be characterized by an identifiable discourse style rooted in the African American Verbal Tradition?

2. If so, does use of this discourse style correlate with use of patterns of BEV grammar?

3. What effect, if any, does use of an African American discourse style have on teacher ratings of black student writing?

4. Given writing with *both* BEV discourse and BEV grammar, does one dimension have greater effect on teacher ratings than the other?

Some responses to these questions emerged from the research of Scott (1981) and Chaplin (1987). Scott controlled for the methodological shortcomings in earlier studies (for example, unequivalent topics, modalities, and audiences) by using African American college freshmen's speeches and essays on identical topics, produced under identical conditions. The essays were edited by freshman composition instructors for BEV, mechanics, spelling, and punctuation. Scott then asked the writing instructors to evaluate edited and unedited versions of the students' essays. When she compared the ratings of edited essays with ratings of corresponding unedited essays, no significant difference was found. Scott concluded that other factors such as discourse patterns were probably influencing the ratings.

Chaplin used 1984 NAEP essays for her work. (Hers is believed to be the only other research on African American student writing in NAEP.) She compared African American and European American eighth- and ninth-grade students in NAEP and African American students in the 1986 New Jersey High School Proficiency Test in an attempt to identify discourse patterns differentiating black and white students. She focused on the construct of field dependency–independency, that is, the thinker's–writer's relationship to the event, idea, phenomenon, or "field" under discussion. The field dependent thinker's–writer's style demands involvement with and a lack of distancing from the phenomenon being studied, analyzed, or communicated about. There is a tendency to see things whole, rather than segmented. The field independent thinker's–writer's style demands distance from and a lack of involvement with the field. There is a tendency to view things in parts or segments.

African American psychologists have long theorized that African Americans employ a field dependent style and European Americans a field independent style (e.g., Wilson, 1971; Williams, 1972; Simpkins, Holt, and Simpkins, 1976). Cooper (1979) did the pioneering research on linguistic correlates of field dependency, bringing together the insights of African American psychologists and communication scholars. While the notion of differing cognitive styles, varied along racial–cultural lines, has caused controversy, it is imperative to understand that we are not talking about cognitive style in the "genetic inferiority" sense used by Bereiter and Englemann (1966) or Jensen (1980). Rather, field dependency–independency emanates from different cultural orientations and world views, a view in concert with the theoretical frameworks of Von Humboldt (1841), Sapir (1929), Vološinov ([1923] 1973), Whorf (1956), Vygotsky (1962), and more recently Hymes (1974). It can be argued that we may not sufficiently understand the exact nature of the field dependency–independency constructs, yet a great deal of research substantiates that these constructs are reliable indicators of differing cultural experiences and cosmologies. Critically, and futuristically as US society becomes increasingly diverse, we must arrive at a genuine acceptance of the fact that difference does not mean deficiency.

Chaplin used black and white teacher raters to assess the African American and European American students' use of field dependency–independency as a discourse style in their essays. Her analysis led to the following observation: "[F]or more of the Black than White student writers, there was an identifiable field dependent style" (Chaplin, 1987, 26). Without being given an imposed structure or racial identification of the student writers, Chaplin's readers identified two discourse features in the black student writing that marked field dependency: cultural vocabulary–influence and conversational tone. According to Chaplin, cultural vocabulary–influence represented culture-specific words, idioms, and phrases, the language that has "helped them to shape reality" and thus "become a part of their writing" (48). Conversational tone she defined as producing an essay that reads like "recorded oral language or a conversation" (37). Although Chaplin states that there were more similarities than differences in the black and white students' writing, she does conclude that "conversational tone, cultural vocabulary, and Black Vernacular English were used more often by Black . . . students" (1990, 18).

In terms of implications for writing instruction, Chaplin advises that, since "Black students . . . seemed . . . less able to distance themselves from cultural influences," such instruction "should be conceived within the context of an understanding and appreciation of the Black experience" if we are to "maximize the potential that Black students have for writing development" (1990, 21). Chaplin's work has buttressed my own claims about a discernible African American discourse style of writing which I began to explore in analyzing the 1969 and 1979 NAEP essays. Those explorations were extended and developed, and the use of a black discourse style became the focal point in the present study.

Sample and Methods

In developing the methodology for this study, I felt it critical to compare African American student writers with one another, rather than with European American student writers. The research literature is quite definitive about the existence of an African American Verbal Tradition, with varying degrees of survival within the race (see e.g., Herskovits, 1941; Dillard, 1972; Lincoln, 1990; Thompson, 1983; Labov, 1972; Asante, 1990; Smitherman, [1977] 1986; Gates, 1988b). Our focus here was to analyze the degree to which this tradition survives in the writing of black students across a generational time span, rather than to assess the degree of borrowing from this tradition by European American students. Further, although black students are often disproportionately represented in "basic" writing courses, I felt it imperative to analyze a variety of black student writers, not just those deemed "basic" or "remedial." Because there is diversity of performance within race, writing norms can be derived from African American student performance.

In our study of 1969 and 1979 NAEP essays, we analyzed black discourse, using holistic scoring for field dependency. The discourse analysis involved only the sample of imaginative–narrative essays and employed general, impressionistic ratings of field involvement by a social psychologist, a graduate student in English, and me. We rated the essays holistically using a "field involvement score" based on the rater's assessment of the degree of distance of the writer from his or her subject matter. Some of the stylistic–linguistic features that this measurement involved were the presence of interaction between the writer and others, dialog in the essay that clearly involved the writer, the attribution of human qualities to nonhuman things, and other signals that the writer was in the environment of the communication context he or she created.

For the present work, using 1984 and 1988/89 NAEP essays, we extended and refined that earlier methodology. Several writing instructors experienced in teaching African American students and one other sociolinguist, who specializes in Black English Vernacular studies, worked with me to construct a model of African American discourse to use in analyzing the essays. First, all became conversant with work on field dependency–independency, including Cooper's and Chaplin's studies and my 1985 NAEP study. Then each instructor independently read the same 25 essays, noting any features that struck him or her as discernibly African American. Next, the group members came together to discuss and compare our lists. We repeated this same procedure twice, thus ending up with a model based on independent assessment, discussion, and 85 percent agreement about the black discourse features in 75 essays in the NAEP sample. Each time we came together for discussion, we found ourselves coming up with similar concepts, different labels and terminology to be sure, but essentially the same characteristic conceptual features. We established the following set of criteria for African American discourse in black student writing:

1. Rhythmic, dramatic, evocative language. *Example:* "Darkness is like a cage in black around me, shutting me off from the rest of the world."

2. Reference to color–race–ethnicity (that is, when topic does not call for it). *Example:* "I dont get in trouble at school or have any problems with people picking on me I am nice to every one no matter what color or sex."

3. Use of proverbs, aphorisms, Biblical verses. *Example:* "People might have shut me off from the world cause of a mistake, crime, or a sin . . . Judge not others, for you to will have your day to be judge"

4. Sermonic tone reminiscent of traditional Black Church rhetoric, especially in vocabulary, imagery, metaphor. *Example:* "I feel like I'm suffering from being with world. There no lights, food, water, bed and clothes for me to put on. Im fighten, scared of what might happened if no one finds me. But I pray and pray until they do find me."

5. Direct address–conversational tone. *Example:* "I think you should use the money for the railroad track . . . it could fall off the tracks and kill someone on the train And that is very dangerius. Don't you think so. Please change your mind and pick the railroad tracks. For the People safelty O.K." [From letter-writing, persuasive task]

6. Cultural references. *Example:* "How about slipping me some chitterlings in tonite"

7. Ethnolinguistic idioms. *Example:* ". . . a fight has broke loose"; "It would run me crazy . . ."

8. Verbal inventiveness, unique nomenclature. *Example:* "[The settlers], were pioneerific"; "[The box] has an eye look-out"

9. Cultural values–community consciousness. Expressions of concern for development of African Americans; concern for welfare of entire community, not just individuals, as for example several essays in which students expressed the view that recreational facilities would have to be for everybody, "young and old, and the homeless among Blacks"

10. Field dependency. Involvement with and immersion in events and situations; personalizing phenomena; lack of distance from topics and subjects.

The research team used holistic scoring to rank each essay in terms of the degree of African American discourse in the essay. We used a 4-point Likert-type scale, from 1 ("highly discernible African American style") to 4 ("not discernible African American style"). Each of the 1984 imaginative essays (N = 432) and a subsample (N = 435) of the 1984 and 1988 persuasive essays were coded independently by two members of our research team. In the case of a discrepancy in coding, a third member coded the essay. The total number of essays coded was 867. For 780 of the essays, or in 90 percent of the discourse sample, the two raters agreed independently on the discourse score assigned to the essay. (For sample essays from 1969 through 1988, see Sample Essays, pp. 211–15.)

Each of the essays had also been given a primary trait score or a holistic score, or both by NAEP teachers—raters trained and experienced in holistic scoring and general writing assessment. A holistic score is an assessment of overall writing competency, what NAEP describes as "a global view of the ideas, language facility, organization, mechanics, and syntax of each paper taken as whole" (Applebee et al., 1990, 84). Further, with holistic scoring, papers are evaluated relative to one another, rather than against specific criteria, as is the case with primary trait scoring. In 1969 and 1979, NAEP raters used a 4-point scale for both types of scoring. In 1984 and 1988, NAEP raters used a 6-point scale for holistic and a 4-point scale for primary trait scoring.

In primary trait assessment, papers are evaluated according to features of specific writing tasks. This score reflects the measure of student success in accomplishing the assigned purpose of the writing (Applebee et al., 1990, 6). Here, matters of mechanics, grammar, and syntax are subordinated to fluency and execution of the writing task.

For analysis, our team's discourse scores and NAEP's rater scores were compared to ascertain the degree of correlation, if any, between use of an African American discourse style and the primary trait and holistic scores assigned to an essay by raters.

Next, the discourse scores were analyzed to examine the correlation, if any, between the production of BEV syntax and the use of a black oral discourse style. BEV syntax was measured by the percentage of realization of patterns established in the literature as BEV grammatical patterns.

Results

Let us begin with a summary of the findings relative to discourse analysis and primary trait and holistic scores in NAEP 1969 and 1979. Analysis indicated the following:

1. There was no statistically significant decline in field dependency from 1969 to 1979. This finding contrasted with the significant decline in BEV syntax in the narrative mode over the decade (Smitherman and Wright, 1983a).

2. There was no correlation between use of BEV syntax and field dependency; that is, high users of BEV syntax do not necessarily use field dependent style, nor are those writers who use low BEV syntax predictably field independent.

3. There was no correlation between rater score and field dependency. By contrast, BEV syntax correlated significantly and negatively with rater score for both primary trait and holistic scoring. Even when all variables (sex, year, essay type, field dependency score) were factored into equation, BEV syntax remained the most significant predictor of rater score.

Next, we turn to the 1984 and 1988 results of discourse analysis, BEV syntax, and rater scores. As detailed above, our present NAEP study used a fully developed, explicit set of criteria for identifying varying degrees of black discourse in the 1984 imaginative essays and the 1984 and 1988/89 persuasive essays. Correlations were run between (1) the discourse score and BEV syntax, and (2) the discourse score and holistic and primary trait scores.

In the case of the first relationship, results tend to support the tendency we observed in 1969 and 1979, namely, that BEV syntax and BEV discourse are *not* co-occurring variables. No correlation was found between a discernibly African American discourse style and the production of BEV syntax. In fact, of the three sets of essay data subjected to discourse analysis, *correlations were found between BEV grammar and non-African American discourse style.* Although only one of these analyses reached statistical significance, it is interesting to note that the correlations are all positive. That is, when overall BEV syntax was high, the discourse scores tended to be high also. A high discourse score on our rating scale indicated an essay that *did not have a discernibly African American discourse style,* thus suggesting that the production of BEV grammar goes up as the writing becomes less "black" rhetorically. Although we must propose this as an observed trend, not a conclusion (see Table 11.8), it is interesting to note that this observation coincides with that of researchers who posit that "talking black" does not have to encompass features of BEV grammar (e.g., Taylor, 1992; Hoover, 1978; Smitherman, 1986a).

In the second possible relationship—between discourse score and holistic and primary trait scores—results for 1984 and 1988/89 were highly significant, in contrast to the 1969 and 1979 findings. In the 1980s, *the more discernibly African American the discourse, the higher the primary trait and holistic scores; the less discernibly African American the discourse, the lower the primary trait and holistic scores.* This finding was statistically significant for all three data sets and for both holistic and primary trait scoring (see Table 11.9). What the nega-

TABLE 11.8   Correlations between BEV syntax and discourse style, 1984 and 1988

Essay year and type	R-value	P-value
1984 Imaginative	.0361	.45*
1984 Persuasive	.1436	.05**
1988 Persuasive	.0044	.95*

* = Not statistically significant.
** = Statistically significant at .05 or less.

TABLE 11.9   Correlations between BEV discourse and holistic and
primary trait scores, 1984 and 1988

Essay year and type	Scoring method	R-value	P-value
1984 Imaginative*	P	−.1660	.001**
	H	−.1783	.000**
1984 Persuasive	H	−.3260	.009**
1988 Persuasive	P	−.1967	.002**
	H	−.3924	.000**

P = Primary trait.   H = Holistic.
* = Imaginative task not given in 1988.
** = Statistically significant at .05 or lower.

tive correlations in Table 11.9 indicate is that the higher the discourse score, the lower the rater's score. As mentioned, a high discourse score indicates an essay written in a non-African American discourse style. As it turns out, these essays were assigned lower rater scores, whether assessed by using primary trait of holistic scoring criteria. This finding held regardless of the degree of BEV grammar in a given essay, at least with primary trait scoring.

As an illustration of this finding, note the opening sentences in the two essays below. The writers are responding to NAEP's 1984 imaginative essay prompt, a picture of a box with a hole in it and an eye looking out, requiring the writers to "imagine" themselves in the picture and to describe the scene and their feelings in a "lively and interesting" way. Essay 582200 begins this way (see Sample Essays for entire essay):

> Well, a boy is in a box outside, may be in his or her back and looking through a square hole. He or she look like hear she is hiding from someone. Maybe he or she is 5 year old and some one is trying to find him/her to beat him or her up.

In terms of its degree of African American discourse, we rated this essay a 4, that is, distinctly non-black style. NAEP raters gave the essay a primary trait score of 1, and a holistic score of 2, both low scores. By contrast, essay 590877 begins this way (refer to Sample Essays, p. 213 for entire essay):

> I see little kids playing around me some on the swings, and some on the sliding bord. The kids are enjoying themselfs. As for me I'm in this box because I'm afraid of all of the other kids in the park.

We gave this essay a black discourse score of 1, that is, distinctly black style. NAEP raters gave the essay a primary trait score of 3 and a holistic score of 5, both high scores.

Now, clearly both of the above essays begin with departures from Edited American English. Yet the latter essay exhibits greater fluency and power, and it is clear that this writer is on her or his way somewhere towards a product that will be rhetorically effective. In sum, what our analysis of essays by several hundred African American student writers indicates is this: given a paper with both BEV grammar and BEV discourse, the greater the degree of black discourse, irrespective of the degree–amount of BEV grammar, the higher will be the rating in primary trait scoring, that is, scoring for fluency–accomplishment of the rhetorical task.

Finally, the imaginative–narrative essay continues to be black students' strong suit. These essays were consistently assessed higher by NAEP raters than were the 1984 or 1988 persuasives. Further, the imaginatives also exhibited higher levels of African American Verbal Tradition style, as indicated by the fact that greater numbers of these essays received discourse scores of 1 or 2 by our research team than was the case with our discourse rating of persuasives.

Conclusions and Implications

The title of this essay contains an age-old black proverb whose message speaks to the power of blackness in skin color, rhetorical fluency, and cultural affinity. For 1984 imaginative and 1984 and 1988 persuasive NAEP essays, a team of experienced writing instructors was able to identify a discernible black discourse style and establish criteria for rating the "blackness" of student essays. The team achieved a 90 percent agreement for 867 essays. Results indicated that students who employed a black expressive discourse style received higher NAEP scores than those who did not. In the case of primary trait scores, this finding held regardless of the frequency of BEV syntax (fairly low anyway, and continuing to decline over time; see Smitherman, 1992d).

There are several clear implications here for writing instructors and others concerned about African American students' written literacy. First, capitalize on the strengths of African American cultural discourse; it is a rich reservoir which students can and should tap. Second, encourage students toward the field dependency style, which enables them to produce more powerful, meaningful, and highly rated essays. Third, design strategies for incorporating the black imaginative, storytelling style into student production of other essay modalities. Fourth, de-emphasize your and your students' concerns about BEV grammar; overconcentration on these forms frequently suppresses the production of African American discourse and its rich, expressive style.

As cultural norms shift focus from "book" English to "human" English, the narrativizing, dynamic quality of the African American Verbal Tradition will help students produce lively, image-filled, concrete, readable essays, regardless of rhetorical modality—persuasive, informative, comparison–contrast, and so forth. I am often asked "how far" does the teacher go with this kind of writing pedagogy. My answer: as far as you can. Once you have pushed your students to rewrite, revise; rewrite, revise; rewrite, revise; and once they have produced the most powerful essay possible, then and only then should you have them turn their attention to BEV grammar and matters of punctuation, spelling, and mechanics.

Finally, if you are worried about preparing your students for the next level ("Well, that might be okay in *my* classroom, but then what about when they pass on to Mrs. X's class . . ."), consider the NAEP results reported here from the perspective of the teacher-raters of the 1980s and beyond. They contrast sharply with those teacher-raters in the 1969 and 1979 NAEP, where African American discourse style had no effect on rater scores. The fact that rater scores in 1984 and 1988 *positively correlated with black discourse styles* speaks favorably for the social and educational efforts of groups such as the Center for Applied Linguistics, the National Council of Teachers of English, the Conference on College Composition and Communication, and others who, over the past twenty years, have worked to sensitize teachers to the linguistic–cultural norms of the African American speech community. Many people now appear to be receptive to and subliminally aware of the rhetorical power of the African American Verbal Tradition, and in some quarters they even consciously celebrate it. Public schools and college teachers, too, now appear to understand that "the blacker the berry, the sweeter the juice."

Sample Essays

Informative, 1969

Essay 344

I remember going to the mounment when in washington. It was a tall building in which the class walk up the way up to the top, and look out the window which was somewhat very small, I didn't mind because I saw washington as it really was. After being up there for a long period of time and the teacher felt that the class had had plenty of rest, we decide to walk down the stairs. Then we went to the capital and just happen that congress was in section that day. So we listen to them for about 10 minutes. From the capital we went to the white house where the guide give us a guide the house.

Informative, 1988

Essay 540770

The unquestionable difference between food on the frontier and food today is technology. All of today's conveniences: microwaves, food processors, and even refrigeration have made food preparation and food usage far different from that of early American pioneers.

As our nation developed, so did its innovative and technological ideas. The pioneers settled on undeveloped land that yielded on certain crops and livestock. Now, we are living in a nation where almost any food is available For instance, pioneers would have never thought of eating kiwi fruit from Australia or even Lobster from Alaska.

With the increase in technology came the modernization of transportation. With varied uses of travel many type of food are now available that were unthinkable in early American life. Also with the increase in technology came convenient methods of preseration or food, namely refrigeration.

In short, the reasons for the vast array of differenes between foods on the frontier and food today are modernization and technological advances.

Imaginative, 1969

Essay 32

But, mother I am telling you the hole truth about Henry laid egg in the Chevy May be he not that kind of thing that go around eat of little thing you were say, But also you doesn't like him.

Essay 53

I am a sad sad bird. Nobody wants me because I am so weird-looking. But some day just like the Negro they will realize that I am something. May be I do have a long beck. They shouldn't juge me that way. I might look dumb to them but I have some sense. They just wont give me change to show it. They just left me out here all by myself. The don't realize. that I'm blood and skin. I'm just as good as any other bird.

Field dependent essay, a discernible black style; NAEP rater score (2), low score.

Imaginative, 1979

Essay 148

Last night a very odd-looking bird appeared in the neighborhood. Then suddenly upon seeing this odd-looking bird a kaos arose before serveral families. This was one of the biggest controversies in several years due to the fact that this town almost became a ghost town. It came to be that the appearance of this bird in the town was a runaway from the California state zoo. And their authorities had come to search for this bird and was offering a reward well over the town's income for a whole year. This incident was news making in more than thirty-eight states throughtout the country. The reason the odd bird's valuability was that it was the only of its kind left in existence. And it was carrying youn'g ready for a full life in a matter of two to three weeks. Nevertheless money to those authorities who were searching for this odd looking bird, was no object. Although the bird wich was last seen in the small village was not found there, the town's fame and popularity rose to everyone. The town was far away from being a ghost town.

Field independent essay, not a discernible black style; NAEP rater score (3), high score.

Essay 149

It was the last of its kind, the only one left. The Ornithologists did not know what to do. Cloning? No, it had only been accomplished with lower forms such as frogs and othe amphibians. Cryogenics? That won't work either, complete cell preservation is still a mystery. What can be done? The scientists thought, discussed and tried to brainstorm their way to an answer. Nothing. 'So this is what our road to the future is. A road to destruction is what it is. So this is where technology is taking us. We are the only species of animal blessed with the gift of creative thought. We are given the responsibility of life on this planet And this what we do. We can't leave well enough alone. One by one we're wiping out the inhabitants of this planet. Well gentlemen, I've come to my decision,' With that Dr Avers PhD, naturalist, etc., etc., steps over to the window, throws it open, and releases the bird. Everyone watches in silence, with mixed feeling as the last of a dying species comes to grips with freedom and with powerful wing strokes gracefully drifts into the horizon.

Imaginative, 1984

Essay 582200

Well, a boy is in a box outside, may be in his or her back and loking through a square hole. He or she look like hear she is hiding from someone. Maybe he or she is 5 year old and some one is trying to find him/her to beat him or her up. There for a hour the person in the box stay there and it is getting dark. The person looking for the kid in the box knows where the kid is a waiting for that person to come out.

NEAP primary trait score (1), holistic score (2), both low; discourse score (4), not a discernible black style.

Essay 590877

I see little kids playing around me some on the swings, and some on the sliding bord. The kids are enjoying themselfs. As for me I'm in this box because I'm afraid of all of the other kids in the park. In a distinance I see a baseball field and some men playing and over by the park is a Basketball court where other kids are playing. And in the picnic grounds theirs a family having a picnic. The kids are playing catch with their father while the mother I think is setting up the picnic area. In another section of the park theirs a crowd of people watching these two guys "break" dancing. "Break" dancing is a new form of dance combining some gymnistics with some regular dance moves. It is a real sight to see. Also I see some girls on the sidewalk jumping rope double dutch style that's when you use two ropes. The girls are very good to. It is a hot day so I see that the swimmin pool is doing good today. I would be over their myself if I wasn't shy. It's a very hot in this box but I'm so afraid to come out. I see that a fight has broke loose by the swings. Two little kids are fighting over one see all the other kids have already taken all the other swings and their two kids and only one swing left. I think that the kids have settled their argument now.

    Now here comes a big black man over by me now. He says that my mother is here to pick me up so I could go home By.

NAEP primary trait score (3), holistic score (5), both high; discourse score (1), a highly discernible African American style.

Persuasive, 1984

Essay 050238

I think that if the ABandoned RailRoad track was not there. that we can use the money that we have saved could go on the things we need for the community center. So that the children can have many & more things to do. The

RailRoad could Be destroyed so that they can make a play ground out of It. And the warehouse could have some toys In It Also Just in case it get cold or Rain. Therefore they could have toys Inside and outside.

NAEP holistic score (2), low score; discourse score (4), not a discernible black style.

Persuasive, 1988

Essay 520462

How are you doing? Fine I hope!

I'm writing you this letter in reference to you making your purchase in buying the warehouse.

I think that in buying the old warehouse, we could paint it and fix it up and make it out of a gym for the kids during the week and on weekends and on Fridays we could have bingo and maybe once or twice a month on Sundays we could give a super.

During the week we could have the children come here after school and do their homework and then let them play a little basketball, until about 5:30 p.m.

On Fridays at about 7:00 we could set up for Bingo and sell the cards 8 for $10 and that way we could help pay for the pot and have 14 games and cherry betts.

Every first or last Sunday in the month we could give a super for the community and sell each plate for $3 to $5.

If you have any questions, please feel free to call me at 288-8263.

Sincerely,

Ms. Zenitta

NAEP holistic score (4), high score; discourse score (1), a highly discernible black style.

Essay 541082

I live about one mile or two from the big old warehouse that's for sale. Most of the time I am at home reading, doing homework, or watching television. But on weekends if I am not out with my friends I have nothing else to do. I think the big old warehouse would be a good place to renovate and turn it into a center for young people who have to go home to an empty house after school, latchkey kids, who need counseling, or just don't have nothing better to do on weekends, but sit around the house or go out and start trouble.

Sometimes I go home to an empty house and I'm scared or just down right bored. I wouldn't mind having a place to go where I can talk to other people my age or play with the little kids who are there.

The warehouse could even have counselors to help young people who have trouble in their homes, are on drugs, drink too much, or pregnant teenagers who have no one to share their feelings with.

I have seen some young people, even kids the age of six or seven stealing or starting fights or just hanging out late on school days and weekends because their parents are never home to take care of them. Maybe if they had a place to go; A place where they could do activities or have a chance to show the talent that they have things would be a little different.

I hope you think about everything I've said carefully before you make your decision. If you have any questions please feel free to call me at 465-8429 anytime after 4:00 p.m.

Sincerely yours,

WORKS CITED

Applebee, A., Langer, J., and Mullis, I. (1985), *Writing Trends Across the Decade, 1974–84*, Princeton, NJ: Educational Testing Service.

Applebee, A., Langer, J., Mullis, I., and Jenkins, L. (1990), *The Writing Report Card 1984–8*, Princeton, NY: Educational Testing Service.

Asante, M. K. (1990), "African Elements in African American English," in J. Holloway (ed.), *Africanisms in American Culture*, Bloomington: Indiana University Press, 19–33.

Bereiter, C., and Engelmann, S. (1966), Teaching Disadvantaged Children in Pre-School, Englewood Cliffs, NJ: Prentice Hall.

Blackwell, J. E. (1981), *Mainstreaming Outsiders: The Production of Black Professionals*, Bayside, NY: General Hall.

Chaplin, M. (1987), "An Analysis of Writing Features Found in the Essays of Students in the National Assessment of Educational Progress and the New Jersey High School Proficiency Test," unpublished manuscript, Rutgers University, Department of English, Camden, NJ.

Chaplin, M. (1990), "A Closer Look at Black and White Students' Assessment Essays," *Iowa English Bulletin*, 38, 15–27.

Cooper, G. (1979), "The Relationship Between Errors in Standard Usage in Written Compositions of College Students and the Students' Cognitive Styles," unpublished doctoral dissertation, Howard University, Washington, DC.

Dillard, J. L. (1972), *Black English*, New York: Random House.

Gates, H. L. (1988), *The Signifying Monkey: A Theory of Afro-American Library Criticism*, New York: Oxford University Press.

Herskovits, M. (1941), *Myth of the Negro Past*, Boston: Beacon Press.

Hoover, M. (1978), "Community Attitudes Towards Black English," *Language in Society*, 7, 65–87.

Hymes, D. (1974), *Foundations in Sociolinguistics*, Philadelphia: University of Pennsylvania Press.

Jensen, A. R. (1980), *Bias in Mental Testing*, New York: Free Press.

Labov, W. (1972a), *Sociolinguistic Patterns*, Philadelphia: University of Pennsylvania.

Labov, W. (1972b), *Language in the Inner City*, Philadelphia: University of Pennsylvania.

Labov, W., and Harris, W. A. (1986), "De Facto Segregation of Black and White Vernaculars," in Sankoff, D. (ed.), *Diversity and Diachrony*, Amsterdam: John Benjamins, 1–4.

Lincoln, C. E. (1990), *The Black Church in the African American Experience*, Durham, NC: Duke University Press.

National Assessment of Educational Progress (1980), "Writing Achievement, 1969–79" (Report No. 10-W-01), Denver, CO: Education Commission of the States.

Sapir, E. (1929), *Language: An Introduction to the Study of Speech*, New York: Harcourt, Brace.

Scott, J. C. (1981), "Mixed Dialects in the Composition Classroom," in Montgomery, M. (ed.), *Language Variety in the South: Perspectives in Black and White*, Montgomery: University of Alabama Press.

Simpkins, G., Holt, G., and Simpkins, C. (1975), *Bridge: A Cross-Culture Reading Program Field Test Report*. Boston: Houghton Mifflin.

Smitherman, G., ([1977] 1986), *Talkin and Testifyin: The Language of Black America*, Boston: Houghton Mifflin; reissued, with revisions, Detroit: Wayne State University Press.

———. (1983), "American English in its Death Throes: Is We Sick?" *North Carolina English Teacher*, winter, 4–7.

———. (1986a), "Talkin and Testifyin: Black English and the Black Experience," in *Les Temps Modernes*, (ed.) Santamaria, U., December, 112–29. [Article translated into French, in special journal issue on Black Americans.]

———. (1986b), "Upside the Wall: The Afro-American Mural Movement," with Donaldson, J. R., in *The People's Art: Black Murals, 1967–78*, (ed.) Burnham, I., Philadelphia: Afro-American Historical and Cultural Museum.

———. (1992), "Black English, Diverging or Converging?: The View from the National Assessment of Educational Progress," *Language and Education*, 6(1).

————. (1994), " 'The Blacker the Berry, the Sweeter the Juice': African American Student Writers and the NAEP," in *The Need for Story: Cultural Diversity in Classroom and Community*, (eds.) Dyson, A. H., and Genishi, C., Urbana: National Council of Teachers of English, 1994.

Taylor, O. (1992, June), Presentation at African American English in Schools and Society Conference, Stanford University, Stanford, CA.

Thompson, R. F. (1983), *Flash of the Spirit: African and Afro-American Art and Philosophy*, New York: Random House.

Vaughn-Cooke, F. (1987), "Are Black and White Vernaculars Diverging?" *American Speech*, vol. 62, pp. 62–72.

Vološinov, V. N. ([1929] 1973), *Marxism and the Philosophy of Language*, translated by L. Matjka and I. R. Tutnik, Cambridge: MIT.

Von Humboldt, W. ([1810] 1963), "Man's Intrinsic Humanity: His Language," in Cowan M. (ed.), *Humanist Without Portfolio*, Detroit: Wayne State University Press.

Vygotsky, L. S. (1962), *Thought and Language*, Cambridge: MIT.

Whiteman, M. (1976), "Dialect Influence and the Writing of Black and White Working-Class Americans," unpublished doctoral dissertation, Georgetown University, Washington, DC.

Whorf, B. (1956), *Language, Thought and Reality: Selected Writings of Benjamin Lee Whorf*, Carroll, J. B. (ed.), Cambridge: MIT Press.

Williams, R. L. (1972), *The Bitch 100: A Culture-Specific Test*, St. Louis: Washington University.

Wilson, R. (1971), "A Comparison of Learning Styles in African Tribal Groups with African American Learning Situations and the Channels of Cultural Connection: An Analysis of Documentary Material," unpublished doctoral dissertation, Wayne State University.

Wolfram, W. (1990), "Re-examining Vernacular Black Speech," *Language*, vol. 66, 121–35.

Wright, S. (1984), "A Description between the Oral and Written Language Patterns of a Group of Black Community College Students," unpublished Ph.D. dissertation, Wayne State University, Detroit.

12

Students' Right to Possibility: Basic Writing and African American Rhetoric

KEITH GILYARD AND ELAINE RICHARDSON

Background

In 1974, a special issue of *College Composition and Communication* contained both a resolution asserting students' right to their own language and attendant explanations of the sociolinguistic and pedagogical premises that shaped the resolution. The combined statement, revolving around a core concept of linguistic equality, supported certain progressive work around questions of language, identity, hegemony, and inclusion—with much of the focus on African American students—that was unfolding inside composition studies generally and the basic writing wing in particular. Although the document and sentiment behind it have remained important, especially during the latest publicized skirmish in the decades-old Ebonics controversy, the SRTOL is still controversial.

Predictably, conservatives have never embraced it and seek to undermine its expression whenever it appears to threaten their sense of order and, perhaps, control. For example, in an attempt to maintain the status quo, they discourage vernacular usage in schools, usually with an argument that they are preparing so-called minority students for success in the market place, all while many of the most successful people in the market place are running off with fresh stacks of pretty little green ones accumulated to the advertising beat of hip hop.

Even some on the other end of the political spectrum, who support the document, criticize its framers and others who have since defended it. Patrick Bruch and Richard Marback, for instance, do seek to "reinvigorate the statement's hope for democratic literacy instruction and democratic social transformation" (269). They are, however, disappointed with talk of repertoire expansion and code-switching that derives from the SRTOL, considering such discussion to be merely liberal, overly restrictive, and indicative of some unwillingness to link questions of literacy to specific social justice efforts. However, they have no way to prove this alleged political bashfulness (backwardness?)

From *Insurrections: Approaches to Resistance in Composition Studies*, ed. Andrea Greenbaum (Albany: State University of New York Press, 2001), 37–51.

because they offer no assessment of practices that derive from the discussions of which they are critical. One would have to explore the educational context in which code-switching is employed to make an informed judgment as to whether it is simply a ploy of liberal pluralism or truly a radical stratagem. Cornel West certainly employs a good measure of code-switching during his public articulations of prophetic pragmatism, the philosophical premise that undergirds Bruch and Marback's work.

But there is no need for too big a fight here. The left has perhaps proved as adept at squabbling among itself as anything else. We are actually supportive of a platform more radical than liberal, but we would have everyone be wary of making totalizing statements relative to SRTOL and its aftermath. We should bear in mind that collaboration on a document like SRTOL does not necessarily mean that its composers were of identical theoretical persuasion, nor does the existence of SRTOL imply that strict uniformity exists among the practitioners supportive of the manifesto. Both of these points, as Steve Parks notes in his historical study, are sometimes obscured. While some originators and subsequent advocates have been content simply to articulate and promote goals of bidialectalism and assimilation, other central figures, such as Geneva Smitherman, have embraced a greater activism. As Smitherman reminds us, putting standard speech in the mouth of Black students "ain done nothin to address the crises in the Black community." Furthermore, in *Black English*, one of the key texts informing the SRTOL resolution, J. L. Dillard argued that English departments accept quality work in African American Vernacular English (AAVE), a proposal that also ranges beyond simplistic notions of code-switching (278–79).

There was never a shortage of ideas about how SRTOL could be implemented beyond a liberal pluralist paradigm, just a shortage of empirical models. We thus offer one. In doing so we shift the terms of engagement somewhat; we extend the notion of "Students' Right to Their Own Language" to a question of "Students' Right to Possibility." We acknowledge language rights at the outset, and this allows us to place our emphasis on the ways of knowing and becoming that our students exhibit—and that we help them exhibit—as they negotiate the structures of academic schooling.

A curriculum designed to implement the principles of the SRTOL as it concerns the teaching of writing to African American students obviously needs to address the central question of to what extent African American speech styles can be instrumental to the development of critical academic writing. Attempting to answer this question takes us beyond appreciation of AAVE and recognition of its equality to other language varieties to a consideration of AAVE's role in a creative, intellectually engaging, persuasive, and at times revolutionary discourse.

The Study[1]

The research reported here derives from four basic writing classes taught at two major universities spanning winter 1996 to winter 1998. Essays were collected from fifty-two students. Because of limited access to African American students in the institutions in which this work was carried out, the same course was taught repeatedly over several semesters, using the same course materials and research procedures. Students were solicited through campus advertisements that announced a writing course featuring Afrocentric topics. When students inquired about signing up for the course, the researcher explained course objectives, gave students syllabi, and obtained permission to use their writing in any report of the research done on the course. The student-subjects received writing instruction over a one-quarter, ten-week time frame, or a fifteen-week semester, using African-centered materials and instructional stimuli.

THE STUDENTS

The subjects of this study were fifty-two African American first-year students—thirty females and twenty-two males—who placed into basic writing. For purposes of this research, any student of African descent living in America for at least ten years was considered a member of AAVE culture. In line with the emphasis on possibilities that extend beyond rights associated with surface features, AAVE discourse is given precedence over syntax, with "discourse" being employed to suggest units of meaning beyond the sentence level. In addition, AAVE discourse is defined here as the language practices that have been largely used and developed by people of African descent in the United States as a survival and self-advancement strategy. We think of discourse, therefore, in the sense that Jim Gee does:

> All school activities, and thus all literacy activities, are bound to particular Discourses. There is no such thing as "reading" or "writing," only reading or writing *something* (a text of a certain type) in a certain way with certain values, while at least appearing to think and feel in certain ways. We read and write only within a Discourse, never outside all of them. (xviii)

A main focus of this experimental curriculum is for African American students to identify themselves as being situated within African American Vernacular discourse. They certainly are members of other discourse communities as well, but none speaks to their African Americaness as directly. Confronted with a pervasive racism, which is embedded in dominant texts or official discourses, most African Americans feel a need to reaffirm their African American selves, individually and collectively. This is often accomplished primarily through language, as is evident in the rich tradition of African American literacy. Hence, students are being asked to see themselves in this tradition as a means of developing their critical consciousness and literacy skills.

INSTRUMENTATION

Seven instruments were used to collect the data: (1) a holistic assessment scale; (2) a demographic questionnaire; (3) a language/writing attitude questionnaire; (4) the African Self-Consciousness Scale (ASC); (5) an AAVE Syntax Scale, (6) a Black Discourse Scale, and (7) field notes. The data reported here do not deal with ASC or AAVE Syntax scales so they will not be discussed any further. The present analyses deal most directly with the assessment of the students' writing and use of Black discourse features in the writing. These Black discourse patterns were also used to determine the level of AAVE in the students' writing samples. The primary data reported here focus on discourse and rhetorical analyses of an out-of-class essay, non-impromptu, where students had time to work outside of class on the essays for at least two weeks. This set of essays has been subjected to discourse/rhetorical analysis and compared with other studies of culturally different student writing with respect to the presence or absence of selected discourse features. Black discourse was assessed by measuring the frequency and distribution of such features as they occurred in students' texts. Discourse features were coded based on a modified version of Smitherman's (p. 191 in this book) typology. The researcher and an assistant independently coded essays and then met to compare and synthesize their findings. Forty-seven essays were given a discourse rating from five to one on a continuum from Black to European-styled discourse, with five representing a highly Black discourse-styled essay and one a European discourse-styled essay. Features of Black discourse that occurred in the data from this study are the following:

1. Rhythmic, dramatic, evocative language. Use of metaphors, significations, vivid imagery. Example: "Our history through the eyes of white America after it has been cut, massacured and censored is pushed down Blacks throath."

2. Proverbs, aphorisms, Biblical verses. Employment of familiar maxims or Biblical verses. Example: ". . . there is a time and place for everything."

3. Sermonic tone reminiscent of traditional Black church rhetoric, especially in vocabulary, imagery, metaphor. Example: "The man should once again be the leader of the household as God intended and the female . . . the helpmate."

4. Direct address, conversational tone. These two are not necessarily the same, but often co-occur. Speaking directly to audience. Also, can be a kind of call/response. Example: "Would you rather be respected as Aunt Jemima and Sambo or Queen Nzinga . . . ? As yourself or someone else . . . ?"

5. Cultural references. Reference to cultural items/icons that usually carry symbolic meaning in the AAVE communities. Example: "There are still those Uncle Toms . . . out to get you."

6. Ethnolinguistic idioms. Use of language that bears particular meaning in Black communities. Example: ". . . Black english is a 'Black Thang' you wouldn't understand. . . . That's on the real!"

7. Verbal inventiveness, unique nomenclature. Example: ". . . [W]e will begin dealing with this deep seeded self-destruction and self-hate. . . ."

8. Cultural values, community consciousness. Expressions of concern for the development of African Americans; concern for welfare of entire community, not just individuals. Example: "Before Blacks can come together in racial harmony they need to strengthen their own people. Trying to unite . . . will only cause more problems if we have not taken care of our own business."

9. Field dependency. Involvement with and immersion in events and situations; personalizing phenomena; lack of distance from topics and subjects. Example: "... [w]e should first try to accomplish better race matters within ourselves. We can do this by patronizing and supporting our Black community."

10. Narrative sequencing. Dramatic retelling of a story implicitly linked to topic, to make a point. Reporting of events dramatically acted out and narrated. Relating the facts and personal sociopsychological perspective on them. Example: "I have learned ... some things that never crossed my path in thirteen years of miseducation. ... This was very important for me because I ... felt that [my] writing was wrong and far beyond improving. ..."

11. Tonal semantics (repetition of sounds or structures to emphasize meaning). Example: "European views are the rules. ..." "We are victimized ..." [structure repeated four times in subsequent sentences].

12. Signifying. Use of indirection to make points. May employ oppositional logic, overstatement, understatement, and/or reliance on reader's knowledge of implicit assumption that is taken to be common knowledge (shared worldview). Example: "In light of having limited means of getting first hand information we then have had to rely on books and the media to provide us with an unbiased account of information ... we know how honest the media is."

13. Call/response (structural). Writer returns repetitiously to the prompt as a structural device, checking for constant connection with the question or text at hand. A repeated invocation of the language from the prompt, manifested as a refrain. Example: "... be a member of the AAVE Culture and literate. ..." "Black and literate. ..." "... Blacks being literate" (repeated four times).

14. Testifying. Telling the truth through story. Bearing witness to the righteousness of a condition or situation. Example: "I use [the works of Angelou and Douglass] to liberate myself from my hardships to come."

15. Topic association. A series of associated segments that may seem anecdotal in character, linked implicitly to a particular topical event or theme, but with no explicit statement of the overall theme (Ball 1992).

Essays were analyzed for actual occurrences of the above-mentioned features and given an overall rating. The typology above is based on Smitherman (p. 206), except where indicated. All of the examples, however, were gleaned from students' essays.

Quantitative analyses focused on correlation of writing assessment scores and Black discourse scores. The demographic and language attitude questionnaires along with field notes are used to supplement analyses of texts and students' experiences in the course.

PROCEDURES

The research population of African American college students received training that involved four components: (a) instruction in academic writing/rhetorical practices incorporating rhetorical and discursive practices of African American Vernacular English (AAVE) culture, (b) examination of the African

American literacy tradition through exploration of values, beliefs, and history as presented in African American texts and media, (c) the writing process (prewriting, drafting, revising, editing, etc.), and (d) writing workshops. A fundamental aspect of the course was introducing students to Black discourse patterns from an analytical point of view. Students studied excerpts from Smitherman's *Talkin and Testifying*, especially the section on Black modes of discourse. They also studied examples from Smitherman's typology and other articles; they analyzed rap lyrics and studied various media and texts that exemplified Black discourse styles. Rhetorical devices were examined in several enslavement narratives and other literature by African Americans such as Sister Souljah's *No Disrespect*. Activities and assignments were developed which encouraged students to experiment with these Black discourse and rhetorical patterns.

HOLISTIC WRITING ASSESSMENT, DEMOGRAPHIC, AND LANGUAGE ATTITUDES SCALES

The holistic writing assessment scale consists of eight categories, with 4.0 representing a well-developed and well-written essay that successfully attempted a thorough response to the prompt, moving to various scores, 3.5, 3.0, etc., representing different levels of idea development and command of the written code, ending at 0.0, which represents a poorly written response that did not address the task. AAVE was not specifically mentioned on the scoring rubrics. The demographic/informative questionnaire functioned to provide socio-cultural information. The language/writing attitude questionnaire was used to uncover the subjects' perceptions of themselves as writers and to obtain subjects' language attitudes, the writing process, and the course experience and was administered pre and post curriculum.

RATER INFORMATION

For each student in the research population, a panel of experts assessed writing samples. Each essay received two ratings using the holistic writing assessment scale. The ratings were averaged. The raters were experienced composition professionals who regularly taught college-level writing both to students of color and others. All were members of the National Council of Teachers of English (NCTE) or the Conference on College Composition and Communication (CCCC). Twenty raters participated in this study, twelve women and eight men. Two of the women were of European American descent. Nine of the women were African American. One woman was of Asian descent. There were four European American male raters, three African American male raters, and one Latino male rater. The average level of teaching experience for the raters was 18.2 years of college-level instruction. The least experienced rater had taught writing for four years. The most experienced rater had taught writing for forty-nine years.

PROMPT

Students were asked to compose an essay in response to a prompt that revolved around the African American rhetorical tradition, as discussed in Bormann (1971):

> Perhaps the greatest distinction between current Black rhetorics and the rhetoric of abolition is that the main audience for the latter had to be the white community, because in the 1830s and the 1840s the great bulk of the Blacks were slaves and could not be reached by the words of the speakers and writers. Today a rhetorician planning a persuasive campaign for reform of race relations can decide to adopt a strategy of unity with the entire society, white and nonwhite, as did Martin Luther King and his followers and as did some leaders of the biracial Congress of Racial Equality (CORE), or they may choose to adopt a strategy of divisiveness and appeal primarily to the Black audience.

Students were asked to interpret the passage by Bormann, certainly controversial in and of itself, and explain a contemporary approach to a persuasive campaign to reform race relations in this country. They were encouraged to use whatever sources from the course readings they needed to support their arguments and to incorporate Black discourse and rhetorical patterns. Students specifically were asked to compose college-level responses, using their best prose, including Black discourse styles.

QUANTITATIVE ANALYSIS

One of the tenets of the African-centered writing curriculum is that form and content are inseparable. In other words, language use reflects ideology. African Americans often write from a deeply felt sense of what their experiences as African Americans has revealed to them, and they frequently feel compelled to employ Black discursive and rhetorical strategies. One of Smitherman's (p. 210) findings was that African American students who used more Black discourse scored higher than those students who did not. Following Smitherman's lead, an analysis was conducted to determine whether essays received higher essay scores with greater use of Black discourse features. In order to examine the relationship of AAVE discourse use and essay ratings, a bivariate analysis was conducted using essay mean scores and Black discourse mean scores. The results, shown in the table below, are statistically significant.

The Relationship between Black Discourse Usage and Essay Scores

Essay (Admin 2)	Scoring Method	R-Value	P-Value
Rhetorical/Argumentative	Holistic	.85	.000*

*Statistically significant at .01 or lower

As was found in Smitherman (p. 210), there was a positive correlation between the use of Black discourse and higher scoring essays. In other words, student texts were not down-graded because of the use of Black discourse features, a fact that suggests that teaching African American students—especially or including basic writers—to develop their voices within the context of their own literacy and rhetorical traditions can help them to avoid the tangled discourses famously alluded to by Mina Shaughnessy in *Errors and Expectations.*

The most frequently used Black discourse features were "cultural values," "community consciousness" and "field dependency." The nature of the prompt, its basis in the Black experience, seems to have influenced the students' heightened involvement. Among the many Black discourse features, it is interesting to note the employment of field dependency. Generally, field dependency functions in opposition to the "objectivity" and "neutrality" that characterize academic discourse. Field dependency is the hallmark of the Black style, a signature feature. It is as salient a Black discourse feature as "zero copula" is for AAVE syntax.

QUALITATIVE ANALYSIS

Instead of analyzing a single text or concentrating on a single student, we will look here at several samples from various students' texts in order to convey a feel for the Black discourse-styled texts produced.

Student #1 Winter 97

By feeding into the stereotypes that America has created the African American race will never advance being ignorant, militant, and extremely violent because all that is just adding fuel to the fire. Instead we need to take that same energy and convert it into something positive and productive for the upliftment of our race. By creating wise, well researched criticism America will [have] no choice but to listen especially if the information that is being presented is reaching through to miseducated Americans, (not only the African-Americans) and is *turning them on to the light*. Causing positive ruckus is far more beneficial than negative ruckus and you can't go to prison for speaking the truth. That's a right we are protected under by the Constitution. *By enlightening the darkened* we will be threatening the "secure" establishments America has created to prolong oppression.

There are several Black discourse patterns that can be discerned above. One pattern above is rhythmic, dramatic, evocative/imagistic language use. Notice the play above on "light." The "miseducated Americans" are those Blacks and non-Blacks who have bought into racial stereotypes. The rhetor has turned this stereotype upside down and inside out, revealing another Black language pattern, signifying. The "darkened" or the "miseducated" will be "en*light*ened." The quality of light has been traditionally associated with "knowledge," "goodness," and, hence White folks. Darkness has traditionally been associated with a "state of ignorance," or "evil," and consequently, Black folks. But here, the Blacks possess or will possess the qualities of knowledge and light. This is an instance of signifying, also known as semantic inversion.

Student #2 Winter 97

Unity consists of several movements that need to take place within the African American community. I believe first and foremost we, as a people, must deal with the disease of Black on Black crime. We must cry out to our young brothers out there who are destroying themselves, and everyone around them, by murdering one another. I remember very recently hear a quote on the radio stating that the number one killer of young, Black men today is young, Black men. When we begin to really take militant steps in an effort to stop the murder rate in our communities, then we will begin dealing with this deep seeded self-destruction and self-hate that has planted its poisons into the hearts and souls of our young adults. . . .

There are several Black discourse patterns that can be identified from the above essay excerpt. This essay demonstrates "direct address/conversational tone)" in that it assumes an immediacy with the audience. The rhetoric is directed toward Black people. For this reason, the writer uses the pronoun "we" and the ethnolinguistic idiom "brothers," which is a lexical item for Black men. Also interesting is the rhetor/writer's incorporation of a narrative interspersion as a testimony to Black-on-Black crime. The most interesting Black discourse pattern here though is the use of rhythmic dramatic, evocative/imagistic language: ". . . [W]hen we begin dealing with this deep seeded self-destruction and self-hate that has planted its poisons into the hearts and souls of our young adults. . . ." "Deep seeded" is itself an instance of "verbal inventiveness." The standard term that this item brings to mind is "deep seated." However, the writer here creates "deep seeded" as it is more in line with the writer's meaning expressed through the metaphor of poison garden. This garden has been grown through the seeds of "self-hate" and "self-destruction" that have been planted in Black communities.

Student #3 Winter 97

Trust and honor make up the soul of African-Americans. Is that trust and honor still with us? Where did it go? During a time when we were lost in a strange land some four centuries ago the only face to bring comfort was that of another African lost in the same wilderness far from home, far from our roots. Within those last four hundred years we have struggled to gain our freedom and our African hearts. The price we paid for this American freedom was our ability to trust and the fire to come together as one. Our satisfaction with freedom in America overshadowed our dream to be Africans again. Four hundred years of losing our languages, morals, and originality has reduced us to rearrange our ways to seek the same gods that caused Europeans to bring us to this country, such as money, cars, and a million dollar home. I say, head for the underground railroad one more time African, because you are not free if you can't love your brother.

The above writer/rhetor is clearly adopting the rhetorical strategy of directing his/her rhetoric to a Black audience. The discourse evidences no nonstandard Black vernacular syntax but is yet styled in AAVE discourse. Notice the conversational tone/direct address, the use of the questions, and the admonition, "I say, head for the underground railroad one more time African, because you are not free if you cannot love your brother." This sentence contains evocative-imagistic, ideographic language use in its employment of the "underground railroad" symbol. The underground railroad symbolizes a freedom from thinking of oneself in terms of European ideals. Further, the essay uses the common Black discourse pattern of cultural values/community consciousness.

Student #6 Winter 97

To me this [the rhetoric of divisiveness—focus on a Black audience] sounds like a wonderful rhetorical strategy. Unfortunately, this strategy will only take us so far. I believe Blacks in this nation will not come together because there is too much jealousy and greed between our people.

Our people struggle with the concept of working together and having unity. The economic situation has most of the money in the hands of white people. The only way to solve problems we have between various cultural backgrounds is to work with other whites.

Divisive rhetoric is like a bunch of Black people knocking on the door of the White house. On the other side of the door, are a bunch of white people. The scenario becomes that you will never get in no matter how much you knock unless the white person on the other side of the door opens it. My point is that divisive rhetoric will get Blacks to the door, but not inside the door.

The above writer/rhetor is arguing for and employing the rhetoric of unity which in Bormann's terms is directing his/her rhetoric to a racially mixed (White, Black, multicultural) audience and is styling her/his discourse to reflect this. This essay, however, is very problematic because of its inherent contradictory premises. The writer argued against Black unity (divisiveness rhetoric), but at the same time used an analogy with Black people united. "Divisive rhetoric is like a bunch of Black people knocking on the door of the White house. . . ." In any case, the writer employs a conversational tone and a familiarity with his/her audience.

Student #7 Winter 97

The diverseness rhetoric would not work for this plan of action, because the decisions needed to be made would have to be made with all Americans in mind. I'm not saying that diverseness would not work in easing race relations, But it is not the means I would choose to fix whats been brokien for so long. Race, Race is a term a ignorant word, it has nothing to do with people it was [a] term used for seperating people, and I think this is what caused all of this trouble in the first place. Let me explain, if you use race to catagorize someone, there must be a dominant race of people. A white person made up race so who do you think thinks they're the dominant race, that's right you guessed it. Unity is the key, once White America is turned into everybody America, this place will finally be what everybody makes it out to be, a great country.

This writer/rhetor is arguing for the rhetoric of unity, directing his/her rhetoric to a racially mixed (White, Black, multicultural) audience. The writer seeks to deracialize the problem while at the same time showing that the problem is white domination of America. The writer employs conversational tone as a rhetorical strategy to create credibility with his/her reader, hoping to persuade readers to his/her point of view.

The above excerpts from students' papers demonstrate various levels of written literacy development. Not all of the student writers had realized their writing potential, but they certainly were on their way, spurred on by Black discourse strategies such as field dependency. To report on the students' long-term gains is beyond the scope of this essay, but further data, which will be reported in subsequent publications, does exist to support the instructional design implemented. Black discursive style, rather than a quality to be merely appreciated, is essential to the development of a Black, formal, public voice.

To get a sense of the students' perception of the curriculum, it may be helpful to look at student reflections on ways in which the learning about AAVE and the Black literacy tradition was beneficial to them:

Student #20 Fall 96

It helped me develop a better understanding of our language and possibly why other people may not get it. I was exposed to some excellent literature.

Student #15 Fall 96

The course helped me understand more about the AAVE culture and language.

Student #21 Fall 96

This course has helped me to recognize the difference between standard english and Black english and to be able to write according to my audience.

Student #3 Fall 96

This course has helped me to identify my weakness in writing. I also feel more comfortable about my writing style and the Black discourse I use because now have control over it.

Student #14 Fall 96

I have become more aware about the language of my people. I learned that to talk Black is not to talk improper; it is just a different way of talking. I learned to take more pride in my people and my ancestors.

Student #6 Fall 96

It has opened my eyes to the struggles of African Americans. I learned to write in the language of Wider Communication and Black English at the same time. It has been very useful, and will continue to be as I pursue my English degree.

Student #12 Fall 96

I have learned to coincide my voice with the voice of the work I am critiquing to come up with a proper analysis of the subject.

Student #19 Fall 96

I honestly feel that I learn and comprehended so much information because I was learning about my people. In addition I was learning with my peers. I am happy that Sister [. . .] was the instructor of this course. She knew the course material very well therefore it was easier for the class to learn. She was able to teach from her heart and soul. You don't find many instructors like that. This class has not only given me the opportunity to learn more about my culture, I have also had more confidence towards all my classes because of my new found identity.

CONCLUSION

By making the African American rhetorical tradition the centerpiece of attempts to teach academic prose to African American students, especially those characterized as basic writers, we believe that we increase the likelihood that they will develop into careful, competent, critical practitioners of the written word. Such students seem to become more vested in improving their writing when it is directly and functionally connected in this manner to issues and exercises that are of immediate concern to them. This approach does not "essentialize" Black students, to anticipate a criticism that always seems just around the corner these days when ethnic identity is discussed. Neither is it an argument for limiting the enormous benefits of studying African American rhetoric to a strictly African American population. Rather, this method serves as recognition that the path to broad articulations for those who have generally been alienated from the so-called mainstream often runs through intensive valuing of and practice in the particular. Nor, obviously, do we suggest that African American students be allowed to settle for texts that are inaccessible to the larger community. The point is to pursue our best chance of placing greater numbers of strong, critical Black voices in dialogue with each other and the larger community, resulting—potentially at least— in better political possibilities. For writing teachers in their roles as teachers, the best opportunity to contribute to this process involves both embracing the doctrine of "students' right," still one of our most important statements related to concerns of grammar, *and* making curricular use of the political tensions and expressive traditions inherent in overall Black discourse.

NOTE

1. The quasi-experimental teaching was performed by Elaine Richardson.

WORKS CITED

Ball, Arnetha. "Cultural Preference and the Expository Writing of African-American Adolescents." *Written Communication* 9.4 (1992): 501–32.
Bormann, Ernest, ed. *Forerunners of Black Power: The Rhetoric of Abolition.* Englewood Cliffs, NJ: Prentice-Hall, 1971.
Shaughnessy, Mina P. *Errors and Expectations.* New York: Oxford UP, 1977.
Smitherman, Geneva. *Talkin and Testifyin: The Language of Black America.* Boston: Houghton Mifflin, 1977. Detroit: Wayne State UP, 1986.
———. " 'The Blacker the Berry, the Sweeter the Juice': African American Student Writers." *The Need for Story: Cultural Diversity in Classroom and Community.* Ed. Anne Hass Dyson and Celia Genishi. Urbana, IL: National Council of Teachers of English, 1994. [Pages 191–216 in this book.]
Souljah, Sister. *No Disrespect.* New York: Times/Random House, 1994.

13

"I Want to Be African": In Search of a Black Radical Tradition/African-American-Vernacularized Paradigm for "Students' Right to Their Own Language," Critical Literacy, and "Class Politics"

CARMEN KYNARD

At a time when ev'rybody and they momma, black and white academics alike, call everything black folk said and did in sixties social justice movements essentialist, Steve Parks's 2000 book *Class Politics: The Movement for the Students' Right to Their Own Language* came along and blew up a new spot, giving us a different context and paradigm. *Class Politics* uses the 1974 resolution from the Conference on College Composition and Communication (CCCC) called "Students' Right to Their Own Language" (SRTOL) to reassess institutional and pedagogical reform. Parks resuscitates the civil rights movement, Black Power, the New Left, the antiwar movement, and women's liberation for composition studies. Right from jump, he lets you know that "composition studies owes its current status to the counterhegemonic struggles waged around access to higher education" (3). He even takes it straight to Mina Shaughnessy and lets you know that without that history, she would not have had an audience for her ideas. This is not that same ole song and dance about access coming from the supercourageous explorers out there in the big bad higher education jungle, stomping through the ever-wilder brush of antiremediation legislation, giving the suffering natives that good ole dosage of the academic discourse serum that the empire has purposely kept from them, so that we can now act like we have significantly—both ideologically and pragmatically—undone literacy paradigms in the academic empire.[1] Naw, Parks don't go there to this kind of jungle madness and I give him his props for that. Nonetheless, Parks has taken some deserved hits. The Black Caucus—both collectively and in terms of its individual, historical leaders—has quite forcefully contended that his book erases its presence as well as Geneva Smitherman's work in shaping the politics of CCCC and SRTOL (Scott and Kinloch; Gilyard, "Holdin").

By revisiting the work of the Black Caucus and the radical rhetorics connected to Black Power and the black radical tradition, I hope to rebuild a frame where the picture of an African-American-vernacularized paradigm for critical literacy and social justice can emerge. I am not interested so much in

From *College English* 69.4 (2007): 360–90.

inserting new pictures into existing structures; the frameworks must also change. Today the possibilities for SRTOL, always imagined and yet never fully achieved, fall squarely in line with our inadequate responses to the anti-systemic nature of sixties social justice movements. The legacy of SRTOL and its current possibilities can only be understood inside of the calls for change forwarded by the Black Power Movements that exist outside of our current imaginations of and workings toward a linguistically diverse, ethno-middle class that can code-switch to match "codes of power" (Lisa Delpit's term) instead of undoing them.

"HOLDIN IT DOWN" II/TOO

Before SRTOL, the fields of composition-rhetoric and linguistics advocated the legitimacy of all language variations alongside the social inadequacy of nonstandardized forms. As Geneva Smitherman argues in "CCCC's Role in the Struggle for Language Rights" (see p. 58 in this book), the turning point was the 1968 murder of Martin Luther King, which occurred during the CCCC Annual Convention in Minneapolis. This "loss of innocence" was most dynamically captured by Ernece Kelly's speech, "Murder of the American Dream" (Smitherman p. 63). Kelly's speech stands as the central rhetorical and metaphorical connection to critical black student protests and the urban uprisings of the moment (what we sometimes call "the riots of the sixties.") In the speech, she argues:

> I grew more Black as the Conference proceeded, and as I watched the awful resistance of white participants to the challenges to recognize their biases and to work to defeat them. I had to grow Blacker as I realized the awful blindspots which prevented some whites here from seeing Blacks as humans who could contribute to a conference or to a classroom. I am tired, very tired of being the object of studies, the ornament in professional or academic groups, the object to be changed, reshaped, made-over. I feel sure that thousands of Black students would echo those words. (107)

This speech marks the origins of the NCTE Black Caucus (BC) and, thus, the origins of a Black Power sensibility in NCTE. BC members opened the doors of the convention and welcomed inside the uprisings in the streets. Twelve years later, in 1980, Kelly was still blowin' up NCTE's spot. At the 1980 NCTE Annual Convention in Cincinnati, Kelly announced to the BC that the convention site was a subsidiary of the Nestlé Corporation, which was pimping its free, unhealthy milk formula to mothers in Third World countries.[2] These combined events signaled a BC stance on the concerns of global human rights and dignity that have continually shaped NCTE (M. W. Davis 33–34). In 1985, Kelly also outlined the political stance that the BC would represent in regards to apartheid in South Africa, this time not simply opening the doors of the convention onto U.S. streets, but onto the streets of Soweto too.[3]

When we go back to Kelly's 1968 speech, we also see a pedagogy and praxis for connecting to the black student protests of the time.[4] After the conference, she continued working with her students on a newspaper called *Black Libre* and a conference with the Association of Afro-American Educators. It is clear that black student-composers and black teacher-compositionists were engaging a praxis that fell outside of what white compositionists and CCCC were making central in the field at the time. That becomes even clearer in the Autumn 1971 issue of the *Negro American Literature Forum*, guest-edited by Kelly, which opens with black "students rapping about the broken promises they experienced in college" (Kelly, "Guest" 79). Among them were two PhD candidates, a second-year student at a four-year school, and a community college student, all rapping with Kelly. These black students/protesters were co-lateral meaning makers for the kind of English/composition studies that Kelly centralized in this issue. There, their unique rhetorics were not the mere makings of "nonstandard forms" but a knowledge-production system that would continue to challenge the structure and epistemologies of the educational systems that had previously excluded them.

Alongside these student protesters, Kelly brought in a posse of scholars whose political and vernacular impulses would match the charge of the journal. Thus, the same issue edited by Kelly that showcased her students also featured the article "A Nigger Mess" by Vivian Davis, another founding member of the BC. In her article, Davis warns about the dangers of black faculty who were brought into white schools, a central demand made by the black student protesters of the time, to represent a racial quota system when their ideologies and pedagogical models served white supremacy rather than Black Power. Also in this issue we find Smitherman's piece "Black Idiom," where she reminds her readers that black style is revolutionary when it moves black audiences to new levels of social awareness and solidarity. These scholars, their connections to the BC, and their connections to the political activisms of the time centered the emergence of the SRTOL. In many ways, we are stuck facing the same issues that Davis addressed in 1971 about the importation of ideologies and pedagogical models that merely serve white supremacy. With different words and formulations, the social inadequacy of nonstandard forms is still central to theoretical positions that claim the legitimacy of all language variations, even if this time some variations are just better for certain places at certain moments.

Keith Gilyard's essay "Holdin It Down: Students' Right and the Struggle over Language Diversity" has addressed these historical issues more fully (see also his "African American Contributions to Composition Studies"). Inspired by this history of SRTOL, I have returned to the story of Black Power because it shapes a central arena in which to carve out an alternate politics and praxis of critical literacy/SRTOL that we have still not achieved. My historicization of the impact of these movements is influenced by the work of Rod Bush, who argues that "with the co-optation of the labor leadership into the ruling coalition and the repression of the Left in the post-war period, the Black Movement became the principal anti-systemic social movement in the United States" (65). As such, this movement is not a subchapter in the story of 1960s social movements, nor is it a mere extension onto the history of socialism, class struggle, or class politics. It is *the* catalyst of it all, including as Parks has brilliantly shown us, SRTOL.

BLACK SOCIALISM/BLACK ENGLISH

Parks's *Class Politics* quite brilliantly establishes the Black Power Movement as one of the central twinnings to the scholarly understandings of Black English that would be articulated in higher education and, thereby, in SRTOL. This happens in Chapter 3, where Parks appropriately gives us a new name: "Black Power/Black English." That chapter focuses most specifically on Stokely Carmichael, citing Carmichael's major ideas as articulated with Charles Hamilton in *Black Power: The Politics of Liberation*; writings by Martin Luther King whereby Parks shows how and why the political paradigms of the civil rights movement and integration differed from Black Power; and a discussion of the revolutionary understandings of class exploitation and the fierce internationalism of the Black Panther Party. There are three themes in this chapter that twin "Black Power/Black English" and that I hope to revisit here, not merely as critique but as a rebirth. Here is a summary of the three themes that I will address as I see/read them:

1. Activists and artists like Langston Hughes, Amiri Baraka, Stokely Carmichael, and the Black Panther Party present Black English and the situation of African American masses predominantly in terms of class struggle under the terms of Marxism and socialism.

2. Smitherman redefines African American culture away from the radical protest movements and unrest of the 1960s and disconnects her language politics from the kind of progressive work of socialist and left organizations working for African American empowerment as embodied in the Black Power movement.

3. William Labov's image of black speakers provides the basis for organizational alliances with left, socialist constituencies that Smitherman's African-centered focus did not.

Parks's project here is to lay out the various competing theories around Black Power and Black English that CCCC would negotiate in constructing SRTOL and, eventually, deradicalizing it by locating it within ethnicity paradigms rather than a class critique. My project, however, is to place Black Language, Black Power, the history of a Black Radical tradition[5]—and thereby, Smitherman's work—inside of a position where African American vernacular cultures, critical literacy, and full-scale battles against structured racism and class oppression function coterminously. As a result, the political impulse of these particular three themes by Parks must necessarily be rewritten.

Borrowing from the ideas of Sylvia Wynter, I argue that Black Power offered a new perspective on Black English that, quite contrary to our current incessant critiques of essentialism, situated the language of the masses of black folks as a critical source of knowledge, not where the people are statically controlled as the "folk" and "anthropological natives" to be recorded, but instead where they are part of "the movements of people who are logically excluded, as 'the waste products of all modern political practice' [. . .] with their exclusion being indispensable to the reproduction of our present order [. . .]" (120). Such a position demands that we not "sanitize this original heretical dynamic into the Liberal-universalist mainstream" (114) of much of our present understanding of language and literacy, as Parks also argues. Such a position, however, also demands that we also not sanitize the wor(l)ds of black speakers as merely the markers of a set of "oppositional politics" against capitalism and U.S. culture. As Parks shows, Labov's work was the hot-ticket item during the birth of SRTOL for the New University Conference (NUC), a group that advocated for student activists and saw themselves as the New Left reorganizing the academy (Parks 54, 115). Parks argues that the NUC saw Labov's definitions of Black English as more nested with the political possibilities for Black Power and an interracial class movement on college campuses than Smitherman's work was (115). While it is never quite clear what or how Parks thinks of this dangerous appropriation, whereby Black English becomes a type of grand mascot, the nature of such definitions of Black English also deserves a kind of scrutiny and critique that Parks does not offer. As the mascot for class struggle, black culture and language are reduced to "a coping mechanism" or "oppositional response" to oppression (Kelley, *Yo Mama's* 35). Robin Kelley critiques the aspects of Labov's work that Parks suggests the NUC privileged. Kelley compares Labov's work with Howard Seals's 1969 self-published pamphlet *You Ain't the Man Yuh Mamma Wuz*, which presents a richer representation of black language and culture. I won't go into all of Kelley's critiques here in his appropriately titled chapter, "Looking for the 'Real' Nigga: Social Scientists Construct the Ghetto," but the significance is in its critiques of Labov's conception of black culture in singular, "cardboard typologies who fit neatly into [. . .] definitions of the underclass and render invisible a wide array of complex cultural forms and practices" (17).[6] Such typologies simply cannot form the basis of a black radical position on class, literacy, education, and life under white supremacy. Ultimately they have become part of what Wynter calls "universalism." Using Black English for such aims means that the NUC was part of the deradicalization of SRTOL and a type of white paternalism just as much as any ethnicity paradigm that Parks criticizes.

Much of Parks's third chapter centers not only the work of Stokely Carmichael, but also the Student Nonviolent Coordinating Committee (SNCC) and the Black Panther Party (BPP). What is missing, however, from these discussions is that the Black Power Movement did not privilege any one, uniform position on class, or on race and gender for that matter. Instead we need to think of these as what Bush calls antisystemic movements, which he explains in the following way:

> The Black Movement, because of the class position of its constituency and the consciousness that African Americans have developed in their struggle for justice and equality in the United Sates, should be the central component of an anti-systemic movement in the United States. (20)

Thus complicated polemics arise. When Carmichael did his tour of "Third World" nations in 1967, he portrayed black urban rebellions as part of an international socialist movement, a rhetoric that Parks examines brilliantly. However, Carmichael was also adamant that blacks' reactions were racial rather than part of their class oppression.[7] At the Organization of Latin American Solidarity in Cuba in 1967, Carmichael announced that Black Power not only addressed class exploitation but also cultural integrity, which he believed had to be restored and maintained. His world travels convinced him that Pan-Africanism was the ideology that blacks in America must assume for liberation. Thus, from jump he was already promoting a discourse within SNCC about a common African heritage, a subject of hot debate that was always on the table in complicated ways.

In the same year as Carmichael's travels, Huey Newton of the BPP drafted Carmichael to serve as the party's field marshal but was then imprisoned.[8] Carmichael was asked to speak at the Free Huey Newton rallies, where he announced that "Communism is not an ideology suited for black people, period, period. Socialism is not an ideology fitted for Black people, period, period" (Carson 282). He argued that neither of these ideologies addressed racism and that blacks needed "an African ideology" that spoke to their "blackness" (282). As he put it: "[I]t's not a question of right or left, it's a question of black" (282). Eldridge Cleaver and Bobby Seale did not agree with this but they kept Carmichael on as a national spokesperson because he was needed as the primary attraction for public events and fundraisers. Even when the BPP leadership did not agree with what the cat was saying, they knew they needed to free Huey, and Carmichael had the rhetoric that could bring that on.[9] To be sure, Carmichael has always maintained a critique of capitalism, as in this 1994 argument he makes (as Kwame Ture):

> There is no question that Africans throughout the world are oppressed by racist capitalism. It is crystal clear that conscious people of African descent will instinctively recognize their priority in life to liberate their people [. . .]. The conscious seek to serve, the educated seek at best individual achievement. The only motivating force of education in the capitalist system is profit, individualized at the richest level [. . .]. This reality is driven home by the fact that our ancestors were chattel slaves. If, in a capitalist system, human beings are commodities, then everything they produce, including education, is also a commodity. (89)

However, Carmichael has never sacrificed Africa on the altar of class politics and we must understand this as part of a complicated African American rhetorical and political tradition. Clay Carson further argues:

> [S]erious differences emerged during the spring of 1968 as black leaders attempted to formulate programs to achieve the goal of black power. Even the militants disagreed about whether the goal of the black struggle should be black capitalism or African communalism, whether the strategy should emphasize electoral politics or revolution. The major line of

cleavage within the black militant community was between cultural nationalists who urged blacks to unite around various conceptions of a black cultural ideal, and self-defined political revolutionaries who were more likely than the cultural nationalist to advocate armed struggle to achieve political or economic goals. (286)

My purpose in presenting this history is not to say that the BPP and SNCC were so divided that they did not have any kind of class ideology or political platform. I am simply trying to present a more dynamic, multidimensional, and complex process for how class, culture, African origins, race, and black activism/radicalism were framed. These conversations were and are always in process and highly contested.[10]

The language of socialism and class struggle did not constitute the "Black English" of Carmichael and the BPP, as Parks suggests might have been the case (107). Had Parks said something like this to Carmichael in 1967 or any time thereafter, my main man Stokely might have slapped the mess outta him. In the end, Parks comes dangerously close to appropriating Black English away from Black Power just like the NUC and ethnicity theorists. Examinations of the politics of the BPP, the Black Radical tradition, or SRTOL are certainly not new, so there is no excuse for recentering Labov's limited understanding of black working-class people's oppression and culture, stripping away Black Nationalism from the BPP's class politics, and calling all of this "socialism" and "Black English." There is important work then to be done in triplet-ing Black English, Black Power, and SRTOL. As Joseph Peniel urges, however, "Black Power Studies" is not merely an academic research area with which to accumulate expertise/exchange value in the academic marketplace. Endemic to this work is the call to examine the role of black vernacular intellectuals and what their scholarship can do so that these categories (scholarship, vernacularity,[11] and intellect) become renovations. Otherwise, we will be stuck filling quota calls for African American representation/representatives and native informants issued by existing bourgeois structures, as Vivian Davis of the BC so forthrightly warned in 1971. This work also means challenging the nature of knowledge in the American university and the world/ language it constitutes. It means redefining what it means to be revolutionary in the context of radical social change as it effects the masses as opposed to using language education to become part of the newly incorporated post-1960s ethno-middle-classes who can swing back to the hood every now and again and use their old "home languages" to jive-talk with the brothers and sisters left behind on the street co'ners.

Smitherman's text "Black Power Is Black Language," which Parks criticizes, was published in 1972, a year after her piece in Kelly's edited collection, and given the historical chronology that I have provided here it seems that Smitherman may have been more supportive of socialism than Carmichael was by that point. According to Parks, Smitherman's article "rhetorically positioned [Black Power] as nonthreatening to the political status quo of coalition politics, mass marches, and nonviolence" and did not "effectively" manage to translate "the most radical language politics of the Black Power Movement into the classroom" (111). As such, Smitherman's work should not be placed "in alignment with the Black Panthers or the Socialist elements of the Black Power Movement" (111). Parks identifies "Black Power Is Black Language" as the central text in which Smitherman moves away from the radical protests of her time because of the following sentence: "[P]erhaps then we may convince them [the students] that the pen is mightier than the Molotov Cocktail" (91). But Parks's story fails to capture the context of Smitherman's essay. Smitherman's essay is part of a book that collects a history of African American rhetorics in visual forms including art, photographs, and graphic designs; poetics from Mari Evans to Amiri Baraka; and polemical essays about various political issues facing the masses. It functions as almost the quintessential Black Arts Movement piece—written by blacks, for blacks—the sister movement not examined by Parks. Smitherman's comment about Molotov cocktails is not an attempt to suggest that teachers should convince black youth that they should not be takin it to the streets. It is the closing sentence of an essay where she is arguing that writing, new black arts writing by students, shaped by and from African American language, can be "a weapon capable of the most devastating destruction" (91). This is a rhetorical move that she was not doing in her works geared for white audiences. It is also a critical move in composition studies, where she links the Black Arts Movement, its alternate conception of what the aesthetic is and does outside of the Western bourgeois "order of being, aesthetic, knowledge, and correlated program of truth" (Wynter 163), to what and why students write in schools. When all is said and done, the classroom, its language pedagogy, and students' texts—in both content and form—can truly be as explosive, as socially transformative and social-action-based, as the insurrections on the streets. Unfortunately, Parks distorts these politics and moves the most prominent African American compositionist outside of CCCC's radical, progressive politics around SRTOL, the very resolution that she helped create. The BPP, the Black Power Movement, and Smitherman are moved completely outside of a long-standing trajectory of black nationalism—relegated, quite paternalistically, to nothing more than the provincial, unlearned shallowness of ethnic separatism, an argument that is also not new given James Sledd's 2000 account of Smitherman's work.[12] Equally disconcerting is the simultaneous ventriloquism whereby Black English speaks class struggle, with such formulations now becoming part of what Wynter has called the "demise" of the Black Arts Movement (Wynter 160–64).

If we are going to locate SRTOL inside of Black Power, we must also remember that the Black Power Movement was also a "revolt of culture that was powered by a reawakened racial consciousness" (Van Deburg 75). A year after her 1972 "Black Power Is Black English" article, Smitherman published "God Don't Never Change," a piece inspired by Amiri Baraka's argument that "God Don't Never Change" does not mean "God Does Not Change." We must remember that it was as a poet/wordsmith/vernacular-intellectual-activist that Baraka founded the Revolutionary Communist League (RCL), the movement with "the deepest roots in the black cultural politics of the 1960s" and "Marxist-Leninist-Maoist" tradition (Kelley, *Freedom* 102).[13] The point is that Parks calls up Baraka but does not see these language and aesthetic politics as part of Baraka's socialism, SRTOL, or Black Power.

One might also ask here if socialism is necessarily antiracist in its positions on Ebonics and black speakers who do not sound like white middle-class folk. As an example, Helen Halyard quite forthrightly and publicly denounced Ebonics as the "incorrect English" of black urban youth and racistly recast them as linguistically inferior because of their economic impoverishment.[14] Of course, we cannot associate all of socialism with Halyard's foolishness, but the marriage of an African American discourse on socialism and the politics of Black English in scholarly texts is not readily available. The African American presence in Marxism, communism, and socialism is a very long and complicated history. As William Watkins has argued, there have indeed been many examinations of this history (e.g., Kelley, *Hammer* and *Freedom Dreams*; Robinson; Hutchinson), but there has been very little work about the history/legacy of a Black Marxian critique of education.[15] By extension, there is even less work in this regard as it intersects with language arts/literacy pedagogy, making it all the more important to look critically at what we might call a socialist origins or class analysis for SRTOL as it is historicized in, and intersected by, a Black Power/Black English dynamic. The version that we find in Parks's chapter, as an example, does not seem aligned with the kind of socialist trajectory that can trace itself to folks like Paul Robeson, the African American international socialist, who said that he always wanted to carry one central idea in his music, plays, and film: "I want to be African."[16]

Perhaps an interesting point of comparison for illuminating a Black Power position in CCCC and SRTOL would have been for Parks to compare Smitherman to someone like Angela Davis rather than with Carmichael. As someone whose experiences merged with SNCC, the BPP, and the Communist Party of the U.S.A. (CPUSA), Davis's ongoing stance that black liberation could never be achieved apart from an international workers' movement against imperialism, capitalism, and racism seems to be a more socialist platform than Carmichael's. Yet Davis herself still argues, alongside her oppositional stance to the black cultural nationalists of the BPP, that she needed to embrace some of its elements. As she argues:

> But, at the same time, I needed to say "black is beautiful" as much as any of the intransigent anti-white nationalists. I needed to explore my African ancestry, to don African garb, and to wear my hair natural as much as the blinder-wearing male supremacist cultural nationalists. ("Black Nationalism" 291)

She also reminds us that black was always her point of reference as a member of the CPUSA through the all-black collective in Los Angeles called the Che-Lumumba Club (291).

Such a project of looking at African Americans who fold out racist oppression in terms of class struggle under the terms of Marxism and socialism is very important. It is fundamentally linked to the beef that Davis has with many of us young folks on the scene today who have no understanding of how Marxist thought has shaped radical concepts of revolution (as in: young folk who wanna give all kinda props to Davis, with pictures of her afro serving as a widely circulated cultural icon, yet know nothing about how Davis's ideas about racial equality have been shaped by the Frankfurt School). I have also added Davis into the mix for a specific reason: she wrote one of the classics on the lives of working-class black women and their aesthetic, political movements—*Blues Legacies and Black Feminism: Gertrude "Ma" Rainey, Bessie Smith, and Billie Holiday*—which centers black working-class women outside of a bourgeois, liberal humanist framework of feminism/aestheticism, giving a complex reading of class alongside aesthetics and discursive styles. She unequivocally locates blues "on an African cultural continuum" where Nommo is very important (49). Let's remember that Smitherman's definition of Nommo in her 1972 article, "Black Power Is Black Language," was one of the thorns in Parks's side, what he unequivocally locates as taking Smitherman away from a socialist paradigm and the radical politics of Black Power.[17] Davis's book is interesting in regard to Nommo and black working-class women's languaging reality because she sees Black English as embodying a challenge to cultural oppression under racism; at the same time, she also locates West African languaging systems, the Nommo, that coax out new meanings and twist literal meanings into new constructs. For instance, Davis gives the example of a 1956 Billie Holiday interview with Tex McCleary, who asked about her favorite "happy" song. Billie responded that it was "Yesterdays," a song that most folk thought was a "sad" song. McCleary then asked Billie to speak out the words of the song as if to give him a content lesson. Yet the boundaries between Billie speeching this song and her singing it were fluid. Her speechifying did not produce the sad message that McCleary seemed to think she was missing. In fact, Billie had changed the song's message and meaning, whether she was doing song or talk. In other words, she made bad mean good. The context that Billie gave to those lyrics was what counted, and not the surface content that McCleary was stressing—a content that Billie often did not control (Davis, *Blues* 173–74). Black English and its shaping of the blues aesthetic, as Davis is showing here, gave these women— a core of working-class black women—the ability to control the meanings and messages in their work by providing the tools to rewrite them. Smitherman was making these very same arguments in 1971 and 1972. And just as Billie could move with ease inside the speech-music continuum, making both sides and all in between do what she wanted and needed, black students can move that speech-written continuum in the same way. This is the power of African American language; this is what Smitherman brought to SRTOL. This is not to say that all scholars who place Africa and Nommo in their work are radical or have a radical Afrocentric approach that shapes their understanding of class struggle, capitalism, and imperialism. Yet, Parks leaves no possibility that any of this could be possible.[18]

The BPP and their "Red Dreams of Black Liberation"[19] certainly identified a Marxist commitment in their rhetoric and program and dismissed some forms of black cultural nationalism. But, as Kelley argues, it is more accurate to say that they just had their own kind of cultural nationalism (*Freedom* 94), what you might call a type of "Black Maoism" (Prashad 142).[20] It was never a monolithic expression and philosophy, anyway; I mean, after all, Maulena Karenga, who does not seem to encompass the prototypical Panther Parks creates, was part of the BPP too.[21] As Kelley reminds us, while the BPP ten-point program was certainly influenced by Marxist-Leninist positions, Malcolm X was still the biggest ideological influence on its shaping (*Freedom* 94). Instead of seeing socialism as the Black English of these Black Power movements, we must see Black English as the rhetorical and ideological tool in which Marxist, Leninist, Maoist, communist, and socialist positions were battled out and reshaped for black liberation to reach the black masses. I am not suggesting that a socialist paradigm was not operative for the BPP and cannot be operative for a politics of Black English. My point here is that socialism did not simply shape black freedom struggles; those freedom struggles also shaped socialism.

I point here to George Washington Woodbey, a Baptist minister and African American socialist who was born a slave in Tennessee in 1854. His major goal was to make complex ideas surrounding socialism clear to the black masses. He was particularly credited for bringing his congregations to their feet in sermons that were finished off with fiery orations on socialism. Not only did he make Afro-Christianity and socialism compatible, a stance he took the heat for from black and white socialists alike, but he also convinced Christian followers to use socialism to direct their lives and understandings of the world (James 53). The point is that African American rhetoric was right there from jump in African Americans' commitment to socialism, right down to them "holy-rolling, bench-walking, spirit-getting, tongue-speaking, vision-receiving, intuitive-directing, Amen-saying, sing-song preaching, holy-dancing, and God-sending" sermons (Smitherman, *Talkin* 212).

While images of Malcolm X takin it to the Harlem streets are readily produced in many of our imaginations, brothers and sisters way before then took it to Harlem's street pulpits too. Hubert Harrison, "the father of Harlem radicalism," might be regarded as undertaking the first sustained analysis of a class position on race for black people, thus launching what you might call an African American rhetoric of socialism. Harrison adopted the phrase "Race First," which would be used by Marcus Garvey as the essence of the UNIA, in response to Woodrow Wilson's policy of "America First" and the socialist slogan/position of "Class First" (Richards and Lemelle 9–10). Harrison's historical moment also coincided with a rising number of black college students at HBCUs who had African American/socialist magazines in their hands as they engaged a wave of student activism inspired by the New Negro Movement, like the famous Fisk student rebellions in the 1920s (James 51–56). Perhaps most compelling for me is how African American language and African

American rhetorics merge with a Black Radical tradition, Afro-Socialists, if you will, to "talk that talk," get the crowd to wave ya hands in the air like ya just don't care, and shut down the structural racism that plagues life opportunities. Black students and black activists have continually used Black Englishes to move their audiences in order to shape an African American rhetoric of class exploitation.

It is much too simplistic to lodge Black Power solely in the BPP, which serves to limit the reaches of this as a movement before the existence of the BPP, during, and after. As Peniel has shown in his comprehensive work, street corner speaking, study groups, and hosts of community organizations all shaped and were shaped by Black Power—before, during, and after the 1960s:

- student groups who held study sessions and rallies, like the Afro-American Association, Revolutionary Action Movement (RAM), Student Organization for Black Unity (SOBU)/Youth Organization for Black Unity (YOBU);

- community organizers like the Freedom Now Party (FNP), the Group on Advanced Leadership (GOAL) in Detroit, the Republic of New Afrika (RNA), UHURU (Wayne State University), the League of Black Revolutionary Workers, the Patrice Lumumba Coalition, the Community Self-Defense Program, the New African Peoples Organization, the Black Workers Congress, the Congress of African People, and the African People's Socialist Party;

- meeting sites and "think tanks" like Drum and Spear Bookstore, the Institute of the Black World (IBW), and Malcolm X Liberation University, Peoples College;

- periodicals and newspapers like *Muhammad Speaks* (early 1960s and 1970s), *RAM Speaks*, *Black America* (also under RAM), *Soulbook*, *Razor's Edge*, *The African World* (historical predecessors would include the African Nationalist Pioneer Movement's *The Street Speaker* and *The Black Challenge*, etc.); and

- activist/community teachers like Queen Mother Audley Moore, Ethel Johnson, and Grace Lee Boggs. (Peniel; Bush)

All of these historical and contemporary institutions have been crucial. We have yet to really wed them to the impulse of SRTOL in theory or practice.

"THE REVOLUTION WILL NOT BE [CODE-SWITCHED]" (OR POWER-CODED)

At the end of *Class Politics*, Parks argues that "one way to read the history of SRTOL is that it has created two mutually opposing positions": teachers are responsible for teaching Standard English; or teachers should not teach Standard English (242). This is no neutral, factual statement that just falls freely and unideologically from the sky; it is Parks's created history. African Americans in 4Cs who see themselves linked to the history and legacy of SRTOL do not talk about the history this way; surely Smitherman does not. Parks's important point here, however, is that such a polarization is inaccurate as there were never two poles for activists and progressive organizations. Strangely, no African American directly connected to SRTOL, 4Cs, or the Black Caucus is discussed in the conclusion (back in the day, we called such occurrences: things that make you go hmmm . . .), but my point here is not to ask for an integration policy. The frame that holds Parks's picture is not one that can encase the radical origins of the Black Caucus/Black Power/black presence in 4Cs that gets represented in the 1971 *Negro American Literature Forum* under the editorship of Ernece Kelly, later captured by SRTOL. Unfortunately, Parks goes on to re-create the very binary that he says never really existed in the first place with his use of the work of Lisa Delpit, which he argues "almost directly refers to the SRTOL debate" (243). Delpit never directly mentions SRTOL in her work so Parks himself connects her statement with SRTOL and sixties language politics. Nonetheless, these are important points to revisit that go beyond Parks's text since, perhaps, Delpit's book has been "written in response to the historical situation produced by 1960s language politics" (Parks 243). Unfortunately, that response is more problematic than it has ever been socially transformative. While Delpit's text has indeed helped us to see that standardized English is simply one code among many, her positions are completely strangleheld by the "code of power," a term that she popularized and that she often reifies. What we get is a paradigm for economic uplift that black students can be taught to linguistically manipulate and master (which, is ironically, the makings of the integrationist, ethnicity paradigm that Parks himself has critiqued . . . and has shown to be the basis of the beef of the BPP and Black Power in the wake of the wide-scale urban rebellions that engulfed the country on the assassination of Martin Luther King).[22]

The subsection called "Community Studies" in the conclusion to *Class Politics* (called "Ozymandias—Creating a Program for SRTOL") serves as a critical lens into the problematic issues around African American language that get reinscribed by Delpit. Parks uses two extensive quotations from Delpit that presumably support his "program for SRTOL" and then goes on to summarize and analyze some of her ideas. Parks sees Delpit's classroom examples as critical literacy, as "critical instruction" about how "the poverty of working class and minority students" is maintained, how students' own cultures relate to the culture of power, how different writing exercises can employ "standard" and "non-standard" Englishes (obviously separable in this binary) (Parks 244). And herein lies the problem. I see very little of this kind of literacy paradigm described in Delpit's book and, instead, often see there language lessons for white middle-class etiquette, some of it downright offensive and colonizing. How can two people have such radically different readings of Delpit? What accounts for the distinctions in our (class) politics that produce such divergent, opposite understandings of Delpit's classroom, language praxis, and stance on racism as it affects "minority" children? And how and why do those divergent political grounds shape programs for SRTOL that can never be coterminous?

Let me step it back here and break down my own opposing read of Delpit that I am arguing moves us away from SRTOL and a Black-Powered presence in composition studies rather than toward it. Be very clear here: when I say that Delpit moves away from a Black Power presence, I mean that as a negative thing. This move away is directly connected to the creation of a college-educated black middle class or elite, who as Bush argues are not linked to the demands for Black Power and systemic change because they "are essentially locked into a comprador relationship with the white-dominated but multiracial elite of the U.S. national and world-system" (23). It is not within the scope and purpose of my essay to look at Delpit's entire book, so I will simply limit my critique here to the sections of *Other Peoples' Children* where Parks has obtained his two most extensive quotations. Parks includes the following line from Delpit's text: "When I speak therefore of the culture of power, I don't speak of how I wish things to be but how they are" (qtd. in Parks 243). This line is particularly interesting because it comes at a point in "The Silenced Dialogue," perhaps Delpit's most famous chapter from the book, where she is discussing an experience with a Native American student.[23] Delpit's subsection begins with what she calls one of the problematic, typical statements coming from liberals: that students have a right to their own language and culture and that schools must be pushed to offer children the opportunity to express themselves in their own language styles (37). Okay, good enough: she is not embracing ethnoclassism via language arts pedagogy. But that ain't really where she takes the argument. Her immediate example is of an undergraduate in her senior-level education course who was writing an autobiography. The student submitted a paper that had many problems in spelling, sentence structure, and paragraphing. Delpit argues that it is criminal to pass the student without attending "to obvious deficits in the codes needed for her to function" (38). However, Delpit also inadvertently suggests, by the way the subsection is framed, that the student's Native American cultural style has been allowed to shape her childhood schooling, not the power code, and that this cultural style has now impeded her production of "correct" spelling, full paragraphs, and complete sentences (see Lu for an excellent discussion of how and why such assumptions are simply too rushed and immature). We are to assume that the student's written fluency in her home/community codes has prevented her fluency in another code, namely standardized English. As readers, we do not get to know the student, do not know if she has ever experienced herself as the type of student, as Gilyard describes himself, for whom "the struggle to be fluent was the most important challenge" (McGee 25), nor can we be sure that Delpit knows this student very well either.[24] Further discussion about the student's rhetorics, purpose, and style is even more eclipsed because we never hear anything about the content of her writing. This erasure of what the student is saying puts Delpit right in the fire of Malea Powell's criticisms about constructing "marginal others" whom we do not get to hear; we do not know what they are saying, because we are only told about them (7).

Unfortunately, there is no evidence that Delpit knows anything about this student's culture, history, or linguistic repertoires, or at least she does not discuss these. I have in mind the work of Charles Coleman in "Our Students Write with Accents—Oral Paradigms for ESD Students," where he shows how the language features and patterns of African American English (AAE) shape students' writings because he has studied AAE. The point is that you need to understand something about a student's linguistic background to make the kind of claims about cultural codes that Delpit does and nowhere do we get such a discussion. Furthermore, as Coleman argues, the point is not to enact a repair model where the very ways we explain standardized grammars are too simple to extrapolate the issues that students may be facing. I will quote Powell again here and dare make the argument that Powell has presented a literacy theory far more complex than the issues of surface grammar that get called the "code":

> I am offering here [. . .] a very different configuration in which it is the rhetor's very relationship with oppressive discourse that opens a space for possibility. Practicing this kind of relational mixed-blood rhetoric, then, means following the Academy's, the discipline's, "rules" by transgressing them, not just to oppose them but to transform them, to change utterly the grounds upon which our scholarship exists [. . .]. (9–10)

It is critical to remember that much of Delpit's book centers on Native American children though there is very little public recognition of this, especially in the section of her book that I am focusing on here. Delpit tells of an elementary school teacher whose students critique language discrimination but who also learn to separate their Native American "Heritage Language" from Standard English in sometimes offensive ways (41–42). Students are taught to keep the two registers completely separate through class activities such as dressing up, using ornate utensils and tablecloths, and speaking "Formal English" for fancy class dinners, as if perhaps performing for one of those commercials where people dress in ball gowns and ask one another to "pass the Grey Poupon please." They can use their home languages, casual dress, fingers and/or plastic utensils, however, for an outdoor picnic. This is not about teaching critical literacy in a white supremacist world; this is about teaching hyperbourgeois forms of etiquette. Home languages are the commodities that have "exchange value" only in local communal settings; Standard English has the "higher exchange value" (it is literally coupled with more expensive utensils) because it can (and must) be applied to high-paying, professional settings. Meanwhile, Athabaskan language (though it is not clear whether Delpit speaks it) is short and metaphoric; academic language is wordy (Delpit 41–42). Another village teacher has students practice formal letter writing about the Alaska Land Claims Settlement Act (Delpit 45). We know that students are using such texts to learn grammar and formal writing rules, but are they really deeply engaging polemical issues? Helping students analyze structures of oppression and then getting them to mimic forms is not critical literacy. As Allan Luke reminds us, structures of power are never static or fully transparent with rules to follow about genres, texts, and skills. "Codes of power" must be subjected to an unrelenting analysis on the part of teachers and students. It is not as simple as an unchanging, stock set of rules to follow. Of course, these teachers might be doing more critical activities related to meaning rather than to form, but Delpit has not privileged that kind of discussion in her representation of these classrooms, all of which Parks has suggested can be a "program for SRTOL."

It is hardly Scott Lyons's dynamic notion of "rhetorical sovereignty" that these "other people's children" explore in these classroom examples. Lyons defines rhetorical sovereignty, "our highest hopes for literacy at this point," as

> the inherent right and ability of peoples to determine their own communicative needs and desires in this pursuit, to decide for themselves the goals, modes, styles, and languages of public discourse. Placing the scene of writing squarely back into the contingency of the Indian rhetorical situation, rhetorical sovereignty requires of writing teachers more than renewed commitment to listening and learning; it also requires a radical rethinking of how and what we teach as the written word at all levels of schooling, from preschool to graduate curricula and beyond. (449–50)

Although the notion of "codes of power" has been insightful, the examples in the chapter of *Other People's Children* from which Parks borrows his quotations and summary reduces language and language rights to grammar and form. Those examples could never achieve the kind of societal transformation that Lyons makes central to his language politics and are certainly not linked to the life and work of people like Amiri Baraka and Langston Hughes, whom Parks has highlighted in his book.[25] Furthermore, Parks's embrace of Delpit's text is almost reminiscent of the type of Booker T. Washington saga that white conservatives and progressives loved in the previous century for the ways that it sought to work within the system. As Delpit herself says, "Now I am certain that if we are trying to effect societal change, we cannot do so from the bottom up, but we must push and agitate from the top down" (40). Such top-down formulations are what Bush calls the "political counterpart" to "liberal universalism" (10). This is a different praxis than, for instance, what Manning Marable argues for in *The Great Wells of Democracy*:

> Fundamental change within our system will largely have to occur not from the top down, but from the bottom up [. . .]. [There are] tremendous capacities for social change that are reflected in the activities of ordinary black Americans—including the Hip Hop generation, prisoners and those impacted by the destructive effects of massive incarceration, activists in community-based organizations in disadvantaged neighborhoods, and people involved in faith-based institutions that are actively engaged in social justice projects. (xiv)

While Delpit's larger project may be crucial in its opening up of a space for critique of the racelessness in progressive pedagogies that do not interrogate social inequality and instead merely reinscribe bourgeois liberal humanism, her pedagogical politics are nonetheless linked to the very same bourgeois educational models, strange bedfellows for a definition of SRTOL otherwise linked to socialism and class-based struggles. The very nature of the most radical of those 1960s social movements, in all of their contradictory and varied impulses, was not simply to protest existing conditions but to compel participants to imagine something radically different from the way things were.

A politics grounding an acquiescence to a "culture of power" is ill-suited to the pulse of sixties social justice movements and SRTOL. This articulation of a "culture of power" seems to be the contemporary, trying-to-be-poststructuralist correlate to the "culture of poverty" discourse that has permeated social science literature (Bush). While a notion of a "culture of power" seems to be flipping the script on this body of social science literature, making the elite the object of six-and-seven-$-figured grant-funded study this time around, both paradigms are problematic. Both locate power, attainment, and lack as behaviorally defined, where in our case language becomes a set of behaviors to acquire power. Such ideas about a "culture of power" achieve the same as the ideas underneath a "culture of poverty," namely a "peculiar pattern in class analysis that cripples rather than strengthens the attack on the structural inequality deeply embedded in the capitalist system" (Bush 11). Behavioral analyses are simply not systemic. As a theoretical construct, all that "culture of power" stuff, as it is currently used, is just way too played out now. It has not said or done a lot about interrogating racialized class exploitation facing black masses, particularly that facing black youth, nor has this heuristic done much to interrogate how current modes of capitalist production shape institutions of higher education and, thereby, their literacy politics and practices and their effect on African American language users (Duncan). Equally alarming is the way that continual warnings about minding the culture of power actually reify it, since power is not naturally free-floating without a continual language used to describe, explain, or reimagine it. In other words, the "code" and "culture" of "power" are ones that we ourselves create and re-create because we continue to extrapolate where it is, what it looks like, and how to write/speak/think inside of it.

Parks seems to further embrace Delpit's argument that without the explicit teaching of Standard English, poor and minority children will leave school without the necessary "skills to succeed in the marketplace" (243). He goes on to tell us that his students at Temple need to enter the culture of power because "it is not an option to simply resist" (247). Here again, we learn or hear nothing about these students; they are just an amorphous, nameless, raceless, genderless mass presumably marked as nonwhite and/or non-middle-class since they are not part of the "culture of power." Here we must wonder why Black English has been defined away from its young users, in this case perhaps some of Parks's students, who cannot use it as part of the discourse that can "resist" or mediate "our inherited material conditions and our capacities to engage, even alter, these same surroundings" (Longaker 473). Meanwhile, Parks himself can claim Black English as the socialism of the BPP! (More things that make you go hmmm . . .) It seems strange then that after criticizing Smitherman for not taking on socialism and class struggle Parks can center Delpit for a SRTOL program that will get children some skills for *"the marketplace."* When we go back to Smitherman's 1972 essay, "Black Power Is Black Language," the one that is presumably antisocialist, we see a different notion of reading the workplace. Smitherman says: "To conceptualize the educational process in terms of preparing students for the 'world of work' is to make our institutions of higher learning training mills in which the daily output is one student-robot capable of fitting into the vast machinery of technological times" (89). Of course, Parks is not enacting the kind of factory-line, robotic literacy/educational theory that Smitherman criticizes in this quotation, but Delpit won't help him move too far away from it.

It also seems strange that a moment that was all about "alternative discourses" as endemic to social change would be written within the reclamoring for simplistic notions of standard written English that rounds out Parks's text in his concluding chapter. What we can take from Delpit in relation to alternate forms of writing and SRTOL does not come from what she says, but rather how she says it. Delpit's texts do not follow the genre set forth by semi-detached university observers/note-takers who construct dense, unengaging academese where every sentence has four or five authors listed in parentheses at the end, and where black children are language specimens to be studied. And you don't get those cut-and-dried, cookie-cutter subsections like: abstract, keywords, review of the literature, method, data collection, findings, discussion, implications, notes. With Delpit, you read a direct address within a set of personal references and interrogations. There is even some good ole African American signifyin' up in the joint, especially on white folks who do process theory (which is why they are still mad at her). And there ain't none of them ego-inflated discussions of methodology where people add the word "critical" onto their framework as if that has somehow created a radical lens into race and class. Delpit certainly experiments with alternative and cultural styles in her own academic writing, especially with the use of narrative, and I would argue that this is also why she has such a large following: she is accessible, human, and chit-chatty wit cha. That is not a criticism of her flava, since I really like it, so much so that I can look deeper into her arguments that continually annoy me. The point is this: if we look at literacies and writing as something much more complex than the morphosyntactic structures of standardized English, then we can see that Delpit's own writing does not match the "codes of power" for writing in the academy. Yet, she has been successful in this world anyway. Her own rhetorics represent a very specific, cultural phenomenon—a black womanist rhetoric of teaching and education—and those rhetorics let this sister get heard, even in academe! Why not advocate this same possibility for our students?

Of course other people's close readings of Parks's "Community Studies" section will be different from mine, especially those by people who are not users/theorists/teachers/"unleashers" of African American literacies (Ball and Lardner). That said, no kind of sentence picking inside of descriptions of the "culture of power" will give you the kind of paradigm that moves past the dominant "market rhetorics" (a notion that I am borrowing from Mark Garrett Longaker) that shape how the purposes of African American language have been set. No amount of socialist wishing will make a Delpitized SRTOL program one that can challenge racialized class exploitation. Some people will not see that as the goal of writing, but those that do gotta get it right . . . and then get it radicalized. As Longaker argues, "[W]riting teachers can adopt and promote teaching methods that do not leave us always responding to some perceived demands from postindustrial or global industry" (475). We end Parks's book without a radical program for taking up SRTOL that understands and incorporates African American rhetorics as a crucial process for the kind of knowledge production that has moved us toward social justice and critical literacy as introduced by the Black Power movements, the kind of knowledge production that has created real and alternative means of demanding and achieving human dignity, racial equality, and educational equity. In this regard, Richard Wright's argument has the most power for our teaching:

> Those groups that have suffered the most from the conditions of marginalization and disempowerment have the most to teach about the roles of language as ideology, as synergy, as catalyst, as force, as weapon in the ongoing and unrelenting struggle for liberation. More than any other, African American rhetoric is rich in traditional forms of expression as well as in its variable transformations over time, in response to the changing character of domination and the conditions of existence that it seeks to impose. (95)

The point of SRTOL is to fully inhabit the little bit of theoretical space that we have left to enact what Smitherman was advocating through SRTOL as the embodiment of a black arts/Black Power paradigm: that black styles are revolutionary, for the time and place in which they socially arise, when they move black working-class audiences to new levels of social awareness, solidarity, and political activism, and push past the socially prescribed norms of being and thinking (and therefore, speaking and writing) of the moment.

MAKIN A WAY OUT OF NO WAY ALL OVER AGAIN

The polarization between multiple literacies and Standard English that Parks sees too many scholars connecting to SRTOL has been continually bypassed in the work of African American compositionists. Elaine Richardson describes very powerfully her students' blackademic theorizin and stylin in her 2003 book *African American Literacies* and in her 2001 article with Keith Gilyard, "Students' Right to Possibility: Basic Writing and African American Rhetorics" (p. 217). Theresa Redd does the same in her 1995 essay "Untapped Resources: 'Styling' in Black Students' Writing for Black Audiences," where she shows how African American students' texts are fundamentally reshaped in content and style when they are asked to write for black audiences. Arnetha Ball has created a rich record of African American students' narrativizing in their writing that moves beyond sentence-level detections of "dialect." And you can always roll into a session at CCCC and hear Halima Toure, teacher educator and compositionist, and Jon Yasin, hip-hop style chronicler and compositionist, throw down what they are doing in their work with teachers and students. Youngbloods are in the house too: the classroom praxis uncovered in Valerie Kinloch's descriptions of her students' ideas and writing, represented in her 2005 *CCC* article, "Revisiting the Promise of Students' Right to

Their Own Language: Pedagogical Strategies" (p. 429), has been continually unfolded for us at CCCC and at the NCTE Annual Convention. There is also one of my favorite essays, "Nobody Mean More to Me than You and the Future Life of Willie Jordan," by June Jordan, where we see students shaping texts in African American English based solely on their awareness of what they do in language and what they want language to do, as well as of local and global racial oppression. The text is not simply about language but about what students decided to do with it in the context of their spirited fight against South African apartheid and U.S. apartheid, as represented by the murder of a student's family member by police. If you go back to Helen Whiting and Septima Clark, you will see that this kind of literacy instruction was always on the radar even when white journals would not go there.[26] We have never been without precedent for a praxis for SRTOL in classrooms.

By now, it might seem that I have absolutely no love for Parks, but nothing could be further from the truth. It cannot be stressed enough that I am wholly indebted to him for opening up a very critical space in which to link and think through SRTOL, Black Power, black arts, black language, and the work of Geneva Smitherman. He uses class struggle to give us a new discourse in which to speak on the issues that have gotten horribly silenced in these postmodern erasures where much time gets wasted arguing in antisocially critical terms about what is essentialist and what is not. The explorations that I have made in this article, from George Washington Woodbey to Angela Davis, are ones that Parks has helped to put in motion. It is important to see just how and why Parks's text moves past hyperbourgeois, academicized postmodernisms that are utterly divorced from human conditions and the struggle against class exploitation and structured racism. I got nothing but love for Parks for that. Thus, the critiques that I have made here are not meant to be text-based analyses of any single book. The book, as always, is simply part of much larger writing.

I will round out this entire piece now by stepping back to the beginning, to the spark that set the whole thing off: radical student protest paving the way for new possibilities in rhetorics of social equality and equitable educational systems. I will let the story of a Young Lords Party (YLP) member, Miguel Melendez (with the YLP being a vital component of African American Freedom struggles in higher education in New York City) carry the momentum here at the end.[27] As a former SEEK student at Queens College in 1967, Melendez found his politics completely changed during the summer before returning to Queens College after his first year as a SEEK student. Residents of El Barrio, like people in major cities across the country, began to take to the streets in large-scale urban rebellions and uprisings. As a college student, Melendez became part of New York City Mayor Lindsay's program of sending college students of color into the neighborhoods to calm young people. This bureaucratic peacemaking strategy was in no way designed to alter the system. These native informants who had, it was hoped, learned in college how to "code-switch" into the "power code" (but still had their own street/mother tongue/community codes to take back home) would, in the ideal version of the Lindsay program's imagined results, be able to placate the politically charged masses, since in learning all that "language" of the power code, they had also taken on its ideologies. That's not how it went down, though. When those college students entered the community of El Barrio, they began to articulate something different: "an emerging Puerto Rican nationalism and militancy" alongside the cats in the street (Melendez 74). These were not students hopelessly ambivalent and confused about how to fit back into their communities after their first year of a writing curriculum where "resistance" was simply not their option. Nor were these students who had no means to invent their own politics of language, style, and radical action. When Melendez went back to Queens College, which he would eventually leave, things were different and learning would never be quite the same again, despite the Lindsay-esque purposes that were imposed onto it. As he states,

> I returned to the QC campus that fall, feeling I had developed a cultural identity defined by my Barrio roots. [. . .] I began to have qualitatively different conversations. I was for the first time in my life experiencing the world as a Puerto Rican. I always knew I was ethnically Puerto Rican but after that summer in El Barrio I became politically aware of my pride in being Boricua. (74)

And so goes the beginning of the makings of a vernacular intellectual, a student activist, a Young Lord in New York City.

With the momentum of Melendez's story, we can continue to scrutinize student activism, and "Students' Right to Their Own Language" in literacy studies. No radical approach to understanding and dismantling racialized capitalism, politicizing Black English and language possibility/variety, and building multiracial coalitions that battle for critical literacy in classrooms can do any of the following:

- erase the presence and history of Black Caucuses formed inside of the social justice movements from the vision based on a horizon "not circumscribed by the narrow horizons of the dominant (especially ruling) group" (Bush 21);

- reduce (Black) English(es) and their urban allies (all those other "nonstandard" varieties from people of color) to incorrect grammar from hoodrats who know no better but can be rescued from it when their class oppression is wiped out;

- relegate black political traditions to a simple yin-and-yang between class struggle or cultural expression/nationalism;

- posit that Black English and its users exist solely to critique racist class exploitation as if that is all black people were brought onto this capitalistic earth to utter from their mouths;

- position students as incapacitated by democratic dialogue and critical literacy that intersects with cultural styles, "Black vernacular intellectual" traditions (Farred), and "home language";

- argue that students must first acquire a monolithic standard of academic discourse provided by their bourgeois, mainstream-perspective-bearing teachers and then position "academic discourse"/"codes of power" and African

American Vernacular as incompatible rhetorics that are contrasted instead of merged; or

- frame the world and political options according to "cultures of power" that reify power rather than dismantle it, through work that consciously uproots white supremacy and class oppression.

These antiblack, antihuman, and antilanguage inclinations exist, even in places where you would not expect them. Those of us who are students of a black vernacular, those of us who are students of a black freedom struggle against the class oppression of all of us, and those of us who are students of a long-standing, protracted battle to rewrite knowledge, "access," and (higher) education must do the work that it will take to decenter these inclinations from the places that would deny our education and thereby, our freedom.

Certainly, there is a kind of tightrope to walk here. The balance is achieved on the one side when we understand the structural racism facing African American masses and subject that to an unyielding historical materialist critique. The process of gathering the "marketplace skills" (with Standard English as a required commodity that "minority children" must acquire and trade) and rules of "cultures of power" is not, however, the same as engaging this critique, no matter how crucial these things are for students to master. We also need to balance the other side on the tightrope by uncovering the forces that reflect the cultural, rhetorical principles and linguistic philosophies that have shaped African American communities. But the most important thing about walking a tightrope is gettin ovuh to the other side. I will go back to Angela Davis here, to highlight what that other side looks like. As she has continually argued, on behalf of Marx's eleventh thesis on Feuerbach: "Philosophers have interpreted the world in various ways. The point, however, is to change it" (qtd. in Davis, "Black Nationalism" 293). And it don't stop.

NOTES

1. I am referring here to compositionists' critiques of Mina Shaughnessy's metaphors of exploration and new frontiers, the miracle workers with no precedence, in the field of basic writing. Bruce Horner critiques these metaphors in "The Birth of Basic Writing." Drawing from Ira Shor's similar critique, Horner warns that such a notion creates a blindness to history.

2. The free samples that the corporation was providing required that water, often contaminated in these parts of the world, be added, causing many babies' deaths.

3. As Marianna White Davis shows, there were three objectives that the Caucus approved: (1) THAT NCTE break any formal connections with South Africa; (2) THAT Caucus members not support any entertainers who performed in South Africa; and (3) THAT Caucus members participate in all anti-apartheid activities.

4. As Kelly further asks in her 1968 speech:

Why aren't there Blacks helping to plan this conference who have access to the papers which deal with the Black aesthetic and its relationship to composition or the Black image and why it does or does not rest in the anthologies we use or the richness and values of the language of the Black ghetto? Yes such ideas have been dealt with and their complexities examined. Why weren't these papers presented here?

5. I am borrowing the term *the black radical tradition* from Cedric Robinson's book *Black Marxism*. This tradition is historicized on the basis of a collective political praxis and worldview born from the uniqueness of generations of struggle against slavery, segregation, and current-day exploitation of the black masses that would launch the seminal rebellions of slave revolts, maroonage, and today, black nationalisms.

6. This line of thought should not be new to compositionists. Gilyard makes similar critiques of Labov at the close of *Voices of the Self.*

7. Carmichael's increasing and insistent emphasis on racial struggle created a great deal of conflict inside of SNCC, especially with Jim Forman, who wanted class analysis to remain a central aspect of black political strategizing. Factional conflicts in SNCC about class politics were never settled, with Carmichael increasingly de-emphasizing Marxian notions of class conflict; this also shaped SNCC's and Carmichael's interaction with the BPP in California. Even though Forman was perhaps SNCC's most vocal and diligent advocate of a Marxian analysis in SNCC, he still felt that Marxist groups were trying to ideologically colonize SNCC, did very little when Angela Davis and Franklin Alexander were expelled for being part of the Communist Party, and felt that socialist groups were trying too hard to recruit blacks away from SNCC instead of working with their own racist, white brethren. Though Forman seemed more aligned with the class politics of Oakland's BPP, Carmichael was the militant black spokesperson in demand by the BPP and everybody else.

8. At this time, the BPP central spokesperson was Eldridge Cleaver, a leader who had been involved with the Nation of Islam as well as Malcolm X's Organization of Afro-American Unity, and was then married to Kathleen (Neal) Cleaver, a former SNCC activist.

9. I would suggest Keith Gilyard's book on John Oliver Killens, where he contends that Killens, like Langston Hughes and others, could not "ignore appeals to Black nationalism and reasonably hope to capture the attention of the Black masses" (6). This rhetoric and politics have shaped Carmichael and the BPP also.

10. As Vijay Prashad shows, these stances did not compromise the compelling need, for instance, for Carmichael to give the keynote statement at the Arab Student Convention in 1968 or for the BPP to take up the cause of Iranian students set for deportation from the United States because of their anti-Shah activities.

11. When I speak of vernacularity, I mean "the discursive turning away from the accepted, dominant intellectual modality and vocabulary and the adoption of a new positioning and idiomatic language. It also signals a turning toward, not in a nostalgic but in a considered and deliberate fashion, and (re)connection to an originary—but not necessarily umbilical—community" so that a scholar is ideologically remade (Farred 11).

12. James Sledd, a pioneer in fighting racism in language education, dismisses Smitherman's work as ethnic separatism rather than as a demand for social justice and equality. In a 2000 review called "Race, Class, and Talking Proper: The Ebonics War Continues" in the *Texas Observer*, Sledd discussed Smitherman's collection of essays *Talkin That Talk: Language, Culture, and Education in African America.* Sledd finally lets the cat out of the bag regarding his take on Smitherman: she is really just an ethnic separatist. This criticism that Sledd harbors is not directed at simply one book, because *Talkin That Talk*, the book Sledd is reviewing, is almost like the Geneva Smitherman Reader. The collection draws together her most important articles and essays, ranging from 1972 to 1999 and including an autobiographical piece, "From Ghetto Lady to Critical Linguist." Sledd goes on to note that when Smitherman discusses Ebonics, he recognizes its features in his "own familiar speech." Again, he makes no specific references to Smitherman's text but her work does not merely discuss sentence-level grammatical patterns or pronunciations. It is, of course, nice to know that Sledd shared so many patterns of Ebonics with his black brethren. I never heard him speak, and I am no linguist, but I would love to have heard this white man from Texas deliver a speech like Malcolm X or Chuck D, though I do recognize that Africanized language shapes that of the white South. But because he does not speak about larger discourse patterns, it seems he has missed Smitherman's points. Sledd ends his review with the following:

> Few linguists have listened to my heresy in the past, but some students of black talk might listen now if I offered the sauce-for-the-gander judgment that fashionable Afrocentrism is not much different and certainly no more reprehensible than flying the Stars and Bars over the South Carolina statehouse. Both are devices to enhance insider self-esteem [. . .] absurd as ancestor worship, the most absurd custom of "good Southern families."

Sledd's point here is that Ebonics exists only because it serves Afrocentrics. While I appreciate Sledd's concern for racial integration, the neutralizing of a Jim Crow colonial system by saying that any Afrocentrist—and they are always a monolithic and singular group—could achieve the same goals as a KKK segregationist is tired and played out. The tangible results and symbolic meanings (i.e., all those lynch ropes around black necks) of those "good Southern families" waving their Confederate flags on the Old Dixie statehouse of South Carolina is not the history of Afrocentrists that Sledd claims it to be, no matter how much some Afrocentrics might actually want to re-create that kind of history against white folk. That's just not how U.S. racism has worked. Nor am I impressed with these claims that really have at their heart a plea for blacks to relinquish notions of culture and African roots. I am reminded here of the work of Diane Ravitch and her public castiga-tions of Afrocentrics, who she said were sending black children to school to only study their own race, as if that has ever happened. This type of racism has only moved many more black people toward Afrocentrism, even those who might disagree with some of its central tenets, because those theories and scholarship never get represented within the kind of complicated, ideological, or his-torical discourses that are employed, for instance, when we talk about the Renaissance and the Enlightenment. Sledd has it wrong then. As the new student of black talk he mentions, I *had been* ardently listening to him *before* in the dozen or more of his works that I had read. I wouldn't be now. It is unfortunate that he rounded out his impressive decades-long scholarship by not know-ing us "new students of black talk" at all, seeing us as nothing more than Old-Dixie flag-waving black Confederates.

13. Robin Kelley's treatment in *Freedom Dreams* and "Black Like Mao" of these activists and scholars, including Nelson Johnson and Abdul Alkalimat, is very important. It has been important for me to at least superficially give a thumbnail sketch, as best I can understand it, of the history of a radical black left. Given my baptism in these fires and my struggles to understand and be politi-cally reinvigorated by all of this, I was disappointed to read Parks's chapter, which seemed to dis-tort more than illuminate black radical thinkers and their ideological movements.

14. In 1997, Helen Halyard, the assistant national secretary of the Socialist Equality Party in the United States, spoke to student audiences at Wayne State University, the University of Michi-gan, Michigan State University, and the University of Pennsylvania, where she castigated Ebonics as the poor speech of the inner city. She said:

> The very poor English spoken in *all* impoverished neighborhoods, black, white, or His-panic, is a product of social decay [. . .]. The black nationalists have seized upon the misuse of grammar to be found in more impoverished neighborhoods in order to invent a new language that they claim is racially determined. (Italics mine)

This is nothing more than saying that black children speak incorrectly and that black scholars, the economically privileged "charlatans" whom she links back to President Nixon, have just invented an excuse for inner-city youth's improper use of grammar. Halyard goes on to say that the Black Power movement fell because blacks took jobs in universities and corporate America and since they now feel threatened, they have retreated into a "pseudoscientific jargon" surrounding Ebon-ics "to preserve all the rot of society [. . .]. Thus, street slang becomes a distinct language and impoverished inner city ghettos the basis for a separate culture."

15. As Watkins argues, "Black and White pedagogy have been as disconnected as Black and White history" (123). He also argues that the white radical intelligentsia have often overlooked the black radical tradition in education because these ideas were seen as a provincial domain for the liberations of blacks only. This tradition is also deep-rooted, from DuBois to the African American Communists who were active in teacher unions and curriculum change in 1950s Harlem.

16. In 1934, Robeson was studying African languages in England and wrote and spoke about how he found a kinship with those languages in terms of rhythm and intonation. In "The Culture of the Negro" he says that going to Africa was like a homecoming for him, and in another essay in that same year he also argued that black religion, dance, and song are traced unequivocally to Africa; it is only racist historiography that suggests otherwise. That essay, "I Want to Be African," is also where he argues that the central aim of his work is to be understood as African. After visit-ing Africa, he adamantly argued that blacks in the United States must be more conscious of their African traditions. He continued to attack the racist historiography that erased African roots in "Songs of My People" in 1949. Furthermore, for him, the racism that wiped out the roots of Africa in understanding African American history was closely connected to imperialism. As he writes in 1955 in "African and the Commemoration of Negro History":

> I believe the misrepresentation of the African and the distorted picture of the American Negro still so prevalent in our American culture, stemming as they do from the basic cause of economic exploitation, cannot be attacked or rooted out separately. Each myth is propped up by the other; both must be destroyed. When that happens, the true worth of the Negro—whether in Africa or the Americas—and his place in the mainstream of the world's culture will be properly understood [. . .]. (394)

All of these various essays can be found in *Paul Robeson Speaks* (Foner).

17. Davis's argument is that the blues both preserve and transform the West African philoso-phy of Nommo, that process of naming things, forces, and modes. The tradition of Nommo also reinvents Christian religion, and thereby the secular, because the power of the word is not exer-cised by God alone. Human beings are endowed with this creative and transformative power.

Davis, thus, situates the blueswomen in the sacred-secular continuum that Smitherman was talking about in the 1970s, where someone like Ma Rainey refigures the blues as prayer. It is also interesting to note that blues singers were associated with the Devil; someone like Robert Johnson was considered to have signed away his soul to Legba, or Elegua, the Yoruba Orisha of the Crossroads. This shows the interesting intersection of Christianity, African religious philosophies, and secular music. Davis sets field hollers, works songs, spirituals, and the blues inside an African philosophy where speech patterns are aesthetic forms also.

18. There has been a complex, varied system of thought in which Africa has centered black political expressions way before twentieth century. As Kelley argues in *Freedom Dreams*,

> to criticize us for myth making or essentialism misses the point [. . .]. [W]e dreamed the ancient world as a place of freedom, a picture to imagine what we desired and what was possible [. . .]. [It] provided black people with a language to critique America's racist state and build a new nation, for its central theme wasn't simply escape but a new beginning, dreams of black self-representation, of being on our own, under our own rules and beliefs, developing our own cultures, without interference. (15)

By the late 1800s, someone like Edward Wilmot Blyden had flipped his original 1850s proposals of a black mission to Christian-civilize Africa to an assertion that it was traditional African culture that should be developing blacks (17). His ideas were not without problems, but it is important to see how Africa represented for him a place free of exploitation. The imagining of Africa as a place that would keep black folks whole anchors a visual, musical, dance, literary, and philosophical system that includes Countee Cullen, Claude McKay, Aimé and Suzanne Césaire, Nicolás Guillén, Jayne Cortez, Lois Mailou Jones, Meta Warrick Fuller, John Biggers, Faith Ringgold, John Coltrane, Dizzy Gillespie, Peter Tosh, Afrika Bambaataa, Rock Steady Crew, Katherine Dunham, and Pearl Primus. A very rich and wide body of scholarship has centered African influences, continuities, and retentions in the black cultural spheres of the "New World": Robert Farris Thompson's *Flash of the Spirit: African and Afro-American Art and Philosophy* in 1984, Patricia Jones-Jackson's *When Roots Die* in 1987, Henry Louis Gates's *Signifying Monkey: A Theory of Afro-American Literary Criticism* in 1988, Joseph Holloway's *Africanism in American Culture* in 1990, Marion Kraft's *The African Continuum and Contemporary African American Writers: Their Literary Presence and Ancestral Past* in 1995, Paul E. Lovejoy's *Identity in the Shadow of Slavery* in 2000, Therese Higgin's *Religiosity, Cosmology, and Folklore: The African Influence in the Novels of Toni Morrison* in 2001, Keith Cartwright's *Reading Africa into American Literature: Epics, Fables, and Gothic Tales* in 2002, and Amy Levin's *Africanism and Authenticity in African American Women's Novels* in 2003. We would also do well to remember that W. E. B. DuBois's 1920s *Darkwater: Voices from the Veil* situates Africa as a place of spiritual wholeness, a central rhetorical and organizing principle to critique a corrupted Europe and its imperialism.

19. The phrase "Red Dreams of Black Liberation" is the title of one of Kelley's chapters in *Freedom Dreams*. The connections in particular between Maoism and the Black Panther Party as well as countless other black radical organizations are more complex that I can render. For an excellent overview of these organizations' politics—how and why they turned to China for a Marxist model that could challenge white and Western visions of class struggles while simultaneously incorporating a new politics of black arts—see "Black like Mao: Red China and Black Revolution" by Robin D. G. Kelley and Betsy Esch.

20. Prashad also makes it clear that this Third World solidarity was not new. He reminds his readers that Ho Chi Minh hung out in and was inspired by the Garveyite halls of Harlem in the 1920s. This is very much in line with the way the BPP inspired a multicolored left like the Young Lords Party, the Brown Berets, the American Indian Movement, the Red Guard Party, and the I Wor Keun, who all worked with one another.

21. The location of a socialist agenda for the BPP was largely informed by Chinese and Cuban revolutions which, according to Huey Newton, allowed the BPP to discard the aspects of Leninist and Marxist traditions he thought did not match a black reality. Cleaver was of the same mindset in believing that these political orientations would not do with regard to fighting and understanding racism.

22. This section is also inspired by Gilyard's critique of Lisa Delpit in "African American in Process." After an African-American-signified title like that, there is little left to say, so my comments here only scratch at the surface of the issues Gilyard addresses.

23. Delpit's chapter "The Silenced Dialogue: Power and Pedagogy in Educating Other People's Children" first appeared in the *Harvard Educational Review* in 1988.

24. Gilyard's full quotation in that interview deserves mentioning here in that it provides an alternative view to Delpit's of how one's politics of surface features evolve:

But I really had an understanding of how important it was to struggle to be fluent and that the struggle to be fluent was the most important challenge facing a writer. And that when and as you are achieving fluency, you strived to be clear because you were trying to make the most sense with your message. Again, growing up in New York and knowing a lot of writers, I understood that getting the stuff correct in terms of presentation was the last phase. I saw professional writers working with editors. So I never would have come to composition from what they would call the current-traditional paradigm because I would have been outside of that already as a creative writer. (25–26)

25. In fact, Delpit's examples look more like what Lyons discusses as a Quasi Native Education, as defined by the report of the Indian Nations at Risk Task Force, "Toward True Native Education: A Treaty of 1992." A Quasi Native Education attempts to make American hegemonic models merely more relevant to Native students and communities but still upholds the divisions between school and the students' culture. True Native Education, which rejects such divisions, is what Lyons calls for to achieve rhetorical sovereignty.

26. Black teachers like Helen Whiting were publishing in the 1930s about their experiences engaging African American children with what we would today call "culturally relevant teaching," to borrow from the contemporary term coined by Gloria Ladson-Billings. Susan Noffke notes that African American teachers like Whiting and Septima Clark were also noted for using African words and African-derived language systems (Ebonics!) in their teaching even then, while Clark was also organizing her students and the community to conduct door-to-door petitions in 1917 that eventually forced the city of Charleston to hire black teachers. Arguments for these kinds of teachers and teaching could be found in *The Negro History Bulletin*, created by Carter G. Woodson in 1937. Student projects were described in this journal, which included community-related investigations incorporating the arts, African history, and current events related to African Americans. Woodson's journal as well as DuBois's *Crisis* explicitly centered issues of "cultural and language diversity" at a time when major white journals like *Progressive Education* left these things undertheorized, if theorized at all. What this demonstrates is that there was already a public discourse about Ebonics and critical literacy in African American venues that was more complex than calls for the teaching of "code-switching."

27. The YLP is critical to contextualizing open admissions at CUNY. Miguel Melendez's *We Took the Streets: Fighting for Latino Rights with the Young Lords* is an excellent place to start, especially since Melendez speaks of his college experiences at CUNY. Melendez describes his early days as a SEEK student as follows:

On campus, I felt self-conscious, but I knew I had to get through the academic plunge somehow. Black and Latin students were an obvious minority; we were for sure a new sight in the student lounge and cafeteria. We stuck together and didn't give a shit. We knew we had as much right to be there as anyone else, and we were just beginning to understand our rights and stand up for them. We reclaimed our right to have access to higher education, and eventually demanded and received black and Puerto Rican studies programs in every single CUNY institution.

The "SEEK students," as we were referred to with an air of disdain, organized our own political activities and rallies on campus. Sure, we wanted an end to the war, but we were also insisting on an end to colonialism in Puerto Rico, Africa, Latin America, and Asia. We also wanted social justice (education, housing, health care, full and equal employment) for all national minorities within the United States.

At one of those rallies I got a chance to see and meet a young poet reciting a poem entitled, "Jibaro, My Pretty Nigger." The title alone got my attention. [. . .] I was left with one of those chills that begins in the middle of your back and travels to your hairline.

[. . .] Over the next couple of weeks I would learn that his name was Felipe Luciano [. . .] He had [. . .] formulated a very political and social persona. He could talk and persuade with style and vocabulary [. . .]. He had been paroled and now attended Queens College.

After spending several months fighting for common causes on campus, Felipe and I became good friends. The spring semester of 1967 came to a close at Queens College. Although I survived that year and was returning in the fall, I did begin to question the Eurocentric approach to higher education. I was getting bored. (70–71)

WORKS CITED

Ball, Arnetha F. "Cultural Preference and the Expository Writing of African American Adolescents." *Written Communication* 9 (1992): 501–32.

———. "Evaluating the Writing of Culturally and Linguistically Diverse Students: The Case of the African American English Speaker." *Evaluating Writing.* Ed. C. R. Cooper and Lee Odell. Urbana, IL: NCTE, 1999: 225–48.

———. "Language, Learning, and Linguistic Competence of African American Children." *Linguistics and Education* 7 (1994): 23–46.

———. "Text Design Patterns in the Writing of Urban American Students: Teaching to the Strengths of Students in Multicultural Settings." *Urban Education* 30 (1995): 253–89.

Ball, Arnetha F., and Ted Lardner. *African American Literacies Unleashed: Vernacular English and the Composition Classroom.* Carbondale: Southern Illinois UP, 2005.

Bush, Rod. *We Are Not What We Seem: Black Nationalism and Class Struggle in the American Century.* New York: New York UP, 2000.

Carson, Claybourne. *In Struggle: SNCC and the Black Awakening of the 1960s.* Cambridge, MA: Harvard UP, 1981.

Cartwright, Keith. *Reading Africa into American Literature: Epics, Fables, and Gothic Tales.* Lexington: UP of Kentucky, 2002.

Coleman, Charles. "Our Students Write with Accents: Oral Paradigms for ESD Students." *CCC* 48 (1997): 486–500.

Davis, Angela. "Black Nationalism: The Sixties and Nineties." *The Angela Davis Reader.* Ed. Joy James. Oxford: Blackwell, 1998. 289–93.

———. *Blues Legacies and Black Feminism: Gertrude "Ma" Rainey, Bessie Smith, and Billie Holiday.* New York: Vintage, 1998.

Davis, Marianna White. *History of the Black Caucus of the National Council of Teachers of English.* Urbana, IL: NCTE, 1994.

Davis, Vivian. "A Nigger Mess." *Negro American Literature Forum* 5 (1971): 94–97.

Delpit, Lisa. *Other Peoples Children: Cultural Conflict in the Classroom.* New York: New P, 1995.

DuBois, W. E. B. *Darkwater: Voices from the Veil.* New York: Harcourt, 1920.

Duncan, Garrett Albert. "Urban Pedagogies and the Ceiling of Adolescents of Color." *Social Justice* 27.3 (2000): 29–42.

Farred, Grant. *What's My Name: Black Vernacular Intellectuals.* Minneapolis: U of Minnesota P, 2003.

Foner, Eric, ed. *Paul Robeson Speaks.* New York: Citadel, 1978.

Gabbin, Joan, June Patton, James Francois, and Salim Al-Nurridin. "Black Rap." *Negro American Literature Forum* 5 (1971): 80–84, 108–14.

Gates, Henry Louis. *The Signifying Monkey: A Theory of Afro-American Literary Criticism.* New York: Oxford UP, 1988.

Gilyard, Keith. "African American Contributions to Composition Studies." *CCC* 50 (1999): 626–44.

———. "African American in Process." *Lets Flip the Script: An African American Discourse on Language, Literature, and Learning.* Ed. Gilyard. Detroit: Wayne State UP, 1996. 87–96.

———. "Holdin It Down: Students' Right and the Struggle Over Language Diversity." *Rhetoric and Composition as Intellectual Work.* Ed. Gary Olson. Carbondale: Southern Illinois UP, 2002. 115–27.

———. *Liberation Memories: The Rhetorics and Politics of John Oliver Killens.* Detroit: Wayne State UP, 2003.

———. *Voices of the Self: A Study of Language Competence.* Detroit: Wayne State UP, 1991.

Gilyard, Keith, and Elaine Richardson. "Students' Right to Possibility: Basic Writing and African American Rhetorics." *Insurrections: Approaches to Resistance in Composition Studies.* Ed. Andrea Greenbaum. Albany: SUNY P, 2001. [Pages 217–28 in this book.]

Halyard, Helen. "Ebonics and the Danger of Racial Politics: A Socialist Viewpoint." *World Socialist Web Site.* 21 Apr. 1997. 12 Aug. 2004 http://www.wsws.org/polemics/1997/apr1997/ebonics1.shtml.

Higgin, Therese. *Religiosity, Cosmology, and Folklore: The African Influence in the Novels of Toni Morrison.* New York: Routledge, 2001.

Holloway, Joseph. *Africanism in American Culture.* Bloomington: Indiana UP, 1990.

Horner, Bruce. "The 'Birth' of Basic Writing." *Representing the Other: Basic Writers and the Teaching of Basic Writing.* Ed. Horner and Min-Zhan Lu. Urbana, IL: NCTE, 1999. 3–29.

Hutchinson, Earl Ofari. *Blacks and Reds: Race and Class Conflict 1919–1990.* East Lansing: Michigan State UP, 1995.

James, Winston. "Being Red and Black in Jim Crow America: Notes of the Ideology and Travails of Afro-America's Socialist Pioneers, 1877–1930." *Souls* 1 (Fall 1999): 45–63.

Jones-Jackson, Patricia. *When Roots Die: Endangered Traditions in the Sea Islands*. Athens: U of Georgia P, 1987.

Jordan, June. "Nobody Mean More to Me Than You and the Future Life of Willie Jordan." *On Call: Political Essays*. Boston: South End, 1985. 123–39.

Kelley, Robin. *Freedom Dreams: The Black Radical Imagination*. Boston: Beacon, 2002.

———. *Hammer and Hoe: Alabama Communists during the Great Depression*. Chapel Hill: U of North Carolina P, 1990.

———. *Yo Mama's Disfunktional: Fighting the Culture Wars in America*. Boston: Beacon, 1997.

Kelley, Robin, and Betsy Esch. "Black like Mao: Red China and Black Revolution." *Souls* 1.4 (Fall 1999): 6–41.

Kelly, Ernece. "Guest Editor's Note." *Negro American Literature Forum* 5 (1971): 79.

———. "Murder of the American Dream." *CCC* 19 (1968): 106–08.

Kinloch, Valerie Felita. "Revisiting the Promise of Students' Right to Their Own Language: Pedagogical Strategies." *CCC* 57 (2005): [pp. 429–52 in this book].

Kraft, Marion. *The African Continuum and Contemporary African American Writers: Their Literary Presence and Ancestral Past*. New York: Lang, 1995.

Ladson-Billings, Gloria. *The Dreamkeepers: Successful Teachers of African American Children*. San Francisco: Jossey, 1994.

Levin, Amy. *Africanism and Authenticity in African American Women's Novels*. Gainesville: U of Florida P, 2003.

Longaker, Mark Garrett. "Market Rhetoric and the Ebonics Debate." *Written Communication* 22 (2005): 472–501.

Lovejoy, Paul E. *Identity in the Shadow of Slavery*. New York: Continuum, 2000.

Lu, Min-Zhan. "An Essay on the Work of Composition: Composing English against the Order of Fast Capitalism." *CCC* 56 (2004): 16–50.

Luke, Allan. "Genres of Power? Literacy Education and the Production of Capital." *Literacy in Society*. Ed. Ruqaiya Hasan and Geoff Williams. New York: Longman, 1996. 308–38.

Lyons, Scott. "Rhetorical Sovereignty: What Do American Indians Want from Writing?" *CCC* 51 (2000): 447–68.

Marable, Manning. *The Great Wells of Democracy: The Meaning of Race in American Life*. New York: Perseus, 2002.

McGee, Sharon James. "I Have Fun Playing with Language: An Interview with Keith Gilyard." *Writing on the Edge* 14.2 (2004): 23–37.

Melendez, Miguel. *We Took the Streets: Fighting for Latino Rights with the Young Lords*. New York: St. Martin's, 2003.

Noffke, Susan. "Multicultural Curricula: 'Whose Knowledge?' and Beyond," *The Curriculum: Problems, Politics, and Possibilities*. Ed. Landon Beyer and Michael Apple. Albany: SUNY P, 1998. 101–16.

Parks, Stephen. *Class Politics: The Movement for the Students' Right to Their Own Language*. Urbana, IL: NCTE, 2000.

Peniel, Joseph. "Dashikis and Democracy: Black Studies, Student Activism, and the Black Power Movement." *Journal of African American History* 88 (2003): 182–203.

Powell, Malea. "Blood and Scholarship: One Mixed-Blood's Story." *Race, Rhetoric, and Composition*. Ed. Keith Gilyard. Portsmouth, NH: Boynton, 1999. 1–16.

Prashad, Vijay. *Everybody Was Kung Fu Fighting: Afro-Asian Connections and the Myth of Cultural Purity*. Boston: Beacon, 2001.

Redd, Teresa. "Untapped Resources: 'Styling' in Black Students' Writing for Black Audiences." *Composing Social Identity in Written Language*. Ed. D. Rubin. Hillsdale, NJ: Erlbaum, 1995. 221–40.

Richards, Sandra, and Sidney J. Lemelle. "Pedagogy, Politics, and Power: Antinomies of the Black Radical Tradition." *Black Protest Thought and Education*. Ed. William Watkins. New York: Lang, 2005. 5–32.

Richardson, Elaine. *African American Literacies*. New York: Routledge, 2003.

Robeson, Paul. "Africa and the Commemoration of Negro History." Foner 394.

———. "I Want to Be African." Foner 88–91.

———. "Songs of My People." Foner 211–17.

Robinson, Cedric. *Black Marxism: The Making of the Black Radical Tradition*. Chapel Hill: U of North Carolina P, 1983.

Scott, Jerrie Cobb, and Valerie Kinloch. Rev. of *Class Politics: The Movement for the Students' Right to Their Own Language*, by Stephen Parks. *JAC* 21 (2001): 705–10.

Shor, Ira. "Our Apartheid: Writing Instruction and Inequality." *Journal of Basic Writing* 16 (1997): 91–105.

Sledd, James. "Race, Class, and Talking Proper: The Ebonics War Continues." *Texas Observer* Online. 21 July 2000. 1 July 2004 http://www.texasobserver.org/article.php?aid=779.

Smitherman, Geneva. "Black Idiom." *Negro American Literature Forum* 5 (1971): 88–91, 115–17.

———. "Black Power Is Black Language." *Black Culture: Reading and Writing Black.* Ed. Gloria Simmons and Helene Hutchinson. New York: Holt, 1972. 85–93.

———. "CCCC's Role in the Struggle for Language Rights." *CCC* 50 (1999): [pp. 58–82 in this book].

———. "Introduction: From Ghetto Lady to Critical Linguist." *Talkin That Talk* 1–10.

———. *Talkin That Talk: Language, Culture, and Education in African America.* New York: Routledge, 2000.

Smitherman, Geneva, and Teun A. van Dijk. *Discourse and Discrimination.* Detroit: Wayne State UP, 1988.

Thompson, Robert F. *Flash of the Spirit: African and Afro-American Art and Philosophy.* New York: Random, 1984.

Ture, Kwame. "The Higher Education of Africans and the Pursuit of Western Capitalism." *Journal of Blacks in Higher Education* 5 (Autumn 1994): 89.

Van Deburg, William. *Black Camelot: African American Culture Heroes in Their Times, 1960–1980.* Chicago: U of Chicago P, 1997.

Watkins, William. "A Marxian and Radical Reconstructionist Critique of American Education." *Black Protest Thought and Education.* Ed. William Watkins. New York: Lang, 2005. 107–36.

Wright, Richard L. "The Word at Work: Ideological and Epistemological Dynamics in African American Rhetorics." *Understanding African American Rhetoric: Classical Origins to Contemporary Innovations.* Ed. Richard Jackson II and Elaine B. Richardson. New York: Routledge, 2003. 85–98.

Wynter, Sylvia. "How We Mistook the Map for the Territory and Re-imprisoned Ourselves in Our Unbearable Wrongness of Being, of Desestre: Black Studies toward the Human Project." *Not Only the Master's Tools: African American Studies in Theory and Practice.* Ed. Lewis R. Gordon and Jane Anna Gordon. Boulder, CO: Paradigm, 2005. 107–69.

14

Writing, Rhetoric, and American Cultures (WRA) 125 — Writing: The Ethnic and Racial Experience

STACI PERRYMAN-CLARK

COURSE DESIGN

Course Description

According to the Michigan State University (MSU) course catalog, WRA 125—Writing: The Ethnic and Racial Experience is a themed-based Tier I (first-year) writing course that focuses on "drafting, revising, and editing compositions derived from readings on the experience of American ethnic and racial groups to develop skills in narration, persuasion, analysis, and documentation." WRA 125 is one of many courses offered in the Tier I Writing Program. For course content, most instructors who teach sections of this course select one specific racial or ethnic group on which to focus, and self-design course readings and other materials corresponding to these groups accordingly. Therefore, most instructors find it useful to add more specific versions of the course in addition to the one identified in the course catalog. My specific description reads as follows:

> As we use an Afrocentric lens, we'll study more specifically, African American Vernacular English (AAVE), African American Language (AAL)/ Ebonics, and African American Rhetoric (AAR). As students, you will be introduced to Ebonics/AAL and AAR as systems of speaking and writing, equally legitimate to Standard Academic English (SAE), the writing that you typically do in school. In this class, each of you will have the opportunity to write in SAE, AAL/Ebonics, or other language varieties and languages. While many of you may or may not be familiar with AAL/Ebonics, it is my hope that you all will have a clearer grasp on the language usage of African Americans, and how this language fits in college composition classrooms.

From *Composition Studies* 37.2 (2009): 115–34.

Institutional Context

MSU is a large, Midwestern, Land-Grant University. There are approximately 46,045 students total: 36,072 undergraduate and 9,973 graduate and professional. [Fifty-four] percent of its students are women, and 46 percent are men. There are approximately 4,800 faculty and staff. The average high school GPA for incoming freshmen (middle 50 percent of class) is between 3.4 and 3.8. The average SAT combined score is between 1020 and 1240, and the average ACT composite score is between 23 and 27 (http://www.msu.edu/thisismsu/facts.html).

WRA 125 is a first-year writing course that is housed in the Tier I Writing Program at MSU. Our Tier I Writing Program is unique because while it is a writing program, it is not housed in the English Department. The history of the department in which it is housed, Writing, Rhetoric and American Cultures (WRAC), is also distinctive because the department recently underwent a name change. Prior to 2003, the Department was called American Thought and Language. Tier I Writing's disciplinary orientation was not rhetoric and composition, or English studies; instead, Tier I Writing was historically taught as a history-focused course on Western civilization. Because there are still many faculty and instructors who specialize in History and American Studies, some instructors choose to focus on themes related to these disciplines. Many instructors who also teach WRA 125 often approach topics related to racial and ethnic groups with an emphasis on History or American Studies. For the course I designed, however, I chose an emphasis on scholarship associated with Composition Studies.

Teaching Rationale

Because my section WRA 125 is situated within the context of an Afrocentricity, I find it useful to clarify exactly how I understand an Afrocentric approach pedagogically. My conceptual framework primarily relies on Molefi Kete Asante as a lens. Asante defines Afrocentric education as

> a frame of reference wherein phenomena are viewed from the perspective of the African person. The Afrocentric approach seeks in every situation the appropriate centrality of the African person (Asante, 1987). In education this means that teachers provide students the opportunity to study the world and its people, concepts, and history from an African worldview. . . . Because all content areas are adaptable to an Afrocentric approach, African American students can be made to see themselves as centered in the reality of any discipline. ("Afrocentric" 171)

I understand Afrocentric education to be valuable not only because first-year writing students study alternative cultural traditions and communicative practices (like those engaged by African Americans), as opposed to studying mainstreamed forms of communication (like Standard English and the classical rhetorical tradition), but also, because I understand Afrocentricity as a pedagogical approach that is inclusive to all racial/ethnic, and gender groups. In

African American Literacies, Elaine Richardson acknowledges that an "African American-Centered or Afrocentric orientation . . . generally has a negative popular reputation because certain scholars' revisionist claims about African civilization or theories . . . could be termed separatist" (32). The way I understand Afrocentricity, however, is not separatist or exclusive to other cultural traditions. While African worldviews, concepts, and people may be at the center or focus of scholastic inquiry in my first-year writing courses, space is still made available for other rhetorical and cultural traditions to be included. With each assignment and required reading, I particularly encourage students to make overt connections between African American communicative practices and literacies, and their own literacy experiences as they investigate personal literacy practices, online literacy practices, and disciplinary literacy practices.

In Sociolinguistics and Composition Studies, Afrocentric pedagogy is also situated within the context of language acquisition and practice (Richardson; Gilyard and Richardson p. 217 in this book; Holmes). Such a focus often includes a discussion of Ebonics and African American dialect. Alice Ashton Filmer states that "an awareness of the sociolinguistic pressures facing African-American students is difficult for most outsiders, even sympathetic ones, to grasp without careful attention to the lived experiences of black people" ("African American" 265). Asante adds that "sociolinguistics or racism and cultural imperialism have to be challenged and neutralized in order to produce an area of respect where African Americans assume more than a marginal role in their own discourses" (*Manifesto* 7). Thus, a first-year writing course, I believe, must work to counter and teach students about linguistic prejudice. As Leah Zuidema cautions, while most scholars and practitioners in composition may be familiar with the CCCC Students' Right to Their Own Language (SRTOL), most organizations stop short of teaching students about SRTOL and linguistic prejudice (p. 341).

For each major assignment, I permit students to choose the language varieties that *they* determine most appropriate for each writing situation. The major writing assignments that I designed consist of the following: a linguistic literacy autobiography, a cultural literacy analysis assignment, a disciplinary literacies analysis, and a multigenre literacies project. For the literacy autobiography assignment, students compose a linguistic literacy autobiography that analyzes their spoken and written languages/language varieties at home and school. The linguistic literacy autobiography assignment uses Keith Gilyard's *Voices of the Self: A Study of Language Competence* and Geneva Smitherman's "From Ghetto Lady to Critical Linguist" (in *Talkin that Talk: Language and Education in Black America*) as lenses. While literacy autobiographies and personal narratives are common genres associated with first-year composition courses, I place greater emphasis on its relationship to Afrocentricity and Ebonics.

The next assignment moves from individual communicative practices to the communicative practices of particular online communities. For the cultural literacy assignment, students are to investigate the representation of AAVE in digital spaces. More specifically, they should formulate an argument on how AAVE is appropriated and/or discussed in online and digital spaces. For this assignment, students analyze a personal website, a popular culture website, and an academic website in order to understand how discussions and/or appropriations of Ebonics change, or do not change, depending on the website's mode, audience, and purpose. To complete this assignment, students read essays and articles that combine African American Rhetoric with technology (including Adam Banks's "Taking Black Technology Use Seriously: African American Discursive Traditions in the Digital Underground"; portions of Lisa Nakamura's *Cybertypes: Race, Ethnicity, and Identity on the Web*; and Carmen Kynard's " 'Wanted: Some Black Long Distance [Writers]': Blackboard Flava-Flavin and other AfroDigital Experiences in the Classroom"). Students also read essays on Black feminism and how visual images and linguistic representations of African American women are manipulated in digital environments (including Stephen Knadler's "E-Racing Difference in E-Space: Black Female Subjectivity and the Web-based Portfolio" and Regina Spellers's "The Kink Factor: A Womanist Discourse Analysis of African American Mother/Daughter Perspectives on Negotiating Black Hair/Body Politics").

The third assignment shifts the focus from online communities (broadly conceived) to disciplinary communities. In the disciplinary literacies assignment, students conduct research in academic journal articles published in Composition and then formulate an argument about how these conversations in the field have changed over time. To complete this assignment, students were assigned articles on Ebonics, language rights, and pedagogy between 1974 (beginning with the SRTOL Resolution) and 2000 to read in class. Once we discussed these articles as a class, students conducted research in academic journals related to Composition Studies. After they conducted this research, they composed arguments that assess the state of Ebonics in rhetoric and composition, and how discussions of Ebonics may or may not have changed over time. While research on Ebonics intersects with several fields, students were given the option to use research in fields related to Composition in order to formulate their arguments, as long as the sources were focused on the uses of Ebonics in writing.

The last assignment gives students the opportunity to synthesize key themes from the course (and their previous essays) while demonstrating creativity. The final multigenre essay asks students to take a theme from one of their previous major projects and compose a multigenre project based on that theme. In the past, some students have used multigenre essays to compose websites of AAVE resources for students. Others have prepared print-based packets with handouts and guides for elementary or high school teachers teaching AAVE. Many students select platforms consistent with their majors. If a student's major is in communications, (s)he might select a magazine to design. If the student specializes in K–12 education, (s)he might select a guide to design for teachers.

Critical Reflection

One of my first goals for the course was to initiate a class discussion of the term *Afrocentricity*. During the first week of the course, I asked students to conduct a search on the term. Students were then asked to come to class prepared to discuss their results. Although I did not specify which results they were to discuss, most students chose to record results that gave a working definition for Afrocentricity, so, for our class discussion on the search results, I asked students to identify [1] what Afrocentricity means, [2] where they searched for the term, and [3] why they chose to search in that particular place. Unpacking Afrocentricity became a useful space for introducing students to research and academic search engines. Based on students' searches, they gathered the following definitions for Afrocentricity:

- an intellectual perspective of African people
- a way to show Africans' contributions to Western culture
- something that seeks to discover and interpret information through a different filter from Eurocentric scholarship
- a worldview that emphasizes the importance of African people and culture

The majority of students chose to search in the following electronic locations: Wikipedia, Google, and World Ages Archive. When students were asked why most of them chose to search in these locations, they identified the following reasons:

- Google is easy to use, and thus, very convenient;
- Wikipedia was the first result that came up on Google; and
- Wikipedia is a good place to find factual information.

After addressing the students' decisions based on their responses to the previous questions, we discussed how different search engines and databases yield different results and how some search engines and databases may or may not be more reliable than other engines. For example, after discussing the results that students came to class with, I had students conduct a search again for *Afrocentricity* using Google, Google Scholar, and JSTOR. From these results, students concluded that Google Scholar may be more reliable than Google because it provides results from academic papers, journals, books, and other publications written about Afrocentricity, while Google displays a broad range of results that may or may not be as credible or evaluated by scholars. Issues of credibility become more complex when comparing JSTOR and Google Scholar, however. Based on our searches in JSTOR, students concluded that there is a trade-off: it may be easier to find peer-reviewed articles on JSTOR than Google Scholar since JSTOR contains a database of mostly peer-reviewed articles from academic journals written about Afrocentricity. Google Scholar also contains peer-reviewed publications, but it is often more difficult to exclude papers that have not been peer-reviewed by scholars and experts of a particular discipline from its search results. But Google Scholar has an advantage over JSTOR because it yields the most recent results, while JSTOR only stores articles published prior to a certain year.

Students also produced valuable work with particular research-related skills for their first essays. For an invention exercise to be used with the literacy autobiography assignment, students were asked to keep field notes where they recorded their daily communications, the language or language variety they used with these forms of communication, and the technological media used, if applicable. In students' literacy autobiographies they often wrote about these linguistic differences in relation to computer-based technologies. For example, many students discussed linguistic differences in relation to IM chats or writing on someone's Facebook wall. When it came time to reflect on these differences on students' blogs (the platform for students to post invention exercises related to each major assignment), many students were unsure whether or not they should use Standard English or "digital language" to discuss their linguistic choices since they were working in digital spaces. Some students claimed that because their class blogs discuss literacy and academic issues, they felt compelled to use some variety of Standard English in order to prove their credibility and ability to respond "intelligently" to academic audiences. (We complicated this notion of a standard and issues of intelligence, correctness, etc. in subsequent class discussions.) Others attempted to draw on other varieties of English, including texting or digital language because of the genre in which they were writing. Since they were in fact composing on a blog, and since blogs are digital, they argued that digital and/or text message language should be acceptable.

Students' responses to the literacy autobiography assignment were fascinating to read because they demonstrated how students made linguistically-based decisions and accounted for the decisions that were made. Consider the following example from one student's literacy autobiography, where he describes the ways in which he code-switches depending on particular contexts. He writes,

> We've all seen comedy sketches that point out one African American who works in the office building among his white coworkers. After a board meeting, everyone starts slapping high fives giving pats on the back and say encouraging things like "Good job" and "Way to go." When the congratulations get to the lone African American in the office his coworkers switch to Ebonics and say things like "Dats what I'm talkin' bout, brotha," as if he doesn't understand Standard English.

When the student writes, "Dats what I'm talkin' bout, brotha," he does so deliberately and purposefully in order to show the necessities of being able to code-switch between Ebonics and Standard English. This demonstrates how he understands the situations that he determines require Ebonics for certain communicative contexts. Such purposeful decisions are often stated explicitly in his and many other students' essays.

While the intellectual work that students did with the first assignment was quite engaging to read, there were significant challenges associated with the second assignment. Because the second assignment asks students to make an argument about the representation of Ebonics/AAVE in digital spaces using a popular culture, academic, and personal website, many students' main arguments were too broad, vague, or less valid. Because the Web is such a large place to explore, it was extremely challenging for students to draw definitive conclusions about the representation of Ebonics on the Web. Thus, many students merely concluded that Ebonics was represented differently on these three sites, an accurate, but weak, thesis that was less sophisticated than I was looking for. Another problem with this assignment derived from the categories I ascribed to the websites. Many students were unsure how to make sense of categories that did not fit neatly into any of the three categories provided, and some sites fit in more than one category. A final problem with this assignment was that students could not make a representative argument based on such a small sample of websites. In retrospect, I see significant flaws in the design of this assignment and take responsibility for the less sophisticated work produced as a result. Perhaps next time I won't provide fixed categories, nor will I set the assignment up for students to make a representative argument. Instead, I might allow students to do rhetorical analyses on the uses of Ebonics on a specific site (or sites) that they choose as they self design their own theses and arguments.

Because of the disappointment associated with the second assignment, I was at times apprehensive about assigning the third, since I believe the third assignment to be the most challenging in the sequence. As previously stated, for the third major writing assignment, students were asked to make an argument about how Composition Studies addresses issues of Ebonics, language rights, and pedagogy. What is interesting about this topic is how through discussions of Ebonics, students learned more about the field. When I first introduced this assignment, students completed an activity that prompted them to use JSTOR and Google Scholar to look for sources on Ebonics and Composition Studies. To complete this task, students were asked to record the keyword searches they used when searching for sources, the types of sources they found, and any additional trends they noticed when searching, just as they had done when searching the term *Afrocentricity*. These trends then prompted us to discuss various elements of scholarly discourse and the field's discourse. Based on their findings, students used the following keywords in various combinations: AAVE, Composition Studies, Ebonics, college. After gathering a list of keyword searches, students explained why they tried different keywords. Some students noted that Ebonics and AAVE are often used interchangeably in the field, and by relying on one term, they might miss key articles that used the other term. Other students insisted that they needed to put in "Composition Studies" to exclude sources that discuss Ebonics in other related disciplines like Sociolinguistics and Education. Others indicated that if they only searched for "Composition Studies" the results would be too broad; they only wanted sources that discussed both Ebonics and Composition Studies.

Like the Afrocentricity search activity, the Ebonics/AAVE and Composition Studies search activity also prompted us to discuss the different genres of scholarly discourse. Students noted that in JSTOR the majority of their results were journal articles, essays, and book reviews. With Google Scholar, however, students noticed that books, edited collections, book reviews, journal articles, essays, electronic resources, and academic papers (including papers that I presented at conferences) were all included. With these observations we discussed the conventions of published books, published articles, and sources that were not peer-reviewed. Because Google Scholar results generated academic papers and conference papers, and because the third assignment specifically asks students to draw from sources published in academic journal publications, students were to proceed with caution and review sources carefully. One student asked if academic books could be included in his sources, since the assignment specifically asks for journal articles. The student accurately identifies book publications that are also credible, scholarly sources that should be used. If students were to make an argument about the field, then only referring them to journals may be misleading because it excludes book-length projects and edited collections, both of which are needed to make an argument about the state of the field.

Although the third assignment taught students many of the conventions associated with academic discourse and scholarship, my feelings toward their essay responses were mixed. I was pleased with the ways that students made sense of Ebonics-based discourse in the field. They were able to pick up relatively quickly on scholarship that assesses the strengths and limitations of SRTOL, in addition to scholarship that calls for more pedagogical models on Ebonics and changes in teachers' attitudes. What I wanted to see more of, however, was the generation of their *own* new knowledge. Many students relied on summaries of disciplinary-specific themes related to Ebonics, as opposed to building on these summaries to show where the field's conversations need to go next. And when students added knowledge and critique of the field, many did not provide substantial evidence to support these claims. For example, some students argued that the field still uses racist practices in relationship to Ebonics-speaking students when it demonstrates how Ebonics is primarily appropriate for oral-based genres, but many of these students did not provide sufficient support to prove that this was the case. Other students who adapted similar arguments did not sufficiently develop them. I attribute this focus on summary to a portion of the essay prompt that suggests students begin by summarizing their sources. The next time I assign this, I'll devote more attention to development and moving from summary to analysis. Despite these issues, I was generous in my assessment of their work because the task was so challenging and it was the first time that many of my students had read or engaged anything in the field this way.

As an instructor I often like to front-load my assignments so that students complete the most difficult work first. Therefore, I wanted the final multi-genre project to be more creative and fun. This project was designed so that students could take a theme from one of their previous assignments and explore it through different genres; that way any additional reading that students would be required to complete would be minimal. I always appreciate reading these assignments at the end of the semester because they are all so drastically different from each other. And with this assignment, students also made particular linguistic choices based on the genres in which they write, just as they had done with their literacy autobiographies. Consider the following excerpt from a student's poem, where she writes about Ebonics while incorporating many of its rhetorical, phonological, and syntactical features that we studied throughout the semester: "Hey how y'all doin / Dey be some great thangs happenin / I learned Ebonics in ma WRA class / Now, I be speakin it like crazy / Do you wanna try it out? / It be fun, trust me / Although ma teacher be interesting / She goofy wit dose projects sometimes / Dey be fun though / It be killin me so bad . . ." In the first line, "doin" is an Ebonics-based phonological feature where /in/ is used for *ing* (Smitherman, *Testifyin* 17). In the second line, multiple Ebonics-based phonological features are present. The student first substitutes the /d/ sound for the /th/ sound. Next the vowel plus /ng/ in *thing*, for example, is rendered as *thang*. And she also substitutes the /in/ for /ing/ again. With regard to syntax, she makes use of the habitual *be* verb. The fourth, sixth, and eighth lines include the habitual *be* verb again. The eighth line is one of a few occasional examples of signifying, an African American rhetorical pattern that employs an "oppositional logical" or "reliance on reader's knowledge of implicit assumption that is taken to be common knowledge" (Gilyard and Richardson p. 221). The student signifies when she makes reference to the instructor's (my) "goofy" demeanor. Such a reference assumes that readers are familiar with either the individual teacher's disposition in the class or the disposition of nerdy or goofy English/composition teachers in general. The final two lines include additional incorporations of the habitual *be*, and the next to last line substitutes the /d/ sound for the /th/ sound (Smitherman, *Testifyin*). This student's excerpt is meaningful because it demonstrates her knowledge of many of the rules governing Ebonics, in addition to her ability to execute them correctly and appropriately in different writing situations across genres.

Both the study of Afrocentricity and Ebonics/AAVE/Composition Studies open up a repertoire of disciplinary and scholarly conversations about how the academy operates. Students learned more from applications of Ebonics and Afrocentric pedagogy besides the cultural and communicative practices of African Americans. They learned how Ebonics is talked about in Composition Studies, how things get published in the academy, and how to do secondary research on scholarly sources. They also became more familiar with the various genres of published scholarship. Introducing students to conversations about scholarship, the academy, and how things operate provides students with glimpses of how writing is situated in disciplinary contexts. As demonstrated through students' work with the term *Afrocentricity*, students can learn much about disciplinary practices through an exploration of Afrocentric pedagogy and African-based communicative practices.

What was still unclear from this course, however, was how students now understand the concept of Afrocentricity. Although students became more and more knowledgeable about Ebonics, the relationship between African

American cultural practices, worldviews, etc. was less apparent to students. And even though we spent the beginning of the course trying to unpack and apply concepts of Afrocentricity, an explicit discussion of Afrocentricity in the context of language remained underexplored. The next time I teach this course I want to encourage students to make overt connections between the conceptual frameworks that inform how they understand Afrocentricity and Ebonics. In doing so, hopefully as a writing teacher, I will gain a better sense of how they understand Afrocentricity at the beginning and end of the term. Despite these limitations, I was pleased that students learned many skills associated with research, the field, and the academy while learning about the communicative practices of African Americans.

WORKS CITED

Asante, Molefi Kete. "The Afrocentric Idea in Education." *Journal of Negro Studies* 60.2 (1991): 170–80.
———. *An Afrocentric Manifesto*. Cambridge, UK: Polity, 2007.
Banks, Adam. "Taking Black Technology Seriously: African American Discursive Traditions in the Digital Underground." *Race, Rhetoric and Technology: Searching for Higher Ground*. 2005. Rpt. in Craig et al. 93–112.
Craig, Collin, Staci Perryman-Clark, and Nancy C. DeJoy, eds. A *Reader for Writers*. Boston: McGraw-Hill, 2008.
Filmer, Alice Ashton. "African American Vernacular English: Ethics, Ideology, and Pedagogy in the Conflict between Identity and Power." *World Englishes* 22.3 (2003): 253–70.
Gilyard, Keith, and Elaine Richardson. "Students' Right to Possibility: Basic Writing and African American Rhetoric." *Insurrections: Approaches to Resistance in Composition Studies*. Ed. Andrea Greenbaum. Albany: SUNY P, 2001. [Pages 217–28 in this book.]
Holmes, David. *Revisiting Racialized Voice: African American Ethos in Language and Literature*. Carbondale: Southern Illinois UP, 2004.
Knadler, Stephen. "E-Racing Difference in E-Space: Black Female Subjectivity and the Web-Based Portfolio." *Computers and Composition* 18.3 (2001): 235–55.
Kynard, Carmen. "'Wanted: Some Black Long Distance [Writers]': Blackboard Flava-Flavin and other AfroDigital Experiences in the Classroom." *Computers and Composition* 24 (2007): 329–45.
"MSU Fast Facts." Office of the President: Lou Anna K. Simon. Michigan State University. 18 Apr. 2008. Web. 8 Aug. 2008.
Nakamura, Lisa. "Cybertyping and the Work of Race in the Age of Digital Reproduction." *Cybertypes: Race, Ethnicity, and Identity on the Internet*. 2002. Rpt. in Craig et al. 396–432.
Richardson, Elaine. *African American Literacies*. New York: Routledge, 2003.
Smitherman, Geneva. *Talkin that Talk: Language and Education in Black America*. New York: Routledge, 2000.
———. *Talkin and Testifyin: The Language of Black America*. 1977. Detroit: Wayne State UP, 1986.
Spellers, Regina. "The Kink Factor: A Womanist Discourse Analysis of African American Mother/Daughter Perspectives on Negotiating Black Hair/Body Politics." *Understanding African American Rhetoric: Classical Origins to Contemporary Innovations*. Ed. Ronald Jackson and Elaine Richardson. New York: Routledge, 2004. 223–43.
Zuidema, Leah. "Myth Education: Rationale and Strategies for Teaching against Linguistic Prejudice." *Journal of Adolescent Literacy* 48.8 (2005): [pp. 341–52 in this book]. Rpt. in Craig et al. 351–66.

SYLLABUS

General Course Catalog Description

Drafting, revising, and editing compositions derived from readings on the experience of American ethnic and racial groups to develop skills in narration, persuasion, analysis, and documentation.

Specific Course Description

Welcome to WRA 125! While the title of this class is highly generic, we will examine writing the American, ethnic, and racial experience, using an Afrocentric framework to explore the field of Composition Studies.

As we use an Afrocentric lens, we'll study more specifically, African American Vernacular English (AAVE), African American Language (AAL)/Ebonics, and African American Rhetoric (AAR). As students, you will be introduced to Ebonics/AAL and AAR as systems of speaking and writing, equally legitimate to Standard Academic English (SAE), the writing that you typically do in school. In this class, each of you will have the opportunity to write in SAE, AAL/Ebonics, or other language varieties and languages. While many of you may or may not be familiar with AAL/Ebonics, it is my hope that you all will have a clearer grasp on the language usage of African Americans, and how this language fits in college composition classrooms.

Since this is a Tier I Writing course, you will be expected to write. While we'll study the use of AAL/AAVE as a language and Composition Studies as a discipline, you will also practice producing various pieces of writing. Our course goals are also consistent with the shared learning outcomes passed by the Tier I Writing Program Committee. By the end of the course, hopefully you will have achieved the following goals as a student:

- To engage reading, writing, and research as epistemic and recursive processes;
- To understand AAVE/AAL/Ebonics as a valuable linguistic system, equally legitimate to Standard English;
- To understand the rhetorical value of legitimating AAVE/AAL/Ebonics and other languages/language varieties, in addition to recognizing the choices behind language variety appropriation;
- To begin negotiating the use of different linguistic systems through audience expectations;
- To identify and use the appropriate conventions depending on genre and/or audience expectations;
- To collect, analyze, and share information (both orally and written) through the research process;
- To develop arguments and present ideas to others in clear, effective, and persuasive prose in a variety of genres; and
- To begin developing analyses of both verbal and visual texts in print-based and digital environments.

Texts, Readings and Other Materials

1) Craig, Collin, Staci Perryman-Clark, and Nancy C. DeJoy, eds. *A Reader for Writers*. Boston: McGraw Hill, 2008. (Located at the MSU Bookstore)

2) *A Brief McGraw-Hill Handbook*. Boston: McGraw-Hill, 2008. (Located at the MSU Bookstore)

3) JSTOR (links to JSTOR articles can be found through Angel or http://www.lib.msu.edu)

4) Additional Course Readings from websites (links are posted on course website under "Readings")

Some of the readings will be available from our Tier I Writing Reader, *A Reader for Writers*. This can be purchased at the MSU Bookstore. Other readings will be available online through JSTOR web links accessed in ANGEL. You will be able to locate several of the readings through JSTOR, an electronic database accessible from (http://ANGEL.msu.edu). If you are unfamiliar with navigating pdf files or electronic databases, we will work together as a class to ensure that each of you can access the required readings. It is also highly recommended that you bring a laptop to class with you to work on peer projects and other group work.

Work Policies and Requirements

Reading
Reading things carefully is an important form of participation in this course. You'll be asked to respond to readings in various ways throughout the term — in class discussions, in class activities, and through your writing assignments. You must — to enable your own learning, as well as to contribute to the learning environment of others — come to class having done the assigned reading. Note that reading assignments are due on the DAY they appear on the syllabus. If I notice students aren't doing the readings, I will conduct in-class pop quizzes. As an instructor, I prefer not to do this; however, I want to make it clear that completing all required readings is necessary for doing well in this course.

Revisions and Development Workshops
Since this course assumes that good writing develops with revision, we will spend some time in class working on drafts of essays. On days when you see "Reader Review" on the syllabus, be sure to bring a hard copy version and/or (depending) an electronic version (in MS Word as a doc file — NOT docx or wps — only to access in the labs) of your work in-progress for other members of your group to see. Also be expected to attend all of these workshops classes (see attendance policy below). I will not accept final drafts from any student who does not submit a rough draft.

Revising Graded Work
You can submit revisions for two projects for reevaluation after they've been returned with grades — within certain constraints (revisions for the final project will not be accepted) :

1. Opportunities for revision will be time-limited — that is, you must submit rewrites for papers within a week of the day you get them back from me.

2. For me to accept a revised paper, you must submit to me (an MS Word attachment is fine) a REVISION MEMO in which you explain to me how you understand the work that still needs to be done, and in which you describe a plan for how you'll go about doing it.

3. You must include your revision memo, as well as your graded and commented-on original version of the paper, along with your revised version of it.

Technology Components

In addition to course readings and writing assignments, you will be expected to produce work using the following technological mediums:

1) ANGEL (see http://ANGEL.msu.edu): Most of the course work and assignments will be accessible through ANGEL, where you can download and read them by the assigned due date. Your rough drafts must also be posted as a .doc file ONLY in drop boxes on ANGEL by 8 a.m. on the as signed due dates. At various times during the semester, you will be asked to post responses to course readings in the discussion forum. At other times, you will be asked to discuss course readings using ANGEL Chat.

2) Web logs (Blogs): For Developing Work exercises (more on this later) that will help you brainstorm ideas for each of your individual essays, you will be asked to post work to your own personal Blog spaces. In class, we will learn how to create and post responses to our blogs through Blogger. Occasionally, you will also post responses to readings, and are encouraged to read classmates' blogs and comment on their responses.

3) MSU Library http://www.lib.msu.edu/: Because Assignments 2–4 will require you to do research, especially with electronic sources, the MSU library will provide you links to available databases. In addition, for those readings available in ANGEL, you will be required to access many of them through JSTOR. JSTOR is an academic database where you can access various academic journals. The link to JSTOR can be accessed both from ANGEL and MSU's library website under Commonly Used E-Resources.

4) Email: Frequently, I will send notes, directions, and other reminders about class activities and assignments through email. It is expected that you check your MSU email (through http://mail.msu.edu) frequently to make sure you are up-to-date on course materials and expectations. If you use another email location (like Yahoo! or Gmail), please make sure your settings forward mail from mail.msu.edu to that location.

Evaluation

We'll be using a point system to determine grades. Here's how things will break down:

Project 1	25 pts.
Project 2	50 pts.
Project 3	75 pts.
Project 4	100 pts.
Attendance/participation/in-class activities	100 pts.
Developing Work	80 pts.
IAR analyses	30 pts.
Online Participation (on blogs and discussion forums)	50 pts.
Total	**510 points**

This is the grading scale: 94–100% / 4.0; 87–93% / 3.5; 80–86% / 3.0; 75–79% / 2.5; 70–74% / 2.0; 65–69% / 1.5; 60–64% / 1.0.

Assignments

Library Modules
Library Modules are electronic exercises to be completed through ANGEL. They are tutorials that will help you understand research, and how to find and evaluate sources more effectively using library resources. These lessons are to be completed by the assigned due dates on the course schedule. Completion of these exercises will be reflected in your attendance/participation course grade.

Developing Work (500 words; 10 pts./each)
Developing Work (DW) Exercises are inventive spaces for working with ideas for all four of your major projects. For each project, you will complete two DW exercises. Responses to these DWs will be posted on your course blogs (details to come). These responses should be roughly 500 words, typed with careful attention paid to editing, since this work will become available to a broader audience beyond the class.

IAR Analysis (500 words; 30 pts./each)
For each unit, you will be asked to provide an Invention, Arrangement, and Revision analysis of one reading discussed in class. Sometimes you will provide your IAR analyses on your course blogs; other times, you will discuss these analyses in ANGEL class discussions.

Reflective Essays (1 page)
Reflective essays are to be turned in as a cover letter with your submission packet for projects 1–3 (project 4 will require a separate reflection prompt). For these essays you will discuss the Invention, Arrangement, and Revision strategies you used to create your texts. (Note: As part of your submission packets for each project, you will also turn in rough drafts of the marked-up copies of your essays where you received feedback during peer review.) Your project will NOT be graded unless you turn in a cover letter that discusses your IAR choices.

Project 1: Literacy Autobiography (4–6 pages; 25 pts.)
As a lens for completing this assignment, we will look to excerpts from Keith Gilyard's *Voices of the Self*. In this book, Gilyard constructs a literacy autobiography, where he analyzes his use of AAL/AAVE and compares it to the language that is used in school. In light of this, you will be asked to create a literacy autobiography that includes a discussion of the differences between your home language and school language.

Project 2: Cultural Literacy (5–7 pages; 50 pts.)
For this unit we will shift gears from analyzing our personal literacies, to examining alternative modes for writing in online spaces. Here, we'll incorporate evidence from academia, popular culture, visual, and digital environments in order to investigate attitudes toward AAVE/AAL and AAVE/AAL's

appropriation in these spaces. You will ultimately create an expository essay that argues how the general public and academia appropriate or portray AAVE/AAL through digital media.

Project 3: Disciplinary Literacy (5–7 pages; 75 pts.)
In unit 3, you will move from cultural literacy to disciplinary literacy, where you'll discuss Composition Studies as a discipline. We will read select pieces from scholars in Composition Studies to examine how both fields deal with AAVE/AAL. You will create an expository research essay that argues how both the scholars we've read, in addition to scholars you research on your own, confront/deal with, or discuss AAVE in Composition Studies.

Project 4: Multigenre/Remix (Lengths may vary; 100 pts.)
For the final unit, you will select a theme/thesis or research question that deals with issues we've covered (from units 1–3) throughout the term. Using this theme/thesis, you will compose a multigenre essay where you'll investigate recurring themes regarding AAVE/AAL. We'll work extensively on how to craft an effective research question and where to look for research. You may also consider experimenting with manipulating both standard and nonstandard languages within this essay. Further guidelines will be given later.

List of All Required Readings

Ball, Arnetha. "Expository Writing Patterns of African American Students." *English Journal* 85.1 (1996): 27–36.

Banks, Adam. Chapter 4. *Race, Rhetoric, and Technology: Searching for Higher Ground.* Mahwah: Erlbaum, 2005. (pp. 93–112 in *A Reader for Writers*)

Conference on College Composition and Communication. "Students' Right to Their Own Language." *College Composition and Communication* 25 (1974): 25.

Craig, Collin, Staci Perryman-Clark, and Nancy C. DeJoy, eds. *A Reader for Writers.* Boston: McGraw-Hill, 2008.

Gilyard, Keith. "Rapping, Reading and Role-Playing." *Voices of the Self: A Study of Language Competence.* 1991. Rpt. in Craig et al. 25–40.

———, and Elaine Richardson. "Students' Right to Possibility: Basic Writing and African American Rhetoric." *Insurrections: Approaches to Resistance in Composition Studies.* Ed. Andrea Greenbaum. Albany: SUNY P, 2001.

Knadler, Stephen. "E-Racing differences in E-Space: Black Female Subjectivity and the Web-Based Portfolio." *Computers and Composition* 18.4 (2001): 235–55.

Kynard, Carmen. " 'Wanted: Some Black Long Distance [Writers]': Blackboard Flava-Flavin and other AfroDigital experiences in the classroom." *Computers and Composition* 24.3 (2007): 329–45.

Nakamura, Lisa. "Cybertyping and the Work of Race in the Age of Digital Reproduction." *Cybertypes: Race, Ethnicity, and Identity on the Internet.* 2002. Rpt. in Craig et al. 396–432.

Nembhardt, Judith. "A Perspective on Teaching Black Dialect Speaking Students to Write Standard English." *The Journal of Negro Education* 52.1 (1983): 75–82. (pp. 433–42 in *A Reader for Writers*)

Ramsey, P. A. "Teaching the Teachers to Teach Black-Dialect Writers." *College English* 41.2 (1979): 197–201.

Redd, Teresa, and Karen Schuster-Webb. *Teacher's Introduction to African American English: What a Writing Teacher Should Know.* Urbana: NCTE, 2005. (Ch. 1–2.)

Richardson, Elaine. "African American-Centered Rhetoric, Composition, and Literacy: Theory and Research." *African American Literacies.* London: Routledge, 2003.

Spellers, Regina. "The Kink Factor: A Womanist Discourse Analysis of African American Mother/Daughter Perspectives on Negotiating Black Hair/Body Politics." *Understanding African American Rhetoric.* Ed. Ronald Jackson and Elaine Richardson. New York: Routledge, 2004. 223–43.

Smitherman, Geneva. "It Bees that Way Sometime: Present-Day Sounds in Black English." *Talkin and Testifyin: The Language of Black America.* Detroit: Wayne State UP, 1977.

———. "Introduction: From Ghetto Lady to Critical Linguist." *Talkin that Talk: Language and Education in Black America.* New York: Routledge, 2000. Rpt. in Craig et al. 53–64.

———. "CCCC's Role in the Struggle for Students' Language Rights." *College Composition and Communication* 50.3 (1999): 349–76.

Zuidema, Leah. "Myth Education: Rationale and Strategies for Teaching against Linguistic Prejudice." *Journal of Adolescent Literacy* 48.8 (2005): 668–75. Rpt. in Craig et al. 351–66.

Schedule

DAY 1—Course Introductions; Syllabus; Language Attitude Questionnaire

DAY 2—Introduce Assign. 1; Create Blogs; Discuss Afrocentricity; **DUE: Come to class with search results from "Afrocentricity"**

DAY 3—**MLK Day—NO CLASS**

DAY 4—Watch and discuss American Tongues; Discuss Zuidema; Discuss IAR using Zuidema; Read Zuidema: "Myth Education"

DAY 5—Discuss Smitherman and Redd/Schuster Webb; Discuss IAR; Contrastive Analysis exercises; **Read Smitherman: "It Bees That Way"; Read Redd/Schuster Webb (Chs. 1–2); IAR of one Reading due on Blog**

DAY 6—Discuss Gilyard; Discuss DW1a; Practice doing contrastive analysis for literacy autobiographies; **DW1a Due; Read Gilyard Chs. 2–3; Bring literacy logs to class**

DAY 7—Q/A session for paper 1; Practice Peer Reviewing and creating a focus for paper 1; **Read Smitherman: "From Ghetto Lady"; DW1b Due**

DAY 8—Peer Review workshop (review attendance policy); **Rough Draft due in drop box by 8 am; Library Module 1: Searching with a Purpose Due**

DAY 9—Introduce Assignment 2; Brainstorming topics; Preliminary web browsing; **Submission Packet for Assignment 1 Due by class time**

DAY 10—Discuss Banks; Work with www.BlackPlanet.com; Discuss Kynard; **Read Banks: "Talking B(l)ack"; Read Kynard: "Wanted"**

DAY 11—Preliminary web browsing; Discuss Nakamura; **Read Nakamura: "Cybertyping"; DW2a Due**

DAY 12—Discuss Spellers; Discuss Knadler; Web browsing and constructing thesis; **Read Spellers: "The Kink Factor"; Read Knadler: "E-racing"**

DAY 13—**In-Class Conferences; DW2b due**

DAY 14—Assignment 2 Check-In; Oral Reports on Additional sources; **Report on 2–3 articles you found in research on Ebonics in Digital Spaces; Library Module 2: Identifying Credible Websites Due**

DAY 15—Rubric for Assignment 2; Expectations for assignment 2; **IAR for one reading Due on Blog**

DAY 16—Peer Reader Review; **Rough Draft due in drop box by 8 am**

DAY 17—Introduction to Composition Studies as a discipline; Practice doing keyword searches; **Library Module 3: Popular, Scholarly, Trade Due; Submission Packet for Assignment 2 Due by class time**

DAY 18—Discuss what writing teachers should do to help students write; Discuss Ramsey; Discuss Nembhardt; **Read Ramsey: "Teaching the Teachers"; Read Nembhardt: "A Perspective on Teaching"**

DAY 19—Discuss SRTOL; Oral reports on Oakland Ebonics case; Oral Reports on Black English Case; **Skim CCCC Students' Right to Their Own Language (SRTOL) Position Statement (click on link that opens as a PDF after reading the background)**

DAY 20—Discuss Ball; Discuss Richardson; Looking for Additional sources; **Read Richardson and Gilyard: "Students' Right to Possibility"; Read Ball: "Expository"**

DAY 21—Work on Annotated Bibliographies; **Read Brief McGraw-Hill Handbook on Annotated Bibliographies (196–198); DW3a Due**

DAY 22—Discuss Smitherman and Canagarajah; **Read Smitherman: "CCCC's Role in the Struggle"; Read Canagarajah: "Safe Houses"**

DAY 23—**DW3b + Annotated Bib due; Be prepared to discuss 1–2 sources you're using in paper 3**

DAY 24—Rubric for Paper 3; Peer Reader Review; **Rough Draft due in drop box by 8 am**

DAY 25—Introduce Assignment 4; Looking at Sample MGE's; Brainstorming/Recapping themes; **Submission Packet for Assignment 3 Due by class time**

DAY 26—MGE Work; Work drafting genres; Identifying Genres and Conventions

DAY 27—**DW4a Topic Proposal Due on Blog; CONFERENCES; NO CLASS; continued work on MGE**

DAY 28—**CONFERENCES; NO CLASS; continued work on MGE**

DAY 29 — **DW4b Draft of 1 genre due (in print);** Continued work time on genres; In-class conferencing and consulting

DAY 30 — Assignment 4 Check-in; Continued work time on genres

DAY 31 — Continued work on genres

DAY 32 — Rubric for Assignment 4; Peer Reader Review; **Rough Draft due**

DAY 33 — EXAM PERIOD; **FINAL MGE DUE DURING EXAM PERIOD**

PART FOUR

Pluralism, Hybridity, and Space

15 The Place of World Englishes in Composition: Pluralization Continued

A. SURESH CANAGARAJAH

"The task, as we see it, is to develop an internationalist perspective capable of understanding the study and teaching of written English in relation to other languages and to the dynamics of globalization. At a point when many North Americans hold it self-evident that English is already or about to be the global lingua franca, we need to ask some serious questions about the underlying sense of inevitability in this belief—and about whose English and whose interests it serves"

—Horner and Trimbur 624.

I n their award-winning essay "English Only and U.S. College Composition," Bruce Horner and John Trimbur trace the pedagogical and cultural developments that have led to the conception of English writing in the United States as a unidirectional and monolingual acquisition of literate competence. While these assumptions have been motivated by the modernist ideology of "one language/one nation," the authors envision that postmodern globalization may require us to develop in our students a multilingual and polyliterate orientation to writing. They outline the shifts in curriculum, policy, and research that will promote such a broadened pedagogical orientation in the future. However, as a teacher of writing for ESL and multilingual students, I am left with the question: what can I do to promote this pedagogical vision in my classroom now? I am concerned about the implications of this policy change for the texts produced by students in my current writing courses. Though the policy changes Horner and Trimbur advocate are admittedly "long term ideals" (623), teachers don't have to wait till these policies trickle down to classrooms. They have some relative autonomy to develop textual practices that challenge dominant conventions and norms before policies are programmatically implemented from the macro-level by institutions (see Canagarajah, *Resisting Linguistic Imperialism*). The classroom is a powerful site

From *College Composition and Communication* 57.4 (2006): 586–619.

of policy negotiation. The pedagogies practiced and texts produced in the classroom can reconstruct policies ground up. In fact, the classroom is already a policy site; every time teachers insist on a uniform variety of language or discourse, we are helping reproduce monolingualist ideologies and linguistic hierarchies.

This is an essay on pluralizing composition from the specific angle of emergent World Englishes. It explores the textual and pedagogical implications of the policy changes outlined by Horner and Trimbur. We may consider this article as taking off where Horner and Trimbur leave us. (The epigraph with which this essay begins is literally the final statement of their article.) Since their project is historical. Horner and Trimbur only account for the ways in which monolingual norms evolved in composition. It is not their intention to outline the pedagogies developing under the pressure of multilingual communicative practices or to fashion such pedagogies anew. Though I attempt to accomplish these objectives, I undertake a humbler task first: I outline some ways of accommodating in academic writing diverse varieties of English. This project can accompany, inspire, and even facilitate the more radical project (for which Horner and Trimbur call) of engaging with multiple languages in English composition.

THE IMPLICATIONS OF GLOBALIZING ENGLISH

Before I articulate the ways in which World Englishes[1] can find a place in academic writing, it is important to understand their new status in contemporary society. There are many developments that challenge the privileged place of what have been called "native" varieties—i.e., what I call the Metropolitan Englishes (ME), spoken by the communities that traditionally claimed ownership over the language in England, the United States, Canada, Australia, and New Zealand. Since the 1980s, Kachru has persistently argued that World Englishes (WE) are rule governed, with well-established norms and communicative functions suitable for their new environment. Others have taken an ideological tack to this argument and demonstrated how these varieties evolve from ways in which local communities appropriate the language according to their social practices to resist the colonizing thrust of English (see Canagarajah, *Resisting Linguistic Imperialism*; Pennycook). A more recent argument is that appropriating English according to the preferred interests and identities of the speaker is both a condition for gaining voice and also the most effective way for developing proficiency in that language (Peirce). The nativization, resistance, and voice arguments notwithstanding, even in postcolonial communities like my own Sri Lanka, it is either "standard American" or "standard British" English that is treated as the target for conversational and literate purposes in educational institutions. Though the stigma attached to WE is changing, these varieties are still treated as unsuitable for classroom purposes. However, the intensified globalization of English in postmodern society further challenges this unequal and hierarchical relationship between English varieties. If earlier arguments haven't radically changed the status of English

varieties in literacy and education, recent social and communicative developments should.

To begin with raw statistics, the demography of English is changing.
According to the British applied linguist David Graddol, the "native" speakers[2] "lost their majority in the 1970s" (58). Two different projections for year
2050 give the distribution of the speakers as follows:

	Graddol	Crystal
English as sole or first language:	433 million	433 million
English as additional/second language:	668 million	462 million

Even according to Crystal's conservative estimate (see *English as a Global
Language*), multilingual users of the language will be about 30 million more
than the "native" speakers. Graddol is stating the obvious when he proclaims.
"[I]n future [English] will be a language used mainly in multilingual contexts
as a second language and for communication between nonnative speakers"
(57). This changing demography of English has profound implications for
language norms. At its most shocking, this gives the audacity for multilingual
speakers of English to challenge the traditional language norms and standards
of the "native speaker" communities. My fellow villagers in Sri Lanka would
say, "Who the hell is worrying about the rules-schools of Queen's English,
man?" After all, multilingual speakers have a much larger speech community
with which to use their varieties. Their reference point is not British or American communities anymore. They know that there are millions of people around
the world who use varieties like their own and are open to negotiating differences with sensitivity and skill. Therefore, they are now using their own varieties with greater confidence.

These changes are encouraging a reconsideration of the native/nonnative
distinction between varieties. They compel us to think of English as a plural
language that embodies multiple norms and standards. English should be
treated as a multinational language, one that belongs to diverse communities
and not owned only by the metropolitan communities. From this point of
view, "standard" Indian English, Nigerian English, and Trinidadian English
would enjoy the same status as British English or American English, all of
them constituting a heterogeneous system of Global English (Brutt-Griffler;
Crystal, *Language Revolution*; McArthur; Modiano). This perspective will also
make us reexamine the distinction native/nonnative when it comes to speaker
identities. Should we call a person who has been speaking Sri Lankan English
since his birth a nonnative speaker of English? Granting even my multilingualism, the use of the term *nonnative* is difficult to apply to me in relation to
English. To use the terminology developed by applied linguists (see Hamers
and Blanc), I may be called a *balanced bilingual* who has acquired *simultaneous
bilingualism* in a case of *childhood bilinguality*. That is, I have acquired Tamil
and English in parallel, with equal facility, since my earliest days of linguistic development. Therefore, I am tempted to ask in Babu English,[3] "Honored
Sirs and Madams, I humbly beseech you, which language am I a native of?"

Only the color of my skin would influence someone to call me a nonnative speaker of English—not my level of competence, process of acquisition, or time of learning. Therefore, it is more appropriate to use terms such as *expert* and *novice* that don't invoke considerations of blood, family, or race to describe proficiency (see Rampton). We should recognize that there are expert users of Sri Lankan English as there are of American English. If each of us can acknowledge that we are novice speakers of the other's variety, we will make efforts to develop competence in it (if necessary for our purposes) without expecting the other to defer to our own variety as the universal norm.

Contemporary social and economic developments in transnational life would force us to argue that English varieties shouldn't be treated as relevant and functional only within their respective communities of origination—i.e., Indian English for India, and Nigerian English for Nigeria. Just as composition was stultified by the monolingual norm of the nation-state framework, the nativization, resistance, and voice arguments for WE won't go far enough if they are made on behalf of self-contained local communities. Local Englishes are now traveling—just as American English travels through CNN, Hollywood, and MTV. Often it is CNN that carries the diverse Englishes of reporters, politicians, and informants—not to mention musicians and film stars—into the houses of the most reclusive middle class families in the West. Furthermore, diaspora communities have brought their Englishes physically to the neighborhoods and doorsteps of American families. If they are not working with multilingual people in their offices or studying with them in schools, Anglo Americans are exposed to WE in other ways. The new work order involves an international network of production, marketing, and business relationships. Personnel from the outsourced company who call us in Indian English from Bangalore or Madras are the least of the links in this network. As industrial, business, and marketing agencies across the world communicate with each other, they are compelled to conduct transactions in different varieties of English. At its most intense, the Internet presents a forum where varieties of English mingle freely. There are online journals, discussion circles, and websites that anyone in the world can go to for information. But without a willingness to negotiate Englishes, we get little from these resources. Scholars studying transnational interactions in English show the creative strategies multilingual speakers use to negotiate their differences and effectively accomplish their purposes, often with no deference to native speaker norms (see Firth; Seidlhofer). ME/monolingual speakers come off as relatively lacking in these negotiation skills in comparison with WE speakers (Higgins), with dire implications for their ability to succeed in such transactions.

Developments like this show that in order to be functional postmodern global citizens, even students from the dominant community (i.e., Anglo American) now need to be proficient in negotiating a repertoire of World Englishes. In the case of second language teaching, we already have a body of research that reveals the limitations of curricula that favor only one variety of English—the North American, Australian, or British standard that has traditionally dominated education. In Toronto, Somali immigrant students learn "hip-hop English" more effectively outside the classroom, disregarding the established code of the school (Ibrahim). For these students, hip-hop English serves more functions in peer-group social interaction and self-presentation. In schools in London, Bengali students learn Jamaican English through inter-action with their friends while absconding from classrooms that insist on standard British English (Harris et al.). Since Jamaican English serves more functional purposes for networking in their immediate environment, students tap into their intuitive language competence and personal learning strategies to master a variety that is not formally taught to them.

A more ironic example comes from Eva Lam's ethnographic study of a Chinese American student in California. Almon is frustrated by the negative identities provided for his "broken English" in school. Therefore, he is tongue-tied in the classroom. However, on the Internet, Almon is loquacious. He uses his own English with multilingual speakers of that language (who also come with diverse varieties of their English). Since he has a global speech commu-nity to relate to on the Internet (different from the "native English commu-nity" imposed by the teacher in the classroom), and a language that he owns collectively with this multilingual community of English speakers, his attitude and usage show significant changes. Being the founder of the fan group for Japanese pop singer Ryoko, and the host of an internationally popular home page, Almon engages in a range of discourses (i.e., pop culture, religion, ther-apy, and netspeak) and a variety of genres (i.e., biographical, expressive, and narrative writing in his homepage) all in English with his Internet buddies who display varying proficiency levels. The researcher has evidence of a visi-ble improvement in Almon's English as he engages quite effectively in these communicative interactions.

Lam brings out the many ironies in this situation when she concludes:

> Whereas classroom English appeared to contribute to Almon's sense of exclusion or marginalization (his inability to speak like a native) which paradoxically contradicts the school's mandate to prepare students for the workplace and civic involvement, the English he controlled on the Internet enabled him to develop a sense of belonging and connectedness to a global English-speaking community (476).

It is not surprising that classroom language based on "native" norms is irrel-evant to what students regard as more socially significant needs in their everyday lives. This is confirmed by the choices made by Ibrahim's Somali students and Harris et al.'s Bengali student. Furthermore, a classroom based on "standard" English and formal instruction limits the linguistic acquisition, creativity, and production among students. When Almon is engaged in pur-posive communication in socially valued encounters, he produces texts of a range of genres, uses the language actively, and learns collaboratively with his peers. Thus it is outside the classroom that students seem to develop com-municative competence and negotiation strategies for "real world" needs of multilingualism. Classes based on monolingual pedagogies disable students in contexts of linguistic pluralism. We also learn from this example that taking ownership of English, or appropriating the language by confidently using it to serve one's own interests according to one's own values, helps develop fluency in English. This observation confirms what many teachers have known all along: valuing students' own languages—in this case, nonprestige varieties of English—helps in the acquisition of other dialects, including the socially valued dominant varieties. As we recognize now, the vernacular is an asset in the learning of mainstream languages (see Cummins). Valuing the varieties that matter to students can lessen the inhibitions against dominant codes, reduce the exclusive status of those codes, and enable students to accommodate them in their repertoire of Englishes.

If it is important then to develop proficiency in the range of new Englishes gaining importance in contemporary society, how do we proceed with pedagogical practice? My colleagues in TESOL are busy these days redefining their teaching activity (see Canagarajah, "Introduction"; Holliday; Kumaravadivelu). We realize that rather than developing mastery in a single "target language," students should strive for competence in a repertoire of codes and discourses. Rather than simply *joining* a speech community, students should learn to *shuttle* between communities in contextually relevant ways. To meet these objectives, rather than focusing on correctness, we should perceive "error" as the learner's active negotiation and exploration of choices and possibilities. Rather than teaching grammatical *rules* in a normative and abstract way, we should teach communicative *strategies*—i.e., creative ways to negotiate the norms relevant in diverse contexts. In such a pedagogy, the home/first language may not be a hindrance (or "interference," as labeled in traditional TESOL discourse), but a resource (as we find through Almon's experience).

Would such changes mean that speakers of English will soon lose the ability to communicate with each other as diverse varieties are legitimized for educational and social purposes? Would all this simply perpetuate the ancient curse of Babel—as some linguists fear (see Crystal, *Language Revolution* 60)? Here, some of the intuitive strategies that multilingual people use for communication come to our rescue. According to speech accommodation theory (see Giles), multilingual people always make adjustments to each other as they modify their accent or syntax to facilitate communication with those who are not proficient in their language. Furthermore, they come with psychological and attitudinal resources, such as patience, tolerance, and humility, to negotiate the differences of interlocutors (see Higgins). A refusal to deal with difference (or cooperate with an interlocutor) is not congenial for communication—even when the language of both speakers is the same! Other interpersonal strategies of repair, clarification, gestures, and back channeling are also wisely deployed to negotiate speech difference (see Firth; Gumperz). Indeed such cooperative values and strategies are intuitive to multilingual people who have had to always engage with diverse language groups in their environment since precolonial times (see Khubchandani). At any rate, the different varieties of English still belong to the same grammatical system. Some linguists are of the opinion that the underlying grammatical and syntactic structure (i.e., the deep structure, in Chomskian terms) is the same across the diverse varieties of English (Pullum). From this point of view, speakers don't have to be experts in another variety of English in order to speak to other communities. They simply need the metalinguistic, sociolinguistic, and attitudinal preparedness to negotiate differences even as they use their own dialects. Ideally, this will approximate the Biblical experience of Pentecost—the archetypal metaphor of unity in diversity—as speakers communicate with each other without suppressing (in fact, while celebrating) their differences. While proceeding toward this ideal, we must still acknowledge that such interactions take place in contexts marked by power differences (as I will illustrate below), with unequal roles and responsibilities for speakers, which those from minority communities have to negotiate with ideological clarity and linguistic creativity.

FOCUSING ON COMPOSITION

In the context of the sociolinguistic changes in the global use of English and the pedagogical changes to address them in applied linguistics/TESOL, we shall now turn to examine the place of English in composition. What is the place of WE in college writing? Relative to the developments in TESOL, its place is still unequal and pejorative. Though some of the positions we adopt in composition classrooms are not explicitly proposed or theorized, we do have an unwritten rule that stratifies the codes in the following way. If at all, we permit WE only in certain well-defined contexts:

WE for literary texts; ME for "serious" texts.

WE for discoursal features; ME for grammar.

WE for informal classroom interactions; ME for formal production.

WE for speaking; ME for writing.

WE for home; ME for school.

WE for local communication; ME for international communication.

Let me elaborate. Teachers may prescribe an Achebe, Raja Rao, or Walcott, who uses local varieties, as a literary reader, but when students write an essay on these texts they have to use ME (see also Lu). At best, we may permit the use of WE for personal or creative writing. Even here, we'll appreciate if the authorial voice is in ME, switching to WE only for the voices of characters in the text. This dichotomy, in fact, characterizes our use of readings in the classroom. While we may use postcolonial literary texts as supplementary reading, we use texts that use only ME for discipline-based or expository reading. (This practice is partly dictated by exigency: publishers have already "sanitized" academic texts written in WE. Therefore, texts that feature other varieties from non-Western communities rarely reach the educational institutions here.) To move to the second form of stratification, even the most progressive of compositionists (e.g., Schroeder, Fox, and Bizzell) may permit WE preferences in style, tone, and discourse (at what we may call the extra-sentential or rhetorical level), while insisting on ME for the sentential level of grammar, syntax, and spelling conventions. [Note that some compositionists (see Elbow, "Vernacular Literacies") consider the normative variety for writing as a neutral code, Standard Written English (SWE), which is not native to any community. However, I think that SWE is closer to the standard varieties of traditional "native speaker" communities and distant from WE varieties like my own Sri Lankan English. SWE is simply the textual realization of ME in composition. Hence my preference to label the normative variety for writing as ME.]

Outside the text, we have other ways of segregating the codes. We may accept WE for informal classroom activities (student text discussions whether in groups or as peer critiques; student-instructor conversations; and "low stakes" written assignments such as peer commentary, e-mail, and online discussions) but insist on traditional norms for graded formal assignments (essays and examinations). For some instructors, this arrangement translates as WE for speaking and ME for writing, motivated by the assumption that writing is formal and requires the established code.[4] These forms of stratification, together with the other two discussed in the previous paragraph, resemble what many progressive practitioners have proposed as a pragmatic pedagogical strategy of using the local variants as a means for transitioning to the established code. Widely discussed as a pedagogical option for African American students (see Baugh; Heath; Delpit), this practice has been extended to the teaching of other language-minority communities in more recent times (see Heller and Martin-Jones; Lucas and Katz; Pease-Alvarez and Winsler).

The final two forms of stratification, at a more macro social level, are based on well-known arguments made by liberal linguists. Local variants for home and the dominant variety for school is behind the practice favored in Heath's *Ways with Words* (see also Baugh; Labov; Wheeler). Others in TESOL (e.g., Widdowson) have argued for the use of local variants for intracommunity purposes, while metropolitan norms are used when communities interact at the institutional and/or international level. Scholars adopting this position would tolerate WE being taught in postcolonial communities for local usage; but they would insist on ME for formal, institutional, and international usage (Widdowson). Needless to say, the message conveyed to students in even such presumably progressive positions is that local Englishes should have only a restricted place in one's repertoire.

The above approaches for accommodating local varieties in the classroom provide for many teachers the way to practice the CCCC resolution of Students' Right to Their Own Language (SRTOL). The extent of the students' right here seems to be letting them use their English at home and in their local communities, and for informal purposes and low-stakes writing needs in the classroom. But shouldn't SRTOL also mean that students have the right to use their vernacular for formal purposes? It appears that SRTOL is interpreted as a policy of tolerance (i.e., permitting nonvalorized codes to survive in less-prestigious contexts), not promotion (i.e., making active use of these vernaculars or developing them for serious purposes). Another concern is that SRTOL doesn't seem to extend to the use of all varieties of English. Though the statement itself doesn't make the identity of variants covered clear, the supplementary document by the committee reveals that the authors are thinking primarily of African American Vernacular English (AAVE) and what they call "Chicano" English (see CCCC, *Students' Right* p. 19 in this book). There are understandable reasons why the SRTOL committee mentions only the English of the African American and Chicano communities. In traditional language rights discourse, *national minorities* (those with a history as long as the dominant groups and/or enjoying a sizeable demography and spread) have been given preferred treatment in language rights, while *ethnic minorities* and recent immigrant groups (with a more limited history, spread, and number) are treated as inconsequential (May). But this practice has been questioned lately, as the orientation to language rights based on the nation-state has become outmoded, just as the borders of countries have become porous under the influence of globalization. Now, as even Anglo American students are compelled to develop proficiency in multiple Englishes in order to shuttle between communities in the postmodern world, we must take a fresh look at the treatment of WE in SRTOL.

TOWARD MULTILINGUAL WRITING MODELS

I am glad that some composition scholars are disturbed by the inconsistencies in the current practices and attitudes toward English in composition pedagogies. Peter Elbow would go further and call this state of affairs a "contradiction" ("Vernacular Literacies"126). He is among the few who have started thinking and writing actively to resolve the dilemmas present in implementing SRTOL. Mindful of the concern that minority students shouldn't be further disadvantaged by being excluded from attaining proficiency in established traditional varieties of English while being empowered to use their own (a criticism raised by minority scholars themselves), Elbow adopts a two-pronged approach: "A good strategy for handling contradiction is to introduce the dimension of time: to work for the long-range goal of changing the culture of literacy, and the short-range goal of helping students now" ("Vernacular Literacies" 126). He proposes to accomplish this by letting minority students use their own varieties for their early drafts but teaching them copy editing skills and/or getting them help from copy editors so that their final product conforms to the expectations in the academy.[5] This way, he would help students to acquire SWE in order to prosper in the dominant culture of literacy and succeed in education and society. However, by keeping other varieties alive in the composition classroom and helping students develop written competence in them in low-stakes activities, he would be working toward the long-term goal of full acceptance for all dialects.

Though this is a pragmatic resolution that is sensitive to the competing claims in this debate—i.e., the importance of challenging the inequalities of languages and the need to master the dominant codes for social and

educational success—I have experienced certain difficulties in implementing this approach. I have found that minority students are reluctant to hold
back their Englishes even for temporary reasons. In my ethnography of both
African American and ESOL students, I have discovered the strategies students covertly adopt to bring their Englishes into formal academic writing in
a curriculum that encourages their varieties in everything other than formal/
graded assignments (Canagarajah, "Safehouses"; *Resisting Linguistic Imperialism* chapter 7). The desire to use one's vernacular even in formal texts is easy
to understand. Everything from language socialization approaches and Bakhtinian theories of discourse to poststructuralist linguistics teaches us that to
use a language meaningfully is to appropriate it and make it one's own (see
Peirce). Proficiency requires adapting the new language for one's own values
and interests. To use a language without any personal engagement, even for
temporary utilitarian and pragmatic reasons, is to mimic not speak. It means
"acting white" for my African American students and "putting a show" for
Sri Lankan students.

     In the light of such student resistance, we become alert to some ambi-
guities in Elbow's model. Despite its attempts to accommodate diversity, the
model still falls under the dominant unidirectional monolingualist paradigm in writing. Other varieties of English are accepted only as tentative, dis-
pensable moves toward ME norms. The editing of the other Englishes in the
final product may also lump these varieties into the category of "errors" to be
avoided, in the eyes of students, and lead to the gradual loss of their home
language. What I propose is a modification of Elbow's proposal. In the place
of his notion of time, I like to invoke the notion of space. I am interested in
exploring how we can accommodate more than one code within the bounds
of the same text. In an essay that is written in ME, I would also teach students
to bring in their preferred varieties for relevant purposes. In textual terms,
this strategy will result in a hybrid text that contains divergent varieties of
English. To use another metaphor to capture the difference, while Elbow and
the other scholars (reviewed in the previous section) propose a model of *code
switching*, I propose a model of *code meshing*.[6] While they separate the codes
and prioritize ME for formal purposes, I consider merging the codes. Code
meshing is not new to academic writing. As I will illustrate with a close textual analysis in the next section, some African American scholars have already
used AAVE in rhetorically compelling ways in academic texts that feature
SWE (see Young for a recent discussion of this strategy). Note also that some
radical scholars have used the term *code switching* broadly to signify the same
practice that I call code meshing here—see Anzaldúa (in Lunsford) and my
use (in *Resisting Linguistic Imperialism*). Various other metaphors have been
used to describe this strategy—i.e., appropriation (Canagarajah, *Resisting
Linguistic Imperialism*), third spaces (Kramsch and Lam; Belcher), and "talking
back" (hooks). Though code meshing was used in classical rhetoric as a high-
brow activity (i.e., inserting Greek or Latin without translation into English
texts), I am presenting this notion as a popular communicative strategy in

multilingual communities and developing it even for cases outside such elite bilingualism.

Code meshing calls for multidialectalism not monodialectalism. Holding that knowledge of the vernacular is solely sufficient for minority students would ignore the reality of multilingualism demanded by globalization. It would also segregate minority students into vernacular speech ghettos. My proposal demands more, not less, from minority students. They have to not only master the dominant varieties of English, but also know how to bring in their preferred varieties in rhetorically strategic ways. It is not even sufficient to learn different English varieties and use them in appropriate contexts (as proposed by code switching models); now minority students have to learn to bring them together to serve their interests.

This discursive strategy of code meshing is also motivated by pragmatic sociolinguistic considerations. If all speech events are language games, the rules of the game that all the players currently share need to be acknowledged. This is important even if the current rules favor one group more than the other and may have come into force as a result of that group's dominant status. If we suddenly bring in new rules, we could be disqualified from that game. At the most charitable, this will be construed as a different game altogether, and we could be asked to play that game elsewhere. This is not necessarily a favorable outcome for minority scholars in academic communication. I don't want my text written in Sri Lankan English ruled nonacademic or treated as addressing only Sri Lankan scholars. I don't want my use of Sri Lankan English to make my text a different genre of communication for a different audience. Such a response will result in reducing the relevance and significance of my text. I want to still engage in the game of academic writing as it is played in the mainstream. By inserting the oppositional codes gradually into the existing conventions, I deal with the same audience and genre of communication but in my own terms. To be really effective, I need to work from within the existing rules to transform the game. Besides, I need to socialize the players into the revised rules of the game. The qualified use of alternate codes into the dominant discourse will serve to both play the same game and also change its rules.

It could be objected that this approach is yet another temporary strategy that defers the full pluralization of academic texts and legitimization of WE for a later time. I can hear my South Asian colleagues saying: "But your approach is looking like the very same one as Elbow's, no?" I agree. "However," I would reply, "there are small, small differences that make big, big significance." The advantage in my proposal is that minority students get to see their own variety of English written in academic texts. They don't have to edit out all vernacular expressions. Furthermore, we satisfy the desire of minority students to engage with the dominant codes when they write, and make a space for their own varieties of English in formal texts. Elbow's approach keeps these codes separate and unequal, and compels minority students to postpone critical literacy practices. Moreover, my approach enables students to personally engage in the process of textual change, not to wait for time to do the trick for them.

The reason that Elbow doesn't consider code meshing is probably because he believes that only one grapholect can be present in a text at any one time. He says: "Literacy as a culture or institution almost always implies just one dialect as the only proper one for writing: the 'grapholect'" ("Vernacular Literacies" 128). However, this assumption doesn't hold true for many non-Western communities. We have enjoyed a long tradition of constructing texts that are not only multilingual but also multimodal. According to Walter Mignolo, colonization attempted to suppress such dynamic local literacies and introduced univocal texts. In what he calls the "grapho-centric" literacy tradition, Western communities held that texts should use *words* (not images, symbols, icons, space, color, or other representational systems), *written* words (not spoken words or other modalities of communication), and words from *one language* (not from multiple languages). As this tradition of literacy took hold, other literacy practices were treated as lacking precision and rigor and given pariah status. A consideration of multimodal and multilingual literacy traditions will show us that making a textual space for other Englishes may come easily for students from these communities.

The art of multimodal indigenous textuality has not died, despite its denigration since European colonization. Mario de Souza demonstrates how the *kene/dami* textualities work for the Kashinawa in Brazil. In a multimodal text that involves paintings, alphabets, and drawing of figures and lines within the same "page," this Indian community produces texts that demand complex processes of interpretation. The alphabets and graphics relate to each other in dynamic combinations to produce meanings for insiders. De Souza presents fascinating recent examples of such texts from a teacher-development program in which local instructors produce these texts for their university professors. My own community of Tamils has practiced the well-known *manipralava* textuality from before colonization (see Viswanathan). When Sanskrit was considered the elite language for religious and philosophical purposes, local scholars mixed Sanskrit with Tamil in writing for their community. This way, we both elevated the respectability of the vernacular and democratized Sanskrit. Even now, local people adopt this strategy for in-group communication. However, now we mix mostly English, as this is the dominant colonial language in our context. For example, it is quite common for academic texts in Sri Lanka and India to involve a prominent mixing of English and Tamil (see, for example, Sivatamby). Sometimes, qu 'ations from primary sources are in English, while the commentary is in Tamil. In other cases, foreign words are inserted into Tamil syntax as writers change the script midsentence to accommodate English technical terms or phrases. It is rare for authors to translate or transliterate these marked codes. They expect the readers to perform a veritable bilingual reading. Nor is this a form of elite literacy. Even popular literature now involves English/Tamil mixing. Short stories written by Tamil refugees in the West (in journals like *kaalam* in Toronto and *eksil* in Paris) feature code meshing.

Though such local traditions of multivocal literacy have been practiced from precolonial times, they gained new ramifications during and after the colonial encounter. Despite the official policy in many colonial regimes to impose the grapho-centric and largely monolingual traditions of writing, hybrid literacies were developing subversively in the local communities out of this cultural contact. Mary Louise Pratt calls these the "literate arts of the contact zone." Gloria Anzaldúa has also spoken recently about the ways she draws from the postcolonial tradition of mixing Native Indian, Spanish, and English languages (see Lunsford). While such texts exemplify typical processes of intercultural mediation, they are also ideologically powerful. Contact zone literacies resist from the inside without the outsiders understanding their full import; they appropriate the codes of the powerful for the purposes of the subaltern; and they demystify the power, secrecy, and monopoly of the dominant codes. More importantly, they display immense creativity as the subalterns negotiate competing literacies to construct new genres and codes that speak to their own interests. Code meshing in academic writing would be another example in the continuing tradition of contact zone textualities.

Such literate arts of the contact zone are still alive (albeit hidden) in post-colonial classrooms. Students and teachers who are expected to adopt English only (or monolingual) pedagogies practice bilingual discourse strategies that enable them to develop more relevant classroom interactions, curricular objectives, and learning styles. Ethnographies in contexts as diverse as Hong Kong, Kenya, Tanzania, Malta, Singapore, Malaysia, Brunei, Sri Lanka, and even England and North America point to the strategic role of code mixing in language learning (see the collection of articles in Heller and Martin-Jones). In some of these classrooms, the mixing involves two varieties of English (see Lin and Martin, for examples from Singapore, South Africa, India and Hong Kong). Literacy practices of codes meshing are also not unusual—students mix codes to negotiate the meaning of English texts and to compose stories or journals in expressive, creative, or reflective writing (Hornberger). Much of this research literature demonstrates that rather than hampering the acquisition of English, the negotiation of codes can indeed facilitate it. Some applied linguists do argue that code switching is detrimental to language learning and literacy as it would lead to a fossilization of mixed forms and, eventually, create a deficient *interlanguage* (see Bhatt for a critique). But such scholars are influenced by the notion that language acquisition ideally involves a unilateral movement within a single language, treating the context of acquisition as an idealized homogeneous language environment. Sridhar points out that language acquisition in real life often takes place in multilingual contexts with an engagement with many codes. In such engagement, Cummins argues that one language can play a positive role in the development of another.

While such pedagogical realities have previously not been acknowledged by educational policy makers—as it has been an embarrassment to the dominant pedagogies which prefer the purity of the instructional code and validity of monolingual approaches—it is becoming difficult to hide in scholarly literature or suppress in classrooms a practice that is so pervasive. It is not surprising that some local scholars have started arguing for consciously developing strategies from traditional multilingual approaches (like the *manipravalava* tradition[7]) for local literacy education (Rajan; Viswanathan). They propose that reading and talking about Shakespeare or Wordsworth in Tamil can enable students to adopt a critical detachment from the original texts. What would amount to a translation strategy can also provide different perspectives on the texts, as students perceive them from the spectacles of competing languages.[8] While these scholars recommend this approach only for text reception, my proposal for code meshing sees a place for it in text construction as well with similar benefits.

Though code meshing is a complex discursive act for our students (one that involves a polydialectal competence—i.e., familiarity with standard varieties, expert use of local variants, and the rhetorical strategies of switching), the examples above suggest that multilingual communities have a long tradition of using such communicative practices. Therefore, students from these communities can draw from their textual histories and literacy cultures to make a space for WE in academic texts.

TEXTUAL POSSIBILITIES: AN EXAMPLE

How do we proceed in implementing the above literacy orientation in composition classrooms? In my classes, I like to provide models from the writing of minority scholars to show what multilingual students can achieve in their writing.[9] It is interesting that African American scholars like bell hooks and Geneva Smitherman have made considerable headway in infusing their own dialects into academic writing. It is a reflection of an understandable bias in composition circles that the black vernacular is permitted, even glorified in certain composition circles, but WE is not tolerated in academic writing. As noted earlier, perhaps AAVE and certain North American class and regional dialects are validated because they come from "native English speaking" communities; WE varieties are not given the same treatment because they come from multilingual speech communities. However, it is a blessing to be able to cite as precedent the advances made by African American writers and to create further spaces for new Englishes in academic writing.

Smitherman's "The Historical Struggle for Language Rights in CCC" is a good example of a minority scholar employing a range of dialects to represent her voice and identity in formal academic writing. Interestingly enough, the article takes stock of the pedagogical advances made since SRTOL.[10] For the most part of the paper, Smitherman uses the established code and the conventions of scholarly publication—i.e., citations, footnotes, and scholarly evidence. The essay is also very balanced in representing the alternate positions to the ones she herself holds on SRTOL. Her writing thus wins academic credibility among readers. The instances of AAVE use are few, but carefully deployed to construct her desired voice for this article.

Curiously, most of the cases of AAVE begin to appear in the middle section of the article where Smitherman narrates the dialogue and debate that accompanied the formulation of the resolution. AAVE is not used much in the opening of the paper where she provides the background and reviews the scholarly developments leading to SRTOL. This structure serves to build Smitherman's status as a proficient academic writer and earn the reader's respect before introducing the atypical codes later in the writing.[11] Such a strategy is different from her earlier practice in 1974 (see "Soul N' Style") when she used AAVE more prominently, starting from the very beginning of the article (including the title) and sustaining its use throughout the text. Furthermore, it is significant that in most occasions of AAVE in the SRTOL article. Smitherman doesn't use quotation marks to flag them as distinct or strange. Using quotation marks would have distanced the author from the language, invoking the traditional biases. Consequently, most readers would now process these switches without pausing to consider them unusual. This ambiguity also results from the fact that some elements of AAVE have become mainstreamed. We are losing the ability to classify certain items as categorically "nonstandard." The deft mixing of codes in this article confronts readers with their own biases—i.e., what do we consider as unsuitable for academic writing, and why?

Consider the first occasion of AAVE use when Smitherman writes: "In his scathing critique, with its signifyin title, 'Darkness is King,' Lloyd took Knickerbocker to task . . ." (p. 59). (Knickerbocker's paper, which derides ungrammatical expressions in student writing, is entitled "The Freshman is King.") An in-group motif from folklore (see Abrahams), "signifyin" has now received near global currency. After Henry Louise Gates' *Signifying Monkey* and other publications like Smitherman's own book, *Talkin and Testifyin*, this reference to instigating has become familiar for even speakers of WE like me. Though this is a mere lexical switch, what might be considered a single cultural borrowing, it indexes a whole vernacular speech event. This is an example of the way gradual but bold uses of the vernacular lead to their becoming naturalized and widely shared over time, losing their stigmatized status.

Note also the lexical items underlined in the following statements:

> At the time, my womanist consciousness was just developing, and so I was not very vocal in this hours-long debate, for which I was soundly <u>blessed out</u> by one of the women when we took a bathroom break . . . The debate was finally resolved when Elisabeth McPherson, genius that <u>my girl</u> was, proposed that we cast the wording in the third person plural (Smitherman, p. 69; emphasis mine),

Or

> As I listened to their arguments, all I could think about was the <u>dissin</u> and <u>doggin</u> I had endured during the "Students' Right" years, and <u>I</u> kept saying "no way" (p. 74; emphasis mine).

These too are in-group expressions that have gained wider currency now. They especially belong to the urban vernacular, distinct from the more marked rural (Southern) speech that we will see later. These lexical items also evoke special attitudes and feelings. That the author refers to being "blessed out" suggests that she is taking this as an in-group chastisement that should be accepted and treated as unoffensive. The next usage, "my girl," indicates the close relationship between the interlocutors. The other two nouns "dissin and doggin" reflect the tone and attitude toward the insulting speech of the out-group members. The context invoked in all these uses provides rhetorical justification for these switches. The switches index the type of relationships and feelings referred to.

Another category of fairly unshocking AAVE use is in the stylistic choice of emotive, repetitive, and rhythmic expressions valued in oral communication. This lexical choice violates the established register in academic prose. Such language may be considered too informal for academic writing, but it certainly serves to evoke the desired voice of the author. Consider the satirical humor in the following:

> Not content with <u>knocking</u> Knickerbocker <u>upside the head</u>, Lloyd also <u>slammed</u> the journal and the organization . . . (p. 59).

or

> As an organizational position, the *Students' Right* resolution represented a critical mechanism for CCCC to address its own internal contradictions at the same time as <u>marching, fist-raising, loud-talking</u> protesters, spearheaded by the Black Liberation Movement, <u>marred</u> the social landscape of "America the beautiful" (p. 65).

The rhyme ("knocking Knickerbocker") and rhythm ("marching, fist-raising, loud-talking") evoke a voice that is more oral and nonacademic. There is also the hyperbole of some word choices here that may be considered very unacademic (i.e., *slammed, marred*). All of these lexical choices represent a speaker from a high-involvement culture and jar against the conventions of a low-involvement communicative genre (Tannen). Furthermore, the language certainly suggests the author's identification with the acts described here. In fact, the language is rhetorically appropriate for acts and attitudes that are oppositional to the dominant values of the academy.

In some cases, the author doesn't have to use her own words, but she makes her cited authorities evoke a divergent discourse to accomplish her purposes. She does this by carefully choosing the quotations from her sources. She writes, "Lloyd even goes so far as to say that linguistics 'is a promised land for the English teacher'" (p. 61). The phrase "promised land" has special resonance for the African American community. Apart from the importance of the Bible in vernacular culture, we know that the metaphor of a promised land has enjoyed currency in black consciousness ever since Claude Brown's book. Through this allusion, Smitherman is also appropriating the field of linguistics for the oppositional causes of enlightened instructors who wish to challenge the popular biases of the dominant community. The same rhetorical strategy is used again when Smitherman cites a verse from the Bible: "But we also knew that without 'vision, the people perish'" (p. 66).

However, in the second part of the above quotation, Smitherman quickly shifts to the most direct grammatical display of vernacular English in this article: "Besides, as I commented to a fellow comrade (a psychologist, who was one of the founders of the Association of Black Psychologists), what else was we gon do while we was waitin for the Revolution to come?" (p. 66). In the more striking uses of AAVE (as here), Smitherman embeds them in a clear dramatic context that provides a different frame for deviations from SWE. In the case above, it is clear that the usage reflects the language of the persona who uttered that statement and the in-group solidarity enjoyed with the interlocutor in that speech event. In using AAVE grammar, the author is being true to the context and the interlocutors. Thus, the rhetorical context disarms criticism. We find a similar narrative context in the examples that follow. Discussing the divergent responses to the resolution, she writes "A few simply said that CCCC had done lost they cotton-pickin minds. . . . [Then, after discussing more favorable responses, she continues:] A few simply asked CCCC why it took yall so long. . . . Such ideas elicited strong reactions among CCCC professionals (irrespective of whether they supported the resolution or not) and moved the intellectual production of knowledge in the field to a whole nother level" (p. 70; emphasis mine). Indeed the language gives evidence of the "strong reactions" elicited by the proposal. The mention of "cotton-pickin" makes the stupidity one notch worse. "A whole nother level" indicates that the production of knowledge was not just moved to the next level but to a totally different dimension. These statements alternate with more scholarly views from others, presented in very staid prose, showing that the author is switching codes with remarkable control over a repertoire of Englishes. In addition to the switches between SWE and AAVE, we must note that there are different dialects of AAVE orchestrated here. While the examples in the previous paragraph are largely from the urban vernacular, the ones in the latest example are largely rural and southern.

If the above switches are motivated by the changing rhetorical and speech situations, we find a similar *situational switch* in the acknowledgments section. Smitherman gives "a shout out" to one of her graduate student assistants (p. 80). This language is motivated by the youthful persona addressed. A more senior scholar will not appreciate this manner of acknowledgment. For the only other person thanked in this section, the author writes "I would like to express my gratitude and a special thanks to Dr. _____, . . . for his most capable assistance and archival work" (p. 80). The more formal language suits the senior scholar addressed in this statement (indicated by the title, "Dr."). Apart from the situational motivation, there is additional reason why the switch to vernacular is rhetorically permissible here. In certain low-stakes environments in the text, the vernacular is generally treated as unobjectionable. There is considerable latitude in using nonstandard elements in such peripheral sections of the academic essay. Other low-stakes sections are dedications, titles, and conclusions (see Thaiss and Zawacki).[12] Such textual spaces can therefore be exploited to bring in the alternate codes and discourses desired by the author—and students should be taught to discern these spaces.

Ironically, in the only case where Smitherman flags an expression, she does so not to mark the unusual usage behind the peculiar item but to evoke the widely shared usage of a well-known expression. She says, "(I report with pride that I was the first to introduce 'cussing' into committee discourse, to the relief of one of my male comrades)" (p. 69). She uses quotation marks probably to neutralize what appears to be a shocking *metaphorical switch* here. (Metaphorical switches—unlike the previous situational switches—violate the established code for the situation to evoke alternate values and meanings.) Similarly, the only case where she provides a gloss is to introduce an item that is recent and probably an in-group expression among a subcultural group—black teenagers: "In the 1998 celebration of African American History Month, a television commercial for Mickey D's (Ebonics for McDonald's) featured a White father and his young son browsing through a gallery with paintings of African American heroes and she-roes" (p. 73). Smitherman's gloss for "Mickey D's" indicates that the nickname is perhaps new to the older generation of AAVE speakers. ("She-roes" doesn't warrant a gloss, as its meaning is clear from the context.) At any rate, the example shows that Smitherman is variating the AAVE used—not only between regions, i.e., urban and rural, but also between age groups, i.e., adult and teen talk.

It must be noted that all these instances of AAVE don't amount to much in an article running to about thirty pages. But they are sufficient to change the ethos of the text. More importantly, they demonstrate what Smitherman argues for in this article: "It has been said that politics is the art of compromise. And compromise we did. After the lengthy debates and verbal duels, we finally produced a document that we all felt we could live with" (p. 69). This text is again a compromise—something we can all live with—until more spaces are available for other Englishes when academic literacy gets further pluralized. This position registers a shift in strategy for Smitherman herself. She has apparently moved away from the strategy of using AAVE for the whole essay (as in her two-page 1974 article "Soul N' Style."). To give further insight into this new strategy, she later says (before concluding): "The documented spirit of resistance in the *Students' Right* and CCCC *National Language Policy* is an important symbol that change is possible—*even within the system*" (p. 79; emphasis added). The careful deployment of vernacular items within an SWE text is an example of this strategy of resistance from within. Even if it takes more time for AAVE to gain a legitimate place of its own in academic writing, one doesn't have to wait indefinitely as Elbow's approach would make us assume. The change is already under way in Smitherman's text. The few instances of meshed codes have moved this text to a whole nother level.

PEDAGOGICAL POSSIBILITIES: AN EXAMPLE

If Smitherman's practice hints at some textual strategies for using other Englishes in academic writing, Min-Zhan Lu suggests pedagogical strategies for encouraging multilingual students to bring in their variants of English into the composition classroom. Her 1994 article in *CCC* still remains a rare documentation of teaching strategies for validating alternate codes at the micro-textual and grammatical (as distinct from rhetorical) level. Lu explores the peculiar usage "can able to" in the essays of a Chinese student from Malaysia (e.g., "As a Hawaiian native historian, Trask can able to argue for her people"; "If a student can able to approach each situation with different perspectives than the one he brought from high school, I may conclude that this student has climbed his first step to become a 'critical thinker.'"). Since the modals *can* and *may* are used according to their conventional meaning in other places of the student's writing, it is clear that "can able to" is used with a unique meaning of its own. In fact, Lu finds later that "can" and "be able to" have interchangeable meanings in the student's first language. More importantly, the student points out to the teacher (with the help of her English dictionary!) that "be able to" has an additional meaning of "have permission to" that is not connoted by "can" in English. Therefore she puts together both structures to coin "can able to."

What motivates this student to use this structure? Since the student has personally experienced a lot of pressure from her family against undertaking higher education (because of her status as a woman and her community's norms), she is cognizant of the struggles one has to go through to think critically and act independently. To express this need to achieve independence despite community constraints, she uses "can able to"—a structure that connotes for her "ability from the perspective of the external circumstances" (Lu 452). She is also inspired by her understanding of Trask's ability to still speak for her people despite the constraints of being a minority historian. The student therefore tries to communicate the possibility for action by struggling against external limiting constraints. When the instructor makes this grammatical usage a point of discussion for the whole class, the other students state that it is the dominant American ideology of individual transcendence and personal power that makes speakers treat "can" and "able to" with similar connotations. The Malaysian student wants to convey a different orientation to ability, and is thus forced to fashion a new usage for her purposes.

An important lesson here for teachers is that not every instance of non-standard usage by a student is an unwitting error; sometimes it is an active choice motivated by important cultural and ideological considerations. The assumption that multilingual students are always bound to err in a second language denies them agency. The Malaysian student is not blind to the differences between Chinese and English. She insists on using the peculiar structure because she is struggling to bring out certain ideas that are important to her. This example further shows the dangers of jumping to the conclusion that any peculiarity in English is to be explained by the influences from the student's first language. In being thus judgmental, teachers sometimes ignore the creativity of the students who negotiate unique meanings. Teachers may suppress other explanations for why a structure may sound unusual—i.e., explanations that testify to students' rhetorical independence and critical thinking.

Many pedagogical benefits derive from discussing this grammatical deviation without prejudice or preconception. To begin with, the writer and the rest of the class now understand grammar as ideological. The choices we make hide or emphasize the values we want to convey to our readers. In trying to find out from our students the reasons why they use a peculiar structure, teachers will acknowledge the serious considerations motivating their language usage. Such discussions enable students to use grammar meaningfully, rather than opting for stereotypical choices. In the process, students also develop a metalinguistic awareness of the values and interests motivating grammar. These skills are far more significant for developing writing competence, compared to enforcing a blind conformism to the dominant grammatical conventions.

Understanding student motivation for using unusual grammar structures doesn't exhaust our responsibilities in writing instruction. Can such a structure that is peculiar to SWE be promoted in the essay? How far should students go in deviating from the dominant dialects? Lu provides a multifaceted answer, opening up different possibilities. She narrates that at a later point of the course she got the whole class to explore alternative grammatical structures to convey the Malaysian student's meaning while being mindful of the dominant grammatical conventions of academic writing. After more thought, the writer resorted to using "may be able to" in deference to SWE usage. This strategy ensured that she was within the bounds of established conventions, while also conveying her unique perspective. Other students considered possibilities such as adding an "if" clause to "be able to," or even using "can able to" with a parenthetical explanation or a footnote about the need for this unusual usage. The latter strategy—footnoting—is a form of compromise as it acknowledges that the writer is aware of using the structure in a peculiar way for a unique rhetorical purpose. (Besides, the footnote is a valued convention of academic writing.) On the other hand, another multilingual writer, a student from Vietnam, argued that he would use "can" and "be able to" interchangeably because their connotations of agency inspired modes of resistance and individual empowerment against the fatalism of his own community. The "standard" grammar structure thus became an ideologically favored option for a minority student—a structure he uses not mechanically but with critical thinking. Lu concludes this grammar instruction by noting that the structure "can able to" took on a life of its own in her class. After being playfully used in class discussions, "it became a newly coined phrase we shared throughout the term" (454). The exercise thus dramatizes the process by which English is nativized—and, in fact, how certain cases of peculiar usage become "standardized"—once their meanings and purposes are socially shared.

There are many pedagogical benefits from teaching students to negotiate grammar for their rhetorical purposes. Students must be trained to make grammatical choices based on many discursive concerns: their intentions, the context, and the assumptions of readers and writers. Students must understand that in certain special cases they may have to try out a peculiar structure for unique purposes (making sure that they subtly indicate to the audience that they are using this with the full awareness of the established conventions). This doesn't mean students are free to use the vernacular for all contexts of communication. Negotiating grammar means being sensitive to the relativity of style and usage in different communicative situations. Overzealous teachers who impose correctness according to SWE norms may stifle the development of a repertoire that will help students style shift according to differing communicative contexts. Furthermore, when the standard dialect is inadequate or inappropriate for our purposes—which is not surprising as its grammar does index dominant ideologies and interests—we may negotiate meaningful usage and, in the process, reshape the rules. This is certainly not an instantaneous or individual process. It is important to engage with the linguistic system, with the understanding that there is always the tension between stability and change, dominant usage and emergent conventions, and sociolect and idiolect in any language. Rather than being treated as a sign of a lack of proficiency, such negotiation should be treated as a mark of independent and critical writing.[13]

CONCLUSION

It is time now to take a step back from these microtextual and micropedagogical forms of intervention to ask what difference these activities will make in pluralizing composition. As the theorization of Anzaldúa and Pratt, and the practice of hooks and Smitherman show, code meshing in English writing has a politics of its own. Though not directly confrontational as to reject the dominant codes or to flaunt the vernacular codes in established contexts, multilingual students will resist ME from the inside by inserting their codes within the existing conventions. This activity serves to infuse not only new codes, but also new knowledge and values, into dominant texts. Such subtle Gramscian "wars of position" are important in order to gain spaces for a more direct "war of maneuver." There is value in making gradual cultural and ideological changes in the notions of textuality and language among educationists and policy makers, building a coalition of disparate social groups and disciplinary circles, and winning small battles in diverse institutions toward an acceptance of hybrid texts, before we mount a frontal assault by using nonlegitimized codes in high-stakes writing. In making this sobering concession, we have to keep in mind that textual resistance cannot by itself sustain the larger institutional changes needed to legitimize WE. Even the ability to initiate textual changes is often dependent on the extratextual power authors bring with them. We have to admit that Smitherman is able to use AAVE so confidently in her writing because of her standing as a distinguished scholar in academic circles and her achieved status as a spokesperson for language rights in professional associations. Many other black scholars and students cannot succeed in using AAVE if they don't enjoy the relative status in their contexts of communication. Despite the authority she brings to writing, Smitherman herself is strategic in making qualified uses of AAVE in her texts and in taking measured steps of meshing in her writing career.

Certain forms of struggle are indeed waged better when they are conducted over time, in response to the changing contexts and discourses in the field. On this point, Elbow and I are in agreement: we both rely on time to make a difference. There is already evidence of the beneficial effects of time. To argue for a postcolonial spatial orientation to written texts, we now have evidence from an unexpected quarter. In the context of the Internet and digital media, we see the mixing of not only different varieties of English but also of totally different languages. To be literate on the Internet, for example, requires competence in multiple registers, discourses, and languages, in addition to different modalities of communication (sound, speech, video, photographs) and different symbol systems (icons, images, and spatial organization). To capture these changes for textual processing and production, scholars have now started using the term *multiliteracies* (see Cope and Kalantzis) and are explicating the new acts of reading and writing involved (Warschauer). In fact, many composition scholars prefer the term *designing* over *composing* in recognition of the spatial and multimodal nature of writing (see Faigley). These changes in text construction make it easy to envision that different varieties of English may find a "natural" place in the evolving shape of the text.

Talking of time, this is the moment for me to come clean about my own evolving positions on WE in writing. Having criticized the field of composition and other progressive scholars for their limitations in accepting WE in academic writing, I must confess that I have myself held such positions in the past. The extent to which my radicalism extended previously was to argue for alternative tone, styles, organization, and genre conventions in formal academic writing.[14] I have steered clear of validating nativized varieties at the intrasentential level. In retrospect, it occurs to me that I was playing it safe in my argument. I didn't want to jeopardize my case for pluralizing academic writing by extending it to the controversial terrain of grammar. But a combination of developments in theoretical discourses, social changes, communicative advances, and pedagogical rethinking (reviewed in this article) tell me that now is the time to take my position to its logical conclusion. The moment is ripe to extend my argument of pluralizing English and academic writing into the "deep structure" of grammar. Still, I must confess that I am myself unsure how to practice what I preach (other than the few instances where I shamelessly copy Smitherman's strategies above). Throughout my life, I have been so disciplined about censoring even the slightest traces of Sri Lankan English in my own academic writing that it is difficult to bring them into the text now. Therefore, this article is only a statement of intent, not a celebration of accomplishment. It only aims to make some space for pedagogical rethinking and textual experimentation on the place of WE in composition. As for practice, I am hereby humbly announcing that I'll be joining my esteemed students in the classroom for learning how to accommodate local Englishes in academic writing.

Acknowledgments: I wish to thank Geneva Smitherman for encouraging me to undertake a close reading of her writing strategies. My colleagues Bridgette Davis and Shondel Nero commented on my interpretation of the AAVE items in Smitherman's texts. John Trimbur and an anonymous reviewer raised useful points to make my argument more complex.

NOTES

1. Since I question the distinction native and nonnative varieties, I am using World Englishes to encapsulate the emergent varieties that differ from the traditional "native" varieties I refer to as Metropolitan English (ME). I go on to argue that we have to develop a nonhierarchical model of plural English where all the varieties (including minority dialects such as AAVE and Chicano English) enjoy equal status. To capture the latter notion, I use the label Global English to connote "a family of languages" in the sense of Crystal (*Language Revolution*). Standard Written English (SWE) is, for me, the realization of ME in composition. I will use the label SWE when I refer to the work of composition scholars who prefer to use it, especially in Anglo American pedagogical contexts.

2. Though I go on to argue that we have to adopt more proficiency-based categories like expert/novice to distinguish speakers, and abandon categories based on birth or blood, I retain the use of "native" and "nonnative" when I discuss the work of scholars who use that framework.

3. This is a highly formal and inflected variety of English originally used by locals to talk to colonial administrators but still used in South Asia to address someone deferentially.

4. After making a case for accepting diverse varieties of English in European academic communication, Stephen Barbour still ends up arguing that multilingual authors have to use the established varieties for writing. He argues that since the rich paralinguistic clues of speaking are not available for interpreting writing, multilingual authors have to get the help of editors and translators to eliminate the localisms in their English.

5. Though he discusses primarily the case of AAVE in this article, Elbow is thinking of applying the same position to other varieties of WE. In a recent conference presentation, he illustrates his approach with examples from students of Hawaiian English (see, "Should Students Write").

6. We must distinguish *code meshing* from *code mixing*, which refers to the inclusion of single lexical items ("borrowings") that have become naturalized in the borrowing language. Code meshing, however, can include mixtures of larger structural and rhetorical units and may still symbolize something "marked" in the dominant language of the text

7. *Manipravalava* refers to mixed-code writing. This term originally referred to the mixing of Tamil and Sanskrit in written texts by Tamil scholars at a time when Tamil didn't enjoy the prestige for being used in learned discourse. Sanskrit was the medium for such purposes then. By mixing, Tamil scholars raised the status of their vernacular and subtly resisted the power of Sanskrit.

8. Such scholars attempt to give complexity to translation approaches in composition, although translation was discredited in ESOL after the days of grammar translation method (Richards and Rodgers) and in Composition after the days of using classical texts in teaching (Horner and Trimbur).

9. Curiously, the two best examples for this purpose come from L1 contexts of composition studies. This ironic state of affairs is probably because TESOL still defers to L1 composition for norms in writing pedagogy (see Matsuda). Also, TESOL has traditionally treated academic writing as a pure and sanitized domain of linguistic correctness, under the influence of positivistic applied linguistics. TESOL has not been too daring in working out new textual or pedagogical options.

10. Although this essay is a version of a publication in a refereed journal, *CCC* ("CCCC's Role"), it is probably a solicited essay for a commemorative issue. As a historical review essay and a contribution to a collection of essays in an edited book, the version I analyze has some latitude in style compared to empirical essays in refereed journals. However, the strategies Smitherman employs are transferable to other "refereed" publishing contexts.

11. Elbow ("Vernacular Literacies") would agree with this strategy. He advises his minority students that using "nonstandard" varieties in the beginning of the article would alienate the readers. He trains them to open with established codes before using their preferred varieties.

12. In the more conservative pages of the *TESOL Quarterly*. Smitherman uses AAVE prominently in the safe space of the title (see "Dat Teacher Be Hollin at Us"). Except for glossed uses of "homiez" and "capping," this is the only place where she flaunts AAVE authorially in this article — clearly a strategic choice.

13. While Lu's essay is an example at the micro-level of negotiating a single grammatical item in the writing of a single student, Elbow ("Vernacular Literacies," "Inviting the Mother Tongue") suggests more protracted strategies for the writing process that can help students negotiate divergent grammars.

14. For examples on developing alternate literacy pedagogies, see Canagarajah ("Safe Houses") for African American students and *Resisting Linguistic Imperialism* for Sri Lankan Tamil students; my attempts to culturalize my own academic discourse are narrated in "The Fortunate Traveler."

WORKS CITED

Abrahams, Roger D. *Afro-American Folk Tales: Stories from the Black Traditions in the New World.* New York: Pantheon, 1985.

Barbour, Stephen. "Language, Nationalism, and Globalism: Educational Consequences of Changing Patterns of Language Use." *Beyond Boundaries: Language and Identity in Contemporary Europe.* Ed. Paul Gubbins and Mike Holt. Clevedon, UK: Multilingual Matters, 2002. 11–18.

Baugh, John. *Black Street Speech: It's History, Structure and Survival.* Austin: U of Texas P, 1983.

Belcher, Diane. "An Argument for Nonadversarial Argumentation: On the Relevance of the Feminist Critique of Academic Discourse to L2 Writing Pedagogy. *Journal of Second Language Writing* 6.1 (1997): 1–21.

Bhatt, Rakesh M. "Expert Discourses, Local Practices, and Hybridity: The Case of Indian Englishes." *Reclaiming the Local in Language Policy and Practice.* Ed. A. Suresh Canagarajah. Mahwah, NJ: Lawrence Erlbaum, 2005. 25–54.

Brutt-Griffler, Janina. *World English: A Study of Its Development.* Clevedon, UK: Multilingual Matters, 2002.

Canagarajah, A. Suresh. "Safe Houses in the Contact Zone: Coping Strategies of African American Students in the Academy." *College Composition and Communication* 48.2 (1997):173–96.

———. *Resisting Linguistic Imperialism in English Teaching.* Oxford. UK: OUP, 1999.

———. "The Fortunate Traveler: Shuttling Between Communities and Literacies by Economy Class." *Reflections on Multiliterate Lives.* Ed. Diane Belcher and Ulla Connor. Clevedon, UK: Multilingual Matters, 2001. 23–37.

———. "Introduction." *Reclaiming the Local in Language Policy and Practice.* Ed. A. Suresh Canagarajah. Mahwah, NJ: Lawrence Erlbaum, 2005. xiii–xxx.

Cope, Bill, and Mary Kalantzis. Ed. *Multiliteracies: Literacy Learning and the Design of Social Futures.* London and New York: Routledge, 2000.

Crystal, David. *English as a Global Language.* Cambridge: CUP, 1997.

———. *The Language Revolution.* Cambridge. UK: Polity, 2004.

Cummins, Jim. "Interdependence of First- and Second-Language Proficiency in Bilingual Children." *Language Processing in Bilingual Children.* Ed. E. Bialystok. Cambridge: CUP, 1991. 70–89.

Delpit, Lisa. *Other People's Children: Cultural Conflict in the Classroom.* New York: New Press, 1995.

De Souza, Lynn Mario. "A Case among Cases, a World among Worlds: The Ecology of Writing among the Kashinawa in Brazil." *Journal of Language, Identity, and Education* 1.4 (2002): 261–78.

Elbow, Peter. "Inviting the Mother Tongue: Beyond 'Mistakes,' 'Bad English,' and 'Wrong English.'" *JAC* 19.2 (1999): 359–88.

———. "Vernacular Literacies in the Writing Classroom? Probing the Culture of Literacy. *ALT/DIS: Alternative Discourses and the Academy.* Ed. Christopher Schroeder, Helen Fox, and Patricia Bizzell. Portsmouth, NH: Boynton/Cook, 2002. 126–38.

———. "Should Students Write in Nonmainstream Varieties of English? Using Orality to Reframe the Question." Paper presented at the CCCC Convention, San Antonio, March 25, 2004.

Faigley, Lester. "Rhetoric/design/sustainability." Paper presented at the CCCC Convention, San Antonio, March 26, 2004.

Firth, A. "The Discursive Accomplishment of Normality. On 'Lingua Franca' English and Conversation Analysis." *Journal of Pragmatics* 26 (1996): 237–59.

Gates, Henry Louis. *Signifying Monkey: A Theory of African-American Literary Criticism.* Oxford, UK: OUP, 1988.

Giles, Howard. Ed. "The Dynamics of Speech Accommodation." *International Journal of the Sociology of Language* 46, 1984. (Special topic issue.)

Graddol, David. "The Decline of the Native Speaker." *AILA Review* 13 (1999): 57–68.

Gumperz, John J. *Discourse Strategies.* Interactional Sociolinguistics 1. Cambridge: CUP. 1982.

Hamers, Josianne, and Michel H. A. Blanc. *Bilinguality and Bilingualism.* Cambridge: CUP, 1989.

Harris, Roxy, Constance Leung, and Ben Rampton. "Globalization, Diaspora and Language Education in England." *Globalization and Language Teaching.* Ed. Deborah Cameron and David Block. London: Routledge, 2002. 29–46.

Heath, Shirley Brice. *Ways with Words.* Cambridge, MA: CUP, 1983.

Heller, Monica, and Marilyn Martin-Jones. Eds. *Voices of Authority: Education and Linguistic Difference.* (Contemporary Studies in Linguistics and Education volume 1.) Westport, CT, and London: Ablex, 2001.

Higgins, Christina. "'Ownership' of English in the Outer Circle: An Alternative to the NS/NNS Dichotomy." *TESOL Quarterly* 34.3 (2003): 615–44.

Holliday, Adrian. *The Struggle to Teach English as an International Language.* Oxford: OUP. Forthcoming.

hooks, bell. *Talking Back: Thinking Feminist, Thinking Black.* Boston: South End Press, 1989.

Hornberger, Nancy H. "Multilingual Language Policies and the Continua of Biliteracy: An Ecological Approach." *Continua of Biliteracy: An Ecological Framework for Educational Policy, Research, and Practice in Multilingual Settings.* Ed. N. H. Hornberger. Clevedon, UK: Multilingual Matters, 2003. 315–39.

Horner, Bruce, and John Trimbur. "English Only and U.S. College Composition." *College Composition and Communication* 53 (2002): 594–630.

Ibrahim, Awad El Karim M. "Becoming Black: Rap and Hip-Hop, Race, Gender, Identity, and the Politics of ESL Learning." *TESOL Quarterly* 33.3 (1999): 349–70.

Kachru, Braj B. *The Alchemy of English: The Spread, Functions, and Models of Non-native Englishes.* Oxford: Pergamon, 1986.

Khubchandani, Lachman M. *Revisualizing Boundaries: A Plurilingual Ethos.* New Delhi, India: Sage, 1997.

Kramsch, Claire, and Eva Wan Shun Lam. "Textual Identities: The Importance of Being Nonnative." *Non-native Educators in English Language Teaching.* Ed. George Braine. Mahwah, NJ: LEA, 1988. 57–72.

Kumaravadivelu, Braj. "Toward a Post-method Pedagogy." *TESOL Quarterly* 35.4 (2001): 537–60.

Labov, William. *Language in the Inner City: Studies in the Black English Vernacular.* Philadelphia: U of Pennsylvania P, 1972.

Lam, Eva Wan Shun. "L2 Literacy and the Design of the Self: A Case Study of a Teenager Writing on the Internet." *TESOL Quarterly* 34.3 (2000): 457–82.

Lin, Angel, and Peter Martin. Ed. *Decolonization, Globalization and Language-in-Education Policy and Practice.* Clevedon, UK: Multilingual Matters, forthcoming.

Lu, Min-Zhan. "Professing Multiculturalism: The Politics of Style in the Contact Zone." *College Composition and Communication* 45.4 (1994): 442–58.

Lucas, Tamara, and Anne Katz. "Reframing the Debate: The Roles of Native Languages in English-only Programs for Language Minority Students." *TESOL Quarterly* 28.4 (1994): 537–62.

Lunsford, Andrea A. "Toward a Mestiza Rhetoric: Gloria Anzaldúa on Composition and Postcoloniality." *Crossing Borderlands.* Ed. A. A. Lunsford and L. Ouzgane, Pittsburgh: U of Pittsburgh P, 2004. 33–66.

Matsuda, Paul Kei. "Situating ESL Writing in a Cross-Disciplinary Context." *Written Communication* 15.1 (1998): 99–121.

May, Stephen. *Language and Minority Rights: Ethnicity, Nationalism and the Politics of Language.* Harlow: Pearson Education, 2001.

McArthur, A. "The English Languages?" *English Today* 11 (1987): 9–13.

Mignolo, Walter D. *Local Histories/Global Designs: Coloniality, Subaltern Knowledges, and Border Thinking.* Princeton: Princeton UP, 2000.

Modiano, Marko. "Standard English(es) and Educational Practices for the World's Lingua Franca." *English Today* 15.4 (1999): 3–13.

Pease-Alvarez, Lucinda, and Adam Winsler. "Cuando el Maestro no Habla Espanol: Children's Bilingual Language Practices in the Classroom." *TESOL Quarterly* 28.4 (1994): 507–36.

Peirce, Bonny Norton. "Social identity, investment, and language learning." *TESOL Quarterly* 29.1 (1995): 9–32.

Pennycook, Alastair. *The Cultural Politics of English as an International Language.* London: Longman, 1994.

Pratt, Mary Louise. "Arts of the Contact Zone." *Profession* 91. New York: MLA, 1991. 33–40.

Pullum, Geoffrey K. "Description, Normativity, and Standards: Not in Conflict." Paper presented in the 119th MLA annual convention, San Diego, CA, Sunday, 28 December 2003.

Rajan, Rajeswari Sunder. "Fixing English: Nation, Language, Subject." *The Lie of the Land: English Literary Studies in India.* Ed. R. S. Rajan. Dehli: OUP, 1992. 7–28.

Rampton, Ben. "Displacing the 'Native Speaker': Expertise, Affiliation and Inheritance." *ELT Journal* 44.2 (1990): 97–101.

Richards, Jack C., and Theodore S. Rogers. *Approaches and Methods in Language Teaching: A Description and Analysis.* Cambridge: CUP, 1986.

Schroeder, Christopher, Helen Fox, and Patricia Bizzell. *ALT/DIS: Alternative Discourses and the Academy.* Portsmouth, NH: Boynton/Cook, 2002.

Seidlhofer, Barbara. "Research Perspectives on Teaching English as a Lingua Franca." *Annual Review of Applied Linguistics* 24 (2004): 209–39.

Sivatamby, Karthigesu. YaaLpaaNa camuukaTai viLanki koLLal—aTan uruvaakkam asaiviyak-kam paRRiya oru piraarampa usaaval. [Understanding Jaffna Society: A Preliminary Inquiry into its 'Formation' and 'Dynamics.'] *Prof. S. Selvanayagam Memorial Lecture* 8. Sri Lanka: University of Jaffna,1992. Mimeograph.

Smitherman, Geneva. "Soul N' Style." *English Today* 63.3 (1974): 14–15.

———. *Talkin and Testifyin: The Language of Black America.* Detroit: Wayne State UP, 1990.

———. "'Dat Teacher Be Hollin at Us'—What Is Ebonics?" *TESOL Quarterly* 32.1 (1998): 139–43.

———. "CCCC's Role in the Struggle for Language Rights." *College Composition and Communication* 50.3 (1999): [pp. 58–82 in this book].

———. "The Historical Struggle for Language Rights in CCCC." *From Intention to Practice: Considerations of Language Diversity in the Classroom.* Ed. G. Smitherman and V. Villanueva. Carbondale: Southern Illinois UP, 2003. 7–39.

Sridhar, S. N. "A Reality Check for SLA Theories." *TESOL Quarterly* 28.4 (1994): 800–05.

Students' Right to Their Own Language. Special issue of *College Composition and Communication* 25 (1974): [pp. 19–57 in this book].

Tannen, Deborah. *Spoken and Writing Language: Exploring Orality and Literacy.* Norwood, NJ: Ablex, 1982.

Thaiss, Christopher, and Terry Myers Zawacki. "Questioning Alternative Discourses: Reports from Across the Disciplines," *ALT DIS: Alternative Discourses and the Academy.* Ed. Christopher Schroeder, Helen Fox, and Patricia Bizzell. Portsmouth. NH: Boynton/Cook, 2002. 80–96.

Viswanathan, Gauri. "English in a Literate Society." *The Lie of the Land: English Literary Studies in India.* Ed. R. S. Rajan. Oxford: OUP, 1993. 29–41.

Warschauer, Mark. "The Changing Global Economy and the Future of English Teaching." *TESOL Quarterly* 34.3 (2000): 511–36.

Wheeler, Rebecca S. "Welcoming the Languages of the Home *and* the School." Paper presented in the 119th MLA annual convention, San Diego, CA, Sunday, 28 December 2003.

Widdowson, Henry G. "Proper Words in Proper Places." *ELT Journal* 47.4 (1993): 317–29.

Young, Vershawn Ashanti. "Your Average Nigga." *College Composition and Communication* 55.4 (2004): 693–715.

16

"They're in My Culture, They Speak the Same Way": African American Language in Multiethnic High Schools

DJANGO PARIS

The title of this article comes from an interview I conducted with Miles,[1] an African American high school student I came to know during a year I spent doing an ethnographic study in his youth community. Miles was commenting on the linguistic reality of his multiethnic high school, describing the ways his Latino/a and Pacific Islander peers shared in his culture and his language. In this article, I explore the deep linguistic and cultural ways that Miles was right: that youth in his multiethnic urban high school employed linguistic features of African American Language (AAL) across ethnic lines. I begin by describing some of the characteristics of AAL and then show how language sharing in AAL happened and how youth across ethnic groups made sense of it. I also discuss the ways knowledge about AAL use in multiethnic contexts might be applied to language and literacy education and how such linguistic and cultural sharing can help us forge interethnic understanding in our changing urban schools.

To examine the ways youth shared in AAL across ethnicity and to facilitate a discussion of the educational and social implications of this sharing, I provide ethnographic and sociolinguistic data I collected over the 2006–2007 school year at South Vista High School. South Vista High is a public charter high school serving students from the city of South Vista, a working-class community of color in a major metropolitan area of the West Coast. South Vista was a predominantly African American city as late as 1990, but even then the city was beginning to experience dramatic demographic shifts. By the dawn of the twenty-first century, the Spanish-speaking Latino/a population had become a significant majority of the city's population.

The youth of South Vista were living through this change. Carlos, a Mexican American youth I worked with, put it this way: "It used to be all black people. It was a black city. . . . There was some Latinos, but over time they started moving away, and then more Latinos started moving in" (3/12/07).[2] During the year of my research, 17 percent of the students at South Vista High

---

From *Harvard Educational Review* 79.3 (2009): 428–47.

were African American, 10 percent were Pacific Islander, and 73 percent were Latino/a—mainly Mexican or Mexican American.[3]

The interviews and field notes I draw on here are the result of nine months of close fieldwork I conducted with a group of eight focus youth and the sixty young people in their peer networks. These focus youth included African American, Latino/a, and Pacific Islander young women and young men. I spent more than 400 hours participating with and observing these young people and conducted three semistructured, *ethnolinguistic* interviews with each focus youth over the school year.[4] I employed grounded theory to categorize major themes of youth language use and understanding and used sociolinguistic methods to look more closely at features of AAL in everyday talk.

My own interest in the nexus of ethnic and linguistic difference and school learning is fueled by my years teaching English in multiethnic schools as well as by my own identity as a black/biracial scholar with a black Jamaican immigrant father and a white American mother. My research relationships with these youth—as young people of color, as immigrants, and as speakers and hearers of many Englishes—were far from impersonal; in varying ways, these experiences were also part of my coming-of-age. Although here I focus on AAL in multiethnic high schools, the interviews and field-notes I present should be seen in light of my ethnographic work with these youth across community contexts, from home to church, classroom to basketball court, hip-hop show to soccer match. The AAL I observed, participated in, and recorded in these spaces, of course, was anchored in a historical context of oppression, resistance, and achievement. I attempt to attend to this context as I discuss AAL use across ethnicity at South Vista High.

THE NEED FOR INTERETHNIC LANGUAGE RESEARCH IN SCHOOLS

AAL is the most studied variety of English in the world, with over forty years of sociolinguistic scholarship investigating when, how, where, with whom, and why AAL has been and continues to be spoken by many African Americans (e.g., Baugh, 1983; Labov, 1972; Smitherman, 2006). These decades of scholarship have given us a rich understanding of the grammar, phonology, lexicon, and rhetorical traditions of AAL.[5]

Research into using AAL as a resource for classroom learning is also vast (Rickford, Sweetland, & Rickford, 2004). We know how to contrast AAL grammar with Dominant American English (DAE) grammar so that students come to see and attend to differences depending on social context and purpose (Godley, Sweetland, Wheeler, Minnici, & Carpenter, 2006).[6] We know much about the ways in which the features of spoken AAL carry into writing (Ball, 1995, 1999). We also know what it looks like to teach African American AAL-speaking students to maintain cultural competence while acquiring DAE (Alim, 2004; Ladson-Billings, 1995; Lee, 1995). We have a particularly robust and growing literature on the connections between hip-hop, AAL, and classroom learning (Alim, 2004, 2006; Kirkland, 2008; Mahiri, 2001; Morrell & Duncan-Andrade, 2002). And finally, we know quite a bit about how to train teachers to use AAL as a resource for classroom learning (Godley et al., 2006; Kirkland, 2008).

Yet research on AAL has remained focused solely on African Americans despite demographic change in our communities and schools. There is good reason for our focus on black speakers of AAL: AAL is a black-originated English that is intimately connected with a history of oppression, resistance, and rich linguistic and literary achievement in African America (Rickford & Rickford, 2000). And it is a language used by many African American young people in our schools and communities. However, demographic shifts coupled with the continued residential segregation of poor communities of color have increased the numbers of black and brown students who share the same communities and classrooms (Ball, 2006; Klein, 2004; Ladson-Billings, 2006; Massey, 2001). Understanding how AAL operates in such multiethnic schools will help us understand where our vast knowledge of AAL should be applied. It will also shed light on opportunities for a *pedagogy of pluralism*—a stance to teaching both within and across differences—in multiethnic schools.

This research is an attempt to push educational research further into the realm of interethnic youth communication. Building on seminal theoretical work focused on contact in multiethnic and multilingual contexts (Anzaldúa, 1987, 1999; Bakhtin, 1981; DuBois, 1903, 1965; Pratt, 1987, 1991), I have come to conceptualize *multiethnic youth space* as a social and cultural space centered on youth communication within and between ethnicities—a space of contact where youth challenge and reinforce notions of difference and division through language choices and attitudes. Very little research has brought social language knowledge and methodology to the multiethnic youth spaces so common in contemporary urban schools. Rampton's (1995) ethnographic and sociolinguistic study of language use in a multiethnic youth community in Britain provides a rare investigation into how language and ethnicity function among adolescents in such multiethnic space. Although not based in schools, Rampton's (1998) work moves beyond the study of in-groups and toward an understanding of what he later termed *plural ethnicities*. For Rampton, individuals can adopt plural ethnicities that challenge singular ethnicities in contexts where ethnic groups blur lines of linguistic and cultural ownership. In his analysis, he looked to understand the social rules of *language crossing*, moments when youth would cross into the languages of their peers during interactions.

Although Rampton referred to all instances of youth employing their out-group peers' languages as "crossing," my own analysis has pointed to some moments when AAL was crossed into and other times when it was shared. While language crossing may or may not be ratified by traditional in-group speakers, I refer to *language sharing* as those momentary and sustained uses of the language that are ratified—when use of the language traditionally "belonging" to another group is ratified as appropriate by its traditional speakers. Such sharing occurred at South Vista when African American students ratified the AAL use of their Pacific Islander and Latino/a peers. As I will show, this ratification can be expressed in several ways. Most often at South Vista, ratification occurred through African American AAL speakers continuing an interaction in AAL with their Latino/a or Pacific Islander peers and, by continuing an interaction, implicitly inviting their out-group peers to continue the language sharing. Another way AAL use was ratified as sharing was more simply when African American students did not protest, mock, or otherwise comment on the AAL use of their out-group peers, thereby implicitly deeming it as authentic.

While crossing and sharing have major implications for how we think about language, ethnicity, and schooling in multiethnic contexts, it is important that I avoid overstating what such practices can achieve in an unequal society. Although language is one primary marker of ethnicity and identity, other major markers of race, like skin color, play heavily into systems of discrimination, racism, and privilege. For this reason, I back away from Rampton's "plural ethnicities" and favor more specific terms of practice, such as *linguistic dexterity*—the ability to use a range of language practices in a multiethnic society—and terms of mind, such as *linguistic plurality*, consciousness about why and how to use such dexterity in social interactions. Such terms recognize the importance of interethnic practices without falsely implying that they surmount systemic barriers.

AAL GRAMMAR, LEXICON, AND RITUAL INSULT AMONG BLACK YOUTH AT SOUTH VISTA

All of the African American students I came to know at South Vista were bidialectal AAL speakers: their everyday speech both inside and outside the classroom showed major features of AAL, but they could also shift, to varying extents, into more dominant varieties of English. The research literature has long noted that many African Americans can and do systematically use features of AAL in their everyday speech (Baugh, 1983; Rickford & Rickford, 2000; Smitherman, 1977). Miles said this quite succinctly as we sat on a bench near the athletic field informally talking one afternoon, "*Every black person is bilingual*" he told me. "You gotta be because I was taught that it's harder for us, and you have to use their language to get by." (I use italics throughout the data examples to highlight youth perspectives on AAL as well as AAL features.) Of course, not all African Americans can or do speak AAL. Like any language variety, it is socially and culturally learned and used. Only people who learn AAL and have reason to use it do so. Although this learning is often tied to race for reasons of solidarity and segregation, it is not always racially linked, as I will show at South Vista. Given Miles's statement, it was not surprising that my fieldnotes, formal interviews, and recordings of informal conversations with black youth were laden with lexical, grammatical, and phonological features of AAL as well as larger rhetorical traditions of AAL. I will provide a few brief examples here to give some voice to the prevalence of AAL use among South Vista's black youth. I will then follow this section by showing Latino/a and Pacific Islander youth engaging in the same structures, words, and rhetorical traditions as their African American peers.

I begin my analysis by recalling one afternoon when I was talking with African American youth Anthony as we headed over to basketball practice. I had been playing ball with the boys' and girls' teams for two months, and Anthony called me "Coach" as we walked. When I told him that he could just call me Django, Anthony replied, "But you ø like a second coach to me" (12/15/06). In our exchange, Anthony omitted the copula "to be," saying "you ø like" instead of the DAE "you *are* like." Basically, the option of omitting the copula "to be," a major feature of AAL grammar, is available to speakers when using the present tense of "is" and "are."[7]

Other major features of AAL grammar were commonplace among the African American youth I came to know. In a conversation I had with Terrell about a bootleg CD he was purchasing from a friend, he explained, "He *BIN* had it, he ø just waitin for me to have the money" (5/8/07). In addition to a copula omission, Terrell used the remote verbal marker *stressed been* in "He *BIN* had" to denote the fact that his friend had possessed the CD for some time and still had it. Part of a complex tense (when an action occurs) and aspect (how an action occurs) system, this feature is one of many that highlight how AAL semantics can differ significantly from DAE.

My ethnographic interviews with African American youth Miles and Rochelle also illustrated common AAL features. In one interview, Rochelle stated, "When *people call me out my name*, I don't really *be listening*" (12/4/06). Here Rochelle used a hallmark of AAL grammar known as the *habitual be*, in "I don't really *be* listening" for the DAE "I'm not usually/always listening." Rochelle's use of the habitual be is another example of the AAL tense and aspect system. In addition to the habitual be, Rochelle also used the AAL expression "people call me out my name," a phrase meaning when people insult or slander you (see Smitherman, 2006).

In addition to demonstrating AAL grammatical structures, verbal interactions between African American youth at South Vista were also laden with the AAL lexicon. One afternoon I was shooting hoops with African American youths Sharon and Miles. Miles was wearing his white socks up high, a retro look used by many NBA players.

DJANGO: You got the old school look.

SHARON: No, he do that because he ø *hella ashy*.

MILES: No, it's like Baron Davis.

SHARON SHAKES HER HEAD: You ø ashy. *She walks off.*

In addition to the AAL optional *absence of third-person singular "s"* (or, here, "es") in "do" for the DAE "does," Sharon also omitted the copula. Yet grammar was not at the center of this interaction; the exchange hinged on the term *ashy*. Although there is much debate about what constitutes the entire AAL lexicon, *ashy* is considered a long-standing AAL lexical item. It is a generally negative term for dry skin that is uncared for. Sharon was calling Miles out for not taking care of his skin with moisture lotion. He protested that he looked like Baron Davis, a pro player, but Sharon was not having it. She even increased the stakes by calling Miles "hella ashy," using the regional adjective "hella" for "extremely."

Beyond AAL grammar and lexicon, the African American youth I worked with at South Vista participated in broader rhetorical traditions of black language. One common speech act was *the dozens*, also known in the literature as *capping*.[8] An extended form of *signifying*, or using "verbal hyperbole, irony, indirection, metaphor, and the semantically unexpected" (Smitherman, 2006, 70), the dozens are a form of ritual insult involving verbal wordplay centering on humorous insults to family members, friends, and the other participants. They are intended to be funny, often played to an audience. The following interaction that occurred in biology class shows Miles and Derek engaged in playing ritual insults on each other. The class was studying DNA duplication when Miles asked a question.

MILES: Why do people get mutations, deformities?

TEACHER: Sometimes they don't copy right.

MILES: Then you end up short like Derek. *The class laughs.*

DEREK RETORTS: Or dark like Miles. *More laughter.*

MILES: Or like Sharon. *More laughter. Sharon cuts her eyes at Miles, grinning. Miles shrinks back a bit, deciding he better not go further.* (2/28/07)

Miles asked an apparently straightforward question, yet he asked the question seemingly to set up his planned cap on Derek's diminutive stature (as Derek was the shortest boy in tenth grade). Miles's comment was certainly unexpected, a sort of verbal juke that brought some laughter. Yet Derek knew how to play as well and capped back, remarking on Miles's dark skin (which was dark in the broader spectrum of African American skin pigment), only for Miles to pass it off on Sharon, who had a skin color similar to Miles. Sharon, although verbally silent, participated in the exchange by *cutting* her eyes, a gesture of displeasure recognized in the African Diaspora that can be as loud as words. While the crack about skin color may seem particularly mean-spirited and is certainly laden with the pain of racist history, African American wordplay and humor has often served the function of flipping the painfully real white and internalized oppression into the humorous (Carpio, 2008; Rickford & Rickford, 2000). The fact that the relative darkness of skin has historically had an impact on and continues to affect how African Americans view each other and are positioned by the dominant white culture is no laughing matter; yet to make it so simultaneously masks the internalized shame and gives momentary relief from it. It is also important that I point out that all of the people in the class, including the Latina teacher and myself, were people of color, which could have made such a joke more possible.

The use of AAL grammar and lexicon and participation in speech acts like signifying worked to sustain African American students' positions as members of the local and broader AAL speech community. Although social purposes and contexts vary in these examples, they were each acts of linguistic identity that placed youth within a tradition and a cultural community of "every black person" being "bilingual." Rochelle and Miles, for example, often spoke of "our" or "my" language in our discussions about AAL. And yet, as I will show, both Miles and Rochelle also understood that AAL was not theirs alone in South Vista. While these few moments taken from hundreds of examples in my fieldwork show that AAL was alive and well among the African American youth of South Vista, my goal here is to illuminate something far less studied but nevertheless central to understanding the role of oral language in division and unity in multiethnic schools: how do Pacific Islanders and Latinos/as also participate in AAL with black youth, and how do young people of all backgrounds make sense of this AAL sharing?

SHARING AAL AT SOUTH VISTA: GRAMMAR, LEXICON, AND RITUAL INSULT

It was an afternoon walk I had taken often during my months at South Vista. On any given day I would stroll over to the gym for basketball practice with any number of South Vista youth. On this afternoon I was walking with Samoan youth Soa and Latina youth Cynthia. There was an ease to our conversation that reflected many months of spending time together in the classroom and community. My ethnographic work, laden with rich interactions, had taken me from biology class to English class, from the basketball court to the home, and to many other school and community spaces. As we walked to the gym, we joked about a male ball player, Derek, who, despite his very small frame, was a favorite among many of the young women at South Vista.

CYNTHIA: Derek's a *gangsta.*

DJANGO: A small *gangsta. We all chuckle.*

CYNTHIA: He *be teachin* everybody how to be *gangsta.*

DJANGO: What he *be teachin?*

SOA: He taught me how to smoke weed. *They bust up laughing.*

DJANGO: Ok, that is something. *I smile shaking my head.* (2/5/07)

Cynthia started the interaction with the hip-hop lexical item *gangsta* (an action or state of being that rejects dominant rules, or an action or state of being that shows prowess or wealth).[9] I could not resist a small cap myself. Cynthia, a bilingual Latina, continued by employing the habitual be, a major grammatical feature of AAL. I continued the participation, at which point Soa came with the unexpected and funny weed comment. While it is not my purpose here to debate the dangers or merits of Soa's comment (the teachers and administrators were aware of the prevalence of marijuana use), to be "gangsta" at South Vista meant resisting dominant rules of many kinds— cultural preferences both about how to speak and act and also about what to do. While I struggled at times with some of the choices made by the young people I worked with (e.g., truancy and substance use), I also worked to recognize these choices from youth perspectives. Linguistic resistance to DAE norms was certainly one major choice, a choice Cynthia made here by indexing youth identity through AAL grammar and lexicon.

AAL grammar and lexicon and the local hip-hop lexicon were also shared across ethnicity within the youth space of the classroom. Back in biology class, Latina youth Sierra and Samoan youth Ela got into the mix. The class was testing the effect of light on earthworms by blasting flashlights on the squirming organisms. The worms, which do not cherish bright light, thrashed about. "He ø *goin dumb*," observed Sierra. After some chuckles, Ela agreed, "*Hyphy*" (1/10/07). In this interaction, Sierra omitted the copula and compared the worm's thrashing to a local dance known as "going dumb." In a typical version of this dance, the dancers let their limbs go loose and shake wildly, dipping up and down. Ela's agreement to Sierra's comment came through the more general term *hyphy*, a regional movement of bass-heavy club tracks, dance moves, and local lexicon led by rappers such as E-40 and the deceased father of hyphy, Mac Dre.

My ethnographic interviews with Mexican/Mexican American and Pacific Islander youth showed the use of many important AAL features (see table 16.1). Although there was considerable variation in the amount of AAL used by youth in interviews, they all did, in fact, use features of AAL.[10]

Carlos, Rahul, and Ela, for example, all used the habitual be. Coupled with instances from my observations, this use of the tense/aspect system of AAL shows the ways many nonblack youth had picked up an alternative sense of time and action in their everyday English—how they had come to embody Jordan's (1985) wonderful statement about the relationship between AAL grammar and mind: "The syntax of a sentence equals the structure of your consciousness" (163). In addition to the habitual be, Carlos, Carla, Rahul, and Julio used the *existential it's* (Rickford & Rickford, 2000) in phrases like Carla's "*It's* some girls" for the DAE "There is/there are some girls." They also employed the regularization of verb agreement patterns characteristic of AAL and other nondominant varieties of English as in Carlos's "Some dudes that *was* stealing cars."

Ela is a particularly interesting case of language sharing. Ela, who frequently used the habitual be, zero copula, multiple negation, regularization of verb agreement patterns, and absence of third-person singular "s," had arrived in South Vista from Samoa when she was twelve years old, only three years before our work together. Although these had been formative teenage years, for her to pick up and use grammatical features so often in her everyday English said a lot about the strong pull of AAL on Pacific Islander youth.

Beyond AAL grammar, participation by Pacific Islander and Latino/a youth in the AAL lexicon was pervasive in the multiethnic youth space of South Vista. Consider the following fieldnote excerpts documenting uses of "ashy" in multiethnic exchanges. The first example occurred in an exchange among Latina student Gloria, African American student Miles, and me.

I am sitting talking with Miles on the front benches. Gloria, who is wearing short pants, comes up to us and announces, "My legs are all *ashy*." Miles takes no notice of her comment, just glancing down at her legs. (3/20/07)

TABLE 16.1   AAL Features of Latino/a and Pacific Islander Youth

Student	Feature	Examples
Carla	Zero copula	Next year my classes ø gonna be different
	Existential it is	*It's* some girls
Julio	Regularized agreement	People generally call you by the race *you is*
	Existential it is	*It's* really like nothing to do on my block
Carlos	Zero copula	You ø sorry
	Regularized agreement	Some dudes that *was* stealing cars
	Habitual be	Cause *they be tripping* about that
	Existential it is	*It was* a lot of black people
Ela	Regularized agreement	That's how the teachers in Samoa *is*
	Third-person singular "s"/ Zero copula	Every time he wake up, he ø always turning
	Habitual be	My big *mouth be saying*, "Uh uh, uh uh"
	Multiple negation[11]	*I don't got no "F." I don't got no "B"*
Rahul	Existential it is	*It's* times you have to use it
	Regularized agreement	When you *was* growing up
	Zero copula	They ø keeping me on check
	Habitual be	We *be talking* about cars
	Third-person singular "s"	He just *come* in my room
	Multiple negation	*I can't split no rhymes*

Another example of "ashy" was used in an extended exchange between Samoan youth Soa and African American youths Sharon and Ricky.

> Soa and Sharon are sitting against a fence watching the boys play football. The girls are laughing and clowning the boys. I am standing with them and watching as well. Ricky runs out onto the field to play, tearing off his hoodie and throwing it down as he enters the field.

SOA: Ricky, you better not take that off, your arms *is hella ashy! She is too far away to see if they are, in fact, ashy.*

SHARON SHAKES HER HEAD: He ø ashy. *They laugh and I laugh with them.*

> Soa launches into recounting what happened during geometry class. Ricky was near her, and she looked over at his arms and "they was hella ashy." She told him, "You better get some lotion." He went and asked African American student Rashida for lotion. Rashida told him he was hella ashy and gave it to him. We all laugh at the story. (4/5/07)

The word *ashy*—used in the first example by a Mexican American to refer to herself and in the second example by a Samoan and an African American to refer to an African American—was common in interethnic youth exchanges. These examples show sharing of one of the most secure items in the AAL lexicon, a word that has long been seen as an exclusively in-group term. While there is a long tradition of AAL-originated words (or meanings) making their way into mainstream popular use, the ratified sharing of "ashy" showed a particularly deep linguistic connection between the youth of color at South Vista.

Beyond the lexical item "ashy," Soa was also participating in ritual insult and verbal barbs characteristic of speech acts such as signifying and the dozens. I witnessed many occasions when Latino/a and Pacific Islander youth entered these speech acts at South Vista. Early in the basketball season, I sat next to Mexican American student Julio and Miles as we stretched on the gym floor before practice.

MILES: Mexican girls don't got no booty. It's all flat like. *He smiles and shakes his head.*

JULIO FEIGNS INDIGNATION: Yes they do, they got booty! *He is also smiling.*

MILES PERSISTS: They don't got enough food in Mexico to have booties. They got to do the J-Lo and get it pumped in.

JULIO RETORTS: What about African girls, they don't got food neither.

MILES HAS THE LAST WORD: It's in the bone structure, though, they just got booty. *And both bust up.* (11/8/07)

These "Mexican" versus "African" or "black" dozens sessions were common between Latino and African American males who shared social networks. In this session, the subject (or subjection) was women's bodies, although it was often wealth, employment status, and residency status. Here, Miles capped on what he deemed to be the unattractive bodies (specifically, rear ends) of an entire population of women. Julio protested. Miles, quick with the verbally unexpected, got two caps in. The first was that there wasn't enough food in Julio's homeland. The second was that the popular Latina star Jennifer Lopez, renowned in popular media for her attractive body (and, specifically, rear end), had to have surgery to be so good looking. Julio came back with a comment about the lack of food in Africa, but Miles had an answer for that, too, ending the exchange by taking up the racist/sexist mythology of black female body structure.[12]

It would be easy to continue in this vein, analyzing the racist/sexist content of this exchange, and objectification was paramount to this content. I see no analytic "out" for Miles and Julio on this count, save the point that both seemed to feel a racialized-sexualized allegiance to women from their own ethnic backgrounds. A possible additional saving grace was Miles's comment about "bone structure," which can be seen as another example of flipping pain and racist myth into an (objectified) appreciation. It seems he saw a sexualized beauty in the black female body and was attempting here to argue for the superiority of such beauty. But there were other themes about national origin and poverty that provide an important subtext to the turning of pain and shame into humor. While I found myself struggling to listen to this particular exchange (though I did have to laugh at the genius of the J-Lo comment). it also represents Julio's participation with Miles in AAL verbal wordplay that explicitly discussed difference.

One interpretation of such speech events could be that they were playing out community and national tensions between Latinos/as and African Americans, divisions that relate to the struggle for the scarce resources of the oppressed. I believe such an interpretation would be a dominant, divide-and-conquer read, though. Given an understanding of the role of ritual insult in building and sustaining relationships between people, and between people and their language, I am convinced that such loaded insult sessions provided the opposite function; that is, they helped make humor out of shame and pain by unifying Latino/a and African American youth in shared practice and marginalization. In doing so, these sessions resisted both popular conceptions of African American/Latino/a relations and, by invoking stereotypical rhetorics of body, skin, wealth, and gender, also resisted a racist legacy by showing such stereotypes as ridiculous or flipping them into compliments.[13] Both young men spoke of humor in separate interviews when I asked them about these kinds of interactions.

> JULIO: I be like, "You wanna work in my cotton field?" And he be like, "When you gonna cut my grass?" It's just jokes; it's like an inside joke or something like that. But, I mean, it's not to offend no one. It's just a way we get. (1/26/07)
>
> MILES: We have—not like arguments—but you know, friendly—They be like, "Black people this" and I be, "Mexican that," and then, you know, they'll go back, and it's funny. We're having fun. (11/27/06)

I also observed young Pacific Islander and Latina women participating in AAL ritual insult with their black peers.[14] In one exchange, Ela capped on Miles as they worked in biology class to create Punnett squares (a diagram used to determine the probability of the genetic makeup for offspring). Miles was trying to create his diagram using a ruler; Ela sat at the table behind him, and I was behind Ela.

> MILES: It's crooked. *He shakes his head looking down at his Punnett square.*
>
> ELA: It would be. *She chuckles and keeps working on her diagram.*
>
> MILES: *I'ma* get you! *Watch your back, Ela.*
>
> ELA: *I'm a* get Django on you.
>
> MILES: *He ain't gonna do nothin',* he ø scared. *He peers back at me with a smile.*
>
> DJANGO: Please. *I shake my head, staring in mock intensity at Miles.*
>
> ELA: Looks like you ø scared. *She laughs at Miles who nods in defeat.*[15] (2/7/07)

Ela seized a moment of weakness by Miles to insult far more than his diagram. Her cap carried the broader meaning that Miles himself was crooked and unfit. Miles, within the play of the game, felt this insult and took a rather direct intimidation approach. Ela assessed all the verbal and physical tools available in her environment and chose to use me as a counterattack. Miles tried to call her bluff, but I was willing to play, too. My assist was just what Ela needed to finish Miles off. Not only was he "crooked," he was also now "scared."

* * *

While it is a significant research contribution to simply document the use of AAL grammar, lexicon, and speech acts in the everyday English of Latino/a and Pacific Islander youth, such use alone did not tell me much about the ways AAL worked within the ethnic geography of difference, division, and unity at South Vista. Nor was it evident whether such uses were instances of general crossing into AAL or whether they were ratified by the African American in-group as shared practices. In my interviews with youth across groups, I came to understand the processes involved in AAL use—that it was, by and large, seen by all parties as a shared linguistic repertoire across youth space. I also came to understand how youth explained what AAL was and why so many youth used it as something of a lingua franca in multiethnic youth space.

Youth Understandings of AAL Sharing

African American youth were keenly aware that their language was used by Latinos/as and Pacific Islanders. Though this participation was generally seen as unproblematic and caused far more social cohesion than social fissures in youth space, during a midyear interview Rochelle expressed reservations about some Latino/a AAL use.

> DJANGO: Does it bother you when you hear the Mexican kids talking kinda black like that?
>
> ROCHELLE: Yeah.
>
> DJANGO: It does? Like when all of them do it, or just some of them? Like some of them it's OK, some of them it's not?
>
> ROCHELLE: Some is okay because some be half-black, and some dudes be trying to talk like that just to get the attention. It's not funny. They ø gonna get beat up. (2/9/07)

Rochelle was aware that Latino/a youth participated in AAL, and her explanation of when such use was ratified by African American AAL speakers was complex. Rochelle sanctioned some AAL speech by "half-black" Latinos/as as authentic. She did not mean racially mixed youth (Rochelle did not have any Latino/a–black biracial youth in her peer network) but, rather, those Latinos/as she deemed "real" AAL speakers versus those who were feigning prowess for attention. Those who were faking, warned Rochelle, might be physically threatened. Although Rochelle's comment was atypical, and I never knew such violence to take place at South Vista (or even a comment or argument over inauthentic AAL use), these possible inauthentic uses show that some AAL participation by Latino/a and Pacific Islander youth might be perceived by African American youth as unratified language crossing rather than the more generally approved language sharing.

During an interview, Miles expressed a more general sentiment felt across ethnic groups at South Vista about AAL sharing. When I asked him what he thought about AAL use by nonblack youth at South Vista, Miles spoke of a community socializing process in multiethnic youth space.

> MILES: I'm not trippin. They're my homeboys, most of them. I'm cool with it. I don't think they're trying to steal anything. They're just being themselves because they were born here and raised here, but they were also born and raised in their house, so they can—they get the best of both worlds, I guess. (11/27/06)

Miles saw AAL use as a shared part of South Vista youth space. In fact, for Miles, such sharing promoted friendship across ethnicity, promoted Latino/a AAL speakers to be his "homeboys." Miles did not feel these ratified speakers were taking his language. Instead, he saw them as "being themselves," youth who grew up in an AAL-speaking environment with African American peers. Though by saying "most of them" Miles left open the possibility that some participation could be inauthentic, the general thrust of his understanding was that AAL sharing was part of a community socializing process involving sustained linguistic and cultural contact between South Vista's ethnic communities. Even though Miles understood this, he also displayed some envy about the Spanish-speaking abilities of his peers. They got to speak his language, the shared language of multiethnic youth space, and also got to know the omnipresent Spanish, spoken by 70 percent of his school and community.[16] They got "the best of both worlds."

This was not the only time that Miles described this view of the community socializing process of AAL sharing. In a later interview, he furthered this notion:

> MILES: There's a lot of us in there that talk [AAL], well, not a lot, but you know, it's like for you who dress like they're black, you know, with the Girbauds, the long T's, you know. And there's some and they just speak slang like regular black people. It's like they were grown up here and it makes it cool at the same time. (3/26/07)

This statement falls in line with the socializing view of sharing. As he said, "They were grown up here." Yet Miles also provided two further understandings. One is the way he tied AAL use to other cultural ways of being, other identity markers of blackness in youth space. Here Miles used clothing as a prime marker. Girbaud, the hottest urban jean designer of the year, and long T-shirts were ways of indexing participation in black cultural discourse. This way of dressing coupled with "slang" made Latino/a and Pacific Islander AAL speakers "like regular black people." Pacific Islander and Latino/a youth I interviewed also attached AAL sharing to particular cultural activities. Julio, for instance, described his participation on the predominantly African American basketball team as a forum for speaking AAL. Fijian-Indian youth Rahul, who wrote and performed raps, talked of his role as an emcee as sharing in linguistic practices across race. These uses, attached to particular activities, were generally ratified as appropriate by the African American in-group. It seemed such ratification hinged on the speaker showing prowess in the given activity. Rahul's ability to rap, for example, was deemed considerable by the black peers he rhymed with, as was Julio's relative skill on the basketball court by the African American players on his team.

Miles, like Rochelle, expressed a feeling of ownership and solidarity about his culture; yet he also realized he shared that culture with the large and increasing number of Latinos/as and Pacific Islanders who "were grown up here." This was an awareness about AAL that Pacific Islander and Latino/a youth at South Vista also expressed. Ela, for instance, was clear that she and her Samoan peers used AAL as their everyday English, as she told me during an interview.

> DJANGO: When you're not talking Samoan—when you're talking with your friends in English—how would you describe the way you guys talk?
>
> ELA: We talk ghetto a lot. Ghetto—like kids talk. They're like, "Man, he be cursing me—he's talking ghetto." (1/16/07)

Ela used the habitual be to give life to her description of what she called "ghetto." Other than "slang," "ghetto" was the most common term used by youth across groups to describe AAL. "Ghetto" at South Vista and in the broader urban youth and hip-hop culture was an adjective describing something as urban. Depending on context, "ghetto" could be positive, negative, or relatively neutral. Ela's use here was rather neutral to describe an everyday way of talk among peers.

Mexican American student Carlos also viewed AAL as the most common English used across youth space. When I asked him directly whether African Americans had a different way with words, he shared this view:

> DJANGO: Would you say that African American people in general have a way of talking? You said they only talk English. Do they talk English like everybody else or is their English different in any way?
>
> CARLOS: No, well they actually talk like everybody from South Vista, they talk slang, at least a little that you could tell, but they speak like that, too. So everybody here speaks the same in terms of the English. (1/22/07)

As Carlos considered my question, he came to the conclusion that "everybody here speaks the same in terms of English," since everybody speaks "slang." During a later interview, he provided maybe the most succinct statement of AAL linguistic socialization at South Vista. When Carlos came to South Vista from Michoacán, Mexico, in 1999, he spoke very little English. As he shared his personal story of learning English mainly from black youth in his first South Vista middle school, he expressed this general statement: "What happens is, like, when kids are coming—*like English learners*, since they're around black people sometimes, *they learn the slang instead of, like, the English-English"* (3/12/07).

Like Miles, Carlos realized that youth learning English in South Vista were likely to learn English within the long-standing African American community of South Vista. While Miles spoke of those Latino/a and Pacific Islander youth who were born in South Vista, Carlos added the perspective of immigrants, like himself and Ela, who learned to share in black speech as they learned to navigate a new city, a new country, a new language, and a new, hybrid identity.

AAL, EDUCATION, AND PLURALISM IN MULTIETHNIC SCHOOLS

At South Vista, many bilingual Latino/a and Pacific Islander youth worked to simultaneously forge identities as members of their particular ethnic communities *and* as members of broader youth culture. AAL was a major player in this work, and it offers important lessons for multiethnic schools and understandings of pluralist cultural spaces. While the use of Spanish, Samoan, or Fijian by the ethnic in-group often maintained ethnic solidarity and division (Paris, 2008, 2010), AAL served the opposite function: AAL was a shared practice that challenged notions of difference and division rather than reinforced them. Employing the words, the grammar, and the speech acts of black language provided a space of local youth prestige against the backdrop of shared marginalization in a white language– and white culture–dominated society. It was a shared counterlanguage that resisted the dominant norms of school and society.

In an interview one day, Miles proclaimed, "We all gotta stay together. We're the minorities" (1/19/07). Pluralism in multiethnic communities of color—what Miles called staying "together"—needs both within- and across-group practices to sustain it. AAL was the primary linguistic practice of cultural togetherness, though youth of all backgrounds also understood the need to maintain linguistic practices, like Spanish or Samoan, that were particular to their home and ethnic communities.[17] Yet, even as AAL was a tool of inter-ethnic solidarity, it was somewhat troubling that black youth were the only group without an ethnic and linguistic safe haven within this multiethnic youth space. While most Latino/a and Pacific Islander youth could retreat into the important space of their own linguistic and cultural heritage, when African American youth used AAL, wore black-originated clothing styles, or listened to black-originated music, it was likely that youth of other ethnic groups understood their meanings and practices and would join in.

This tension certainly goes beyond language. Current demographic shifts in South Vista and other urban communities forecast a shrinking urban territory for the African American population (Zhou, 2001). With the shrinking numbers at South Vista came fewer exclusively owned practices. This tension was playing out in the lives of Rochelle and Miles and their Pacific Islander and Latino/a peers. They theorized about what it meant and, ultimately, saw the speaking on the wall: AAL would be shared just as their community had come to be shared. Remember that, just a generation before, South Vista had been a predominantly black community. In the face of demographic changes, AAL was echoing across social space from previous eras, and South Vista's African American youth were, in a sense, carriers of the linguistic and cultural torch for the black city their parents had known only decades before. These young people were passing their language into youth space and, through sharing it, ensuring its interethnic survival and importance in the community.

However, there is still a troubling tension between AAL as interethnic unifier and the lack of an ethnic safe haven for black youth. While African American youth did take a certain amount of pride in others being part of their language and their culture, they also struggled with the false linguistic shame of often seeing their shared practices as simply "slang."[18] Perhaps this tension would not seem so troubling if all the youth knew more about the structure and history of AAL. Adopting a *pedagogy of pluralism* would seek to use youth practices of AAL (as well as other heritage languages) in multiethnic schools to embrace, problematize, and extend understandings of interethnic language sharing *and* understandings of ethnic and linguistic solidarity. Such a pedagogical orientation puts schools in position to be sites of critical language learning that could bolster the pride of African American youth about their linguistic heritage, while simultaneously fostering more conscious respect from youth of other ethnic backgrounds. To be clear, I do not mean to imply that youth were not aware of the local and (through hip-hop) global prestige of AAL, but rather I am arguing that more consciousness could have increased respect for the language and its heritage speakers.

Still, AAL *was* a unifier in youth space. It worked to help youth, both consciously and unconsciously, move across divisions predicated on ethnic difference and seek common ground in an oppressive world. Unfortunately, South Vista High did not treat AAL as a unifier; in fact, the school did not seem to treat AAL much at all. Although I witnessed one attempt to use rap as a cultural entry point in an English class, the caring, dedicated, and well-qualified teachers of South Vista did not use the AAL lexicon or grammar as a resource for classroom learning during my year of observations. While I did not witness the old-school corrections of AAL speech that haunted previous eras ("No, it's not 'she in school'! It's 'she *is* in school'!"), and I found that South Vista's teachers were generally receptive to difference, there was no mention that a grammar was happening across ethnicity inside and outside the classroom. This omission saddened me. We dedicate entire classes to learning English, but teachers, their curriculum, and the broader structures of teacher preparation and linguistic ignorance are ill-equipped to use the Englishes of our students as critical resources in learning. Teacher education must contend with the demographic and linguistic realities of changing urban communities, and AAL will remain a central player in these changes.

Most simply, my work with the youth of South Vista suggests that we must reconsider where our vast linguistic and educational knowledge of AAL should be used. To date, this knowledge has mainly been applied to African

American speakers of AAL. South Vista illuminates other urban youth who could benefit from using AAL as a resource for critical language and literacy learning. Although the teachers in South Vista taught in a predominantly Latino/a school, the student demographics belied the linguistic reality. If teachers had been encouraged to listen, they would have realized that AAL knowledge was required, just as knowledge of other heritage languages, like Spanish and Samoan, was required in order to understand and utilize their students' linguistic resources in the classroom. They would have also been treated to an amazing tapestry of practices that reached across groups to claim a linguistic and cultural plurality that often resisted traditional visions of racial strife in schools and communities. Such plurality sometimes seeped into classroom space but usually operated below the official script of classroom learning. Yet it begged to be given official space to foster and extend youth understandings of plural schools and plural communities. Such a classroom space would embody a pedagogy of pluralism, using youth language practices to explore the importance of ethnic difference and interethnic unity, helping youth and communities to build coalitions both within and across differences.

Our schools and communities are changing. Yet, as Miles knew, "We gotta stay together. We're the minorities." AAL use and understanding at South Vista was one aspect of the rich linguistic dexterity and plurality of our young people. Schools must take advantage of these resources to foster togetherness in the face of a difficult, unequal, and increasingly multiethnic society.

NOTES

1. All names are pseudonyms.

2. In this article, I follow *HER* policy using lowercase letters for the names of racial groups (e.g., "black," "white"). In other writing, I capitalize the names of racial groups to highlight the significance of the socially constructed categories of race in schools and society.

3. The majority of Latino/a and Pacific Islander students at South Vista were to some extent bilingual.

4. I use the term "ethnolinguistic" to describe interviews with both the ethnographic aims of gathering insider perspectives and the sociolinguistic aims of collecting everyday language use (Paris, 2008).

5. Although this is not a paper on the linguistics of AAL, I will give brief linguistic explanations of features to provide evidence of the ways the language was used across ethnicity.

6. I use "Dominant American English" instead of the commonly used "Standard English" to foreground unequal power relationships between the dominant variety of English and other varieties of English.

7. See Green (2002) and Rickford and Rickford (2000) for a complete discussion of all grammatical and phonological rules in this section, unless otherwise noted.

8. See Smitherman (2006) for the most current essay on *signifying* and *the dozens.*

9. I should note that the AAL lexicon and hip-hop lexicon have a close relationship, with many hip-hop terms finding a place in the vocabulary of AAL speakers, just as many AAL terms have always been a part of hip-hop culture. Alim (2006) calls the relationship between the AAL lexicon and the hip-hop nation lexicon a "familial one," denoting this strong dialogic relationship. See Smitherman (2006) for a thorough treatment of the term *gangsta* in black and hip-hop culture.

10. AAL features in these interviews also show the persistence of AAL use beyond everyday youth interactions, as I was the primary interlocutor.

11. All of the Mexican/Mexican American students I interviewed used multiple negation structures often. I do not represent them here since such constructions are also a feature of Chicano English (Fought, 2006).

12. Such racist, sexualized mythology about black female bodies in nineteenth-century European "anthropology," which sought to prove racial superiority through phenotype, is documented in prose and photography in Willis and Williams (2002).

13. See Carpio (2008) for an extended argument on the use of stereotypes in the humor of African American literature, stand-up comedy, and visual art as a resistance to the legacy of slavery.

14. This is an important point, as the study of the dozens and ritual insult has been dominated by analysis of male black exchanges (analyzed by male researchers) until recently (Morgan, 2002; Smitherman, 2006).

15. *I'ma*, an AAL feature for first-person future action, represents a complicated morphological transformation from the DAE "I'm going to."

16. See Paris (2010) for a full discussion of Spanish at South Vista.

17. See Paris (2010) for a full discussion of the less extensive but important use of Spanish words and phrases by African American and Pacific Islander youth. For various reasons, including the small numbers of speakers, Samoan and Fijian languages were not used by youth from other ethnic groups in my research (Paris, 2008).

18. This is an internalized shame that continues to haunt many in the African American community (Baugh, 1999; Rickford & Rickford, 2000).

REFERENCES

Alim, H. S. (2004). *You know my steez: An ethnographic and sociolinguistic study of a black American speech community.* Durham, NC: Duke University Press.

Alim, H. S. (2006). *Roc the mic right: The language of hip hop culture.* New York: Routledge.

Anzaldúa, G. (1987, 1999). *Borderlands/La frontera: The new mestiza.* San Francisco: Aunt Lute Books.

Bakhtin, M. M. (1981). Discourse in the novel. In M. Holquist (Ed.), *The dialogic imagination: Four essays* (pp. 257–422). Austin: University of Texas Press.

Ball, A. (1995). Text design patterns in the writing of urban African American students: Teaching to the cultural strengths of students in multicultural settings. *Urban Education, 30*(3), 253–289.

Ball, A. (1999). Evaluating the writing of culturally and linguistically diverse students: The case of the African American vernacular English speaker. In C. Cooper & L. Odell (Eds.), *Evaluating writing* (pp. 225–248). Urbana, IL: National Council of Teachers of English.

Ball, A. (Ed.). (2006). *With more deliberate speed: Achieving equity and excellence in education—realizing the full potential of Brown v. Board of Education.* National Society for the Study of Education. Malden, MA: Blackwell.

Baugh, J. (1983). *Black street speech.* Austin: University of Texas Press.

Baugh, J. (1999). *Out of the mouths of slaves: African American language and educational malpractice.* Austin: University of Texas Press.

Carpio, G. (2008). *Laughing fit to kill: Black humor in the fictions of slavery.* New York: Oxford University Press.

DuBois, W. E. B. (1903, 1965). *The souls of blackfolk.* New York: Avon Books.

Fought, C. (2006). *Language and ethnicity.* Cambridge: Cambridge University Press.

Godley, A., Sweetland, J., Wheeler, R., Minnici, A., & Carpenter, B. (2006). Preparing teachers for dialectally diverse classrooms. *Educational Researcher, 35*(8), 30–38.

Green, L. (2002). *African American English: A linguistic introduction.* Cambridge: Cambridge University Press.

Jordan, J. (1985). Nobody mean more to me than you, and the future life of Willie Jordan. In *On Call: Political Essays* (pp. 157–172). Boston: South End Press.

Kirkland, D. (2008). The rose that grew from concrete: Postmodern blackness and new English education. *English Journal, 97*(5), 69–75.

Klein, H. (2004). *A population history of the United States.* Cambridge: Cambridge University Press.

Labov, W. (1972). *Language in the inner city.* Philadelphia: University of Pennsylvania Press.

Ladson-Billings, C. (1995). Toward a theory of culturally relevant pedagogy. *American Educational Research Journal, 32*(3), 465–491.

Ladson-Billings, C. (2006). The meaning of Brown . . . for now. In A. F. Ball (Ed.), *With more deliberate speed* (pp. 298–313). Malden, MA: Blackwell.

Lee, C. D. (1995). A culturally based cognitive apprenticeship: Teaching African American high school students skills in literary interpretation. *Reading Research Quarterly, 30*(4), 608–630.

Mahiri, J. (2001). Pop culture pedagogy and the end(s) of school. *Journal of Adolescent and Adult Literacy, 44*(4), 382–385.

Massey, D. (2001). Residential segregation and neighborhood conditions in U.S. metropolitan areas. In N. Smelser, J. Wilson, & F. Mitchell (Eds.), *American becoming: Racial trends and their consequences* (pp. 391–434). Washington, DC: National Academies Press.

Morgan, M. (2002). *Language, discourse and power in African American culture.* Cambridge: Cambridge University Press.

Morrell, E., & Duncan-Andrade, J. (2002). Promoting academic literacy with urban youth through engaging in hip-hop culture. *English Journal, 91*(6), 88–92.

Paris, D. (2008). *"Our culture": Difference, division, and unity in multiethnic youth space.* Unpublished doctoral dissertation, Stanford University.

Paris, D. (2010). "The second language of the U.S.": Youth perspectives on Spanish in a changing multiethnic community. *Journal of Language, Identity, and Education, 9*(2), 139–155.

Pratt, M. L. (1987). Linguistic utopias. In N. Fabb, D. Attridge, A. Durant, & C. MacCabe (Eds.), *The linguistics of writing: Arguments between language and literature.* Manchester, England: Manchester University Press.

Pratt, M. L. (1991). Arts of the contact zone. *Profession, 91*, 33–40.

Rampton, B. (1995). *Crossing: Language and ethnicity among adolescents.* New York: Longman.

Rampton, B. (1998). Language crossing and the redefinition of reality. In P. Auer (Ed.), *Code switching in conversation: Language, interaction and identity* (pp. 290–317). London: Routledge.

Rickford, J., & Rickford, R. (2000). *Spoken soul: The story of black English.* New York: John Wiley and Sons.

Rickford, J., Sweetland, J., & Rickford, A. (2004). African American English and other vernaculars in education: A topic-coded bibliography. *Journal of English Linguistics, 32*(3), 230–320.

Smitherman, G. (1977). *Talkin and testifyin.* Detroit: Wayne State University Press.

Smitherman, G. (2006). *Word from the mother: Language and African Americans.* New York: Routledge.

Willis, D., & Williams, C. (2002). *The black female body: A photographic history.* Philadelphia: Temple University Press.

Zhou, M. (2001). Contemporary immigration and the dynamics of race and ethnicity. In N. Smelser, J. Wilson, & F. Mitchell (Eds.), *American becoming: Racial trends and their consequences* (pp. 200–242). Washington, DC: National Academies Press.

Acknowledgments: My deepest thanks to the young people I learned from in South Vista. Thanks as well to Arnetha Ball, Andrea Lunsford, John Rickford, and Guadalupe Valdés for their comments on earlier versions of this article. I alone am responsible for any faults herein.

17

From "Bad Attitudes" to(ward) Linguistic Pluralism: Developing Reflective Language Policy among Preservice Teachers

GAIL Y. OKAWA

> Up until these last few months, I didn't really think about the language that I spoke or the languages that others spoke. . . . I thought that my use of language was correct and everyone that didn't speak the way I did was wrong. Much of this way I once thought was influenced by my parents, my community, and my own closed-mindedness.
>
> —ALLEN, *Language Autobiography*

Over the last forty years, more and more English language arts teachers in the United States have taught students from backgrounds culturally and linguistically different from their own. This was a diversity prompted in the 1950s by movements toward educational equity and desegregation and, more recently, by new patterns of immigration from Latin America, the Caribbean, Africa, Asia, and eastern Europe. Such language differences between teacher and student and among students resulted initially in theories of "verbal deprivation" among psychologists such as Arthur Jensen (1969), and Carl Bereiter and Siegfried Englemann (1966)—gross misunderstandings about standard and nonstandard dialects that were countered by linguists such as Geneva Smitherman (e.g., 1977, 1981), William Labov (1982), James Sledd (1983), and professional organizations such as NCTE's Conference on College Composition and Communication.[1] Since 1981 exclusionist forces such as U.S. English and its precursors have responded to linguistic diversity by promoting English Only policies throughout the nation. Many opponents see these policies as constitutional violations (e.g., ACLU 1996; CCCC 1993; Daniels 1990; and especially González 1990) and not too thinly veiled attempts to use linguistic chauvinism and imperialism to racist ends (Daniels 1990; Louie 1998; Stroud 1997).

From *Language Ideologies: Critical Perspectives on the Official English Movement.* Ed. Roseann Dueñas González. (Urbana, IL: National Council of Teachers of English, 2000), 276–96.

Such forms of what González (1990) refers to as "'linguicism,' or racism on the basis of language" (50) are not unlike methods used in the Hawaiian Islands from 1924 to 1948 with the establishment of an English Standard school system.[2] Whether derived from dialects or languages, linguistic differences have revealed our deepest—often our most unexamined yet aggressive—feelings of ethnocentrism.

As of December 18, 1996, we have had to add "Ebonics" to the list of controversies—not the pan-African meaning that Robert Williams originally intended to convey by the term in 1973, nor even the African American Vernacular English (AAVE) that it might linguistically designate, but rather the conflicting emotional responses among both African Americans and non–African Americans that the word evokes. Perhaps widespread English Only attitudes had intensified the climate of intolerance leading up to the most recent Ebonics controversy.

Nowhere are the repercussions of such controversies felt more acutely than by students in the nation's classrooms. Previous and current language-attitude research involving teachers and preservice teachers reflects negative attitudes toward and linguistic stereotyping of limited-English-proficient (LEP) and AAVE speakers (Gere and Smith 1979; Hughes 1967; Shuy 1973; Williams 1970; Williams, Hopper, and Natalicio 1977; Bowie 1994; Byrnes and Kiger 1991, 1994). The case of *Lau v. Nichols*, in which non-English-speaking Chinese students sought equal educational opportunities from the San Francisco Unified School District, provides a classic example of how "sink or swim" attitudes and instruction have created educational inequality for LEP children, such that these practices were declared a violation of the Fourteenth Amendment by the U.S. Supreme Court in 1974 (Jiménez 1992, 251–55; see also Crawford 1996). Similarly, the *King Elementary School Children v. Ann Arbor School District* case in the late 1970s brought to light how African American children were being ill-treated because of their home language, leading to the decision by Judge C. W. Joiner in 1979 to extend the *Lau v. Nichols* ruling to "children who speak a minority dialect of English" (Jiménez 1992, 255; see also Labov 1982; Smitherman 1981). The autobiographical narratives of scholars such as Keith Gilyard (1991), Victor Villanueva, Jr. (1993), and Haunani-Kay Trask (1993) further reflect the psychic costs paid by students from linguistic and cultural minority groups and amplify our responsibility as teachers in the process. Despite precedent-setting laws and ample evidence of damage done, the "bad attitudes" persist among the most recent generations of would-be teachers.

In this context, how do we encourage informed language attitudes and decisions among inservice and preservice teachers based on linguistic knowledge rather than on language myths? How can we provoke a questioning of negative attitudes—blatant and latent discrimination—among those potentially or currently in the teaching force? Such questions have continued to plague me over the past few years. Having worked with hundreds of education students, I have observed that ignorance of language as systematic social behavior with historical roots is one of the greatest co-conspirators of linguistic chauvinism and internalized linguistic imperialism. This ignorance produces language attitudes that shore up the English Only movement, fuel the Ebonics controversy, and provoke other forms of linguistic intolerance or shame among aggressors or victims, colonizing or colonized. As U.S. school populations continue to grow more diverse, and as linguistically diverse students grow in number, it is increasingly imperative that pre- and inservice teachers in the English/language arts field recognize the social and political consequences of our daily decisions regarding language. We need to understand how we ourselves make language policy on a daily basis—and how individually culpable we are in silencing or encouraging the linguistic growth of our students.

"BAD ATTITUDES": SOURCES AND CONSEQUENCES

I teach an English course called Introduction to Language at a state university in what some automobile manufacturers have referred to as the "heartland of America." Located in the heart of a small midwestern city in the Rust Belt, the university is a commuter campus, and students with few exceptions stop by, pick up their education, and return to the surrounding provincial communities where English Only and standard English are often upheld, whether or not these varieties are actually spoken.

Intro to Language is an infamous sophomore-level course required of and designed primarily for preservice (mainly elementary) education majors. When I began this teaching assignment upon arrival at the university over six years ago, I had developed my syllabus, in a kind of vacuum, as an introduction to language in social context. I had designed the course to provide prospective teachers with knowledge of language as dynamic, socially constructed, and changing; with an understanding of language acquisition; and with experience as language observers and "researchers." We would study how language is influenced by culture, class, geography, and gender, producing its myriad varieties and controversies, as well as matters of language policy. A generic introduction to language. After teaching fifteen sections of this course on a ten-week quarter system, however, I have become more familiar with the region and its students and now adapt course material to this particular linguistic and social context.

The institution's approximately 12,000 students are predominantly Euro-Americans from the city and surrounding suburban and rural communities. Many of them are children, grandchildren, and great-grandchildren of the steel mill workers who immigrated to the area from eastern and southern Europe during steel's heyday. Students in my classes have cited such cultural and linguistic heritages as Italian, Slovak, Polish, Greek, Croatian, and Hungarian, in addition to Irish, Scottish, English, German, and French, with the occasional student of color being African American or Puerto Rican. Between 1977 and 1981, many mills shut down, leaving thousands jobless and leading to the closing of hundreds of businesses. The consequences of these events continue to be felt two decades later. In analyzing the challenges they have encountered while teaching at the same university in the early 1990s, Sherry Linkon and Bill Mullen (1995) describe in *Radical Teacher* the socioeconomic and political context:

> Economic depression and the strong, steadfastly separate ethnic cultures of Youngstown have contributed to the development of a generally divisive, conservative culture in the region. By far the strongest and most hostile division has developed between whites and blacks. Historically, this may be traced to the role African Americans played as company-imported strikebreakers and competitors in the labor pool as early as the 1930s. More recently, the division reflects de facto segregation caused by white flight. . . . [W]hite students, many of whom attended all-white suburban high schools, often encounter blacks for the first time in the classroom and on campus. (27–28)

In addition to Euro-Americans and African Americans, Latinos primarily of Puerto Rican background have had a presence in the region since the 1940s.

In the classroom, many of these tensions play out in negative attitudes toward different languages and dialects, views which are inseparable from unexamined social attitudes toward those of different races, ethnicities, and classes. The repercussions of such intolerance are often manifested in prescriptive approaches to language; overconcern with standard English, grammar, and correctness; frustration with speakers of other languages and/or dialects; and a suspiciousness of any kind of difference.

In so highly charged a social context, my own outsider status further complicates the classroom dynamics. Although a third-generation American not unlike many of my students, I am a Japanese American woman from Hawai'i and look unfamiliar to many, even "foreign," perhaps "alien" to some, for the relative invisibility of Asians and Asian Americans in this community leads to ready stereotyping. Some students, for example, have encountered only foreign-born Asian professors "with accents" and assume they will also have difficulty understanding me (cf. Okawa 1998, 1999). Then, too, as Glenn Omatsu (1995) asserts, "anti-Asian racism has been a defining feature of American labor history" (33) and, in a region steeped in labor culture and attitudes, my Asian background may factor in negatively for some students as well.

While developing a newfound understanding of my students through my classes over the years, I have become increasingly committed to confronting language attitudes as a fundamental concern of the course—not only to identify them, but also to see where they originate. By deconstructing their attitudes and understanding where they come from, students may realize that they have choices in perpetuating or changing their attitudes, especially in the context of teaching young children. Language attitudes thus become an increasingly visible text of the class as students interrogate their experience and assumptions through reading, class discussion, and writing assignments.

THE COURSE: TOPICS AND READINGS

The stated approach to the course is fairly general and nonthreatening:

> Our goal will be to understand *language as a phenomenon that is alive and changing*, not rigid and exclusionary. We will examine its role in our lives:
> - how we, as human beings, acquire it and use it,
> - how we shape (and are shaped by) language, socially, culturally, and politically
>
> Through lecture, discussion, and group work, we will seek to understand language from a multicultural perspective.

To guide prospective teachers in understanding language through a multicultural lens as a dynamic, changing phenomenon, I use a historical approach to explore how we might arrive at a particular point in our language development in a given social context. The U.S. experience becomes a case in point: We begin with a macro-level framework of linguistic and cultural "acquisition" in this country's language history, which exemplifies the pervasiveness of multilingualism and the concept of language variation, despite the emergence of English as the lingua franca (Molesky 1988; Heath 1980). Through our brief study of the layering of languages, beginning with the hundreds of tongues spoken by native peoples, "colonial languages" such as English, Spanish, French, and German (Molesky 1988), African languages such as Hausa, Ibo, and Yoruba (Smitherman 1977), and numerous immigrant languages and dialects during different waves of immigration, we learn that English has not been the only language in and of the United States and that in many ways there is more than meets the eye in the students' backgrounds as well. In discussing "language maintenance," "shift," "loss," and "death," using examples from the American Indian experience of conquest and the students' ethnic/linguistic heritages, some students begin to see the homogenizing effects of assimilation in their family language histories. They discover both their heritages and losses. Jeanine,[3] for example, describes the process of language shift and loss in her family over several generations:

> My great grandfathers came to Ellis Island searching for the American dream, a better life. When they arrived in this ethnocentric world they learned that the Italian language was thought to hold less intelligence than English does. As a result, they changed their names to sound more American. . . .
>
> As a small child I began to speak Italian fluently but was strongly discouraged by my great-grandparents [from doing] so. I thought I was doing something terribly wrong when I spoke Italian, since I was scolded. From that point on, they never spoke Italian in front of me unless they were speaking about something they did not want me to know about—Christmas presents, swear words, or other family members' turmoil. The family suffered a language loss because my dad and aunt were not allowed to speak Italian either. They learned it, though, from listening to their parents and grandparents speak. Recently I asked my grandparents

why they did not want anyone in the family to speak Italian besides them. They said that they did not want me to have to suffer [as] they did because of the way I spoke when I was going to get a job. They continued to say that people are thought to be more important and intelligent if they speak "standard English." They wanted their family to be accepted and respected in an English-speaking society that thought speakers of other languages were less intelligent.

In effect, we must reverse the course of unquestioned assimilation and break down the polarizing identity of "whiteness" outlined by Linkon and Mullen. At the same time, the actual regional and cultural variations in American English—as well as stereotypes and attitudes about them—are introduced in a visually and audibly explicit way as we view examples in the video "American Tongues."

Having sketched out the country's language history to illustrate the increasing complexity of U.S. multilingualism, I move the class to a micro-level study of individual linguistic and cultural acquisition, and assign readings on some basic language-acquisition research in this context of language varieties. In this way, students can begin to see the relationships between culture and language, between environment and linguistic behavior; they become familiar with the universality of the process—and the particularity of the circumstances—of acquiring the grammars (phonology, syntax, semantics, pragmatics) of any given language variety. As they learn how any child acquires language, they come to understand how inextricable culture and language are; as they see how they themselves become language users within a socio-cultural context, they can appreciate more readily how this happens with others. They also learn about ethnocentricity and how naturally they may become ethnocentric through language and about language.

We examine more closely the relationships between different cultures and language, using Shirley Brice Heath's (1983) seminal research in *Ways with Words*, particularly her work on questioning, which was carried out in the black community of Trackton and the white community of Roadville. Through the research described in "Questioning at Home and at School: A Comparative Study" (Heath 1982), many students see how cultural context and assumptions may shape our use and expectations of discourse differently—in this case, the discourse routine of questioning/answering—and appreciate the profound implications that such differences in assumptions may have for students and teachers in a classroom setting.

In order to understand more clearly the intersections among language, culture, and identity, we explore examples from the African American language experience, primarily because the city's schoolchildren are predominantly African American. Again, I use a historical framework to give students a context for current language practices. We watch "Black on White" (1986) an hour-long documentary from the Story of English series, which traces the origins of Black English (BE, now AAVE [African American Vernacular English]) and the influences of BE on dialects spoken by other Americans. We read Smitherman's (1998) "It Bees Dat Way Sometime" and William Labov's (1994)

"The Study of Non-Standard English" to make salient the film's point about the rule-governed nature of this language variety and to dispel myths of "verbal deprivation."

Perhaps more important for prospective teachers, we read Keith Gilyard's *Voices of the Self: A Study of Language Competence* (1991) so that the students, many of whom will do internships and student teaching in urban schools, become aware of the complexities of a bidialectal child's language experience. Through Gilyard's autobiographical narrative and analysis, they can see language acquisition, communicative competence, code switching, and language politics, among other things, at play in concrete terms. They see Keith becoming Raymond as he switches codes and identities to survive his different environments. In this case, my best-laid plans seem to have the desired effect, for some students explicitly comment on the insights they have gained through this reading. In an overview of the course one quarter, Lonnie, a Head Start teacher, wrote:

> I really think that it was essential to read Gilyard. It is important to know that language varieties, [such] as Black English, are rule-governed and have structure. Gilyard's book also showed how teachers can affect a student's learning through their acceptance of all aspects of the student.

Others, like Helen, refer more broadly to major epiphanies regarding the language varieties of others:

> This class has changed everything I once believed about Black English. I now see it with specific rules of grammar and its own unique system. The key I suppose is not to judge the language but to find a common place for when to use it. I am aware [that] I was very ethnocentric and felt like other people just did not understand "how to speak." After reading Gilyard and seeing the way his mom used code switching, I see that it simply is an issue of when to use one's native language. All in all, because of the awareness this class has raised in me and the various authors who dedicated their lives to bring language awareness to people, I have changed [the] beliefs I once held about Black English as well as language as a whole. I feel I can be a more inspiring teacher because of this experience. . . . My value judgements had to do with my parents, friends, and teachers and just being ignorant [of] language's complexity.

Even those who struggle to some degree with understanding and mastering various linguistic concepts may conclude that *Voices of the Self* is interesting, even enjoyable reading, that "[Gilyard] was a good example of everything we learned." This terrain is not traveled without difficulty, however, for negative attitudes can be entrenched, and some students resent the attention paid to Black English, dismiss it on their evaluations as my "bias," or show their disapproval in other ways.

To emphasize the significance of social, political, and geographical context in language development from another perspective, I also draw a parallel between the history and experience of Black English speakers and that of Hawai'i Creole English speakers. While West Africans were brought to

North American plantations enslaved and generally isolated from others who spoke the same languages to prevent insurrection, Asians from China, Japan, Korea, and the Philippines were brought to the Hawaiian Islands—along with thousands from Portugal and Puerto Rico, fewer from Norway, Germany, and other European countries (Takaki 1983)—as contract labor. These groups were segregated by language and ethnic group to discourage pan-ethnic resistance to harsh plantation conditions. In both situations, a white English-speaking oligarchy maintained a position of authority so that speakers of different native languages adapted to the English-speaking environments using pidgin English forms.[4] Pidgin English speakers and their Creole-speaking descendants in both the Islands and the mainland United States have been stigmatized, especially with regard to education, although Dell Hymes (1971) referred to pidgin languages as "creative adaptations" epitomizing the very "interdependence of language and society" (3). On this topic, we discuss both Gilyard's code switching and the development of pidgin and Creole forms as creative linguistic phenomena exemplifying "verbal agility" (my term for verbal acumen), metalinguistic awareness, and the inherent relationships between language and identity.

Hawai'i's creole vernacular, still referred to regionally as Pidgin English, serves as a clear example of how language is influenced by social class and region and leads into our discussion of the students' regional dialects. Here their natural ethnocentricity is tested again. Discussions about language and gender usually stir some interest and prompt candid examples as we look at how gender may influence our language use, sense of linguistic identity, and treatment in a classroom.

When we look specifically at language attitudes in terms of language change and language policy in the later weeks of the quarter—particularly in light of the controversy on dialect differences that prompted the *Students' Right to Their Own Language* document (CCCC, *Students' Right*, p. 19 in this book) and the national uproar on Ebonics, and controversies on multilingualism versus English Only that prompted the CCCC *National Language Policy* statement (1993)—I point out how language attitudes produce language policy on a large scale. More important, some prospective teachers in my classes make connections between teachers' language attitudes and students' self-esteem, identity, and language development. They begin to understand the gravity of their own attitudes in future classroom policymaking—how teachers set language policy with each decision they make regarding their students' and their own language use.

DEVELOPING A REFLECTIVE LANGUAGE POLICY

In essence, the course asks the questions, how is language a dynamic, human phenomenon and how did we get to this point of multilingual complexity as a nation and as individuals? Over the ten weeks, the course provides basic tools for the students' investigation. Their personal exploration culminates in a language autobiography,[5] an opportunity to synthesize, internalize, and situate much of their learning about language in their own experience, to do "some research and much contemplation," according to Denny, a particularly thoughtful student. I provide the following guidelines for this writing assignment:

> This project asks you to explore your personal language development in a reflective narrative. You will need to dig into your language "roots" like a detective and cover the following topics: (a) your family language history, (b) your own acquisition of language, (c) your language development, and (d) the development of your own language attitudes and awareness. You may need to interview family members in your search.

In the course of this autobiographical narrative and other writing, many students identify their "bad attitudes" themselves, in terms of closed- or narrow-mindedness, stereotyping, prejudices, immaturity, ignorance, and/or ethnocentricity on the one hand, and shame or embarrassment on the other. Indeed, both African American and Euro-American students may find that they have been victims of linguistic ignorance and intolerance in very different ways. Miriam, for one, realizes that she had internalized social attitudes stigmatizing Black English speech:

> One thing I have acquired from this class is a sense of pride concerning my race's language. I must admit, I started the quarter with a hidden shame of my language. A shame born from a lack of knowledge regarding my history. Black English has widely been rejected by society for a long time. That rejection has fostered a prejudice toward and within the Black race itself. We have been made to feel not only shame of our language but also of how we speak our language. I believe this is the reason that we as Black people are skeptical to admit [that] "when we let our hair down," the majority of us do speak Black English.
>
> A lot of Blacks, including myself, try unsuccessfully to code switch. This code switching can take considerable effort if we are placed in a particular situation. This class has taught me that my language is something to be proud of. It is a language, not ignorant lazy speech produced by a group of people. It is who I am.
>
> Gilyard held the answer for me. I must strive to be "two-way strong." I must continue to master standardized English, but hang on to my heritage as well. This is the motivation I will take from this class and place in the hearts of my students. If students are educated early about their own language history, they may not form as many prejudiced judgments regarding someone else's language.

Others, like Avis, an African American woman in her forties, find the experience of writing their language autobiography to have a more generalized effect of healing. In class one day, Avis observed that the language autobiography, which she had struggled with and worked on tirelessly, helped her to "see herself" in a new and meaningful way.

From another perspective, Allen, a secondary English major of Euro-American background from one of the small communities outside Youngstown, refers in his language autobiography to his own intolerance:

Up until these last few months, I didn't really think about the language
that I spoke or the languages that others spoke. Like many others, I had a
very [simplistic] view on what I thought the appropriate language in
society should be. I thought that my use of language was correct and
everyone that didn't speak the way I did was wrong. Much of this way I
once thought was influenced by my parents, my community, and my
own closed-mindedness. . . .

    Although my parents provided a good basis for learning and under-
standing the English language, the town in which I grew up kept me
closed-minded to how others spoke. Aside from one black family, Lee-
tonia, my hometown, is an entirely white community. Everyone that I
grew up with speaks the same and virtually acts the same. The only time
I was subject to different dialects was when I occasionally caught *Mr.
Belvedere* on television. It sounds funny now but because *Mr. Belvedere*
was a comedy, I thought that other dialects were humorous. My idea was
that the language I spoke should be the only language. My friends and I
felt others were stupid or ignorant if they spoke differently than we did.
W. F. Bolton describes this type of view as a form of ethnocentricity. . . .

By exploring his family language history and his own language development,
Allen comes to understand the nature and origin of his attitudes toward his
language and those of others outside his community. Recognizing his inherited ethnocentric views, he can go about the business of exercising choice in
any given situation:

    After taking nine weeks of English 651, I no longer have the same ethno-
centric view that I once had. This class has taught me a lot about my language history and about how immature my views of others' language
were. It has taught me more about language in nine weeks than I've
learned in twenty-one years of growing up. I now see others' language as
being different, but equal. I also see them to be far from ignorant.

    Keith Gilyard's book, *Voices of the Self: A Study in Language Compe-
tence*, provided an example for me. Since the book [is] autobiographical, I
could put myself in his shoes. Sometimes it was hard for me to relate to
the examples being set forth in the classroom. All the articles and authors
we've covered didn't provide the illustration that I needed. Gilyard's
tribulations and triumphs in the classroom were instrumental to my
changed feelings. Since I aspire to become a high school teacher, I want to
be able to reach every child, not just the ones I share the same dialect with.

With such insights about prescriptive approaches to their own language and
its dialectal variations (and realizing that they have been victims of prescrip-
tivism themselves, in some cases), students can begin to understand linguistic
chauvinism/protectionism/restrictionism in more personal terms. Perhaps
Jeanine put it best:

    The attitudes I had were that anyone who spoke English even remotely
differently [from] myself must have been lacking some important education. That people who spoke differently were less intelligent or [that they
were] funny. It was not until this class that I realized how off-target my

language attitudes were. In addition, how stupid I was to think that just because they spoke differently they must be less intelligent. I was too quick to judge and now feel my awareness has heightened. I feel that I have become a "cultural relativist." This view can only make me more aware of the responsibility I have to educate my students and debunk the social myth that just because you speak differently you are less intelligent. My attitudes have grown since I discovered and resurfaced the roots behind the closed-minded attitudes. . . . [A]s you resurface the roots of your language attitudes you can begin to change them. We grow up in an ethnocentric world and this is where we learn how to speak and develop our linguistic skills. I believe it is important to learn where your ethnocentric behavior stems from.

Developing a sociolinguistic knowledge base gives students a rationale from which to make informed decisions so that they finally may be more able to comprehend the issues and implications surrounding the English Only controversy as well as the anti-exclusionary and pluralist purpose of the CCCC *National Language Policy* (CCCC 1993) statement, passed by the CCCC membership in March 1988 and, more recently, by the NCTE membership in November 1998: "This policy would enable everyone to participate in the life of this multicultural nation by ensuring continued respect both for English, our common language, and for the many other languages that contribute to our rich cultural heritage." Moreover, they can be more receptive to its three-pronged approach to language:

1. To provide resources to enable native and nonnative speakers to achieve oral and literate competence in English, the language of wider communication.

2. To support programs that assert the legitimacy of native languages and dialects and ensure that proficiency in one's mother tongue will not be lost.

3. To foster the teaching of languages other than English so that native speakers of English can rediscover the language of their heritage or learn a second language. (n.p.)

Most students say they have "never thought about these things [issues] before"; some wish they had never had to; some say the course should be required of all university students. With all of this said, my greatest hope is that when these students go into their own classrooms, they will have the background:

- to become language observers/researchers (as Heath [1982] and others have encouraged us to do)

- to identify verbal agility more than correctness among their students

- to select literature that celebrates dialects, languages, and verbal agility

- to use autobiographical narrative to develop students' self-esteem and unique voices, and to develop teachers' understanding of students' language experiences

- to respect the language rights and identities of their students, to recognize how they set language policy every school day

In an (ungraded) overview for a recent class, Chris candidly describes her growing awareness of dialects and languages in terms of her future as a teacher:

> It's really fascinating to find out how languages actually evolved. More importantly, and for this I am truly grateful, I found out something so crucial for future teachers like myself: how important it is to understand languages and how important they are to a person's identity. I didn't know I was closed-minded when I started this class, but I think I was. I'm ashamed to say I would have probably accepted only standard English in my classroom and discouraged the use of any other language. Now, thankfully, I have been made aware that other dialects and different forms of speech are not wrong just because they are different from my own. You have taught me that I should acknowledge and respect every student's language, and realize that it can be used to teach in a variety of ways. I believe the concepts in this class will prove invaluable to me, not only in the classroom, but in everyday life.

In a relatively nonthreatening learning environment based on descriptive deconstructions of language behavior, students can often confront threatening and uncomfortable issues—admit to ignorance and ethnocentricity—and act on that understanding. For Jeanine, Lonnie, Helen, Denny, Miriam, Allen, Chris, and their students, these reflections can become a profound beginning of revised attitudes about language, identity, and culture.

NOTES

1. In response to the controversy over students' language varieties and the role of those language varieties in education, a specially appointed committee of the CCCC was charged in 1971 with preparing a position statement on students' dialects. The document, *Students' Right to Their Own Language* (see p. 19 in this book), took the following strong stand on the issue:

> We affirm the students' right to their own patterns and varieties of language—the dialects of their nurture or whatever dialects in which they find their own identity and style. Language scholars long ago denied that the myth of a standard American dialect has any validity. The claim that any one dialect is unacceptable amounts to an attempt of one social group to exert its dominance over another. Such a claim leads to false advice for speakers and writers, and immoral advice for humans. A nation proud of its diverse heritage and its cultural and racial variety will preserve its heritage of dialects. We affirm strongly that teachers must have the experiences and training that will enable them to respect diversity and uphold the right of students to their own language. (p. 19)

The resolution on language was adopted by the CCCC membership in April 1974.

2. "Linguistic chauvinism" refers to the belief in the superiority of one's own language, while "linguistic imperialism" refers to the policy of imposing one language or dialect in dominance over another. As Fuchs (1961) maintains, racial and linguistic elitism among the white English-speaking sugar plantation oligarchy became the basis for Hawai'i's English Standard school system, wherein linguistic segregation served as a veneer for racist school segregation for almost a quarter of a century. Linguist Charlene Sato (1985) asserts that "the major effect of this system was the further stratification of Hawaiian society along ethnic lines by means of discrimination along linguistic ones. By institutionalizing linguistic inequality in this way, the ES (English Standard) schools legitimized the negative stereotyping of HCE (Hawai'i Creole English) speakers" (264).

3. In order to ensure student anonymity, pseudonyms have been used for a all student names.

4. See Dillard (1972) and Smitherman (1977) on the historical background of Black English/African American Vernacular English; see Carr (1972), Reinecke (1969), Sata (1985), and Takaki (1983) on the development of Hawai'i Pidgin English and Hawai'i Creole English.

5. Note on writing assignments: Writing assignments are based on theories of reflection from Paulo Freire's work (1970); concepts of "situated (vs. universal) knowledge" from feminist theorists such as Haraway (1991); and the extensive body of literature on narrative and autobiographical writing in education (see Cazden and Hymes [1978]; DiPardo [1990]; Graham [1991]; Haroian-Guerin [1999]; and Rosen [1986])—how this writing develops both reflection and "situatedness" among writers. During some terms, I ask students to keep a Language Experience Journal that will enhance their reflective and observational skills. They write two types of journal entries: (1) entries that ask students to write reflections on their personal language learning, behavior/use, and attitudes, and to relate them to their readings and class discussion; and (2) entries that ask them to describe and analyze examples of language use they observe in others. During other terms, I ask students instead to keep a Language Log, running entries of terms and concepts with examples and observations similar to those kept in the Language Experience Journal.

WORKS CITED

American Civil Liberties Union. 1996. "English Only." *ACLU Briefing Paper* [Online]: http://www.aclu.org/library/pbp6.html. January 14, 1999.

Bereiter, Carl, and Siegfried Englemann. 1966. *Teaching Disadvantaged Children in the Preschool.* Englewood Cliffs, NJ: Prentice-Hall.

"Black on White." 1986. The Story of English Series. Dir./Prod. William Cran. Chicago: Films Incorporated.

Bowie, Carole. 1994. "Influencing Future Teachers' Attitudes toward Black English: Are We Making a Difference?" *Journal of Teacher Education* 3(1).

Byrnes, Deborah A., and Gary Kiger. 1991. "Teacher Attitudes about Language Differences." ERIC document 340 232.

———. 1994. "Language Attitudes of Teachers Scale (LATS)." *Educational and Psychological Measurement* 54(1).

Carr, Elizabeth. 1972. *Da Kine Talk: From Pidgin to Standard English in Hawaii.* Honolulu: University Press of Hawaii.

Cazden, C., and D. Hymes. 1978. "Narrative Thinking and Story-Telling Rights: A Folklorist's Clue to a Critique of Education." *Keystone Folklore* 22: 22–35.

Conference on College Composition and Communication. 1974. *Students' Right to Their Own Language* [Special issue]. *College Composition and Communication* 25: [pp. 19–57 in this book].

———. 1993. *The National Language Policy* [Brochure]. Urbana, IL: NCTE.

Crawford, James. 1996. "Summing Up the *Lau* Decision: Justice Is Never Simple." In *Revisiting the Lau Decision—20 Years After: Proceedings of a National Commemorative Symposium Held on November 3–4, 1994, in San Francisco, California.* Oakland, CA: ARC Associates. Available: http://ourworld.compuserve.com/homepages/JWCRAWFORD/summing.htm.

Daniels, Harvey A., ed. 1990. *Not Only English: Affirming America's Multilingual Heritage.* Urbana, IL: National Council of Teachers of English.

Dillard, J. L. 1972. *Black English: Its History and Usage in the United States.* New York: Random House.

DiPardo, Anne. 1990. "Narrative Knowers, Expository Knowledge: Discourse as a Dialectic." *Written Communication* 7(1): 59–95.

Freire, Paulo. 1970. *Pedagogy of the Oppressed.* Trans. Myra B. Ramos. New York: Continuum.

Fuchs, Lawrence. 1961. *Hawaii Pono: A Social History.* New York: Harcourt, Brace & World.

Gere, Ann, and Eugene Smith. 1979. *Attitudes, Language, and Change.* Urbana, IL: National Council of Teachers of English.

Gilyard, Keith. 1991. *Voices of the Self: A Study of Language Competence.* Detroit: Wayne State University Press.

González, Roseann Dueñas. 1990. "In the Aftermath of the ELA: Stripping Language Minorities of Their Rights." In Harvey A. Daniels, ed., *Not Only English: Affirming America's Multilingual Heritage.* Urbana, IL: National Council of Teachers of English. 49–60.

Graham, R. J. 1991. *Reading and Writing the Self: Autobiography in Education and the Curriculum.* New York: Teachers College Press.

Haraway, Donna. 1991. *Simians, Cyborgs, and Women: The Reinvention of Nature.* New York: Routledge.

Haroian-Guerin, Gil, ed. 1999. *The Personal Narrative: Writing Ourselves as Teachers and Scholars.* Portland, ME: Calendar Islands.

Heath, Shirley Brice. 1980. "Standard English: Biography of a Symbol." In Timothy Shopen and Joseph M. Williams, eds., *Standards and Dialects in English.* Cambridge, MA: Winthrop. 3–32.

———. 1982. "Questioning at Home and at School: A Comparative Study." In G. Spindler, ed., *Doing the Ethnography of Schooling.* New York: Holt, Rinehart, and Winston. 105–33.

———. 1983. *Ways with Words: Language, Life, and Work in Communities and Classrooms.* New York: Cambridge University Press.

Hughes, Anne E. 1967. *An Investigation of Certain Sociolinguistic Phenomena in the Vocabulary, Pronunciation, and Grammar of Detroit Pre-School Children, Their Parents and Teachers.* Unpublished doctoral dissertation, Michigan State University, East Lansing.

Hymes, Dell. 1971. Preface. In Dell Hymes, ed., *Pidginization and Creolization of Languages.* New York: Cambridge University Press. v–viii.

Jensen, Arthur. 1969. "How Much Can We Boost IQ and Scholastic Achievement?" *Harvard Educational Review* 39: 1–123.

Jiménez, Martha. 1992. "The Educational Rights of Language-Minority Children." In James Crawford, ed., *Language Loyalties: A Sourcebook on the Official English Controversy.* Chicago: University of Chicago Press. 243–57.

Labov, William. 1982. "Objectivity and Commitment in Linguistic Science: The Case of the Black English Trial in Ann Arbor." *Language in Society* 11: 165–201.

———. 1994. "The Study of Non-Standard English." In Virginia P. Clark et al., eds., *Language: Introductory Readings.* New York: St. Martin's Press. 555–62.

Linkon, Sherry, and Bill Mullen. 1995. "Gender, Race, and Place: Teaching Working-Class Students in Youngstown," *Radical Teacher* 46: 27–32.

Louie, Tom. 1998. "The Facts Behind the Debate on Bilingual Education." *Peacework* Magazine 290 (November): 8–9.

Molesky, Jean. 1988. "Understanding the American Linguistic Mosaic: A Historical Overview of Language Maintenance and Language Shift." In Sandra Lee McKay and Sau-ling Cynthia Wong, eds., *Language Diversity: Problem or Resource?* New York: Newbury House. 29–68.

Okawa, Gail Y. 1998. "Re-seeing Our Professional Face(s)." *English Journal* 88: 98–104.

———. 1999. "Lotus Blossom and the Rust Belt." Paper presented at the Conference on College Composition and Communication, Atlanta, GA, March 26.

Omatsu, Glenn. 1995. "Racism or Solidarity? Unions and Asian Immigrant Workers." *Radical Teacher* 46: 33–37.

Reinecke, John. 1969. *Language and Dialect in Hawaii: A Sociolinguistic History to 1935.* Honolulu: University of Hawaii Press.

Rosen, H. 1986. *Stories and Meanings.* London: National Association for the Teaching of English.

Sato, Charlene. 1985. "Linguistic Inequality in Hawaii: The Post-Creole Dilemma." In N. Wolfson and J. Manes, eds., *Language of Inequality.* New York: Mouton. 255–72.

Shuy, Roger. 1973. "Language Variation in the Training of Teachers." In Johanna S. DeStefano, ed., *Language, Society, and Education: A Profile of Black English.* Charles A. Jones Publishing.

Sledd, James. 1983. "In Defense of the 'Students' Right.'" *College English* 45: 667–75.

Smitherman, Geneva. 1977. *Talkin and Testifyin: The Language of Black America.* Boston: Houghton Mifflin.

———. 1981. "'What Go Round Come Round': *King* in Perspective." *Harvard Educational Review* 51: 40–56.

———. 1998. "It Bees Dat Way Sometime." In Virginia P. Clark et al., eds., *Language: Readings in Language and Culture.* New York: St. Martin's Press. 328–43.

Stroud, Kim. 1997. "English-Only Laws Reflect Prejudice, Not Patriotism." *Detroit Free Press.* June 30. 9A.

Takaki, Ronald. 1983. *Pau Hana: Plantation Life and Labor in Hawaii.* Honolulu: University of Hawaii Press.

Trask, Haunani-Kay. 1993. *From a Native Daughter: Colonialism and Sovereignty in Hawai'i.* Monroe, ME: Common Courage Press.

Villanueva, Victor, Jr. 1993. *Bootstraps: From an American Academic of Color.* Urbana, IL: National Council of Teachers of English.

Williams, Frederick. 1970. "Psychological Correlates of Speech Characteristics: On Sounding 'Disadvantaged.'" *Journal of Speech and Hearing Research* 13: 472–88.

Williams, Frederick, Robert Hopper, and Diana S. Natalicio. 1977. *The Sounds of Children.* Englewood Cliffs, NJ: Prentice-Hall.

PART FIVE

Critical Language Perspectives and Reimagining SRTOL in Writing Classrooms

18

Myth Education: Rationale and Strategies for Teaching against Linguistic Prejudice

LEAH A. ZUIDEMA

Language is a protective shield for prejudice—or ignorance.

—MACNEIL, 2003

*L*inquistic prejudice is one of the few "acceptable" American prejudices. In polite society, we don't allow jokes that we consider racist or sexist, and we are careful not to disparage a person's religious beliefs. Language is another matter. In *English with an Accent*, Lippi-Green (1997) wrote,

> [W]e regularly demand of people that they suppress or deny the most effective way they have of situating themselves socially in the world. *You may have dark skin*, we tell them, *but you must not sound Black. You can wear a yarmulke if it is important to you as a Jew, but lose the accent. Maybe you come from the Ukraine, but can't you speak real English? If you didn't sound so corn-pone, people would take you seriously. You're the best salesperson we've got, but must you sound so gay on the phone?* (63–64)

Many of us feel free to make judgments about others because of the ways that they use language. We make assumptions based on the ways that people speak and write, presuming to know about their intelligence, their competence, their motives, and their morality (Wolfram, Adger, & Christian, 1999). As Davis (2001) explained, we assume that because we know a little about how people speak or write that we also understand "what they wear, what they eat, how they feel about certain things including birth, death, family, marriage and what they believe about the world and their place in it" (1). We act as though dialects and accents are windows to people's souls, and sometimes we dare to ignore or dismiss entire groups of people because of what we assume their linguistic habits reveal about them.

Employers might assume, for example, that an employee who speaks American English with a midwestern or northern accent is more intelligent (and thus more competent) than an employee who uses Appalachian English.

From *Journal of Adolescent and Adult Literacy* 48.8 (2005): 666–75.

Teachers might assume that a student who uses so-called standard English is more respectful of authority and more intelligent than a student who uses Ebonics. Landlords might assume that a person whose first language is English will take better care of a rental property than a tenant who speaks English with a Spanish accent.

These assumptions are not inconsequential thoughts. People act on their ideas, and, as a result, prejudice becomes active discrimination. Employment, promotions, grades, recommendations, and business agreements are just a few of the things that might be affected (negatively or positively) by reactions to the ways a person uses language in speech or writing. Even people who live—by choice or by happenstance—in relative isolation from racial, ethnic, religious, or cultural diversity might engage in linguistic prejudice.

Detrimental portrayals of language variation on the radio, on television, in films, and on the Internet all provide opportunities to cultivate negative attitudes, which can emerge as prejudicial judgments and behaviors when people encounter language variation in real life (whether on the telephone, in writing, or face to face). Individuals' private prejudices might move them to take public action so that their condemning opinions are transformed into corporate policies; educational paradigms; and local, state, and federal laws— prejudice in practice, one might say.

Robert Phillipson called this "practical" prejudice *linguicism*, and his definition encompasses the process I have outlined. Linguicism is the assembly of "ideologies, structures, and practices which are used to legitimate, effectuate, and reproduce an unequal division of power and resources (both material and immaterial) between groups which are defined on the basis of language" (as cited in Daly, 1995, para. 4). It is difficult to fight linguistic prejudice because the general public may be slow to condemn it or may even be skeptical about its existence because linguicism is such an insidious process. In addition, while most modern linguistics scholars acknowledge the existence of linguicism, their views have little influence on the general public (Smitherman, 2000). The burden of preventing linguicism and countering its effects must fall elsewhere.

Some literacy educators have, appropriately, taken up the challenge of teaching against linguistic prejudice. As Delpit (1998) argued, it is "possible and desirable to make the actual study of language diversity a part of the curriculum for all students" (19). *Standards for the English Language Arts* (International Reading Association & National Council of Teachers of English, 1996) stated that students should "develop an understanding of and respect for diversity in language use, patterns, and dialects across cultures, ethnic groups, geographic regions, and social roles."

It is unfortunate that many schools and teachers have not incorporated such study into their curricula. Perhaps this shouldn't be a surprise; after all, even the International Reading Association (IRA) and National Council of Teachers of English (NCTE) devote relatively little attention to the need for *all* students to study language variation. For example, while IRA and NCTE publications and position statements emphasize teachers' responsibilities to accept and accommodate diverse students' languages, no official statements have been made about teaching students themselves to be accepting of linguistic diversity. Even the frequently cited (and recently reaffirmed) Conference on College Composition and Communication's resolution *Students' Right to Their Own Language* (p. 19 in this book) stops short of declaring the need to teach students about peoples' rights to their own languages.

In a similar manner, a search of *Journal of Adolescent & Adult Literacy* issues dating back to May 2000 uncovered no articles focused on students' attitudes toward or knowledge about linguistic diversity. The March 2001 themed issue of *English Journal* (titled "And Language for All") includes several articles about teaching students whose own language is stigmatized, but it largely ignores the "mainstream" students. The exception is Wilson's (2001) article on language study for preservice teachers. Wilson asserted, "Students who feel smug about their use of Standard English will benefit from understanding the linguistic strengths of speakers of other dialects" (32). Aside from Wilson's article, the issue is devoted entirely to students whose use of stigmatized language in speech and writing often results in their own marginalization. These students are, of course, deserving of a themed issue dedicated to their educational needs. But to ignore the "smug" students is a grave mistake, for these are the people who hold—or, as adults, will hold—much of the power that allows linguistic stigmatization and discrimination to continue.

TEACHING AGAINST MYTHS

If we really want to fight linguicism—and what Daniels (1983) referred to as "some of the basest hatreds and flimsiest prejudices" (9) that linguicism masks—we cannot leave the task to urban or so-called multicultural schools. All schools must heed the call to arms, and English language arts classrooms are among the most appropriate venues for taking action against linguicism. Because the classroom "is a major player in shaping language attitudes, and the classroom that is particularly crucial for the formation of ideas about language is that of the K–12 level" (Smitherman, 2000, 396), English language arts teachers should create opportunities to shape informed, positive student attitudes about language diversity for all students.

Helping adolescent learners create informed opinions about language diversity depends on educating them about the misinformation on this topic. This misinformation can be divided into three broad categories: myths about language, myths about others, and myths about the self. These myths can and should be addressed across the curriculum; for instance, social studies courses are well suited for confronting myths about others. Language study, however, needs to be the starting point and primary focus in English language arts courses. After all, studying language and its use (in writing, literature, and speech) is the principal discipline of the English language arts classroom. Dispelling some of the myths about language can result in a change of attitude toward others and the self.

Following are clarifications of some of the most persistent misconceptions about language, accompanied by strategies that can help students to learn about the true nature of linguistic diversity. Instead of relying solely on lectures and readings, the activities are designed so that students can act as "critical co-investigators in dialogue with the teacher" (Freire, 1970, 68). To facilitate this research process, students should collect samples of speech and writing throughout their study, choosing specimens that demonstrate both stigmatized and admired usages. Students can observe the language patterns of amateurs as well as language professionals such as teachers, politicians, media spokespersons, and published writers, and they can preserve their artifacts with pen and paper and audio or video recorder. As learners confront new ideas about language, they should examine their linguistic data collections in order to verify the truth for themselves. Not all students will subscribe to all language myths; it is important for teachers to discern which misconceptions are most prevalent among particular student groups and to shape the curriculum accordingly.

Myth 1: English Must Obey the Rules of Grammar

Linguists would argue that this statement could be either true or false, depending on one's definition of *grammar*. If, by *grammar*, one means the internal patterns that a given language naturally follows, or descriptions of these inherent patterns, then it is true. In English, for example, it is breaking the rules to attach an article after a noun (e.g., Cat *the* in hat *the*). Scholars did not gather at a conference to decide on this arrangement; no government established this pattern as a law. It is simply the way English works, and when people ignore this or other innate patterns of the language, it causes confusion. When we define *grammar* as the organic patterns of a language, or descriptions of these patterns, it is correct to state that English must obey grammatical rules.

Many nonlinguists, however, define *grammar* as the rules of taste (which linguists refer to as *usage*). Most people believe that observing the rules of taste is the same as knowing the grammar of a language. These prescriptive rules of taste assume great importance, so that many English speakers and writers are familiar with admonitions such as "Don't say 'ain't,'" and "Ask 'may I?'—I know that you can," and "Don't end a sentence with a preposition." Most people will admit, however, that breaking these kinds of socially imposed rules does not actually impede anyone's understanding of the message a person is attempting to communicate. When we define *grammar* as prescriptive standards of taste, it is possible to say that English does not need to obey the rules in order to be effective.

Helping students to distinguish between the two definitions of grammar can be difficult, but I find that using an analogy is often effective. I prefer to use a discussion starter such as this one paraphrased from Lippi-Green (1997, 15): "A taxi must obey the laws of physics, but it can disobey state laws. How is English like a taxi?" Some students see the analogy right away; to help the others, I ask as many of the following questions as necessary:

- Is it possible for a taxi to disobey the laws of physics? What are the consequences of trying to break these laws? Who makes the laws of physics? How can these laws be changed?

- How is it possible for a taxi to disobey our state laws? Why might this happen? What are the consequences? Who makes our state laws? For what purposes? How can these laws be changed?

- How do state laws (as they pertain to taxicabs) differ from the laws of physics? Why are they different?

- In the English language, what are some rules that work in the same way that the laws of physics work for taxis? (We call these rules *grammar.*) What are the consequences of trying to break these grammar rules? Who makes the grammar rules of English? How can these grammar rules be changed?

- What are some English-language rules that work in the same way that state laws work for taxis? (We call these rules *usage.*) How is it possible to disobey these usage rules? Why might this happen? What are the consequences? Who makes usage rules? For what purposes? How can usage rules be changed?

- How does the analogy work? Is the analogy completely parallel? What are the limitations to the analogy?

A follow-up question such as "Who decides what is 'good' or 'standard' English?" helps students to consider the authority and motivations of those who control—or seek to control—language use.

It is important to introduce students to the distinctions between natural grammar and taste-based grammar early in efforts to teach against linguicism. Understanding that English must obey some kinds of grammar rules while having the freedom to disregard others is key to correcting other common misconceptions about language variation.

Myth 2: Some Dialects and Languages Don't Have Grammatical Rules

This is an argument that is frequently used to disparage stigmatized language systems such as Ebonics, Appalachian English, and Hawaiian Creole English. Instead of viewing these systems as patterned and rule governed, many people call them "slang" or "street talk" or resort to cruel labels that show blatant disrespect for the speakers themselves. The best way for students to learn that stigmatized languages and dialects really are rule governed is to discover it for themselves through a series of guided activities.

Wolfram et al. (1999) developed an excellent sequence, "Illustrative Exercises of Grammatical Patterning," to help adolescent learners ascertain the logical, rule-governed nature of such configurations as the *a*- prefix used in some Southern dialects and the invariant *be* from Ebonics. For example, in exercises on the use of the *a*- prefix, students examine matched sentence pairs and use their intuition to answer questions such as, "Does it sound better to say, 'A-building is hard work' or 'He was a-building a house?'" After analyzing a number of similar sentence pairs, learners are prompted to determine which inherent patterns or rules govern the use of the prefix. Whether students speak the mainstream English that some linguists refer to as the Language of Wider Communication (LWC) or rely primarily on stigmatized dialects or languages, exercises in grammatical patterning help them to realize that all language systems are rule governed. Understanding this concept helps students to see through false (but common) claims about the supposed stupidity or laziness of those who use stigmatized dialects and languages. In addition, realizing that speaking a prestigious variety or dialect of a language (e.g., being a literal smooth talker) does not make a person more intelligent or hard working reminds learners about the folly of assigning credibility to a source based only on that person's use of language.

Language-patterning exercises can convince students that systems such as Appalachian English do indeed have organic grammatical rules, but some learners may fail to realize that stigmatized languages and dialects also observe their own taste-based rules of grammar. The challenge for teachers is to find ways for students to observe or experience the rich complexities of dialects and languages that are unfamiliar to them. Ideally, students would interview speakers fluent in LWC as well as a stigmatized system such as Appalachian English, asking the speakers to provide examples of the ways that they adjust their pronunciation, vocabulary, and syntax when they are using the dialect for varied audiences and contexts.

It is unfortunate that time, geography, and other factors frequently prevent such interviews, but students can still have opportunities to see and hear the patterned, complex nature of several varieties of English in documentaries such as *The Story of English* (Cran, 1997) or its sequel series, *Do You Speak American?* (Cran, 2005). The film *American Tongues* (Alvarez & Kolker, 1986) is nearly 20 years old, but it too engages students who are trying to understand that all American varieties of English are governed by natural as well as taste-based grammars. Teaching literature that incorporates accurate portrayals of specific dialects, particularly if they are used for a range of audiences and situations, is also an effective means for students to learn more about the grammaticality of stigmatized language systems and about the code-switching techniques employed by many speakers of stigmatized languages. For examples of literary characters discussing the ways they shift—or are expected to shift—their language use for various audiences, see chapter 6 of *A Lesson Before Dying* by Ernest J. Gaines (1993) or chapter 12 of *To Kill a Mockingbird* by Harper Lee (1960/1988).

Myth 3: Standard English Is Better Than Other Varieties

Learners who understand the fallacies of the first two myths are also prepared to unpack this third myth. They acknowledge that judgments about "good" and "bad" language use are subjective social constructions. They recognize the falsehood in the argument that nonstandard varieties don't have "rules" or are random and therefore worthless. However, this complex myth also hinges on other misconceptions that need to be addressed.

One of these errors is the belief that good English is the everyday spoken language of the most educated and intelligent people. Most LWC speakers recognize that their own language use does not often meet the ideals of so-called standard English. However, many of these same speakers also believe that with enough education and practice, they—like educated speakers "somewhere else"—will be able to let loose a flurry of grammatically perfect prose every time they open their mouths. In actuality, standard English is an abstract ideal based not on speech but on the model of written language (Lippi-Green, 1997).

One way for students to investigate this idea is by analyzing their collected speech and writing samples to determine which ones are most likely to showcase formal standard English. Learners soon discover that the best English is usually found in writing and in speech based on writing, such as news broadcasts. Students also should analyze the differences between their own written and spoken language patterns. These activities help students to understand that most people, no matter how well educated, cannot hope to consistently speak with the polish of revised and edited writing—the kind of language use which is idealized as standard.

Another problem with the myth that standard English is good English is that standard English is a moving target. Wolfram et al. (1999) explained, "There is really no single dialect of English that corresponds to a standard English. . . . The norms for standard English are not identical in all communities. Furthermore, there are two sets of norms—the informal standard and the formal standard" (14–15). Students need to realize that no matter how standard their English is, all speakers are perceived by some listeners to have an accent. Learners can research the moving target concept by contrasting what a variety of sources (including dictionary and textbook writers) mean when they refer to standard English.

Most students know intuitively that formal standard English is not the best choice for every communicative situation, yet they are so used to having their own grammar corrected that they cannot help but believe that non-standard English is bad. Need evidence? Consider how often teens and even adults use perfectly appropriate conventions of casual conversation and then, remembering they are speaking with English teachers, apologize in embarrassment for their "bad grammar." Baron (1990) rightly stated, "We must own up to the fact that the teaching of English to speakers of English has promoted much of the linguistic insecurity and fear of grammar that we observe today" (211–212). It is important for students to hear English teachers acknowledging that a nonstandard register or even another dialect or language is sometimes the most appropriate and effective choice. Hearing the message isn't enough; students also need opportunities to consciously explore and reflect with their teachers about effective uses of systems other than formal standard English.

Smith (2001) suggested an activity that is useful to this end. Smith instructs his students to research and write about the unique vocabulary, pronunciation, syntax, and other linguistic features of the speech communities in which they participate. Students may choose communities defined by vocation, age, interests, beliefs, gender, or other identifying features. Smith explained that this assignment helps

> students see that just because a speech community is different or unique does not make it "wrong," dumb, or stupid. My students discovered they all took part in different speech communities with special linguistic forms unique to their group, age, gender, occupation, geography, situation, etc.

As they strive to appreciate the value of certain nonstandard uses of language, some learners also benefit from experiencing what it means for ideas to be lost in translation. Students should select information that they would normally discuss in their unique speech communities and "translate" the information into the vocabulary, pronunciation, and syntax of another less familiar speech community. To help LWC speakers gain an even greater appreciation for the pressures that speakers of stigmatized language systems face when they are pressured to conform to unfamiliar varieties of English, student volunteers may attempt—perhaps before an audience, if they are willing—to do their translating orally or in a timed, unrevised writing. For a less intimidating approach, introduce students to literature that portrays the difficulties of learning and translating from another language to English, such as An Na's young adult novel *A Step From Heaven* (2001) or many of Pat Mora's poems in My *Own True Name: New and Selected Poems for Young Adults* (2000)—particularly "Learning English: Chorus in Many Voices." Reflection upon these kinds of translating activities with analytical discussion helps students to recognize that the worth of a given language system is tied to its appropriateness and effectiveness for a given context, purpose, and audience, not to inherent qualities such as syntax.

Myth 4: English Is Not as Good as It Used to Be, and It Is Getting Worse

"There seems to be a widespread feeling that the English language is a fragile object and is constantly under siege," wrote Wolfram et al. (1999, 100). Some students may argue that acknowledging the value of stigmatized language systems will change the English language, eventually resulting in its decline or loss. Students are correct to notice that English—like other "live" languages—is constantly changing. Some words or phrases become linguistic fads; others fall into disuse or "misuse." Rules of taste change, and the pronunciations, uses, conjugations, and spellings of words are altered over time to adjust to new contexts, speakers, purposes, and audiences. We call this adaptability "survival of the fittest" when we discuss other kinds of evolution; it is evidence of the resilience of language and not a matter for concern.

Students need to see for themselves that changes in language and language standards are evidence of flexibility and no cause for worry. One way to make this possible is for learners to examine parallel texts in Old English,

Middle English, and early and recent Modern English (Wolfram et al., 1999). (See, for example, Catherine Ball's webpage tracing historical translations of "The Lord's Prayer" at www.georgetown.edu/faculty/ballc/oe/pater_noster .html.) Learning about the history of English, including its interaction with French, Latin, Ebonics, Hawaiian Creole English, and Spanish, also helps students to understand how and why the language changes; the documentary *The Story of English* (Cran, 1997) is useful in this regard. Students who harbor doubts that English can survive change may be convinced by Daniels's (1983) humorous, instructive chapter "Something New and Ominous," which relates highlights from "the history of linguistic insecurity and intolerance and the periods of [erroneous] doomsaying which they regularly generate" (33). Examples from Daniels's chapter can help students to see that worries about language decline are not new, and that changes and flexibility are what help to keep English alive and thriving.

TEACHING AGAINST THE MISEDUCATION OF MYTH EDUCATION

It is not enough to dispel widely held myths about language variation; we also need to expose how myths and misconceptions are perpetuated so that students can participate in efforts to resist, subvert, and combat linguicism. Lippi-Green (1997) wrote a blistering indictment of the powerful institutions that enable "language subordination":

> Standard language ideology is introduced by the schools, vigorously promoted by the media, and further institutionalized by the corporate sector. It is underscored by the entertainment industry and underwritten in subtle and not so subtle ways by the judicial system. (73)

It is imperative that students learn to identify and critique prejudicial portrayals of languages, dialects, speakers, and writers. Projects such as the following provide opportunities for learners to conduct primary-source research and critical analysis of real-life attitudes toward linguistic diversity.

Students can examine music lyrics, radio broadcasts, television shows, films, entertainment magazines, novels, Internet sites, and video games to uncover the prejudices of particular segments of the entertainment industry. Lippi-Green (1997) outlined her students' research of negative portrayals of language variation in Disney animated films in her chapter "Teaching Children How to Discriminate: What We Learn from the Big Bad Wolf." This chapter works well as a model for adolescent learners researching the ways in which pop culture sources link stigmatized as well as admired language varieties with people's abilities, morals, attractiveness, and so on.

Students can collect samples of linguistic prejudice propagated by the news media in television, Internet, and radio news commentary as well as in printed editorials (Wilson, 2001). Students can also record instances when the news media present myths as truths instead of checking the scientific facts with actual linguists. I've found Morris's (1998) article "Toward Creating a TV Research Community in Your Classroom" to be an especially helpful resource for designing media-based, primary-source research projects with high school and college students.

Students can interview employers and their employees, as well as "personnel officers in actual workplaces about their attitudes toward divergent styles in oral and written language" (Delpit, 1998, 44). Another option is for students to create written surveys that people can complete anonymously. Students can use their findings to debate the legality and implications of responses to linguistic diversity in the workplace. To complicate the debate, teachers may wish to share the results of research indicating that some listeners show a decreased ability to understand a person when they believe (based on appearance) that the speaker is of an ethnicity other than their own (Lippi-Green, 1997). Students might also be surprised to learn that the Equal Employment Opportunity Commission's *Guidelines on Discrimination Because of National Origin* outlaw "denial of equal employment opportunity" based on an individual's use of "linguistic characteristics of a national origin" (as cited in Lippi-Green, 153). The exception (per the Civil Rights Act of 1964) is when "an individual's accent . . . interferes materially with job performance" (as cited in Lippi-Green, 154). Also, students may be interested to know that workplace discrimination based on an individual's regional (versus national) linguistic origin is not prohibited by law.

Students can research court cases concerning discrimination that stems from linguistic prejudice. Lippi-Green (1997) outlined several of these cases in her chapter "Language Ideology in the Workplace and the Judicial System." She found that the judges "were willing to depend on their own expertise in matters of language in a way they would never presume to in matters of genetics, or mechanical engineering, or psychology" (160). Students can test Lippi-Green's claim about the behaviors of judges or look at the impact of judicial decisions on discrimination laws or employment and education policies. They might also investigate efforts to pass laws making English the official language of the United States, evaluating the rhetoric and rationale behind such policies as well as the implications of English-only legislation. Students can begin with an investigation into U.S. English, Inc., one of the main proponents of the English-only movement, at www.us-english.org. Counterarguments to the English-only movement are presented on the NCTE website in the Conference on College Composition and Communication's position statement on the National Language Policy at www.ncte.org/about/over/positions/category/div/107643.htm.

Students can consider the roles of schools in perpetuating linguistic prejudice. Opening our own practices for critique takes courage, trust, and careful leadership. If we partner with our students to go beyond critique—if we take action with them in changing our scholastic responses to language variation—we can communicate more clearly than in any other project we pursue together that we are committed to teaching and acting against linguistic prejudice.

TAKING POSITIVE ACTION

Students are sure to make disturbing findings in research projects such as these. We can help students to take positive action in response to their learning and make their research efforts more consequential by offering writing assignment options that work toward eliminating the propagation of linguistic prejudice and the practice of language-based discrimination. Students can compose fiction, poetry, and creative nonfiction that reflect on linguicism; they can write articles that expose linguistic prejudice; and they can write letters, proposals, public service announcements, and other documents that seek to combat linguicism. Publishing students' writings or delivering them to the intended audiences can empower students as activists in their world and make their learning meaningful in a way that writing for the teacher alone cannot do.

The ubiquitous problem of linguistic prejudice deserves significant attention in all schools. We ought to incorporate language study at all levels in freestanding units or in partnership with literature, grammar, speech, and composition studies. While language study is not likely to eradicate language-based discrimination, it may serve to diminish our students' and our own willingness to use language "as both a channel and an excuse for expressing some of our deepest prejudices" (Daniels, 1983, 5). Consistent, widespread education about the true nature of language may help to put an end to popular regard for linguicism as one of the last "acceptable" prejudices.

REFERENCES

Alvarez, L., & Kolker, A. (Producers/directors). (1986). *American tongues* [Motion picture]. United States: Center for New American Media.

Baron, D. (1990). Watching our grammar: The English language for English teachers. In G. Hawisher & A. Soter (Eds.), *On literacy and its teaching: Issues in English education* (pp. 208–223). Albany: State University of New York Press.

Conference on College Composition and Communication. (1974, Fall). Students' right to their own language. *College Composition and Communication, 25.* Retrieved June 26, 2004, from http://www.ncte.org/library/files/About_NCTE/Overview/NewSRTOL.pdf [Pages 19–57 in this book.]

Conference on College Composition and Communication. (1988). The national language policy. Retrieved June 26, 2004, from http://www.ncte.org/about/over/positions/category/lang/107643.htm

Cran, W. (Director). (1997). *The story of English* [Motion picture]. United States: Home Vision Entertainment.

Cran, W. (Director). (2005). *Do you speak American?* [Television series]. New York: WNET.

Daly, M. (1995). The classic *Linguistic Imperialism* . . . being the book that all English speakers should read. *New Internationalist Magazine, 271.* Retrieved June 25, 2004, from http://www.newint.org

Daniels, H. (1983). *Famous last words: The American language crisis reconsidered.* Carbondale: Southern Illinois University Press.

Davis, V. J. (2001, November 17). *Remembering the self in the academy: Rhetorical strategies for students of color.* Paper presented at the annual convention of the National Council of Teachers of English, Baltimore.

Delpit, L. (1998). What should teachers do?: Ebonics and culturally responsive instruction. In T. Perry & L. Delpit (Eds.), *The real Ebonics debate: Power, language, and the education of African American children* (pp. 17–26). Boston: Beacon Press.

Freire, P. (1970). *Pedagogy of the oppressed* (M. B. Ramos, Trans.). New York: Seabury.

Gaines, E. J. (1993). *A lesson before dying.* New York: Vintage.

International Reading Association & National Council of Teachers of English. (1996). *Standards for the English language arts.* Retrieved January 31, 2005, from http://www.reading.org/resources/issues/reports/learning-standards.html

Lee, H. (1988). *To kill a mockingbird.* New York: Warner. (Original work published 1960)

Lippi-Green, R. (1997). *English with an accent: Language, ideology, and discrimination in the United States.* New York: Routledge.

MacNeil, R. (2003, November 21). Keynote address presented at the annual convention of the National Council of Teachers of English, San Francisco.

Mora, P. (2000). *My own true name: New and selected poems for young adults.* Houston, TX: Arte Publico.

Morris, B. S. (1998). Toward creating a TV research community in your classroom. *English Journal, 87*(1), 38–42.

Na, A. (2001). *A step from heaven.* New York: Speak.

Smith, J. (2001, November 25). Re: [ncte-hs] against linguistic prejudice. Message posted to ncte-hs electronic mailing list, archived at http://www.ncte.org/library/files/list_archive/ncte_hs/2001/nov2001/msg00217.asp

Smitherman, G. (2000). *Talkin that talk: Language, culture, and education in African America.* London: Routledge.

Wilson, M. (2001, March). The changing discourse of language study. *English Journal, 90*(4), 31–36.

Wolfram, W., Adger, C. T., & Christian, D. (1999). *Dialects in schools and communities.* Mahwah, NJ: Erlbaum.

RECOMMENDED READINGS ON THE GRAMMAR, VOCABULARY, AND RHETORIC OF EBONICS AND OTHER STIGMATIZED LANGUAGE SYSTEMS

Gilyard, K., & Richardson, E. (2001). Students' right to possibility: Basic writing and African American rhetoric, p. 217 in this book.

In addition to discussing strategies for teaching writing to Ebonics speakers, this chapter outlines 15 rhetorical features that occur frequently in Ebonics discourse. Examples of these rhetorical features include rhythmic language, proverbs, and sermonic tone.

Rickford, J. R., & Rickford, R. J. (2000). *Spoken soul: The story of black English.* New York: John Wiley & Sons.

The authors systematically discuss the grammar of Ebonics, making frequent and helpful use of excerpts from actual conversations to explain the rules for plurals, possessives, pronouns, tense, and more.

Smitherman, G. (2000). *Black talk: Words and phrases from the hood to the amen corner.* New York: Houghton Mifflin.

Smitherman's dictionary goes beyond cataloging definitions: It also provides history, opinions about the role of Ebonics in American education and culture, and an emphasis on significant words and phrases.

Smitherman, G. (2000). *Talkin that talk: Language, culture and education in African America.* New York: Routledge.

Smitherman, a respected scholar of Ebonics who frequently uses Ebonics grammar, vocabulary, and rhetoric in her academic writing, argues for defining Ebonics as a language and traces its historical development.

Wolfram, W., Adger, C. T., & Conna, C. (1999). *Dialects in schools and communities.* Mahwah, NJ: Erlbaum.

The authors focus on pronunciation and grammatical structures, commenting on linguistic patterns and how they are manifested in a number of varieties of English. For example, in a section on "Final Cluster Reduction," the authors explain how and why "best apple" can become "bes' apple" in Ebonics as well as Hispanic English and Vietnamese English.

19

Pedagogies of the "Students' Right" Era: The Language Curriculum Research Group's Project for Linguistic Diversity

SCOTT WIBLE

We affirm the students' right to their own patterns and varieties of language — the dialects of their nurture or whatever dialects in which they find their own identity and style. [. . .] The claim that any one dialect is unacceptable [. . .] leads to false advice for speakers and writers, and immoral advice for humans. A nation proud of its diverse heritage and its cultural and racial variety will preserve its heritage of dialects. We affirm strongly that teachers must have the experiences and training that will enable them to respect diversity and uphold the right of students to their own language.

—COMMITTEE ON CCCC LANGUAGE STATEMENT,
"Students' Right to Their Own Language"

Although many compositionists and other language arts professionals greeted the "Students' Right" policy with high enthusiasm, still a great degree of lingering confusion existed: "Well, then, if I don't correct the grammatical errors, what do I do?" as one well-meaning instructor queried.

—GENEVA SMITHERMAN, "CCCC's Role in the
Struggle for Language Rights"

With its 1972 "Students' Right to Their Own Language" resolution and accompanying 1974 background statement, the Conference on College Composition and Communication (CCCC) prompted the question, "[W]hat should the schools do about the language habits of students who come from a wide variety of social, economic, and cultural backgrounds?" (*Students' Right* p. 20 in this book). As Geneva Smitherman recalls, however, many compositionists felt the "Students' Right" documents left them with few specific strategies to take to the classroom.

This initial unsettled reception has influenced our current perceptions of the document, as composition scholars continue to debate the relevance of

---

From *College Composition and Communication* 57.3 (2006): 442–78.

the "Students' Right" policy to our disciplinary concerns. For example, in the introduction to their 2005 collection *The Hope and the Legacy: The Past, Present, and Future of "Students' Right to Their Own Language,"* Patrick Bruch and Richard Marback explain that compositionists past and present variously characterize the "Students' Right" resolution "as a failed attempt at coalition, as an indirect influence, as a unique historical moment, and as an important inspiration" for literacy educators (xii). Even with these disagreements, the most consistently reached conclusion among compositionists is that the students' right to their own language is a theory that rarely, if ever, has materialized in the writing classroom. Michael Pennell, for example, suggests the "Students' Right" resolution and background statement may be little more than "rhetorical ghosts with no substance below the ink and paper that [they] embody" (229). In fact, as the CCCC Language Policy Committee reported in its recent survey of members of the CCCC and the National Council of Teachers of English (NCTE), many compositionists have never even seen the ink and paper—let alone the substance—of the "Students' Right" policy, as two-thirds of survey respondents were unfamiliar with the resolution (14–15).

In most present-day work around issues of linguistic diversity and language policy, then, compositionists seem to agree that the conversations informing the "Students' Right" theory did not lead to pedagogical transformation inside the classroom. In this essay, I seek to complicate this notion by recovering the work of the Language Curriculum Research Group (LCRG), a research collective that in the late 1960s and early 1970s created a textbook manuscript and trained writing instructors in order to answer the era's pressing question, "What should teachers do about students' varied languages?" The research group, based at Brooklyn College and the Borough of Manhattan Community College, created a Standardized-English-as-a-Second-Dialect (ESD) course for African American and Puerto Rican students[1] whose writing displayed features of the Black English Vernacular (BEV) dialect.[2] Over a five-year period, the LCRG received financial support as well as professional legitimacy from prestigious Ford Foundation grants totaling over $250,000.[3] Because of charged political and educational discourses of the mid-1970s, however, publishers shied away from adopting the group's textbook manuscript. By not publishing, the LCRG and its project perished. Indeed, few present-day scholars—and even fewer of the group's contemporaries—have cited the LCRG's work, a fact that has only reinforced assumptions that the "Students' Right" theory did not usefully inform teachers' practices.[4]

Studying the history of the LCRG can contribute to the ongoing conversation among compositionists who are trying to understand more fully the educational and linguistic politics of the "Students' Right" era. I argue we can deepen our understanding of the "Students' Right" legacy by analyzing actual pedagogies, such as the LCRG's, that emerged from the scholarly discussions informing it. By drawing upon archival materials from the Ford Foundation, the LCRG's unpublished textbook manuscript and teachers' manual, and interviews with Carol Reed, a founding member of the LCRG, this essay challenges perceptions of the "Students' Right" document as a progressive theory divorced from the everyday practices and politics of the composition class-room. Through this recovery of the LCRG's work, scholars can see that the "Students' Right" ideal did in fact inspire teachers to invent pedagogies enabling students to leverage their linguistic diversity as a means for access-ing academic literacies. Learning about the LCRG challenges our ideas about the range of scholarly work that has gone on in the name of the "Students' Right" theory, for we see not only the group's successes in helping students to use their own languages as resources for their academic writing and explora-tion, but also how the LCRG's efforts to transform our pedagogical and politi-cal commitments have nearly disappeared from our disciplinary memory.

To make this argument, I first present a brief overview of the LCRG's work in order to underscore the timeliness as well as the broad scope of its project. I then articulate the significance of the LCRG within composition stud-ies by focusing on three aspects of the group's project that it created in order to enact a "Students' Right" pedagogical theory. I analyze, in turn, the LCRG's Ford Foundation grant proposal and the ESD exercises in its textbook manu-script, which show how the group members bridged sociolinguistics research on BEV with composition studies; the reading materials, writing assignments, and classroom projects incorporated into the textbook manuscript in order to make BEV and African American culture significant subjects of study in the writing classroom; and the LCRG's efforts in teacher training, through which the group prompted teachers to reflect on their attitudes toward racial and linguistic difference. In the final section of this essay, I attend to the reasons why the LCRG's project has escaped our disciplinary memory. Specifically, I analyze how aggressive public resistance in the mid-1970s crippled the LCRG's efforts to create progressive literacy education for African American students. Recounting the effects of this conservative educational discourse should strengthen our commitments to reinvigorating the "Students' Right" ideal and force us to examine carefully the assumptions that have guided both past and present efforts to improve literacy education for students of all linguistic heritages.

A BROAD STRATEGY FOR CURRICULAR REFORM

The LCRG's founding members, Carol Reed and Sylvia Lowenthal of Brook-lyn College and Milton Baxter of the Borough of Manhattan Community Col-lege, formed the research group in 1969 to address concerns they had while teaching composition in the Search for Education, Elevation, and Knowledge (SEEK) program in the City University of New York (CUNY) system. SEEK offered academic support and instruction for students who entered CUNY through the school's open admissions policy. Traditional methods of teaching grammatical correctness frustrated many of the African American students and teachers in SEEK. According to Reed, instructors assumed these stu-dents made grammatical errors simply because they did not know the rules of Standardized English (SE) grammar and mechanics.[5] Teachers therefore gave students "intensive doses of 'more of the same'" (Reed, "Why" 10), namely, repeated exposure—couched as "enrichment"—to the rules of SE grammar as well as countless examples of SE prose (Reed, Baxter, and Lowenthal 1).

Reed, Baxter, and Lowenthal, each trained in sociolinguistics, questioned this pedagogical approach.[6] They believed many African American students' writing reflected "cross-dialect interference," whereby aspects of BEV's grammatical and syntactical code appeared in their efforts to write SE prose (Reed, Baxter, and Lowenthal 3). Several linguistic studies had already shown that children internalize the basic behavioral patterns of their first language by the time they reach schooling age, so the LCRG felt students would benefit from having the patterns of BEV made explicit. This knowledge, the researchers suggested, would better prepare students to identify where BEV grammar and syntax "interfered" when they tried to compose SE (3–5). This hypothesis, which drew heavily upon the sociolinguistics theories of William Stewart, served as the foundation for the group's ESD composition instruction.[7] In 1969, Reed, Baxter, and Lowenthal began to create exercises and writing assignments for a composition textbook that would allow students to learn about the language varieties of their communities as well as how to edit their prose to reflect the SE conventions expected by most teachers in college courses.

The group presented its initial classroom strategies and textbook exercises at several professional conferences, but it was at the 1969 NCTE convention that the group received a big break. Marjorie Martus of the Ford Foundation attended Reed's presentation, and, as Reed would later explain, Martus sensed from attendees' enthusiastic responses that all composition teachers needed to know about the LCRG's project (telephone interview, 9 Nov. 2003). Martus encouraged Reed to apply for a foundation grant that could support the LCRG's efforts to develop its textbook manuscript and ultimately to publish and distribute it to interested writing programs throughout the United States. Reed, Baxter, and Lowenthal readily accepted this invitation, and on March 24, 1970, they submitted their grant proposal to the foundation, titling it "A CUNY Demonstration Project to Effect Bidialectalism in Users of Nonstandard Dialects of English."

Ford Foundation officials awarded the research group an initial $64,456 grant to support textbook development, in large part because they agreed with the LCRG's assessment that literacy educators needed specific pedagogical strategies to use in their classrooms (Ward 6). The Ford Foundation certainly understood the value of sociolinguistics research on BEV, having already supported the Center for Applied Linguistics' work in this area. The LCRG convinced foundation officials that it could—indeed, needed to—translate this research into pedagogical methods in order to help those CUNY instructors who, as Mina Shaughnessy would later describe them, felt "marooned" in their composition classrooms during the early years of open admissions, with "no studies nor guides, nor even suitable textbooks to turn to" (3).

The LCRG, which grew by 1971 to include Paul Cohen, Samuel Moore, and Jacqueline Redrick, used its Ford Foundation grant money to address this situation on several fronts.[8] First, the group members researched several semesters' worth of their students' writing so they could focus their efforts on addressing only those BEV features that appeared most frequently in students' attempts to write in SE. Second, they developed, piloted, and revised their textbook manuscript for ESD first-year composition courses. Half of the units in this manuscript allowed students to compare and contrast BEV and SE toward the ends of acquiring the "code" of written SE as well as the rhetorical modes they could use in their college writing. The remaining materials made African American language practices explicit subjects of study in the composition classroom. Students learned about theories concerning BEV's origins and development, read various examples of the use of BEV by African American journalists and artists, wrote essays about their experiences with and attitudes toward BEV, and conducted ethnographic research on the use of BEV in their own communities. Third, the LCRG researchers offered an overview of their pedagogical methods and textbook manuscript in papers presented at a variety of conferences, including conventions of the CCCC, NCTE, the College Language Association (CLA), the College English Association (CEA), Teachers of English to Speakers of Other Languages (TESOL), and the Linguistic Society of America (LSA). The LCRG's project was well received at conferences, as evidenced by Moore's report to the Ford Foundation following his presentation at the 1972 CCCC convention: "Because [my] presentation outlined methods and gave examples of actual materials designed to attack the problem effectively, much interest was generated in what we are doing here at Brooklyn College" (1). Fourth, the group created a multifaceted approach for preparing educators to teach ethically and effectively to African American students whose writings reflected ESD language-learning situations. Specifically, the group wrote a teachers' manual to accompany the textbook manuscript, arranged sessions in which Brooklyn College education majors tutored the LCRG's SEEK students, and conducted workshops for CUNY instructors to learn about the pedagogical implications of sociolinguistics research on BEV. Many workshop participants valued the LCRG's insights and suggestions, and the workshops were well attended, with the names of prominent scholars such as Shaughnessy, Patricia Laurence, and Kenneth Bruffee appearing on workshop sign-up sheets the LCRG filed in its annual reports ("LCRG-CUNY Teacher-Training"; Bruffee).

On the basis of these successes, the LCRG in 1973 began trying to spark publishers' interest in its textbook manuscript. The research group sent its manuscript to six commercial publishers, including Harcourt Brace Jovanovich, Prentice Hall, and Houghton Mifflin, as well as the Center for Applied Linguistics. During this period, however, "back-to-basics" critics warned that experiments in literacy education for minority students were eroding traditional academic standards. The charged atmosphere led many administrators and teachers to curtail progressive educational programs, and textbook publishers consequently refused to touch the LCRG's textbook manuscript. In June 1974, the Ford Foundation stopped funding the LCRG, leading foundation officer Richard Lacey to conclude that the researchers "were tackling a terribly important problem without enough horses" (memorandum to Marjorie Martus, 12 July 1974).

BRIDGING THE GAP BETWEEN SOCIOLINGUISTICS AND COMPOSITION

As African American scholars who were speakers of BEV, specialists trained in sociolinguistics, and teachers of first-year composition, the LCRG researchers were well positioned to develop writing instruction responsive to the language diversity of students entering universities during the early years of open admissions. The group knew that writing instructors should hear how sociolinguistics research on BEV could usefully inform their teaching. Just as significantly, the researchers also considered their BEV-speaking students to be an important, interested, and intellectually capable audience for this research. Reed would remark in a 1973 *TESOL Quarterly* article that her students were "ready and willing (if not downright *eager*) to [. . .] make practical use of an interesting body of knowledge about factors influencing their own linguistic behavior" ("Adapting" 292). The LCRG's grant proposal, along with its textbook manuscript's instructional units on grammar and mechanics, illustrate one aspect of the group's contribution to conversations that informed the "Students' Right" vision for theoretically sound language arts pedagogy. These materials not only show how the group used sociolinguistics research to meet composition instructors' need for methods to teach SE prose, but they also demonstrate how such research helped to get students more engaged in the composition course, building on students' own ideas about what they wanted to learn and do with writing.[9]

The LCRG was clearly indebted to the sociolinguistics research of Stewart, William Labov, and Walt Wolfram, which catalogued and analyzed the systematic nature of BEV's syntax, phonology, and morphology, but the LCRG distinguished its project by tailoring this research to meet the specific needs of writing instructors. The LCRG members felt sociolinguists too often pursued "misdirected priorities in descriptive research," in that they focused their energies too narrowly on identifying, describing, and classifying as many features of the spoken BEV dialect as they could (Reed, Baxter, and Lowenthal 8–10). The LCRG researchers therefore tailored their descriptions of BEV grammar and syntax in order to meet the needs of their nonspecialist audience of composition instructors and students.

Just as significantly, the LCRG believed writing instructors would pay closer attention to this research if it presented precise analyses of how students' *speech* specifically influenced their *writing*. Therefore, at the outset of their project, the LCRG researchers conducted an exhaustive study of their students' writing through which they identified the features of the spoken BEV code that appeared most often in their students' attempts to write SE prose (Reed, Baxter, and Lowenthal 8). Through this examination, the LCRG helped teachers to distinguish between those features in students' writing that represented "errors" common to many SE writers (such as the *who/whom* distinction) and those features that resulted specifically from "cross-dialect interference" (such as *they/their* distinctions, as in "They are at they mother house," or the zero copula, as in the BEV "He at home now" versus the SE "He is at home") (LCRG, "Teachers' Manual" 24).[10] The LCRG used its research on students' writing, then, to determine what compositionists needed to know about sociolinguistics research on BEV in order to teach writing effectively to linguistic-minority students.

On the basis of these initial investigations into how best to apply sociolinguistics research to composition instruction, the LCRG created its contrastive analysis exercises. These materials made up a significant part of the ESD writing instruction found in the textbook manuscript. Half of the units presented grammatical rules for BEV, such as those for subject-verb agreement, negation, and pronoun usage, and juxtaposed them with SE usage rules. In the exercises that followed, students read passages in BEV, as well as some that showed hypercorrection, and edited them to meet SE conventions.[11] For example, in a chapter on pluralization rules, students changed BEV usages to their SE equivalents and identified the SE grammatical rules that led them to make the changes. Exercises of this type included the sentence, "I know because it has happened to me a few time but I just have to live with it" ("Students' Manual" 115). Given this sentence, students had to distinguish between BEV and SE pluralization rules; in the former, the quantifier *few* signals pluralization, while in the latter, the noun itself, *times*, needs to signal the pluralization.

The LCRG also added nuance to these exercises in order to stress to students that "correct" SE usage did not determine a writer's effectiveness. This emphasis is most readily apparent in the textbook manuscript's use of prose passages and poems as materials for contrastive analysis. For example, in a unit on pronoun usage, students read poems from the Black Arts Movement, Don L. Lee's "The Revolutionary Screw" and "Re-Act for Action" and David Nelson's "Know Yourself," and then identified where and how each of these poets used reflexive pronouns, such as Nelson's splitting of reflexive pronouns in the lines "Do you know the ugliness of *your still becoming Black self* / Do you know the warm beauty of *your true Black self*" (73–76, emphasis added). Accompanying questions asked students to analyze how each particular usage suited the poet's aim, audience, and message (71–72). These types of exercises emphasized effectiveness over correctness. In so doing, they confirmed students' own perceptions of how language functioned in their social worlds outside of school, where friends and relatives lauded for their ways with words commonly "broke" SE grammar rules to achieve their rhetorical goals.

With the systematic ESD approach of their writing textbook, the LCRG researchers contributed to the conversations informing the "Students' Right" policy by articulating specific ways sociolinguistics research on nonstandardized dialects of English could usefully inform writing instruction. Moreover, the LCRG's textbook manuscript made SE conventions a concern only for the latter stages of the writing process. Students were taught to write first, recognize areas of cross-dialect interference second, and only then, when editing their drafts, to change these features into the SE grammatical code. Nevertheless, in certain respects, the group's sentence-level translation exercises seemingly reproduce the traditional aims of the composition course, in that the curriculum characterizes SE prose as the "polish" other educators and employers expected to see in "good" writing. As we will see in the next section, however, the reading materials and writing assignments of the LCRG's textbook manuscript challenged English language arts educators' assumptions about how BEV could invigorate African American students' intellectual work.

VALUING THE BLACK ENGLISH VERNACULAR
IN COMPOSITION CLASSROOMS

As the previous section illustrated, the LCRG aimed "to effect bidialectalism in users of nonstandard dialects of English" (to quote its grant proposal title) by creating exercises to improve students' abilities to write SE. The textbook manuscript's attention to the surface features of BEV and SE characterized most bidialectalist pedagogies of the era, which took compositionists' primary responsibility to be teaching students to write according to the SE conventions other teachers and employers would expect to see in formal writing. Another aspect of the LCRG's project, however, created an equally significant set of aims for the first-year composition course. Student-centered research projects as well as culturally relevant writing assignments and reading materials from the textbook manuscript suggest that the LCRG's project pushed students and teachers to analyze and work with language at deeper levels than just its surface features. These aspects of the LCRG's pedagogy addressed what Reed called the "compulsory miseducation" that African American students— indeed, all students and teachers—endured through traditional language- arts curricula, which taught them to devalue BEV and consider African Amer- ican communities verbally "impoverished" ("Adapting" 294).

As they tried to make BEV central to academic exploration and writing, the LCRG researchers joined an emerging group of African American compo- sitionists and sociolinguists who argued that conventional bidialectalist peda- gogies limited the range of what students could envision themselves doing as writers. Ernece B. Kelly made one of the earliest criticisms of compositionists' work relative to dialect difference with her talk at the 1968 CCCC convention, which she delivered in the immediate aftermath of the assassination of Martin Luther King, Jr. Kelly denounced the discipline's willful ignorance of Black English and challenged the assumptions on which bidialectalist pedagogies were based:

> Here in Minneapolis we meet to discuss composition. Here we meet to discuss the dialects of Black students and how we can upgrade or, if we're really successful, just plain *replace* them. [. . .] Why aren't there Blacks here who will talk about the emergence of an image among Blacks which does not permit them to even bother with the question of whether or not the white man understands their dialect? [. . .] Why aren't there Blacks helping to plan this conference who have access to the papers which deal with the Black aesthetic and its relationship to composition or the Black image and why it does or does not rest in the anthologies we use or the richness and values of the language of the Black ghetto? (106–07)

A number of sociolinguists echoed Kelly's critique, maintaining that the "project to effect bidialectalism" constituted an unethical aim for English language arts instruction. James Sledd, Wayne O'Neil, and Geneva Smitherman in particular argued that even though bidialectalists used the term "dialect difference" to suggest that "correctness" was always relative, they still connoted "dialect deficiency" because, as Sledd explained, they considered students' nonstandardized dialects to be appropriate only for uses that middle-class white society granted little intellectual or cultural worth, such as rapping with friends (450–51). Smitherman extended this critique, claiming that bidialectalist pedagogies forced students to attend to the relatively insignificant surface features of language and, consequently, devote less attention to crafting powerful, meaningful prose: "[T]eaching strategies which seek only to put white middle-class English into the mouths of black speakers ain did nothin to inculcate the black perspective necessary to address the crises in the black community" (*Talkin and Testifyin* 209). These scholars collectively urged compositionists to focus their efforts on teaching students to use writing as a tool for analyzing and producing new knowledge about the world, no matter the dialect.

The LCRG's project, however, defies easy categorization with other bidialectalist pedagogies that focused solely on the surface features of white middle-class English. Admittedly, with its emphasis on contrastive-analysis exercises and "translation" between BEV and SE, the LCRG's textbook manuscript does lead students to view SE writing as *the* medium for academic work. In fact, the LCRG researchers make the very distinction Sledd criticizes when, in the textbook manuscript's introduction, they explain to students that SE represented a formal style of language appropriate for school, job applications, and addresses to professional groups, while the BEV dialects of their communities were most suitable for talking with family, rapping with neighbors, or writing letters to friends (16). Through statements such as this one, along with the repeated emphasis on moving from BEV rough drafts to SE final copies, the LCRG's textbook manuscript reproduced traditional requirements for the first-year composition course, whereby teachers demanded SE proficiency from students in order to grant them credit for the course.

Several other aspects of the LCRG's textbook manuscript, however, show that the researchers also believed the composition course needed to account more fully for the lived experiences, worldviews, and languages of African American students. To work toward these ends, the LCRG created research projects through which students treated BEV as a legitimate object of inquiry in the writing classroom. In one such project for their own courses, the LCRG's SEEK students used tape recorders to chronicle effective BEV speech in their communities (Reed, Baxter, and Lowenthal 18). Along with these tapes, the LCRG's students composed ethnographies in which they identified the wide range of linguistic strategies and interpersonal behaviors that BEV speakers used to communicate meaning (Reed, telephone interview, 7 Dec. 2003). Such class projects pushed the LCRG's students to produce more substantial work than they would within bidialectalist courses. Rather than "seek[ing] only to put white middle-class English into the mouths of black speakers," in Smitherman's words, the LCRG allowed its African American students to compose academic research to address an important issue facing their communities. Specifically, the LCRG incorporated data from students' tapes and ethnographies into the textbook manuscript (Reed, Baxter, and Lowenthal 18), thus enabling the student-researchers themselves to help improve literacy education for African Americans.

In the textbook manuscript, meanwhile, the LCRG gained students' interest by centering discussions and writing assignments on their own experiences with language difference in their schools and in their communities. For example, the first essay assignment asked students either to analyze how they "change [their] speech for different occasions" or to narrate situations in which they "have to talk 'uppity'" (15). The research group effectively linked English language arts instruction to students' social worlds, as these essay assignments allowed students to discuss their own ideas and attitudes toward language diversity. Moreover, these prompts encouraged students and teachers to grapple with the politics of language use that bidialectalist pedagogies often left unexamined.

Reading materials in the textbook manuscript likewise countered the widespread perception that many African American students came to school from linguistically deprived communities. The LCRG meant for the wide range of readings to illustrate that BEV has "its own continuum" of rhetorical styles, ranging "from the street to the pulpit" ("Teachers' Manual" 23). For this reason, the textbook manuscript included toasts[12] by poet and jazz musician Gil Scott-Heron; raps by Frankie Crocker and Lou Rawls; excerpts from the autobiographies of Malcolm X and Billie Holiday; a student essay responding to public criticism of CUNY's open admissions policies; articles from African American newspapers; recipes from soul-food cookbooks; and poems from the Black Arts Movement, such as Helen King's "Reflections of a 69th Street Chicago Pimp after Reading a Really Good Black Poem." The LCRG also devoted over twenty textbook pages to instruction on African American narrative styles. Readings in this section were followed by comprehension questions asking students to make links between BEV use and African American worldviews. In one example, students read "The Fall," an African American toast in which the protagonist narrates his exploits of lawlessness and, even after being jailed, boasts, "I hope the game [on the streets] is still the same / when I finish up next fall" ("Students' Manual" 354). Questions followed asking students to analyze various aspects of the toast, including "Are there special speech acts [in the toast] characteristic of Black delivery style?" and "In what ways does the toast represent a 'blatant disregard and even contempt for white cultural norms'?" (355). By giving such materials concrete space within its textbook manuscript, the LCRG effectively built on Kelly's call for compositionists to deal with "the richness and values of the language of the Black ghetto" (107). The LCRG's textbook manuscript helped students to move beyond bidialectalist pedagogy's attention to making their academic writing "formal." These reading materials and analytical prompts gave students opportunities to learn about the many powerful rhetorical patterns and strategies African Americans had used to build distinctive language traditions.

Through these kinds of materials, the LCRG reinforced the need for compositionists to understand and respect the social contexts within which students learned and used BEV. The LCRG textbook manuscript linked language and culture in this way to redress the way most English language arts curricula ignored the variety and complexity of black worldviews and, in turn, devalued many African American cultural forms (Reed, "Adapting" 294). To be sure, there were teachers who included in their syllabi texts by prominent African American writers such as Richard Wright, Gwendolyn Brooks, and James Baldwin. The LCRG argued, however, that such courses too often narrowly taught students to evaluate African American writers' prose and poetry according to traditional conventions of style and to analyze these texts' characters with reference only to Eurocentric social values and worldviews (LCRG, "Teachers' Manual" 20–23).[13] The LCRG instead shaped compositionists' ideas about the linguistic politics of writing instruction by showing how teachers' best intentions to value BEV in the classroom would be meaningful only if teachers and textbooks valued the social contexts of BEV use, as well.

PROMPTING TEACHER REFLECTION ON RACIAL AND LINGUISTIC DIFFERENCE

The LCRG's project was well-received by English language arts educators, but the researchers knew the discipline's assumptions about linguistic diversity would not change if teachers only viewed these activities and assignments as more efficient means for ridding students' writing of BEV. Therefore, the research group created a teachers' manual and offered tutorial sessions for preservice educators and workshops for inservice compositionists to address directly how normative ideas about race, language, and the aims of education informed dominant approaches to writing instruction. Within each of these sites for teacher training, the LCRG encouraged English language arts educators to see how their practices in linguistically diverse classrooms were shaped by social attitudes concerning cultural and linguistic difference.

The LCRG's teachers' manual prompted reflection on how, particularly for white SE-speaking teachers, acknowledging BEV in the classroom necessarily changed the relationship between students and teacher. The researchers emphasized this fact within the manual's introductory material. The group discussed the rationale and methodology for its course and also answered ten common questions teachers had about BEV in general and its role in the classroom in particular. Among the most significant questions were "What attitudes can be found in the black community regarding BEV?" (39–46); "Are BEV and SE mutually intelligible?" (61–63); and "Must a teacher be fluent in BEV in order to use a bi-dialectical approach?" (59–60). The LCRG responded to these questions but then asked teachers to see that the best answers could only emerge from their interactions with students. To foster these relationships, the LCRG created the textbook manuscript's essay assignments, described in the previous section, for which students wrote about their everyday experiences with language. The teachers' manual also included many similar open-ended discussion questions meant "to tap the students' intuitions about their dialect" (30). The LCRG explained of its intentions with this design, "The students, therefore, are the primary sources of BEV data, and the teacher—in recognition of this—ought to gain an appreciation of BEV from them as much as from the curriculum materials presented in the manual" (30).

Framing the teachers' manual this way encouraged teachers to position themselves as students of BEV, too, open to learning from their own students' language practices. In so doing, the LCRG strategically troubled many teachers' desire to enter the classroom feeling that they knew all there possibly was to know about the subject. While the LCRG certainly used sociolinguistics research to create a theoretical foundation for compositionists' approaches to language diversity, its teachers' manual nevertheless asked instructors to see that social interaction and reflection across racial and linguistic difference was how meaningful knowledge about BEV got created.

The LCRG created small, controlled environments for such cooperative learning and reflection through a partnership with Brooklyn College's School of Education. The research group arranged collaborative-learning sessions that paired upper-division education majors with the BEV-speaking students enrolled in the LCRG's composition courses (Reed, Baxter, and Lowenthal 25–30). In these mutually enriching sessions, the preservice teachers helped the SEEK students to revise their essays and edit them using the grammatical concepts they were learning in the textbook manuscript. Other activities allowed the composition students and education majors to learn more about language practices in African American communities. For example, in some sessions the pair read toasts. The pair would first edit these toasts to reflect conventions of SE. Then, just as the composition students did in the textbook manuscript exercises, the group would discuss how these toasts commented on America's mainstream cultural norms and how specific narrative techniques helped the storyteller to make his or her point (Reed, telephone interview, 7 Dec. 2003). Such activities encouraged both the first-year composition students and the education majors to explore the interconnectedness of African American language practices and worldviews. In addition to these weekly tutorials, all participants met with Fred Hill, an educational administrator with a background in sensitivity training and behavior therapy, who facilitated discussions and reflections on how power, race, and language affected interactions in these tutoring sessions (Reed, Baxter, and Lowenthal 28–29). Collectively, these tutorials and discussions deepened the preservice teachers' understanding of African American linguistic traditions and heightened their sensitivity to their students' rhetorical sophistication and critical sensibilities. Just as significantly, by arranging these sessions, the LCRG offered both future teachers and present SEEK students opportunities to explore their attitudes about racial, ethnic, and linguistic difference and to reflect on how these beliefs influenced the learning atmosphere in college.

In its workshops for CUNY instructors, meanwhile, the LCRG provoked a more thorough interrogation of how composition curricula were too often grounded on discriminatory assumptions about the value of nonstandardized dialects. As the group explained in its teachers' manual, English language arts instruction promoted the "general tendency in American society to assimilate divergent cultural and linguistic heritages into a kind of homogeneous mainstream culture, to the exclusion, in particular, of the culture in which BEV is found" (22). The LCRG used its workshops to help teachers see that they should not focus instruction solely on BEV's linguistic features but needed also to explore the cultural contexts—the spaces, the audiences, the values, the content—that shape BEV, rather than relegating it "to the status of 'street language'" (22). Similarly, the LCRG helped CUNY instructors to recognize BEV as an entire communicative system, complete with gestures, body language, and intonation patterns that speakers and listeners used to create meaning. Baxter explained the need for this aspect of training in his 1976 *College English* article, "Educating Teachers about Educating the Oppressed," suggesting, "[W]hen educators envision the classroom use of a dialect such as BEV, they have in mind BEV-speaking students who will utter their dialect patterns with SAE mannerisms, gestures, pitch ranges, intonation patterns, etc.—no doubt to facilitate the teachers' understanding of BEV" (680). The LCRG's workshops therefore provided a space for helping teachers, many of whom came from different linguistic and cultural backgrounds than those of their students, to understand and interpret the various tools their students often used to communicate meaning. This emphasis throughout the CUNY workshops prompted instructors to recognize the range of cultural and interpersonal elements they needed to attend to in order to create meaningful language-learning situations for linguistic-minority students.

Given these aims, the LCRG devoted significant portions of the workshop to the difficulties and demands of introducing the textbook manuscript and BEV within the composition classroom. The researchers knew that African American SEEK students had endured twelve years of what Reed called "indoctrination" in the belief that they seemingly had no significant linguistic heritage ("Adapting" 294). Workshop participants thus were warned that many BEV-speaking students would resist the acknowledgment of their language in the college classroom, particularly when white teachers tried to use the textbook manuscript. Reed explained, "The student will most likely resent the teacher's calling attention to what he regards as an embarrassing deficiency. He will most likely be wont to suspect racist motives, interpreting his teacher's intent as some subtle new attempt to trap him into admitting what he secretly suspects is proof of his linguistic inferiority" (294–95). Since there was potential for student resistance, the LCRG used the workshops to suggest strategies for introducing the ESD curriculum. For example, they suggested teachers assign books such as Edward T. Hall's *The Silent Language* and Robert A. Hall Jr.'s *Linguistics and Your Language* to help students appreciate the concepts of cultural and linguistic relativity (295–96). An even stronger strategy, discussed earlier, came from the LCRG researchers' own SEEK classrooms;

teachers could begin courses with student ethnographies on language practices in their communities, underscoring their commitment to making BEV and African American culture significant subjects of study in the composition classroom. The LCRG repeatedly emphasized — in its teachers' manual, in its published articles, and in its workshops — that how teachers introduced the BEV-centered curriculum, as well as how they engaged students' responses to this approach, would greatly affect students' motivation to do the intellectual work the course demanded of them.

The LCRG's work in teacher training shows why teacher education concerning linguistic diversity must answer more than just the always pressing "What do I do?" question. The research group understood that sociolinguistics research and classroom exercises alone would not push educators to affirm BEV's relevance to students' writing and academic inquiry. The teachers' manual, tutoring programs, and workshops consequently became spaces in which the LCRG cultivated habits of self-awareness and self-reflection among English language arts teachers. Letters written to the LCRG by workshop participants suggest that many teachers found these experiences essential for their professional development. For instance, Elaine Avidon, course coordinator for Herbert H. Lehman College, wrote, "One of our faculty members participated in your workshop this past weekend at the Conference on English in the Community Colleges. It was clear to her after listening to you, and it's clear to us after listening to her, that we need to hear more about your work in Black English" (1; see also Berlinger, Sealy).

These programs heightened teachers' awareness of how normative assumptions about race and language shaped their interactions with students. They also prepared educators to teach students not only to recognize but also to value and build on the language resources they brought to the classroom. More important, these programs allowed instructors to envision how their interactions with students across linguistic difference transformed their understanding of sociolinguistics research and the aims of writing instruction.

Losing the Battle against "Back-to-Basics" Reform

As its period of annual funding from the Ford Foundation drew to a close in June 1974, the LCRG researchers had already enjoyed numerous successes. Colleagues had given them good feedback about their teacher-training programs. Many students noted in course evaluations that the LCRG course was "better than any other writing course" they had ever taken ("Student Course-Evaluation"). And linguist Beryl Bailey, head of Hunter College's Black and Puerto Rican Studies Program, concluded her 1972 review of the LCRG's textbook manuscript with this assertion: "This project represents the serious efforts of a responsible and energetic group of researchers to fill a breach in the new dimensions which Open Admissions has thrust upon higher education in New York City" (5). On the basis of these positive evaluations, the LCRG circulated revised drafts of its textbook manuscript and teachers' manual to external reviewers as well as to six commercial publishers. This push to publish its materials and reach a broader audience would not succeed. In the mid-1970s, a highly charged discourse constricted mainstream conceptions of productive and appropriate literacy education, effectively limiting the chances for projects such as the LCRG's to flourish.

Although not the first to do so, Merrill Sheils issued the most visible warning of a literacy crisis with her now infamous 1975 *Newsweek* cover story, "Why Johnny Can't Write." Sheils alerted readers that literacy in the United States, according to statistics, was declining each year. She made a specific argument about the source of these problems, implicitly targeting the CCCC's "Students' Right" resolution. Sheils strategically juxtaposed examples of college students' tangled, sentence-fragmented prose with passages from the CCCC's document. In so doing, she encouraged readers to see teachers' affirmation of students' linguistic differences as a sign that well-established standards of correctness were being ignored, even deemed irrelevant, in order to make all students feel welcome in school. She explained:

> The point is that there have to be some fixed rules, however tedious, if the codes of human communication are to remain decipherable. If the written language is placed at the mercy of every new colloquialism and if every fresh dialect demands and gets equal sway, then we will soon find ourselves back in Babel. In America [. . .] there are too many people intent on being masters of their language and too few willing to be its servants. (65)

Sheils conflated ungrammatical, incoherent prose with urban nonstandardized dialects to force a specific conclusion: the "new" students of open admissions, through their demands for culturally relevant education, had wrested away teachers' authority to impose objective standards, corrupted the integrity of writing instruction for all students, and, ultimately, cheapened the significance of a college degree. In his reading of Sheils's work, John Trimbur suggests that as she lamented the blurring of lines separating "masters" from "servants," Sheils tried to reassert literacy's traditional authority to "draw lines of social distinction, mark status, and rank students in a meritocratic order" (279). Given this implicit argument, one can see that to Sheils and other critics, pedagogies like the LCRG's represented academic permissiveness in the name of improving minority students' self-esteem.

A "back-to-basics" educational movement built on this belief that colleges no longer instilled the "American" values of hard work and discipline. This discourse intensified criticism of the LCRG and its work. The ministers, politicians, businesspeople, and parents who led the grassroots back-to-basics movement saw the literacy crisis as evidence of a more widespread social decline illustrated most prominently in the civil disturbances of the 1960s (Brodinsky 522). The back-to-basics supporters in particular believed that the civil rights movement's demands for equal access had been translated into student demands for a light workload and easy credits. Central to the back-to-basics movement's vision for restoring significance to U.S. education were a sternly disciplined, teacher-centered pedagogy; academic criteria, not social criteria, as the basis for promotion through the curriculum; and the elimination of experimental and innovative programs in favor of textbooks that provided frequent drilling and promoted traditional social values (Shor 78–79). The Scholastic Aptitude Test (SAT) even came to reflect the influence of back-to-basics reform; amid clamor about declining SAT scores, testing officials in October 1974 added a thirty-minute section to test students on their knowledge of SE grammar (Parks 196–97). This emphasis on SE and the movement toward educational "basics" directly affected the LCRG. The LCRG's pedagogy seemed to confirm critics' belief that teachers had lowered their standards of "good" writing to accommodate students' nontraditional literacies. The emphasis on basic SE grammar and standardized testing, they argued, reinstated clear-cut measures of quality and reestablished literacy's ability to ensure that hard-working students could achieve economic and social status.

Some English language arts educators in the CUNY system made similar arguments about the need for professors to reclaim authority from students and reinstate rigorous writing standards. For instance, in a 1974 CCC article, Joan Baum of CUNY's York College exhorted her colleagues to quit using "textbooks and workbooks that strain for relevancy and slick contemporaneity" in their quest to meet the apparent needs and interests of open admissions students (295). This approach would not solve students' writing problems, she argued, because these students were "not underprepared in feeling, but in thinking" (295). She instead demanded that publishers recommit to producing "slim essential monographs" that covered issues in logic and academic forms, which in Baum's opinion were "the particular demonstrated needs" of open admissions student (295). Baum labeled her ideas as "traditional, even reactionary" (294), given that she called for removing politics from writing instruction. Her argument in effect characterized pedagogies as misguided, even uninformed, when they allowed students to write *about* their social worlds and *in* the languages they used to negotiate everyday life. In so doing, she, like many others, ignored the theoretical foundations on which scholars such as the LCRG researchers were working. Moreover, she failed to acknowledge a significant assumption grounding the theory of students' right to their own language—"traditional" approaches to writing instruction had done a disservice to most African American students in the first place.

The controversy sparked by Sheils and fueled by the back-to-basics movement's causal analysis that culturally relevant pedagogies led to declining educational and social values created alarm among publishers about the potential marketability of the LCRG's textbook manuscript. In a letter to Martus at the Ford Foundation, Baxter explained that every publisher the group contacted was unwilling to publish the textbook manuscript "in these unstable economic times" because they sensed there was "a 'limited' market for curriculum materials addressed to an all-black audience" (1). Meanwhile, Allene Grognet, publications director of the Center for Applied Linguistics, predicted that "the sales potential of these books could be fairly large, but not through the regular educational channels" (1). She believed they would be used most widely in alternative sites of education such as adult education, vocational retraining, and church and community action schools. This characterization of the LCRG's textbook manuscript as material for "alternative" education underlined the pervasiveness of the normative educational philosophy wherein concentrated attention to the languages and literacies of African American students was not viewed as central to the university's academic mission. No less significant were bottom-line concerns. Publishers might have been able to sell large quantities of textbooks to these alternative markets, but they were not the mainstream—and hence, more profitable—markets publishers value most.

When Richard Wright and Walt Wolfram, both sociolinguists affiliated with the Center for Applied Linguists, reviewed the LCRG textbook manuscript in June 1974, they expressed similar concerns about how students and teachers might react to the textbook's attention to BEV. They recommended changes that would narrow its focus to teaching students to write SE. Wright in particular felt "[t]he heavy usage of Black pride materials" (2) needed to be eliminated because it encouraged BEV-speaking students "to 'be themselves' while living in ignorance of the role/function of language in the larger world community" (1). Moreover, he felt that "[w]ith all the glorification of BEV through poetry, narratives, etc., the student might come to wonder exactly what the course is all about" (2). The textbook needed to focus more narrowly on "the teaching [of] and sensitivity to SE," he argued, and to include far more models of SE prose (2). Wright therefore called for the LCRG to condense its discussion of BEV and the politics of dialect difference into a preface, whereas in the LCRG's draft these ideas were at the heart of most readings, comprehension questions, and writing assignments. Wright felt that if the preface contained the textbook manuscript's sole efforts "to win converts to a more humanistic view of BEV" (2), the body chapters would be free to focus on the business at hand in first-year composition—teaching SE, the standard of correctness students would need to meet in order to open "linguistic avenues to wider audiences, both nationally and internationally" (1).

The LCRG maintained that publishers' and sociolinguists' predictions about the textbook's likely reception were unjustified. The researchers repeatedly told Ford Foundation officials that these evaluations were never confirmed with classroom observations of the textbook manuscript being used in pilot courses. Indeed, Lacey, the Foundation's program officer for the LCRG's project, noted, "Although [the LCRG] invited publishers to visit classes, publishers' representatives have tended to rely on their own or outside professional opinions of the worth of their materials without seeing firsthand the work of the group with students at Brooklyn College and Manhattan Community College" (memorandum to Martus, 29 July 1974, 2). Had reviewers observed students and teachers using the textbook manuscript in CUNY classrooms, they might have perceived a disconnect between Wright's assertions and the ideas guiding the LCRG's approach. For example, whereas Wright felt the LCRG needed to teach linguistic-minority students not to "liv[e] in ignorance of the role/function of language in the larger world community"

(1), the essay prompts and discussion questions in the textbook manuscript allowed students to explore what they already knew from their everyday experience—that language could be used not only to create greater social and economic opportunities but also to discriminate. Moreover, the LCRG knew that such discussions did not distract students from the "real" work of learning SE grammar but instead were central to helping them prepare to negotiate the demands they undoubtedly would face throughout their academic and professional careers.

In order to contradict publishers' and reviewers' assessments of the likely reception and effectiveness of the textbook, the LCRG presented Ford Foundation representatives with end-of-course evaluations written by both students and teachers who had used the ESD materials in their courses. These documents showed that even those SEEK students who initially resented having to take a writing course for BEV speakers eventually left the semester feeling proud of their language and their communities ("Student Course-Evaluation"). On the basis of its findings as well as its disagreements with reviewers, the LCRG refused to surrender editorial control of its project. The researchers wanted to ensure the textbook manuscript continued to focus on both SE *and* BEV as a means for making composition classrooms into spaces where students and teachers examined the connections between language, culture, and power.

Ultimately, the LCRG could not overcome these public perceptions that BEV's presence in the classroom drained educational resources and hastened academic decline. The Ford Foundation, in its highly visible position, felt pressured to dissociate itself from a project the mainstream press characterized as threatening the values and standards of public education. Consequently, in a letter to the LCRG on July 18, 1974, Lacey stated that the Ford Foundation could no longer "justify continued involvement" in its project, "especially given the increased national attention recently directed to the problems you have addressed" (1). The Ford Foundation had discontinued funding the LCRG on June 30, 1974.

The pressures preventing publication of the LCRG's textbook manuscript complicate our common assumptions about why the "Students' Right to Their Own Language" ideal never materialized in widespread classroom practice. Present-day compositionists tend to think that the "Students' Right" era saw no theoretically based pedagogical projects develop, or that, if such projects were created, they just weren't effective. The LCRG's project proves otherwise. The textbook manuscript went unpublished because of resistance to the LCRG's efforts to reconcile what Min-Zhan Lu describes as the "discrepancy between the academy's account of what student writers can/should be allowed to do and the student writers' counter accounts of what they can do/are interested in and capable of doing" (18). Back-to-basics reformers restored faith in authoritarian pedagogy and narrowed many publishers' and teachers' visions of what linguistic-minority students needed to learn in writing classes, and this political and social conservatism has in turn affected the way we see the "Students' Right" document.

The LCRG's project shows us that the "Students' Right" era was not long on theory yet short on praxis. As Reed argued at the 1981 CUNY Association of Writing Supervisors Conference, the racially charged analyses of a literacy crisis led many teachers to become "timid and fearful of any curriculum materials" focusing on dialect differences ("Back" 9). The market for the textbook manuscript shrank, "successfully stifling efforts to disseminate new and effective teaching strategies to English teachers in inner-city classrooms across the country" (9–10). Back-to-basics discourse characterized racial- and ethnic-minority students as undeserving beneficiaries of CUNY's open admissions policies. Many professors, reviewers, textbook publishers, and political commentators agreed and therefore paid no attention to the LCRG's aim to teach African American students to write SE academic prose. Instead, the group's "heavy usage of Black pride materials" and its valuing of BEV's presence in the classroom fueled fears that innovative educators had allowed the "new" African American students of open admissions to be masters, not servants, of their language and their education. This controversy undoubtedly contributed to the LCRG's failure to publish its textbook manuscript, leaving the discipline of composition with no textual history of the LCRG's work.

CONCLUSION

Through its textbook manuscript, teachers' manual, and training workshops, the LCRG created a composition course in which students could enact their right to their own language. Despite the project's significant breadth, however, the absence of the group's work in composition histories speaks volumes about the imperative, in Smitherman's words, to "publish—or your ideas perish" (personal interview, 26 March 2004). Certainly, the LCRG's project met pressing disciplinary needs, a fact underscored by the Ford Foundation's substantial monetary support as well as the feedback the researchers received from colleagues. Ultimately, though, the group's efforts to strengthen composition's commitment to linguistic diversity were dismissed by publishers concerned with managing bottom lines amid feverish back-to-basics discourse. Since the researchers could not effectively respond to the fears of administrators, teachers, and publishers, the LCRG's textbook manuscript remains unpublished, and the ideas it advanced remain unaccounted for in present-day work on linguistic diversity in composition.

The way in which another form of basic-writing pedagogy gained a foothold at CUNY during this period further underscores how political conservatism sealed the fate of the LCRG curriculum. As seen in the previous section, back-to-basics discourse successfully opposed "political" pedagogies, particularly those like the LCRG's that countered the "miseducation" of minority students, against the university's standards of academic excellence. Bruce Horner, in his analysis of the material and institutional conditions of CUNY's early open admissions years, shows how compositionists, already marginalized within CUNY, ensured their institutional existence in the face of this discourse. Specifically, compositionists argued they would prepare SEEK

students to fit into the academic system rather than challenge the narrow definition of "academic excellence" that functioned to make higher education an
exclusive community (207–08). As Horner suggests, compositionists reinforced their argument by teaching students basic writing "skills," and focused
their research efforts on developing, in Shaughnessy's words, "more efficient
and challenging ways of teaching grammar and mechanics" (qtd. in Horner
209).[14] Basic-writing pedagogy survived, Horner argues, because it preserved
the back-to-basics movement's distinction between academics and society's
political and economic concerns.

In some respects, the LCRG's project fit this dominant approach to writing
instruction, for half of the textbook manuscript crafts a more efficient approach
for teaching BEV-speaking students to write SE prose. However, because the
textbook manuscript's reading materials, writing assignments, and research
projects brought linguistic politics into the composition classroom, more widespread adoption of the LCRG's project could have threatened the already
tenuous position of CUNY's writing programs. Horner's analysis illustrates
how material and institutional conditions, by enabling one pedagogy/research
agenda among many to secure a dominant position within the discipline,
effectively narrowed the range of what many scholars see as possible within
basic-writing classrooms. Recovering the history of the LCRG's project forti-
fies Horner's claim about the ways material, institutional, and political conditions affect our theoretical and pedagogical visions for enabling students to
do critical intellectual work.

In addition to this conservative atmosphere, the project's chances for survival may also have been lessened by the LCRG's focus on curricular reform
to the extent that it did not also address other factors affecting marginalized
students' participation in higher education. Certainly, the LCRG's emphasis
on curricular reform was essential, given the dominant focus at CUNY on
developing "more efficient and challenging ways of teaching grammar and
mechanics." The research group reinvigorated public education's democratic
values as it helped linguistic- and racial-minority students to deepen their
knowledge about their linguistic heritages and, in so doing, to develop an
intellectual base that traditional education had systematically denied them.
As Mary Soliday argues in her study of the politics of remedial education,
however, progressive pedagogical projects open themselves to conservative
critiques when, much as the LCRG did, scholars only address the cultural
conflict that marginalized students face as they work their way into the academy. While Soliday acknowledges the significant insights gained through
such analyses, she nevertheless warns they can also serve the purpose of critics who argue that open admissions students and the remedial instruction
developed for them perpetuate low standards and drains the university's
resources (105–06). Soliday's work, then, asks us to see how the LCRG's project could have been strengthened with analysis of how other material conditions affected students' access to campus, textbooks, and the time and space
needed for academic work, as well as how public underfunding of higher
education exacerbated these difficulties curtailing open admissions students'

access to college (19). By focusing solely on the need for curricular reform, the LCRG allowed back-to-basics supporters to sidestep discussions about the politics and economics of education and instead to target these very curricular projects that seemingly favored social promotion over academic integrity.

As we attend to students' material concerns, we also must better understand how the group's textbook manuscript, the CCCC's "Students' Right" resolution, and journals from this era created a limited representation of what Smitherman calls "the linguistic-cultural complexity of the composition classroom" ("CCCC's Role" p. 76). The almost exclusive attention to African American students and BEV in these materials signals that future recovery work needs to account for the presence of other students who faced linguistic and ethnic discrimination in open admissions classrooms. Victor Villanueva, for one, has prompted compositionists to begin to talk about the language politics of the "Students' Right" era in broader terms than just Standardized English and the Black English Vernacular. Consider his description of growing up in Williamsburg and Bedford-Stuyvesant, just blocks from the Brooklyn College campus:

> I was born in Brooklyn. Raised there with Black kids and Asian kids and one Mexican kid and Boricuas. My first language was Spanish; my first English was the English of the neighborhood, Black and Spanglish, or even a Black Spanglish. When I was 15, the family moved to California. I've been in the West (except for two years in Kansas City and trips abroad) ever since — with Mexican kids, Chicano kids, vato kids, pachuco kids, Indian kids, Asian kids, Black kids, and White kids. And the nonsense that Ricans have to endure in New York is the same nonsense that all the other kids of Color endure. (Qtd. in Smitherman and Villanueva 1)

Part of the motivation for revisiting the "Students' Right" document in the twenty-first century, Villanueva argues, is to account more fully for the Puerto Rican, Dominican, Cuban, African, and Jamaican students whose presence in composition classrooms of the 1970s has been elided in our disciplinary histories.

As mentioned in the introduction to this essay, the LCRG's grant proposals in fact stated that the researchers created the ESD curriculum for both African American and Puerto Rican students who spoke BEV, but the textbook manuscript and teachers' manual focused exclusively on African American language practices and cultures. It is unclear how, if at all, the LCRG prompted students to investigate how Puerto Rican and African American cultures intersected and diverged in the communities where students lived. Future work in recovering pedagogical projects submerged by dominant educational discourses of the 1970s could help us to understand more precisely how "Black English Vernacular" might have functioned as a blanket term that elided other forms of cultural and linguistic difference in college classrooms.[15] Such studies would direct compositionists' attention to the specific educational pressures that faced linguistic-minority students from Latino, Asian American, Caribbean American, Native American, and rural white communities whose language varieties have not been valued in the academy. Just as important, analyses of how "Students' Right"–era compositionists and sociolinguists responded to this language diversity can encourage present-day scholars to resee our discipline as one with a history of engaging, learning from, and drawing upon multiple language traditions.

Recovering the history of these projects gains special importance given recent efforts in composition to reinvigorate the "Students' Right" resolution. The CCCC Language Policy Committee emphasized the need for such efforts upon confirming that a majority of English language arts educators feel inadequately prepared to address the learning needs of linguistic-minority students (18–22). For that reason, the committee called for the CCCC to draft a "'Students' Right' document for the twenty-first century [. . .] that would reflect the last quarter century's advances in research on language and linguistic diversity" (33).

The fate of the LCRG's project also demonstrates the need for "advances" in research on linguistic diversity to be considered more broadly than by our discipline's customary measure of publication. Historical investigations such as this one should lead scholars to reconsider the widespread doubt, as Bruch and Marback describe it, that "the words of the ["Students' Right"] resolution have been anything more than empty" ("Critical Hope" xiii). These studies can also problematize the common perception, as Smitherman characterizes it, that the "Students' Right" resolution failed to bring change because "it was informative in terms of theory [but . . .] did not go far enough in praxis" ("CCCC's Role" p. 72). As we have seen, the LCRG researchers applied theory in a variety of ways. The textbook manuscript materials respected students' nonstandardized dialects, emphasized the rhetorical histories behind students' languages, and enabled students to build upon their linguistic resources in order to negotiate the demands of academic writing. The teacher-training workshops and teachers' manual prompted writing instructors to explore how their attitudes toward racial and linguistic difference had been shaped by social norms and how these attitudes in turn influenced their expectations of students' work.

This study of the LCRG therefore asks compositionists to view the CCCC's "Students' Right" resolution in a new light, as a heuristic scholars have used and continue to use for inventing ethical and productive responses to linguistic diversity. The "Students' Right" document surely has never been mistaken for an annotated syllabus telling teachers how to work through each class period and assignment. But, as this essay shows, the theory of students' right to their own language has prompted teachers to listen to students' experiences with and ideas about language, to enable students to begin creating their own scholarly identities through researching and writing about the languages of their communities, and to negotiate the institutional and political resistance to positioning marginalized dialects, languages, and cultures at the center of the composition curriculum. And there are other important, yet largely ignored, projects from the "Students' Right" era that we would do well to recover, such as the curricula developed by the Psycholinguistics Project

Staff working for the Chicago Board of Education and by writing instructors working for the Baltimore City Public Schools; the Bridge readers coauthored by Gary Simpkins, Grace Holt, and Charlesetta Simpkins; and the unpublished instructors' manual of activities and classroom assignments compiled for the CCCC by Smitherman, Elisabeth McPherson, and Richard Lloyd-Jones. The history of the LCRG as well as these other projects should inform "a 'Students' Right' document for the twenty-first century" because such historical analysis leads us to attend more carefully to how material, institutional, and political contexts can affect efforts to reform teacher training and situate linguistic and cultural diversity at the center of English language arts education.

Acknowledgments: I thank Cheryl Glenn and Jessica Enoch for sharing their insights and suggestions as they read countless drafts of this essay, as well as Keith Gilyard and Elaine Richardson for their encouragement to look to the archives in order to better understand our discipline's theories, policies, and responses concerning language diversity. I am also indebted to Deborah Holdstein and the CCC referees, who helped me to sharpen my analysis of how the Language Curriculum Research Group's work speaks to present-day concerns in composition studies. The expertise of Jonathan Green, research associate at the Ford Foundation, made it possible for me to navigate the foundation's archival materials. I thank the Ford Foundation for its permission to quote from its grant files. Finally, for her willingness to give generously of her time—on her birthday, no less—I offer warm thanks to Carol Reed.

NOTES

1. The LCRG stated in its initial Ford Foundation grant proposal that its curriculum materials were meant to help both black and Puerto Rican students whose writing reflected influences of the Black English Vernacular dialect (Reed, Baxter, and Lowenthal 1). The reading materials in the textbook manuscript, however, come almost exclusively from African American writers, the lone exception being Pedro Pietri's "Unemployed," a poem from his 1973 collection *Puerto Rican Obituary*. To reflect this emphasis on writings by African Americans and about African American culture, I have decided not to continue using the phrase "African American and Puerto Rican students" throughout this essay. That said, I discuss the implications of both the LCRG's elision and my own in the conclusion of this essay. I thank the CCC reviewer who directed my attention to this omission of Puerto Rican students as well as the consequences for our discipline's understanding of the educational and linguistic politics of the "Students' Right" era.

2. I use the designation "Black English Vernacular" in the present article in order to reflect the terminology used by many sociolinguists and compositionists during the period under discussion. In its teachers' manual, in fact, the LCRG foregrounded the significance of terminological distinctions about the language of African Americans. The project staff explained, for example, that the word "vernacular" in the term "Black English Vernacular" signaled that not all African Americans spoke the dialect (44). The researchers also encouraged teachers to let students invent their own labels for the language, since "Black English Vernacular," "Black English," "Inner-City Dialect," and "Nonstandard Negro English" were all created by non-blacks, a fact that often "was sufficient to create suspicion among Blacks about the terms and what they represented" (44).

Each of the terms in this designation has been subject to analysis and criticism since the 1970s. While linguist John Baugh made one of the earlier efforts to reintroduce "African American" as a term of self-reference instead of "black," the Reverend Jesse Jackson has been more widely credited for promoting the use of this designation in a 1988 speech honoring Dr. Martin Luther

King. Jr.: "Just as we were called colored, but were not that, and then Negro, but not that, to be called black is just as baseless. Every ethnic group in this country has reference to some cultural base. African Americans have hit that level of maturity" (qtd. in Baugh 86). Ernie Smith has critiqued the use of the term "English" to refer to the language varieties of African Americans because, he argues, even though African American Language varieties have borrowed extensively from English vocabulary, the pidgin and creole languages from which they developed were based on the grammar of Niger-Congo African languages, not of English (50–54). Smith thus contends that Eurocentric scholars "reveal an ignorance" of African American Language's origins by "using vocabulary as their basis for classifying Black American speech, while using grammar as their basis for classifying English" (57–58). Robert Phillipson, meanwhile, argues that although the technical meaning of the term "vernacular" is used to classify those languages "made up of the words and patterns grown on the speaker's own ground, as opposed to what is grown elsewhere and then transported," this term nevertheless stigmatizes those languages to which it is applied because it is almost always used, "both in its technical sense and in popular speech, to mean a localized nonstandard or substandard language in contrast to literary, cultured, or foreign language" (40). Finally, Geneva Smitherman began to use the term "language" instead of "dialect" in the mid-1970s in part to avoid the pejorative connotations almost always attached to the term. More significantly, she writes, "as I got deeper into the study of my Mother Tongue, it became starkly clear that the speech of Africans in America is so fundamentally different, in so many ways, from the speech of European Americans that it seems to get right up in yo face and *demand* that you address it as a 'language'" (*Talkin that Talk* 14).

Given this rich analysis concerning these designations, I will follow the contemporary practice of many present-day scholars by using the term "African American Language" when I do not directly refer to the texts and ideas of the LCRG and its contemporaries.

3. The LCRG also received funding from the following sources: the City University of New York Research Foundation's Faculty Research Award Program ($15,000); Brooklyn College's Search for Education, Excellence, and Knowledge Program's released-time funds ($15,000); the New York State Higher Education Opportunity Program ($5,000); and the New York Board of Higher Education ($25,539). All told, the LCRG received over $311,000 in funding from 1969 to 1974.

4. Among the LCRG's contemporaries who did cite the group's work, if only briefly, are Mina Shaughnessy, who provides a footnote mentioning the group's work on cross-dialect interference (157n14). and Robbins Burling, who presents excerpts from a controversy about the LCRG project that erupted in the pages of the *Crisis* in 1971 (109–10). Present-day discussions of the LCRG can be found in Keith Gilyard's "African American Contributions to Composition Studies," in which he surveys this same 1971 controversy (637–38), and Elaine Richardson's *African American Literacies*, in which she describes the theoretical foundations of the LCRG's textbook manuscript (14–15).

5. I use the term "Standardized English" instead of "Standard English" throughout this essay, following Romy Clark and Roz Ivanič, who do so in order "to emphasise that [the dialect's] privileged position is the result of an ideologically shaped process, not an objective fact" (211).

6. Lowenthal, with an MS in speech pathology and audiology, and Reed, who held an MA in German language and literature, both participated in the Linguistic Society of America's 1969 summer institute, where their course of study included descriptive linguistics and second-language learning. Milton Baxter, meanwhile, was working toward a PhD in linguistics at New York University, consulting in the Black English Linguistics Department at Brooklyn College, and entering a new teaching position at the Borough of Manhattan Community College.

7. In 1970, Reed worked part-time with Stewart at Columbia University's Teachers College, teaching about BEV to inner-city teachers enrolled in his "Introduction to American Negro Dialects" course. For a description of early pedagogical approaches to what he labeled a "quasi-foreign language situation," see Stewart.

8. Cohen and Redrick, both of whom held master's degrees in linguistics, joined the LCRG in 1970. One year later, Moore became both a member and the coordinator of the LCRG. Unlike the other researchers, Moore trained in the education field, earning a master's degree in education from Columbia University's Teachers College, where he focused on the philosophy of education and curriculum building.

9. When the LCRG used the term "Standard English" throughout its materials, it referred almost exclusively to the standardized *written* code of English. Not only did the researchers acknowledge that spoken standards differed from written standards, but they also wanted teachers to attend only to students' writing habits, not their speech. Being BEV speakers themselves, the researchers believed interference with students' speech in effect told them to reject a significant aspect of their identities ("Teachers' Manual" 57–59).

While the LCRG constructed its project, however, linguists were developing terminology to differentiate the spoken and written standards of English: Standard American English (SAE) and Edited American English (EAE), respectively. This distinction was meant to counter the argument made by E. D. Hirsch Jr. in *The Philosophy of Composition* that if one learned to speak Standard English, he or she would necessarily be able to write it (39). Although the CCCC's 1974 "Students' Right" background document reflects the then-emerging SAE-EAE distinction, I use the abbreviation SE in this essay to reflect the LCRG's practice throughout its materials for referring to written Standard English.

While the LCRG was developing its ESD curriculum, several linguists had begun to argue that learning to write Standard English was not analogous to learning a second dialect. For example, Carol Chomsky and Irene Moscowitz each showed that one's ability to write Standard English is correlated more closely with one's reading ability than with his or her spoken dialect (Hartwell 104). As Patrick Hartwell explains, this research connecting reading to writing would eventually erode support for bidialectalist and Standard-English-as-a-Second-Dialect pedagogies, based as they were on the claim that students' spoken dialects "interfered" with their writing (104–05).

10. The zero copula and the invariant *be* have been two of the most frequently studied aspects of African American Language. The term "copula" refers to the linguistic units *is* and *are* that couple, or join, a sentence's subject and its predicate; "zero copula," then, refers to sentences created without this joining unit, as with the absent *is* in the sentence "He at home now." The invariant *be*, meanwhile, describes habitual action or activities performed regularly, as illustrated in this sentence from the LCRG's teachers' manual: "When Nixon *be* saying that he is going to help Blacks, he really don't mean it" (48). As John Russell Rickford and Russell John Rickford note, even though quantitative sociolinguistic analyses of the zero copula and the invariant *be* demonstrate that African American Language is systematic, many people viewing the language from outside the culture fail to recognize that numerous rules govern its use, leading to uninformed conclusions that African American Language is ungrammatical or that its speakers are lazy and uneducated (109). For a succinct overview of grammatical rules governing African American Language, see Rickford and Rickford, Chapter 7.

Indeed, many educators and policymakers have misinterpreted, ignored, and in some cases outright rejected sociolinguistic analysis, using the zero copula and invariant *be* to support their arguments that African Americans were cognitively deficient relative to European Americans. Thomas J. Farrell, in his 1983 "IQ and Standard English," argued that black children's lower scores on IQ tests resulted from differences in grammar between their language and that of white students (477). Specifically, he claimed that because Black English did not fully conjugate the verb to *be*, Black English speakers, especially black children, could not develop the most complex forms of abstract thinking: "[T]he emergence of the verb 'to be' [. . .] affords a far more flexible sense of time than what was previously possible conceptually when action verbs alone dominated the language. The development of the copulative verb is very important because a language with only action verbs is not likely to develop propositional thinking" characteristic of the abstract thought articulated within Aristotle's science of logic (475). Farrell argued that if the grammar of one's language did in fact determine one's patterns of thinking, black students needed to learn the grammar of Standard English in order to develop fully their capacity for abstract thinking (477).

Baugh was among the many linguists and compositionists who criticized Farrell's invocation of the "difference as deficit" theory as well as his failure to acknowledge the influence of cultural and economic factors on students' IQ scores (12; 163n1). He noted that while access to written Standardized English literacy has often been restricted to those with political and economic power, "the cognitive interplay of *langue* and *parole*, so central to abstract thought, is available to all normal children in language acquisition" (12).

11. Hypercorrection occurs when a writer applies grammatical rules to irregular words to which these rules don't apply. For example, the common rule for SE pluralization calls for adding an *-s* to a noun. Hypercorrection might occur when a writer uses *-s* to mark plural nouns in cases where words do so by internal vowel changes instead; hypercorrection, then, would explain the pluralization of *woman* as *womans*. The LCRG had concluded from its extensive research on student writing that hypercorrection reflected the forms students most often wrote in, rather than fully BEV dialect writing ("Teachers' Manual" 196–97). As a result, several student essays in the textbook manuscript showed hypercorrection, and students were to revise these essays according to SE grammatical conventions.

12. Smitherman defines toasts as epic-poem tributes to a hero who displays fearlessness, defiance, and open rebellion in the face of white power (*Talkin and Testifyin* 157).

13. For one extended example of a pedagogy grounded on Eurocentric approaches to African American writers' rhetorical styles, see Fleischauer.

14. The original source of this quotation is Shaughnessy, "Basic Writing and Open Admissions," intradepartmental memorandum to Theodore Gross, 10 Dec. 1970, City College Archives, City College of New York. I cite this quotation indirectly in order to acknowledge its central importance to Horner's analysis of how attention to grammar and mechanics came to dominate the field of basic writing.

15. An example of such elision within composition scholarship can be seen in Marian E. Musgrave's 1971 *CCC* essay "Failing Minority Students: Class, Caste, and Racial Bias in American Colleges." In this article, Musgrave presents an important critique of how first-year composition courses "seldom meet the needs of minority group students, and in fact often destroy these students" (24), adding, "I am talking as much about Indians, Puerto-Ricans, Eskimos, Cubans, Mexican-Americans, poor whites, and Cajun French as I am about Blacks" (24). As she unpacks biased assumptions about "black dialects," however, Musgrave notes in passing, "for 'black' read Appalachian, Spanish-American, etc." (26), but then never articulates the similarities and differences in the biases faced by students from these linguistic communities.

WORKS CITED

Avidon, Elaine. Letter to Carol Reed. 26 Apr. 1972. PA70-444. Ford Foundation Archives.
Bailey, Beryl L. "Report to the Ford Foundation on Project Initiated by the Language Curriculum Research Group." June 1972. PA70-444. Ford Foundation Archives.
Baugh, John. *Out of the Mouths of Slaves: African American Language and Educational Malpractice.* Austin: U of Texas P, 1999.
Baum, Joan. "An Exhortation for Teachers of English in Open-Admissions Programs." *CCC* 25 (1974): 292–97.
Baxter, Milton. "Educating Teachers about Educating the Oppressed." *College English* 37 (1976): 677–81.
———. Letter to Marjorie Martus. 6 Oct. 1976. PA70-444. Ford Foundation Archives.
Berlinger, Manette. Letter to Carol Reed. 11 May 1972. PA70-444. Ford Foundation Archives.
Brodinsky, Ben. "Back to the Basics: The Movement and Its Meaning." *Phi Delta Kappan* 58 (1977): 522–26.
Bruch, Patrick, and Richard Marback. "Critical Hope, 'Students' Right,' and the Work of Composition Studies." Introduction. Bruch and Marback vii–xvii.
———, eds. *The Hope and the Legacy: The Past, Present, and Future of "Students' Right to Their Own Language."* Cresskill, NJ: Hampton, 2005.
Bruffee, Kenneth A. Letter to Carol Reed. 2 June 1972. PA70-444. Ford Foundation Archives.
Burling, Robbins. *English in Black and White.* New York: Holt, 1973.
CCCC Language Policy Committee. *Language Knowledge and Awareness Survey.* Urbana, IL: NCTE Research Foundation, 2000.
Clark, Romy, and Roz Ivanič. *The Politics of Writing.* London: Routledge, 1997.
Committee on CCCC Language Statement. "Students' Right to Their Own Language." Spec. issue of *CCC* 25.3 (1974): [pp. 19–57 in this book].
Farrell, Thomas J. "IQ and Standard English." *Coherence and Cohesion: What Are They and How Are They Achieved?* Spec. issue of *CCC* 34 (1983): 470–84.
Fleischauer, John F. "James Baldwin's Style: A Prospectus for the Classroom." *CCC* 26 (1975): 141–48. Ford Foundation Archives. Ford Foundation Research Center, New York, NY.
Gilyard, Keith. "African American Contributions to Composition Studies." *A Usable Past: CCC at 50, Part 2.* Spec. issue of *CCC* 50 (1999): 626–44.
Grognet, Allene Guss. Letter to Richard Lacey. 2 July 1974. PA70-444. Ford Foundation Archives.
Hall, Edward T. *The Silent Language.* Garden City, NJ: Doubleday, 1959.
Hall, Robert A. *Linguistics and Your Language.* Garden City, NJ: Anchor, 1960.
Hartwell, Patrick. "Dialect Interference in Writing: A Critical View." *Research in the Teaching of English* 14 (1980): 101–18.
Hirsch, E. D., Jr. *The Philosophy of Composition.* Chicago: U of Chicago P, 1977.
Horner, Bruce. "Discoursing Basic Writing." *CCC* 47 (1996): 199–222.
Kelly, Ernece B. "Murder of the American Dream." *CCC* 19 (1968): 106–08.
Lacey, Richard A. Letter to the Language Curriculum Research Group. 18 July 1974. PA70-444. Ford Foundation Archives.
———. Memorandum to Marjorie Martus. 12 July 1974. PA70-444. Ford Foundation Archives.
———. Memorandum to Marjorie Martus. 29 July 1974. PA70-444. Ford Foundation Archives.
Language Curriculum Research Group. "Final Report to Ford Foundation." 15 July 1975. PA70-444. Ford Foundation Archives.

———. "Students' Manual for Teaching Standard English Writing to Speakers Showing Black English Influences in Their Writing." Ms. 1972. PA70-444. Ford Foundation Archives.

———. "Teachers' Manual for Teaching Standard English Writing to Speakers Showing Black English Influences in Their Writing." Ms. 1973. PA70-444. Ford Foundation Archives.

"LCRG-CUNY Teacher-Training Workshop Sign-up Sheet." N.d. Appendix. Language Curriculum Research Group. "Final Report to Ford Foundation." 15 July 1975. PA70-444. Ford Foundation Archives.

Lu, Min-Zhan. "Composing Postcolonial Studies." *Crossing Borderlands: Composition and Postcolonial Studies.* Ed. Andrea A. Lunsford and Lahoucine Ouzgane. Pittsburgh: U of Pittsburgh P, 2004. 9–32.

Moore, Samuel A. Letter to Marjorie Martus. 28 Mar. 1972. PA70-444. Ford Foundation Archives.

Musgrave, Marian E. "Failing Minority Students: Class, Caste, and Racial Bias in American Colleges." *CCC* 22 (1971): 24–29.

O'Neil, Wayne. "The Politics of Bidialectalism." *College English* 33 (1972): 433–38.

Parks, Stephen. *Class Politics: The Movement for the Students' Right to Their Own Language.* Urbana, IL: NCTE, 2000.

Pennell, Michael. "Implementing 'Students' Right to Their Own Language': Language Awareness in the First Year Composition Classroom." Bruch and Marback 227–44.

Phillipson, Robert. *Linguistic Imperialism.* Oxford: Oxford UP, 1992.

Reed, Carol. "Adapting TESL Approaches to the Teaching of Written Standard English as a Second Dialect to Speakers of American Black English Vernacular." *TESOL Quarterly* 7 (1973): 289–307.

———. "Back to Square '2': Starting Over in the 80's." *Writing Problems after a Decade of Open Admissions: Proceedings of the Fifth Annual CUNY Association of Writing Supervisors (CAWS) Conference, April 3, 1981.* Ed. Carol Schoen. New York: Instructional Resource Center, 1981. 7–10.

———. Telephone interview. 9 Nov. 2003.

———. Telephone interview. 7 Dec. 2003.

———. "Why Black English in the College Curriculum?" Afro-American Institute of Brooklyn College Lecture Series. Brooklyn. 10 Nov. 1971.

Reed, Carol, Milton Baxter, and Sylvia Lowenthal. "A CUNY Demonstration Project to Effect Bidialectalism in Users of Nonstandard Dialects of English." Proposal to the Ford Foundation. 24 Mar. 1970. PA70-444. Ford Foundation Archives.

Richardson, Elaine. *African American Literacies.* London: Routledge, 2003.

Rickford, John Russell, and Russell John Rickford. *Spoken Soul: The Story of Black English.* New York: Wiley, 2000.

Sealy, Rose. Letter to Samuel A. Moore. 31 May 1972. PA70-444. Ford Foundation Archives.

Shaughnessy, Mina P. *Errors and Expectations: A Guide for the Teacher of Basic Writing.* New York: Oxford UP, 1977.

Sheils, Merrill. "Why Johnny Can't Write." *Newsweek* 8 Dec. 1975, U.S. ed.: 58–62+.

Shor, Ira. *Culture Wars: School and Society in the Conservative Restoration, 1969–1984.* Boston: Routledge, 1986.

Simpkins, G., G. Holt, and C. Simpkins. *Bridge: A Cross-Cultural Reading Program.* Boston: Houghton Mifflin, 1977.

Sledd, James. "Doublespeak: Dialectology in the Service of Big Brother." *College English* 33 (1972): 439–56.

Smith, Ernie. "What Is Black English? What Is Ebonics?" *The Real Ebonics Debate: Power, Language, and the Education of African-American Children.* Ed. Theresa Perry and Lisa Delpit. Boston: Beacon, 1998. 49–58.

Smitherman, Geneva. "CCCC's Role in the Struggle for Language Rights." *A Usable Past: CCC at 50. Part 1.* Spec. issue of *CCC* 50 (1999): [pp. 58–82 in this book].

———. Personal interview. 26 Mar. 2004.

———. *Talkin and Testifyin: The Language of Black America.* Detroit: Wayne State UP, 1977.

———. *Talkin that Talk: Language, Culture, and Education in African America.* London: Routledge, 1999.

Smitherman, Geneva, and Victor Villanueva. Introduction. *Language Diversity in the Classroom: From Intention to Practice.* Ed. Smitherman and Villanueva. Carbondale: Southern Illinois UP, 2003. 1–6.

Soliday, Mary. *The Politics of Remediation: Institutional and Student Needs in Higher Education.* Pittsburgh: U of Pittsburgh P, 2002.

Stewart, William A. "Foreign Language Teaching Methods in Quasi-Foreign Language Situations." *Teaching Standard English in the Inner City.* Ed. Ralph W. Fasold and Roger Shuy. Washington, DC: Center for Applied Linguistics, 1970. 1–19.

"Student Course-Evaluation Questionnaire." 4 Mar. 1975. Appendix. Language Curriculum Research Group. "Final Report to Ford Foundation." 15 July 1975. PA70-444. Ford Foundation Archives.

Trimbur, John. "Literacy and the Discourse of Crisis," *The Politics of Writing Instruction: Postsecondary*. Ed. Richard Bullock and Trimbur. Portsmouth, NH: Boynton, 1991. 277–95.

Ward, F. Champion. "Request for Grant Action." 22 June 1970. PA70-444. Ford Foundation Archives.

Wolfram, Walt. "Reaction to: For Teaching Standard English . . ." July 1974. PA70-444. Ford Foundation Archives.

Wright, Richard. "Reaction to *For Teaching SE* . . ." July 1974. PA70-444. Ford Foundation Archives.

20 From Language Experience to Classroom Practice: Affirming Linguistic Diversity in Writing Pedagogy

KIM BRIAN LOVEJOY, STEVE FOX,
AND KATHERINE V. WILLS

Teachers of college writing are responsible for helping students develop their abilities to write for varied purposes and audiences, communicate their ideas clearly, and use language effectively in academic settings. In today's classrooms, we encounter students with widely varying literacy backgrounds and skills, students who are linguistically and culturally diverse, most often defined in terms of racial and ethnic (nonwhite) background but also including white students whose home language is a non mainstream variety of English. Clearly, language differences are more commonplace than they were in the 1970s when "Students' Right to Their Own Language" was first adopted by the Executive Committee of the Conference on College Composition and Communication.[1] Indeed, as Peter Elbow (2004: 123) asserts in a special issue of the *Journal of Teaching Writing* devoted to linguistic varieties, "Linguistic difference is now unavoidable—especially for most teachers at all levels." Elbow echoes a reality about linguistic diversity that researchers in writing and composition have examined over the last half century, and it is surprising—even disheartening—that our pedagogy has not advanced to keep pace with these changes.[2] Arnetha Ball and Ted Lardner (2005), in their most recent attempt to redirect and revitalize our teaching practices, focus attention on the role of writing program administrators, who are in positions to lead and support efforts toward "unleashing" the literacies of linguistically diverse students. For a profession that has long been committed to equal access and social justice, a "sustained reform" of our pedagogy, as Ball and Lardner advocate, is the challenge that teachers must face if our goal is to make learning accessible to all students. Toward this reform, this article not only affirms but demonstrates how language experiences and reflection can create paths that lead to renewed pedagogy and classroom practices that embrace linguistic diversity.

Teachers of writing and composition continue to struggle with the implications of home and community languages as part of classroom pedagogy,

From *Pedagogy* 9.2 (2009): 261–87.

and most composition programs do not have explicit language policies or program initiatives that address linguistic diversity in the classroom. While teachers generally agree that linguistic and cultural differences represent a significant change in their work with students, many teachers have not begun to understand the role of linguistic diversity in education (in the teaching of writing, specifically) and the pedagogical implications of multiple varieties of English. On the one hand, most teachers understand the need to accept the language of their students on the grounds that it is the language of nurture, the students' home language. On the other hand, many of those same teachers who respect language diversity are unwilling to invite the students' language into the classroom. Often they understand the students' own language as serving purposes outside the classroom, and they are reluctant to explore or even consider the relationship between home/community varieties and the variety targeted in schools and universities—edited American English.[3] Such attitudes toward language and dialects are shaped by what John Trimbur (p. 136 in this book) calls the "relentless monolingualism of American linguistic culture," a force that silences not only other languages but also dialects of English often mistakenly thought to be "wrong" or "bad English." As educators, however, we are compelled to raise questions and explore alternative views of language if we believe some students struggle as language learners and writers because of home or community circumstances beyond their control. In today's linguistic environment, it no longer makes sense to teach writing as though *all* students share a common language or dialect. It is time to give serious thought to how our students' language varieties figure into instruction in the teaching of writing.

In contrast to teachers in the 1970s who had few materials to reform their pedagogy in light of a changing student landscape, today we have an impressive body of research to help us examine our beliefs about language and to shape our pedagogy. Maria Reyes de la Luz and John J. Halcon (2000) offer unique insiders' perspectives on the cultural and linguistic strengths or Latino/a students, providing rich ethnographic data to show that nurturing ethnic and cultural identities is the most effective pedagogy for critical literacy and success in educational settings. Drawing on theories of rhetoric and composition and on her own literacy experiences in a predominantly white educational system, Elaine Richardson (2003) reports on the effects of an African American composition curriculum on the student-participants' writing development, showing how knowledge about the language and literacy of African Americans in the teaching of academic writing can improve the literacy experiences of college students. In her recent book *Hiphop Literacies* (2006), Richardson explores the literacies of popular culture, again with the aim of broadening our understanding of literacies and valuing the wealth of knowledge our students bring to the classroom. Katherine Kelleher Sohn (2006), in an ethnographic study of Appalachian college women, reiterates the importance of respecting home dialects and ways of knowing and demonstrates the students' uses of speaking and writing to reach a fuller awareness of their identity. Eleanor Kutz, Jackie Cornog, and Denise Paster (2004: 66) describe a writing curriculum in which students explore their own language uses with the "tools of ethnographic research," transferring their analytical skills to a wide range of discourse types and styles—from home and community varieties to academic discourse. Despite the depth and breadth of these studies, Ball and Lardner (2005) remind us that teachers are not easily persuaded to alter their existing pedagogy and change their classroom practices. Geneva Smitherman (qtd. in Ball and Lardner 2005: 147), too, has expressed her own quandaries about such resistance:

> People listen to the information about the competence of language, they take it in and then—like cognitive dissonance—they exhibit language behaviors that are totally contrary to the information. There has to be something going on in the deep recesses of the minds of individuals such that the information that they have gained has no access to, or effect on, their behaviors. People have been given the information—the facts— but they still behave in the same old ways.

So how can teachers begin to reflect on issues of linguistic difference that affect growing numbers of our students and do so in a way that transforms pedagogy? How do we bring these issues to other writing teachers in order to influence sound pedagogy at the program level?

As teachers of college writing, we share the common goal of making learning accessible to our students, and we would like to see our writing program move in the direction of a more inclusive pedagogy, providing we can offer other teachers a clear sense of what we can achieve by addressing language differences in the classroom. Our aim is to collaborate on a way to approach linguistic diversity in the teaching of college writing. In order to change the way teachers think about language and diversity, it is important, certainly, that teachers share knowledge of the language policies adopted by our professional organization and the key research that supports those policies. It is equally important that teachers begin to reflect on their own language experiences, to engage in conversations about language with their colleagues, and to share these experiences with students. Each of us has lived different and relevant language experiences, some of privilege and some of prejudice, and these experiences provide a window through which to view the language and diversity issues that we face in the classroom and in society. In this article, we describe some of our own language experiences, ones we could as well share with our students. We show how these language experiences lead to specific teaching practices that we have used as a way of valuing students' language, moving them forward in their learning about writing and language, and teaching all students the rich meanings embedded in linguistic differences. We conclude with an assessment of our pedagogy and classroom practices, and how we can build on them to improve our teaching as well as shape the contour of our writing program. Our hope is that other teachers and writing program administrators will find our work instructive and purposeful in respect to their own efforts to make learning in the writing classroom a positive and productive experience for all students.

FROM LANGUAGE EXPERIENCE TO CLASSROOM PRACTICE

Katherine's Classroom

Kindergarten was not a safe place for me to grow linguistically. For the first day of schooling my Greek immigrant parents, Calliope and Vasilios, dressed me in an all-American outfit reminiscent of Dale Evans—the female western singer and television and radio personality of that era—a tan-colored skirt with buckskin fringe, a matching fringed vest, and a small tin star completed the outfit. My parents bubbled with pride as they walked me to University City K–6 Elementary School in St. Louis, Missouri, to begin half-day kindergarten.

That afternoon when I had returned home, my family and I gathered at the gold-flecked Formica kitchen table. My mother ladled three bowls of chicken avgolemono (egg and lemon) soup: three lemony tendrils of steam rose from the bowls. My father lifted me to his lap as he asked me in his demotic Greek dialect what I had learned during my first day in school: *Ti emathes sto scholio semera?*

I twirled the fringe of my cowgirl skirt and looked at my father's gray eyes as I assuredly said: "You stupid." After a stunned pause, my father, who had always been an exemplary student of human nature, asked me where I had heard that phrase, "You stupid."

I explained to him in Greek that a few of my kindergarten classmates pelted me with these words. No teacher had interceded. My dad patiently explained that my classmates were calling me stupid because I did not speak English yet and they could not understand me. The following day, as my father remembers it, I picked up a sycamore branch in the playground and whacked anyone who called me stupid. Needless to say, I was not easily daunted as a six-year-old minority language user because I understood my linguistic difference as a marker of my superiority, not inferiority. I was on my way to being a bilingual first grader.

To this day, my kindergarten experience flavors my practice of language diversity in the classroom as an assistant professor and teacher of college writing. One lesson I want all my introductory college writing students to learn is that language diversity need not be a reflection of inherent intelligence or writing potential. I tease out attitudinal differences that so many incoming freshmen have about what constitutes *proper* language use. I not only assign essays to help students with their college writing, I inform undergraduates about language diversity. For example, many freshmen confuse a foreign accent with grammatical precision, assuming that if someone sounds different, he or she must be speaking in structurally incorrect English. I explain that speakers with accents might have better syntax and grammar than native English users: they just have an accent. Or some students might believe that because a fellow student speaks Ebonics he or she can not code-switch to Standard English dialect, thereby being bidialectical (Wheeler and Swords 2006: 21). I might even ask students to consider Smitherman's (2004: 191) language-dialect debate: Is Ebonics a language in itself and not a dialect of

Euro-English? In addition to having my students write academic essays and read popular stories from readers, I ask them to consider differences between dialects and languages. I share my seminal language experience from kindergarten while making transparent my pedagogy, hoping to create a safe(r) writing and speaking environment.

Below I provide a case study in the form of quotations from class writings and interviews with first-year student "Roxanne Dell," a student in W131: Introductory Composition. The home language reflection assignment significantly helped Roxanne understand her literacy experience and then gain more confidence as she applied her writing skills in college. Roxanne had never considered how her personal language history shaped her language skills and affective attitudes.

Roxanne's parents were from Indianapolis, but her six brothers and sisters were born in different states. Until Roxanne was nine years old, she and her family lived in campgrounds traveling around Indiana, Kentucky, Georgia, Florida, and elsewhere.

INTERVIEWER: Before you took my class, had you reflected on your language experiences?

STUDENT RD: No. I had never thought about it before the question came up in [W131] class. . . . It was pretty amazing how it does all connect: my problems, my struggles, my hardships in middle school and high school . . . I see how not being in a stable home . . . I didn't have a place to call my school because we traveled all the time.

Roxanne reports that she feels much more confident and she has learned much from the W131 class. "In my literacy paper, I came to realize that everyone has a literacy experience that had an effect on their life [*sic*]. I never really thought about it but my literacy experience has a big impact on my life. Being raised by parents who loved to travel from state to state . . . , I now realize how all the transience has influenced my learning abilities as a child." Furthermore, Roxanne gained insights into the diversity of language experiences of her classmates: "In the beginning, I thought mine [home language experiences] would be different from everyone else's. I realized that there are plenty of other people that struggle and have literacy experiences that have had a big impact on their lives. Quite a few of them are, I guess you could say, negative . . . I feel I was not the only person struggling." Like Roxanne, when students are asked to reflect on their home language experiences, they begin to recognize and accept their and others' linguistic histories.

Once students reflect on their own home language experiences and contextualize them among their classmates' experiences, I assist students in better understanding the social, regional, and historical contexts of their language use. By making more transparent the scaffolding of their language use, students gain confidence in discussing their writing and speaking education and "miseducation." Walt Wolfram (1999: 47) presents a rationale for systematic and scientific incorporation of information about linguistic diversity through educational systems and public communication. He argues the following:

"(a) Beliefs and attitudes about language diversity are intense and entrenched; (b) there is widespread misinformation and 'miseducation' about dialects that pervade the understanding of this topic in American society; and (c) there is a critical need for informed knowledge about language diversity and its role in education and public life."

Like Wolfram, I agree that teaching edited American English coupled with dialect awareness would be more effective than teaching edited American English alone, if only to avoid dialect discrimination and raise each student's awareness of his or her idiosyncratic dialect (49). Wolfram supplies several activities and exercises for working through the myths of dialect; however, in my first-year composition courses, I prefer to contextualize dialect within class readings, student writing, and instructor writing. Because many of my students are from rural Indiana, they use regionalisms affectionately labeled "Hoosierbonics" by a colleague. I ask my students to compare Hoosierbonics to Hebonics, or Jewish vernacular, often used in the television show *Seinfeld* (Bernstein 2006, cited in Wolfram 1999). They quickly apprehend the fluid and even positive connotations to dialects.

In a graduate screenwriting course, I encouraged students to create dialogue that authentically reflects dialects from varied social classes, ethnic backgrounds, and regional locales. Chris Smith (a pseudonym), an aspiring fiction and screenwriter, had this insight after I shared my home language history: "I remember you talking about your family being Greek. . . . It is helpful to know that even [people with] PhDs face various cultural challenges. That was helpful to me because then I could see my characters being on various levels educationally. It helped me to understand my characters . . . that all characters exist as they are, not as we would want them to be. You don't want to make them something just so you can clarify their English." Having heard my home language narrative in the screenwriting class, Chris felt much more at ease incorporating his home language, derived from southeastern Kentucky, into his screenplay about his characters who move from the Appalachian hills to a midwestern city.

Chris reflected on the concept of home languages as it related to his screenwriting: "You really realize how different each culture is. It [my home culture] is a very separate, very distinct culture from the culture that exists two hours away in Lexington, Kentucky, and then two more hours away in Louisville, Kentucky, and then drastically different two more hours away in Indianapolis, Indiana."

Even though the dialects and language diversity of my students might be situated in Hispanic, Asian, or Indian languages or rural and urban vernaculars, students are at least surprised, often intrigued, and occasionally reassured when I share that I, too, have learned many dialects, ethnolects, sociolects, codes, and languages without having to compromise my identity or authenticity: schoolbook French; schoolbook Spanish; American slang; American Broadcast English; St. Louis, Missouri, General American; business dialect; edited American English; academic English; Hoosierbonics; Chicagoese; Valspeak; first-generation English; ESL; and demotic Greek, to name a few.

I direct multilingual language users or those who are uncomfortable with multilingualism in the American classroom to the 2000 U.S. census (U.S. Census Bureau 2003) that found almost 60 million people, or about 20 percent of the American population, speak and write in more than one language—and the trend toward multilingualism is expected to continue to grow. In my courses, I try to dismantle the inveterate notion among most of my freshman writers that they just need to learn the one proper way to speak and write *perfect* English.

Perhaps if my kindergarten teacher had been encouraged to deal with language diversity in her elementary education teaching program, she could have used my kindergarten mini-trauma as an introduction to a lesson on language and tolerance. In any case, I share these moments with my students today as part of my pedagogical scaffold (Schön 1983, 1987).

Kim's Classroom

I developed my interest in English language varieties after my course work in sociolinguistics in graduate school, where I was first introduced to the formal study of language, its structure, and its uses. Having struggled with school language through most of my education, I was intrigued by the distinction between *prescriptive* and *descriptive* grammars, or how we *ought* to use language versus how we *actually* use it. This distinction presented a different view of language than the one I had intuited from my school experiences. I had not thought about kinds of grammar before then, though I was well aware of my own difficulties with grammar in school. In elementary and secondary school, for example, I was frequently assigned grammar exercises that were unhelpful and frustrating, for me as well as my parents. Through college and even into graduate school, features of my oral dialect and idiolect (e.g., using the past tense of "go" as a past participle, as in I'*d went*) appeared in my writing and speaking in situations where a more formal variety was expected. Grammar was not something I began to grasp until I got into graduate school, where the structure of the language finally began to make sense to me. It was my course work in sociolinguistics that answered many of the questions I had about my language experiences in school.

I was fortunate to have working-class parents who valued education and who offered assistance when I needed it. My mother was usually the one to help with the details of homework assignments. My father, on the other hand, was helpful in the ways he touted education. He worked as a letter carrier for the postal service, and his interactions with people on his route often became the topics of conversations at the dinner table, lessons from the world outside. His love of reading was an early influence on my emerging literacy: books and the idea of writing things down, in a quiet work space I could call my own, appealed to me. However, I was not a particularly good reader or writer. I recall the times in sixth grade when I would meet in the library after school and read with my teacher because she had recognized a weakness in my reading ability. I was a slow reader. When I wrote papers, it was a painstaking task to get words into sentences that would carry my meaning. Writing with fluidity was as unnatural to me as reading from right to left, and I almost always got my papers returned with excessive marking of sentence errors. It was always about grammar and sentence style; rarely were comments directed to the content and meaning of my compositions. I was fortunate to have had a professor in college and two in graduate school who took an interest in my development as a writer. I probably would not be a teacher today if it were not for my persistence and their dedication. My college professor was the first teacher I can remember talking to me about something I had written—a paper about the bastard son Edmund in Shakespeare's *King Lear*. I learned to write because these teachers were interested in helping me to develop my ideas and to communicate them—by questioning, probing, insisting on clarity, teasing out connections and parallels, and talking about the craft of writing.

Interestingly, learning to write in a second language was as problematic as learning to write in my first language. I grew up in an English-French community just seventy miles south of Montreal, and I was required to take French in elementary school. I can remember the trepidation I experienced at the thought of learning in another language, but I was consoled by the fact that my mother spoke French fluently, having been raised in a bilingual home and having attended the same school when half the school day was taught in French. Though she never attempted to teach her children French, she spoke French with her three sisters, with the neighbors, and with people she would run into at the market. It was a language she used almost as much as she did English. Nevertheless, when I had to complete homework assignments in French and sought my mother's help, either with grammar or compositions, I got the same response from my teacher as I did when I wrote in English, the same red marking of my papers. My French teacher, in fact, told me not to ask for my mother's help. "She speaks a different dialect, Canadian French," the teacher would say, an admonition that made little sense to me. I understood that what I was learning in French was different—*a prestige variety*, the teacher said—but it didn't mean anything to me at the time because I didn't know the differences or why they would matter to anyone. When I wrote in French or in English, I was doing my best to communicate, to put sentences together in a way that conveyed my meaning; my teachers responded as though grammar and style dictated meaning, and because I was weak in these areas, I was, in effect, a meaning-less writer.

We are supposed to learn to write in school—to develop our abilities to compose in writing while also learning the intricacies of form and style. But when many students step into the classroom even today, they are taught the style and conventions of edited American English, often without substantive instruction in composition, in writing to convey and sustain meaning. Romy Clark and Roz Ivanič (1997), for example, suggest that teachers' insistence on correctness, while understandable in some kinds of writing, is often misplaced and damaging, affecting not only students who struggle with mechanical aspects of writing but also teachers who perpetuate language myths that they believe will ensure their students' success in society. These technical aspects of writing, Clark and Ivanič argue, are often generalized and used as criteria of quality, leading to judgments of intelligence and moral worth. Rather than focusing attention immediately on the conventions of academic writing, I want my students to understand grammar as "sociolinguistic practice" (Wolff 2005), for writing serves many functions and roles, including those of context, purpose, and social identities, all of which affect the choices we make as writers. This view of grammar suggests that students first *compose* their writing and attend to larger features of texts (e.g., focus, development, purpose, context) in their own language. Learning the conventions of academic writing is important and necessary, but students should also learn the importance of their own language or get to experience what they already know and can do with language. Donald Wolff (2005: 97–98), writing about grammar and conventions in *The Outcomes Book*, recalls a student he taught in a university course "designed for the weakest dialect writers," and this student achieved A work by the end of the term. However, when he congratulated her on her achievement, she said that she appreciated the grade but wanted "to avoid writing in the future." Although Wolff initially felt he had succeeded by helping the student achieve the university's standards, he writes, "I felt that I had failed, for my emphasis on academic prose had killed whatever joy she might have had in writing by making it grunt work. I take this as an emblem for a very real danger in stressing academic writing and its concomitant correctness." Enabling students to learn academic writing in the context of their own language was the intended outcome of the "Students' Right" policy. However, though it was clearly an important influence on the writing-as-process movement (Bruch and Marback 2005), the students' own language was never fully explored and used as a means of learning a new language variety. As educators, if we can agree that the *composing* features of writing should take precedence over grammar in writing instruction, then our pedagogy should be directed at how we can best enable students to trust their own language when they write.

Because of my own language experiences, I set out to discover as much as I can about the students' home/community language, and I naturally tend to identify more with unconfident or struggling writers than I do with reasonably confident ones. It's as though I know their fears and frustrations about writing even before they can articulate them. But I continually remind myself that the instruction and experiences I offer college students must be suited to their needs as writers, whatever those needs might be, and not just to the needs of the struggling writer. I teach in a mixed classroom of mainstream and non-mainstream students, some older, nontraditional students, but mostly white college-age students with increasing numbers of African American, Asian American, and Latino/a students. The challenge in mixed classrooms is teaching in a way that moves everyone forward in their development as writers, and in a class about writing and learning to write, the topic of language is rich in possibilities for raising awareness of difference and creating optimal environments for learning.

Despite the differences among students in my writing classes, students seem to share attitudes toward language, often reflecting misconceptions and untruths, language myths derived largely from their school experiences. For example, they express the belief that "standard" English is necessary and important in society and that any other variety of English is wrong, incorrect, lazy, or bad. They know from their own experiences that their language is functional and purposeful in their worlds outside the classroom, but they don't see its relevance to writing and to the acquisition of "standard" English. They see their own language as substandard and therefore irrelevant to school writing. Nancy Mack (2006: 56–57) reports that marginalized students "perceive themselves as lacking verbal aptitude" and "fear that their language habits are a potential target for humiliation at the university." Rosina Lippi-Green (1997) writes about how commonly held myths about language lead to language subordination. My interactions with students in class confirm that many have not had opportunities to talk openly about their language varieties in their study and practice of the English targeted in school. They lack fundamental teaching about language and its uses, and their language attitudes are often barriers to their learning.

For these reasons, I aim to give my students a broader conception of language than what they would typically learn in a traditional classroom. I want them to experience the language varieties within the class itself and to experience their own language as a meaning-making vehicle.[4] In self-sponsored writing activities, they express themselves in their own language to communicate meaning, in whatever form or style they choose. In the following excerpt, for example, Brett writes about his home language, his personal and community identity, and the disconnection he felt with "proper" English in school:

> I fight Authority and Authority always Wins! I remember first coming into this institution knowing that I will have to write papers, talk in front of people, and the worst of all read! Why? To me, learning to speak correctly was never presented to me as something as a necessity. Especially in the environment I grew up in. My friends and I grew up in working-class neighborhoods, and we spoke how we felt and were never corrected. In other words, a standard English was never spoken at home nor encouraged. When I graduated high school I had only passed junior general English. I flunked the English courses that were designed to prepare students for college level academics. . . . Growing up, I just couldn't bring myself to speak that way nor did I really know how. I felt that speaking proper really wasn't who I was. I was roughneck, a thug, a kid who'd go fishing, get drunk, smoke some weed, and most of all hang out at "Smoky's Corner." . . . My mom would refer to this place when she was scolding me for my rebellious behavior. "Your Dad and 'em would act that way when they were over at Smoky's Corner," she would harp. I didn't care! I loved it. I loved it all—this hickish–white trash persona. I call it the John Mellencamp syndrome. How could I be that way if I spoke proper? I fought authority, remember? Unfortunately to my dismay, I forgot about the end of the chorus—authority always wins. I accept my dialect, but I also accept the fact that I need to know the "standard."

I liked the fact that Brett was comfortable writing about his dialect and identity as a young man, bringing his own background and experiences into juxtaposition with the culture of the university. He demonstrates a good deal about his writing abilities in this piece—the way he frames the piece with references to authority, his use of questions to engage readers, the concrete details characterizing his identity, and the language he captures when he quotes his mother.

I insist that what my students produce must be meaningful, substantive, and coherent, and if the intended readers are outside my circle of experience, I ask questions of the text and the writer to be sure their writing fulfills its promise. Rather than insisting on "proper" form and style, on the conventions of writing we value in formal settings, I tell them it's more important that they hear the words on the page as they're read. Many students are preoccupied and stifled by form. I like to show them a passage from Richard Rodriguez's autobiography *Hunger of Memory* (1983: 1): "Once upon a time, I was a 'socially disadvantaged' child. An enchantedly happy child. Mine was a childhood of intense family closeness. And extreme public alienation. Thirty years later, I write this book as a middle-class American man. Assimilated." This kind of writing would not pass muster in most schools today, though it clearly possesses a powerful and richly evocative form and its meaning is intensely clear. This is one kind of writing I want my students to experience as both readers and writers. I want them to produce pieces of writing that others can read and react to, and allowing them to eavesdrop in reader response groups provides the motivation and incentive for them to revise and continue writing, especially when the writer begins to comprehend that his or her words mean something to readers.

For an assignment asking students to describe a culture they inhabit that may not be known or familiar to others, Andy, an African American student, began her paper this way: "There's this place I know where only cool cats go, artists, musicians, poets you know. A funky junky place where bop blows cool on smoke-stained eyes 'round ten round tables and forty square chairs in the long, narrow space, with fifty orange candles to give a glow to the place." She titled the paper "Funky Junky Smokin' Bar," which happened to be the place she liked to go when she needed to work on her art sketches. While most students used an expository frame to describe their culture, writing from the perspective of an observer rather than a participant, Andy chose a participant role, first describing her surroundings: "Juke box playing some crazy Miles shit. Swivel right. Check the stage; no music till nine. Look down at the bar top, scribbles and scratches, quotations, orations in black sharpie pen. Look up at the beat young mystery behind the bar; she's somebody's prose. Eyes follow mystic Yowza! butt to the mixing station to draw me a long pour wicked libation." Readers soon discover that she too is an artist in this bar, with her sketchpad in hand, waiting for the moment when her creative thoughts begin to flow. As she describes the surroundings, she conveys her inability to put lines on the empty page in front of her out of fear and a fast-approaching deadline. Finally, something happens—"The place is getting louder. Up on stage piano's undressed . . . Show time"—and it triggers an onslaught of ideas:

> Becoming part of the beat, mind mirrors sound, creation___alive! Rainbows into moving colors, voice moving in my head___*Do this, do that, shape this, curve that.* . . . I feel I see I fly free! White page gone, colors, lines. . . . Now this funky junky place got people all out in space. Claude caressing the ivory keys, melodic abstract inspirations, Frank's horn blows and blasts, bellows and bleats his pain. Glasses clickin', people smokin' and drinkin'. A sax man moanin' "Can't find a gig blues," sculptor blowin' hard about paying his dues, while this dude's in his notebook riff'n' with his pen, and another in my sketch pad scratchin' and scribblin' again and again, and home is a funky junky smokin' bar with ten round tables and forty square chairs and fifty orange candles and bop___blowin'___cool.

When I met with this student in conference, I could have coached her to adopt a more academic style and stance, but I chose instead to capitalize on what she was attempting to achieve in the paper. There is a clever, inventive use of language in the paper, with its rhythms, rhymes, and alliterations, which I wanted to validate as effective and communicative. She intentionally used a poetic style because it seemed to better represent the aura she was attempting to capture in her description. I encouraged her to expand on her description of the culture, capturing sensory details, and to accentuate the narrative embedded in the description since she had assumed a participant role. She envisioned her college peers as her audience and wanted to display her sketches as illustrations in her text, giving the narrative another dimension.

This kind of instruction in a writing classroom can release the creative energies of the writer, and it serves to model the way language works. Moreover, with these written pieces, as well as published pieces like the Rodriguez excerpt, teachers can find ways of talking about language to debunk the myths that freeze writers. With the diversity we are seeing in our classrooms, we must create space and opportunities for students to experiment with their natural, home language, making meaning and communicating powerfully, while also understanding the reality of a complex world that values "standards" in the language of wider communication. Certainly in every classroom the language of edited American English is a primary goal of writing instruction, but when taught in the context of a language-rich curriculum, it's easier for students to see how they can begin to incorporate their own realities, their own language, into the dominant discourse of schools and society.

Steve's Classroom

My first teaching job was in a context of language oppression. I was assigned to teach English in a church-sponsored secondary school in Hong Kong, in 1977, as a young MA graduate. I had signed up for the Southern Baptist equivalent of the Peace Corps. I learned that my assigned school was one of the relatively few schools in Hong Kong to use Chinese as the medium of instruction. Most Chinese students in Hong Kong, a British colony, studied all their subjects (except for Chinese language and literature) in English. The most prestigious university, Hong Kong University, used English as well. My mentor at the secondary school, a veteran missionary teacher, felt strongly that Chinese students should study in their own language. Consistent with her beliefs, she had become fluent in Chinese herself, attended a Chinese Baptist church, and adapted to Hong Kong Chinese culture.

For my students at that secondary school, English was a ticket to success in business and government, or sometimes an essential tool if they ended up emigrating to the United States, Canada, or England. But they struggled with English, and they struggled to overcome the barriers of an English-based, exam-oriented educational system. Few of them were admitted to an institution of higher learning in Hong Kong. Many of them were from lower-income, working-class families. Language was implicated in matters of socioeconomic class, social mobility, educational and occupational success, prestige, and status.

What I learned in Hong Kong has stayed with me. Teaching basic and first-year English at a community college in a midwestern city, teaching basic English at a major state university, and for the past sixteen years teaching a variety of writing courses at an urban commuter campus in Indianapolis, I have seen how education is held out to students as a way out of dead-end jobs, as a ticket to success in U.S. society, as a path to self-fulfillment. A key ability in this journey is mastery of edited American English. I have served as the gatekeeper of that English, as an elder who initiates others into this privileged community, as a representative of mainstream language. To some students, no doubt, I have been like a missionary from another culture—a dominant, successful, powerful culture that, no matter how beneficent the intentions of its purveyors, remains a sometimes oppressive culture.

I am not parroting politically correct jargon or spouting empty rhetoric. I am not trying to compensate for my sense of guilt at my part in this cultural and social drama, nor do I wish to lay a guilt trip on other English teachers. English language and writing instruction can be a source of liberation, too, for both students and teachers. But we have to see it for what it is, in all its manifestations. We have to see the "violence of literacy" (Stuckey 1990) as one aspect of the power of literacy in order to approach our task free of illusions, and we must be ready to inquire into our students' language backgrounds and contexts.

Because of those early teaching experiences and my learning about language and writing in graduate school, I often use a literacy or education narrative, at times a literacy or language autobiography, as an early assignment in a course. Both my students and I need to explore what language has meant for them in the past before we discover what it might mean for them in the future. English is a tool they can use, but they must recognize how it has been used to shape them. To be honest, they and I have not fully understood this reality. Too often, we simply plow ahead, soldiers in a parade-ground exercise or at times a march into battle, not questioning our orders or the justification for the war we are engaged in. A document such as "Students' Right to Their Own Language," when read afresh, strikes me as the Emancipation Proclamation might have struck some soldiers and citizens during the U.S. Civil War.

Students' literacy narratives often lead them to new awareness about the possibilities of writing; they are liberated from internalized constraints and limiting self-perceptions. Deborah, a returning adult student, discovered herself as a writer, as she notes in this reflective statement accompanying her writer's collage:

> The theme or point of this collage is my discovery that writing is not something just for other people. It made its own way forward as I read the parts of the different writings from the first workshop. I could see my stubbornness to think this might not be for me, then I could see the exploration of the possibilities, and finally I came to the realization that everyone has something to say as a writer just as everyone has something to say as a person. This is probably very simple to most people and yet I was not able to see it until now.

Other students, like Linda, realize that they flourish as writers when given certain freedoms:

> I intensely despise writing research papers that are supposed to fit a formal format of strict dialogue. Staying within the correct outline of the paper format is dull. I find those papers to be stark and dry without any originality. . . . In my Appreciation to Literature class I was able to write essays in my own personal style. I absolutely loved it and never wanted to stop writing; I would stay up all night and morning typing those papers.

Inviting students to bring other varieties of language into the classroom and into their writing is not easy, especially in first-year composition or even advanced writing courses, which often focus on professional, academic, journalistic, business, or technical writing. Those contexts constrain language use and have their own conventions for style, organization, and editing. Such writing tends to be done in mainstream settings where edited American English is the norm.

One way to invite students to use their home languages and other varieties of language is through multigenre writing. Since learning about multigenre papers from Tom Romano at a conference of writing teachers in Indianapolis (see Romano 2000), I have used this approach in various courses, including advanced expository writing (an upper-level course required of secondary English education majors and chosen as an elective by English majors and other students), the senior capstone seminar for English majors, and first-semester composition. Whatever their topics—and they have included biographies and memoirs of celebrities, authors, and relatives; explorations of issues in education, politics, and culture; quilting, state parks, house music, mentoring programs, and dance programs in public schools—students explore them in a collage of different genres, including dialogue, e-mail, letters, brochures, personal essays, news articles, feature articles, interviews, plays, anecdotes, short stories, poems, résumés, photo captions, speeches, recipes, instructions, profiles, and song lyrics. Some of these genres allow and in fact invite familiar, colloquial, and creative uses of language. Writers must think about their audience and purpose, both for the paper or project overall and for individual sections within it. An instant message conversation between two young people must reflect the language appropriate to such a genre and scenario, but must also work within the larger framework of the multigenre project to reach its intended audience, which might be a broader readership that needs to understand youth culture but isn't fully privy to its conventions. Thus, a student can use one or more of her languages (or dialects or idiolects, whichever term you prefer) in a deliberate manner, enjoying the freedom and power that comes from purposeful communication. Other students, the instructor, and often readers outside the university (such as family members and friends) can enjoy the wide repertoire of language employed in a way they might not appreciate if the student wrote a more "monolingual" essay, whether that be in edited American English or a nonstandard variety of English.

In future courses, I will more thoroughly integrate various elements of this language-sensitive approach to writing instruction. I would like to have students explore their own language and literacy histories and present fluencies; read, think, and write about issues that arise from language variety, such as bilingual education, multilingual societies, intercultural communication, and the impact of language on culture and thought; and experiment with language and style in multigenre papers.

In first-year composition last year, I began such an approach by having students read Rodriguez's *Hunger of Memory* and June Jordan's essays about language (see Jordan 2002) and having them do a writer's collage (a form of literacy narrative taken from Peter Elbow and Pat Belanoff's text, *Being a Writer* [2002]) and a multigenre collage. Students enjoyed writing in the collage and multigenre formats, and some did interesting things with style, but their language variety was mostly in terms of register, not dialect. Reading Rodriguez and Jordan helped students think about language and education in new ways, though I would say most students who chose to write about these issues argued against any radical changes in how language was used in U.S. schools. Students did empathize with Rodriguez's difficulties learning English in school while speaking Spanish at home, and for some students, their emotional response to his narrative outweighed any rational response to his own complex argument against bilingual education. Hannah wrote, "It is sad when English became the primary language they spoke in the home. I know that it is good to practice the language that you are striving to become better at, but also you do not want to lose your values from home, your native tongue." Even students who wrote papers arguing against bilingual education mostly drew on Rodriguez's story rather than his arguments for supporting evidence. For example, one student cited Rodriguez's family's desire for their children to assimilate: "His parents wanted Richard and their other children to speak English and to succeed in school so badly they were willing to sacrifice their way of life, their 'family language' as Rodriguez refers to it."

Similarly with Jordan's arguments about Black English: students resisted her logical points but were moved by the story of Willie Jordan (June Jordan's student, no relation) and his brother's killing by the police. However, some students found Jordan's essay convincing, such as Randi: "I also thought it was really neat to see them write out their spoken language. It made me want to try and write it out. I think it is a good idea for these students to be trying that, I do not see anything wrong with them taking ahold of their language and running with it. That is who they are and no one should change it." Moreover, students learn something about language choices available to writers from Rodriguez and Jordan. As one student wrote, "Reading *Hunger of Memory* and *Some of Us Did Not Die* gave me the opportunity to analyze the choices of other writers. Sometimes Richard Rodriguez wrote in a way that I didn't think was grammatically correct. I learned about artistic license and that a person doesn't have to follow the rules of grammar as long as he knows why he's doing it."

Beyond my own classroom, I would like to work with others in our university writing program to develop language policies and teaching strategies that effectively implement the principled policies we adopt. As the director of a National Writing Project site, working with teachers of kindergarten to college students, I would like to help them explore these issues in their own contexts, deepening their understanding of how language works and strengthening their commitment to an informed, democratic, just educational practice.

In some ways I am not so far removed from my teaching experience in Hong Kong. In the U.S. educational system today, standardized examinations are employed by a top-down system to impose control on teachers and students alike. The ruling class imposes its will, often in a heavy-handed manner (witness English-only statutes, immigrant bashing, and the conflict between poor urban youth and their more privileged teachers and administrators). Yet just as the reigning system in Hong Kong was threatened by the looming handover to the People's Republic of China in 1997, so the system in the United States today is threatened by demographic and political changes. As writing teachers, we are almost inevitably seen as missionaries from another, powerful culture by many of our students and their families, especially when we teach in diverse urban and rural settings (though no university is cut off from these social changes). How will we respond? We could help build linguistic fences around our schools. We could resign our missionary posts, but we would lose our ability to influence our institutions. Or we could respond as my mentor teacher in Hong Kong did, respecting students' right to their own *languages* and the many languages available to them, offering them linguistic choices, and even learning some of their languages.

RECOMMENDATIONS FOR PEDAGOGY AND PRACTICE

A number of important themes emerge in our descriptions of language experiences and classroom practices. As we think about how we can assist other teachers to reflect on their own writing pedagogy, we offer these themes as guides to other teachers' inquiries into the dynamics of linguistically diverse classrooms.

Our objective has been to show that reflecting on our language experiences is not only a way to design classroom practices but also a way to understand the struggles for language rights among those with the least power in our society and, equally important, to see our way through our profession's language policies to the pedagogical reforms that will change students' lives. This process of writing and reflecting on language experiences, as well as interacting with each other, is the seedbed for reenvisioning our pedagogy and how we use class time, what we want our students to experience, and what we value as educators. In this article, we recount different language experiences and their impact on the classroom practices we enact with our students. Katherine's early childhood experience shapes the classroom activities that engage her students and enables her to connect with language policies like that articulated in Students' Right (1974), to find meaning in its message, and to educate her students about language choices. Kim's personal struggles with written language as a white, working-class student help him to connect with students from diverse backgrounds whose discourses and practices differ from those of the academy. The language-rich environment of the classroom is the ideal setting for learning about linguistic identities and for introducing the discourse of academic writing. Steve describes a language experience while teaching in another country and his interactions with another teacher whose sensitivity to language changed Steve's own perceptions. His experience teaching in Hong Kong provides a critical language perspective that informs his reading and understanding of our profession's language policies. As we will point out later in this discussion, each teacher's language experiences create the pathways to understanding linguistic diversity and the pedagogy to communicate that understanding to our students.

Recognition and acceptance of linguistic differences in the classroom are fundamental to our understanding of social context. The linguistic experiences of students vary significantly, even in classrooms that are predominately white and middle-class. At our institution, most students are native speakers of English, but increasing numbers are bilingual and bidialectal learners. The language experiences we describe in this article illuminate the linguistic diversity that exists in every classroom, whether it be related to ethnicity, gender, class, or location. Indeed, the social context of the classroom — the linguistic identities of our students and the space in which these various identities can express themselves and flourish — is key to understanding who our students are and how we can help them develop their abilities. Zemelman and Daniels (1988: 51) write about the social context of the classroom as "our most powerful available tool in literacy development." Our attention to the differences in our students' literacy backgrounds is critically important to ensuring their success as learners. We believe that "safety" and "trust" are important elements of successful writing classrooms — that students need to feel safe if they are going to write and show growth in their writing. This is especially true for students who have struggled because of their language differences. Eileen

Kennedy (2003), for example, invited her Creole-speaking students to write in Creole, but at first she wasn't successful because her students had never done it before, had never been asked to, and some didn't know how (there were no orthographic standards). However, when she began to relate her own experiences with language prejudice and to gain their trust, they began to experiment with their language and tell their stories. Kennedy reports that enabling her students to write in their home language was instrumental in helping them acquire the conventions of edited American English. Both Katherine and Kim have experienced classrooms where their home language was not valued, and all three of us have found some of our students opening up as writers when they discerned the classroom environment as safe and accepting of all language varieties.

Besides recognizing and accepting these differences, it is also important to explore their value in learning and teaching. Certainly one way to value our students' backgrounds and experiences is through their critical engagement with course readings that reflect their worlds, as Valerie Felita Kinloch (p. 429) so aptly demonstrates. For students learning to write, a pedagogy that validates their home and community language varieties taps into their personal resources for learning and enables them to connect with the curriculum. These are the varieties that are often barred from the classroom, that represent our students' own textual worlds, and that can form the basis for instruction in academic writing. L. S. Vygotsky's (1978) "zone of proximal development" supports the view that students who use nonmainstream varieties are more likely to succeed in learning more formal varieties if they can build on what they already know and do as language users. Likewise, students who are raised in homes and communities where they hear mainstream English (or a variety closer to the language of schools) can enrich their learning experience—their ability to write effectively—by understanding how language defines and expresses different individual and cultural realities. As we have attempted to show, our own language experiences can inform our teaching and help us to appreciate how a changing classroom climate invites new conceptions of what literacy means in twenty-first-century America.

Self-sponsored writing, literacy histories/autobiographies, multigenre writing, and imaginative writing are effective ways to teach composing skills while valuing students' own language and experiences. Although an important goal of first-year composition is to help students do effective academic writing in university courses, the best *academic* writing is done by those who develop fluency as writers in many genres and for a variety of purposes and audiences. We believe students will be more successful as writers when they examine their attitudes toward writing and language and when they explore the possibilities of writing, even in a playful manner. All three of us have students do some kind of literacy autobiography or literacy narrative as a way of taking stock, of reflecting on the sources of their writing attitudes and abilities. Inviting students to include their language experiences in such literacy histories can lead to important insights. Reading literacy and language narratives (including those of the instructor) allows students to see that their experiences are not unique; they can be encouraged by comparing their experiences to those of published writers, and they can become more open to the language varieties of their classmates.

Because we also believe in inviting students to bring their home and outside languages into their writing, we offer writing assignments that might not seem strictly academic. Self-sponsored writing has been touted by writing teachers for many years, but it is especially important in a linguistically diverse classroom. The students in Kim's classroom write on subjects of their own choosing, on subjects they know about, and sometimes in language varieties particular to those subjects and settings.

Multigenre assignments create space for students' creativity and ingenuity while also doing intellectual work in the academy. Even if other instructors never assign such multigenre papers, students in a writing class often become engaged by research questions and the opportunity to communicate their learning in a variety of genres. Steve hopes his students will carry this excitement about intellectual inquiry and interesting communication into other classrooms or professional settings. He also wants to see if students can be invited to use more varieties of language in multigenre papers.

Imaginative writing assignments, such as the screenwriting Katherine writes about above, allow student writers to explore authentic language as they create characters and their dialogue. Although creative writing classrooms might be considered exempt from the rules that govern writing and language use in other classrooms, in fact even creative writing teachers must consider their students' language backgrounds and help students understand what readers will accept and when they can expand the possibilities of written language, challenging their readers. And within first-year writing courses, imaginative writing (perhaps as part of multigenre papers) may have a valuable role to play. Within an imaginative text, a student can explore varieties of language and even juxtapose those varieties.

Language education is important to both mainstream and nonmainstream students. If all students are going to develop healthy and informed attitudes toward language differences, we need to talk about language differences and what they signify. As students and teachers alike reflect on their language experiences related to gender, class, region, ethnicity, as well as color, they learn to be better readers and communicators. They heighten their awareness of the plethora of dialects. Teaching awareness and respect for different dialects, speech communities, home languages, L1s and L2s, and so on does not obviate the need to teach edited American English; rather, the teaching of language diversity enhances students' and teachers' rhetorical toolbox and makes for more effective communication to a wider variety of audiences.

Heightening language awareness is not just for students. Many K–16 teachers would benefit from teacher training and self-reflection about language. Smitherman and Villanueva (2003: 4) call for the inclusion of "a course on language awareness and American dialects" in the training of English teachers at all levels. Similarly, Kim Brian Lovejoy (2003: 95) states, "To meet the challenge of diversity, English teachers must begin to fill the gaps in knowledge created by teacher preparation programs that emphasize literary study with little, if any, attention to the teaching of writing in diverse cultures." Teacher education programs, literature and composition graduate programs, and professional development for veteran teachers can improve learning through instruction in language diversity. Our pedagogy should be aware of the social conditions and classroom demographics surrounding us.

We need to explore the pedagogical implications of our profession's language policies and to sustain our progress toward pedagogical reform. As Scott Wible (p. 353) points out in his historical article on the Language Curriculum Research Group (LCRG) of the late 1960s and early 1970s, teachers have developed classroom strategies for honoring and building on students' multiple languages and literacies. In the case of the LCRG, their work came into conflict with a resurgence of back-to-basics reform and political and social conservatism. Recently, a number of books, articles, and conference presentations have begun exploring classroom implementation of the "Students' Right" policy. Once again, such promising work could remain marginalized or suppressed by the latest version of the "back to the basics" educational movement. In a climate that emphasizes standardized testing under the guise of advocating educational success for all students, policies and practices that highlight language diversity may meet with a chilly welcome. Another problem is teacher ignorance and apathy. Even with a required linguistics course or two, or multicultural emphases in methods courses, how many teachers have enough knowledge about language diversity, and enough confidence, to create innovative classrooms that use language diversity to promote acquisition of multiple discourses and critical thinking about those discourses? Policies alone will not reach many of these teachers, or will not touch them deeply enough to create lasting change.

We think many teachers would find effective the process we narrate in our language and teaching stories above: reflecting on their own language experiences, followed by conversations with colleagues, and then moving into their classrooms with this heightened awareness. Such "consciousness raising" may provide more fertile ground for implementing particular teaching strategies offered by monographs and articles and developed by teachers themselves in their local contexts. The process of remembering, reflecting, reading, and applying will be recursive, entered into at different points, and reentered as needed. The authors of this article try to help our students engage in similar reflection and conversation to affect their writing and language practice. We also want to invite teachers in our programs and departments to reflect on their experiences and have such conversations. We may find it easier to integrate policies and practices when we make personal connections to our own and others' language experiences.

Making our profession's language policies and the underlying theories more personal and local must be done with a firm grounding in linguistic and rhetorical knowledge, and with attention paid to political, social, and economic factors. As Wible (p. 373) cautions, "By focusing solely on the need for curricular reform, the LCRG allowed back-to-basics supporters to sidestep discussions about the politics and economics of education." Teachers should be encouraged to make new knowledge through teacher research projects. Changing professional practices is difficult enough; changing professional assumptions, attitudes, and goals seems quixotic. Renee Blake and Cecilia Cutler (2003), in a study of five secondary schools in New York City and their teachers' attitudes toward linguistic differences, found that schools' philosophies that promoted linguistic diversity influenced teachers' disposition and sensitivity toward students whose language varieties differed from the mainstream. This institutional infrastructure is a necessary component of teacher reform. Like all revolutionary change, however, changing the way we view language diversity in the classroom will require reaching individual teachers one by one, in small groups. As the authors of the "Students' Right" policy state, "We affirm strongly that teachers must have the *experiences* and training that will enable them to respect diversity and uphold the right of students to their own language" (p. 19; emphasis added). If teachers can put themselves into the "Students' Right" statement, they are more likely to bring the statement into their classrooms by engaging students in diverse uses of language and thus enabling them to express their meanings in multiple ways. This broader conception of language and literacy is premised on teachers' sensitivity to differences in their classrooms that serve the purposes of education for all students.

NOTES

1. "Students' Right to Their Own Language" was passed by the membership of the Conference on College Composition and Communication Conference in April 1974, and the resolution, along with supporting background material, appeared as a special issue of *College Composition and Communication* in the fall of the same year (see pp. 19–57 in this book). The resolution challenged teachers to rethink how they use and respond to students' language and advocated the teaching of edited American English within the context of other Englishes. For a discussion of this resolution and its history, see Smitherman 2003. See also the Linguistic Society of America's 1996 "Statement on Language Rights" (lsadc.org/info/lsa.res.rights.cfm).

2. See, for example, Smitherman and Villanueva 2003, Redd and Webb 2005, and Nero 2006.

3. Because of the diversity of our linguistic and cultural heritage, we prefer to use "edited American English" instead of "standard English," which perpetuates the myth of a universal American standard. As Bean et al. (2003: 37) report, "The rise of 'world Englishes' around the globe is causing diverse varieties of English to be widely used, published, and sanctioned, thereby creating contexts in which the idea of a 'standard English' is recurrently questioned and critiqued."

4. Julie Hagemann (2001) provides a sociolinguistic explanation for an overt pedagogy that values the home language of nonmainstream students, but she places all emphasis on code-switching, making students aware of their own language and how it varies from edited American English. She argues that doing so makes students less defensive about their language and more open to learning the conventions of academic English. While this approach offers teachers a useful strategy, we would argue that it is equally important to create opportunities for students to use their own language in writing situations in which code-switching would be inappropriate and unnecessary.

WORKS CITED

Ball, Arnetha E., and Ted Lardner. 2005. *African American Literacies Unleashed: Vernacular English and the Composition Classroom*. Carbondale: Southern Illinois University Press.

Bean, Janet, et al. 2003. "Should We Invite Students to Write in Home Languages? Complicating the Yes/No Debate." *Composition Studies* 31.1: 25–42.

Bernstein, Cynthia. 2006. "More than Just Yada, Yada, Yada: Jewish English." In *American Voices: How Dialects Differ from Coast to Coast*, ed. Walt Wolfram and Ben Ward, 251–57. Malden, MA: Oxford.

Blake, Renee, and Cecilia Cutler. 2003. "AAE and Variation in Teachers' Attitudes: A Question of School Philosophy?" *Linguistics and Education* 14.2: 163–94.

Bruch, Patrick, and Richard Marback. 2005. *The Hope and the Legacy: The Past, Present, and Future of "Students' Right to Their Own Language."* Cresskill, NJ: Hampton.

Clark, Romy, and Roz Ivanič. 1997. "Issues of Correctness and Standardisation in Writing." In *The Politics of Writing*, ed. Romy Clark and Roz Ivanič, 187–216. New York: Routledge.

Elbow, Peter. 2004. "Alternative Languages: Losers Weepers, Savers Keepers." *Journal of Teaching Writing* 21: 123–38.

Elbow, Peter, and Pat Belanoff. 2002. *Being a Writer: A Community of Writers Revisited*. New York: McGraw Hill.

Hagemann, Julie. 2001. "A Bridge from Home to School: Helping Working Class Students Acquire School Literacy." *English Journal* 90: 74–81.

Jordan, June. 2002. *Some of Us Did Not Die: New and Selected Essays of June Jordan*. New York: Basic Books.

Kennedy, Eileen. 2003. "Writing in Home Dialects: Choosing a Written Discourse in a Teacher Education Class." *Quarterly* 25.2. www.writingproject.org/cs/nwpp/print/nwpr/571.

Kinloch, Valerie Felita. 2005. "Revisiting the Promise of 'Students' Right to Their Own Language': Pedagogical Strategies." *College Composition and Communication* 57.1: [pp. 429–52 in this book].

Kutz, Eleanor, Jackie Cornog, and Denise Paster. 2004. " Beyond Grammar: Building Language Awareness in the Writing Classroom." *Journal of Teaching Writing* 21: 65–82.

Lippi-Green, Rosina. 1997. *English with an Accent: Language, Ideology, and Discrimination in the United States*. London: Routledge.

Lovejoy, Kim Brian. 2003. "Practical Pedagogy for Composition." In Smitherman and Villanueva 2003: 89–108.

Mack, Nancy. 2006. "Ethical Representations of Working-Class Lives: Multiple Genres, Voices, and Identities." *Pedagogy* 6: 53–78.

Nero, Shondel J., ed. 2006. *Dialects, Englishes, Creoles, and Education*. Mahwah, NJ: Lawrence Erlbaum.

Redd, Teresa M., and Karen Schuster Webb. 2005. *A Teacher's Introduction to African American English: What a Writing Teacher Should Know*. Urbana, IL: NCTE.

Reyes de la Luz, Maria, and John J. Halcon, eds. 2000. *The Best for Our Children: Critical Perspectives on Literacy for Latino Students*. New York: Teachers College Press.

Richardson, Elaine. 2003. *African American Literacies*. New York: Routledge.

———. 2006. *Hiphop Literacies*. New York: Routledge.

Rodriguez, Richard. 1983. *Hunger of Memory: The Education of Richard Rodriguez*. New York: Bantam.

Romano, Tom. 2000. *Blending Genre, Altering Style: Writing Multigenre Papers*. Portsmouth, NH: Boynton/Cook.

Schön, Donald. 1983. *The Reflective Practitioner*. New York: Basic Books.

———. 1987. *Educating the Reflective Practitioner*. San Francisco: Jossey-Bass.

Smitherman, Geneva. 2003. "The Historical Struggle for Language Rights in CCCC." In Smitherman and Villanueva 2003: 7–39.

———. 2004. "Language and African Americans: Movin On Up a Lil Higher." *Journal of English Linguistics* 22.3: 186–96.

Smitherman, Geneva, and Victor Villanueva, eds. 2003. *Language Diversity in the Classroom: From Intention to Practice*. Carbondale: Southern Illinois University Press.

Sohn, Katherine Kelleher. 2006. *Whistlin' and Crowin' Women of Appalachia: Literacy Practices since College*. Studies in Writing and Rhetoric. Carbondale: Southern Illinois University Press.

Stuckey, J. Elspeth. 1990. *The Violence of Literacy*. Portsmouth, NH: Boynton/Cook.

"Students' Right to Their Own Language." 1974. Special issue of *College Composition and Communication* 25: [pp. 19–57 in this book].

Trimbur, John. 2006. "Linguistic Memory and the Politics of English Only." *College English* 68: [pp. 127–39 in this book].

U.S. Census Bureau. 2003. *Language Use and English-Speaking Ability: 2000*. www.census.gov/prod/2003pubs/c2kbr-29.pdf. Accessed 10 August 2006.

Vygotsky, L. S. 1978. *Mind and Society: The Development of Higher Mental Processes*. Cambridge, MA: Harvard University Press.

Wheeler, Rebecca S., and Rachel Swords. 2006. *Code-Switching: Teaching Standard English in Urban Classrooms*. Urbana, IL: NCTE.

Wible, Scott. 2006. "Pedagogies of the 'Students' Right' Era: The Language Curriculum Research Group's Project for Linguistic Diversity." *College Composition and Communication* 57: [pp. 353–80 in this book].

Wolff, Donald. 2005. "Knowledge of Conventions and the Logic of Error." In *The Outcomes Book: Debate and Consensus after the WPA Outcomes Debate*, ed. Susanmarie Harrington, Keith Rhodes, Ruth Overman Fischer, and Rita Malenczyk, 97–103. Logan: Utah State University Press.

Wolfram, Walt. 1999. "Dialect Awareness Programs in the School and Community." In *Language Alive in the Classroom*, ed. Rebecca Wheeler, 47–66. Westport, CT: Praeger Greenwood.

Zemelman, Steven, and Harvey Daniels. 1988. *A Community of Writers: Teaching Writing in the Junior and Senior High School*. Portsmouth, NH: Heinemann.

21

The Reflection of "Students' Right to Their Own Language" in First-Year Composition Course Objectives and Descriptions

STUART BARBIER

Recently, three publications revisited the Conference on College Composition and Communication's 1974 "Students' Right to Their Own Language" (SRTOL) Resolution (p. 19 in this book): Geneva Smitherman's essays "CCCC and the 'Students' Right to Their Own Language'" and "CCCC's Role in the Struggle for Language Rights" (p. 58) and Stephen Parks' book *Class Politics: The Movement for the Students' Right to Their Own Language.* While both authors explore the history of the SRTOL resolution, they differ in their approaches to and interpretations of this history. Smitherman, focusing on composition theorists, highlights "CCCC's historical role in the struggle for language rights" ("CCCC's Role" p. 58) and concludes that even though it "has not always stepped decisively and swiftly to the challenge," CCCC can be proud of its "record as advocate for those on the linguistic margins" (p. 58) and "can win" (p. 80) the continuing struggle. Parks positions his historical review within student, class, and coalition politics (8, 17), concludes that the SRTOL is "the symbol of a time past" (204) that has "never garnered wide support" (203), and argues that "perhaps a new statement is needed" (17). Both authors made me wonder what the actual status of the SRTOL resolution is within colleges today. Is there any evidence of support for the resolution or lack thereof? Is there any sign that composition teachers can win the struggle? Both of these questions—and their implications—are important.

My interest in the issue at the heart of these questions was initially sparked when I was a graduate student and intensified when I was hired to teach writing at Delta College, a community college in mid-Michigan. One of the objectives for Delta's first-year composition course states that students are to "employ the conventions of standard written English." This objective is one of six classified under the overall outcome of being able to "write a formal college composition for a specific audience and purpose." This struck me as a possible contradiction; if an audience and purpose are better served by using African American Language (AAL), for example, why should this language

From *Teaching English in the Two-Year College* 30.3 (2003): 256–68.

not be used? Does the term "formal academic composition" necessarily exclude AAL? Further study of the issue led me to Smitherman's and Parks' publications, among others, which led me to question the status of standard English in composition departments at other schools, as expressed in written first-year composition course objectives and descriptions. In other words, do such objectives show support for the resolution? If not, can this be changed? To answer these questions, I decided to undertake a study and propose a change to the standard written English (SWE) course objective at my own institution, a proposal that ultimately passed, and one that I would encourage other institutions to make.

In order to make this study manageable and to make comparisons to my own college easier (to help support my resolution to my division), I chose to look specifically at other community colleges in Michigan. First, though, I reconstructed the history of the SWE statement at Delta College. How did it come about? Was it the focus of debate?

The History of the Standard Written English Objective at Delta College

Delta College formalized its course outcomes and objectives (O/Os) in 1996–97 after the vice president of instruction and learning services mandated that each academic division in the college write and approve what they felt each course should require and accomplish. Prior to this, instructors were mostly on their own to set such requirements. Now, while instructors still write their own syllabi and choose their own texts and materials, they have to include (and presumably meet) the departmentally mandated O/Os. In the English Division, different committees were formed to write the O/Os for the various courses. The committee to write the O/Os for English 111, Delta's first-year composition course, was headed by Sylvia Robins, associate professor of English. In an interview, she stated that the wording for the SWE objective came from a workshop she attended at Delta at the time conducted by Notre Dame's Barbara Walvoord, the noted researcher in assessment. In the workshop, Walvoord shared her "Policy for the Use of Edited Standard Written English Conventions," a one-page handout she provides students that sets out why she requires SWE and what she means by it. In the first part of the handout, she explains that language constantly changes, and that different variations exist for different groups separated by geographical region or culture. She states that no variation is " 'better' in any absolute sense—just different." She further states:

> However, a common societal pattern is that the ruling class imposes its form of language on everyone else. In the U.S., the "standard" is the form of the white middle and upper classes. Forms developed by people who have been economically, culturally, or geographically separated are often incorrectly considered "bad" English. But actually such forms are different, not "bad." Each form has its own rules and its own uses.

> One of the tasks of a good education is to make you aware of these facts about language. Another task of education, however, is to prepare you to function effectively in the world where readers generally expect you to control Edited Standard Written English (ESWE). Thus, in this class, too, you must use ESWE. (1)

According to Robins, there was "hardly any debate" in the division about adopting the SWE objective. No mention was made in the English 111 O/Os about a student's right to his or her own language, nor was an outcome or objective developed that was related to making students (82 percent of whom are European American and 7.1 percent African American [Delta College 6]) aware of the reason SWE is required. In this regard, Parks seems to be correct in calling the SRTOL resolution "history." Does this mean, though, that the resolution is "history" at other institutions or that the struggle cannot be won?

Before answering these questions, I feel it would be helpful to review a bit of the history behind the SRTOL resolution for those who may be unfamiliar with it.

THE CCCC's "STUDENTS' RIGHT TO THEIR OWN LANGUAGE" RESOLUTION

In a special issue of *College Composition and Communication* (Fall 1974), the Conference on College Composition and Communication presented the "Students' Right to Their Own Language" resolution adopted in 1974, background information informing the resolution, and a bibliography for further reading. The resolution states:

> We affirm the students' right to their own patterns and varieties of language—the dialects of their nurture or whatever dialects in which they find their own identity and style. Language scholars long ago denied that the myth of a standard American dialect has any validity. The claim that any one dialect is unacceptable amounts to an attempt of one social group to exert its dominance over another. Such a claim leads to false advice for speakers and writers, and immoral advice for humans. A nation proud of its diverse heritage and its cultural and racial variety will preserve its heritage of dialects. We affirm strongly that teachers must have the experiences and training that will enable them to respect diversity and uphold the right of students to their own language. (see p. 19 in this book)

As Smitherman puts it, this resolution "was short, but powerful" and "had the effect of a bomb being dropped right in the midst of the English profession" ("CCCC" 376). This is not surprising, as, according to John Rickford, "any attempt to give vernacular varieties recognition or legitimacy in the schools is likely to be met with massive misunderstanding and vociferous public opposition—reactions negative enough to kill it" (266). The resolution was a major attempt to recognize other varieties and resulted from many years of work. But as Parks points out, the resolution passed with a low vote total, seventy-nine to twenty, a result of changes in the rules that allowed for a majority vote of those present and a quorum of only fifty (198).

Leading up to this resolution was a flurry of activity in language issues (though Parks would argue that it was a "slow process" [6]). Smitherman argues that the CCCC "organization has consistently provided a forum for scholars as well as activists to raise up the issue of language rights. The historical record of CCCC mirrors the contradictions of language policy, politics, and power that exist in the larger society" ("CCCC" 337). She then traces this history, beginning in 1951 with Lloyd's views on how a focus on grammatical correctness caused students to be embarrassed about their dialects (cited in Smitherman, "CCCC's Role," p. 58). Smitherman explains that the articles appearing in the 1950s and 1960s still advocated teaching the "social inadequacy of nonstandard forms" ("CCCC" 380), but in the late 1960s and early 1970s articles began to advocate "the creation of educational policies to redress the academic exclusion of and past injustices inflicted upon Blacks, Browns, women, and other historically marginalized groups" (381). However, it was the special issue of *CCC* in December 1968 discussing African American language, Smitherman contends, that instigated the "Students' Right to Their Own Language" policy resolution (384).

The "Students' Right" resolution set out to eliminate the contradiction between theory and practice. As Smitherman points out. "since linguistic research had demonstrated the linguistic adequacy of 'nonstandard' dialects, why wouldn't the 'system' accept them? To reject them was tantamount to making them deficient" ("CCCC" 384). Thus scholars had to advocate "the wider social legitimacy of all languages and dialects, and to struggle, wherever one had a shot at 'being effective,' to bring about mainstream recognition and acceptance of the history and language of those on the margins" (384). Smitherman concisely discusses the reactions to the resolution, both positive and negative. Other researchers who provide important insight into the issue include Keith Gilyard and Elaine Richardson (p. 217), John Baugh, Hanni Taylor, Sara Jonesberg, and Arnetha Ball. For example, echoing Smitherman, Ball points out that "the past three decades have been active ones for educators and scholars who have devoted their work to the goals of educational parity in a pluralistic society. Because of their accomplishments, the writing profession is undergoing a period of change and reform" (245). How widespread is this change and reform, though? Do English departments reflect "Students' Right to Their Own Language" in their first-year composition course objectives and descriptions? Specifically, how many community colleges in Michigan, besides Delta, have a standard English statement among the outcomes of their first-year composition course?

SAMPLE AND METHODS

To conduct this study, I first went to the Michigan Department of Education's Web site listing Michigan Community Colleges (www.mde.state.mi.us/school/colleges/community.shtml). The site listed twenty-nine, each with a linked Web site. I then went to the twenty-nine Web sites and looked for first-year composition course descriptions and outcomes. I found four Web sites that included that information and printed the information. For twenty-three of the remaining schools, I identified someone in the English department (or its equivalent) to e-mail; for two I had to e-mail the Web site "information" address for the name and e-mail address of English faculty members, both of whom I was then able to e-mail (a copy of my e-mail is reproduced in Appendix 2). After twelve days, I had received responses from all but eight schools. I sent the same e-mail to a second contact at the eight schools, whom I identified by revisiting the schools' Web sites. After four more days, I called the English departments of the seven schools that still had not replied. I either received the name of another contact from the person who answered the phone, or I left a message on the department's answering machine. Ultimately, twenty-four of the twenty-nine schools replied (82.8 percent). I printed all of the replies and organized the information into five categories:

1. those schools with an explicit standard English statement;

2. those with an "academic/educated discourse" statement;

3. those with an "appropriate conventions" statement;

4. those with a "grammar/mechanics" statement, without an explicitly mentioned language variation; and

5. those with no departmentally mandated English variation statement.

RESULTS

Of the twenty-four community colleges in Michigan that responded to my question about the presence of a standard English statement in their departmental first-year composition course descriptions; statements of course outcomes, objectives, competencies, or requirements; and/or standard syllabi, eight (33.3 percent) indicated that they had an explicit standard English statement (Category 1); three (12.5 percent) an "academic/educated discourse" statement (Category 2); three (12.5 percent) an "appropriate conventions" statement (Category 3); four (16.7 percent) a "grammar/mechanics" statement without an explicitly mentioned language variation (Category 4); and six (25.0 percent) no English variation statement (Category 5). Notably, all three schools that had an "appropriate conventions" statement (Category 3) also had a "grammar/mechanics" statement elsewhere in their documents and could thus have been put in Category 4, making Category 4 contain seven (29.2 percent); however, it seemed that the "appropriate conventions" statements took precedence. Also notably, no school mentioned African American Language. Last, one response indicated that the school "supports the Writing Program Administrators (WPA) Outcomes for First-Year Composition," which were then listed; I interpreted this to be a departmental mandate. Table 21.1 summarizes these results (Appendix 1 presents the actual statements by category and college).

In short, 45.8 percent of the respondents (eleven) had an explicit language variety statement (Categories 1 and 2). The statements that fall into the third category could be variously interpreted as "appropriate conventions" could imply conventions appropriate to whatever language variety is being used

TABLE 21.1   Language Variety Statements

Category	Number of Schools	Percent of Schools
1: Explicit SE Statement	8	33.3
2: Academic/Educated Discourse Statement	3	12.5
3: Appropriate Conventions Statement	3	12.5
4: Grammar/Mechanics Statement	4	16.7
5: No Statement	6	25.0

(thus the statement does not prescribe a particular language variety). Given that each of the schools in this category also included grammar/mechanics statements, one might think that standard English was implied; however, one can also use grammar/mechanics properly in any language variety. One might think this also for the four schools that included a grammar/mechanics statement (Category 4). Thus, 54.2 percent (thirteen—three in Category 3, four in Category 4, and six in Category 5) of the schools could be said to either reflect or subscribe to the "Students' Right" resolution, at least on the surface (this in itself would be an area for future study). Still, eleven (45.8 percent), including my college, do not subscribe to the resolution (Categories 1 and 2). If one interprets the grammar/mechanics statements to imply standard English, the number of schools which seem to subscribe to the resolution would decrease to nine (37.5 percent), and the number that do not would increase to fifteen (62.5 percent). To see which number is most accurate, one could poll the faculty members' interpretations of the "appropriate conventions" and "grammar/mechanics" statements. Last, it should be noted that my contact at one of the schools that fell into Category 5 (no mandated statement) indicated that some faculty members included standard English statements in their syllabi. However, my contact also stated that one faculty member stopped using such a statement (she did not remember when or why), and that one instructor indicated that he thought "there was one, at least back in the 1970s or 1980s, because of the court cases involving the appropriateness of Black English" (personal communication 19 Nov. 2001).[1] What is not clear in this instructor's response is whether a standard English statement was *added* or *dropped* because of the court cases.

Besides illuminating the language variety statements or lack thereof, some of the results of the study also indicated that the underlying spirit of the "Students' Right" statement was being followed in other ways, if perhaps not explicitly. For example, one community college included general education goals in its first-year composition course syllabus (which are to appear in all instructors' syllabi, according to my contact at the college) (personal communication 16 Nov. 2001). Two of these goals found in an instructor's syllabus online were that "Students will assess the impact of prejudices on their attitudes and behaviors," and "Students will develop basic cross-cultural understanding, and ability to communicate with people from different cultures"

(Holmes). This college, however, also mandated standard English earlier in its syllabus. Another college, one that fell into Category 3 (appropriate discourse), also included the outcome, "Understand the relationship among language, knowledge, and power" (personal communication 28 Nov. 2001). Additionally, one of the colleges that fell into Category 2 (academic/educated discourse) included the objective that students "demonstrate an increased understanding of individuals of varying cultural and social backgrounds" (personal communication 6 Dec. 2001); one would hope that this understanding would include language issues). Last, a third college contact explained at length why his school did not have any statement about language variety (Category 5):

> Down here, that phrase [Standard Written English] pretty much has been interpreted as possible code words which could send the wrong message to our African American and Hispanic students, of whom we have not many, but still more than in the past. [. . .] At the college, we have had surprisingly little if any pressure from nativist groups to teach "Standard Written English," and I doubt seriously that our faculty would pay much attention to such pressure. (Personal communication 20 Nov. 2001)

Thus, anecdotal evidence also points to some support for the CCCC resolution.

CONCLUSIONS AND IMPLICATIONS

That 82.8 percent of my contacts in Michigan community colleges responded to my question may speak to the high level of interest teachers still have in the "Students' Right" statement (future studies could look at larger numbers and types of colleges and universities, perhaps even looking for regional variations). One respondent, Joe Eklund, explicitly expressed his interest:

> I'm pleased to see that the issue of dialect variation is alive and well. I recall that in the 1970s the "Students' Right to Their Own Language" was a hot topic. The oversimplification of the issue then was the fierce battle between those who knew in their hearts that "standard" English was merely a social construct of the ruling classes stuffily imposed on the fluid and dynamic natural phenomenon of human speech versus those who recognized that all that is just academic B.S. and that if students wanted to pass their other courses and get a decent job, they damn well better learn to talk right, etc. [. . .] well, you get the idea.

Eklund interestingly and admittedly simplistically sets out the essentials of the debate; the issue of "Students' Right" does not have to be an either/or issue, however. There is room for more than one language variation. As Smitherman points out,

> Now, don't nobody go trippin cause ain none of dese proposals suggesting that schools shouldn't teach "standard English" or more precisely, the US Language of Wider Communication—note I said "wider," not "whiter" communication. *All* students need to know this language if they are going to participate fully in the global world of the twenty-first century. In a similar fashion, Freire argued that it "would be very fool-

ish" and "made no sense . . . for Cape Verdians [and other colonized people] to cut themselves off from the language of the colonizer." My point has to do with how you teach the LWC and the social and political messages that should accompany language and literacy instruction. My further point is that mastery of the LWC is necessary, but insufficient to be a citizen (or, especially, a leader) in the global, diverse world of the twenty-first century and beyond. ("Ebonics" 161)

Jonesberg similarly asserts that because of the way power is distributed in the United States, "certain kinds of 'getting ahead' require knowing how to operate in [. . .] LWC" and because of this teachers are obligated to "open up LWC to all of our students, help them become fluent in it and be able to use it with comfortable facility" (53). Thus, dropping standard English statements does not mean students will not be using/learning it. It is the teacher's responsibility to teach students how to determine what variety will be appropriate. Also, teachers should help students understand the political and social issues involved.

In conclusion, given what many of the above researchers have stated, and given that, according to my study, more than half of the Michigan community colleges seem to support the "Students' Right" resolution in words (broadly interpreted), it seemed to make sense for the Delta College English faculty to alter the wording of the SWE course objective from "employ the conventions of standard written English" to "employ the appropriate writing conventions." This would enable the instructor and students to discuss what "appropriate" means, as well as the underlying political and social issues. I proposed this to the faculty, and with a vote of fifteen to ten, it passed. Also, with a vote of nineteen to six, we added the new objective (borrowing from Northwestern Michigan College and the WPA outcomes) that students be able to "understand the relationship among language, knowledge, and power." It would seem, then, that Parks' assertion that the resolution is merely history is not entirely correct; there is partial support, as my study showed, at least in words. Future studies are needed to show whether there is more widespread support across various institutions as well as whether there is an alignment between words and deeds. In other words, what happens in the classrooms of those institutions that profess an alignment to the SRTOL resolution? As for Smitherman's assertion that we can win, my study shows that progress can be made. It's not that Parks would disagree with this; he feels that winning depends on forming an alliance among faculty, students, and activists (academic as well as nonacademic) to "implement the best of the politics of the SRTOL" (252). This is a big undertaking, especially for those faculty teaching multiple sections of first-year composition. What I did seems to be a good start, however, and I would encourage faculty to explore these issues at their own institutions.

NOTE

1. Unless my contacts gave me explicit permission to do so, I have not identified them by name in the text or on the Works Cited page; instead, I include the date of the personal communication in the text where appropriate.

APPENDIX 1: RESULTS BY CATEGORY

Category 1: Explicit SE Statement

Community College	Statement
Delta	Employ the conventions of standard written English
Glenn Oaks	Demonstrate competency in standard English grammar, mechanics, and sentence structure
Kalamazoo Valley	Demonstrate the ability to write acceptable sentences in standard English, following the conventions of sentence structure, punctuation, and capitalization; the ability to choose words appropriately and to use standard American spelling; the ability to vary writing style, vocabulary, and sentence structure for different audiences and for different purposes
Kirtland	Use the conventions of mechanically sound, grammatically correct, syntactically accurate standard written American English
Lake Michigan	The ability to write compositions using formats and conventions of American standard English [. . .] (standard grammar, punctuation, spelling, and mechanics)
Monroe County	Demonstrate the rules of edited American English (two faculty contacts identified this as "Standard Edited American English")
Mott	Use a variety of sentence lengths and structures [and . . .] use standard English grammar, punctuation, and spelling
Muskegon	The student is expected to write effectively in standard English and to demonstrate an understanding [. . .] that good writing always includes . . . correct grammar and spelling

Category 2: Academic/Educated Discourse Statement

Community College	Statement
Alpena	Demonstrate ability to produce clear, accurate, and correct academic discourse
Kellogg	Demonstrate the ability to write essays that utilize [. . .] educated usage
Southwestern Michigan	To anticipate and address the expectations of a generally educated audience. To appreciate how mechanics and grammar reflect a certain level of audience awareness and concern.

Category 3: Appropriate Conventions Statement

Community College	Statement
Bay de Noc	[Under learning outcomes:] Use appropriate conventions for spelling, sentence structure, punctuation, and grammar; [under requirements:] Demonstrate competency in mechanics
Montcalm	[Under learning outcomes:] Use appropriate conventions for spelling, sentence structure, punctuation, and grammar; [under objective:] By taking this course, you will [. . .] learn to revise your writing until it is [. . .] clear and mechanically sound
Northwestern Michigan	Develop knowledge of genre conventions ranging from structure and paragraphing to tone and mechanics [and, later in the list] control such surface features as syntax, grammar, punctuation, and spelling

Category 4: Grammar/Mechanics Statement

Community College	Statement
Bay Mills	Show a command of basic sentence structure and demonstrate a proficiency with certain grammatical rules and punctuation
Lansing	[Under style:] Choose effective words for tone and levels of usage; write clear and concise sentences; [under mechanics:] write essays with rare disruption from errors in grammar, punctuation, spelling, [word choice], and manuscript form
North Central Michigan	Students should be able to write and revise [. . .] by [. . .] improving their knowledge and application of grammatical conventions
Schoolcraft	Avoid spelling, usage, and typographical errors [. . .] Are relatively free from mechanical errors, including run-on sentences, fragments, and agreement errors

Category 5: No Departmentally Mandated Statement

Community College	NO RESPONSE Community College
Gogebic	
Grand Rapids	Henry Ford
Macomb	Jackson
Mid Michigan	St. Clair County
Oakland	Washtenaw
West Shore	Wayne County

APPENDIX 2: SAMPLE E-MAIL TO COMMUNITY COLLEGE CONTACTS

Dear Professor (last name of contact),

As part of a language course I am taking at Michigan State University, I am researching whether first-year composition courses at Michigan community colleges include any requirements related to using a particular variety of English. For example, the first-year composition course at Delta College, where I teach, includes the departmentally mandated outcome to "write a formal college composition for a specific audience and purpose," under which is the objective to "employ the conventions of standard written English."

Does your English department have such a statement? If so, how is it worded? If not, do your colleagues include such a requirement in their syllabi or paper assignments? If so, how do they word it?

I would appreciate your help.

Sincerely,

(name)

(title), Delta College

WORKS CITED

Ball, Arnetha. "Evaluating the Writing of Culturally and Linguistically Diverse Students: The Case of the African American Vernacular English Speaker." *Evaluating Writing: The Role of Teachers' Knowledge about Text, Learning, and Culture.* Ed. Charles R. Cooper and Lee Odell. Urbana, IL: NCTE, 1999. 225–48.

Baugh, John. *Beyond Ebonics: Linguistic Pride and Racial Prejudice.* Oxford: Oxford UP, 2000.

Delta College. *Delta College Catalog 2002–2003.* University Center, MI: Author, 2002.

Eklund, Joe. Personal communication. 20 Nov. 2001.

Gilyard, Keith, and Elaine Richardson. "Students' Right to Responsibility: Basic Writing and African American Rhetoric." *Insurrections: Resistance in Composition.* Ed. Andrea Greenbaum. New York: SUNY P, 2001. [Pages 217–28 in this book.]

Holmes, John B. "Syllabus." Personal Web site. 2001. 15 Nov. 2001 http://puma.kvcc.edu/jholmes/ENG110/syllabus.htm.

Jonesberg, Sara Dalmas. "What's a (White) Teacher to Do about Black English?" *English Journal* 90 (Mar. 2001): 51–53.

Michigan Department of Education. "Michigan Community Colleges." 2001. 14 Nov. 2001 http://www.mde.state.mi.us/school/colleges/community.shtml.

Parks, Stephen. *Class Politics: The Movement for the Students' Right to Their Own Language.* Urbana, IL: NCTE, 2000.

Rickford, John. "Ebonics and Education: Lessons from the Caribbean, Europe and the U.S.A." *Ebonics and Language Education.* Ed. Clinton Crawford. New York: Sankofa, 2001. 263–84.

Robins, Sylvia. Personal interview. 20 Nov. 2001.

Smitherman, Geneva. "CCCC and the 'Students' Right to Their Own Language.'" *Talkin That Talk: Language, Culture, and Education in African America.* Ed. Geneva Smitherman. New York: Routledge, 2000. 337–99.

———. "CCCC's Role in the Struggle for Language Rights." *CCC* 50 (1999): [pp. 58–82 in this book].

———. "Ebonics, *King,* and Oakland: Some Folk Don't Believe Fat Meat Is Greasy." *Talkin That Talk: Language, Culture, and Education in African America.* Ed. Geneva Smitherman. New York: Routledge, 2000. 150–62.

"Students' Right to Their Own Language." Spec. issue of *CCC* 25 (Fall 1974). [Pages 19–57 in this book.]

Taylor, Hanni. *Standard English, Black English, and Bidialectalism: A Controversy.* New York: Lang, 1989.

Walvoord, Barbara. "Policy for the Use of Edited Standard Written English Conventions." Handout in the workshop "How to Make the Grading Process Time-Efficient and Effective for Learning and How to Use the Grading Process for Departmental and General Education." Delta College. University Center, Michigan. 1997.

22 Critical Language Awareness in the United States: Revisiting Issues and Revising Pedagogies in a Resegregated Society

H. SAMY ALIM

I entered the language and literacy battlefield in the *thick* of the Oakland "Ebonics controversy," which eerily revisited many of the same racial and cultural stereotypes raised by "The Black English Case" in Ann Arbor (*Martin Luther King Elementary School Children v. Ann Arbor School District Board*) nearly two decades earlier. While the media and public discourse attacked Black Language (BL) and Black people for so-called "deficiencies," a generation of young Hip Hop Headz (including me) spent hours crafting linguistic skillz and pushin the boundaries of the English language in *rhyme ciphers, battles,* and *freestyles*. Wasn't no way in the world you could get me to see BL as deficient!

"ME AND YOU, WE GON WORK IT OUT": THE NEED FOR CRITICAL, INTERDISCIPLINARY DIALOGUE BETWEEN EDUCATORS AND SOCIOLINGUISTS

Having been in the communities and classrooms where BL was spoken, I saw ways to develop language pedagogy for speakers of BL by putting the full scope of language and literacy knowledge "to work for the people," as one of my professors always used to say, and I attempted to become equally knowledgeable in sociolinguistic theory and methodology and educational policy and practice. Incorporating sociolinguistic theory and methodology with educational concerns requires dialogue, which in some ways has been underdeveloped between these two fields because linguists may sometimes be perceived as "intellectual snobs" who are afraid of getting their hands dirty in the complex world of classrooms, while educators are sometimes perceived as "advocates," not intellectuals, whose research is either "too teachery" or "too touchy-feely."

Recent works (e.g., Adger, Temple, & Taylor, 1999; Lanehart, 2002) have demonstrated interdisciplinary scholarship, and Lanehart's (2007) most recent work exemplifies the willingness of some sociolinguists to become involved

From *Educational Researcher* 34.7 (2005): 24–31.

in education research, as she urges the field to put aside old debates about the historical origins of BL and focus more of its energy on the urgent, pressing educational needs of today's classrooms. I have written this article in this spirit of dialogue—or as Bay Area rapper Jubwa of Soul Plantation says in a critical rap about racial politics in America, "Me and you, we gon work it out!"

"THE DOE FLOW WHERE THE WHITE MAN GO": LANGUAGE AND RACIAL POLITICS IN U.S. EDUCATION

As scholars concerned with educational issues, the year 2004 gave us pause to reexamine the successes and failures of 50 years of court-ordered desegregation since *Brown v. Board of Education of Topeka, Kansas* (1954). This landmark civil rights decision, which many refer to as "the single most honored opinion in the Supreme Court's corpus" (Balkin, 2001), effectively overruled *Plessy v. Ferguson* (1896), which required separate but equal facilities for Blacks and Whites. In the years of struggle leading up to the case, many Blacks and their supporters, knowing that "the doe flow where the White man go" (i.e., White facilities were usually better funded and better resourced by local and state governments than Black ones), argued that the doctrine of "separate but equal" was inherently unequal and that de jure segregation helped to reinforce the ideology of White supremacy.

The year 2004 was cause for a double pause for scholars of educational linguistics who were also revisiting 25 years of language and racial politics since the Black English Case (*Martin Luther King Elementary School Children v. Ann Arbor School District Board*). Just as AERA chose *Brown* as the primary sub-theme for its annual conference, NWAV (New Ways of Analyzing Variation, the annual conference for quantitative sociolinguists) chose *King* as its primary conference theme. *King* was a federal Court case on behalf of fifteen Black, economically oppressed children residing in a low-income housing project on Green Road in Ann Arbor, Michigan. The plaintiffs argued that the school board had not taken the social, economic, cultural, and linguistic backgrounds of the students into account in the effort to teach them how to read in "standard English" (Smitherman, 1981). Thus, they argued, the students did not have access to equal educational opportunities, also a primary concern for *Brown*. While school desegregation rulings have sometimes mentioned the effects of "language," and while language education rulings have sometimes mentioned the effects of "desegregation," both types of case lie right at the nexus of language and racial politics in U.S. education. As Judge Joiner ruled:

> This case is a judicial investigation of a school's response to language, a language used in informal and casual oral communication among many blacks but a language that is not accepted as an appropriate means of communication among people in their professional roles in society. . . . The problem posed by this case is one which the evidence indicates has been compounded by efforts on the part of society to fully integrate blacks into the mainstream of society by relying solely on simplistic

devices such as scatter housing and busing of students. . . . Some evidence suggests that the teachers in the schools which are "ideally" integrated such as King do not succeed as well with minority black students in teaching language arts as did many of the teachers of black children before integration. The problem, of course, is multidimensional, but the language of the home environment may be one of the dimensions. It is a problem that every thoughtful citizen has pondered, and that school boards, school administrators and teachers are trying to solve. (Judge Charles W. Joiner's "Memorandum Opinion and Order" in *Martin Luther King Elementary School Children v. Ann Arbor School District Board*, decided July 12, 1979)

These two cases (*Brown* and *King*) have often been discussed separately in the scholarly literature, but a joint discussion of the cases should prove useful in improving access to equal educational opportunities for linguistically profiled and marginalized students.

This article seizes the current moment in U.S. educational history to call for a critical interdisciplinary dialogue between educators and sociolinguists. Given its timely nature (in commemoration of *Brown* and *King*),[1] I focus on how language and literacy scholars have attempted to address the linguistic consequences of the African slave trade (Baugh, 2000a). These linguistic consequences, as we most recently witnessed in the heated Ebonics controversy of Oakland, California (where the Oakland School Board called for teachers to respect the legitimacy and richness of BL while teaching "standard English"), remain causes of concern in American public discourse. By revisiting the central issues facing scholars who study the language and literacy practices of Black Americans, we can review what has been tried and call for what needs to be done. I conclude by urging educators and sociolinguists to revise pedagogies in what has become a resegregated society (Orfield & Yun, 1999).

DESEGREGATION AND DIVERGENCE: *BROWN* AND *KING* IN A RESEGREGATED AMERICA

Seven months after the *King* decision, linguist Geneva Smitherman, with the institutional support of the Center for Black Studies at Wayne State University, hosted a national invitational symposium to discuss the effects of the case on the future education of Black youth. Speaking before an audience of more than "300 high powered professionals" from educational, linguistic, psychological, and legal backgrounds (Smitherman, 1981, 23), Dr. Annamarie Gillespie-Hayes of the Training Institute for Desegregated Education captured the urgency that Black Americans felt about obtaining equal access to educational opportunities: "Twenty-five years after *Brown v. Board of Education*, the desegregation of schools 'with all deliberate speed' has resulted in more deliberation than speed in the dismantling of dual school systems. The crucial word for Black people in the *Brown* mandate was "speed," while the Southern school boards accentuated 'deliberation'" (Gillespie-Hayes, 1981, 259). Witnessing the massive White American resistance to court-ordered desegregation, Gillespie-Hayes and others chose to focus on an educational program that privileged *content* over *configuration*. Whether they knew it or not, the greatest irony of the *Brown* decision would be that students at the turn of the century would once again be separated by race in U.S. schools, only this time the segregation would be due to a complex array of social, economic, and legal issues (Frankenberg & Lee, 2002).

The resegregation of American society—not just of Blacks and Whites, but of all communities from each other, particularly Blacks and Latinos—has resulted in a situation where most Black and Brown children in the United States attend racially segregated schools (de facto segregation is in full effect in almost every major urban area). As noted by Balkin (2001), the increasing resegregation of U.S. cities is strongly correlated with poverty levels: "Although only 5 percent of segregated white schools are in areas of concentrated poverty, over 80 percent of black and Latino schools are" (6). Turner Middle School in Southwest Philadelphia was 99.4% Black, with the majority of students living below the poverty line in the late 1990s when I worked there. I have also taught in California schools where not a single White student attended. Teachers throughout the United States can testify to the presence of de facto segregation, as there has been a gradual relaxing of the need to comply with court-ordered desegregation since the 1970s (Prince, forthcoming; also see Balkin's discussion of *Board of Education of Oklahoma City v. Dowell*, 1991; *Freeman v. Pitts*, 1992; and *Missouri v. Jenkins*, 1995).

What might (re)segregation have to do with language education? In the context of a resegregated society, sociolinguists (Labov & Harris, 1986) argued that Black and White speakers of English were not participating in the same processes of linguistic change. If true, this meant that rather than Black and White dialects of English converging, they were actually diverging. In the press, this had immediate and "newsworthy" social implications, as Americans in the post–Civil Rights Era had come to see themselves as a nation of citizens devoted to equal opportunity for all. So, whereas the Kerner Commission (the National Advisory Commission on Civil Disorder) feared the development of "two separate societies, one Black, the other White," some sociolinguists feared the development of two separate languages, one Black, the other White (see the debate among top sociolinguists in Fasold's 1987 special issue of *American Speech*). This would mean that the language of some Blacks in resegregated America would be growing farther and farther away from the "language of schooling," possibly halting Black American educational progress.

In the *King* decision, Judge Joiner explicitly makes the connection between language barriers and segregation. *King* represents the first test of applicability of 1703(f), the language provision of the 1974 Equal Educational Opportunity Act, to speakers of BL (Smitherman, 1981, 2000). The critical clause reads:

No state shall deny equal educational opportunity to an individual on account of his or her race, color, sex, or national origin, by—

. . . .

> (f) the failure by an educational agency to take appropriate action to overcome language barriers that impede equal participation by its students in its instructional programs. (20 U.S.C. 1703[f])

In his "Memorandum Opinion and Order" (1979), Judge Joiner sought to go beyond *Brown*'s use of social science research: "The court believes that research results . . . are better received as evidence in the case, on the record and subject to cross-examination, than simply by reading the reports and giving consideration to what appears in those reports as was done in *Brown v. Board of Education*." It is clear from the ruling that Judge Joiner relied heavily on the research results of educational psychologists and linguists. He ruled:

> The evidence clearly suggests that no matter how well intentioned the teachers are, they are not likely to be successful in overcoming the language barrier caused by their failure to take into account the home language system, unless they are helped by the defendant to recognize the existence of the language system used by the children in their home community and to use that knowledge as a way of helping the children to read standard English.
>
> The failure of the defendant Board to provide leadership and help for its teachers in learning about the existence of "black English" as a home and community language for many black students and to suggest to those same teachers ways and means of using that knowledge in teaching the black children code switching skills in connection with reading standard English *is not rational in light of existing knowledge on the subject* [emphasis added].

Sociolinguistic testimony that dually attributed the continued existence of BL to external, social factors (such as the historical and enduring isolation of Blacks from "mainstream" America and its institutions) and internal, community factors (such as the recognition of BL as an important cultural symbol of Black ethnic identity and group solidarity) influenced Judge Joiner's decision, which is critical to my arguments in this article.

Before *King*, several desegregation cases mentioned the distinctiveness of BL (Bailey, 1981). The year that attorneys Gabe Kaimowitz and Kenneth Lewis filed the federal *King* case in Ann Arbor (on July 28, 1977), the famous Detroit desegregation case was decided not too far away. That case, *Bradley v. Milliken*, recognized the external, social factors that help to maintain BL: "Children who have been thus educationally and culturally set apart from the larger community will inevitably acquire habits of speech, conduct, and attitudes reflecting their cultural isolation. They are likely to acquire speech habits, for example, which vary from the environment in which they must ultimately function and compete, if they are to enter and be a part of that community." Recognizing a long-standing truism about speech—that language is the property of the community, not solely the individual—the Judge continued: "This is not peculiar to race; in this setting, it can affect children who, as a group, are isolated by force of law from the mainstream" (433 U.S. 287). Not only was the court recognizing these factors in the maintenance of BL, they also suggested that any such isolated linguistic group—be they Spanish-dominant Mexicans in some Los Angeles communities or Arabic-dominant Palestinians in some northern New Jersey communities—"must be treated directly by special training at the hands of teachers prepared for the task" (433 U.S. 287; see also Bailey, 1981 for a thorough legal analysis).

In the aftermath of the *King* decision, in which Judge Joiner deemed as irrational the failure of the school board to use existing knowledge to teach language arts, and the Oakland Ebonics controversy (Baugh, 2000a; J. Rickford & R. Rickford, 2000), in which the majority of the American public deemed statements like the *judge's* to be irrational, it seems like "what go around come around"—and around and around. The cycle of hysteria that surrounds the right of Black students to their own language begs two important questions for scholars: "What are the rational ways by which teachers can take BL into account when teaching Black students?" and "What is the state of 'existing knowledge' on the subject?" After we revisit what scholars have contributed, I suggest an important way in which we can revise our pedagogies, not only to take the students' language into account but also to account for the inter-connectedness of language with the larger sociopolitical and sociohistorical phenomena that help to maintain unequal power relations in a still-segregated society.

RESPECT DA DIALECT: SOCIOLINGUISTIC APPROACHES TO LANGUAGE AND LITERACY DEVELOPMENT

Some sociolinguists have been concerned with the educational implications of language research for quite some time, even becoming vocal advocates in times of educational "crisis" for students who speak languages other than the dominant norm. Before considering the studies that address BL and literacy development, it is important to note that linguists have been heavily involved in the vast array of language issues in schools since the 1960s. Their involve-ment includes early attempts to use linguistic knowledge to teach reading (Fries, 1962) and more recent efforts to produce research in support of bilin-gual education and policy, which has come under increasingly vehement attack in the last decade, coinciding with the dramatic rise of the Latino popu-lation in many areas of the United States (Crawford, 1992; Krashen, 1996; Stanford Working Group, 1993; Valdes, 2001; Zentella, 1997). Sociolinguists have also supported bidialectal programs for native Hawaiians and speakers of "Hawaiian Creole English" (Benham & Heck, 1998) and called for the sup-port and development of academic language and biliteracy in social contexts (Enright-Villalva, 2003; Hornberger, 1989). More directly, some have provided evidence, legal testimonies, and policy recommendations in the firestorms surrounding BL in schools (Baugh, 1998, 2000a; J. Rickford & R. Rickford, 2000; Smitherman, 1981, 2000).

Since the Oakland Ebonics controversy, John Rickford has continually revised and made available to the public (see www.stanford.edu/~rickford) his synthesis of sociolinguistic approaches to "working with vernacular varieties of English in schools" (see J. Rickford, 2000). In trying to answer the question that was on the mind of concerned teachers of Black students—How might the vernacular of African American children be taken into account in efforts to help them do better in schools?—John Rickford (2003) outlined four major sociolinguistic efforts towards that end: (a) the linguistically informed approach, (b) contrastive analysis, (c) dialect readers, and (d) dialect awareness programs.

The "linguistically informed approach" is characterized primarily by William Labov's work on reading failure, from his early explorations of the topic (1967) to his current, expansive research agenda to develop "Individualized Reading Programs" (2001; Labov & Baker, 2003) in elementary schools in Philadelphia and California (with Bettina Baker, John and Angela Rickford, John Baugh, and others). Labov begins with one fundamental premise: Teachers should distinguish between mistakes in reading and differences in pronunciation. For instance, if a Black child reads, "I missed my chance" as "I miss my chance," teachers should not view this as a decoding error, but rather as an utterance that is consistent with the pronunciation patterns of BL. It is not clear whether teachers are, in fact, failing Black students for these types of "errors." Nor is it clear how such awareness on the part of teachers will help develop a more responsive reading pedagogy, particularly in areas of comprehension (see A. Rickford, 1999). However, a thorough analysis of the kinds of possible decoding errors that Black students *do* make, and efforts to produce Individualized Reading Programs can only be helpful. We now know more about Black children's decoding skills than we have in the past, and that is certainly promising.

The "contrastive analysis" approach can be used to distinguish the differences between "standard English" and BL. John Rickford (2003) reports that this approach has been used successfully by Taylor (1989) in Chicago, by Parker and Crist (1995) in Tennessee and Chicago, and by Harris-Wright (1999) in Dekalb County, Georgia. A vivid example of the potential success of this approach in teaching "standard English" writing skills is noted in the work of Taylor (1989), who showed that students taught by this method had a 91.7% decrease in their use of third-person singular without the final *s* (a well-studied feature of BL), while those taught by more traditional means only had an 11% decrease. Contrastive analysis, along with other strategies from second language acquisition methodology, has also been used in the comprehensive Academic English Mastery Program in the Los Angeles Unified School District, which serves more than fifty schools, thousands of teachers, and tens of thousands of students (LeMoine & Hollie, 2007).

"Dialect readers" introduce reading in the home and community language of the students and then later make the switch to "standard English." This approach has sparked heated debate here in the United States. Despite research that demonstrated that the well-known dialect reader program, "Bridge" (Simpkins & Simpkins, 1981), advanced the reading abilities of Black students, the publishers of the program discontinued the product because of community outrage against the use of BL in schools. This incident underscores the need for community education on BL. More reading gains like these could be lost as a result of misunderstandings between school administrators and local communities. Black students achieved 6.2 months of reading gain in a 4-month period, while a control group taught by traditional methods actually lost ground in that same period.

The final approach is the "dialect awareness" approach spearheaded by Walt Wolfram and his colleagues at North Carolina State University (Wolfram, Adger, & Christian, 1999). Dialect awareness programs seek to infuse the fundamental principles of linguistic variation into school curricula. The program excites students about the inherent variability of language and meets standards proposed by the International Reading Association and the National Council of Teachers of English, indicating that students should "develop an understanding of and respect for diversity in language use, patterns, and dialects across cultures, ethnic groups, geographic regions, and social roles" (National Council of Teachers of English & International Reading Association, 3). One of the most exciting aspects of dialect awareness programs is that they encourage students to become ethnographers and collect their own speech data from their local communities. Although the educational effectiveness of these programs is not truly tried and tested (most attempts are short-term, making it difficult to measure student progress), teachers interested in developing language and other skills (e.g., data analysis, oral history projects) view this approach positively. Dialect awareness programs represent one potential way to reduce dialect discrimination in schools and society.

DISRUPTING THE "NATURAL" SOCIOLINGUISTIC ORDER OF THINGS: THE NEW LITERACY STUDIES AND CRITICAL LANGUAGE AWARENESS

The sociolinguistic approaches described above have one fundamental similarity with the New Literacy Studies (see Hull & Schultz, 2002)—both groups of scholars are working to provide evidence that will disprove the notion that the language and literacy practices of students from linguistically marginalized groups are "deficient." Labov (1972) made this statement early on:

> The view of the black speech community which we obtain from our work in the ghetto areas is precisely the opposite from that reported by Deutsch or by Bereiter and Engelmann. We see a child bathed in verbal stimulation from morning to night. We see many speech events which depend upon the competitive exhibition of verbal skills—sounding, singing, toasts, rifting, louding—a whole range of activities in which the individual gains status through his use of language. . . . We see no connection between verbal skill in the speech events characteristic of the street culture and success in the schoolroom. (212–213)

Many scholars have used another sociolinguistic framework, the ethnography of communication, to drive home the main message that students on the margins of school success often possess "different, not deficient" language and literacy practices in their home communities. This "mismatch," they argue, is one cause of schools' failure to reach these pupils. Most notable in this area is Heath's (1983) classic, decade-long study of how families from Black and White working-class communities socialized their children into different "ways with words," or varying language and literacy practices, some of which were closer to school norms than others. Subsequently, scholars have taken on research agendas that aim to "bridge" the out-of-school language and literacy practices of Black students with classroom practice (Ball, 2000; Dyson, 2003; Foster, 2001; Lee, 1993), while others have examined the inventive and innovative language and literacy events of Black youth involved in Hip Hop Culture (Alim, 2004a, 2004b), spoken word poetry (Fisher, 2003), and other verbal activities (Mahiri & Sutton, 1996; Richardson, 2003).

The New Literacy Studies (NLS) scholars, such as Gee (1996) and Street (1993), position themselves at the crossroads of sociolinguistics, linguistic anthropology, and critical linguistics. Like linguistic anthropologists, the NLS view literacy—in fact, *literacies*—as situated within the social and cultural practices that are constitutive of everyday life (Hull & Schultz, 2002). Exploring what Ball and Freedman (2004) refer to as "new literacies for new times," the NLS pull away from the generally noncritical American sociolinguistic tradition by drawing from contemporary social and cultural theorists, such as Bakhtin, Bourdieu, Derrida, Foucault, Heidegger, and Gramsci, among others and thus more closely align with the British tradition of Critical Language Awareness (Fairclough, 1995; Wodak, 1995). Critical Language Awareness views educational institutions as designed to teach citizens about the current sociolinguistic order of things, without challenging that order, which is based largely on the ideology of the dominating group and their desire to maintain social control. This view of education interrogates the dominating discourse on language and literacy and foregrounds, as in the NLS, the examination and interconnectedness of identities, ideologies, histories/herstories, and the hierarchical nature of power relations between groups. Research in this area attempts to make the *invisible visible* by examining the ways in which well-meaning educators attempt to silence diverse languages in White public space by inculcating speakers of heterogeneous language varieties into what are, at their core, White ways of speaking and seeing the word/world, that is, the norms of White, middle-class, heterosexist males (Alim, 2004c). Importantly, a critical approach is not concerned with the study of decontextualized language but rather with the analysis of "opaque and transparent structural relationships of dominance, discrimination, power and control as manifested in language" (Wodak, 1995).

Although American sociolinguistic research certainly has been helpful in providing detailed descriptions of language variation and change, this is where it stops (Lippi-Green, 1997). By viewing the role of language in society through a noncritical lens, the tradition can actually harm linguistically profiled and marginalized students. Most American suggestions about pedagogy on language attitudes and awareness tend to discuss linguistic stigmatization in terms of *individual* prejudices rather than discrimination that is part and parcel of the *sociostructural fabric of society* and serves the needs of those who currently benefit the most from what is portrayed as the "natural" sociolinguistic order of things. Fairclough (1989, 7–8) argues that the job of sociolinguists should be to do more than ask, "What language varieties are stigmatized?" Rather, we should be asking, "How—in terms of the development of social relationships to power—was the existing sociolinguistic order brought into being? How is it sustained? And how might it be changed to the advantage of those who are dominated by it?"

Research conducted by the Linguistic Profiling Project (LPP) at Stanford University (Purnell, Idsardi, & Baugh, 1999; Baugh, 2000b, 2003) attempts to apply findings of studies on language-based discrimination to educational practice by working with Black, Chicano, and Pacific Islander youth in a diverse working-class city in northern California to develop a Freireian critical pedagogy (Freire, 1970) on language. That pedagogy aims to educate linguistically profiled and marginalized students about how language is used and, importantly, how language can be used against them (Alim, 2004d). Questions central to the project are: "How can language be used to maintain, reinforce, and perpetuate existing power relations?" And, conversely, "How can language be used to resist, redefine, and possibly reverse these relations?" This approach engages in the process of consciousness-raising, that is, the process of actively becoming aware of one's own position in the world and what to do about it (as in the Women's Liberation movement or the Black and Chicano Liberation struggles). By learning about the full scope of their language use (through conducting ethnographic and sociolinguistic analyses of their own communicative behavior) and how language can actually be used against them (through *linguistic profiling* and other means; see Bertrand & Mullainathan, 2003), students become more conscious of their communicative behavior and the ways by which they can transform the conditions under which they live. The LPP moves far beyond the traditional sociolinguistic and educational approaches that bear the slogans "respect for diversity," "certain language varieties are appropriate in certain situations and not others," and "all languages are equal," that continually default in the elevation of the "standard language" over all other varieties—or, as Smitherman observed (1977) in a play on the Orwellian notion of inequality—that give students the message that "all languages are equal, but some are more equal than others."

"IT'S NOT A GAME NO MO!": ARMING LINGUISTICALLY PROFILED AND MARGINALIZED STUDENTS

LPP students know what's up. Check out what one seventh-grade Black female said about her own language use in an interview:

> STUDENT: People think I talk too ghetto. They be like, "Yo English is toe [tore] up!"
>
> INTERVIEWER: Why do they say that, though?!
>
> STUDENT: Cuz I say things like, "I ain't gon. . . ." like, "I ain't gon do it," or I won't say "eating," I'll say "ea'in."

The student is well aware of the fact that she uses a variable feature of BL that has yet to be fully described in the literature: the reduced (glottalized) consonant in "ea'in." She is also keenly aware of this variable's social standing—"too ghetto"—as a marker of BL. Results such as these show that this agenda cannot be too narrowly defined by struggle between racial or ethnic groups, but must also be prepared to deal with the many class contradictions that exist within groups. We can frame our discussions in terms of "discrimination," "racism," and "stereotyping," which most schools are now discussing openly.

As we continue our critical interdisciplinary dialogue on education on the anniversaries of *Brown* and *King*, rather than *harming* linguistically profiled and marginalized students, our goal should be *arming* them with the silent weapons needed for the quiet, discursive wars that are waged daily against their language and person. We must revise our pedagogies to confront what Sledd (1996) referred to as "the harsh ways of the world we live in." Our pedagogies should not pretend that racism does not exist in the form of linguistic discrimination. Nor should they pretend that linguistic profiling does not directly affect the personal and family lives of our students who speak marginalized languages (be they Whites from remote regions in North Kakalaka [Carolina], Puerto Ricans from the Bronx *barrios*, or Blacks from the 504 in New Aw'lins). As one of my eighth-grade Chicana students wrote: "My dad felt that he lost his job because he could not speak English good. He was always on time and always worked hard, but his boss never paid attention to him. He would get angry at him when he couldn't say what he wanted to say."

We must confront these matters of language discrimination in schools and society. Like Judge Joiner's ruling 25 years ago, these matters point to contradictions that lie at the nexus of language and racial politics in the United States today:

> The plaintiffs have attempted to put before this court one of the most important and pervasive problems facing modern urban America—the problem of why "Johnnie Can't Read" when Johnnie is Black and comes from a scatter, low-income housing unit, set down in an upper-middle class area of one of America's most liberal and forward-looking cities.

Critical language awareness programs are now being tried in the United States context in an effort to help students read not just the *word* but also the *world*. These efforts are being made because we can't keep frontin in times like these. Like the Bad Boy who stormed the stage at a *Vibe Magazine* Hip Hop industry seminar once put it, "It's not a game no mo!" Educators, sociolinguists, all "thoughtful citizens," me and you, we gon work it out.

NOTE

1. The author was invited to write this article in honor of the 50th anniversary of the landmark civil rights decision in *Brown v. Board of Education of Topeka, Kansas* (1954), and the 25th anniversary of *Martin Luther King Elementary School Children v. Ann Arbor School District Board* (1979), popularly known as the Black English case.

REFERENCES

Adger, C. T., Christian, D., & Taylor, O. (Eds.). (1999). *Making the connection: Language and academic achievement among African American students.* Washington, DC: Center for Applied Linguistics; McHenry, IL: Delta Systems.

Alim, H. S. (2004a). *You know my steez: An ethnographic and sociolinguistic study of style-shifting in a Black American speech community* (Publications of the American Dialect Society, No. 89). Durham, NC: Duke University Press.

Alim, H. S. (2004b). Hip hop nation language. In E. Finegan & J. Rickford (Eds.), *Language in the USA: Perspectives for the 21st century.* Cambridge, UK: Cambridge University Press.

Alim, H. S. (2004c). Hearing what's not said and missing what is: Black language in White public space. In C. B. Paulston & S. Keisling (Eds.), *Discourse and intercultural communication: The essential readings.* Malden, MA: Blackwell.

Alim, H. S. (2004d). *Combat, consciousness, and the cultural politics of communication: Reversing the dominating discourse on language by empowering linguistically profiled and marginalized groups.* Paper presented at the annual meeting of the American Dialect Society, Boston, MA.

Alim, H. S. (2006). *Roc the mic right: The language of hip hop culture.* New York: Routledge.

Bailey, R. W. (1981). Education and the law: The *King* case in Ann Arbor. In G. Smitherman (Ed.), *Black English and the education of Black children and youth: Proceedings of the national invitational symposium on the* King *decision* (pp. 94–129). Detroit: Wayne State University, Center for Black Studies.

Balkin, J. M. (Ed.) (2001). *What* Brown v. Board of Education *should have said: The nation's top legal experts rewrite America's landmark civil rights decision.* New York: New York University Press.

Ball, A. F. (2000). Empowering pedagogies that enhance the learning of multicultural students. *Teachers College Record, 102*(6), 1006–1034.

Ball, A. F., & Freedman, S. W. (Eds.). (2004). *Bakhtinian perspectives on language, literacy, and learning.* New York: Cambridge University Press.

Baugh, J. (1998). Linguistics, education, and the law: Educational reform for African-American language minority students. In S. S. Mufwene, J. R. Rickford, G. Bailey, & J. Baugh (Eds.), *African-American English: Structure, history and use.* London: Routledge.

Baugh, J. (2000a). *Beyond Ebonics: Linguistic pride and racial prejudice.* New York: Oxford University Press.

Baugh, J. (2000b). Racial identification by speech. *American Speech, 75*(4), 362–364.

Baugh, J. (2003). Linguistic profiling. In S. Makoni, G. Smitherman, A. F. Ball, & A. K. Spears (Eds.), *Black linguistics: Language, politics and society in Africa and the Americas.* London: Routledge.

Benham, M. K. P., & Heck, R. H. (Eds.). (1998). *Culture and educational policy in Hawai'i: The silencing of Native voices.* Mahwah, NJ: Lawrence Erlbaum.

Bertrand, M., & Mullainathan, S. (2003). *Are Emily and Greg more employable than Lakisha and Jamal? A field experiment on labor market discrimination* (NBER Working Paper No. 9873). Available from Social Science Research Network, at http://www.nber.org/papers/w9873.pdf

Bradley v. Milliken, 433 U.S. 267 (1977).

Brown v. Board of Education of Topeka, Kansas, 347 U.S. 483 (1954).

Crawford, J. (Ed.). 1992. *Language loyalties: A sourcebook on the Official English controversy.* Chicago: University of Chicago Press.

Dyson, A. H. (2003). *The brothers and sisters learn to write: Popular literacies in childhood and school cultures.* New York: Teachers College Press.

Enright-Villalva, K. (2003). *"Something that people can do": The hidden literacies of Latino and Anglo youth around academic writing.* Unpublished doctoral dissertation, School of Education, Stanford University, Stanford, CA.

Fairclough, N. (1989). *Language and power.* London: Longman.

Fairclough, N. (1995). *Critical discourse analysis: The critical study of language.* London: Longman.

Fasold, R. W. (1987). Are Black and White vernaculars diverging? *American Speech, 62,* 3–5.

Fisher, M. (2003). Open mics and open minds: Spoken word poetry in African Diaspora participatory literacy communities. *Harvard Educational Review, 73*(3), 362–389.

Foster, M. (2001). Pay Leon, pay Leon, pay Leon, paleontologist: Using call-and-response to facilitate language mastery and literacy acquisition among African American students. In S. Lanehart (Ed.), *Sociocultural and historical contexts of African American English* (pp. 281–298). Philadelphia: John Benjamins.

Frankenberg, E., & Lee, C. (2002). *Race in American public schools: Rapidly resegregating school districts.* Report published by the Civil Rights Project of Harvard University. Available at www.civilrightsproject.harvard.edu/research/deseg/reseg_schools02.php

Freire, P. (1970). *Pedagogy of the oppressed.* New York: Seabury Press.

Fries, C. C. (1962). *Linguistics and reading.* New York: Holt, Rinehart, and Winston.

Gee, J. P. (1996). *Social linguistics and literacies: Ideology in discourses.* London: Falmer.

Gillespie-Hayes, A. (1981). More deliberation than speed: The educational quest. In G. Smitherman (Ed.), *Black English and the education of Black children and youth: Proceedings of the national invitational symposium on the King decision.* Detroit: Wayne State University, Center for Black Studies.

Harris-Wright, K. (1999). Enhancing bidialectalism in urban African American students. In C. T. Adger, D. Christian, & O. Taylor (Eds.), *Making the connection: Language and academic achievement among African American students* (pp. 53–59). Washington, DC: Center for Applied Linguistics; McHenry, IL: Delta Systems.

Heath, S. B. (1983). *Ways with words: Language, life, and work in communities and classrooms.* Cambridge, UK: Cambridge University Press.

Hornberger, N. (1989). Continua of biliteracy. *Review of Educational Research, 59*(3), 271–296.

Hull, G., & Schultz, K. (Eds.). (2002). *School's out! Bridging out-of-school literacies with classroom practice.* New York: Teachers College Press.

Krashen, S. (1996). *Under attack: The case against bilingual education.* Culver City, CA: Language Education Associates.

Labov, W. (1967). Some sources of reading problems for speakers of the Black English Vernacular. In A. Frazier (Ed.), *New directions in elementary English* (pp. 140–167). Champaign, IL: National Council of Teachers of English.

Labov, W. (1972). *Language in the inner city: Studies in the Black English Vernacular.* Philadelphia: University of Pennsylvania Press.

Labov, W. (2001). Applying our knowledge of African American English to the problem of raising reading levels in inner city schools. In S. Lanehart (Ed.), *Sociocultural and historical contexts of African American English* (pp. 299–317). Philadelphia: John Benjamins.

Labov, W., & Baker, B. (2003). *What is a reading error?* Available at first author's website: http://www.ling.upenn.edu/~wlabov/

Labov, W., & Harris, W. A. (1986). De facto segregation of Black and White vernaculars. In D. Sankoff (Ed.), *Diversity and diachrony* (pp. 1–24). Amsterdam: John Benjamins.

Lanehart, S. (2002). *Sista, speak! Black women kinfolk talk about language and literacy.* Austin: University of Texas Press.

Lanehart, S. (2007). If our children are our future, why are we stuck in the past? Beyond the Anglicists and the Creolists, and toward social change. In H. S. Alim & J. Baugh (Eds.), *Talkin' Black: Language, education, and social change.* New York: Teachers College Press.

Lee, C. D. (1993). *Signifying as a scaffold for literary interpretation: The pedagogical implications of an African American discourse genre.* Urbana, IL: National Council of Teachers of English.

LeMoine, N., & Hollie, S. (2007). The Academic English Mastery Program. In H. S. Alim & J. Baugh (Eds.), *Black Language, education, and social change.* New York: Teachers College Press.

Lippi-Green, R. (1997). *English with an accent: Language, ideology and discrimination in the United States.* London: Routledge.

Mahiri, J., & Sutton, S. S. (1996). Writing for their lives: The non-school literacy of California's urban African American youth. *Journal of Negro Education, 65,* 164–180.

Martin Luther King Elementary School Children v. Ann Arbor School District Board, Civil Action No. 7-71861, 473 F. Supp. 1371 (1979).

National Council of Teachers of English & International Reading Association. (1996). *Standards for the English language arts.* Newark, DE: Author.

Orfield, G., & Yun, J. (1999). *Resegregation in American schools.* Report published by the Civil Rights Project of Harvard University. Available at www.civilrightsproject.harvard.edu/research/deseg/reseg_schools99.php#fullreport

Parker, H., &. Crist, C. (1995). *Teaching minorities to play the corporate language game.* Columbia, SC: National Resource Center for the Freshman Year Experience and Students in Transition, University of South Carolina.

Prince, D. A. (in press). Structuring access to learning opportunities in American high schools. Unpublished dissertation, School of Education, Stanford University, Stanford, CA.

Purnell, T., Idsardi, W., & Baugh, J. (1999). Perceptual and phonetic experiments on American English dialect identification. *Journal of Language and Social Psychology, 18*(1), 10–30.

Richardson, E. (2003). *African American literacies.* New York: Routledge.

Rickford, A. M. (1999). *I can fly: Teaching narratives and reading comprehension to African American and other ethnic minority students.* Lanham, MD: University Press of America.

Rickford, J. (2000). Using the vernacular to teach the standard. In J. D. Ramirez, T. G. Wiley, G. de Klerk, & E. Lee (Eds.), *Ebonics in the urban education debate.* Long Beach, CA: Center for Language Minority Education and Research.

Rickford, J. (2003). *Sociolinguistic approaches to working with vernacular varieties in schools.* Paper presented at the annual meeting of the American Educational Research Association, Chicago.

Rickford, J., & Rickford, R. (2000). *Spoken soul.* New York: John Wiley & Sons.

Simpkins, G. A., & Simpkins, C. (1981). Cross-cultural approach to curriculum development. In G. Smitherman (Ed.), *Black English and the education of Black children and youth: Proceedings of the national invitational symposium on the* King *decision* (pp. 221–240). Detroit: Center for Black Studies, Wayne State University.

Sledd, J. (1996). Grammar for social awareness in a time of class warfare. *English Journal, 85*(7), 59–63.

Smitherman, G. (1986). *Talkin and testifyin: The language of Black America* (rev. ed.). Detroit: Wayne State University Press. (Original work published in 1977 by Houghton Mifflin, Boston)

Smitherman, G. (2000). *Talkin that talk: Language, culture, and education in African America.* New York: Routledge.

Smitherman, G. (Ed.). (1981). *Black English and the education of black children and youth: Proceedings of the National Invitational Symposium on the* King *Decision.* Detroit: Wayne State University, Center for Black Studies.

Stanford Working Group. (1993, June). *Stanford working group on federal education programs for limited-english proficient students: a blueprint for the second generation* [Working paper]. Stanford, CA: Stanford University.

Street, B. (1993). *Cross-cultural approaches to literacy.* New York: Cambridge University Press.

Taylor, H. (1989). *Standard English, Black English, and bidialectalism.* New York: Peter Lang.

Valdes, G. (2001). *Learning and not learning English: Latino students in American schools.* New York: Teachers College Press.

Wodak, R. (1995). Critical linguistics and critical discourse. In J. Verschueren, J. Ostman, & J. Blommaert (Eds.), *Handbook of pragmatics* (pp. 204–210). Philadelphia: John Benjamins.

Wolfram, W., Adger, C. T., & Christian, D. (1999). *Dialects in schools and communities.* Mahwah, NJ: Lawrence Erlbaum.

Zentella, A. C. (1997). *Growing up bilingual: Puerto Rican children in New York.* London: Blackwell.

23 *Revisiting the Promise of* Students' Right to Their Own Language: *Pedagogical Strategies*

VALERIE FELITA KINLOCH

Black children in America must acquire competence in white English, for the sake of self-preservation, BUT YOU WILL NEVER TEACH A CHILD A NEW LANGUAGE BY SCORNING AND RIDICULING AND FORCIBLY ERASING HIS FIRST LANGUAGE.

—June Jordan, *Moving towards Home*

We all have a right to our own language.

—José, composition student, Fall 2001

With fervor and a sense of urgency, June Jordan writes of the disparity between linguistic distinctions/labels, and linguistic practices/codes, in her essay, "White English/Black English: The Politics of Translation." Of concern for Jordan is how the proliferation of nonstandard *Englishes* and other languages has been met with a lot of silence, one that positions nonstandardizations (i.e., Black English, non-*Englishes* as first languages, working-class, poverty) as the subordinate Other to standardizations (i.e., Edited American English, wealth, power). For when Jordan writes, "Our Black English is a political fact suffering from political persecution and political malice" (36), she is talking about the subordination and relegation of Black English to otherness just as much as she is talking about the extinction of a communicative tongue that has historically represented the lived experiences of African American people. Additionally, Jordan is talking about the social and political histories surrounding oppression, colonization, linguistic silencing, and the struggle for civil rights.

For Jordan, the struggle for civil rights has always been a struggle to erase the categories of right and wrong in language use, as in her lifelong battles against perpetual threats to the readers, writers, and speakers of Black English and other language forms. In other words, to refuse to delegitimize

From *College Composition and Communication* 57.1 (2005): 83–113.

the languages, cultures, and home discourse practices of "minority" people is to interrogate two myths: that Standard English, or Edited American English, is the correct communicative form that should be used by all American English speakers; and that its users, particularly classroom teachers and researchers, must protect the language from nonstandard practices. Such myths reiterate dynamics of "right"/"wrong," "correct"/"incorrect" in the presence of multiple languages while reinforcing linguistic homogenization and the neglect of linguistic diversity. However much such myths abound in the presence of linguistic diversity, composition and literacy scholars must ask ourselves: What are we to do to combat such language myths and how are we to engage in this work in the space of our classrooms?

My purposes in writing this article are directly connected to Jordan's theorization of the preservation of diverse language forms, mainly Black English, in American society. Acknowledging the myths and the ensuing detriments of *a* Standard English in terms of people's social relationships, politics, and access to power, Jordan writes:

> And what is everybody going to do about it? I suggest that, for one, we join forces to cherish and protect our various, multifoliate lives against pacification, homogenization, the silence of terror, and surrender to standards that despise and disregard the sanctity of each and every human life. We can begin by looking at language. Because it brings us together, as folks, because it makes known the unknown strangers we otherwise remain to each other, language is a process of translation; and a political process, taking place on the basis of who has the power to use, abuse, accept, and reject the words—the lingual messages we must attempt to transmit—to each other and/or against each other. ("White English/Black English" 38)

Jordan's concern with both the translation and the transmittance of "lingual messages" speaks to the work of professional organizations whose interests lie at the intersection of theory and practice in the teaching of writing, language, literature, literacy, and communication. One such organization, the Conference on College Composition and Communication, took up the challenge of translating the meanings of a changing national climate—heightened by, for example, the death of Dr. Martin Luther King, Jr., the 1960s and 1970s social movements, and newly formed educational programs—by

> [r]esponding to a developing crisis in college composition classrooms, a crisis caused by the cultural and linguistic mismatch between higher education and the nontraditional (by virtue of color and class) students who were making their imprint upon the academic landscape for the first time in history. In its quest to level the playing field, U.S. society was making it possible for these students from the margins to enter colleges and universities. (Smitherman, "Historical" 19)

In response to such changes, the members of CCCC passed the *Students' Right to Their Own Language* resolution (see p. 19 in this book), proving, in the sentiments of both Jordan and Smitherman, the importance of joining forces in an ever-changing Americanized society.

The history and the promise of the resolution lead to the fourfold purpose of this article: (1) to revisit the historical significance and highlight the pedagogical value of the *Students' Right to Their Own Language* resolution; (2) to offer student-teacher classroom exchanges/vignettes that intersect points of engagement with pedagogical practices supportive of language diversity; (3) to advance strategies for affirming language variations in composition courses; and (4) to propose ways for composition scholars to affirm and support the expressive rights of students.

1. A THEORETICAL DISCUSSION OF *STUDENTS' RIGHT TO THEIR OWN LANGUAGE* (SRTOL)

In April 1974, members of CCCC officially adopted the *Students' Right to Their Own Language* resolution. The original purpose of the resolution was to provide "a position statement on a major problem confronting teachers of composition and communication: how to respond to the variety in their students' dialects" (p. 19). The resolution was powerful, given the social and political movements redefining American life and calling into question issues of justice and liberation for "marginalized" people before, during, and after the 1960s and 1970s civil and social rights movements.[1] During this historical moment, CCCC waged an organizational campaign to address and better account for the language rights of students, particularly students from communities publicly labeled disadvantaged, poor, working-class, and black (for important research on the interrogation of such labels, see Lee). The policy resolution thus reads:

> We affirm the students' right to their own patterns and varieties of language—the dialects of their nurture or whatever dialects in which they find their own identity and style. Language scholars long ago denied that the myth of a standard American dialect has any validity. The claim that any one dialect is unacceptable amounts to an attempt of one social group to exert its dominance over another. Such a claim leads to false advice for speakers and writers, and immoral advice for humans. A nation proud of its diverse heritage and its cultural and racial variety will preserve its heritage of dialects. We affirm strongly that teachers must have the experiences and training that will enable them to respect diversity and uphold the right of students to their own language. (Passed by the CCCC Executive Committee in 1972 and by the membership in 1974; first published in *College Composition and Communication*, Fall 1974, p. 19)

Even before the adoption of the *Students' Right* resolution thirty-one years ago and since the inception of the organization some fifty-five years ago, composition and communication scholars have sought forums in which to discuss issues of language diversity, language rights, and teaching strategies (current examples are the Modern Language Association; the National Communication Association; the American Educational Research Association; and the National Council of Teachers of English). With professional forums provided to language and literacy educators, issues of "students' right to their own language" and "to their own patterns and varieties" (*Students' Right*, p. 19) are widely debated and positions contested. Therefore, it is not surprising that reactions to the resolution were immediate. On one hand, people demanded that the organization rescind the resolution because of its acceptance of students' *stigmatized* language forms in schools. On the other hand, people praised the resolution and its supporting document as helpful strategies in creating student-centered classrooms and in encouraging students to embrace their dialects and language variety (see Smitherman, *Talkin that Talk*). Regardless of the outpouring of public and professional reactions, it is significant that the resolution forced people to examine a new style of pedagogy in the education of previously ignored students during the 1970s, when groups of people outside of academe were protesting and fighting for rights. It was a response, however controversial, to the crisis brewing between the ideals of higher education and the realities of nontraditional students entering academic environments. It was a call, directed toward scholars and community activists, for equality in the education of students of color already labeled "disadvantaged," students entering academic institutions at increasingly high rates.

I believe that the CCCC resolution is valuable in its affirmation of the right of students to language varieties. The resolution is right in calling into question the training and experience of teachers in terms of respecting student diversity in language and geographical location (i.e., home communities). However, the resolution will become less convincing if it remains in the political and social climate of the 1960s and 1970s. While we must remember the fights and struggles of people for civil rights (e.g., the 1963 March on Washington for Jobs and Freedom), for acceptance into academic spaces (e.g., the arrival of nine black students at Little Rock Central High School in 1957), and for entrance into institutions of higher learning (e.g., James Meredith's 1962 admission as the first black student to attend the University of Mississippi), we must also use the memories of those events to educate the very students walking through our classroom doors. We need to revisit the *Students' Right* resolution in responding to the changing landscape of our classrooms, discourse communities, and profession so as to not misrepresent organizational statements and resolutions as decade-specific only. Current professional documents and policies that seek to affirm student differences in dialects and language patterns must consider the work that occurs inside and outside of classrooms as well as the work of literacy education in general.

In considering such work, Geneva Smitherman's 1987 article "Toward a National Public Policy on Language" highlights how "the unfinished business of the Committee on the Students' Right to Their Own Language [. . .] to counteract those reactionary sociolinguistic forces that would take us back to where some folk ain't never left from" (31) speaks to the unfulfilled promise of the resolution. Similarly, in her 1999 article "CCCC's Role in the Struggle for Language Rights," Smitherman asserts that as a result of the resolution "you could no longer ignore language and dialect diversity, whatever position you took, you had to reckonize" it (p. 79), and, while "the struggle for language rights yet continues, CCCC can win" (p. 80). The significance of returning to the promise of *Students' Right*, in a climate of oppositional view-points on language diversity, affirmative action, immigration, and access to academic resources (see California's propositions 187, 209, and 227, for example; see also NCTE's *The Students' Right to Know*), means that composition scholars can continue to "redefine the meanings of literacy and the meanings of inclusion, that composition studies stands to regain [King's "legacy and promise"] in heeding Smitherman's call to begin to celebrate, through engagement, the legacy of rights rhetoric in composition studies" (Bruch and Marback p. 186).

To talk of a rhetoric of rights is to talk of the struggle over and for rights (e.g., racial, civil, linguistic; see Villanueva, "Maybe"; Ball and Lardner) "insofar as oppression and citizenship, language and democracy, and privileged and unprivileged vocabularies are concerned" (Kinloch, "June Jordan" 72). It is also to talk of the redistribution/reallocation of and access to literacy resources for all students, for example high-quality teachers, libraries, writing centers, and educational materials. This rhetoric of rights involves a rethinking of the limitations of a privileged, standardized vocabulary used to theorize racial (in)equality, social (in)justice, and the learning practices of students marked "disenfranchised," "remedial," and "underprepared." It is this type of work that allows educators to better conceive of and use creative pedagogical practices and methods to affirmatively approach linguistic diversity in classrooms; this work can move us closer to winning the struggle for language and cultural rights (see Smitherman, "CCCC's Role" p. 58; Jordan, "White English/Black English").

According to Jordan, moving closer to winning the struggle involves appreciating linguistic diversity. In her many published essays and poems, Jordan embraces such diversity, the human connection to word patterns, and writing by celebrating "language [as] a communal means intrinsic to human life" ("White English/Black English" 37). She does not seek to erase the presence and use of "Standard" English from conversations on the politicization of language or the transmittance of lingual messages in in-school and out-of-school environments. Nor does she seek to replace English in America with Black English, "Russian, Hungarian, and Arabic languages" (37). Jordan's goal is similar to the goal of the CCCC Students' Right committee: "to heighten consciousness of language attitudes; to promote the value of linguistic diversity" (Smitherman, "Historical" 20). Jordan promotes this diversity by acknowledging the very factors of Black English and its system of group identification through the rejection of autonomous structures of what she calls "white English." Jordan's position on language, difference, and identity points to her own interrogation of a rhetoric of rights that has historically excluded people of color from full participation in academic and political decision-making processes. She writes, "And so I work, as a poet and writer, against the eradication of this system, this language, this carrier of Black-survivor consciousness" ("White English/Black English" 37). Her work, as a writer, complements this "verbally bonding system" of linguistic significations, this rights rhetoric (37), inside of her very own classroom.

In "Nobody Mean More to Me Than You and the Future Life of Willie Jordan," Jordan chronicles her students' initial reaction to the Black English of Alice Walker's character, Celie, in *The Color Purple* as "sounding funny" and "not looking right." Her students, whose very linguistic speech patterns shared similarities with those of Walker's character, soon came to translate passages of the novel into Standard English, which taught valuable lessons. First, writers can establish particular identifying factors of characters—"the probable age and sex and class of speakers" (177)—through the manipulation of language. Second, there exist rules, qualities, and guidelines for Black English as for other "verbal systems of communication" (178), including Edited American English. This is but one example of a pedagogy that exposes students to the richness of linguistic systems often deemed nonstandard and incorrect in order for students to be articulate in and appreciative of multiple communicative forms. Jordan's work with student speakers of Black English points to one way of valuing language variances, by heightening the consciousness of language in the face of fixed, monotonous linguistic labels.

2. THE PROJECT: CLASSROOM VIGNETTES AND STUDENT RESPONSES

How, then, can teachers of writing use the lessons from Jordan's classroom interaction with students in ways that promote linguistic diversity? In what ways can the promise of the *Students' Right* resolution be invoked in this discussion as pedagogical strategies are tested and language differences negotiated? In what follows, I use the *Students' Right* resolution and supporting text to highlight the academic work in a college composition course at an open-admissions university in Texas. I am not particularly concerned with debating the rights and wrongs of the resolution and/or with rewriting it.[2] I am concerned with discussing the relationships between students and teachers by using an "interpretive attitude" to highlight the democratic prospects of literacy education and language rights. In *The Constitution of Deliberative Democracy*, Carlos Nino posits the concept of "interpretive attitude" to discuss shared values and commitments, social practices, "deliberative character," and public participation in a democratic state. On adopting an interpretive attitude in democratic relations (in government, education, and the public sphere), Nino writes,

> Democracy is a social practice, consisting of regular conduct and predictable attitudes. These practices make up institutions that in turn are oriented toward a certain goal or value. We cannot participate thoughtfully in the practice, nor can we understand it as intelligent observers, if we do not adopt an interpretive attitude, putting the conduct and attitude in the light of certain goals or values. (9)

Composition scholars could benefit from using Nino's "interpretive attitude" to keep alive the democratic promise of *Students' Right* and to implement its lessons inside classrooms so as to participate in and understand as observers the literacy acts of students. A renewed commitment to the resolution is a commitment to having conversations with students about linguistic systems and democratic values established in communities, classrooms, and other spaces of public participation. For thanks to its democratic promise "SRTOL left its imprint on composition studies, causing the field to develop greater consciousness of language politics, greater sensitivity to the multiple voices of students, and greater appreciation for the language and cultural background of a pluralistic society" (Scott and Kinloch 710).

To use Nino's "interpretive attitude" to further articulate the democratic promise of the *Students' Right* resolution, I describe specific lessons from one composition course, collectively followed by critical analyses, as upholding the need to affirm the rights of students to their own language varieties. It is my belief that educators should experiment with the challenges presented in the resolution to find supplemental ways of educating students whose diversity is either (un)marked by cultural, racial, linguistic, and/or literate practices.[3] Neither the resolution nor the Executive Committee can be blamed for bringing into greater institutional awareness the demands of responding to students' language variety. At the same time, supporting the resolution without using its lessons to either frame or challenge academic practices is detrimental in its oversimplification of linguistic diversity. For it is Smitherman who, on recalling her involvement with the CCCC resolution committee, writes, "The charge to scholar-activists was to campaign for the wider social legitimacy of all languages and dialects, and to struggle [. . .] to bring about mainstream recognition and acceptance of the culture, history and language of those on the margins" (*Talkin that Talk* 384). This charge speaks to Nino's call for an interpretive attitude that recognizes democracy as a social practice grounded in justice, participation, conduct, and acceptance. Nino's own interpretive attitude parallels with my idea of democratic engagement in terms related to the signification of "relationships, conversations, and experiences, grounded in mutual exchanges, people have with one another" as multiple competing discourses are negotiated (Kinloch 10). Insofar as *Students' Right* is concerned, justice, conduct, and democratic engagements surface in classroom interactions with students and teachers just as much as in assessment measures that test students' acquisition of knowledge (legislated national and state testing) and in students' affiliated involvement in home communities (with families and friends, at their jobs, in community centers).

The need to reinterpret Smitherman's fundamental concept of "being on the margins" is just as important today as it was during the adoption of the *Students' Right* resolution. This reinterpretation involves increased public and professional understanding of literacy and language in the academic spaces of classrooms and the habitable spaces of people's communities. Such an understanding would justify a rhetoric of rights predicated upon equity, equality, opportunity, access to quality resources, and investment in an economy of emerging literacies and multiple languages. This could produce democratic engagements supportive of Nino's interpretive attitude inside of composition classrooms.

Classroom Vignette 1

One morning I walked into my composition class in Houston only to meet students looking out of the window at the faculty parking lot and talking about how "the damn bayous always be running over when it rains." Without realizing that I had already entered the classroom, one student remarked, quite interestingly, that the university building was on the margins in much the same ways that they (my students) were on the margins. I interrupted by asking, "What does it mean to be on the margins?" And as they turned to look at me before taking their seats, the same student said, "Why, when I say some-thing about what I understand an author to be saying, do I get crazy looks from people acting like they don't understand me? Do those looks mean my language is on the margins? Probably so 'cause people don't understand my point." Another student, in disagreement with the aforementioned student, remarked, "Being on the margins don' have to mean gettin' certain looks from people 'cause of what you say 'bout a reading. It has more to do with who's talkin' and what language form that person's usin' . . . the more proper or standard or the more you sound like the teacher, the more respect."

And so this is how my class began. A class session not intended to directly focus on "being on the margins" or on "Standard English [and] sound[ing] like the teacher," but one that quickly became involved with language rights and, in the sentiments of another student, "the right to use language to deny being on the margins." Over the next few weeks, we decided to focus more on how students should have a right to their own language and how the classroom can serve as a place where such a right is interrogated for mean-ing in the larger public sphere. Let me offer an example of a classroom engagement:

In advocating for "students' right to their own language," I quickly learned that I needed to advocate for student participation in selecting course readings.[4] My students and I spent one in-class and one out-of-class session devising a list of reading material that, in some way or another, addresses language issues. I compiled suggestions and asked for student volunteers to be responsible for bringing into class a selection from the list. Some students volunteered to bring in chapters from Pat Mora's *Nepantla: Essays from the Land in the Middle* while others volunteered to bring in chapters from Mike Rose's *Lives on the Boundary*, Studs Terkel's *Race: How Blacks and Whites Think and Feel about the American Obsession*, Geneva Smitherman's *Talkin that Talk*, Luis Rodríguez's *Always Running: La Vida Loca*, Victor Villanueva's *Bootstraps: From an American Academic of Color*, and Stephen Carter's *Integrity*, as well as Robert King's "Should English Be the Law?" and Amy Tan's "Mother Tongue." Another student (hereafter referred to as "José"), who had remained silent for some time, offered to bring in and lead class discussion on June Jordan's essay "Problems of Language in a Democratic State." So Jordan's essay led in our class discussion of language rights.

On the day of José's presentation, he opened by reading the following passage from the Jordan essay:

Nevertheless and notwithstanding differences of power, money, race, gender, age and class, there remains one currency common to all of us. There remains one thing that makes possible exchange, shared memory, self-affirmation and collective identity. And isn't that currency known and available to everybody regardless of this and that? And isn't that common currency therefore the basis for a democratic state that will not discriminate between the stronger and the weak? And isn't that indispensable, indiscriminate, or non-discriminating, currency, our language? Isn't that so? (223–24)

José then responded:

If I am to believe what Jordan is saying, then I am to believe that we all have our right to language. If I am to read into her quote a bit of sarcasm, then I should know that our common currency, language, is really not that common because it does not make all of us equal or strong or rich. So the basis of this democracy is the common currency of language—the language of power—and that's not Black English Vernacular or Spanglish or mixing French with English for comprehension or writing in Chinese first before translating into English. For the people in power in this democracy, Standard English is superior to all others. And what Jordan really wants to know is what the hell are we doing about it?

Classroom Vignette 2

During a class session on critical thinking skills, "Maria" said: "I am a critical thinker, . . . tell me what I need to think about and I can be critical. To be critical is to just give 'em what they want, what they've already said. Not too hard when you think about that. Listen to what they're saying and change the language around. That's critical enough."

José then recalled his presentation on the Jordan essay a few days before as he prepared his response to Maria's argument. He said. "You know Jordan is right about the problems of language in a democracy. And if we really read what she's saying here, we can apply it to the ways we think about life and access and opportunity. Who wants to pretend to be a critical thinker by having the information dictated to them? That's not learning and that's not acknowledging our right to our own language and the freedom that comes with this right." A female student, "Claudia," sitting next to José inserted her position, "We don't know how to talk so we don't know how to be critical. If I'm talking with my accent, I get looks from other people, and they automatically tune me out. They're not taking what I say critically and they're sure not taking my accent as part of my language right." (Important to note is that when I mentioned the terms "institutional dialect," "syntax," "phonology," "morphology," and "semantics," Claudia, Maria, José, and others gave me an unforgiving and knowing look. Claudia then said something like, "Yeah, but I'm saying they don't *listen*, they don't want to *hear* me").

Another student, sitting in silence in the back of the room, said, "Well, let's talk. Where do we begin? Can we talk about how all this language rights we are supposed to have places us in a certain class that many of us can't seem to get out of?" To this, I asked students to critically reflect on the Jordan quotation from José's presentation insofar as the reality of class issues is concerned. The reactions to both Jordan's talk of language and the reality of class proved quite insightful. Students began to talk about their own language as reflective of their class status: "I know that one reason my class level is what it is, well, is because of my *verbal* language. If I can fix that, then I can move out of my class," insisted "Anthony," a student in this course. Silence entered the room as heads began nodding in agreement and as I, the instructor, was being looked upon for answers to the dilemmas circulating around language acquisition and, suddenly, class status.

I turned to the Jordan piece and offered an explanatory remark: "In our history, the state has failed to respond to the weak. State power serves the powerful. . . . Apparently the minority problem of language has become a majority problem of low-level reading and writing skills" ("Problems of Language" 224–225). Jordan's discussion of state power and the language of minority peoples parallels the beliefs many of my students have, that power is restricted from people whose language does not represent a standard American form; therefore, class mobility is heavily based on increased language skills. The language skills of many of these students derive from immersion in their culture, mainly the culture of immigrant Spanish-speaking grandparents and parents or working-class black laborers, and as a result class becomes a question of mobility for those who are able to access and utilize Standard English. Students are all too aware of this fact, and their desire for class mobility represents their ongoing struggle to reinvent themselves and their language while they are *inventing the university* (Bartholomae). However much my students attempt to invent the university, they must, at some crucial point, learn the skills necessary to maintain their positions in a university, and such skills include reading and writing competencies, or, as one student eloquently stated, "I can read and I can write. Tell me how I can use my skills to move ahead in the world without being judged on my accent, my pronunciation of certain words, and on race. You do know that language rights are always tied into race, right?" (See also Delpit.)

Classroom Vignette 3

Issues of language and class, as with issues of race, are present throughout the supporting document of the *Students' Right* resolution. One section reads:

> Students who come from backgrounds where the prestigious variety of English is the normal medium of communication have built-in advantages that enable them to succeed, often in spite of, and not because of, their schoolroom training in "grammar." They sit at the head of the class, are accepted at "exclusive" schools, and are later rewarded with positions in the business and social world. Students whose nurture and experience give them a different dialect are usually denied these rewards. As English teachers, we are responsible for what our teaching does to the self-image and the self-esteem of our students. (p. 22)

After reading this passage with my class, I awaited their individual responses. Many of them expressed feelings of rage, not because of what the passage says, but because of the reality of class privilege in this democracy. "Minh," a student in the class, shared with us how her Chinese language was considered an "interference" with her acquisition and mastery of Standard Written and Spoken English: "My twelfth-grade English teacher once said: 'You know, Minh, if you want to one day live in power, then you'll have to work on *downplaying* your accent . . . and you must stop using Chinese words and phrases when trying to express a complete thought. If you must, then translate privately, but never make it a public act. Your speech will determine your class status.'"

Other students in the class became even more enraged after Minh's comment, and wanted to further investigate the *Students' Right* passage in light of one of the course readings on language and class. For the next reading discussion, they unanimously selected bell hooks's "Confronting Class in the Classroom," and Minh volunteered to lead the discussion.

When Minh's presentation day arrived, she asked me to provide an introduction to the piece. Not knowing where my introduction would fit into Minh's discussion, I decided to begin with the following passage from "Confronting Class in the Classroom": "[A]ny professor who commits to engaged pedagogy recognizes the importance of constructively confronting issues of class. That means welcoming the opportunity to alter our classroom practices creatively so that the democratic ideal of education for everyone can be realized" (189). Minh jumped in by talking about the mantra of class issues in the classroom as representative of controversial fields of contact in which, according to Minh, "students can easily be exposed to others and can feel so uncomfortable if the teacher does not provide the space and time for students to talk about their feelings and hear different reactions from other people in the classroom" (hooks's engaged pedagogy). Minh made a connection between hooks's talk of class and the *Students' Right* resolution's talk of students from privileged versus nonprivileged backgrounds by saying: "I was offended when my twelfth-grade teacher told me to *downplay* my accent because of what she thinks is my unprivileged cultural background. Well, I think it's important to know that regardless of language and accent and dialect, we all have a right to our language and the language of social class mobility. I care about my Chinese language and my English language, and I need to know how to nurture them as I move up the class ladder." At the closing of this class session, another student confessed, "I'm black, I'm male, I'm poor, and yet I speak Standard English. Do I give a damn about differences in language and class? Yeah, I do, because language defines class and class defines social and political status, power, and, in some way, it all defines who we are or who we want to eventually be. But will I give up my right to my own language? Now that I know I have a right, no!"

From this class session and for the remainder of the semester, students productively interrogated the fundamental principles outlined in both the Jordan and the hooks essays, and their doing so is demonstrative of how language and class issues can motivate students to critically reflect on their own experience while cultivating their own expressive powers through methods of inventiveness and analysis. They reread the essays, bringing into subsequent class sessions highlighted paragraphs to share with one another; they questioned Jordan's statement, "I believe that somebody real has blinded America in at least one eye. And, in the same way that so many Americans feel that 'we have lost our jobs,' we suspect that we have lost our country. *We know that we do not speak the language*" ("Problems" 232). Additionally, the students made connections between Jordan's emphasis on language being a common currency and hooks's implication that people need to talk about class distinctions by using language. One student even brought into class a quotation from Toni Morrison's *Lecture and Speech of Acceptance, Upon the Award of the Nobel Prize for Literature*, and as he stood tall to read a passage from the text, everyone fell speechless. He stated, "Since we're talking about the power of language this semester, about how students do have a right to their language, and about how we can use language to talk about issues like class, I brought in something to share." He then said, "Toni Morrison writes, 'We die. That may be the meaning of life. But we *do* language. That may be the measure of our lives'" (22).

Lessons from the Vignettes

Clearly, "we do language." In doing language, my students and I confront issues of language abuse inside the writing classroom. When students become silent after reading a text on language and class issues, when they make use of their native languages and dialects (see Elbow) to assert their beliefs the best way they can, when they turn to the course texts in search of a deeper meaning, and when they take classroom work into their homes and communities, bringing back other people's reactions, then we are doing the work required of an engaged pedagogy. We are participating in a rhetoric of rights. We are reading, talking, discussing, sharing, and writing about issues circulating around language rights, but more important we are confronting our own sense of reality, which often gets ignored in classrooms. We are, in the sentiments of Karla Holloway in "Cultural Politics in the Academic Community: Masking the Color Line," confronting the very lived realities comprised in our ever-so-expanding classrooms: "Our classrooms are populated by the 'them' we once studied. Those we theorized about [. . .] not only are in front of the classroom, but are now its students" (611). Holloway goes a step further to assert that educators should

> [e]mbrace to our own ends the identity politics—the perspectives of race, culture, gender, and ethnicity—inherent in language. We can claim the power of our voices, and their complexity, *and their complexions* to assert the dimensions of our concerns, to call attention to our successes in vitalizing the community of the university—both its faculty bodies and its student bodies. (617)

This type of engagement, whereby teachers are embracing the politics of language identity and students are sharing their perspectives on language diversity, represents a vital intersection of Nino's interpretive attitude, Jordan's legitimatization of black English and *languages*, and the adoption of the *Students' Right* resolution: the availability of a public discourse to talk about educational and political concerns is often absent shared democratic values when groups of people do not participate in evaluating and reimagining the possibilities of our commitments. In the sentiments of Nino, an interpretive attitude would mean that we are publicly confronting tensions surrounding, for example, the politicization of language rights, linguistic diversity, and democratized systems. I seek not to oversimplify the case for linguistic diversity in classroom practices by encouraging teachers to wear an interpretive attitude and go on about the business of teaching. What I want to do, as evidenced by my involvement with writing students, is to reimagine our educational commitments, our shared values, in ways that mobilize public and professional attitudes circulating around the education of monolingual and multilingual students. This mobilization, I believe, needs to be grounded in linguistic and cultural negotiation and not in a wrong language/right language debate.

An interpretive attitude allowed me to accept responsibility "for what [my] teaching does to the self-image and the self-esteem of our students" (*Students' Right* p. 22) as students produced classroom work using traditional academic writing, a combination of academic writing with linguistic varieties, and mixed-genre writings.[5] They used their multilingual and bidialectical voices to discuss, debate, and reflect on course readings, to make meanings, and to construct sophisticated written and verbal arguments. By the semester's end, they all embraced *Students' Right*, witnessed how the resolution could indeed be implemented inside a classroom focused on student involvement and student voice, and they all agreed with James Berlin, in "Composition Studies and Cultural Studies" that "[r]hetoric, after all, was invented to resolve disputes peacefully, as an alternative to armed conflict, and it remains the best option in a perilous time" (116).

Our collective endorsement of Berlin's belief in rhetoric, along with our "interpretative attitude," to borrow Nino's phrase, taught us valuable lessons as we established connections between language and struggle, language and cultural and academic selves. Minh articulated her frustration not with language, but with the teachers and academic systems that alienated her cultural and linguistic registers from classroom practices, forcing her to immediately assimilate into "a language of otherness that doesn't acknowledge the history of my people." José, obviously moved by Minh's comment, responded, "If we [students] must master . . . the codes of power . . . standard English . . . academic writing . . . pass all the tests, for the classes and the state, then shouldn't there be an awareness of our conditions, our languages, our lives and literatures, by teachers?" A different student interrupted, "By the whole system, José, by the whole system!"

José, Minh, and the other students were in agreement. José then asked if we could return to hooks's article, "Confronting Class in the Classroom." He pulled out the article along with hooks's text, *Talking Back: Thinking Feminist,*

Thinking Black (as students snickered, "Man, you bought that book? You trying to outdo us?"). He read the selected passages:

> Students who enter the academy unwilling to accept without question the assumptions and values held by privileged classes tend to be silenced, deemed troublemakers. ("Confronting Class" 179)

> To avoid feelings of estrangement, students from working-class backgrounds could assimilate into the mainstream, change speech patterns, points of reference, drop any habit that might reveal them to be from a nonmaterially privileged background. ("Confronting Class" 181)

> Coming to Stanford with my own version of a Kentucky accent [. . .] I learned to speak differently while maintaining the speech of my region., the sound of my family and community [. . .]. In recent years, I have endeavored to use various speaking styles in the classroom as a teacher and find it disconcerts those who feel that the use of a particular patois excludes them as listeners, even if there is translation into the usual, acceptable mode of speech. Learning to listen to different voices [. . .] challenges the notion that we must all assimilate. (*Talking Back* 79)

After his reading, students discussed hooks's journey to enter a world different from her "nonmaterially privileged" world in the South and the struggles that resulted. One student made the connection between hooks's efforts to maintain her home practices and Jordan's argument to embrace the language, culture, family, community, and rights that are ours as we work to erase boundaries of right/wrong, standard/nonstandard. This discussion was met with a peculiar student request: to devise a resolution on student willingness to be a part of an academic community. The following is what resulted:

1. Students, hereafter referred to as "we," are willing to negotiate who we are, the languages we speak, and the codes we use only if this negotiation is embraced in the classroom as "negotiation" and not "abandonment";

2. We are willing to accept and critically engage in academic challenges that promote various theories and conventions as long as we are not prohibited from making our own meaning and producing our own arguments that may, at times, oppose or challenge traditional arguments and positions;

3. We are willing to work, even struggle if need be, to understand the content as long as this struggle includes working with both content and spoken discourse—we don't want to privilege one by devaluing the other. We know this may be hard, so we'll appreciate all attempts;

4. We are willing to embrace the language diversity and variety of the people in this class so we can prepare ourselves to accept the variety of other people we will eventually encounter. We refuse to believe that we are linguistically inferior.

This student-devised resolution allowed other lessons to emerge during the remainder of the academic semester. More specifically, we agreed that to be on or at the margins (see Vignette 1) does not have to mean that students are "linguistically inferior" or "underprepared." My students have helped me to realize that being on or at the margins is to occupy a space of critical inquiry, one that moves beyond labels of inequality, social injustice, and marginaliza-tion and into relationships of reciprocity, linguistic virtuosity, and under-standing: "And humanity tells us that we should allow every [person] the dignity of his [or her] own way of talking" (*Students' Right* p. 38).

Additionally, we learned that invention of the university does not mean that students, and teachers alike, should deny who they are and whence they come (our Class Resolution 1). Nor does it mean that the ways students learn of and eventually come into academic discourse communities of critical inquiry depend on the denial of dialect diversity: "Diversity of dialects will not degrade language nor hasten deleterious changes. Common sense tells us that if people want to understand one another, they will do so" (*Students' Right* p. 38). Students, using various dialects and language forms, can contrib-ute to the mission of pedagogically sophisticated classrooms at the same time that their messages are received and recognized (the student resolution on willingness is a good example of this). My students asked me to honor our resolution, their language rights, as they agreed to honor, with questions, my teaching practices and academic assignments. It was a difficult, yet successful semester.

3. SRTOL, POINTS OF ENGAGEMENT, AND PEDAGOGICAL PRACTICES

The success of the semester unveiled itself as we began to trust one another, thus, divulge critical information about our identities. I remember one stu-dent sharing her journal entry on the consequences of not doing language (a message from Morrison's *Nobel Lecture* speech). As she scrambled through her entry, trying to make sense of her writing in light of the arrows, marginal notes, and scratched-out sentences, she frustratingly stopped and asked to be skipped over. Without hesitation, her writing partner said, "No! Just read it." What she eventually shared with the class was her social location: she was a resident of a local barrio, a first-generation college student, a fluent Spanish and Spanglish speaker, and the only fluent English speaker in her extended family. She then said that to not do language was not a part of her vocabulary and experience, and she could not understand how people could not do and love and feel language, "the only thing that heals the pain."

She sat, and nothing in the room moved, until Anthony's hand went up. He thanked this student for her honest reflection and then informed us of his social location: he was a resident of the third ward, a historic black inner-city community, son of working-class parents, and a user of "any language form I can get my hands on." Anthony's connection to language comes from his interaction with the people, his "street mentors" in his community, who can smooth-talk one minute and theorize the next. Anthony and the other student speakers and listeners reminded me that any classroom teacher who wants to confront language issues circulating around the politics and the teaching of writing must acknowledge, trust, and value students as knowl-edgeable people from various discourse communities.[6] They also taught me that listening to and critiquing students' realities can lead to self-reflection and critical consciousness of differences as an increased sense of agency for students, teachers, and governing systems is established.

In drawing on the plethora of knowledge students have and can bring into the classroom, I turn to Smitherman and her invitation to educators to reflect "How can I use what the kids *already* know to move them to what they *need* to know? This question presumes that you genuinely accept as viable the language and culture the child has acquired by the time he or she comes to school" (*Talkin and Testifyin* 219). Smitherman's assertion legitimizes the varieties of linguistic and cultural diversity that intersect with dynamics of privilege, identity, and schooling. In this way, the dilemma of *Students' Right* becomes a concern for how composition scholars locate meaningful teaching practices inside of classrooms while asking the questions: What else could the resolution say about language variety? How else could the resolution challenge educators to adopt a rights rhetoric of and for student differences/ voices inside classrooms? And how far is too far for educators to go in discussing and advocating the rights and values of students?

The contributions of José, Minh, Anthony, and the other students to class conversations on language prove that, at times, going too far is not going far enough. Their honest responses to class readings, discussions, and journal reflections on topics ranging from "being on the margins," "social class (im)mobility," and "a privileged language" speak directly to the politics of teaching writing in these United States, given our national history with social injustice. So, writes Smitherman,

> One major result of the social movements of the 1960s and 1970s was the creation of educational policies to redress the academic exclusion of and past injustices inflicted upon Blacks, Browns, women, and other historically marginalized groups. Programs and policies such as Upward Bound, open enrollment, Educational Opportunity Programs (EOPs), preferential/affirmative action admissions, and the development of special academic courses ("basic" writing) brought a new and different brand of student into the college composition classroom. ("CCCC's Role" p. 63)

The politics of teaching writing require educators to recall, as Smitherman does, the social movements and educational policies birthed in the 1960s and 1970s so as to complicate our thinking about writing, reading, language, and literacy practices. In "CCCC's Role in the Struggle for Language Rights," Smitherman presents the reality of the new student with a different, albeit nontraditional, Americanized culture. In *Bootstraps: From an American Academic of Color*, Victor Villanueva, Jr., goes a step further in talking about the new student, whether Latina/Latino, Puerto Rican, or African American, as not so new, and not so foreign, and he uses himself and his linguistic fluencies as examples. In this mixed-genre autobiography, Villanueva writes of his multilingual skills—as a speaker of English, Black English (or African American Language), Spanish, and Spanglish—as he reflects on the language of other speakers of color:

He looks at the experiences of the African American speaker of Black English, the Spanish-speaking Mexican American, Puerto Rican, or other Latino, and says, "They lack sophisticated speaking skills in the language of the majority." Then he remembers having spoken Spanish and Black English and the Standard English required at the school, seems like always [. . .] (xiv)

He then chronicles the existing distances (located in assumptions) between teachers and students by recalling an early school experience: "Spanish was taught by Mr. Hauser (trying to teach Spanish to thirty bilingual kids). We didn't know about dialects, prestige, or the like, just about right and wrong. He was wrong [. . .]" (3).

In relation to Villanueva's powerful experiences and Smitherman's talk of the new student is Jordan's insistence that "Black English is not a linguistic buffalo; as children, most of the thirty-five million Afro-Americans living here depend on this language for our discovery of the world" ("Nobody" 175). We can also turn to Min-Zhan Lu's confession that "if I watched myself carefully, I would figure out from the way I read whether I had really mastered the 'languages.' But writing became a dreadful chore. When I tried to keep a diary, I was so afraid that the voice of school might slip in that I could only list my daily activities" (141–42).

Collectively, Smitherman, Villanueva, Jordan, and Lu encourage us all to critically discuss the democratic possibilities of educating students not simply by avowing differences in language and culture but also by problematizing and complicating them as essential components of academic literacy. One way to do this type of work is to reimagine the promise of *Students' Right* through our history's social movements. Another way is to use the resolution to engender multilingual, multicultural, multigenerational perspectives, grounded in critical and creative pedagogies, in the composition class. Either way, we must, according to Lu, "complicate the external and internal scenes of our students' writing [. . .]. Don't teach them to 'survive' the whirlpool of crosscurrents by avoiding it. Use the classroom to moderate the currents. Moderate the currents, but teach them from the beginning to struggle" (147). How do we complicate and moderate, and how can we effectively *do* such work in our classrooms?

I offer the following strategies for engaging in such work in the space of academic classrooms. Some strategies have been tested numerous times and have yielded successful classroom discussions and assignments. Others have been partly tested, depending on the course level, readings, and requirements.

1. Invite students to examine the spatial location and demographic trends of their university community juxtaposed with their home community affiliation(s). I begin by asking students to consider such questions as: How would you describe the university in terms of cultural and linguistic practices, male-female attendance, and location within the surrounding community? What does your descriptive observation say about who you are as a member of this academic community? Would you describe the university and the students as

multilingual and multicultural, and if so, how are you using such terms? What do the terms signify? (This requires students to consider arguments by Banks, Keith Gilyard, and Baugh, for example).

2. Ask students to listen to the languages of other people (the faculty and student bodies of their university community), by paying attention to and documenting the structures and patterns, codes and language shifts of speakers. What do such patterns and shifts indicate about communicative practices, about the ways people interact with one another, and about "academic" and "nonacademic" conventions? How do you linguistically engage with the members and the nonmembers of your discourse community, and what do such implications imply?

3. Ask students to write out the lyrics to popular songs and invite volunteers to play a sample of the selected songs with the class before sharing the written lyrics (we compare what we hear with what we read). In this comparison, we are listening to and reading the words (form and pronunciation) before analyzing, synthesizing, citing, and even rewriting the content as exercises in revision.

4. Engage students in a discussion of how socioeconomic status and geographic location, or region, influence language practices by listening to music samples of various East and West Coast artists. We take note of how meaning is read as comprehensible and is popularized across linguistic and spatial differences. Students could then write a response to the rap lyrics by considering their own positions juxtaposed with the position(s) of the rapper as writer.

5. Invite students into a discussion of phonology, semantics, syntax, accent, and dialect. This can lead to an examination of the *Students' Right* resolution and various theories of language acquisition, grammar, and vocabulary. It follows that students often become so interested in the topic of language development and rights that they explore the language histories of friends and family members through interviews, surveys, and informal conversations. This strategy can be enhanced if connections are established between the composition instructor and an instructor whose research area is in sociolinguistics, the teaching of grammar, and/or the teaching of the English language. This instructor could be invited to lead a class discussion on the history of the language and the connections of the language to speech acts and writing skills.

6. On occasion, I ask students to listen to recordings of selected poetry and prose read by Langston Hughes, noting how he combines the language of the blues with his oration of the language of everyday people. This has proven very successful, especially in encouraging students to explore the nature of mixed genres and the skills involved in code switching. Writing assignments follow.

7. A most important strategy is to create a comfortable, safe environment in which students trust one another enough to share their beliefs about language diversity. This is not always an easy strategy to fulfill, for it means that we must consciously work at getting to know our students in an abbreviated amount of time. To do this, it is helpful to know students by their first names, to support their collective and individual explorations of language, and to ask for volunteers to lead class discussions and be responsible for a major component of the class work. At the beginning of the semester, work into the

culture of the classroom time for freewriting/journal writing. If at the beginning of class, ask students to respond to a topic or a set of topics related to the class readings. Then ask student volunteers to share parts of their entries, sharing that can lead into the class lesson for that day. If at the end of class. remind students that they will be asked to share their responses at the beginning of the next class session, and their sharing can lead into that class lesson. I like to have students see how I consciously connect themes from their journal entries to class lessons and assignments. Throughout the semester, students are invited to return to earlier journal entries as they brainstorm topics for academic essays, prepare for in-class presentations, and work in groups to analyze pressing issues circulating around language rights.

I have discovered that such strategies not only establish connections between class readings/theories and student realities, but they also encourage students who are normally silent to participate in class conversations. Over time, students become less reluctant to use their own language form in the classroom as they attempt to master the negotiation of home practices with academic practices. The struggles of my students to negotiate indicate my lifelong struggle to work at dismantling the social and political dimensions of power, politics, and literacy evident in the larger society (this is a lifelong struggle, indeed). My strategies, then, are influenced by my interpretive attitude (see Nino) to make public the very realities and struggles of students as they become comfortable with their academic identities.

To implement new strategies for working with students means that teachers cannot lambaste their homes or communities or first languages. Experimentation with new strategies points to an awareness of the changing student demographics within the university, changes that require critical conversations about language and writing so choices can be made, arguments supported, context and audience defined, and variations studied. This is the type of work I engaged in with my undergraduate composition students; it is the same type of work I am committed to as I now work with preservice and inservice graduate students and public high school students.

4. CONCLUSION: RETURNING TO *STUDENTS' RIGHT TO THEIR OWN LANGUAGE*

My overall argument, that communicative actions regarding student differences should become a central part of classroom pedagogy, is a difficult one to put into and keep in practice. I am quite aware that this movement is not easy. As an African American educator familiar with home and academic language variations, I realize the power of language, particularly as it constructs identity and positions people in certain classes.[7] I am also aware that the discourses of institutional and public politics are profoundly committed to the markers of white middle- and upper-class socioeconomic values that many of my students attempt to imitate in becoming *insurgent* intellectuals (see hooks and West) of mainstream culture. Nevertheless, as I inform my students, becoming insurgent intellectuals requires a personal investment in the world of and the sharing of ideas, however diverse or not, are the methods by which those ideas are presented. And this claim clearly supports the *Students' Right* resolution regarding the affirmation of language varieties students bring into the classroom.

Or, in the sentiments of two of my students: "So you mean, like, I do have a right to speak the way I be speakin' in class, even while I be learnin' a standard?" and "See, them other teachers don' really wanta hear dat from the get go, so I don' be talkin'. They don' know about affirmin'."

My students represent the lives of people whose language variations should be affirmed and respected. They must learn to believe, as we should, that in their language patterns and varieties can be found sophistication, meaning, and power. I am not afraid to tell my students that I know how to code switch and that my primary form of communication is partly influenced by the Gullah culture of the Sea Islands. I am not afraid to tell them that my family members frequently mix "black" English with "white" English, and that I am able to demonstrate mastery of both language forms. Oftentimes, the next question from my students is an inquiry into how they can achieve such mastery in using both the language forms they already know and the language patterns of mainstream society.

With this inquiry came our acceptance of their language form as powerful and meaningful. This acceptance forced me to invite students to use their "mother tongues" in the classroom, and they invited me to make use of my "mother tongue" when I felt the need to. Asking students to engage in this process reiterates Peter Elbow's argument:

> If we want our students to take on the power of full mainstream literacy, we can never remove the difficulty or even identity anxiety that some of them may experience in having to move past an oral culture (not necessarily to leave it) and take on a culture of literacy. But we can substantially mitigate their anxiety by inviting them to take on *full literacy* in their oral dialect. (372)

I agree with Elbow that our students should be invited "to take on *full literacy* in their oral dialect," which leads me to another valuable lesson: students must be exposed to various forms and expressions of literacy. Lisa Delpit, in *Other People's Children: Cultural Conflict in the Classroom*, asserts, "All we can do is provide students with the exposure to an alternate form, and allow them the opportunity to practice that form *in contexts that are nonthreatening, have a real purpose, and are intrinsically enjoyable*" (54). Encouraging students to use alternate forms of expression in the classroom can demonstrate the richness of languages in communication, engagement, participation, and understanding in literacy learning.

For example, when I first made use of my "mother tongue" in the classroom, I explained to students that there are many ways of saying the same thing; the significance of which expressive form to use depends on defining the audience and the context. Soon thereafter, students who were silent because of perceived language barriers began to share interpretations of class readings—they began to demonstrate proficiency in language and literacy, but, more important, they began to critically understand the power of the "mother tongue" in an academic environment. As declared by Judge Charles C. Joiner in his order that a school district in Ann Arbor, Michigan, could not use children's language as reason to register them into learning disability courses, teachers must "recognize the existence of the language system used by the children in their home community and to use that knowledge as a way of helping the children to learn to read standard English" (*Martin Luther King Elementary School Children v. Ann Arbor School District Board*).

While my composition students can in fact read Standard English, many of them were initially reluctant to engage in discussions for fear that linguistic (in)competence in Standard English would measure their success or failure. In thinking about my students' fear, I recall Henry Giroux's argument that "the discourse of standards represents part of the truth about ourselves as a nation in that it has often been evoked in order to legitimate elitism, racism, and privileges for the few" (190). One way to confront this truth so as to not maintain it is by using *Student's Right* to enact a democratic platform in which theorizations of student differences, incompetencies, and disadvantages become expressions of the contradictions of the struggle for success, acceptance, and competency as measured through schooling. By bringing the resolution into the space that it is meant to occupy—the classroom—we can work to enact a multilingual policy that respects, upholds, and legitimizes every person's right to his or her own language while affording him or her access to "multiple aspects of the communication process [whereby] we can be sure we are dealing with the totality of language, not merely with the superficial features of 'polite usage'" (*Students' Right* p. 33).

Contemporary conversations about and practices of language variation stem from the promise set forth in *Students' Right* that says that teachers "must decide what elements of our discipline are really important to us, whether we want to share with our students the richness of all varieties of language, [and] encourage linguistic virtuosity" (22). It is essential that we, as a profession, privilege the language rights of our students by exposing them to the multiplicity and creativity inherent in expressive forms of literacy. This means that educators should rethink the implications of the resolution in ways that parallel the justice of our classroom pedagogy with the legacy of the resolution. We must do more than theorize about student differences and language variation. We must use a rights rhetoric such as *Students' Right* to encourage students to become active learners and critical thinkers inside and outside of classrooms if we are, in the words of Smitherman, "taking care of business" (*Talkin and Testifyin* 216). Clearly, we can engage in complex discussions of language in composition courses in ways that pay attention to the *Students' Right* resolution, Jordan's argument regarding our common currency, hooks's attention to the language of class, Nino's interpretive attitude, and Smitherman's analysis of language rights if we are ever to repudiate the inequities of social class, language abuse, and racism. Let us affirm the rights of students to their own language by affirming the practices they bring into classrooms as they enhance their critical thinking, reading, writing, and performing skills.

Acknowledgments: I am indebted to Professors Jia-Yi Cheng-Levine, Maisha Fisher, Min-Zhan Lu, Andrea Lunsford, and Erica Walker for their critical and insightful responses to earlier drafts of this article. I would like to acknowledge members of the NCTE Commission on Language and the mentors/mentees of the NCTE grant program, "Cultivating New Voices among Scholars of Color" for their stimulating discussions and critical insights on the *Students' Right to Their Own Language* resolution.

NOTES

1. Examples of events that occurred during this time include Truman's Executive Order 9981 Establishing the President's Committee on Equality of Treatment and Opportunity in the Armed Forces, signed in 1948; the *Brown v. Board of Education* decision, 1954; the Civil Rights Acts, 1957 and 1964; the Voting Rights Act, 1965; the launch of the Poor People's Campaign, 1967; and the *Students' Right* resolution, 1972 and 1974. All such events hold important places in the discussion of a rhetoric of rights as articulated by Jordan, Smitherman, Villanueva, and the CCCC Executive Committee of 1972.

2. In *Class Politics: The Movement for the Students' Right to Their Own Language* (published by NCTE, 2000), Stephen Parks discusses "how class politics, political alliances, and progressive social movements can enhance the foundation of composition studies" through "community-based critical pedagogy" (Scott and Kinloch 705). I believe it is significant to cite him in detail. In the introduction of the book, Parks writes: "My hope, however, is that a history of the SRTOL can serve as a tool in the general effort to establish an effective progressive response to current conservative politics, for the realities that mark the lives of the oppressed can gain political relevancy only through alliances committed to transforming the social terrain; that is, an informed student paper does not by necessity lead to political change. The future must be defined by collective action. Perhaps this history can remind us of that fact" (17). In his examination of class politics, collective action, social movements, and the history of both composition studies and the SRTOL movement, Parks does not "provide an exact model by which such a pedagogy can be directly implemented in classrooms, in communities, or in efforts at organization" (Scott and Kinloch 709). His "history" of composition studies and his call for a community-based critical pedagogy, in relation to the SRTOL movement, overlook the participatory involvement and collective action of African American scholars, an oversight worthy of critical examination.

3. I am concerned with what and how we communicate about language use, acceptance, and standardizations to our students (both speakers proficient only in EAE and speakers labeled "linguistically diverse") and to our colleagues, particularly as we teach academic writing. This teaching, I believe, does not have to occur to the sole exclusion of languages and variances historically deemed "nonstandard" and "nontraditional." This work, of integrating and promoting linguistic diversity in any classroom, is difficult; however, such work can prove useful in students' understanding of the multiple facets of language, writing, communicating, and existing in this diverse, multilingual world.

4. In *Empowering Education*, Ira Shor writes of student participation and curricular negotiations: "The teacher leads and directs the curriculum, but does so democratically with the participation of the students, balancing the need for structure with the need for openness. The teacher brings the lesson plans [. . .] but negotiates the curriculum with the students and begins with their language, themes, and understandings" (16). However difficult it may be, I seek to embrace Shor's assertion by advocating for students' right to their own language and by encouraging student participation in my own classrooms.

5. Because this preliminary study of the historical and pedagogical significance of the SRTOL resolution examines classroom conversations and engagements with course readings, I do not offer substantive data from student writings as a way to demonstrate the "ultimate" effects of my pedagogical strategies. I will take up the challenge of demonstrating the effects of my strategies on student writings in a future study.

6. My own reflections on this course are ongoing: in part, I seek to enhance my own methods of engaging students in the very complex issues highlighted throughout this article; in another way, I reconsider how my actual pedagogical practices speak to the difficulties of student writers on writing. While I attempt to illustrate methods and pedagogical practices throughout this article, I am aware that this article highlights students' thinking (talking, presenting, and engaging with

the texts, with one another, and with the teacher) rather than their doing (the act of writing and the difficulties that may come with this process).

7. I recognize that my own positionality affects my abilities to work with the suggested strategies. The ways in which my students see and react to me—insofar as race, class, age, and academic status are concerned—are oftentimes inviting "of classroom environments supportive of imaginative explorations, freedom of idea expression and generation, and the journeys of the writing process" (Kinloch, "Poetry" 111). It does not, nonetheless, become easy to teach complex thematic issues, to ask students to discuss such issues openly and honestly in the classroom and, subsequently, to have students produce written, academic arguments.

WORKS CITED

Ball, Arnetha, and Ted Lardner. "Dispositions toward Language: Teacher Constructs of Knowledge and the Ann Arbor Black English Case." *CCC* 48.4 (1997): 469–85.

Bartholomae, David. "Inventing the University." *When a Writer Can't Write.* Ed. Mike Rose. New York: Guilford, 1985. 134–65.

Berlin, James. "Composition Studies and Cultural Studies: Collapsing Boundaries." *Into the Field: Sites of Composition Studies.* Ed. Anne Ruggles Gere. New York, MLA: 1993. 99–116.

Bruch, Patrick, and Richard Marback. "Race, Literacy, and the Value of Rights Rhetoric in Composition Studies." *CCC* 53.4 (2002): [pp. 169–87 in this book].

Buress, Lee, and Edward B. Jenkinson. *The Students' Right to Know.* Urbana, IL: NCTE, 1982.

Carter, Stephen. *Integrity.* New York: Perennial, 1996.

Conference on College Composition and Communication. *Students' Right to Their Own Language.* Spec. issue of *CCC* 25.3 (Fall 1974): [pp. 19–57 in this book].

Delpit, Lisa. *Other People's Children: Cultural Conflict in the Classroom.* New York: New Press, 1995.

Elbow, Peter. "Inviting the Mother Tongue: Beyond 'Mistakes,' 'Bad English,' and 'Wrong Language.'" *JAC* 19.3 (Summer 1999): 359–88.

Giroux, Henry. "Pedagogy and Radical Democracy in the Age of 'Political Correctness.'" *Radical Democracy: Identity, Citizenship, and the State.* Ed. David Trend. New York: Routledge, 1996. 179–93.

Holloway, Karla. "Cultural Politics in the Academic Community: Masking the Color Line." *College English* 55 (1993): 610–17.

hooks, bell. "Confronting Class in the Classroom." *Teaching to Transgress: Education as the Practice of Freedom.* New York: Routledge, 1994. 177–89.

———. *Talking Back: Thinking Feminist, Thinking Black.* Boston: South End, 1989.

hooks, bell, and Cornel West. *Breaking Bread: Insurgent Black Intellectual Life.* Boston: South End, 1991.

Jordan, June. "Nobody Mean More to Me Than You and the Future Life of Willie Jordan." *Moving Towards Home: Political Essays.* London: Virago, 1989. 175–89.

———. "Problems of Language in a Democratic State." *Some of Us Did Not Die: New and Selected Essays of June Jordan.* New York: Basic, 2002. 223–32.

———. "White English/Black English: The Politics of Translation." *Moving Towards Home: Political Essays.* London: Virago, 1989. 29–40.

King, Robert. "Should English Be the Law?" *Atlantic Monthly* Apr. 1997: 55–64.

Kinloch, Valerie, "In Search of a Dwelling Place: Personal Writing in Composition Studies." CCCC Convention. San Antonio. 26 Mar. 2004.

———. "June Jordan and the Linguistic Register: A Statement about Our Rights." *Still Seeking an Attitude: Critical Reflections on the Work of June Jordan.* Ed. Valerie Kinloch and Margret Grebowicz. Lanham, Maryland: Rowman, 2004. 71–86.

———. "Poetry, Literacy, and Creativity: Fostering Effective Learning Strategies in an Urban Classroom." *English Education* 37 (2005): 96–114.

Lee, Carol. "Why We Need to Re-Think Race and Ethnicity in Educational Research." *Educational Researcher* 32.5 (2003): 3–5.

Lu, Min-Zhan. "From Silence to Words: Writing as Struggle." *Women/Writing/Teaching.* Ed. Jan Zlotnik Schmidt. New York: SUNY P, 1998. 133–48.

Martin Luther King Elementary School Children v. Ann Arbor School District Board. Civil Action No. 7-71861. 473 F. Supp. 1371. 1979.

Mora, Pat. *Nepantla: Essays from the Land in the Middle.* Albuquerque: U of New Mexico P, 1993.

Morrison, Toni. *The Nobel Lecture in Literature, 1993.* New York: Knopf, 1993.

Nino, Carlos Santiago. *The Constitution of Deliberative Democracy.* New Haven: Yale UP, 1996.

Parks, Stephen. *Class Politics: The Movement for the Students' Right to Their Own Language.* Urbana, IL: NCTE, 2000.

Rodríguez, Luis J. *Always Running: La Vida Loca.* New York: Simon, 1993.

Rose, Mike. *Lives on the Boundary.* New York: Penguin, 1990.

Scott, Jerrie Cobb, and Valerie Kinloch. Rev. of *Class Politics: The Movement for the Students' Right to Their Own Language*, by Stephen Parks. *JAC* 21.3 (Summer 2001): 705–10.

Shor, Ira. *Empowering Education: Critical Teaching for Social Change.* Chicago: U of Chicago P, 1992.

Smitherman, Geneva. "CCCC's Role in the Struggle for Language Rights." *CCC* 50.3 (1999): [pp. 58–82 in this book].

———. "The Historical Struggle for Language Rights in CCCC." *Language Diversity in the Classroom: From Intention to Practice.* Ed. Geneva Smitherman and Victor Villanueva. Carbondale: Southern Illinois UP, 2003. 7–39.

———. *Talkin and Testifyin: The Language of Black America.* Detroit: Wayne State UP, 1977.

———. *Talkin that Talk: Language, Culture and Education in African America.* New York: Routledge, 2000.

———. "Toward a National Public Policy on Language." *College English* 49 (1987): 29–36.

Tan, Amy. "Mother Tongue." *Crossing Cultures: Readings for Composition.* 6th ed. Ed. Anne Knepler, Ellie Knepler, and Myrna Knepler. New York: Longman, 2003. 409–415.

Terkel, Studs. *Race: How Blacks and Whites Think and Feel about the American Obsession.* New York: New Press, 1992.

Villanueva, Victor. *Bootstraps: From an American Academic of Color.* Urbana, IL: NCTE, 1993.

———. "Maybe a Colony: And Still Another Critique of the Comp Community." *JAC* 17.2 (1997): 183–90.

PART SIX

Lingering Questions

24

What Should Colleges Teach? Part 3

STANLEY FISH

I write a third column on the teaching of writing in colleges and universities because three important questions posed by a large number of posters remain unanswered: (1) Isn't the mastery of forms something that should be taught in high school or earlier? (2) Isn't extensive reading the key to learning how to write? (3) What would a composition course based on the method I urge look like?

Questions (1) and (2) can be answered briefly. Question (3) is, as they say, a work in progress.

By all the evidence, high schools and middle schools are not teaching writing skills in an effective way, if they are teaching them at all. The exception seems to be Catholic schools. More than a few commentators remembered with a mixture of fondness and pain the instruction they received at the hands of severe nuns. And I have found that those students in my classes who do have a grasp of the craft of writing are graduates of parochial schools. (I note parenthetically that in many archdioceses such schools are being closed, not a good omen for those who prize writing.)

I cannot see, however, why a failure of secondary education relieves college teachers of a responsibility to make up the deficit. Quite the reverse. It is because our students come to us unable to write clean English sentences that we are obligated to supply what they did not receive from their previous teachers. No doubt this obligation constitutes a burden on an already overworked labor force, but (and this is one of those times a cliché can acquire renewed force), somebody has to do it.

The question of the relationship of reading and learning to write is more complicated. Classical rhetoricians preached the virtue of imitation; students were presented with sentences from the work of great authors and asked to reproduce their form with a different content. I like this exercise because its emphasis is so obviously formal.

But what about just doing a lot of reading and hoping that by passing your eyes over many pages you will learn how to write through osmosis? I'm

From *The New York Times* Opinionator, September 7, 2009.

not so sure. If to wide reading were added daily dinner-table discussions of the sophistication and wit found in many 18th and 19th century novels, I might be more sanguine. And if your experience with words were also to include training in public speaking and debate (itself a matter of becoming practiced in forms), I might say, O.K., you probably don't need a form-based composition course. Unfortunately, however, reading is not the favorite pastime of today's youth and debate societies don't have the cachet they once did; so my insistence that a narrowly focused writing course be required for everyone stands.

How does one teach such a course? What texts can one use? How does one effect the passage from sentences to larger prose units? "How do you determine whether and in what ways [this] approach improves . . . students' writing," asks James Gee. My answers to these questions are provisional. I'm still trying to work them out.

I have reached some conclusions. First, you must clear your mind of the orthodoxies that have taken hold in the composition world. The main orthodoxy is nicely encapsulated in this resolution adopted in 1974 by the Conference on College Composition and Communication: "We affirm the students' right to their own patterns and varieties of language—the dialects of their nurture or whatever dialects in which they find their own identity and style."

Of course, as a matter of law students have the right to any dialect they choose to deploy (although in some small cities where the "English Only" movement has succeeded in the ballot box, linguistic rights have been curtailed). The issue is whether students accorded this right will prosper in a society where norms of speech and writing are enforced not by law but by institutional decorums. If you're about to be fired because your memos reflect your "own identity and style," citing the CCC resolution is not going to do you any good.

Behind the resolution is a theoretical argument. Linguistic forms, it is said, are not God-given; they are the conventional products of social/cultural habit and therefore none of them is naturally superior or uniquely "correct." It follows (according to this argument) that any claim of correctness is political, a matter of power not of right. "If we teach standardized, handbook grammar as if it is the only 'correct' form of grammar, we are teaching in cooperation with a discriminatory power system" (Patricia A. Dunn and Kenneth Lindblom, *English Journal*, January, 2003).

Statements like this one issue from the mistake of importing a sociological/political analysis of a craft into the teaching of it. It may be true that the standard language is an instrument of power and a device for protecting the status quo, but that very truth is a reason for teaching it to students who are being prepared for entry into the world as it now is rather than the world as it might be in some utopian imagination—all dialects equal, all habit of speech and writing equally rewarded.

You're not going to be able to change the world if you are not equipped with the tools that speak to its present condition. You don't strike a blow against a power structure by making yourself vulnerable to its prejudices.

Even as an exercise in political strategy, "having conversations with students about linguistic systems and democratic values" (Kinloch, "Revisiting the Promise of Students' Right to Their Own Language," see p. 435 in this book) strikes me as an unlikely lever for bringing about change; as a strategy for teaching writing, it is a disaster.

And if students infected with the facile egalitarianism of soft multiculturalism declare, "I have a right to my own language," reply, "Yes, you do, and I am not here to take that language from you; I'm here to teach you another one." (Who could object to learning a second language?) And then get on with it.

Of course, I still haven't explained how you get on with it. Not by consulting Strunk and White's *The Elements of Style*, a book cited favorably by more than a few posters. I wouldn't go as far as Randy Burgess does when he calls the famous little book "the worst," but I would say that it is unhelpful because its prescriptions presuppose the knowledge most of our students don't have. What good is it to be told, "Do not join independent clauses with a comma," if you don't have the slightest idea of what a clause is (and isn't), never mind an "independent" one? And even if a beginning student were provided with the definition of a clause, the definition itself would hang in mid-air like a random piece of knowledge. It would be like being given a definition of a dropkick in the absence of any understanding of the game in which it could be deployed.

You have to start with a simple but deep understanding of the game, which for my purposes is the game of writing sentences. So it makes sense to begin with the question, What is a sentence anyway? My answer has two parts: (1) A sentence is an organization of items in the world. (2) A sentence is a structure of logical relationships.

The second part tells you what kind of organization a sentence is, a logical one, and in order to pinpoint what the components of that logic are, I put a simple sentence on the table, something like "John hit the ball" or "Jane likes cake." I spend an entire week on sentences like these (which are easily comprehended by students of any background), asking students to generate them, getting them to see the structure of relationships that makes them all the same on a formal level, getting them to see that the motor of meaning production is form, not content.

Once they see that—and it is an indispensable lesson—they are ready to explore, generate, and practice with the other forms that organize the world's items in increasingly complicated ways. Basically, there is only one thing to be learned, that a sentence is a structure of logical relationships; everything else follows.

I have devised a number of exercises designed to reinforce and extend the basic insight. These include (1) asking students to make a sentence out of a random list of words, and then explain what they did; (2) asking students to turn a three-word sentence like "Jane likes cake" into a 100-word sentence without losing control of the basic structure and then explain, word-by-word, clause-by-clause, what they did; (3) asking students to replace the nonsense words in the first stanza of Lewis Carroll's "Jabberwocky" with ordinary English words in a way that makes coherent (if silly) sense, and then explain what they did, and how they knew what kind of word to put into each "slot." (The answer is that even in the absence of sense or content, the stanza's formal structure tells them what to do and what not to do.)

Notice that the exercises always come in two parts. In the first part students are asked to do something they can do easily. In the second part they are asked to analyze their own performance. The second part is the hard one; it requires students to raise to a level of analytical conscience the operations they must perform if they are to write sentences that hang together.

In the final exercise, . . . the class is divided into groups of four or five and each group is asked to create its own language—complete with a lexicon, and a grammar capable of conveying the distinctions (of number, tense, mood, etc.) conveyed by English grammatical forms. At the end of the semester each group presents a text in its language and teaches the class how to translate it into English, and how to translate English sentences into sentences in the new language, to which the group always gives a name and about which it is always fiercely proprietary.

To my knowledge, there are no textbooks that teach this method— Stephen reports, "until you described it . . . I had never heard of such a course at any college"—although, in some respects, Francis Christensen's "generative rhetoric" of sentences, now considered outmoded, comes close.

What I do is supplement the exercises described above with a standard grammar text filled with the usual terminology, a terminology that will not seem impenetrable and hostile to students who have been learning how language works at a level these texts assume but do not explicate. My current favorites are Geraldine Woods' *English Grammar for Dummies* and Martha Kolln's *Rhetorical Grammar: Grammatical Choice, Rhetorical Effects*. I like the first because its examples are so fanciful ("Lochness loves my singing") that there is no danger of becoming interested in their content. I like the second because of Kolln's emphasis on how grammatical choices fulfill and/or disappoint reader expectations.

I have also assigned J. L. Austin's *How to Do Things With Words*, Richard Lanham's *A Handlist of Rhetorical Terms*, and Lynne Truss's *Eats, Shoots & Leaves*, and I have flirted with using the Rhetorica Ad Herennium and parts of Quintilian and Seneca, if only to show students how old the formal teaching of writing is.

My course is entirely sentence-centered except for one exercise, when I put a sentence on the board—usually something incredibly boring like, "The first year of college presents many challenges"—and ask each student in turn to add a sentence while taking care to look backward to the narrative that has already been developed and forward to the sentences yet to be written by his or her colleagues.

At the end of the semester, I used to send my students into the class taught by Cathy Birkenstein and Gerald Graff, whose excellent book *They Say / I Say* introduces students to the forms of argument in a spirit entirely compatible with my focus on the forms of sentences. (We have taught in each other's classes.)

As to the question of whether this method improves writing, I can only cite local successes in my classes and the anecdotal reports of former students who have employed it in their own classes. I take heart from veteran composition teachers like Lynn Sams, who says that after many years of experimentation, she has concluded that "the ability to analyze sentences, to understand how the parts work together to convey desired meaning, emphasis, and effect is . . . central to the writing process." ("How to Teach Grammar, Analytical Thinking, and Writing: A Method That Works," *English Journal*, January, 2003). Amen.

25 *What if We Occupied Language?*

H. SAMY ALIM

When I flew out from the San Francisco airport last October, we crossed above the ports that Occupy Oakland helped shut down, and arrived in Germany to be met by traffic caused by Occupy Berlin protestors. But the movement has not only transformed public space, it has transformed the public discourse as well.

Occupy.

It is now nearly impossible to hear the word and not think of the Occupy movement.

Even as distinguished an expert as the lexicographer and columnist Ben Zimmer admitted as much this week: "occupy," he said, is the odds-on favorite to be chosen as the American Dialect Society's Word of the Year.

It has already succeeded in shifting the terms of the debate, taking phrases like "debt-ceiling" and "budget crisis" out of the limelight and putting terms like "inequality" and "greed" squarely in the center. This discursive shift has made it more difficult for Washington to continue to promote the spurious reasons for the financial meltdown and the unequal outcomes it has exposed and further produced.

To most, the irony of a progressive social movement using the term "occupy" to reshape how Americans think about issues of democracy and equality has been clear. After all, it is generally nations, armies, and police who occupy, usually by force. And in this, the United States has been a leader. The American government is just now after nine years ending its overt occupation of Iraq, is still entrenched in Afghanistan and is maintaining troops on the ground in dozens of countries worldwide. All this is not to obscure the fact that the United States as we know it came into being by way of an occupation—a gradual and devastatingly violent one that all but extinguished entire Native American populations across thousands of miles of land.

Yet in a very short time, this movement has dramatically changed how we think about occupation. In early September, "occupy" signaled ongoing

From *The New York Times* Opinionator, December 21, 2011.

military incursions. Now it signifies progressive political protest. It's no longer primarily about force of military power; instead it signifies standing up to injustice, inequality, and abuse of power. It's no longer about simply occupying a space; it's about transforming that space.

In this sense, Occupy Wall Street has occupied language, has made "occupy" its own. And, importantly, people from diverse ethnicities, cultures, and languages have participated in this linguistic occupation—it is distinct from the history of forcible occupation in that it is built to accommodate all, not just the most powerful or violent.

As Geoff Nunberg, the long-time chair of the usage panel for *American Heritage Dictionary*, and others have explained, the earliest usage of "occupy" in English that was linked to protest can be traced to English media descriptions of Italian demonstrations in the 1920s, in which workers "occupied" factories until their demands were met. This is a far cry from some of its earlier meanings. In fact, *The Oxford English Dictionary* tells us that "occupy" once meant "to have sexual intercourse with." One could imagine what a phrase like "Occupy Wall Street" might have meant back then.

In October, Zimmer, who is also the chair of the American Dialect Society's New Word Committee, noted on NPR's "On the Media" that the meaning of occupy has changed dramatically since its arrival into the English language in the 14th century. "It's almost always been used as a transitive verb," Zimmer said. "That's a verb that takes an object, so you occupy a place or a space. But then it became used as a rallying cry, without an object, just to mean to take part in what are now called the Occupy protests. It's being used as a modifier—Occupy protest, Occupy movement. So it's this very flexible word now that's filling many grammatical slots in the language."

What if we transformed the meaning of occupy yet again? Specifically, what if we thought of Occupy Language as more than the language of the Occupy movement, and began to think about it as a movement in and of itself? What kinds of issues would Occupy Language address? What would taking language back from its self-appointed "masters" look like? We might start by looking at these questions from the perspective of race and discrimination, and answer with how to foster fairness and equality in that realm.

Occupy Language might draw inspiration from both the way that the Occupy movement has reshaped definitions of "occupy," which teaches us that we give words meaning and that discourses are not immutable, *and* from the way indigenous movements have contested its use, which teaches us to be ever-mindful about how language both empowers and oppresses, unifies and isolates.

For starters, Occupy Language might first look inward. In a recent interview, Julian Padilla of the People of Color Working Group pushed the Occupy movement to examine its linguistic choices:

> To occupy means to hold space, and I think a group of anti-capitalists holding space on Wall Street is powerful, but I do wish the NYC movement would change its name to "'decolonise Wall Street'" to take into

> account history, indigenous critiques, people of colour, and imperialism. . . . Occupying space is not inherently bad, it's all about who and how and why. When white colonizers occupy land, they don't just sleep there over night, they steal and destroy. When indigenous people occupied Alcatraz Island it was (an act of) protest.

This linguistic change can remind Americans that a majority of the 99 percent has benefited from the occupation of native territories.

Occupy Language might also support the campaign to stop the media from using the word "illegal" to refer to "undocumented" immigrants. From the campaign's perspective, only inanimate objects and actions are labeled illegal in English; therefore the use of "illegals" to refer to human beings is dehumanizing. The *New York Times* style book currently asks writers to avoid terms like "illegal alien" and "undocumented," but says nothing about "illegals." Yet the *Times'* standards editor, Philip B. Corbett, did recently weigh in on this, saying that the term "illegals" has an "unnecessarily pejorative tone" and that "it's wise to steer clear."

Pejorative, discriminatory language can have real-life consequences. In this case, activists worry about the coincidence of the rise in the use of the term "illegals" and the spike in hate crimes against all Latinos. As difficult as it might be to prove causation here, the National Institute for Latino Policy reports that the F.B.I.'s annual Hate Crime Statistics show that Latinos comprised *two thirds* of the victims of ethnically motivated hate crimes in 2010. When some*one* is repeatedly described as some*thing*, language has quietly paved the way for violent action.

But Occupy Language should concern itself with more than just the words we use; it should also work towards eliminating language-based racism and discrimination. In the legal system, CNN recently reported that the U.S. Justice Department alleges that Arizona's infamous Sheriff Joe Arpaio, among other offenses, has discriminated against "Latino inmates with limited English by punishing them and denying critical services." In education, as linguistic anthropologist Ana Celia Zentella notes, hostility towards those who speak "English with an accent" (Asians, Latinos, and African Americans) continues to be a problem. In housing, the National Fair Housing Alliance has long recognized "accents" as playing a significant role in housing discrimination. On the job market, language-based discrimination intersects with issues of race, ethnicity, class, and national origin to make it more difficult for well-qualified applicants with an "accent" to receive equal opportunities.

In the face of such widespread language-based discrimination, Occupy Language can be a critical, progressive linguistic movement that exposes how language is used as a means of social, political, and economic control. By occupying language, we can expose how educational, political, and social institutions use language to further marginalize oppressed groups; resist colonizing language practices that elevate certain languages over others; resist attempts to define people with terms rooted in negative stereotypes; and begin to reshape the public discourse about our communities, and about the central role of language in racism and discrimination.

As the global Occupy movement has shown, words can move entire nations of people—even the world—to action. Occupy Language, as a movement, should speak to the power of language to transform how we think about the past, how we act in the present, and how we envision the future.

26 *Where We Go from Here*

ARNETHA F. BALL AND TED LARDNER

Race remains widely discussed in scholarly and public contexts. Academics deconstruct the "social fact" of race (Omi and Winant, "Theoretical"), defining an enforceable fiction the category of difference "race" signifies. Public discourse about race abounds as well, as citizens weigh in not only on affirmative action and racial profiling but also on education reform and school financing, access to health care, urban policy—the list goes on. On the popular front, the sociocultural meanings of hip-hop fashion, language, music, and dance remain to be unpacked as young people across a demographic spectrum embrace ethnic hybridity as normative (Chideya).

With these discourse exchanges continuing apace, we see room for material change in our institutions and classrooms. While race remains a topic of many intellectual conversations, racism remains a problematic experience in day-to-day life. As a system of advantage, racism is harder to talk about, much less do something to remedy, because it is built into institutional routines. Racism is hard for many to see; because the routines seem natural, their consequences appear inevitable. Notwithstanding our best intentions, many of us participate in practices that have discriminatory effects. So there's the rub. Day in and day out, teachers willing to be different *can* make a difference in improving the educational opportunities of AAVE-speaking students. But we have to be willing to be different, to do different, to make a difference.

In chapter 5 [of *African American Literacies Unleashed*], we sought to give teachers something to hold on to and do in their own classrooms. Here we wish to shift our perspective, to think about efficacy and reflective optimism from the perspective of writing program administrators (WPAs), teacher educators, and researchers. We offer suggestions for actions, as well as implications and questions for further research. We organize our remarks to disparate audiences, although we recognize the importance of avoiding the creation of false divisions, particularly between "practitioners" and "researchers." Classroom teachers, WPAs, and teacher educators do indeed act as "researchers,"

From *African American Literacies Unleashed* (Southern Illinois University Press, 2005), 176–96.

employing methodologies that range from informal observation and reflection in situ to narrowly defined, rigorously factored "objective" analyses of survey and other data. So, whether integrated in a teacher's own reflective practice, articulated in terms of a specific writing program, or disseminated as widely applicable findings, we see members of each group making significant contributions.

WRITING PROGRAM ADMINISTRATORS

The dynamics of program administration and organization have been shown to influence a teacher's sense of efficacy. A number of researchers have demonstrated that teachers' sense of efficacy is positively influenced by faculty collegiality, teacher control over important working conditions, having a sense of ownership, and participation in staff development (Ashton and Webb; Little; Raudenbush, Rowan, and Cheong; Guskey).

Opportunities for participation in "extra-role" activities in school have also been associated with teachers' job satisfaction and collective efficacy (Somech and Drach-Zahavy). A message to those at the writing program administration level therefore calls for policies and program development that support these activities. We believe writing program administrators will improve the educational opportunities of AAVE-speaking students (and all students) by seeking to improve teacher efficacy by initiating and supporting collaborations within and across writing program and institutional boundaries, and by situating efforts aimed at broadening teachers' knowledge of AAVE-related pedagogical issues within collaborative staff-development activities.

Collaboration

Isolation is a recurring motif in research on efficacy. Teachers are isolated from one another, isolated from administrators, and, frequently, isolated from students who come from different communities and cultures. Teachers' isolation emerges as a limitation to student achievement. It is a double logic that leads to this result. In reference to cultural discontinuity between school and home, for example, Ashton and Webb explain:

> When teachers are unable to cope with these cultural discontinuities, they feel less effective with these students and their parents. To protect themselves from this threat to their sense of efficacy, teachers may limit their contacts with these families, thereby increasing the likelihood of further discontinuity and, ultimately, alienation of these families from the school. (22)

Ashton and Webb are referring to K–12 teachers in this discussion. Nevertheless, we see similar tendencies at work in college writing programs. College writing teachers have not customarily sought community contacts with parents or families of their students, yet it is interesting to speculate about what might happen if they did.

Moreover, in the organizational culture of universities we are familiar with, teachers typically lack ready opportunities to interact with one another. While the emergence of "learning communities" represents a potential transformation of undergraduate education, purposefully sustained collaborative (and interdisciplinary) interactions focused on teaching are the exception rather than the norm. What one teacher does in his or her classroom has little impact beyond the closed classroom door. What is encouraging is that composition teachers seem to be at the forefront of making changes in ingrained university culture, showing interest in team teaching and interdisciplinary and interinstitutional collaborations. We see an important role for WPAs in leading and supporting these efforts because we see in these efforts the avenues to building teachers' sense of efficacy, and we can cite research that, at least indirectly, supports our claim.

In a study of teachers in thirteen elementary schools, Anit Somech and Anat Drach-Zahavy probed the involvement of teachers in "extra-role behavior" and sought to correlate extra-role behavior with job satisfaction and efficacy. The authors define "extra-role behavior" as "behaviors that go beyond specific role requirements, and are directed towards the individual, the group, or the organization as a unit, in order to promote organizational growth" (650). In the study, twenty-four items were identified as examples of extra-role behavior. Some were oriented toward benefiting other teachers. These included offering colleagues lesson material teachers had prepared for their own classrooms, or working with others to plan assignments or collaborative projects. Some activities were oriented toward benefiting the school overall as an organization, such as organizing social activities for the school, decorating the school, or organizing extra activities with parents. Finally, some behaviors were oriented toward benefiting students, including spending extra out-of-class time to help a student, arriving early for class, or acquiring expertise in new subjects that will improve teaching (654). In the study, teachers were surveyed to assess their job satisfaction, sense of self-efficacy, and sense of collective efficacy (that is, an individual's assessment of their organization or team's ability to do its job). The authors established correlation between extra-role behavior and job satisfaction, self-efficacy, and collective efficacy.

The authors worked from the premise that "behaviors that go beyond in-role duties become a fundamental component for achieving effectiveness in schools" (655). And they find that "job satisfaction, self-efficacy, and collective efficacy [are] key factors that were positively and distinctively related to teachers' extra-role behavior" (657). Discussing their results, the authors note

- strong positive relationship between job satisfaction and extra-role behavior toward students;
- both job satisfaction and self-efficacy were related to extra-role behavior towards the team;
- teachers with higher collective efficacy, compared with those with lower collective efficacy, engaged more frequently in extra-role behavior toward the team. (565, 657)

In their concluding discussions, Somech and Drach-Zahavy suggest that teachers

> find themselves in a profession that isolates them from their colleagues. Strong collegial relations can counteract these feelings. Hence, reducing isolation from peers through joint planning and implementation of activities would be likely to foster extra-role behavior. (657)

We are interested in how university writing teachers may interact with each other and how WPAs can take a role in fostering these collegial interactions that seem to benefit teachers' sense of satisfaction and efficacy in their work. Teachers can feel efficacious to the extent that the professional space created for them by the intersection of program goals and personal commitments is marked by expectations that reflect their voices as competent, well-trained educators.

Writing program administrators often are in a position to commit resources (if only of energy and time at first) to collaborative initiatives involving teachers from a variety of disciplines who are interested in improving student achievement in their courses. Similarly, WPAs are often in a position to link university writing teachers with K–12 teachers. Many state university systems have demonstrated interest, for example, in lowering costs of remedial programs at the baccalaureate level by improving the articulation between high school and college curricula. In Ohio, for example, the Ohio Board of Regents sponsors a long-running program called the Early English Composition Assessment Program. For nearly two decades, it has offered university writing professionals funding to establish collaborations with high school English teachers to help bridge the gap between high school writing instruction and the expectations of university composition programs.

In addition, as administrators with constituencies around the university, WPAs are in a position to broker collaborations between mentoring programs that may be housed in student-support-service programs. At South Seattle Community College, first-generation, low-income, and/or disabled students find tutoring and other vital resources in CLIC, the Collaborative Learning and Instruction Center. CLIC offers eligible students thirty hours per week of access to tutors, advisors, computers, and reference materials, staffed by four part-time tutors and two full-time advisors. According to Sash Woods, CLIC's approach is based on challenging the "false dichotomy between the rigorous and the nurturing":

> There are three aspects to creating this environment. One is broadly sowing resources in a variety of formats so that the conditions exist for truly informed choice. The second is designing an atmosphere of respect in which students are viewed as capable and gifted. Finally, there is planned structuring of diverse opportunities for connections in which learning is generated through relationships.

At Cleveland State University and fourteen other public and private universities in Ohio, the STARS (Student Achievement in Research and Scholarship) mentoring program serves undergraduate minority students of high academic achievement in their quest to pursue graduate degrees (http://www.regents. state.oh.us/stars/). Through four chapters in northeast Ohio, each year about thirty juniors and seniors participate in the STARS program. About fifteen students graduate each year, and virtually all the graduating students move on to graduate school. The STARS program recruits undergraduate minority students of high academic achievement and engages them in undergraduate research and mentoring activities. STARS students participate fully in three major activities: an undergraduate research project, culminating in a formal presentation of research at the annual STARS statewide conference; a mentoring relationship with a professor in the student's major; and a seminar to prepare for graduate school with a series of workshops to guide students through the application process and to orient them to the expectations of graduate study. Writing teachers and tutors have roles to play in each of these mentoring programs, and WPAs are often in the position to foster collaborations between teachers in first-year writing programs and staff and students involved in these support services.

Another site for collaboration that has recently gained attention is service learning. To cite an example, Dr. Mindy Wright, director of the Writing Workshop at Ohio State University, has created a service-learning course that links university students as tutors to children in nearby public elementary schools. One day each week, the university students travel to the partner schools to tutor elementary students in reading and writing. Tutoring work provides the university students opportunities to serve a specific need in the community. At the same time, the community service work gives the university students hands-on experience as a reference for reflection in their exploration of "literacy" in course texts and writing assignments.

As our discussion of extra-role behavior and collaboration would suggest, we think service learning/outreach scholarship benefits teachers' sense of efficacy, rounding their understanding of students' capabilities by seeing students acting in contexts outside the university classroom. Composition teachers acknowledge how service-learning courses offer students nonacademic in addition to academic contexts in which to read and write (Cushman and Emmons). We would add that service-learning or community-outreach projects offer similar opportunities for teachers to resituate their literacy teaching in contexts additional to the university/academic literacy context. Our proposal to WPAs is to consider how service learning may benefit teachers in their programs by giving them the opportunity to enhance their sense of efficacy through these kinds of collaborations.

Staff Development

One of the most critical elements that writing program administrators can promote to help writing professionals become successful teachers of all students is the implementation of policies that support professional development programs that focus specifically on preparing writing and composition teachers to work effectively with diverse student populations. In order for writing classrooms to become places where hearing diverse voices becomes a natural and constant phenomenon, WPAs need to be ready to initiate dialogues in which the presence of diverse voices is appreciated and rewarded. To sustain their efforts, WPAs must participate in continuing education workshops offered at places like CCCC and other professional conferences. We believe they must also engage personally in activities that make their own lives and communities more culturally sensitive and diverse.

The approach that WPAs choose is an important variable. In "Developing Pedagogies: Learning the Teaching of English," Stenberg and Lee describe their efforts to create a "teacher-learner community comprised of members with a range of experience" (340). Articulated as a project of critical inquiry, the "pedagogical inquiry" they describe entails "an ongoing process of discovering—and responding to—revisionary possibilities" (340). In their discussion, Stenberg and Lee draw on the context of TA mentoring to illustrate the need for accounts of pedagogy that "show the processes through which pedagogical development occurs" (341). They seek to "establish teaching as a critical process that parallel[s] writing as a critical process" (343). We believe WPAs can play a role in nurturing teachers' developing confidence in their abilities to teach all students well, particularly as they create a climate around the writing program along the lines Stenberg and Lee describe. Staff development forums where teachers and other stakeholders, including students and staff, can collaborate in reflecting on and rethinking pedagogy, seem more likely to produce the feelings of collegiality and participation that correlate with efficacy. Carmen Werder, P. J. Redmon, Jeff Purdue, and Kathryn Patrick describe such a program, the Teaching and Learning Academy at Western Washington University. The TLA involves fifty faculty from across the disciplines, along with about twenty students and staff members. In biweekly study groups, participants in the TLA meet informally to examine and discuss issues related to teaching and learning on the WWU campus. According to Werder et al., "the real motive for the TLA is not really any particular reform effort, but rather the revitalization of our whole institutional learning culture."

Scholarship in this area has begun to show the possibilities when writing program administrators position the writing curriculum as the object of practical inquiry and reflection for program staff (Phelps). Michael Apple documents a historic dilemma of American teachers in past decades who were systematically "deskilled" by reforms, program demands, or policies that increased external control over the curriculum and pedagogy. At the same time that these teachers were losing their professional autonomy, they were under increased pressure from students and parents in the community to deliver more effective and needs-responsive education. Today's accountability-driven society threatens a return to these trends, which have had a negative effect on teacher efficacy and on writing and composition classrooms populated by African American students. "Standards," Thomas Fox has argued, "often inhibit access" (*Defending* 2). In the ongoing work of a hypothetical writing program, we can imagine what he means. We recollect the litany of complaints, for example, that constitutes the usual feedback from faculty colleagues—within the English department and across the college. The gist is that students don't know how to write: What are they learning in those courses? Why can't they write a coherent sentence? We recollect our own experiences in TA-training programs, including instructions from writing program directors such as "If you turn in a grade sheet with all As and Bs, I will not accept it" (message: Be tough).

Fair enough. We have argued for a conception of reflective optimism— high regard for students' ability to meet standards—as a necessary complement (and corrective) to efficacy (when teachers purchase efficacy by discounting expectations). What too often seems to happen, however, is that appeals made to high standards give insufficient consideration to developing practices that make it more likely for students to meet them. No child left behind? To the extent that anyone can be "for" a slogan, we are for that. It is where policy hits program administration that hard work remains for WPAs. Writing program administrators have a world of burden to contend with, true. Workloads divide their institutional identity. They are half-time faculty on the publish-or-perish promotion track, half-time administrators, on top of which, saddled with high responsibility, they often have limited authority find even more limited budgets.

Acknowledging these built-in constraints, we believe administrators of writing across the curriculum programs, writing centers, and first-year writing programs including basic writing programs should come together with teachers to build consensus on exactly what the educational goal of the program should be and how should these goals differ given the increased numbers of culturally and linguistically diverse students entering the writing program at every level. Different groups may have different goals or expectations for what constitutes "good" teaching or different definitions of what "good" teaching is. These matters should be discussed with all of the stakeholders in the enterprise—including the students who are involved. If they choose to do so, if they are able to muster the resources (human and otherwise) necessary, writing program administrators have a role to play in sustaining reforms that foster efficacy and reflective optimism among writing teachers.

TEACHER EDUCATORS

In our efforts to make a difference in the classroom experiences of AAVE-speaking students, we must also address the challenge at the teacher-training level. Here, professional development programs require radical changes so that composition teachers gain an appreciation for the role they must play in allowing African American students' voices to be heard, legitimized, and leveraged within the writing classroom. A radical shift of priorities in the use of time within teacher professional development programs would eventually have to occur if such perspectives are to take hold among future composition professionals. Teachers must be trained in the selection and allocation of instructional resources, materials, and methodologies that are representative of a wide variety of different ethnic and cultural group experiences.

In chapter 4 [of *African American Literacies Unleashed*], I (Arnetha) shared my own story of growing up in South Central Los Angeles and learning about the language prowess of African American students in my community. I told of the resources my fellow classmates brought to the classroom and of my teachers' inability to use the resources that these poor and under-achieving students brought into the classroom to enrich their curriculum. I then shared my experiences as a teacher in schools that were labeled "multicultural" that had as their common denominator a predominant population of students of color who were socially and economically disenfranchised and who were viewed as a "problem." Finally, I shared my experiences as a teacher educator in one university-based teacher-education program, my eye-opening experiences while working in South Africa, and my subsequent application of the lessons I learned to my own reform-centered teaching in my own teacher-education classroom. It was my cross-national teacher-education experiences that served to crystallize the realization that the greatest challenge facing teacher education today is the need to prepare teachers who are interested in acquiring the attitudes, knowledge, skills, and dispositions necessary to work effectively with diverse student populations and with those who are socially and economically disenfranchised. With that realization, I have created an approach that facilitates the development of teachers who envision themselves as becoming excellent teachers of diverse student populations.

In my early experiences as a teacher educator, I observed numerous cases in which student teachers were able to produce seemingly appropriate answers to examination questions and class assignments without actually making differences in their teaching practices. The teachers were not integrating sound theoretical perspectives into their personal teaching styles in ways that would allow the power of those perspectives to transform their day-to-day teaching practice. I can still recall the look on the face of one student teacher who glibly stated,

> I can discuss topics of interest in my undergraduate teacher education course and never think about them again until another education class brings up the topic. . . . The knowledge in my brain is doing no good because I'm not using it. . . . Teacher education programs can't force any student to internalize the theories that they have "learned" in their class.

After sensing this same attitude from too many students over a period of several years, I knew I had to do something more proactive to address this phenomenon. I began to develop a teaching approach to help teachers develop the attitudes, skills, and dispositions necessary to become *change agents* in schools and to increase their feelings of efficacy and commitment to teaching diverse student populations.

My teaching approach was guided by a desire to discover the process through which teachers—who are engaged in a theory-driven teacher-education program—can move beyond positions of cognitive internalization of theory and best practices toward transformative positions of reflective commitment needed to guide them in their generative development as class-room teachers of diverse students. Vygotsky's discussion of internalization can help us to understand how this learning and development occurs—how the information presented to teachers in teacher-education programs moves from an interpsychological plane (as a social exchange in which teacher edu-cators encourage students' conceptual considerations) to an intrapsychologi-cal plane (where these social classroom activities are embraced by student teachers to become an internal catalyst that generates teacher advocacy, effi-cacy, and commitment). In my teacher-education course, I found that as teach-ers were exposed to theoretical perspectives, challenging discussions, strate-gically designed curricular activities, and extensive thoughtful, reflective, introspective, critical writing, I was able to detect changes in their attitudes toward teaching diverse students. These changes were reflected in the teach-ers' changing discourses as they moved beyond the production of seemingly appropriate communication about theory and practice toward an internaliza-tion and synthesizing of ideas that led them to commitment that transformed their experiences as teachers.

Upon entering my course, students were confronted with the challenge of considering these issues through interpersonal and socially mediated forums, including individual and shared reflections on these issues, extensive written engagement with carefully designed prompts on various thought-provoking topics, and discussions that challenge their preconceived notions on these issues. Exposure to theoretical readings and practical activities takes place during the course to serve as a catalyst to engage students in dialogic conver-sations that can impact their thoughts on issues of diversity. However, I pro-pose that engaging teachers in writing that draws on the two major modes that bring teachers' past, present, and future perspectives together, the pro-cesses of analysis and synthesis, will help teachers begin to conceptualize how to teach diverse students in fresh and exciting ways (Emig 13). As a result of their engagements in thoughtful and reflective writing along with teacher research projects, the teachers are able to bring theory and practice together in ways that crystallize the internalization process. Teaching diverse students begins to take on personal meaning for the teachers and they begin to go beyond the initial ideas and activities presented in class and beyond their own previous levels of functioning to expand upon the concepts, relate them to new situations, and act upon their understanding with personal conviction. In this work, I found that strategically planned and executed teacher-education programs can help teachers to become more effective in their work with AAVE-speaking students. (See Ball, *Carriers*, for an extended discussion.)

RESEARCHERS

For decades, scholars and researchers from many disciplines have explored the educational issues faced by speakers of AAVE in their attempt to negotiate the codes of school-based literacy. A great deal of published work exists going back to the bidialectalism movement in education in the 1960s and, of course, even before then. But certainly since the 1960s, following school desegregation and the Civil Rights and Black Power Movements, no one can deny that volumes of literature have been produced with the aim of fostering improved literacy for African American students whose home language is a variety of AAVE.

While much of the early work focused on convincing others that AAVE was a logical and viable language and on sociolinguistic findings for reading instruction at the elementary level, composition professionals formalized their participation in the debate with the adoption of the "students' right to their own language" resolution at the CCCC in 1974. The Black Caucus of NCTE/CCCC issued a statement supporting this resolution, noting that it is not the students' language that is problematic in academic settings but the teachers' attitudes towards the students' language that constitutes the problem. In their statement, the Black Caucus urged teachers to regard their students' language as a resource. Over thirty years since the "students' right" resolution, we believe that—allowing for the exception of classrooms with exceptional teachers—the teaching corps of composition professionals has yet to live up to the challenge to reconstruct pedagogy to make the most of the literacy potentials of all students.

The primary message that we wish to leave with researchers who focus on scholarship related to rhetoric and composition includes a commendation as well as a challenge. Researchers in writing and composition are to be commended for the work they have done and continue to do to "disrupt the intellectual comfort zones" (Gilyard, *Flip the Script* 19) of those who theorize and practice in rhetoric and composition on issues of race and particularly on issues that relate to AAVE-speaking students. The challenge remains, however, for us to consider how best to move these conversations beyond the pages of our research reports and scholarly recitations, to become conversations of central day-to-day concern to other practitioners, administrators, and teacher educators such that the dialogue with research will result in the implementation of changed practice. We see three areas where such collaborative conversations and research seem important.

Teacher Authority

We need research that better illuminates the culturally nuanced ways teachers exercise or enact authority in their classrooms. How do teachers construct a teaching persona or teaching identity for themselves? How do they negotiate an ethos in relationship with their students? Observations of teachers in the community-based organizations we have discussed, along with themes emerging in studies of teachers who work successfully with African American students (Ladson-Billings), lead us to believe issues of teacher authority in writing and composition classrooms need further exploration. Our curiosity parallels questions raised by Lisa Delpit, for instance, who has challenged an albeit simplified notion of writing process pedagogy. Delpit wanted the pedagogy to be more explicit and directive; we are interested in the teacher's enactment of authority. For example, Anthony Petrosky's study of teaching in rural Mississippi classrooms reveals the prominent role and the strong authority exercised by the teacher. Michele Foster's study of uses of performance by a female African American teacher in an urban community-college classroom similarly suggests a strong central place for her exercise of, or enactment of, authority in the success of her relationships with her students. How do teachers access and make use of authority in writing classrooms? What responsibilities do teachers implicitly or explicitly claim as their part of students' success in the classroom, in the institution, in the community?

Writing Program Assessment

Measured in terms of college grade-point average, persistence in college, and graduation rates, the achievement gap between black and white college students has been widely documented. In "The Black-White Achievement Gap in the First College Year: Evidence from a New Longitudinal Study," Kenneth Spenner, Claudia Buchmann, and Lawrence Landerman suggest this gap appears as soon as students arrive in college. The first-year writing course would be one logical place to examine the causes and perhaps reconstruct the narrative of underachievement. The study summarizes a range of explanations for achievement differences, including "status attainment variations, social and cultural capital differentials, negative stereotype threat, and the racial climate of college classrooms and campuses" (5). The study defines "climate" as "the extent to which prospective interactional ties of a focal environment (i.e., classroom, dormitory, social or institutional group) are perceived as welcoming and integrative, on the one hand, or hostile and exclusive, on the other" (10). "Climate" also refers to "the 'micro-politics' of the classroom such as differential treatment by teachers, school personnel and peers" (10).

Are there writing programs where African American English–speaking students not only survive but thrive because they take centrally into account the factors in achievement outlined in existing research? Are there curriculums in place that work well at making the best use of students' diverse languages and community literacies even as they effectively support students' efforts to crack the codes of academic literacy? Do data exist from any college writing program correlating race and writing achievement? Without falling into a reductionist assessment strategy, can we collect data across institutions that will show comparative levels of proficiency from program to program? We have worked with AAVE-speaking students in writing and composition classrooms for some time. Our impression and our puzzlement about why many of these students perform less successfully than students from other groups was one of the reasons we have come together to write this book. Yet we cannot find research that outright says AAVE-speaking students do as well or do better than other groups of students in a particular college writing classroom. The 1999 National Assessment of Educational Progress confirms that African American high school students are performing less well than their white counterparts. We see a need for similar performance data to be collected among first-year writing programs at the college level. But, more importantly, we see a need for research within and across institutions to show what effective writing programs are doing for AAVE-speaking students.

Teacher Change

Current movements in educational reform have been based on the belief that real change comes only with the support, participation, and leadership of those who will ultimately implement the reform or change: teachers. Unless teachers play the lead role in envisioning, planning, and implementing a reform movement that reenvisions the possibilities for African American students in writing and composition classrooms, efforts toward reform in the writing classroom are unlikely to succeed. In order for reforms to be effective, programs must have teachers who are committed to the reform process and who have the will and the capacity to implement the change.

We have found that teachers who seek a transformed pedagogy must challenge themselves to critically reflect on, analyze, and change the communication patterns through which literacy is practiced in their writing classrooms. Until teachers take race-related differences in language and literacies into account as a normal part (central and routine rather than marginal) of pedagogy and reflection, the needs of AAVE-speaking students will not be redressed, and their abilities and aptitudes for critical engagement and effective expression will remain undercounted. We regard efficacy as the most important change in reconstructing the reality of classroom teachers, offering models found in exemplary practices in community-based organizations where teachers show high efficacy and reflective optimism while at the same time integrating an explicit examination of race into the learning activities students engage in. Referring to the practice of "storying" from critical race theory to show the different possibilities for reality that exist, we likewise employ story to delve into and analyze in our own teaching lives the emergence of these alternative possibilities out of a matrix of professional, community, and personal experiences. We have found that teachers' extraprofessional identity formation plays a critical role in their vision of themselves as effective teachers and as change agents in the lives of their students. Further research in this area seems warranted.

Teachers who seek a transformed pedagogy must challenge themselves to critically reflect on, analyze, and change the communication patterns through which literacy is practiced in their writing classrooms. The vision contained in the "students' right to their own language" resolution has yet to become a broadly understood pedagogical foundation for college writing classes. Indeed, efforts to incorporate it stand out for this reason. Fine work in pedagogical theory by teacher-scholars including Kay Halasek, Jacqueline Jones Royster, Deborah Mutnick, and Laura Gray-Rosendale offer important insights in realizing the vision of the "students' right" resolution. With *African American Literacies*, Elaine Richardson adds vitally to this pool of knowledge.

In the community-based organizations we discuss, we find African American students' preferred modes of expression readily incorporated in the interactive discourse among participants. We believe these modes of expression have a place in the writing classroom as building blocks for bridging African American students' experiences with academic-based literacy. We also regard these modes of expression as a source of knowledge that all students can benefit from as they broaden their abilities to express their ideas in a variety of forms. Including these devices in the writing curriculum is a strategy that is in keeping with other educational approaches that have successfully used the cultural resources of students to enrich the learning experience. Rather than avoid the students' cultural experiences, identities, and interests, other successful programs within the academy and within the extracurriculum have consciously sought them out and used them to inform the curriculum, The results are positive. More research focusing on how AAVE-speaking students and teachers coconstruct a positive writing environment for developing academic literacies is needed.

The teaching practices in the community-based organizations we have discussed give participants abundant opportunities to develop broad capacities to function within their local communities—to talk, write, and develop their abilities to learn and adapt to new information and changes in their lives. This ability to develop participants' capacities is rooted in the powerful sense of efficacy and reflective optimism that program leaders possess. In addition, in each program, aspects of the community, including the participants themselves and their culturally influenced language patterns, were viewed as resources. We also believe that a shared sense of racial solidarity forms the core meaning of these community-based organizations as specifically African American sites of the extracurriculum, and a question remains as to how a similar sense of shared commitment may be activated in college writing classrooms. Or are college writing classrooms always already part of the problem? Perhaps one key to this puzzle can be found by examining the mind-set of writing teachers. Where are they coming from? What shapes their vision of their students? What empowers their faith in their capability to be a meaningful force for positive change in their students' lives?

It is important that the research in writing and composition move forward within an interdisciplinary arena of inquiry that takes significant and positive steps toward building a more powerful theoretical framework for writing research and instruction. Most critically, members of the research community must begin to communicate and collaborate with teachers rather than theorizing among themselves about what needs to happen in classrooms. Many researchers who focus on scholarship related to rhetoric and composition have been away from freshman and basic writing classrooms for many years, and among those who continue to teach in these classrooms, few can boast of having recent extended successful experiences teaching struggling African American students. Perhaps we must look to those who are challenged with the task of meeting the needs of these students on a daily basis to offer us innovations in the areas of scholarship and practice. We must solicit the support of these professionals as teacher researchers and as action researchers with whom we might collaborate and to whom we might extend support.

We also recommend that scholars initiate collaborations between writing professionals in traditional academic settings and those in community-based organizations in order to facilitate the design and implementation of innovative writing programs addressed to authentic audiences that link academic demands with community and cultural resources through the use of interactive technologies. We predict that these are the sites from which modern-day scholarship and classroom innovations will emerge—particularly within those classrooms that have adopted and implemented the principles we propose in this book.

CONCLUSION

The mistakes of silence are few, our grandmothers said, and easily forgotten.

As a rule, we have rarely suffered for following our grandmothers' counsel. But there comes a time we must look with fresh eyes at the world and admit the human dimensions of their fallibility. There comes a time when we acknowledge of our elders that, to paraphrase the poet, even when they were right, they were wrong (Clifton).

As writing teachers responding to complexities, complications, and conundrums when race (and racism) are acknowledged as abiding elements that shape the context of our work, we recognize that we have written and taught the mistakes of silence. Too long. Too often we have let silence take the place of conversation. Too often for our own good, too often for the good of all our students—silence, where lively conversation is needed. We want for our own good as people, as teachers, to understand our situation. We want for ourselves, with and for our students, to understand "race" as a power-infused category of social difference, to name how it operates in our relationships; to our own professional identities, to the literacies we sponsor, and, fundamentally, to each other as citizens and human beings. As one modest step toward that goal, we have focused in this book on teachers' responses to AAVE in the writing classroom.

In 1979, in the Ann Arbor "Black English" case, federal district court judge Charles Joiner's recognition of the need to acknowledge students' language was evident in the way he phrased his ruling, putting teachers' "skilled empathy" at the center of the effort to break down the barriers to learning (Memorandum). We think "skilled empathy" is a good term to use to talk about ways of reconceiving the personal and professional dimensions of teacher change. Open-ended, neither "skill" nor "empathy" is a static entity of finite quantity that a teacher can possess. Instead, skill and empathy can always be improved. Likewise, any step we take toward unleashing literacies and reimagining the possibilities for AAVE-speaking students in writing and composition classrooms is a starting point that moves us away from a state of complacency. This, too, is an effort that can always be improved. At the same time, this, like any starting point, is initially "a promise."

Adding to the call for "skilled empathy," we have found exemplary practices of teachers in community-based organizations that express a powerful sense of teacher efficacy and reflective optimism. These teachers ground belief in the capability of their students in a disposition to develop skills and attitudes necessary to teach AAVE-speaking students effectively. These teachers have developed a strong knowledge base about the cultural heritage and community literacies of their students, using that knowledge to inform curricular and pedagogical practices. Implicitly or explicitly, these teachers situate their students' learning in a context of racial solidarity that stems from participation with issues of race in their private and professional lives.

We know we will begin to see a difference in the educational lives of AAVE-speaking students in writing and composition classrooms when we no longer hear teachers say, "I respect the discourse patterns African American students use in their community, but there is no place for them in this classroom." What we have said in this book is that there is a place for these patterns in the writing classroom. Locating the best place for them will require the development of teachers' sense of efficacy, grounded in reflective optimism and a commitment to becoming agents of change in the writing lives of African American students.

WORKS CITED

Apple, Michael. *Teachers and Texts: A Political Economy of Class and Fender Relations in Education.* London: Routledge and Kegan Paul, 1986.

Ashton, Patricia T., and Rodman B. Webb. *Making a Difference: Teachers' Sense of Efficacy and Student Achievement.* New York: Longman, 1986.

Ball, A. F. *Carriers of the Torch: Addressing the Global Challenge of Preparing Teachers for Diversity.* New York: Teachers College P, 2006.

Chideya, Farai. *The Color of Our Future.* New York: Morrow, 1999.

Clifton, Lucille, "Heaven." *The Terrible Stories.* Rochester, NY: BOA, 1996.

Cushman, Ellen, and Chalon Emmons. "Contact Zones Made Real." *School's Out! Bridging Out-of-School Literacies with Classroom Practice,* ed. Glynda Hull and Katherine Schultz. New York: Teachers College P, 2002. 203–32.

Delpit, Lisa. "The Silenced Dialogue: Power and Pedagogy in Educationg Other People's Children." *Harvard Educational Review* 58, no. 3 (1988): 280–98.

———. "What Should Teachers Do? Ebonics and Culturally Responsive Instruction." *The Real Ebonics Debate,* ed. Theresa Perry and Lisa Delpit. Boston: Beacon Press, 1998. 17–26.

Emig, Janet. "Writing as a Mode of Thinking." *College Composition and Communication* 28, no. 2 (1977): 122–28.

Foster, Michele. "'It's Cookin' Now': A Performance Analysis of the Speech Events of a Black Teacher in an Urban Community College." *Language in Society* 18 (1989): 1–29.

Fox, Thomas. *Defending Access: A Critique of Standards in Higher Education.* Portsmouth, NH: Boynton/Cook Heinemann, 1999.

Gilyard, Keith. *Let's Flip the Script: An African American Discourse on Language, Literature, and Learning.* Detroit: Wayne State UP, 1996.

Guskey, Thomas R. "Teacher Efficacy, Self-Concept, and Attitudes toward the Implementation of Mastery Learning." *Teaching and Teacher Education: An International Journal of Instructional Innovation* 4, no. 1 (1988): 63–96.

Ladson-Billings, Gloria. *The Dream Keepers: Successful Teachers of African American Children.* San Francisco: Jossey-Bass, 1994.

Little, Judith Warren. "Norms of Collegiality and Experimentation: Workplace Conditions of School Success." *American Educational Research Journal* 19 (1982): 325–40.

Omi, Michael, and Howard Winant. "On the Theoretical Concept of Race." In *Race, Identity, and Representation in Education,* ed. Cameron McCarthy and Warren Crichlow. New York: Routledge, 1993. 3–10.

Petrosky, Anthony. "Rural Poverty and Literacy in the Mississippi Delta: Dilemmas, Paradoxes, and Conundrums." *The Right to Literacy*, ed. Andrea Lunsford, Helene Moglen, and James Slevin. New York: MLA, 1990.

Phelps, Louise Wetherbee. "Practical Wisdom and the Geography of Knowledge in Composition." *College English* 53, no. 8 (1991): 863–85.

Raudenbush, Stephen W., Brian Rowan, and Yuk Fai Cheong. *Contextual Effects on the Self-Efficacy of High School Teachers*. Stanford, CA: Center for Research on the Context of Secondary School Teaching, 1990.

Richardson, Elaine. *African American Literacies*. New York: Routledge, 2003.

———. "Race, Class(es), Gender, and Age: The Making of Knowledge about Language Diversity." *Language Diversity in the Classroom: From Intention to Practice*, ed. Geneva Smitherman and Victor Villanueva. Carbondale: Southern Illinois UP, 2003. 40–66.

Somech, Anit, and Anat Drach-Zahavy. "Understanding Extra-Role Behavior in Schools: The Relationships between Job Satisfaction, Sense of Efficacy, and Teachers' Extra-Role Behavior." *Teaching and Teacher Education* 16 (2000): 649–59.

Spenner, Kenneth I., Claudia Buchmann, and Lawrence R. Landerman. "The Black-White Achievement Gap in the First College Year: Evidence from a New Longitudinal Case Study." <http://www.soc.duke.edu/~cbuch/web/spenner_buchmann_landerman.pdf>.

Stenberg, Shari, and Amy Lee. "Developing Pedagogies: Learning the Teaching of English." *College English* 64, no. 3 (2002): 326–47.

Werder, Carmen, P. J. Redmond, Jeff Purdue, and Kathryn Patrick. "Creating a Reflective Space: The Teaching and Learning Academy at Western Washington University."<http://www.evergreen.edu/washcenter/Fall2003Newsletter/Pg38-40.pdf>.

Woods, Sash. "Putting an Asset-Based Perspective into Practice: The Collaborative Learning and Instruction Center at South Seattle Community College." <http://www.evergreen.edu/washcenter/Fall2003Newsletter/Pg41-44.pdf>.

ABOUT THE EDITORS

Staci Perryman-Clark is an assistant professor of Rhetoric and Writing Studies in the Department of English at Western Michigan University, where she also directs the First-Year Writing Program. Her work focuses on creating culturally relevant pedagogies and curricular designs to support all students' expository writing practices. Her published work currently focuses on designing alternative curricular models for undergraduate and graduate courses. Her recent publications include journals published in *Composition Studies*, *Composition Forum*, and *WPA: Writing Program Administration*, with forthcoming publications in *Pedagogy* and *Teaching English in a Two-Year College* (*TETYC*). She has received national honors from both the Ford Foundation and Conference on College Composition and Communication.

David E. Kirkland is an assistant professor of English Education at New York University. His scholarship explores the intersections among youth culture and identity, language, literacy, and power, and urban education. He has utilized critical approaches to qualitative educational research (including critical ethnography and critical discourse analysis) to understand literacy in the lives of a group of urban adolescent Black males. He examined closely the literate lives of young Black men, their language practices and participation structures within wider social and cultural fields that exist beyond school contexts. His work has been featured in several academic publications, including *Reading Research Quarterly*, *Research in the Teaching of English*, *English Education*, and *English Journal*. His current research examines the literate construction of digital iDentities among urban youth participating in online social communities, its impact on youth culture and subjectivity, and its reconfiguring of race and gender.

Austin Jackson is an assistant professor in the Residential College in the Arts and Humanities at Michigan State University. His research and teaching interests include writing and rhetoric, African American Language and literacy, and qualitative research in English education. He serves as director of the My

Brother's Keeper program, a mentoring program for middle school students attending the Paul Robeson Malcolm X Academy (K–8) in Detroit. He has coauthored several publications exploring links between critical approaches to writing pedagogy and student participation in contemporary struggles for critical democracy.

ACKNOWLEDGMENTS *(continued from page iv)*

H. Samy Alim, "Critical Language Awareness in the United States: Revisiting Issues and Revising Pedagogies in a Resegregated Society," *Educational Researcher*, Vol. 34, No. 7 (Oct., 2005), pp. 24–31. Reprinted by Permission of SAGE Publications.

H. Samy Alim, "What if We Occupied Language?," *New York Times* Opinionator, Dec. 21, 2011. Copyright © 2011 New York Times. Reprinted by permission.

Arnetha F. Ball and Ted Lardner, "Where We Go From Here," *African American Literacies Unleashed*, Southern Illinois University Press, 2005, Chapter 6, pp. 176–96.

Stuart Barbier, "The Reflection of 'Students' Right to Their Own Language' in First-Year Composition Course Objectives and Descriptions," *Teaching English in the Two Year College*, March 2003, pp. 256–268.

Ann E. Berthoff and William G. Clark, "In Response to 'The Students' Right to Their Own Language,'" *College Composition and Communication*, May 1975, pp. 216–17.

Patrick Bruch and Richard Marback, "Race, Literacy, and the Value of Rights Rhetoric in Composition Studies," *College Composition and Communication*, June 2002, p. 651–74.

A. Suresh Canagarajah, "The Place of World Englishes in Composition: Pluralization Continued," *College Composition and Communication*, June 2006, p. 586–619.

Conference on College Composition and Communication on Language Policy, "Students' Right to Their Own Language," *College Composition and Communication*, Fall 1974.

Stanley Fish, "What Should College Teach? Part 3," *New York Times* Opinionator, Sept. 7, 2009. Copyright © 2009 New York Times. Reprinted by permission.

Lawrence D. Freeman, "The Students' Right to Their Own Language: Its Legal Bases," *College Composition and Communication* 26 (1975): 25–9.

Keith Gilyard and Elaine Richardson, "Students' Right to Possibility: Basic Writing and African American Rhetoric," *Insurrections: Approaches to Resistance in Composition Studies*, ed. Andrea Greenbaum, State University of New York Press, 2001, Chapter 3, pp. 37–51. Copyright © 2001 the State University of New York. Reprinted by permission. All rights reserved.

Valerie Felita Kinloch, "Revisiting the Promise of 'Students' Right to Their Own Language': Pedagogical Strategies," *College Composition and Communication*, Sept. 2005, pp. 83–113.

Carmen Kynard, "'I Want to Be African': In Search of a Black Radical Tradition/African-American-Vernacularized Paradigm for 'Students' Right to Their Own Language,' Critical Literacy, and 'Class Politics,'" *College English*, March 2007, pp. 360–90.

Kim Brian Lovejoy, Steve Fox, and Katherine V. Wills, from "Language Experience to Classroom Practice: Affirming Linguistic Diversity in Writing Pedagogy," Pedagogy: Critical Approaches to Teaching Literature, Language, Composition, and Culture, Volume 9, Number 2, 2009, pp. 1–287. Reprinted by permission of Duke University Press. www.dukepress.edu.

Gail Y. Okawa, "From 'Bad Attitudes' to(ward) Linguistic Pluralism: Developing Reflective Language Policy among Preservice Teachers," *Language Ideologies: Critical Perspectives on the Official English Movement*, National Council of Teachers of English, 2000, Chapter 12, pp. 276–96.

Django Paris, "'They're in My Culture, They speak the Same Way': African American Language in Multiethnic High Schools," *Harvard Educational Review*, 79:3 (Fall 2009), pp. 428–47. Copyright © 2009 President and Fellows of Harvard College. All rights reserved. For more information, please visit www.harvardeducationalreview.org.

Stephen Parks, "The Students' Right to Their Own Language, 1972–1974," *Class Politics: The Movement for the Students' Right to Their Own Language*. Refiguring English Studies, NCTE, 2000, Chapter 5, pp. 160–202. Copyright © 2013 by Parlor Press. Used by permission.

Staci Perryman-Clark, "Writing, Rhetoric, and American Cultures (WRA) 125—Writing: The Ethnic and Racial Experience," *Composition Studies* 37.2 (2009), pp. 115–34. Reprinted by permission.

Allen N. Smith, "No One Has a Right to His Own Language," *College Composition and Communication*, May 1976, pp. 155–59.

Geneva Smitherman, "African American Student Writers in the NAEP, 1969–88/89 [1992]" from *Black English, Diverging or Converging?: The View from the National Assessment of Educational Progress, Language and Education*, Volume 6, Issue 1, 1992, pp. 47–61, reprinted by permission of Taylor & Francis Group; and Geneva Smitherman, "'The Blacker the Berry, the Sweeter the Juice': African American Student Writers" from *The Need for Story: Cultural Diversity in Classroom and Community*, ed. Anne Haas Dyson and Celia Genishi, NCTE, 1994, pp. 80–101.

Geneva Smitherman, "CCCC's Role in the Struggle for Language Rights," *College Composition and Communication*, Feb. 1999, pp. 349–76.

Geneva Smitherman, "Students' Right to Their Own Language": A Retrospective," *The English Journal*, January 1995, pp. 21–27.

John Trimbur, "Linguistic Memory and the Politics of U.S. English," *College English*, July 2006, pp. 575–88.

Scott Wible, "Pedagogies of the 'Students' Right' Era: The Language Curriculum Research Group's Project for Linguistic Diversity," *College Composition and Communication*, Feb. 2006, pp. 442–78.

Jeff Zorn, " 'Students' Right to Their Own Language': A Counter-Argument," *Academic Questions*, July 6, 2010, pp. 311–26. Reprinted with kind permission from Springer Science+Business Media.

Leah A. Zuidema, "Myth Education: Rationale and Strategies for Teaching against Linguistic Prejudice," *Journal of Adolescent and Adult Literacy* 48.8, May 2005, pp. 666–75. Reprinted by permission of John Wiley & Sons.

INDEX

AAE. *See* African American English

AAL. *See* African American Language

AAVE. *See* African American Vernacular English

Academic English Mastery Program, 421

accents, 70, 242, 284, 327, 341–42, 347, 350, 384, 437, 438, 439, 442

acquisition of language, 24–25, 27, 36

activism, 249–50

admissions, college, 174

affirmative action, 63, 173–74, 177, 180, 184, 185

Affirming Students' Right to Their Own Language (Scott, Kratz, and Straker), 2

African American discourse
  benefit to all students in studying, 228
  samples of, 206
  scholars who are speakers of, 358

African American English (AAE), 242–43

African American History Month, 73

African American Language (AAL).
    See also Black Americans; Black English; code switching
  "Ann Arbor Black English Case" (Ball and Lardner), 79–80
  analysis, "contrastive," between standard English and BL, 421
  Black Radical tradition, 239–40. *See also* Black Power
  described as "slang" and "ghetto," 318–19
  "field dependent" communication style, 204–5

King Elementary School v. Ann Arbor School District Board, 79–80

language versus dialect, 384–85

negative attitudes toward, 183

Oakland Ebonics controversy, 156, 186

online information and, 264–65

phonological features of, 266

research, need for interethnic, 306

Romantic Ethnicity, 157–58

slave trade and suppression of, 128

South Vista youth experience, 317–19, 320–21

spoken features mingled with written, 306

versus Standard English, as empowering for students, 158–59

as unifying language, 320–21

use of and sharing among minority youths, 317–19

African American Literacies (Richardson), 247, 475

"African American Student Writers in the NAEP, 1969–88/89 [1992] and 'The Blacker the Berry, the Sweeter the Juice' " (Smitherman), 191–216

African American Verbal Tradition, 211

African American Vernacular English (AAVE), 218, 287, 296, 299, 478

African Americans
  and affirmative action, reactions against, 174
  essays, samples of, 211–15, 223–28
  field dependency in writing/thinking, 204–5

minorities
  African Americans in South Vista,
    CA, 305–19
  dialects and standard English, 102
  enabling marginalized students,
    424–25
  Latino/a in South Vista, CA, 305–19
  Mexican Americans, 306, 312, 314,
    315, 316, 318
  myths regarding standard English,
    430
  Pacific Islander, in South Vista, CA,
    305–19
  students, and SRTOL, 373–74, 431–32
  "submerged" in English-centric
    classrooms, 20, 69, 96, 145
Missouri v. Jenkins, 418
MLA. *See* Modern Language
  Association
Moby-Dick (Melville), 135
Modern Language Association (MLA),
  84
monolingualism, 127, 135, 137, 382
Montgomery bus strike, 99
Moore, Samuel, 356, 357
Mora, Pat, 348, 436
morphology, 36–37
Morris, B. S., 349–50
Morrison, Toni, 440
Mullen, Bill, 327
Muller, Herbert J., 103
multiculturalism
  education course in languages, 328–30
  teacher development and, 471
*Multilingual Anthology of American
  Literature, The* (Shell and Sollers),
  135
multilingualism, 127, 129, 138
  diversity, worldwide, versus stan-
    dardization, 281–85
  language shift versus language
    maintenance, 146
  pedagogical possibilities, 296–300
  and rights rhetoric, 183–84
  writing models, 287–92
multiliteracies, 300
"Murder of the American Dream"
  (Kelly), 62–65
Mutnick, Deborah, 475
*My Own True Name: New and Selected
  Poems for Young Adults* (Mora), 348

Myrdal, Gunnar, 154
"Myth Education: Rationale and
  Strategies for Teaching against
  Linguistic Prejudice" (Zuidema),
  12, 341–52

Na, An, 348
National Assessment of Educational
  Progress (NAEP)
  Black high school students compared
    to white counterparts, 474–75
  Black English variables, 196–97
  holistic scoring methods, 194, 195
  primary trait scale for Black students'
    writing, 194
  results of 1969–79 testing, 197–201,
    207–10
  Writing Assessment, 191
National Association for the Advance-
  ment of Colored People (NAACP),
  156
National Council of Teachers of English
  (NCTE), 342, 357, 422
  annual meetings, 1970 and 1971, 34
  Black Caucus, 473
  CCCC position statement on stu-
    dents' dialects, 3, 20
  response to CCCC's SRTOL docu-
    ment, 142–44
  social and educational efforts, 211
  "Statement on Usage," 84–85, 96
  survey on knowledge of SRTOL, 354
National Language Policy (NLP), 73–76
  adopted by CCCC, 147–48
  Americans, bilingual and multi-
    lingual as a goal, 76
  English Only movement, 147
  and teachers, 334
National Writing Project, 396
Nationality Act of 1906, 135
NCTE. *See* National Council of
  Teachers of English
Negri, Antonio, 133
Negro American Literature Forum, 231,
  241
Nelson, Donald, 359
Nelson, Sophia, 85, 88
*Nepantla: Essays from the Land in the
  Middle* (Mora), 436
"New Grammar," 60, 61, 62